Journals of the Century

THE HAWORTH INFORMATION PRESS
Serials Librarianship
Jim Cole and Wayne Jones
Senior Editors

E-Serials: Publishers, Libraries, Users, and Standards, Second Edition
by Wayne Jones

Journals of the Century edited by Tony Stankus

Journals of the Century

Tony Stankus, MLS
Editor

The Haworth Information Press®
An Imprint of The Haworth Press, Inc.
New York • London • Oxford

Published by

The Haworth Information Press®, an imprint of The Haworth Press, Inc., 10 Alice Street, Binghamton, NY 13904-1580.

Cover design by Anastasia Litwak.

Library of Congress Cataloging-in-Publication Data

Journals of the century / Tony Stankus, editor.
    p. cm.
Includes bibliographical references and index.
ISBN 0-7890-1133-6 (hard : alk. paper) — ISBN 0-7890-1134-4 (pbk. : alk. paper)
1. Scholarly periodicals—Bibliography—Catalogs. I. Stankus, Tony.

Z6944.S3 J685 2002
[PN4836]
011'.34—dc21
                                            2002024215

CONTENTS

About the Editor   viii

Contributors   ix

Acknowledgments   xv

Introduction to the Journals of the Century Project   1
     Tony Stankus

CLUSTER I: THE HELPING PROFESSIONS   5

Chapter 1. Journals of the Century in Social Work   9
     James W. Williams

Chapter 2. Journals of the Century in Education   19
     Nancy Patricia O'Brien

Chapter 3. Journals of the Century in Psychology   29
     Daniel E. Burgard

Chapter 4. Journals of the Century in Sociology   45
     Lynne Rudasill

Chapter 5. Journals of the Century in Library
    and Information Science   57
     Cheryl A. McCarthy

CLUSTER II: MUSIC, MUSEUMS, AND METHODISTS   77

Chapter 6. Journals of the Century in Music   81
     Alan Karass

Chapter 7. Journals of the Century in the Visual Arts   115
     Alexandra de Luise

Chapter 8. Journals of the Century in Anthropology
   and Archaeology   141
        Gregory A. Finnegan
        Joyce L. Ogburn
        J. Christina Smith

Chapter 9. Journals of the Century in Philosophy   151
        John M. Cullars

Chapter 10. Journals of the Century in the American
   Religious Experience   173
        Donna L. Gilton

CLUSTER III: BUSINESS AND LAW   189

Chapter 11. Journals of the Century in Business
   and Economics   193
        Colleen Anderson

Chapter 12. Journals of the Century in Law   221
        Christopher D. Byrne

CLUSTER IV: WAR AND PEACE   241

Chapter 13. Journals of the Century in Modern History   243
        Edward A. Goedeken

Chapter 14. Journals of the Century in Political Science
   and International Relations   271
        Thomas E. Nisonger

Chapter 15. Journals of the Century in Military Affairs   289
        Robert E. Schnare
        Alice Juda
        Lorna Dodt
        Pam Kontowicz
        Carol Ramkey
        Ron Dial

CLUSTER V: PHYSICAL SCIENCES
AND ENGINEERING   321

Chapter 16. Journals of the Century in the Basic Sciences,
    Part I: Mathematics and the Physical Sciences   325
        Tony Stankus

Chapter 17. Journals of the Century in Engineering
    and Computer Science   373
        Carol S. Robinson

CLUSTER VI: LIFE, HEALTH, AND AGRICULTURE   389

Chapter 18. Journals of the Century in the Basic Sciences,
    Part II: Life Sciences   391
        Tony Stankus

Chapter 19. Journals of the Century in Medicine
    and Surgery   413
        Lucretia W. McClure

Chapter 20. Journals of the Century in Pharmacy, Physical
    Therapy, and Nutrition   427
        Julia Whelan
        Patricia Durisin
        Vivienne Piroli

Chapter 21. Journals of the Century in Agriculture
    and Veterinary Medicine   443
        Sandra Sinsel Leach
        Ann Viera

Index of Journal Titles   459
        Fyiane Nsilo-Swai

Subject Index   493

ABOUT THE EDITOR

Tony Stankus, MLS, is Science Librarian at the College of the Holy Cross. He is the author or more than 100 papers and nine books, including *Biographies of Scientists for Sci-Tech Libraries, Science Librarianship at America's Liberal Arts Colleges,* and *Scientific and Clinical Literature for the Decade of the Brain* (Haworth Press). Stankus is Associate Editor of *Science & Technology Libraries* for manuscripts on serials and writes the "Making Sense of Serials" column for *Technicalities.*

CONTRIBUTORS

Colleen Anderson *(Business and Economics)* is Head of Reference at Bryant College, a New England center for business education in Smithfield, Rhode Island. She holds a master's in librarianship from the University of Rhode Island, and is a candidate for an MBA. She has written on the bond market for the former *RQ* and authored the collection development chapter in Schlessinger and Schlessinger's *The Basic Business Library.* Her most recent work has appeared in *CyberPsychology & Behavior.*

Daniel E. Burgard *(Psychology)* is Instructional Librarian at the Lewis Health Science Library at the University of Texas Health Science Center in Fort Worth. He received his master's in librarianship from the University of Illinois. His previous work has appeared in *Serials Review* and *Online & CD-ROM Review.*

Christopher D. Byrne *(Law)* is Reference and Instructional Services Librarian at the Marshall-Wythe Law Library at the College of William & Mary Law School in Williamsburg, Virginia. He holds a master's in librarianship from the University of Rhode Island and a JD from Harvard. He is a former editor with the *Journal of Law & Public Policy.*

John M. Cullars *(Philosophy)* is Humanities Bibliographer at the University of Illinois at Chicago Library. He has a master's in librarianship and a doctorate in comparative literature (both from Indiana University). His articles and reviews have appeared in *Library & Information Science Research, Library Quarterly,* and *College & Research Libraries.* He has chaired the Western European Specialists Section of the Association of College and Research Libraries.

Alexandra de Luise *(Art)* is Coordinator of Instructional Services at the Benjamin S. Rosenthal Library, Queens College, City University of New York, in Flushing. She has a master's in both librarianship and art history from Rutgers University. In addition to papers in *Art Documentation,* she has compiled the chapter on art periodicals and series for the upcoming art reference book, *Guide to the Literature of Art History,* volume 2, edited by Max Marmor and Alex Ross.

Ron Dial *(Military Affairs)* is an advisor to the *Air University Index to Military Periodicals* and Chief Periodicals Librarian at Air University, Maxwell Air Force Base, Alabama. He holds a master's in librarianship (University of Kentucky) and media technology (Alabama A&M University).

Lorna Dodt *(Military Affairs)* is Command Librarian, Army Material Command, Alexandria, Virginia. She has a master's in librarianship from the University of Washington in Seattle, and is the author of *Military References and Resources,* Third edition.

Patricia Durisin *(Pharmacy, Physical Therapy, and Nutrition)* is Library Liaison to the Department of Physical Therapy, and Coordinator of Public Services, Simmons College Libraries, Boston. She holds a master's in librarianship from Simmons, where she has also team-taught Reference and Information Sources. She is guest editing a forthcoming issue of the *Journal of Library Administration* on Information Literacy.

Gregory A. Finnegan *(Anthropology and Archaeology)* is Associate Librarian for Public Services and Head of Reference at the Tozzer Library at Harvard University, Cambridge, Massachusetts. He holds a master's in librarianship (University of Chicago) and a doctorate in anthropology (Brandeis University). In addition to reviews of books and computing for *College and Research Libraries* and other publications for librarians, he has served as the film review editor for *American Anthropologist.* He is a former chair of the Anthropology and Social Sciences Section of the Association of College and Research Libraries.

Donna L. Gilton *(The American Religious Experience)* is Associate Professor at the University of Rhode Island Graduate School of Library and Information Studies, Kingston. She has a master's (University of Pittsburgh) and a doctorate (Simmons College) in librarianship. The daughter of a minister, and herself a church activist, she has an equal number of papers in the former *RQ* and the *African Methodist Episcopal Review.*

Edward A. Goedeken *(Modern History)* is Humanities Bibliographer at the Iowa State University Libraries in Ames. He holds a master's in librarianship (University of Iowa) and history (Iowa State), and a doctorate in history as well (University of Kansas). In addition to frequent reviews and articles in *The Serials Librarian* and *Library Quarterly,* he authors the biennial survey of articles on American library history in *Libraries & Culture.*

Alice Juda *(Military Affairs)* is Reference Librarian at the Naval War College Library, in Newport, Rhode Island. She holds a master's in librarianship (University of Rhode Island) and teaching (Harvard). In addition to editing the *Naval War College's Library Newsletter,* she is the author of specialized bibliographies on U.S.-Cuba relations, urban warfare, war termination and exit strategies, and humanitarian relief missions performed by the military.

Alan Karass *(Music)* is Music Librarian at the Music Library of the College of the Holy Cross in Worcester, Massachusetts. He has a master's in librarianship from Simmons College and is a degree candidate for another in historical musicology at the University of Connecticut. In addition to contributions to the *Boston Early Music Newsletter* and the *Music Library Association Newsletter,* he is co-editor of *Music Reference Services Quarterly.* He is currently working on the funeral cantatas of Telemann, and holds national office in both the Music Library Association and the American Recorder Society.

Pam Kontowicz *(Military Affairs)* is Librarian and Archivist at the Combined Arms Research Library, Fort Leavenworth, Kansas. She holds a master's in librarianship from the University of Washington at Seattle, and a JD from Marquette University in Milwaukee. She has previously written for *Kansas History.*

Sandra Sinsel Leach *(Agriculture and Veterinary Medicine)* is the Head Librarian at the University of Tennessee Agriculture and Veterinary Medicine Library in Knoxville. She received her master's in librarianship from Emory University, and has numerous papers in the *Quarterly Bulletin of the International Association of Agricultural Information Specialists.*

Cheryl A. McCarthy *(Library and Information Science)* is an Associate Professor at the University of Rhode Island Graduate School of Library and Information Studies in Kingston. She holds a master's in librarianship from URI and a doctorate from Simmons. She has published broadly across all types of libraries with papers in *School Library Journal, College & Research Libraries,* and *Public Libraries.* She is a past president of the New England Library Association and currently an editor with *School Library Media Research.*

Lucretia W. McClure *(Medicine and Surgery)* is Librarian Emerita of the University of Rochester Medical Center and currently Assistant for Special Projects at the Countway Library of Medicine of the Harvard Medical School. She holds a master's in librarianship from the University of Denver. In addition to contributions to the librarians' journal *Against the Grain* and *The Serials Librarian,* she has many papers in the former *Bulletin of the Medical Library Association.* She is arguably the most honored medical librarian of the twentieth century, having been invited to give the Jane Doe Lecture, and having received the Marcia C. Noyes Award, the President's Award, and the first ever Lucretia W. McClure Award for Excellence in Education, all from the Medical Library Association.

Thomas E. Nisonger *(Political Science and International Relations)* is Associate Professor at Indiana University's School of Library and Information Science in Bloomington, where he won the TERA Award for Teaching Excellence. He holds a master's in librarianship (University of Pittsburgh) and a doctorate in political science (Columbia University). He recently published *Management of Serials in Libraries,* and he received the 2001 K. G. Saur Award for the best paper contributed to *College & Research Libraries.* He serves on the editorial boards of *The Serials Librarian* and *Library Collections, Acquisitions, & Technical Services.*

Fyiane Nsilo-Swai *(Title Verifications and ISSN Searching)* is Reference Librarian, D'Alzon Library, Assumption College, Worcester, Massachusetts. Her considerable fact-checking work (over 1,900 entries) was completed while at the libraries of the College of the Holy Cross, as part of the professional field experience required by the University of Rhode Island's Graduate School of Library and Information Studies, where she earned her master's.

Nancy Patricia O'Brien *(Education)* is Head of the Education and Social Sciences Librarian at the University of Illinois at Urbana-Champaign. The second edition of her *Education: A Guide to Reference and Information Sources*, appeared in 2000; the *Dictionary of Education* that she is co-authoring with John Collins of Harvard is due out in late 2002. She won the Distinguished Education and Behavioral Science Librarian Award from the Association of College and Research Libraries in 1997.

Joyce L. Ogburn *(Anthropology and Archaeology)* is Associate Director of Libraries for Resources and Collection Management Services at the University of Washington in Seattle. She holds a master's in both anthropology (Indiana) and librarianship (Chapel Hill). She contributed the anthropology chapter to the *Social Sciences: A Cross-Disciplinary Guide to Selected Sources* and is a member of the editorial board of the librarian's professional journal, *Against the Grain*. She continues as compiler of the *Resources for Anthropology & Sociology Librarians & Information Specialists,* a Web page of the Anthropology and Social Sciences Section of the Association of College and Resource Libraries, a group she formerly chaired.

Vivienne Piroli *(Pharmacy, Physical Therapy, and Nutrition)* was formerly the Periodicals Librarian, and is now Reference and Instruction Librarian at Simmons College Libraries, Boston. She holds a master's in librarianship (Simmons) and history (Harvard), in addition to a higher diploma in education from Trinity College of Dublin, Ireland. She was selected as a participant in the Association of College and Research Libraries Immersion 2001 Institute, and she is active in the New England Library Instruction Group.

Carol Ramkey *(Military Studies)* is Director, Marine Corps University Library, Quantico, Virginia. She has a master's in librarianship from Emory University. She has written for the *Community and Junior College Journal* and is currently working on an article about directing a joint military academic and public library.

Carol S. Robinson *(Engineering and Computer Science)* is Collection Manager and Ocean Engineering Librarian, Barker Engineering Library, Massachusetts Institute of Technology, Cambridge. She holds her master's in librarianship from Simmons. In addition to Web-based guides to civil, environmental, mechanical, and ocean engineering, her work has appeared in *Serials Review.*

Lynne Rudasill *(Sociology)* is Assistant Education and Behavioral Science Librarian and Reference Coordinator at the Education and Social Sciences Library at the University of Illinois at Urbana-Champaign. She received her master's in librarianship from the University of Illinois. Past contributions to the literature include a paper in the *New Review of Information Networking*. Recently, she contributed a chapter to *Powerful Learning, Powerful Partnerships*.

Robert E. Schnare *(Military Studies)* is Director of the Naval War College Library in Newport, Rhode Island. Schnare holds a master's in both librarianship (University of Pittsburgh) and history (University of Connecticut). He is the co-author of *Bibliography of Preservation Literature, 1983-1996*, articles and reviews of library and archives administration, and military procurement policies.

J. Christina Smith *(Anthropology and Archaeology)* is Anthropology/Sociology Bibliographer at the Mugar Memorial Library at Boston University. She has a master's in both librarianship (San Jose State University) and archaeology (UCLA). Her reviews have appeared in the former *RQ*, *Library Journal*, and *College & Research Libraries*. She formerly served as Chair of the Anthropology and Social Sciences Section of the Association of College and Research Libraries.

Ann Viera *(Agriculture and Veterinary Medicine)* is Reference Librarian for Veterinary Medicine at the University of Tennessee Agriculture and Veterinary Medicine Library in Knoxville. She received her master's from Berkeley and has appeared in *Science & Technology Libraries* and the former *RQ*.

Julia Whelan *(Pharmacy, Physical Therapy, and Nutrition)* is Head of Reference and an instructor in the Division of Pharmacy Practice at the Massachusetts College of Pharmacy and Allied Health Sciences, Boston. She received her master's in librarianship from Simmons College. Her information consulting on botanicals in complementary medicine for hospital staffs and medical library associations has been funded by the National Institutes of Health. She has reviewed print and Web guides to the literature of pharmacy and pharmacology for *Choice*, and published in the *Journal of Pharmacy Teaching*.

James W. Williams *(Social Work)* is Social Sciences Subject Specialist and an Assistant Education and Social Sciences Librarian at the Education and Social Sciences Library at the University of Illinois at Urbana-Champaign. He has a master's in librarianship from Florida State University. He is a frequent contributor to, as well as one of the editors of, *The Serials Librarian*.

Amanda Wright-Henk *(Graphs of Regions of Publication and Publishing Sectors)* is Assistant to the Science Librarian at the College of the Holy Cross, Worcester, Massachusetts. A recent graduate of Clark University, she is currently attending the Graduate School of Library and Information Science at Simmons College.

Acknowledgments

I owe an enormous collegial debt to all the contributors, without whose freely given manuscripts I would have had no project to lead.

I owe an additional personal debt to the following, without whose decisive help over the last three years I would have never been able to do those manuscripts any kind of editorial justice!

- Ronna Rae Archbold, MEd, EBSCO Publishing, Ipswich, MA
- Diane Gallagher, MLS, Periodicals Dept., Dinand Library, College of the Holy Cross, Worcester, MA
- Maria Gerrol, Raphaelson & Raphaelson, Worcester, MA
- Meredith Goldsmith, MSW, LICSW, Great Book Valley Health Center, Worcester, MA
- James Hogan, DALS, Director of Libraries, College of the Holy Cross, Worcester, MA
- Mary McQuillan, BA, Finard & Co., Burlington, MA
- Laurie S. Raphaelson, JD, Raphaelson & Raphaelson, Worcester, MA
- Thomas W. Syseskey, MLS, Thomas Moore College Library, Manchester, NH
- Michelle Young, BS, RPT, Jewish Health Care Center of Worcester, MA

Introduction to the Journals of the Century Project

Tony Stankus

PURPOSE AND PLAN OF THE BOOK

For more than a century, libraries have had professionals who made it their business to select, acquire, display, and bind academic, professional, and trade journals, and then to assist library customers in their use. Over the last three years (1999-2001), the Journals of the Century Project set out to honor these serials librarians by having a panel of subject expert librarians offer their views of what they each regarded as the most influential journals in their respective fields over the last 100 years. As befitted their considerable acumen, each of the contributing authors was given considerable leeway in his or her approach to this task. The only mandate was that the authors be highly discriminating rather than all-inclusive. Owing to the courtesy of Jim Cole, the editor, these contributions appeared initially in the four issues that made up Volume 39 of *The Serials Librarian*. We reproduce and review them now in six clusters of individual chapters showing the characteristic pattern each cognate group displayed in terms of the geographic origin of their journals and the sectors of the publishing industry responsible for producing them. An index by title with ISSNs for the print versions of the journals follows.

CLUSTERS OF CHAPTERS WITH GRAPHS AND COMMENTARY

- The Helping Professions (encompassing journals of the century in social work, education, psychology, sociology, and library and information science)

- Music, Museums, and Methodists (encompassing journals of the century in music, visual arts, anthropology and archaeology, philosophy, and the American religious experience)
- Business and Law (encompassing journals of the century in business, economics, and law)
- War and Peace (encompassing journals of the century in modern history, political science and international relations, as well as military affairs)
- Physical Sciences and Engineering (encompassing journals of the century in the basic sciences, Part I: mathematics and the physical sciences, as well as engineering and computer science)
- Life, Health and Agriculture (encompassing journals of the century in the basic sciences, Part II: life sciences; medicine and surgery; pharmacy, physical therapy and nutrition; and agriculture and veterinary medicine)

Cluster Graphs by Regions of Journal Publication

While recognizing that individual articles of great genius can come from anywhere on Earth, the authors of *Journals of the Century* articles basically found that for much of the twentieth century, the United States and western Europe seemed much more productive of journals they regarded as particularly influential. We admit that part of this conclusion may well be due to our own American-centric, Anglophone bias. But it is also based on the observed behavior of smart article authors from around the world. Time and again, foreign authors bypassed their own national journals, and voted for best journal by sending their own manuscripts to those journals with a record of being published and widely read in North America, the UK, and in the more economically prosperous parts of continental Europe. This continued even after the rise of newly industrialized states in Asia, and economic growth and more political stability in Latin America.

We segmented the multinational regional graphs along traditional language affinities, old political alliances, or the administrative status that affected individual countries historically.

- For our purposes, the "Former British Empire" included the UK, Ireland, Canada, Australia, New Zealand, South Africa, India, Pakistan, Jamaica, Hong Kong, and Singapore. We of course realize that these are now quite independent countries, that have, in many cases, become publishing powers in their own right. However, a shared heritage of British publishing practices and academic, commercial, and professional association ties, played a substantial role in their rise to international prominence.

- *"Dutch, Nordic, and Germanic"* refers to publications coming from the Netherlands, any of the Scandinavian countries, Germany, Austria, and Switzerland. These are roughly contiguous and linguistically-related countries, even given that Switzerland is multilingual, and all these countries now publish predominantly in English. More important, they share an affinity as home to some of the most important international for-profit publishing houses.
- *"Romance Europe"* consists of France, Belgium (despite its Flemish-speakers), Luxembourg, Italy, Spain, and Portugal.
- The *"Rest of the World"* consists of Eastern and Balkan Europe, and the rest of Asia, Africa, Latin America, and Oceania.

Cluster Graphs by Sector of the Publishing Industry

For our purposes, the publishing industry graphs are divided along four major sectors, as well as two special situations involving those sectors. The major sectors are the not-for-profit research or professional society, the not-for-profit university press, the not-for-profit government, and the for-profit publisher. Most of the journals in our collection are published by one of these groups acting alone. However, combinations between or among differing sectors are not infrequent. In our graphs, we note two types of collaborative efforts: solely not-for-profit and for-profit. Joint efforts between societies, university presses, or governments that do not include a for-profit firm are termed solely not-for-profit. Joint efforts between any societies, university presses, governments, and any for-profit presses, are termed as including for-profit publishers, regardless of the number of not-for-profit entities involved in the collaboration.

Cluster Commentaries

The "Cluster Commentaries" first explain why given chapters were grouped together. They then deal with publishers who seemed particularly notable or dominant in that cluster, whether in solo or joint publishing ventures. The commentaries are authored by the Project Leader. Although the choice of words are his, and the sentiments he expresses are not necessarily those of the individual chapter authors, the statistics underlying his comments are derived entirely from the choice of journals made independently by those subject experts. No new journals or publishers were added at any point by the Project Leader. It should be noted that the commentaries on publishers often credit the overall parent publishing organization, rather than its component imprints or divisions, even though the chapter authors generally identify the individual imprint. The commentaries use some nomenclatural shorthand: Kluwer, rather than Wolters-Kluwer: Elsevier, rather than Reed-Elsevier: Springer, rather than Bertelsman-Springer. Finally, although our authors and title and index checkers used a good deal of diligence in keeping up with title changes, the titles printed here were often subject to change over the last three years. Frankly, even as you, dear reader, turn these pages, one or more of the 1,900+ titles mentioned is likely being modified.

CLUSTER I:
THE HELPING PROFESSIONS

This cluster is held together by five traits common to most of its component disciplines and their literatures, particularly in their daily application, as opposed to their purely academic study. These are:

- Historically, an abundance of women in the ranks, often working for modest salaries, with those in need of education or counseling.
- An optimistic belief that changes for the better in learning or behavior come through understanding personal characteristics, family background, and cultural contexts.
- A willingness to advocate actively for children, adult clients, or community needs with governing authorities.
- A substantial component of practical, clinical, or community experience during the course of training.
- And, while some disciplines were initially developed in Europe, and concern issues of many different cultures and languages, their modern American practitioners published their own field research, policy statements, and case histories largely in English in domestic journals.

Unsurprisingly for a community of altruists, this cluster has the highest percentage of not-for-profit publishing, and second highest reliance on American sources of any in this book. Publications like Columbia's *Teachers College Record* and *Smith College Studies in Social Work,* along with others from the American Psychological, Sociological, and Library Associations, were completely expected.

What requires more explanation was the rise in the latter twentieth century of numerous for-profit titles. This seemingly counter-intuitive development had to do with the sometimes unexpected consequences of success for the helping professions, the sociology of higher education, and matters of gender politics.

One of the first major influxes of women into the mainstream of higher education was caused by the turn of the century abandonment of the state-sponsored two-year Normal School as the standard model for the training, almost exclusively of women, to be primary school teachers in school systems otherwise administered mostly by men. Normal schools were either upgraded into four-year teacher's colleges, (which then attracted more men) or integrated onto land-grant universities, where the numbers of women on campus increased dramatically. This initial upgrade in years of schooling required also increased the number of women both teaching in high schools, and becoming school principals, two areas of public education where men had previously had more numbers, higher pay, and preferential opportunities for further advancement. Most important, the turn of the century switch from the Normal School model supported the rise of some of the earliest and most important general journals of education, sponsored by the upgraded schools of education or by teachers associations, and paid for by subscriptions from what became an almost entirely college-degree-holding workforce by 1920.

Enrollments in the other helping professions were prompted by immigration-related problems, particularly in the cities. Ironically private colleges for often wealthy, but socially conscious women, played a significant role, often through private charities affiliated with women's clubs or religious organizations. The demand for social services greatly increased with economic problems in the 1930s, and the Roosevelt era saw government agencies employing many members of the helping professions. The baby boom of the 1950s not only exacerbated the needs for teachers and librarians, but also for what used to be called guidance counselors, a profession that greatly expanded into what has since become school psychology. Vast increases in federal funding in the Johnson administration for training in education and social services saw existing programs grow even larger, and the start of many new programs. A great many more faculty (then mostly holding only master's degrees) were hired to staff them, increasing their proportional representation on university campuses. But this success only intensified the suspicions of other academic departments or professional schools that these helping professions departments were "easy" programs, and too reliant on "feel-good" field work that was not critically evaluated. Critics suggested that helping professions programs did not measure up in terms of scholarly rigor. (It would be frankly naïve to suspect that gender had nothing to do with those negative attitudes.)

Partly as a consequence, academic deans did two things that put pressure on existing journals, and furthered the rise of co-publishing with for-profits and for-profit specialty publications.

- They extended the curriculum to incorporate master's degrees for practitioners, as the preferred path for anyone with hopes of professional advancement. This, of course, put strong pressure on the faculties in schools of education and the helping professions to earn doctorates for hiring, promotion, and tenure. That required much more reading of higher level materials for graduate students (namely journal articles), and more publishing outlets for the doctoral-level faculty (more pages in existing journals, or more new journals).
- Second, many academic administrators pushed for more " scholarly" journals, by which they really meant more quantitative, or science-like journals. Consequently, many of the existing professional society journals, which formerly had a balance between technical and practical papers, became increasingly experimental, statistical, and mathematical. This was particularly the case in academic psychology, which always had more of an experimental science tradition, but it also affected sociology. Today a great many psychology professors and sociologists identify at least as much with the scientists or econometricians on campus, as with school teachers, or with social service providers in their local community.

This still left many readers and contributors, particularly practitioners and those professors whose primary job was the supervision of field experiences, crowded out of some of their traditional journals. This opened the door for for-profit presses to set up co-publishing arrangements with overburdened societies, who did not wish to alienate the practitioners entirely. This was particularly the forte of Sage Publications. Yet another firm, The Haworth Press (admittedly the publisher of this book), developed an almost uncanny sense of when a functional specialty or special interest group was growing large enough to demand that the librarians who served them get new Haworth journals tailored to their special interests. Perhaps most cleverly of all, Haworth first founded *The Serials Librarian,* the professional journal for the very librarians who would order those new journals!

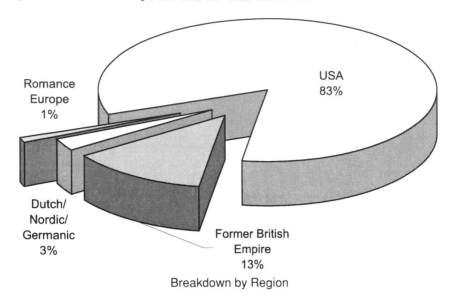

Breakdown by Region

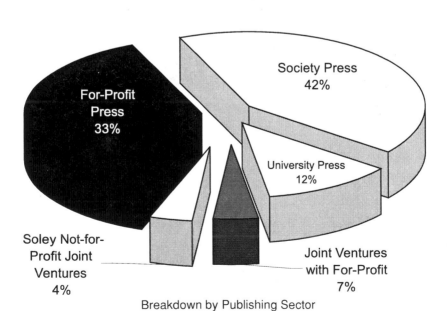

Breakdown by Publishing Sector

Chapter 1

Journals of the Century in Social Work

James W. Williams

Social work is an applied discipline within the social sciences. During the Twentieth Century, journals became crucial for the provision of current awareness, the presentation of new ideas, the exploration of topics in a timely manner, and the building of a disciplinary knowledge base. Practitioners, educators, and students became ever more dependent on the journal literature for information and knowledge as the century passed. To identify the most important social work journals of the Twentieth Century was a challenge.

CRITERIA AND METHODOLOGY OF STUDY

The criteria used to determine the most important social work journals of the Twentieth Century were: (1) longevity of publication (with those journals which underwent title changes, but were, nonetheless, in continuous publication, counted as a single bibliographic entity); (2) affiliation with a professional association or an academic institution, which lends prominence and is suggestive of a certain level of quality; (3) use in studies concerned with the journal literature of social work, reasoning that social work educators and practitioners who study the content of the literature, publication trends, publication by faculty in schools of social work accredited by the Council on Social Work Education, and other topics would consult the most important journals in their field; (4) refereed publication; and (5) designation as a core journal by the National Association of Social Workers' *Social Work Abstracts,* the premier indexing source for social work journals in the United States.

The catalog of the University of Illinois Library at Urbana-Champaign, the *Dictionary Catalog of the Whitney M. Young, Jr. Memorial Library of Social Work, Columbia University,*[1] *An Author's Guide to Social Work Jour-*

This chapter originally appeared in *The Serials Librarian* 39(3): 69-77, 2001.

nals,[2] and the list of journals indexed by *Social Work Abstracts*[3] (from its inception in 1965 to 1999) were consulted to identify potential candidates for inclusion, in addition to those titles with which the author was familiar. Compared to many of the social science disciplines, such as education, psychology, political science, and sociology, the literature of social work is relatively small. Both monograph and serial publications increased in number during the second half of the century, however, especially from around 1970 onward. Else (1978)[4] and Mendelsohn (1982)[5] discussed the proliferation of new social work journals during the 1970s. While more new journals appeared throughout the 1980s and 1990s, the rate of increase was less than during the 1970s.

The *SSCI Journal Citation Reports* were examined and some data from the reports were used.[6] Caution was exercised, however, because *JCR* is not comprehensive. Lindsay and Kirk (1992)[7] reported that only 18 of the 35 serials designated as core journals by *Social Work Abstracts* were included as SSCI source publications, while Green, Baskind, and Conklin (1995) stated, "SSCI reviews less than half of all available social work journals."[8]

A literature review identified seven social work journals which have been used extensively to study various topics of disciplinary interest. Between 1965 and 1999, 15 articles reported on studies which included *Families in Society, Social Service Review,* and *Social Work,* with the authors invariably stating that these titles were chosen for study because they were the major social work journals.[9-23] Among the 15 studies, ten also included *Child Welfare,* eight the *Journal of Social Work Education,* seven the *Journal of Social Service Research,* and six *Social Work Research.* Another three studies confirmed the general preeminence of these journals in social work.

Cnaan, Caputo, and Shmuely (1994)[24] developed a prestige rating for 97 journals from social work and such cognate disciplines as psychology, sociology, law, and public administration, based on a survey of 421 senior faculty at CSWE-accredited graduate schools of social work. Respondents rated their familiarity with and perceived quality of the titles. A formula was devised to combine the separate measures and thereby establish a prestige rating.

The findings indicate that the most prestigious journals in social work are:

> *Social Service Review, Social Work,* and *American Journal of Orthopsychiatry.* . . . The next most prestigious journals . . . are *Social Casework* (now *Families in Society*) and *Social Work Research and Abstracts.*[25]

Green (1995)[26] studied the publications of faculty members in 45 schools or departments of social work that included a doctoral program. The study identified 1,349 full-length articles which appeared in 21 social work and 193 non-social work journals from 1990 through September 1993. Just over one-third (34.8 percent) of the total output was published in seven social work journals: *Social Work, Families in Society, Administration in Social Work, Social Service Review, Research on Social Work Practice,* the *Journal of Social Service Research,* and the *Journal of Social Work Education.*

Baker (1992)[27] used SSCI to study the citation interrelationships of 20 social work journals and derived five clusters of core journals. He concluded the "first and most prominent cluster" to be comprised of *Social Work Research and Abstracts* (now *Social Work Research*), *Social Work, Social Service Review, Social Casework,* and the *Journal of Social Work Education.* Baker noted that SSCI did not include the *Journal of Social Service Research,* an absence which also drew comment from Lindsay and Kirk (1992).[28]

If *Child Welfare,* a specialty journal within the social work discipline, is excluded and the *Journal of Social Service Research* is added, Baker's list matches the titles identified as the most prominent by the literature review. These six journals are, therefore, concluded to have a first-tier importance among social work journals of the century. All six are refereed publications, and all are designated core journals for indexing by *Social Work Abstracts.*

JOURNALS OF FIRST-TIER IMPORTANCE

Published bimonthly by Families International, Inc., in association with the Alliance for Children and Families, *Families in Society: The Journal of Contemporary Human Services* is the oldest social work journal published in the United States. Founded in 1920, it was called *The Family* until 1946, *Journal of Social Casework* from 1946 through 1949, and *Social Casework: The Journal of Contemporary Social Work* from 1950 through 1989. Based on a citation study for the 1980s, Lindsay and Kirk (1992) stated, "This journal makes an important contribution in the development of social work, although the editors are required to balance popular presentations of interesting topics and the less entertaining task of building a scientifically tested knowledge base."[29] The title ranked fourth in prestige in the Cnaan survey. Green found it to be the second largest journal publication source for doctoral social work faculty members, with 75 articles featured between 1990 and 1993.

The *Social Service Review* is edited by the School of Social Service Administration at the University of Chicago and is published by the University of Chicago Press. Founded in 1927, the quarterly journal ranked first in prestige in the Cnaan survey. With 62 articles for the period 1990-1993, it placed at fourth as the publication source for doctoral faculty members.

Social Work: Journal of the National Association of Social Workers is issued bimonthly by the National Association of Social Workers, the major U.S. professional organization for social work practitioners. Founded in 1920, the journal was published under the title *Compass* until 1948 and as the *Social Work Journal* from 1949 to 1955. The present title was assumed when NASW changed its name from the *American Association of Social Workers* to its present title. Bush (1997)[30] gave circulation as 155,000, making this by far the most widely distributed social work journal in the United States. The title ranked second in prestige in the Cnaan survey. Green found it to be the publisher of the most articles from doctoral faculty members, with 121 featured between 1990 to 1993.

The *Journal of Social Work Education* is published three times yearly by the Council on Social Work Education, the major U.S. professional association for social work educators. The journal began publication in 1965 and, until 1984, was called the *Journal of Education for Social Work*. The title ranked sixth in Cnaan's prestige survey and, with 45 articles, was the seventh most popular source for journal publications by social work doctoral faculty.

The final two first-tier journals are comparatively late entrants, with both beginning publication in 1977. Both journals also have a research focus, a reflection of the growing importance of an empirically developed knowledge base to the discipline. The quarterly *Social Work Research* is another publication of the National Association of Social Workers and, until 1994, was issued as a section of *Social Work Research and Abstracts*. The Cnaan survey ranked it fifth in prestige. With 38 articles from doctoral faculty members during the period 1990-1993, it placed ninth as a publication source. The quarterly *Journal of Social Service Research* is a commercial publication from The Haworth Press, Inc. The Cnaan survey ranked it eighth in prestige. With 47 articles, it placed sixth as a source for doctoral faculty publications in the Green study.

JOURNALS OF SECOND-TIER IMPORTANCE FOR DOMESTIC PERSPECTIVE

Another five U.S.-based journals qualify for second-tier importance. Four are long-running publications, being founded between 1922 and 1932, while the fifth is one of the several new journals established in the 1970s.

The *American Journal of Orthopsychiatry* began publication in 1930 and is issued quarterly by the American Orthopsychiatric Association. Although Cnaan displayed a ready acceptance of the journal in the statement quoted above, the title is not generally regarded as a social work journal and is not so classified by SSCI. The journal is, nonetheless, very important to social work. It has been continuously indexed by *Social Work Abstracts* since *SWA*'s establishment in 1965 and has consistently been designated a core journal for indexing since this practice was begun in 1988. The Cnaan prestige study ranked it third. The writer, therefore, decided to accept it as one of the most important journals of the century. The Green study identified it as one of only nine non-social work journals in which doctoral faculty members had published more than ten articles during the period 1990-1993.

Child Welfare: Journal of the Child Welfare League of America is published bimonthly by the league. Founded in 1922 and issued under the title *Bulletin* until 1948, this specialty serial was ranked eleventh in prestige by Cnaan and also placed at eleventh as a source for doctoral faculty members publications in the Green study. *An Author's Guide to Social Work Journals* gave circulation as an impressive 15,000.[31]

Policy & Practice of Public Human Services: The Journal of the American Public Human Services Association is issued quarterly. Founded in 1932 as *Public Welfare News*, it was published from 1943 until 1998 as *Public Welfare* by the association under its earlier name: American Public Welfare Association. Although the journal is not refereed and requests that articles be written in a popular rather than a scholarly style, it was indexed as a core journal by Social Work Abstracts through 1995. At eighteenth spot in the Cnaan prestige survey, it placed in the top one-fifth. Lindsay and Kirk (1992) commented:

> *Public Welfare* has bridged the competing demands of providing material that would be useful to its broad membership group and developing a cumulative knowledge base. . . . *Public Welfare* remains an important forum for the analysis and discussion of issues in public social work.[32]

The disappearance of this title from *Social Work Abstracts* after 1995 is puzzling.

Smith College Studies in Social Work was founded in 1930 and is issued by the Smith College School for Social Work in three numbers yearly. The absence of this title from the Cnaan prestige study was surprising. It continues to be a core journal in Social Work Abstracts and, with 12 articles from doctoral social work faculty members during the years 1990-1993, it placed at seventeenth as a publication source. In their study of impact factors during the 1980s, Lindsay and Kirk (1992) stated, "It is unfortunate that a journal with such history has had virtually no measurable impact on knowledge development."[33] Despite this conclusion, *An Author's Guide to Social Work Journals* gave the acceptance rate as approximately 20 percent.[34]

The fifth and final U.S. publication of second-tier importance is much younger than the other titles in this group. *Administration in Social Work* was founded in 1977 and is issued quarterly by The Haworth Press, Inc. Ranked impressively at ninth in the Cnaan prestige study, the title was the third most frequent publication source for doctoral faculty during 1990-1993, with 66 articles featured.

JOURNALS OF SECOND-TIER IMPORTANCE FOR INTERNATIONAL PERSPECTIVE

Another five English language journals provide an important non-U.S. perspective and, therefore, also qualify for second-tier importance. The quarterly *Australian Social Work: The Journal of the Australian Association of Social Workers* was founded in 1947 and called *Australian Journal of Social Work* until 1971. *The Indian Journal of Social Work* was founded in 1940 and is issued quarterly by the Tata Institute of Social Sciences in Deonar, Mumbia, India. This journal features many thematic issues. *Social Worker,* the official journal of the Canadian Association of Social Workers, was begun in 1932. This quarterly publication was bilingual for many years. In 1995, a separate French language edition began to be issued under the title *Travailleur social. International Social Work,* a U.S.-based journal from Sage Publications, was founded in 1958 and is issued quarterly as an official journal of the International Association of Schools of Social Work, the International Council on Social Welfare, and the International Federation of Social Workers.

With the exception of *The Indian Journal of Social Work*, these titles are core journals in *Social Work Abstracts. The Indian Journal of Social Work* is also indexed in *SWA,* but not as a core journal. The general absence of the four titles from studies of social work literature suggest that U.S.-based social work research is quite insular in nature. Only *International Social Work* was represented in the Cnaan prestige study. In forty-sixth place for prestige, it was near the low end of the upper half. Only *The Indian Journal of Social Work* was among the twenty-one titles identified in the Green study of doctoral publishing, and it had featured just a single article from 1990-1993.

The fifth journal has fared somewhat better with its American audience. *The British Journal of Social Work* was formed in 1971 by the merger of the *British Journal of Psychiatric Social Work* (issued 1947-1970 by the Association of Psychiatric Social Workers) and *Social Work* (issued 1939-1970 by the Council of the Charity Organisation Society). Published bimonthly by the British Association of Social Workers, the journal ranked twenty-eighth in the Cnaan prestige survey, toward the low end of the upper one-third. In the review of impact factors through the 1980s, Lindsay and Kirk (1992) found, "Since 1981, the *Journal* has improved its impact score and . . . emerges as an important social work journal."[35] Impact scores varied between 1991 and 1998, but came within the top ten for four of the years. The journal was designated a core journal by *Social Work Abstracts* for many years. During the course of this study, however, the writer found no issues had been indexed by *SWA* after those for 1993.

NEWER SOCIAL WORK JOURNALS

The expansion of social work literature was mentioned earlier. In addition to the four journals discussed above which were founded during the 1970s, another 14 social work serials which began publication during the decade were readily identified. These include the *Clinical Social Work Journal,* which began publication in 1973; *Human Services in the Rural Environment,* the *School Social Work Journal,* and *Health & Social Work* (a publication of the National Association of Social Workers) which started in 1976; and *Social Work in Education* (another NASW publication), the *Journal of Gerontological Social Work,* and *Social Work with Groups,* which first appeared in 1978.

New social work journals continue to be established, but the pace appears to have slowed. From the list of titles indexed by *Social Work Abstracts,* 11 journals were identified which had begun publication in the 1980s and only six which started during the 1990s. New serials in the 1980s included *Child & Adolescent Social Work,* which was first published in 1984, and *Affilia: Journal of Women and Social Work,* which first appeared in 1986. *Research on Social Work Practice,* a quarterly journal from Sage Publications, debuted in 1991. With 53 articles from doctoral faculty in the Green study, this then very new journal ranked fifth as a publication source.

As the above titles would indicate, many of the newer journals are directed to special areas of practice. These publications provide a needed forum for a selective audience of practitioners and educators. They also contribute importantly to the cumulative knowledge base of social work. While not of the prominence to qualify as journals of the century, social work literature is enriched by their presence. The aforementioned and other journals which first appeared in the latter decades of the Twentieth Century are candidates for being among the most important journals of the Twenty-First Century.

CONCLUSION

A few good quality journals served the profession of social work well for much of the Twentieth Century. These journals have endured because they fulfilled and continue to fulfill the needs of practitioners and educators. Several of the long-running journals underwent one or more title changes, reflecting a decision by editors and/or publishers to meet changing demands and to improve content. As the discipline became more specialized, new journals began to appear to accommodate the diversity among practitioners and educators.

NOTES

1. *Dictionary Catalog of the Whitney M. Young Jr. Memorial Library of Social Work*, Columbia University, New York. Boston, Mass.: G.K. Hall & Co., 1980. 10 volumes.

2. *An Author's Guide to Social Work Journals*. 4th edition. Washington, D.C.: National Association of Social Workers, 1997.

3. *Social Work Abstracts*. Washington, D.C.: National Association of Social Workers. 1(1965)-

4. John F. Else, "Social Work Journals: Purposes and Trends," *Social Work* 23 (4): 267-273, 1978.

5. Henry N. Mendelsohn, "Journal in Social Welfare: A Review," *Serials Review* 8 (1): 9-13, 1982.

6. *JCR: Journal Citation Reports: A Bibliometric Analysis of Social Science Journals in the ISI Database*. Philadelphia, Pa.: Institute for Scientific Information.

7. Duncan Lindsay and Stuart A. Kirk, "The Role of Social Work Journals in the Development of a Knowledge Base for the Profession," *Social Service Review* 66 (2): 303, 1992.

8. Robert R. Green, Frank R. Baskind, and Barbara Conklin, "The 1990s Publication Productivity of Schools of Social Work with Doctoral Programs: The Times, Are They A-Changin'?," *Journal of Social Work Education* 31 (3): 391, 1995.

9. Merlin Taber and Iris Shapiro, "Social Work and Its Knowledge Base: A Content Analysis of the Periodical Literature," *Social Work* 10 (4): 100-106, 1965.

10. Roslyn Weinberger and Tony Tripodi, "Trends in Types of Research Reported in Selected Social Work Journals, 1956-65," *Social Service Review* 3 (4): 439-447, 1969.

11. Michael W. Howe and John R. Schuerman, "Trends in the Social Work Literature: 1957-72," *Social Service Review* 48 (2): 279-285, 1974.

12. Srinika Jayaratne, "Analysis of Selected Social Work Journals and Productivity Rankings Among Schools of Social Work," *Journal of Education for Social Work* 15 (3): 72-80, 1979.

13. Paula Allen-Meares and Bruce A. Lane, "Do Educators and Practitioners Have Differing Views of School Social Work?," *Social Work in Education* 5 (3): 141-155, 1983.

14. Richard M. Grinnell, Jr., "Quantitative Articles in Social Work Journals: A Research Note," *Arete* 8 (1): 33-38, 1983.

15. Richard M. Grinnell and Martha L. Royer, "Authors of Articles in Social Work Journals," *Journal of Social Service Research* 6 (3/4): 147-154, 1983.

16. John S. Wodarski and Michael Brenner, "Variables Influencing Publication in the Field of Social Work," *Journal of Sociology & Social Welfare* 10 (1): 149-166, 1983.

17. Tony Tripodi, "Trends in Research Publication: A Study of Social Work Journals from 1956 to 1980," *Social Work* 29 (4): 353-359, 1984.

18. Allen Rubin and Patricia G. Conway, "Standards for Determining the Magnitude of Relationships in Social Work Research," *Social Work Research and Abstracts* 21 (1): 34-39, 1985.

19. Bruce A. Thyer and Kia J. Bentley, "Academic Affiliations of Social Work Authors: A Citation Analysis of Six Major Journals," *Journal of Social Work Education* 22 (1): 67-73, 1986.

20. Grafton H. Hull and H. Wayne Johnson, "Publication Rates of Undergraduate Social Work Programs in Selected Journals," *Journal of Social Work Education* 30 (1): 54-62, 1994.

21. Bruce A. Thyer, Kim E. Boynton, Leslie Bennis, and David L. Levine, "Academic Affiliations of Social Work Journal Article Authors: A Publication Productivity Analysis from 1984-1988," *Journal of Social Service Research* 18 (3/4), 1994.

22. Irene R. Bush, Irwin Epstein, and Anthony Sainz, "The Use of Social Science Sources in Social Work Practice Journals: An Application of Citation Analysis," *Social Work Research* 21 (1): 45-56, 1997.

23. Sheldon R. Gelman and Margaret Gibelman, "A Quest for Citations? An Analysis of and Commentary on the Trend Toward Multiple Authorship," *Journal of Social Work Education* 35 (2) 203-213, 1999.

24. Ram A. Cnaan, Richard K. Caputo, and Yochi Shmuely, "Senior Faculty Perceptions of Social Work Journals," *Journal of Social Work Education* 30 (2): 185-199, 1994.

25. Ibid., p. 195.

26. Green, Baskind, and Conklin, "The 1990s Publication Productivity of Schools of Social Work with Doctoral Programs," pp. 388-401.

27. Donald R. Baker, "A Structural Analysis of the Social Work Journal Network: 1986-1987," *Journal of Social Service Research* 15 (3/4): 153-169.

28. Lindsay and Kirk, "The Role of Social Work Journals in the Development of a Knowledge Base for the Profession," p. 305.

29. Ibid., p. 301.

30. Bush, Epstein, and Sainz, "The Use of Social Science Sources in Social Work Practice Journals," p. 47.

31. *An Author's Guide to Social Work Journals*, p. 60.

32. Lindsay and Kirk, "The Role of Social Work Journals in the Development of a Knowledge Base for the Profession," p. 301.

33. Ibid.

34. *An Author's Guide to Social Work Journals*, p. 331.

35. Lindsay and Kirk, "The Role of Social Work Journals in the Development of a Knowledge Base for the Profession," p. 300.

Chapter 2

Journals of the Century in Education

Nancy Patricia O'Brien

INTRODUCTION

Education is a discipline with a lengthy history of journal publishing. Since education has an impact on nearly every area of life, the list of education journals exceeds well over 1,000 titles. Selecting a few that represent the key journals of the twentieth century was no simple task. Although a number of factors were considered, the final ones used were longevity, endurance, and being central to the study or practice of teaching and learning. Being indexed in a number of indexing sources was also given consideration as a reflection of importance. A number of studies have been published that discuss education journals, but generally were given limited consideration since so many of them address very targeted subdisciplines (Shulman and Margalit on special education;[1] Keister's review of the leading journals in higher education,[2] for example). John C. Smart's findings on the correlation between quality and citation rates of education journals suggests that the relationship is weaker in education than it is in other disciplines.[3] Accordingly, emphasis was placed on those journals demonstrating longevity and significance rather than high citation rates. Nonetheless, an indication of the impact factor recorded by ISI's *Journal Citation Reports (JCR)* is listed in parentheses after those titles that had a rating. Ninety-nine journals within education and educational research were listed within *JCR;* thirty-seven journals were listed under the category of "psychology, educational"; and, twenty journals were listed separately for special education in *JCR.* While there are a number of exceptional journals that could easily be included in the following list, those that finally were chosen epitomize journals making a lasting contribution over several decades. The following seven categories contain thirty-four journals of major importance to the field of education. Of the many categories and topics that are not included in this list, that lack

This chapter originally appeared in *The Serials Librarian* 39(3): 95-102, 2001.

does not indicate an absence of important journals, but rather that the available journals do not meet the criteria above.

GENERAL EDUCATION

In general education, the *American Journal of Education* (U.S., 1893) has demonstrated over a century of research, theory, and implementation of educational practices in the school setting. Formerly entitled *School and College, School Review,* and *University of Chicago School Review,* this journal is included in the key education indexes and is published by the University of Chicago Press. It has a high impact factor (IF 14) in the *Journal Citation Reports.* Another enduring journal that claims to be the oldest continuously published education journal in the United States, *Education* (U.S., 1880), is currently published by Project Innovation. It focuses on all levels of education, with a particular emphasis on innovative practices and teaching. Essays as well as research articles appear in this long-lived publication. The *Harvard Educational Review* (U.S., 1931) is a frequently cited source (IF 7) and is published by the Harvard Graduate School of Education. It is one of the best known journals in the field and addresses educational issues at all levels of education. Formerly entitled *Harvard Teachers Record,* this journal is widely indexed. The *Peabody Journal of Education* (U.S., 1923) is another journal associated with a reputable school of education, in this instance, the Peabody College of Education at Vanderbilt University. Policy issues and trends in education are presented in each of the thematically focused issues published by Lawrence Erlbaum. With its nearly eighty year history, this journal has affected the practice of teaching and the training of teacher educators. Founded in 1900, *Teachers College Record* (U.S., 1900) is published by Teachers College, Columbia University. Widely indexed, this journal has a reasonably high impact factor (IF 39) and provides a forum for research, analysis and commentary in all areas of education. Like the *Harvard Educational Review,* this journal provides regular and thoughtfully crafted book reviews. Since almost the beginning of the twentieth century, *Phi Delta Kappan* (U.S., 1915) has monitored the issues, policies, and trends in education. With its well known features on legislation and federal actions that affect education, this journal mirrors the current areas of concern within education. Published by Phi Delta Kappa International, *PDK* is a popular source of education information and is regularly cited (IF 30). *Sociology of Education* (U.S., 1927) is published by the American Sociological Association. Cited in several multidisciplinary indexes, it has a high impact factor (IF 6) and contains articles related to educational policy. The focus is on social development and the study of the sociology of education, particularly in the ways that individuals, institutions, and the education process impact one another. This journal was previously published by the American Viewpoint Society from 1927 to 1963 as the *Journal of Educational Sociology: A Magazine of Theory and Practice.*

HIGHER AND ADULT EDUCATION

Adult Education Quarterly: A Journal of Research and Theory in Adult Education (U.S., 1950) began its career midway through the twentieth century as Adult Education. Published by the American Association for Adult and Continuing Education, this quarterly publication provides articles on research and theory in adult and continuing education. Its existence reinforces the importance of lifelong learning within society. *Academe: Bulletin of the American Association of University Professors* (U.S., 1915) has been published by the American Association of University Professors since the early years of the twentieth century and offers reports and articles on current issues within higher education. Also featured are regular analyses on pertinent legislation and an annual report on salaries and the status of the profession. While its impact factor (IF 76) is at the lower end, this journal is frequently consulted and provides a barometer of key topics in higher education. It was previously published as the *AAUP Bulletin* from 1915 to 1978. Published since 1966, the *Chronicle of Higher Education* (U.S., 1966) provides a weekly review of the major events in higher education. Critical to the higher education practitioner, this newspaper offers information about students, faculty, research, legislation, finances, athletics, technology, and more. Published by the Chronicle of Higher Education, this newspaper is the main source for keeping abreast of current events in higher education. The Ohio State University Press publishes the *Journal of Higher Education* (U.S., 1930), a key journal for providing scholarly research and practice papers related to postsecondary education. Topics addressed range from athletics to governance and are as likely to address technical issues as policy matters. A more recent entrant into the arena of higher education journals is the *Review of Higher Education* (U.S., 1977). Issued during its first year as *Higher Education Review,* the journal is currently published by the Johns Hopkins University Press on behalf of the Association for the Study of Higher Education (ASHE). This title is a frequently cited source (IF 12). Indexed in several key sources, the *Review* provides a respected forum for essays, articles and reviews.

COMPARATIVE AND MULTICULTURAL EDUCATION

The official journal of the Comparative and International Education Society, *Comparative Education Review* (U.S., 1957), is published by the University of Chicago Press. Each year a special issue is published in addition to the regular focus on comparative, international, and multicultural education concerns. With a history of frequently cited articles (IF 36) and quality publishing, this journal filled an early niche in the literature and continues to do so. Another multicultural journal that appeared fairly early in the twentieth century is the *Journal of Negro Education* (U.S., 1932). The cover subtitle is "Review of Issues Incident to the Education of Black People." Appropriately published by the Howard University School of Education and indexed in key sources, this journal addresses the education of African Americans in all types of settings and at all levels of education. Despite falling into the lower end of the impact factor ratings (IF 95), this journal fills a unique place in educational publishing. *Language Learning: A Journal of Research in Language Studies* (U.S., 1948) falls into the upper quartile of the impact factor ratings (IF 25), is indexed widely, and has been published for over fifty years. Currently published at the University of Michigan by Blackwell Publishers, this journal presents research articles from multidisciplinary perspectives on bilingualism, literacy, second language acquisition, and language learning and acquisition. Another journal that focuses on second language acquisition, *TESOL Quarterly* (U.S., 1967), is published by the Teachers of English to Speakers of Other Languages (TESOL). Although it has a relatively brief history within the twentieth century, with only thirty years of publishing, it provides a forum for "teachers of English to speakers of other languages and of standard English as a second dialect." Directed to a particular aspect of education, this journal includes research and practice articles and reports of projects related to teaching, communication, language rights, and respecting language diversity within the context of second or other language instruction. It is a widely indexed journal.

CURRICULUM, INSTRUCTION, AND TECHNOLOGY

Technology within education is too pervasive of an area to ignore, but only a few journals have the longevity to be accorded recognition within the context of this article. Published by the Association for Educational Communications and Technology (AECT), *Educational Technology Research and Development* (U.S., 1953) has a history of addressing the current technological questions within education. Its former titles reflect the journal's practice of adapting to mirror the changes in the discipline: *AV Communica-*

tion Review; Educational Communication and Technology; and *Journal of Instructional Development.* Thematic issues, research reports and articles, and development reports are included, so that the contents address the needs of the practitioner or administrator dealing with technological change. Indexed in a few of the key sources, this journal has a moderately high impact rating (IF 73). A University of Chicago Press title that is known for its quality is the *Elementary School Journal* (U.S., 1900). Published since the very beginning of the twentieth century, this title focuses on educational theory and research as practiced and implemented in the elementary and middle school classroom. Widely indexed and highly cited (IF 17), this journal has had a major influence on primary schooling within the U.S. Its earlier titles include *Course of Study, Elementary School Teacher and Course of Study,* and *Elementary School Teacher.* Of those journals focusing on secondary education, *English Journal* (U.S., 1912) has greatly affected the teaching and learning of language and literature. Published by the National Council of Teachers of English (NCTE), this journal incorporates association news with research articles, essays, book reviews, and thematic issues. It is indexed in several sources, and provides a legacy of quality literary instruction at the secondary level. Professional associations provide several key journals within education, such as the *Journal of Adolescent & Adult Literacy* (U.S., 1957). Published by the International Reading Association, this journal was formerly the *Journal of Developmental Reading* and the *Journal of Reading.* Not only does this journal focus on adolescent and adult literacy within the school, its research, theory, and practice articles move beyond that particular setting. As society attempts to address the issue of literacy, it is not surprising to find that this journal has a reasonably high impact rating (IF 51). The elementary level counterpart to the two titles above is published by the National Council of Teachers of English. Previously published as *Elementary English* and *Elementary English Review* and now entitled *Language Arts* (U.S., 1924), the focus of this publication is on preschool through middle grade school children and their language arts learning. Research in these areas is interspersed with association news, making this a useful journal for the language arts instructor. Since literacy is such a major component of education, it is not surprising that another publication of the International Reading Association is also widely indexed and has a fairly high impact rating (IF 49). *Reading Teacher* (U.S., 1948) is a staple within the reading instructor's classroom tools. With a half century of publishing, this journal provides research, theory, and practice articles related to reading and literacy instruction. Regular features, such as reviews of children's books, make this a popular journal for the busy teacher. During its early years (1948-1951), this journal was published as *Bulletin of the International Council for the Improvement of Reading Instruction.* Another content area, science, is covered in a variety of practical and theoretical journals. One that has over eighty years of publishing history is *Science Education* (U.S., 1916). Research articles that are international in scope address science instruction and learning at all levels of education. Given its longevity, comprehensiveness, and high impact rating (IF 20), this journal, published by Wiley, is a significant contributor to the education literature of the twentieth century. Its earlier titles include *General Science Quarterly* and *Summary of Research in Science Education*.

EDUCATIONAL HISTORY AND PHILOSOPHY

In the area of educational history and philosophy, there are several journals that offer background and research articles in the foundations of education. Two of these demonstrate significant contributions and longevity. *Educational Theory* (U.S., 1951) is published by the University of Illinois on behalf of several notable societies, including the John Dewey Society, Philosophy of Education Society, and regional and state philosophy of education and history of education societies. For nearly half a century, this journal has provided a forum for essay and research articles on the historical, cultural, and philosophical foundations of education. *Paedagogica Historica: International Journal of the History of Education* (Belgium, 1961) is published by the Center for the Study of the History of Education at the University of Ghent. Geared toward the serious researcher of educational history, this journal provides a source for information on international research. In addition to research articles, also included are announcements of upcoming conferences, conference reports, and tables of contents from relevant journals. Articles are written in German, English, and French.

EDUCATIONAL PSYCHOLOGY, RESEARCH, AND MEASUREMENT

The American Educational Research Association (AERA) publishes several high quality journals, many of which have high impact ratings. One of these is the *American Educational Research Journal* (U.S., 1964), with a nearly forty year record of publishing original studies of empirical and theoretical research. Well indexed, and with a high impact rating (IF 3), this journal addresses educational research at all levels of education and is nearly ubiquitous in its availability in academic libraries. Even more highly rated (IF 2) is the AERA published journal, *Review of Educational Research* (U.S., 1931). Having a longer publishing record than its sister title above,

RER provides reviews and interpretations of the educational research literature. Widely indexed in a number of multidisciplinary sources, this journal has provided critical, quality articles about the field of education for nearly seven decades. The quarterly lacks advertisements and is directed to the serious researcher of not only the twentieth century but of the twenty-first century. Two journals published by Heldref Publications (the educational publishing division of the Helen Dwight Reid Education Foundation) merit inclusion due to their longevity, impact ratings, and their availability in many indexing and abstracting sources. These are the *Journal of Educational Research* (U.S., 1920) and the *Journal of Experimental Education* (U.S., 1932). The *Journal of Educational Research* addresses issues in elementary and secondary education through research articles, ethnographic studies, replicative projects, and reviews of methodologies. Its impact rating (IF 52) and its presence in several indexes confirm that it has been a key journal for most of the twentieth century. The *Journal of Experimental Education* also has a high impact rating (IF 32) and a publishing history spanning nearly three-quarters of a century. This journal focuses on the improvement of educational practice, at all levels and in many different types of settings. Both qualitative and quantitative research articles are included in this publication that addresses innovative methodologies in educational practice. Listed in the "psychology, educational" section of the *Journal Citation Reports* (IF 5), the *Journal of Educational Psychology* (U.S., 1910), published by the American Psychological Association, has been a long-standing contributor to the study of educational psychology in this country. Every educational level is included in research articles that address cognition, motivation, special needs, learning styles, and other educational psychology topics in this widely indexed journal. A journal that lacks an impact factor rating but has a nearly sixty year history of addressing assessment and measurement is *Educational and Psychological Measurement* (U.S., 1941). Published by Sage and indexed in many sources, this scholarly journal addresses the perennial issues surrounding the use of tests. Taking an early look at the controversies surrounding tests, articles continue to address test development and use, and provide descriptions of test programs, validity studies, and reviews.

SPECIAL EDUCATION

The needs of special populations are of broad concern. This is reflected even in the designation of education resources within the *Journal Citation Reports,* where the field of education is divided into two primary areas: education and educational research, and special education. In the latter area, twenty highly cited journals are listed. The most frequently cited is the *American Journal on Mental Retardation* (U.S., 1876), which also has the highest impact factor. Published by the American Association on Mental Retardation, and formerly entitled *American Journal of Mental Deficiency,* this journal is extensively indexed by medical, psychological, educational, and related indexing services. Since its founding in the last quarter of the nineteenth century, it has addressed the causes, treatment, and prevention of mental retardation. At one time, this journal was also entitled *Journal of Psycho-Asthenics* (1896-1918). *Exceptional Children* (U.S., 1934) is published by the highly respected Council for Exceptional Children. It has the second highest impact factor (IF 2) for citations within special education. Indexed in several sources, this journal publishes research related to the development and education of exceptional children from infancy through adolescence. The focus includes both giftedness and disabilities. This is a quality journal for research on an exceptional population. Its former titles include *Council Review* and *Journal of Exceptional Children*. *Gifted Child Quarterly* (U.S., 1957) has a respectably high impact factor (IF 4) and offers research on gifted and talented children. Published by the National Association for Gifted Children, the journal focuses on the identification, education and nurturing of giftedness. The focus on giftedness is a more recent trend within special education, as can be seen by the publication, dates of journals in this area. In its first year of publication it was issued as the *Gifted Child Newsletter.*

CONCLUSION

Within the limitations of being able to select only a few journals from the discipline of education, the thirty-four titles above are those that have demonstrated longevity and significant contributions to the various subdisciplines of education. The selection of these education journals as outstanding representatives of the twentieth century is based upon both subjective and objective criteria and is open to debate. Nonetheless, they deserve inclusion for the very real impact they have had upon the study of education. Their impact upon the twenty-first century has yet to be seen.

NOTES

1. Shmuel Shulman and Malka Margalit, "Evaluation of Research Trends in Special Education Journals (1979-1982)," *Studies in Educational Evaluation* 11 (1): 75-81, 1985.

2. Stephen D. Keister, "Higher Education as a Field of Study: The Leading Journals," *Serials Review* 16 (1): 59-63, 1990.

3. John C. Smart, "Perceived Quality and Citation Rates of Education Journals," *Research in Higher Education* 19 (2): 175-182, 1983.

Chapter 3

Journals of the Century in Psychology

Daniel E. Burgard

More than any other social science discipline, psychology relies on journals as its primary mechanism for the communication of research findings. Psychology journals grew along with the field itself, beginning the century closely allied with a few key individuals and laboratories and evolving into well structured and tightly defined publications. As psychology diverged from its roots in philosophy, the twentieth century witnessed an explosion of psychological research and publication. Not surprisingly, a related explosion took place in the number and type of journals devoted to publishing research results. At the end of the twentieth century, psychologists find themselves in possession of a rich array of journals ranging from long-standing general titles to very specific and very important niche publications.

Not only do research psychologists love to publish in journals, but they also love to talk about their journals and argue about which are the best. It is not surprising that numerous studies aimed at delineating the best psychology journals were conducted in the past few decades. Hardesty and Oltmanns do an excellent job in reviewing the spate of journal ranking studies which appeared in the 1970s and 80s.[1] The studies reviewed by Hardesty and Oltmanns typically tried to identify the best journals either by looking at how often a journal's articles are cited or by surveying psychologists to gather opinions on the best journals. As noted by Doreian, however, there always was and always will be disagreement over the methodology employed in such studies.[2] Despite their methodological drawbacks, these studies do provide evidence as to which journals were viewed as being the most important to researchers in the field. Additionally, the studies represent a healthy concern of a field for its past and future and, once again, underscore the importance of journals to the field of psychology.

Given the number and variety of available titles and the methodological problems inherent in judging publications, selecting the best psychology journals of the century is no mean task. The attempt reported here relies on a

This chapter originally appeared in *The Serials Librarian* 39(3): 41-56, 2001.

variety of criteria in reaching its verdict. Many of the previously mentioned surveys of psychology journals are used to narrow down the field of possible best journals. Citation data from the Institute for Scientific Information's *Journal Citation Reports* are considered. Any mention of a journal being heavily cited is based on data found in the *Journal Citation Reports* of the past twenty years. Another important consideration is the longevity of a journal's impact on the field. It would be hard to call a five, six, or even ten year old periodical a "journal of the century" regardless of how good it is. What ends up being represented below are the psychology journals which were the most important to the most people most of the time in the twentieth century. These titles mirror the growth and maturation of psychology and can easily stand alongside the best journals from any other research discipline.

One of the first things the reader will notice about the following list of titles is that it contains only English language publications. Louttit documented the steep rise in the percentage of English language publications found in *Psychological Index* and *Psychological Abstracts* in the first half of the twentieth century along with a correspondingly steep decline in the overall percentage of German and French language publications.[3] The amazing growth of the American research enterprise, the elimination of foreign language requirements by American graduate schools of psychology, and the rise of English as the de facto international language of science mitigated against a non-English language psychology journal maintaining a position in the ranks of the elite journals. Certainly, some German and French journals were very important in the early part of the twentieth century, but tumultuous politics through the end of World War II combined with the factors mentioned above doomed these to be mostly of national or regional impact. Given the growing interest in psychology around the world, non-English journals may gain in importance in the twenty-first century, but for now it is hard to find such a title with the credentials to be called a journal of the twentieth century.

A similar limitation of the list is its bias towards items published in the United States. The factors mentioned in the preceding paragraph and the fact that the main literature index, *PsycINFO,* is produced in the United States combine to create a situation where the bulk of American research psychologists focus their interest and knowledge on American journals. Rankings based on reputation and citation figures inevitably lead to lists dominated by psychology journals published in the United States. However, any periodical which is a standard publishing outlet for a country's psychologists could be considered a journal of the century. In some countries, national journals play the specific role of spreading applied research and raising awareness of new research at the local level.[4] Psychologists in many countries rightly feel their journals rank among the best. Koulack and Keselman noted that Canadian psychologists rated both the *Canadian Journal of Behavioural Science* and the *Canadian Journal of Psychology* as being among their top ten journals.[5] It is reasonable to expect that psychologists in other countries might select the *Australian Journal of Psychology, Ceskoslovenska Psychologie,* the *Indian Journal of Psychology, Schweizerische Zeitschrift für Psychologie,* the *South African Journal of Psychology,* or any of the high quality journals of the British Psychological Society as being among their best journals of the century.

The reader will also not find certain very important psychology publications on the list of the century's best journals. This is because they are not frequently issued journals which report the results of research, but are instead annuals, indexes, book review sources, or news organs. Items such as the *Annual Review of Psychology, Contemporary Psychology,* and *Psychological Abstracts* help structure the literature of psychology by synthesizing, reviewing, and categorizing the mass of literature which the field produces each year. Some annual publications, such as *Advances in Experimental Social Psychology,* are dominant in their sub-fields and are highly valued by researchers. The American Psychological Association's monthly newspaper, the *APA Monitor,* also serves a very important function but is not one of the most important journals of the century. The existence of these types of "non-journals" enriches the psychological literature, and their absence from a best journals list should not be taken as a diminution of their importance.

The categories used to partition the best journals into manageable sections are taken from the *Journal Citation Reports.* They are: general, applied, biological/physical, clinical/abnormal, developmental, experimental, mathematical, and social/personality. Psychiatry is not considered in this study, and educational psychology is covered in the "Journals of the Century in Education" chapter. The delineation of categories serves as a useful organizational device which can help bring order to a confusing situation. Since the categories each encompass a different number and variety of journals, more titles were both considered and listed for the larger groups, such as experimental and social/personality.

GENERAL

The journals listed in this category published many or most of the seminal psychology articles of the twentieth century. If one were to undertake the challenge of selecting the single most important psychology journal of the century, it would probably be found among the general titles listed in the following discussion.

The *American Journal of Psychology* was first published in 1887 and is the longest continually published psychology journal in the United States. After its founding by G. Stanley Hall, the *American Journal of Psychology* was owned first by Hall and then by Karl Dallenbach for a combined eighty years until it was presented to the University of Illinois. The University of Illinois Press began publishing the journal in 1968 and continues to do so to this day. Besides publishing some landmark articles of continuing importance,[6] the *American Journal of Psychology* also offered a large number of highly valuable obituaries of notable psychologists. While no longer one of the very highest cited titles, its long tradition of independence and growth along with the field of psychology help make the *American Journal of Psychology* one of the most important journals of the century.

American Psychologist, published by the American Psychological Association since 1946, is the Association's official journal. With a subscription base of over 115,000 at century's end, it has a greater reach than any other psychology journal. *American Psychologist* carried the subtitle "the professional journal of the APA" for eleven years after its inception and was initially meant only to publish professionally relevant items such as Association and Division news, conference reports, and job advertisements. In 1957, the word "professional" was dropped from the subtitle and *American Psychologist* began to publish some articles which reported the results of scientific research.[7] It is both a highly respected and a heavily cited journal, which publishes readable articles and a variety of Association-related items.[8] At the end of the century, *American Psychologist* is clearly a significant journal with a long reach and will continue to offer important articles to a broad range of researchers well into the coming century.

Behavioral and Brain Sciences began in 1978 and is published by Cambridge University Press. Its articles are always very highly cited. In fact, its high citation per article numbers are more typical of a life science journal. *Behavioral and Brain Sciences* generally publishes articles in the areas of cognition, neuropsychology, and behavioral biology. Its articles, however, are cited by research presented in psychology journals ranging from the biological to the social. It currently offers an interesting format whereby articles are published along with commentary from peer researchers. *Behavioral and Brain Sciences* shows how quality research and editing coupled with an interesting format can combine to quickly create a respected publication.

Psychological Bulletin has been among the most important psychology journals since its inception in 1904. In what was probably the deal of the century for psychology journals, *Psychological Bulletin* was part of a package of journals sold by Psychological Review Publishing to the American Psychological Association in 1924 for $5,600. The other journals in the package included *Psychological Review, Psychological Index, Psychologi-*

cal Monographs, and the *Journal of Experimental Psychology.* Currently, Psychological Bulletin publishes integrative and evaluative review articles. Rated among the best journals in numerous surveys of American psychologists and always one of the most cited psychology journals,[9] *Psychological Bulletin* is clearly a journal of the century.

Established by James Mark Baldwin and James McKeen Catell in 1894, *Psychological Review* is probably the only publication which can claim to be one of the very best psychology journals in both 1900 and 2000. As with most journals in 1900, *Psychological Review* published a mix of research articles, laboratory news, and professional items. The founding of *Psychological Bulletin* in 1904 and the *Journal of Experimental Psychology* in 1916, allowed *Psychological Review* to take on its current theoretical emphasis. One of its unique early contributions was the publication of an annual supplement titled *Psychological Index.* The *Index* was important in its own right and served as a catalog of the field until *Psychological Abstracts* grew into the primary psychology index in the mid-1930s. Whether one considers reputation, current citation levels, longevity, or historical impact, *Psychological Review* stands out as one of the century's best psychology journals.

A few newer journals in the general category deserve special mention for the immediate impact they had in the last few years of the century. *Psychological Science* and *Psychological Methods* debuted in 1990 and 1996, respectively, and both quickly found themselves among the most cited psychology journals. *Psychological Science* is the premier publishing endeavor of the American Psychological Society. It has been very successful in publishing a variety of articles written in clear, understandable language. *Psychological Science* fashions itself after the general periodical *Science* and takes on an advocacy role in promoting psychology to public policy decision makers. *Psychological Methods* is a spin-off of the methods section of *Psychological Bulletin.* It publishes articles which are useful to a variety of researchers and likely will continue to be among the most highly cited journals for the foreseeable future. Along with the *Review of General Psychology,* another new American Psychological Association journal, *Psychological Science* and *Psychological Methods* represent a growing realization that a need exists for journals which can bridge subfields and present psychological research of interest to a wide range of psychologists.

APPLIED

The *Journal of Applied Psychology* was founded by G. Stanley Hall in 1917 and is published by the American Psychological Association. It is usually the most cited applied psychology journal and has been rated highly in various studies such as those done by Koulack and Keselman and Meltzer.[10] Currently, the *Journal of Applied Psychology* publishes articles in all applied areas with the exception of clinical psychology, applied experimental psychology, and human factors.

Since its founding in 1954, the *Journal of Counseling Psychology* has published articles on counseling theory and practice. It was financed initially by a group of nearly thirty psychologists and published independently by Journal of Counseling Psychology, Inc., until being sold to the American Psychological Association in late 1965.[11] The *Journal of Counseling Psychology* is typically among the most cited applied psychology journals and was identified by Myers and Delevie as one of the most influential journals for counseling psychologists.[12]

Organizational Behavior and Human Decision Processes offers both theory and research papers concerning human performance and organizational psychology. Titled *Organizational Behavior and Human Performance* from its inception in 1966 through its name change at the end of 1984, it always has been published by Academic Press. Long a heavily cited and highly respected journal, *Organizational Behavior and Human Decision Processes* is widely read but is especially important to industrial and organizational psychologists.[13]

Personnel Psychology is notable for its appeal beyond the walls of academic psychology. Begun in 1948 and independently published by Personnel Psychology, Inc. for its entire history, it has steadfastly maintained the moniker "a journal of applied research." Rated highly by academicians, practicing industrial/organizational psychologists, and other personnel professionals,[14] *Personnel Psychology* publishes psychological research applicable to all types of personnel problems. It offers a "scientist-practitioner forum" which presents lessons learned from dealing with problems faced on a day-to-day basis by personnel workers. Perhaps more so than any other journal of the century, *Personnel Psychology* seeks to present sound research which can be directly and immediately applied in a variety of non-laboratory settings.

BIOLOGICAL/PHYSIOLOGICAL

Highly rated by all the previously mentioned reputation studies, the *Journal of Comparative Psychology* has a long and interesting publishing history. It was formed in 1921 by the union of *Psychobiology* and the *Journal of Animal Behavior*. It was purchased by its current publisher, the American Psychological Association, in 1947 and carried the name *Journal of Com-*

parative and Physiological Psychology from 1947 to 1982. It regained its current name in 1983 when it spun off the journal *Behavioral Neuroscience.* As happened with many other journal consolidations and separations during the century, worries arose that the 1983 split would harm the *Journal of Comparative Psychology.* Some researchers feared it would either become or be typecast as a publishing outlet solely for research using rats as subjects.[15] The *Journal of Comparative Psychology,* however, seems to have survived the split in good health and maintained its status as one of the best journals. Its offspring, *Behavioral Neuroscience,* has become an extremely important journal in its own right and deserves inclusion on the list of the best journals.

Published by Cambridge University Press since its inception in 1964, *Psychophysiology* regularly offers a variety of research articles, methodological articles, and reports about instrumentation.[16] It is always one of the more highly cited journals and is generally concerned with the behavioral intersection of psychology and physiology. Carrying the official designation "International Journal of the Society for Psychophysiological Research," *Psychophysiology* maintains a distinct international presence on its editorial board and publishes articles by authors with diverse geographical backgrounds.

CLINICAL/ABNORMAL

The *Journal of Abnormal Psychology* has been recognized as one of the best journals either by citation or by reputation for most of the twentieth century. It was founded in 1906 and served as the official organ of both the American Psychopathological Association from 1910 to 1925 and the Psycho-Medical Society of England from 1914 to 1921. In recognition of its editor's feeling that abnormal and social behavior emanated from the same basic mental mechanisms, it expanded its name to the *Journal of Abnormal Psychology and Social Psychology* from 1921 to 1925.[17] It was donated by its creator and editor, Morton Prince, to the American Psychological Association in 1925 and began publication under the new auspices in 1926 with the more manageable name *Journal of Abnormal and Social Psychology.* The *Journal of Abnormal Psychology* reverted to its current name in 1965 when the American Psychological Association started the *Journal of Personality and Social Psychology.*[18]

The *Journal of Consulting and Clinical Psychology* started in 1937 as the *Journal of Consulting Psychology* and has long been one of the most respected and most cited journals.[19] It took on its current name in 1968 and is published by the American Psychological Association. The *Journal of Con-*

sulting and Clinical Psychology publishes articles dealing with the diagnosis and treatment of disordered behavior. It complements the *Journal of Abnormal Psychology* which focuses on the developmental and descriptive aspects of behavior disorders.

DEVELOPMENTAL

Child Development began publication in 1930 by the Williams and Wilkins Company but was taken over by the Society for Research in Child Development in 1936. Long published by the University of Chicago Press, it is produced currently by Blackwell Publishers. Its articles are typically the most cited of all the developmental journals and it is held in high esteem by researchers in the area.[20] Along with the Society for Research in Child Development's other publications, the Monographs of the Society for Research in Child Development and Child Development Abstracts and Bibliography, researchers are well served by this journal of the century.

Developmental Psychology is another in the stable of high quality journals published by the American Psychological Association. It started life in 1969 and quickly found its way to the top tier of journals as ranked by members of the American Psychological Association.[21] It publishes articles which advance knowledge and theory about human development across the human life span. While it does not have quite as long a history as the immediately preceding publication, *Developmental Psychology* is an indispensable journal for researchers working in the area and is deserving of being designated a journal of the century.

EXPERIMENTAL

One of the few journals of the century originating outside the United States, *Cognition* is published by Elsevier Science in the Netherlands and has been in existence since 1972. The highly cited articles in *Cognition* range from the experimental to the theoretical and span the whole of cognitive science. *Cognition*'s editorial board consists of scientists from around the globe and a glimpse at the contents of any issue will reveal articles authored by researchers from a wide array of countries. The international flavor of the journal is unmistakable and *Cognition* easily lives up to its subtitle of *International Journal of Cognitive Science*.

Cognitive Psychology began publishing in 1970 and is produced by Academic Press. It emphasizes human cognition and publishes a variety of articles ranging from empirical to theoretical. It usually offers only two to four studies in each quarterly issue, but they are always among the most cited of all psychology articles. With its selective publication yet high citation rates, *Cognitive Psychology* musters an impact which few journals can match on a per article basis.

The *Journal of Experimental Psychology* has a long history of publishing important and useful articles. It published a handful of "psychological classics" or older items still cited long after their publication,[22] and its current articles are heavily cited. The *Journal of Experimental Psychology* began in 1916 with John B. Watson as its first editor and was owned by the Psychological Review Company until 1924 when it was sold to the American Psychological Association. It subdivided into four sections in 1975 and added an applied section in 1995. Today, the *Journal of Experimental Psychology (JEP)* comprises five individually edited and published sections: *JEP: Animal Behavior Processes; JEP: Applied; JEP: General; JEP: Human Perception and Performance;* and *JEP: Learning, Memory, and Cognition.* While the sections are in some cases still growing to fill in their niches, the group of five together deserves to be designated as a journal of the century.

The *Journal of Memory and Language* began life as the *Journal of Verbal Learning and Verbal Behavior* in 1962. Published by Academic Press since its inception, it was rated very highly in Mace and Warner's 1973 survey of psychology department heads.[23] Additionally, the *Journal of Verbal Learning and Verbal Behavior* is well represented in studies listing individual articles heavily cited in both introductory textbooks and other journals.[24] Officially switching to the name *Journal of Memory and Language* in 1985, it has maintained its high standing and remains one of the most cited journals in psychology.

Perception & Psychophysics began publication in 1966 and has continually focused on experimental research in the areas of sensation, perception, judgment, and psychophysics. It has long been a heavily cited journal and has been noted as publishing some articles which had a substantial impact on the psychology of perception.[25] *Perception & Psychophysics* is one of several quality publications owned and produced by the Psychonomic Society.

MATHEMATICAL

Based on reputation studies and citation data from the past twenty years, *Psychometrika* has the most distinguished publishing history in quantitative psychology. The official journal of the Psychometric Society, *Psychometrika* began publication in 1936 and has always been published by the Society. The original subtitle of the journal, "a journal devoted to the development of psychology as a quantitative rational science," gives the reader an idea of its founders' mission. Originally, *Psychometrika*'s creators wanted to buy an existing journal to serve as their publishing outlet, but failing that, decided to start their own journal, which continues to thrive sixty years later.[26] *Psychometrika* still carries its original subtitle on its masthead, thus remaining true to its sixty year mission of developing psychology as a quantitative rational science.

PERSONALITY/SOCIAL

The *Journal of Experimental Social Psychology* has been published since 1965 and was one of the first titles dedicated to the experimental investigation of social interaction. Produced by Academic Press since its inception, the *Journal of Experimental Social Psychology* published many influential articles and has always been a highly regarded journal by psychologists.[27] Its editors are not resting on their laurels, however, and recently added a section which will offer brief reports of promising new research in appropriate areas.

Originally known as *Character and Personality,* the *Journal of Personality* took on its current name in 1945. It was first produced by Duke University Press in 1932 and was taken over recently by Blackwell Publishers. Long one of the most cited personality journals, the *Journal of Personality* also was rated highly in a variety of reputation studies.[28] Its nearly seventy year history of independently publishing high quality research gives the *Journal of Personality* a good claim for being called a journal of the century.

The *Journal of Personality and Social Psychology* has a relatively short but highly interesting publishing history. It was created by the American Psychological Association in 1965 and has been published by the Association since. From its inception, it has been highly regarded, and its articles are always among the most cited of all similar journals.[29] Following editorial changes designed to deal with huge page growth in the 1970s and a subsequent dip in submissions, the current editorial arrangement was settled on in 1980.[30] Currently, the *Journal of Personality and Social Psychology* is produced in three separately edited sections: attitudes and social cognition, interpersonal relations and group processes, and personality processes and individual differences. Its high quality and large yearly page count combine to make the *Journal of Personality and Social Psychology* the publication with the largest current impact in this area.

Personality and Social Psychology Bulletin is the well respected official publication of the Society for Personality and Social Psychology. Although the Society for Personality and Social Psychology is actually Division Eight of the American Psychological Association, the *Bulletin* is owned by the Society. It started publication in 1975 and has been produced by Sage Publications since 1980. Always a highly cited title, *Personality and Social Psychology Bulletin* publishes empirical papers in all areas of personality and social psychology. Similar to the preceding title, it gains in prestige and importance because of its organizational backing and its role as a primary publishing outlet for research conducted by thousands of interested psychologists. A related publication, *Personality and Social Psychology Review,* began in 1997 and is also expected to become a very important title.

CONCLUSION

Attempts to inventory a century's most important items in any category are bound to create some measure of controversy. Indeed, a variety of additional titles could conceivably be added to this list of the twentieth century's best psychology journals. One might want to include some of the highly specialized journals which are overwhelmingly important to researchers in various subfields of psychology. Publications such as the *American Journal of Community Psychology, Human Factors,* and *Memory & Cognition* are mandatory reading for scholars in their respective areas. Additionally, journals in fields outside of psychology are often of primary interest to psychologists. Examples of such titles are *Brain Research* and the psychological acoustics section of the *Journal of the Acoustical Society of America.* These are but a few examples of focused items which can, for any specific researcher, eclipse the importance of the titles identified above as journals of the century. Of course, the general scientific periodicals *Science* and *Nature* often publish very influential articles and are standard reading for many psychologists.

One probably could spend the whole of another century debating what titles should and should not be considered "journals of the century." The items listed above, however, represent only the very most influential journals of the twentieth century. The journals themselves are a direct reflection of the growth and flowering of the field of psychology. Indeed, psychologists are fortunate to have such a rich and varied set of journals serving their field. The historical importance and excellent quality of many current psychology journals are a testament to the researchers who made the field into the well structured scientific discipline it is today. Hopefully, a person writing about the best psychology journals of the twenty first century will find just as fertile a group from which to select.

NOTES

1. Larry Hardesty and Gail Oltmanns, "How Many Psychology Journals Are Enough? A Study of the Use of Psychology Journals by Undergraduates," *The Serials Librarian* 16, no. 1/2 (1989): 133-153.

2. Patrick Doreian, "On the Ranking of Psychological Journals," *Information Processing & Management* 25, no. 2 (1989): 205-214.

3. C. M. Louttit, "Publication Trends in Psychology: 1894-1954," *American Psychologist* 12 (1957): 14-21.

4. E. Sanz, I. Aragon, and A. Mendez, "The Function of National Journals in Disseminating Applied Science," *Journal of Information Science* 21, no. 4 (1995): 319-323.

5. David Koulack and H.J. Keselman, "Ratings of Psychology Journals by Members of the Canadian Psychological Association," *Canadian Journal of Behavioural Science* 7, no. 4 (October 1975): 449-450.

6. Ivan N. McCollom, "Psychological Classics: Older Journal Articles Frequently Cited Today," *American Psychologist* 28, no. 4 (April 1973): 363-365.

7. Ludy T. Benjamin, Jr., "The Founding of the *American Psychologist:* The Professional Journal That Wasn't," *American Psychologist* 51, no. 1 (January 1996): 8-12.

8. Alan Feingold, "Assessment of Journals in Social Science Psychology," *American Psychologist* 44, no. 6 (June 1989): 961-964; David Koulack and H.J. Keselman, "Ratings of Psychology Journals by Members of the American Psychological Association," *American Psychologist* 30, no. 11 (November 1975): 1049-1053.

9. Koulack and Keselman, "Ratings of Psychology Journals by Members of the American Psychological Association," 1049-1053; Kenneth C. Mace and Harold D. Warner, "Ratings of Psychology Journals," *American Psychologist* 28, no. 2 (February 1973): 184-186.

10. Koulack and Keselman, "Ratings of Psychology Journals by Members of the American Psychological Association," 1049-1053; H. Meltzer, "Ratings of Psychological Journals by and for Industrial-Organizational Psychologists," *Professional Psychology* 9, no. 2 (May 1978): 290-300.

11. C. Gilbert Wrenn, "Birth and Early Childhood of a Journal," *Journal of Counseling Psychology* 14, no. 4 (Winter 1966): 485-488.

12. Roger A. Myers and Ari S. Delevie, "Frequency of Citation as a Criterion of Eminence," *Journal of Counseling Psychology* 13, no. 2 (Summer 1966): 245-246.

13. Koulack and Keselman, "Ratings of Psychology Journals by Members of the American Psychological Association," 1049-1053; Mace and Warner, "Ratings of Psychology Journals," 184-186; Meltzer, "Ratings of Psychological Journals by and for Industrial-Organizational Psychologists," 290-300.

14. Koulack and Keselman, "Ratings of Psychology Journals by Members of the American Psychological Association," 1049-1053; Meltzer, "Ratings of Psychological Journals by and for Industrial-Organizational Psychologists," 290-300.

15. Ernest D. Kemble, "On the Mitosis of *JCPP,*" *American Psychologist* 36, no. 11 (November 1981): 1462.

16. Antonio Sanchez-Hernandez, Maria J. Pedraja, Elena Quinonez-Vidal, and Francisco Martinez-Sanchez, "A Historic-Quantitative Approach to Psychophysiological Research: The First Three Decades of the Journal *Psychophysiology* (1964-1993)," *Psychophysiology* 33, no. 6 (November 1996): 629-636.

17. Gordon W. Allport, "The *Journal of Abnormal and Social Psychology:* An Editorial," *Journal of Abnormal and Social Psychology* 33, no. 1 (January 1938): 3-13.

18. Gary R. VandenBos, "The APA Knowledge Dissemination Program: An Overview of 100 Years," in *The American Psychological Association: A Historical Perspective,* Edited by Rand B. Evans, Virginia Staudt Sexton, and Thomas C. Cadwallader, (Washington, D.C.: American Psychological Association, 1992), 347-390.

19. Koulack and Keselman, "Ratings of Psychology Journals by Members of the American Psychological Association," 1049-1053; Mace and Warner, "Ratings of Psychology Journals," 184-186.

20. Craig J. Peery and Gerald R. Adams, "Qualitative Ratings of Human Development Journals," *Human Development* 24, no. 5 (1981): 312-319.

21. Koulack and Keselman, "Ratings of Psychology Journals by Members of the American Psychological Association," 1049-1053.

22. McCollom, "Psychological Classics: Older Journal Articles Frequently Cited Today," 363-365.

23. Mace and Warner, "Ratings of Psychology Journals," 184-186.

24. Daniel W. Gorenflo and James V. McConnell, "The Most Frequently Cited Journal Articles and Authors in Introductory Psychology Textbooks," *Teaching of Psychology* 18, no. 1 (February 1991): 8-12; Murray J. White, "Prominent Publications in Cognitive Psychology," *Memory & Cognition* 11, no. 4 (July 1983): 423-427.

25. Murray J. White, "Big Bangs in Perception: The Most Often Cited Authors and Publications," *Bulletin of the Psychonomic Society* 25, no. 6 (November 1987): 458-461.

26. Paul Horst and John Stalnaker, "Present at the Birth," *Psychometrika* 51, no. 1 (March 1986): 3-6.

27. Koulack and Keselman, "Ratings of Psychology Journals by Members of the American Psychological Association," 1049-1053; Mace and Warner, "Ratings of Psychology Journals," 184-186.

28. Koulack and Keselman, "Ratings of Psychology Journals by Members of the American Psychological Association," 1049-1053; Mace and Warner, "Ratings of Psychology Journals," 184-186; H. Meltzer, "Ratings of Journals By and For Personality Psychologists," *American Psychologist* 33, no. 8 (August 1978): 776-777.

29. Koulack and Keselman, "Ratings of Psychology Journals by Members of the American Psychological Association," 1049-1053; Mace and Warner, "Ratings of Psychology Journals," 184-186; Meltzer, "Ratings of Journals By and For Personality Psychologists," 776-777.

30. Bibb Latane, "*Journal of Personality and Social Psychology:* Problem, Perspective, Prospect," *Personality and Social Psychology Bulletin* 5, no. 1 (January 1979): 19-31; Gary R. VandenBos, "The APA Knowledge Dissemination Program: An Overview of 100 years," 347-390.

OTHER WORKS CONSULTED

Gerald R. Adams and J. Craig Peery, "If You Can Name It, I Can Rank It," *American Psychologist* 35, no.1 (January 1980): 109-110.

Joachim H. Becker, "German-Language Psychological Journals: An Overview," *The German Journal of Psychology* 8, no. 4 (December 1984): 323-344.

H.S. Bertilson and P.L. Knutson, "Classics in Personality and Social Psychology: Older Journal Articles and Books Cited Frequently Today," *Personality and Social Psychology Bulletin* 6, no. 3 (September 1980): 417-420.

H.S. Bertilson, "Classics in Psychophysiology: Older Journal Articles and Books Cited Frequently Today in *Psychophysiology*," *Psychophysiology* 15, no. 6 (November 1978): 604-605.

Edwin G. Boring, *A History of Experimental Psychology*, Second edition (New York: Appleton-Century-Crofts, Inc., 1950).

Louis C. Buffardi and Julia A. Nichols, "Citation Impact, Acceptance rate, and APA Journals," *American Psychologist* 36, no. 11 (November 1981): 1453-1456.

Allan R. Buss and John R. McDermott, "Ratings of Psychology Journals Compared to Objective Measures of Journal Impact," *American Psychologist* 31, no. 9 (September 1976): 675-678.

Hulsey Cason and Marcella Lubotsky, "The Influence and Dependence of Psychological Journals on Each Other," *Psychological Bulletin* 33, no. 1 (January 1936): 95-103.

Rand B. Evans and Jozef B. Cohen, "The *American Journal of Psychology*: a Retrospective," *American Journal of Psychology* 100, no. 3-4 (Fall-Winter 1987): 321-362.

James E. Everett and Anthony Pecotich, "Citation Analysis Mapping of Journals in Applied and Clinical Psychology," *Journal of Applied Social Psychology* 23, no. 9 (May 1993): 750-766.

Paul Fehrman, "Psychology," in *Magazines for Libraries*, 9th edition, edited by Bill Katz and Linda Sternberg Katz (New Providence, N.J., R.R. Bowker, 1997), 1097-1127.

Lorenz J. Finison and Charles L. Whittemore, "Linguistic Isolation of American Social Psychology: A Comparative Study of Journal Citations," *American Psychologist* 30, no. 4 (April 1975): 513-516.

Raymond D. Fowler, "1996 Editorial: 50th Anniversary Issue of the *American Psychologist*," *American Psychologist* 51, no. 1 (January 1996): 5-7.

Eugene Garfield, "Is Citation Analysis a Legitimate Evaluation Tool?," *Scientometrics* 1, no. 4 (May 1979): 359-375.

Randy J. Georgemiller, Joseph J. Ryan, and Kathleen N. Sitley, "Clinical Utility Rankings of Neuropsychologically Related Journals," *Professional Psychology: Research and Practice* 17, no. 3 (June 1986) 278-279.

"Introduction: A Half Century of the American Psychologist," in *The Evolution of Psychology: Fifty Years of the American Psychologist*, edited by Joseph M. Notterman (Washington, D.C.: American Psychological Association, 1997), xxi-xxv.

Walter Kintsch and John T. Cacioppo, "Introduction to the 100th Anniversary Issue of the *Psychological Review*," *Psychological Review* 101, no. 2 (April 1994): 195-199.

Herbert S. Langfeld, "Jubilee of the *Psychological Review:* Fifty Volumes of the *Psychological Review*," *Psychological Review* 50, no. 1 (January 1943): 143-155.

Joel R. Levin and Thomas R. Kratochwill, "The Name of the Journal Fame Game: Quality or Familiarity?," *American Psychologist* 31, no. 9 (September 1976): 673-674.

Gerald M. Murch and Frank Wesley, "German Psychology and Its Journals," *Psychological Bulletin* 66, no. 5 (November 1966): 410-415.

Donald V. Osier and Robert H. Wozniak, *A Century of Serial Publications in Psychology 1850-1950: An International Bibliography* (Millwood, New York: Kraus International Publications, 1984).

Ray Over, "Journal Ranking By Citation Analysis: Some Inconsistencies," *American Psychologist* 22, no. 8 (August 1978): 778-780.

Alan J. Porter, "A Comparison of the Various Ratings of Psychology Journals," *American Psychologist* 33, no. 3 (March 1978): 295-299.

Alan J. Porter, "Use Lists With Caution," *American Psychologist* 31, no. 9 (September 1976): 674-675.

Harriet L. Rheingold, "The First Twenty-Five Years of the Society for Research in Child Development," *Monographs of the Society for Research in Child Development* 50, no. 4-5 (1986): 126-140.

Mark R. Rosenzweig, "Continuity and Change in the Development of Psychology Around the World," *American Psychologist* 54, no. 4 (April 1999): 252-259.

Mark R. Rosenzweig, "Resources for Psychological Science Around the World," in *International Psychological Science: Progress, Problems, and Prospects* (Washington, DC: American Psychological Association, 1992), 17-74.

J. Phillipe Rushton and Henry L. Roediger, "An Evaluation of 80 Psychology Journals Based on the *Science Citation Index*," *American Psychologist* 33, no. 5 (May 1978): 520-523.

J. Phillipe Rushton, "The Impact of British Psychology Journals on Science," *Bulletin of the British Psychological Society* 30 (June 1977): 212-213.

Joseph J. Ryan and Daryl L. Bohac, "Essential Books and Journals in North American Clinical Neuropsychology," *Clinical Neuropsychologist* 10, no. 2 (May 1996): 222-228.

Franz Samuelson, "The APA Between the World Wars: 1918 to 1941," in *The American Psychological Association: A Historical Perspective*, edited by Rand B. Evans, Virginia Staudt Sexton, and Thomas C. Cadwallader (Washington, D.C.: American Psychological Association, 1992), 119-147.

Social Sciences Citation Index Journal Citation Reports (Philadelphia: Institute for Scientific Information, 1977-).

Michael M. Sokal, "Origins and Early Years of the American Psychological Association: 1890 to 1906," in *The American Psychological Association: A Historical Perspective*, edited by Rand B. Evans, Virginia Staudt Sexton, and Thomas

C. Cadwallader (Washington, D.C.: American Psychological Association, 1992), 43-71.

Kayla J. Springer and Ruth B. Gross, "Nominations of "Classic" Literature in Clinical Psychology," *Professional Psychology* 4, no. 1 (February 1973): 79-85.

Robert J. Sternberg and Tamara Gordeeva, "The Anatomy of Impact: What Makes an Article Influential?," *Psychological Science* 7, no. 2 (March 1996): 69-75.

Alison M. Turtle, "The Forerunners and Foundation of the *Australian Journal of Psychology*," *Australian Journal of Psychology* 47, no. 3 (December 1995): 123-127.

Robert H. Wozniak, "A Brief History of Serial Publication in Psychology," in *A Century of Serial Publications in Psychology 1850-1950: An International Bibliography* (Millwood, New York: Kraus International Publications, 1984), xvii-xxxiii.

Chapter 4

Journals of the Century in Sociology

Lynne Rudasill

Selecting the "Journals of the Century" in Sociology not only provides an opportunity to closely review the growth and development of the literature of the field, it also provides an opportunity to look at the maturation of the discipline. Although Lee Braude, Professor of Sociology at the State University of New York College at Fredonia, points to arguments that sociology as a way of studying human behavior can be seen as early as the fourteenth and fifteenth centuries, the development of the field in the United States began in earnest only in the nineteenth century.[1] In the late nineteenth and early twentieth centuries, notable similarities in the development of sociology in the United States and in Europe included parallels in the inception of teaching at institutions of higher education along with the recognition of the discipline as a whole. Whether it was the great names, such as Simmel, Durkheim, and Weber on the eastern shores of the Atlantic, or Sumner, Ward, and Small in the United States, the early advocates of the formalized study of sociology were in the classroom at approximately the same time, and all were considering the precepts that Comte and others had laid before them. Further, early discussions of sociology centered as much around the methodology that would be used within the growing discipline, as the theory and practice of sociology itself.

The history of publishing in the discipline for the twentieth century mirrors that of many of the other social sciences. Albion W. Small, first chair of the first department of sociology in the United States at the University of Chicago, agreed to edit the *American Journal of Sociology* at the end of the nineteenth century. In an article in 1916, Small stated that colleagues who had been contacted to provide possible contributions to the journal had advised him "to reconsider our purpose, as there could not possibly be in the near future enough sociological writing to fill such a journal."[2] Small listed in the same article the sixteen journal titles that were most likely to contain information that would be useful in the study of sociology. The titles in-

This chapter originally appeared in *The Serials Librarian* 39(3): 57-67, 2001.

cluded *Annals of the American Academy of Political and Social Science, American Economic Review, Journal of the American Institute of Criminal Law and Criminology,* and *The Survey: Social Service Weekly.* The only title that would be easily recognized as subject specific to the field would be the *American Journal of Sociology.*[3] In 1932, *Ulrich's Periodicals* was published for the first time, listing by subject the serial publications in various fields. A total of 87 titles were listed for sociology that year. In 1963, 280 titles were listed under the subject heading, and by 1998, approximately 1,500 titles were listed.[4] Clearly Small's naysayers were not looking very far into the future of the subject. Just as the publications in the field grew almost exponentially, the field itself grew and diversified. *Sociological Abstracts* lists over twenty major areas of coverage in its indexing of the sociological literature.[5] Smelser identified sixty-two areas of interest for the membership of the American Sociological Association and fifty-seven areas of interest for the International Sociological Association in 1993.[6] In *Sociology: A Guide to Reference and Information Sources,* Stephen H. Aby identified twenty-two distinct fields within the discipline.[7] Due to the restrictions of space in this article, fewer areas of specialization will be identified. In fact, the journals that have been chosen will be listed under several general rubrics. For our purposes, we have divided the results into the following areas: General Sociological Theory—United States; General Sociological Theory—International; Approaches to Research; Sociological Sub-Fields, Border Disciplines, and Social Problems.

A number of factors were considered in the selection of titles for inclusion here. Citation analysis, reputation, longevity, and perceived importance to the field were the primary criteria. Citation analysis is the simplest way of identifying those journal titles that appear to be of importance. The results of several years of citation analysis from ISI's *Journal Citation Reports* were examined to determine the titles that most consistently can be found to have high impact factors.[8] But citation analysis is not enough. Whether one uses the Institute for Scientific Information's impact factors, strict citation counts, or counts the specific citations in several issues of any particular journal, citation does not tell the entire story. Reputation, or ranking by practitioners in the field, is another means of determining the importance of a journal.[9] However, departments of sociology and individual practitioners have specific areas of interest, making a broad view of the field telescope somewhat. Therefore, although useful in narrowing down the field to a manageable size, these two strategies, whether used individually or in tandem, do not provide the entire picture of a field's literature. Longevity is another contributing factor for qualification on the list of the century's best or most important journals, since a journal that does not consistently provide accurate, germane coverage of the topics in question certainly won't last very long. Longevity cannot, however, be the sole factor because the field has grown and changed so much in the last one hundred years.

In writing about the journals of the century, all three of the above factors are very valuable in determining membership in the club, and they have been used extensively. The ultimate test for inclusion here, however, is the degree to which the journal reflects the development of the discipline. Sociology, as we know it, is really a creature of the twentieth century. It was during the last one hundred years that the field defined itself, its methodology, and its import. Like other more mature social sciences, sociology first determined its methodology, and then began the application of method to better understand society. Along the way, the discipline expanded its venue and began to develop distinct and highly specialized fields of study as well. Some of these fields have broken somewhat with sociology and developed on their own, sometimes developing their own publishing paradigms, and some, less-well defined, have remained under the umbrella of the study of society.

GENERAL SOCIOLOGICAL THEORY—UNITED STATES

The following titles, all published in the United States, are those offered as "Journals of the Century" in the area of general sociological theory and practice:

The *American Journal of Sociology* (ISSN 0002-9602) has been published in the United States by the University of Chicago Press since 1895. Easily the "grand-parent" of all sociological periodicals, this journal is the most prestigious, and probably the most essential, publication for collection by any library that deals with the discipline in a scholarly manner. To follow the tables of contents of the journal over the century is to follow the evolution of the field. The journal began publication when funding for the University of Chicago's University Extension World subsidy was given over to Albion Small for the purpose of establishing a journal of sociology.[10]

The journal scores consistently in the top ten for impact factor in the *Journal Citation Reports* of ISI. Without exception, the title is on the "most important," "most essential," and "highly rated" lists produced in the subject area. The journal contains book reviews in every issue, as well as review and research articles, and frequently supports "theme" issues for topics of importance in the discipline.

The American Sociological Association has been publishing the *American Sociological Review* (ISSN 0003-1224) in the United States since 1936. The flagship journal of the Association, the *Review*, sometimes referred to as *ASR*, emphasizes reports of an empirical and quantitative nature across the broad spectrum of subjects in the field. Usually held in the same high regard as the *American Journal of Sociology,* it too appears in most top ten lists for impact factor and "best" lists. The *American Sociological Review* is another title that is essential for a scholarly collection in the discipline of sociology.

In 1972, book reviews were eliminated from *ASR* and the title *Contemporary Sociology: A Journal of Reviews* (ISSN 0094-3061) began publication. Like its parent, *Contemporary Sociology* is published by the Association in Washington, D.C. and frequently appears on the high impact factor lists. The periodical contains a "Symposium" in each issue in which essays on specific topics are featured. These theme essays look at new movements within the field and resultant publications. The second part of the journal contains shorter reviews organized within general subject categories of the field. After the brief reviews, an indication of other titles received for review and a place for commentary are provided. *Contemporary Sociology* is essential for both collection development and the opportunity it provides to look at the development of sociological theory as it is systematized in the literature. In 1997, the journal turned up as number one in impact factor on the *Journal Citation Reports.*

Social Forces (ISSN 0037-7732) is the next pick as a member of the group of "Journals of the Century" in sociology. It has been published in Chapel Hill by the University of North Carolina Press since 1922 and was first affiliated with the Southern Sociological Society, and now the Institute for Research in Social Science. The journal publishes across a broad range of topics for the sociological community. Qualitative and historical research in the variety of subfields is published as well as more quantitative articles. Book reviews are also present in each issue. The first three volumes of the work were entitled The *Journal of Social Forces. Social Forces* shows very well in the impact area and appears on every "best" list of import.

GENERAL SOCIOLOGICAL THEORY—INTERNATIONAL

The following titles have been chosen for inclusion on the list in the hope that students of the discipline will be made more aware of developments in other geographic areas. The trend toward globalization of economies, media, and politics has already had great impact on the field and, millennial panic notwithstanding, this trend will probably continue. For better or worse, English has become the international language. With this in mind, in combination with the gradual disappearance of foreign language requirements at the graduate level, we have included only titles that contain articles written in English. Unfortunately, this eliminates the addition of titles such as *Cahiers Internatiounaux de Sociologie* and several other titles in Spanish and German.

Sociology: the Journal of the British Sociological Association (ISSN 0038-0385) has been published since 1967 for the Association, currently by Cambridge University Press. Its focus on British studies makes it a good counterpart to the journals published in the United States. General in nature, it works across the range of topics current in Great Britain and includes research and review articles as well as book reviews, a section for most current topics, and notes on research. In an historical review of the first fifteen years of the existence of the British Sociological Association, Joseph A. Banks tells a tale very similar to that of Albion Small. The number of British universities offering degrees in sociology went from six in 1950 to nineteen in 1964 excluding "those Colleges of Advanced Technology which were teaching the subject for London external degrees but were in the process of creating their own degrees as they gradually acquired university status."[11] The growth has been exponential. The journal shows up repeatedly on the impact factor top ten list and is frequently included as a "best" selection.

Acta Sociologica (ISSN 0001-6993) is the official journal of the Scandinavian Sociological Association and is published in Oslo by the Scandinavian University Press. Since 1955, it has been publishing articles in English on mainstream issues in sociology for Europe and the United States. In addition to feature articles of a generally quantitative nature, the journal publishes research notes, reviews, conference reports, and book reviews. Issues are occasionally thematic. The journal scores consistently high in citation analysis.

The *Canadian Journal of Sociology/Cahiers canadiens de sociologie* (ISSN 0318-6431) is one of the newer journals on the list, beginning publication in 1975. It is clearly ethnocentric in nature with its primary focus on providing a publication outlet for Canadian sociologists. Articles cover the entire discipline in both qualitative and quantitative features, and book reviews are included. This title does not generally receive the highest of marks for impact factor, but was included as an example of the recognition that sociology is both global and local in nature. The journal is published by the University of Alberta in Edmonton for the Department of Sociology.

Chinese Sociology and Anthropology: A Journal of Translations (ISSN 0009-4625) and *Soviet Sociology: A Journal of Translations from Scholarly Soviet Sources* (ISSN 0038-5824) are both published by M. E. Sharpe. They are included on this list as further examples of the global-local dichotomy that exists in the field. Together, the two journals provide access to the social science literatures of two of the world's largest nations. Although not commonly found at the high end of the citation analyses, the two are important for communication within the field if any true commonalities are ever to evolve regarding society and societies.

APPROACHES TO RESEARCH

A great deal of the first third of the twentieth century was spent by sociologists debating the way in which sociology should be done. What were the research methods to be? Smelser identifies five types of data by which analysis can be made-experimental data, survey data, archival data, ethnographic data, and data involving comparative studies.[12] The question remains, however, as to what uses these data types may be put. As if collection of data was not enough, the management of the collected data provides another problem. The field tried at first to develop methods that closely reflected those of the other sciences, but over the last several years, more and more discussion of the scientific method has led to the realization that any work done cannot be free of bias, whether personal or cultural. Research in the field, as in many other of the social sciences, can be divided into two camps-quantitative and qualitative/historical. The following titles reflect this division and are important as reflections of the changes in sociological method.

The *Journal of Mathematical Sociology* (ISSN 0022-250X) published by Gordon and Breach in London since 1971 is the epitome of the quantitative research method. The emphasis is on modeling, measurement, and quantitative methods. Computers, computer programming, and statistics are other areas of emphasis for this title. The journal is pricey, apparently following the model of high subscription costs for journals in the natural sciences. It is included on the "Journals of the Century" list as the prime example of quantitative work in the discipline.

Less expensive, but just as devoted to empiricism, is the journal *Sociological Methods and Research* (ISSN 0049-1241) from Sage in the United States. Published since 1972, this journal works to clarify and discuss the quantitative methods used in sociology. It includes both review articles and features. The title is usually found higher up on the impact factor scale than the *Journal of Mathematical Sociology*, but both titles have been included as a reflection of the importance of the views they maintain of the proper sociological method.

The title *Qualitative Sociology* (ISSN 0162-0436) provides us with a counterbalance to the two journals just mentioned. It has been published since 1978, currently in the United States by the Human Sciences Press. It emphasizes research methods that do not rely specifically on numbers. Instead, articles using survey, ethnographic, historical, and comparative data are published. The journal includes feature and review essays. The title is important in its reflection of the more post-modern approach to research that is still ascendant in some areas of the social sciences.

Critical Sociology (ISSN 0896-9205), formerly the *Insurgent Sociologist,* is another title that reflects societal influences on the discipline and its publications. The title began as a newsletter for radicals in the profession in 1969. Under its former title, it developed into a journal giving voice to the work of "activist-oriented" sociologists. With volume 15, the new name was given to the serial as a way of engendering a wider audience. It has been published continuously under the auspices of the Department of Sociology of the University of Oregon and contains three to four feature articles per issue along with review essays and book reviews. It provides a truly alternative view of mainstream sociology.

SOCIOLOGICAL SUBFIELDS

Here we have chosen the specific titles that have proven to best exemplify publication in some of the specific subfields of sociology. These subfields are moving targets and are not all well represented by specific journal titles. Included are topics such as race, ethnicity, and class; population and immigration; family studies; life cycle; gender studies and sex roles; criminology; and rural sociology. Some of these are more well defined than others as fields independent of the discipline of sociology. Criminology and demography are two subfields that have successfully distanced themselves from the broader discipline. They are, however, frequently identified as fields of sociology in most surveys and general texts on the matter. Women's studies is another area that is gradually developing its own venue and paradigm, and some argue that African-American studies is yet another area that first developed under the aegis of sociology.

Very few titles that are associated with subfields in sociology make the more general "best" lists or the high impact factor lists. Listed below are those titles that not only are important to their subject areas, but have managed to garner more widespread recognition as titles that are included as "Journals of the Century."

Race & Class (ISSN 0306-3969), alternatively *Race and Class,* is a British journal that originally began publication in 1959 under the title *Race* (ISSN 0033-7277). The journal has been another example of radical sociology since 1974 when it underwent the change in its name and began focusing on post-colonial societies as well as class distinctions. Occasionally making significant ratings for impact factor, the title was primarily chosen as a reflection of the societal changes affecting sociology in the past century.

It is published by the Institute of Race Relations in London. Another title in the area is *Ethnic and Racial Studies*. Although not chosen for inclusion on the list, it is mentioned here as a more conventional journal emphasizing the comparative study of societies and the problems they face. It provides a mainstream approach to the study of ethnicity, race, and class.

Two titles have been chosen for inclusion in the area of demography and population studies. *Population and Development Review* (ISSN 0098-7921), which began publication in 1975 by the Population Council in New York, is the first. This journal is specifically dedicated to discovering the trends in demography and discovering how these trends are related to development with a view to the manner in which these trends affect human resources and social welfare. In doing so, the journal seeks a general, as opposed to a specialist, orientation and readership and falls under the frequently cited category. Another title in the subject area, *Population Studies* (ISSN 0032-4728), is published in London by the Population Investigation Committee of the London School of Economics. Book reviews and feature articles have an international flavor. It too can be found on the list of high impact factor titles. Other titles that did not quite make "Journal of the Century" include *International Migration Review* and *Human Ecology*, both quite useful in this subfield.

A title that is frequently cited and consistently praised is the *Journal of Marriage and the Family* (ISSN 0022-2445). This publication by the National Council on Family Relations has been issued in the United States since 1938. This "Journal of the Century" includes articles in many family-related areas, including divorce, children and child care, work and family, etc. A comparatively large number of feature articles and reviews (approximately 20 and 10 respectively) can be found in each issue. Themes are not uncommon, and commentary on prior publications is also found between the journal's covers.

Rural Sociology (ISSN 0036-0112) should also be included on the list of "Journals of the Century" for its frequent appearance in citation analysis and on "best" lists. Published by the Rural Sociological Society in the United States, the journal does not limit itself to rural sociology in the strictest sense, choosing to include articles on a wide variety of topics. The published articles are frequently thematic and book reviews are included.

Gender and Society (ISSN 0891-2432) is published by Sage. Publication began in 1987, making it the youngest journal to make the "Journals of the Century" list. It is very representative of many of the issues brought about by the women's movements of the last century and includes articles on topics such as stratification, ethnicity, and other topics which are gender related. It publishes both feature articles, about six per issue, and reviews.

Criminology, like population studies and women's studies, draws a good deal of its theory from the same well as sociology. We will, therefore, include one journal, *Criminology: An Interdisciplinary Journal* (ISSN 0011-1384), on the list of sociological "Journals of the Century." The American Society of Criminology has sponsored the publication of this title since 1963. The disciplines it frequently includes are law, criminal justice, and history as well as other social sciences. Publications include feature articles and commentary on prior issues.

A final entry in this category is not listed as a "Journal of the Century" but perhaps as a journal of note. *Teaching Sociology* (ISSN 0092-055X), a publication of the American Sociological Association, is another very important resource for those engaged in pedagogy. It provides reviews of works that can be used as textbooks, an area that is not widely covered anywhere else, in addition to what one might expect from a "teaching" title. Curriculum aids, as well as information on teaching techniques and theory are published here.

BORDER DISCIPLINES

In a few areas, sociology and other subjects border so closely on one another that they are distinct fields. Three that quickly come to mind here are the sociology of education, the sociology of medicine, and social psychology. Each area has one representative "Journal of the Century."

Sociology of Education (ISSN 0038-0407) is another publication of the American Sociological Association. It has been in production since 1927. The four to six articles found in each issue are primarily quantitative feature articles, although policy-related essays are not uncommon. Occasionally, a thematic issue will be published.

The *Sociology of Health & Illness* (ISSN 0141-9889) is published in Great Britain by Blackwell. Although it has a very European focus, it is frequently found to have high impact ratings in the U.S. as well. In publication since 1979, the journal provides about six articles per issue, space for response, and book reviews.

Social psychology is well represented by the journal *Social Psychology Quarterly* (ISSN 0190-2725), published by the American Sociological Association. It began publication in 1937 as *Sociometry* (ISSN 0038-0431), changed its title to *Social Psychology* (ISSN 0147-829X) for one volume in 1978, and became referred to as the *Quarterly* in 1979. Articles number about six per issue, and some research notes are published. The articles published reflect the quantitative nature of psychological publications, although a variety of perspectives are maintained.

SOCIAL PROBLEMS

For the purposes of this work, we have saved the specific topic of the study of social problems in sociology for last. There is one "Journal of the Century" in this area, but there are several subtopics for which no titles have been chosen. Some of the topics that can be included under social problems drug and alcohol abuse, homelessness, personal violence, and suicide. Frequently, these topics move from theoretical sociology to applied sociology to social work. The topics, therefore, will be left for another article. However, the journal *Social Problems* (ISSN 0037-7791), published by the University of California for the Society for the Study of Social Problems, provides enough broad-based theoretical coverage of the area and receives enough notice to be included on the list for sociology. The journal publishes about seven articles per issue. Themes are frequently used, and news from the association consists most importantly of the presidential address from the annual conference.

So concludes the list of titles chosen as the "Journals of the Century" in sociology. The discipline continues to grow, diversify, and germinate new branches. The publishing history of the past century is rich with new titles, new areas, and new methodologies. What does the future hold? The next "Journals of the Century" list will most likely be published in a format other than paper and will emphasize more electronic access to titles than we are experiencing today. E-journals will very likely be replaced by something even more "out there," and those who come after us will know if the theory of consilience has yet taken hold.

NOTES

1. Lee Braude, "The Emergence of Sociology," *Choice* 32 (October 1994): 237-247.

2. Albion W. Small, "Fifty Years of Sociology in the United States," *American Journal of Sociology* 21, no. 6 (1916): 786.

3. Ibid., p.785-788.

4. *Ulrich's International Periodicals Directory* (New York: Bowker. 1932-).

5. *Sociological Abstracts.* (San Diego: Sociological Abstracts, 1953-).

6. Neil J. Smelser, *Sociology.* (Cambridge, MA: Blackwell Publishers, 1994), 6-7.

7. Stephen H. Aby, *Sociology: A Guide to Reference and Information Sources.* 2nd ed. (Englewood, CO: Libraries Unlimited, 1997), vii-x.

8. Several years of the *Journal Citation Reports* from ISI were used-1998, 1997, 1984, and 1979. For a complete explanation of the concept of impact factor, please see the Reports.

9. Several sources were used for standard lists of journals in the discipline as well as specific "best lists." Please see the list of "Other Works and Cited References" for specifics.

10. Small, "Fifty Years of Sociology in the United States," p. 786.

11. Joseph A. Banks, "The British Sociological Association-The First Fifteen Years," *Sociology: The Journal of the British Sociological Association* 1, no. 1 (1967): 2-9.

12. Smelser, p. 5.

OTHER WORKS AND CITED REFERENCES

Stephen H. Aby, *Sociology: A Guide to Reference and Information Sources*. 2nd ed. (Englewood, CO: Libraries Unlimited, 1997).

Joseph A. Banks, "The British Sociological Association-The First Fifteen Years," *Sociology: The Journal of the British Sociological Association* 1, no. 1 (1967): 2-9.

Pauline Bart and Linda Frankel, *The Student Sociologist's Handbook*. 4th ed. (New York: Random House, 1986).

Janice Beyer, "Editorial Policies and Practices Among Leading Journals in Four Scientific Fields," *Sociological Quarterly* 19, no. 1 (1978): 68-88.

Lee Braude, "The Emergence of Sociology," *Choice* 32 (October 1994): 237-247.

Blaize Cronin et al., "Accounting for Influence: Acknowledgment in Contemporary Sociology," *Journal of the American Society for Information Science* 44, no. 7 (1993): 406-12.

W. Glanzel, "A Bibliometric Approach to Social Sciences," *Scientometrics* 35, no. 5 (1996): 291-307.

Journal Citation Reports (Philadelphia: Institute for Scientific Information, 1976-).

William B. Katz (Ed.), *Magazines for Libraries* (New York: Bowker, 1969-).

Richard F. Larson et al., "Journal Productivity of Ph.D. Sociologists," *The American Sociologist* 7, no. 9 (1972): 9-11.

Sociological Abstracts (San Diego: Sociological Abstracts, Inc. 1953-).

Albion W. Small, "Fifty Years of Sociology in the United States," *American Journal of Sociology* 21, no. 6 (1916): 721-864.

Neil J. Smelser, *Sociology* (Cambridge, MA: Blackwell Publishers, 1994).

Marvin Sussman (Ed.) *Author's Guide to Journals in Sociology & Related Fields*. (New York: The Haworth Press, Inc., 1978).

Ulrich's International Periodicals Directory (New York: Bowker. 1932-).

Chapter 5

Journals of the Century in Library and Information Science

Cheryl A. McCarthy

PURPOSE OF CHAPTER

"We seek knowledge only because we desire enjoyment, and it is impossible to conceive why a person who has neither desires nor fears, would take the trouble to reason" (Rousseau, *Discourse on the Origin of Inequality*). While researching and evaluating library and information science (LIS) journals for this chapter, I approached the challenge with both desire for knowledge as well as fear and trepidation in selecting the most influential LIS journals of the century. The knowledge gained from such a study, however, is valuable for students, educators, and professionals in the field. Previous studies analyzing LIS journals revealed both a proliferation of titles and an increase in the quality of journals in the last quarter century. Thus, choosing the best LIS journals of the century from a universe of over 1,000 titles was daunting. Understandably, any selection of the most influential journals will inevitably be subjective and, hopefully, will stimulate debate.

METHODOLOGY AND CRITERIA

Two distinct purposes characterize LIS journals: some publish research, while others publish professional information for practitioners. When considering the pool of LIS journals, therefore, no distinction was made between scholarly research journals and professional information journals or between refereed or non-refereed journals. The universe of LIS journals was first identified by reference to the 37th edition of *Ulrich's International Periodical Directory, 1999*. For a more selective list of LIS journals, two sources were consulted: Katz' *Magazines for Libraries, Ninth Edition*

This chapter originally appeared in *The Serials Librarian* 39(2): 121-138, 2000.

(1997) and Bowman's *Library and Information Science Journals and Serials: An Analytical Guide* (1985).

Initially, colleagues at the University Library and the Graduate School of Library and Information Studies were polled for their perceptions of the most influential LIS journals in an open-ended survey. Next, a literature review was done to assess evaluative studies of LIS journals and, finally, a preliminary list of LIS journals was created from ratings established in previous quantitative and qualitative studies. In addition, titles (excluding review sources and indexes) were cross-checked for their inclusion in at least two of the following indexes: *Library Literature; Library and Information Science Abstracts; Information Science Abstracts;* and *Social Science Citation Index Journal Citation Reports.*

On the basis of this evaluation, the following categories of titles were eliminated from the pool of journals: (1) all newsletters for limited audiences; (2) all proceedings and bulletins resulting solely from meetings or conferences; (3) all local, state, and regional publications (acknowledging that quality titles such as *Illinois Libraries* exist); (4) all individual library publications (acknowledging that scholarly journals such as *Harvard Library Bulletin* exist); (5) all irregular serials and annuals; (6) all non English-language journals; (7) all journals which are no longer published unless they have migrated to an electronic version (with one notable exception); and (8) all new journals that have been in existence for less than a decade. Thus, new electronic journals of the 1990s were eliminated unless they had migrated from a highly regarded print source. Although e-journals are a relatively new phenomenon, they will be a significant factor to consider in the next century.

Therefore, the journals selected are English-language journals, predominately American, with a national or international audience. In addition, all LIS journals chosen had been evaluated, ranked, and indexed in the literature. Furthermore, to qualify as one of the most influential LIS journals of the century, a journal should be where experts in the field consistently publish research or where professionals consistently go for information.

HISTORY OF LIBRARY
AND INFORMATION SCIENCE JOURNALS

Library Journal, the first American LIS journal, appeared in 1876. In the 1880s the first British library journal, the *Library Chronicle,* began publication and was the precursor to the *Library Association Record.* In the centenary issue of the *Library Association Record* (1999), Diana Dixon quoted James Duff Brown writing in *The Library* in 1899, "Ten years ago one

American and one English periodical served every requirement. Now there are six . . . which are devoted to the craft of librarianship in all its branches." Brown further predicted that "very soon every public library will have its own little magazine or circular in which to describe new books" (Dixon, 1999). Although, at the turn of the century, Brown had anticipated the increase in publications by local libraries, he could not have anticipated the growth and specialization of the profession, nor the corresponding growth of specialized journals in the twentieth century.

One hundred years later, there are 1,003 periodicals plus 552 annuals and irregular serials and 238 related references for a total of 1,793 listings under the heading "Library and Information Science" in the 37th edition of *Ulrich's International Periodical Directory, 1999*. LIS periodicals made a quantum leap in the twentieth century from the six titles published in 1899 to 1,003 periodicals published in 1999 (excluding annuals and irregular serials). After more than doubling in size from 169 to 475 titles between 1946 and 1966, LIS journals nearly doubled again from 475 to 900 titles between 1966 and 1987 (Maguire, 1988). In the last decade of the century, from 1987 to 1999, LIS journals increased by 103 titles. Thus, in the second half of the twentieth century, LIS journals increased by 834 titles or 83 percent. By the end of the 20th century, therefore, the LIS journal literature is extensive and specialized.

While LIS serials have proliferated, so too have journals in other disciplines where LIS professionals publish, read, or go to for selection. As the official publication of the ALA, *American Libraries* enjoys the largest circulation with 58,000 member subscribers, followed by *Library Journal* with about 24,000 subscribers. Most LIS journals, however, have much smaller circulation figures, ranging from several thousand in the general interest areas, to a few hundred in specialized fields.

Why have journals proliferated in the last half of the century? There is a corresponding relationship between the proliferation of journals and the development of the profession itself. Although the first generation of librarians were self-taught scholars, librarians of the first-half of the 20th century were trained in apprentice-like library settings. Following World War II, however, library education migrated to colleges and universities where the first Master's in Library Science, M.L.S. degree, was awarded in 1951. By 1965 ten graduate library school programs offered doctoral degrees (Blake, 1996).

With this shift to academic programs, a corresponding shift occurred in expectations for promotion and tenure of LIS faculty. From the 1950s to the 1970s, the primary responsibility for library school faculty was teaching. By the end of the 1970s, however, faculty promotions began to depend on research. Mary Kingsbury's survey of 59 deans and directors of ALA accredited programs identified "research" as the primary factor for evaluating faculty by the 1980s. She revealed that the quantity of publications was no longer a guarantee for either tenure or promotion (Kingsbury, 1982). Therefore, the demand for the publication of quality LIS research and the need for quality LIS journals has increased during the last quarter century.

LITERATURE REVIEW

Surveying the literature evaluating LIS journals, one finds a range of quantitative and qualitative studies. Though bibliometric and citation studies generate statistical views of top, or "core" journals, a more holistic approach, combining both quantitative and qualitative measures, can better identify core journals that have a significant impact on the profession. Therefore, this study attempts to identify the most influential LIS journals of the century by analyzing previous studies using a variety of methodologies including historical analysis, existing statistical data, surveys and perception studies, bibliometrics and citation analysis, and content analysis.

Historical Analysis. In 1988 Carmel Maguire presented a paper at the 54th IFLA Conference in Sydney, Australia that assessed the value of library journals in an historical context. In her introduction she quoted Dorothy Broderick as saying, "Readers and subscribers have every bit as much responsibility for the quality of a publication as those who put it out" (Maguire, 1988, 318). She concluded that "On every hand there seem to be quantitative and qualitative gaps in our knowledge about the library journals" (Maguire, 1988, 322). A more recent analysis of British LIS journals in 1995 by McDonald and Feather also concluded that quantitative measures, such as citation analysis, can only be partial indicators of quality. Journals, they concluded, must also be evaluated contextually through research assessment (McDonald and Feather, 1995).

Content Analysis. One study in 1987 by a team of researchers (Feehan, Gragg, Havener, and Kester) used a combination of methods including content analysis to analyze a core of 91 English-language LIS journals published in 1984. The authors compared their sample size of "91 core" journals with previous studies that had identified different size core LIS journals. In 1984 Eaton and Burgin identified 61 core LIS journals, while in 1983 Nour identified 42 core LIS journals, and in 1977 Peritz identified 39 core LIS journals. In these studies "core" journals were selected if they were indexed in at least two major LIS indexes. After surveying the contents of all 91 core journals published in 1984, the research team identified substantive research articles. The researchers then selected twenty percent of these articles for random sampling and analysis. They concluded that this study could be replicated for continued research and analysis of LIS journals (Feehan, Gragg, Havener, and Kester, 1987).

Existing Statistical Data. Bobinski in 1986 opted to use existing statistical data to perform "An Analysis of 105 Major U.S. Journals in Library and Information Science." Bobinski analyzed LIS journals based on the following factors: inclusion in indexes, year of initial publication, publisher, frequency of publication, subscription costs, and circulation figures. From *Ulrich's International Periodical Directory, 1984,* Bobinski identified a universe of 845 LIS journals. Bobinski suggests that the rise in the quality of journals in the 1970s and 1980s is reflected in the increase in the number of titles cited in *Social Science Citation Index* as well as in forty-eight other indexes outside the library and information science field. Moreover, Bobinski concludes that three possible causes can be attributed to the increase in quality of LIS journals. He credits the increase in quality of journals to the increased productivity of academic librarians and the research by LIS educators and professionals with doctorates, as well as the growing specialization in the field (Bobinski, 1986).

Surveys. Surveys appear to be the dominant methodology used to assess the rankings of top journals. Two studies used similar surveys a decade apart to analyze how top ranked journals select what they publish. In 1978 O'Connor and Van Orden reported that the thirty-three national library periodicals surveyed had a manuscript rejection rate of 77.3 percent and only a few of those journals employed external reviewers. The authors challenged the ALA as well as other publishers of LIS journals to clearly state the publication's purpose and the criteria for evaluating manuscripts. In addition, they urged journals to adopt a double-blind refereeing system to help improve the quality (O'Connor and Van Orden, 1978).

While replicating the O'Connor and Van Orden study in 1988, John Budd presented survey data from 48 journals showing an improvement in the publications' stated criteria as well as a reduction in rejection rates (60-70 percent) and an increase in the use of referees. This, he concludes, offers hope for better communication in the field through better journals (Budd, 1988).

In addition to surveying publishers, both practitioners and LIS educators have been surveyed for their perceptions of quality journals. In 1985 Kohl and Davis reported data from a survey of deans of ALA accredited library schools and directors of ARL libraries to determine the hierarchy of LIS prestige journals. Kohl and Davis' perception study set a standard that others have followed, referenced, and replicated. Kohl and Davis found fundamental agreement between the perceptions of ARL directors and library school deans on two-thirds of the rankings of 31 LIS prestige journals (Kohl and Davis, 1985). In a similar study in 1990, Blake and Tjoumas surveyed

LIS faculty who specialize in public and school librarianship for their rankings of LIS prestige journals. The survey results show individual LIS faculty members' rankings differ depending on one's specialty (Blake and Tjoumas, 1990). Moreover, when Blake compared the ratings of LIS faculty with district school library media coordinators, there was a significant difference in hierarchy based on the perceived utility of the journal. LIS educators rated research journals higher, while district library media coordinators rated professional information or practice based journals higher. Thus, Blake identified the varied perceptions between LIS faculty and practitioners based on the utility of the journal (Blake, 1991).

Blake replicated the Kohl-Davis study in 1996 finding an apparent dichotomy in results. Blake discovered no common hierarchy in rankings of prestige journals between deans of ALA accredited library schools and ARL Directors. Blake's results revealed "scant evidence of substantial agreement on the relative prestige of these 57 journal titles" (Blake, 1996, 176). Furthermore, he concluded that "the apparent shared hierarchy in the study by Kohl and Davis no longer appears to exist" (Blake, 1996, 176). Thus, Blake finds that the usefulness of the journal to support one's professional responsibilities is the major factor influencing how one ranks the journal. This study raises the question about whether LIS educators are communicating their research results with the practitioners in the field.

Citation Analysis and Bibliometrics. While these survey studies provide a qualitative view of journals, citation-based measurements and bibliometric studies provide a quantified analysis for comparison. Several different researchers chose citation-based measures and bibliometrics to quantify the status of LIS journals (Kim, 1992; Fang, 1989; Rice, 1990, 138-153). Others quantified specific communication patterns in the LIS literature (Borgman and Rice, 1992; Thompson, 1991; Van Fleet, 1993). Another study analyzed citations in both the publications of faculty and course reading lists of faculty at one library school (Esteibar and Lancaster, 1992).

In 1991 Kim analyzed nine citation-based measures compared with the perception study by Kohl and Davis and identified factors associated with the journal's ranking. Kim concluded that a common hierarchy of LIS prestige journals exists between the citation analysis and the perception rankings of LIS journals (Kim, 1991). Kim's study recognizes the significance of citation-based measures in confirming the perceptions of more subjective studies. Combining results from both quantitative and qualitative studies in this paper, therefore, provides a more substantial basis for evaluating the most influential LIS journals of the century.

SELECTION BY DIVISIONS AND SUBDIVISIONS

An analysis of the best LIS journals of the century reveals an interesting phenomenon. While professional associations dominate the list of publishers of the LIS journals founded in the first three quarters of the century, commercial publishers are the sole producers of LIS journals founded in the last quarter of a century (with one exception). The American Library Association combined with its divisions and affiliates publishes the largest number of the "best" LIS journals with a total of twenty titles. Haworth Press and Reed-Elsevier (combined with its divisions) are the top two commercial publishers with a total of ten titles each.

Initially for this article, ten categories of LIS journals were created and then expanded to incorporate five major divisions with twenty-four subdivisions. The five divisions are listed in alphabetical order: (1) General Interest Library Journals; (2) Library and Information Science Research Journals; (3) Special Functions in Library Journals; (4) Specialized Collections in Library Journals; and (5) Type of Library in Library Journals. In division five the subheading, "Special Libraries (Specific Type)," was used to combine significant specialty areas under one listing, but only one title per specialty was allotted.

THE JOURNALS

Is there, then, one best journal of the century? While one shoe does not fit all, neither does one journal serve all library and information science professions. An earlier citation-based study identified the following three LIS subdivisions and named the top journal in each for the decade 1977-1987: in Library Science, *College & Research Libraries;* in Information Science, *Journal of the American Society for Information Science* (JASIS) and in Librarianship, *Library Journal* (Rice, 1990, 138-153). While these titles are arguably the best in their subdivisions, this study has selected a broader scope of twenty-four subdivisions. Each subdivision was chosen as having a unique purpose for a specific group of professionals. Therefore, it is not surprising that the publications by the professional associations of each group are among the best in the field.

While librarians and information specialists know and read the top journals in their specialty, few professionals may be familiar with the range and depth of LIS serials. While one study revealed that the perceived hierarchy of LIS journals may be in the eyes of the beholder (Blake, 1991), library and information science educators and professionals should be knowledgeable in all of the most influential LIS journals of the century. Thus, this article is intended to inform LIS educators, students, professionals, and practitioners in all LIS fields about the range of top LIS journals. While this discussion should inform all LIS professionals, it should also confirm a specialist's perceptions of the best in one's specialty. Although many titles were considered, only three titles for each subdivision were chosen for a total of seventy-two titles. This discussion, therefore, will focus on those selected as the most influential LIS journals of the century and will not include discussion of the non-selects.

GENERAL INTEREST LIBRARY JOURNALS

General Interest American Libraries

Library Journal (1876, Cahners Business Information, U.S.) emerges as the leader in the general interest category for its currency, relevancy of issues to the profession, reviews, and "best" categories. As the first LIS journal of record, *Library Journal* continues to serve the profession admirably and deserves recognition as the best general interest journal as cited in previous studies. Moreover, it is the journal that librarians go to first for professional issues. *American Libraries* (1907, American Library Association, U.S.) is the official journal of the ALA with the largest circulation of 58,000 members and provides excellent coverage of news and current issues. *Wilson Library Bulletin* (1914-1995, H. W. Wilson Co., U.S.) is the only journal selected that is no longer in publication. *Wilson Library Bulletin* was chosen, however, because it was one of the most readable journals in librarianship for eighty years before ceasing publication in 1995. Moreover, some of its features such as the reference reviewing source can be found on the H. W. Wilson Web site.

General Interest International Libraries

Two essential international publications for libraries are published in Germany by K. G. Saur Verlag KG (a division of Reed-Elsevier): *IFLA Journal* (1975, K. G. Saur Velag, Germany); and *Libri: international journal for libraries and information services* (1951, K. G. Saur Velag, Germany). *IFLA Journal* provides articles of international relevance as well as news and reports from the International Federation of Library Associations & Institutions. *Libri* publishes scholarly articles primarily in English with an international perspective for libraries. The third international journal of note is the *International Information and Library Review* (formerly *International Library Review*, 1969, Academic Press Ltd., U.K.) which includes refereed articles on a variety of subjects concerning international and comparative librarianship.

History of Libraries and Librarianship

Libraries and Culture: a journal of library history (Formerly *Journal of Library History, Philosophy, and Comparative Librarianship;* and *Journal of Library History*, 1966, University of Texas Press, U.S.) is the only U.S. publication with a focus on scholarly history of libraries and library collections within the culture. Because of its unique stature, it is the only journal in this category and serves an essential function for preserving the history of the profession.

Library Oriented Reviews and Selection Tools

The staple for librarians is the review source for selection. While no one source can suffice as a library's only selection tool, three titles perform a basic function for keeping libraries current. *Booklist* (formerly *Booklist and Subscription Books Bulletin;* includes *Reference Books Bulletin*, 1905, American Library Association, U.S.) has been an indispensable review source since the beginning of the century for medium and small public, school, and community college libraries. Librarians can use this source with confidence as all titles selected are recommended by the ALA Publishing Committee. *Choice* (1963, Association of College and Research Libraries, American Library Association, U.S.) is the number one review source for academic libraries and is essential for all academic and research libraries. *Kirkus Reviews: adult, young adult, and children's book reviews* (formerly *Kirkus Reviews; Jim Kobak's Kirkus Reviews*, 1933, Kirkus Associates, U.S.) is valuable for public libraries for its previews of new books for adults and children and its identification of potential bestsellers and books in demand.

Magazine and Supplement General Audience Book Reviews

The *New York Times Book Review* (1896, New York Times Co., U.S.) and the *TLS, The Times Literary Supplement* (formerly *The Times Literary Supplement*, 1902, Times Supplements Ltd., U.K.) are the "go to" sources for the sophisticated reader for weekly reviews of the most significant new titles. *New York Review of Books* (1963, NYREV, Inc., U.S.) publishes scholarly essays and reviews and intends to shape opinions as well as ruminate on books and culture.

Technology and Libraries

All three titles chosen are significant for covering all aspects of library technology and should be read by not only systems librarians but all librarians who need to keep current with new technologies. *Computers in Libraries* (formerly *Small Computers in Libraries* 1981, Information Today, Inc., U.S.) keeps librarians abreast of new technology developments in a very readable format. *Information Technology and Libraries* (1968, Library and Information Technology Association (LITA), American Library Association, U.S.) is the official journal of LITA and provides quality refereed articles on all aspects of library technology. *Library Hi Tech Journal* (1983, Pierian Press, U.S.) is most noted for its theme issues.

LIBRARY AND INFORMATION SCIENCE RESEARCH JOURNALS

Information Science

The number one scholarly journal in information science ranked tops in both perception studies and citation studies is *Journal of the American Society for Information Science* (JASIS) (1950, John Wiley and Sons, U.S.). *JASIS* is the official publication of the American Society for Information Science (ASIS). Two additional scholarly journals publishing information science research for an international audience are published in the United Kingdom by divisions of Reed-Elsevier: *Information Processing and Management: an international journal* (1963, Elsevier Science, U.K.) and *Journal of Information Science: principles and practice* (1979, Bowker-Saur, Ltd., U.K.).

Library Research and Education

All three titles are scholarly and should be read by library science educators and students researching the field. The *Journal of Education for Library and Information Science* (formerly *Journal of Education for Librarianship*, 1960, Association for Library and Information Science Education, U.S.) is the scholarly ALISE publication noted for its comprehensive coverage in the field of library education. *Journal of Librarianship and Information Science* (formerly *Journal of Librarianship*, 1969, Bowker-Saur, Ltd., U.K.) is a scholarly British publication noted for its research articles with an international focus on librarianship and information science. *Research Strategies: a journal of library concepts and instruction* (1983, JAI Press,

U.S.) provides scholarly articles both theoretical and applied with a focus on library instruction.

Library Research and Practice

All three journals chosen publish research and are essential reading for the profession. *Library and Information Science Research: an international journal* (1979, Ablex Publishing, U.S.) publishes research articles with an international and theoretical perspective. *Library Quarterly* (1931, University of Chicago Press, U.S.) publishes substantive research including articles with an historical perspective. *Library Trends* (1952, University of Illinois at Urbana-Champaign, U.S.) is noted for its theme approach with different perspectives on various research topics.

SPECIAL FUNCTIONS IN LIBRARY JOURNALS

Acquisitions and Collection Management

Two journals lead the field in collection development including practical applications in *Collection Building* (1978, MCB University Press, U.K.) and a more scholarly approach in *Collection Management* (1975, The Haworth Press, Inc., U.S.). In the area of library acquisitions, *Library Acquisitions: practice and theory* (1977, Elsevier Science, U.K.) tops the list with articles that are international and pragmatic in their approach.

Administration and Management in Libraries

Fiscal management is one of the most pressing issues for library managers and one journal addresses all financial aspects, *Bottom Line: managing library finances* (1987, MCB University Press, U.K.). Two quality journals that address all issues of concern for library management including both theoretical and practical approaches are *Journal of Library Administration* (1980, The Haworth Press, Inc., U.S.), and *Library Administration and Management* (1975, Library Administration and Management Association, LAMA, American Library Association, U.S.).

Cataloging and Classification

Two journals cover the field of cataloging, classification and documentation for specialists. *Cataloging & Classification Quarterly* (1980, The Haworth Press, Inc., U.S.) provides well documented papers covering both practical and theoretical approaches. *Journal of Documentation: devoted to the recording, organization, and dissemination of specialized knowledge* (1945, Association for Information Management, U.K.) is a scholarly ASLIB publication with technical articles for the practitioner as well as theoretical research.

Electronic and Online Resources in Libraries

With new technologies emerging in libraries and with an increasing demand for online resources, libraries need to stay current with developments in the field. Three reliable sources were chosen for their significance and proven record in keeping current. Two sources are published by Online: *Database: the magazine of database reference and review* (1978, Online, U.S.) which focuses on all information technologies for the professional; and *Online: the leading magazine for information professionals* (1977, Online, U.S.) which focuses on information providers and the Internet. A web version is also available. A journal with well documented and refereed articles about new database products and online services and searching is *Online and CD-ROM Review: the international journal of online and optical information systems* (1977, Learned Information Europe, Ltd., U.K.).

Indexing and Abstracting

The oldest and most reliable index of library sources is *Library Literature* (1921, H. W. Wilson Co., U.S.) which is available in print, CD-ROM and online including full text capabilities (www.hwwilson.com). *LISA: library and information science abstracts* (1969, Bowker-Saur Ltd., U.K.) provides the widest coverage in the field with abstracts from over 500 periodicals and books, theses, reports and proceedings. *LISA* is also available online. *Information Science Abstracts* (1965, Information Today, Inc., U.S.) is the only American abstracting tool in the field of information science and thus provides an essential complement to the other two sources. Abstracts from journals, books, and reports are arranged under broad classifications.

Reference and Public Services

As the official publication of the Reference and User Services Association of ALA, *RQ, Reference and User Services Quarterly* (1960, Reference and User Services Association, American Library Association, U.S.) remains the best vehicle for communication with reference librarians and other public services librarians. The recent change in association name reflects the increased emphasis on user services in this vital journal. *The Reference Librarian* (1981, The Haworth Press, Inc., U.S.) is most useful for its thematic and double issues which cover the range of reference services and are also available as monographs. *RSR: reference services review* (1972, Pierian Press, U.S.) is an essential source for the reference librarian especially for its evaluative reviews as well as its bibliographies and articles on reference services, resources, and instruction.

Serials Acquisitions and Management

Two essential titles for all serials librarians especially in academic, large public, and special libraries are *The Serials Librarian: the international journal of serials management* (1976, The Haworth Press, Inc., U.S.), and *Serials Review* (1975, JAI Press Inc., U.S.). While both journals cover a broad spectrum of topics and issues dealing with serials, *The Serials Librarian* offers additional special issues in international topics and North American Serials Interest Group issues as well as double-issues on special topics. The "Serials Report" section provides timely information to keep professionals up-to-date on people, vendors, sources, meetings, and reports from groups such as the Cooperative Online Serials Program (CONSER).

Technical Services

Technical services librarians consult two essential journals to keep current in the field. *Library Resources and Technical Services* (1957, Association for Library Collections and Technical Services, American Library Association, U.S.) is an excellent ALA divisional publication with refereed feature articles covering a variety of subjects from bibliographic access and control to book production quality in scholarly feature articles. *Technical Services Quarterly* (1983, The Haworth Press, Inc., U.S.) keeps technical services librarians informed about all aspects of technical services operations and trends in the field.

SPECIALIZED COLLECTIONS IN LIBRARY JOURNALS

Archives and Rare Books

The leading source of scholarly articles for archivists is *American Archivist* (1938, Society of American Archivists, U.S.). The articles cover philosophy, theory, history, and professional issues for archivists. *Rare Books and Manuscripts Librarianship* (1986, Association of College and Research Libraries, American Library Association, U.S.) was initiated by the Rare Books and Manuscripts section of ACRL only a decade ago. This journal helps professionals working with these special collections while also communicating the importance of these collections for research. *Records Management Quarterly* (1967, Association of Records Managers and Administrators, U.S.) is a practical approach to a variety of issues from automation systems to electronic records management including case studies written by practicing records managers. This is a valuable information tool to learn more about this important field.

Government Documents

As the official publication of the Government Documents Round Table (GODORT) of the ALA, *Documents to the People* (1972, ALA, U.S.) is essential reading to keep current with U.S. government documents and the profession of document librarians. Two scholarly journals are essential for research and information on all issues especially promoting U.S. and international government information: *Government Information Quarterly: an international journal of policies, resources, services, and practices* (1984, JAI Press, U.S.); and *Journal of Government Information: an international review of policy, issues, and resources* (Formerly *Government Review*, 1974, Elsevier Science, U.K.).

TYPE OF LIBRARY IN LIBRARY JOURNALS

Academic Libraries

The best journal with scholarly research representing both theoretical and practical concerns of academic librarians is *College and Research Libraries* (1939, Association of College and Research Libraries, ACRL, American Library Association, U.S.). A companion volume to *C&RL* also published by ACRL is *College and Research Libraries News* (1966, Association of College and Research Libraries, ACRL, American Library Association, U.S.). It is the basic news source of the ACRL including reports, meetings, and brief readable articles of interest to academic librarians. *Journal of Academic Librarianship* (1975, JAI Press, U.S.) provides well documented research articles on major issues from management to technology concerns of academic librarians. An excellent review of the professional literature is also provided.

General Public Libraries

Two journals focus on the major concerns of public librarians. *Public Libraries* (1970, Public Library Association, American Library Association, U.S.) is the official PLA publication with regular monthly features addressing practical issues such as service, law, research, reports and continuing education. *Public Library Quarterly* (1979, The Haworth Press, Inc., U.S.), on the other hand, provides more in-depth and well-documented feature articles on a variety of significant topics including management and technology.

Public Libraries and Youth Services

Horn Book Magazine: about books for children and young adults (1924, Horn Book, U.S.) is the only source that has continued to serve children's literature for seventy-five years with serious and thoughtful in-depth reviews, interviews, and essays and is ranked as the best review source for children's literature. Two additional superb journals provide well-documented and thoughtful articles on youth services and professional issues: *Journal of Youth Services in Libraries* (formerly *Top of the News*, 1946, Association for Library Service to Children/Young Adult Library Services Association, American Library Association, U.S.); and *VOYA: voice of youth advocates* (1978, Scarecrow Press, U.S.). *VOYA* focuses primarily on the concerns of young adult librarians.

School Libraries

Cahners Business Information claims to be number one in publishing professional business serials. With the publication of *Library Journal* and *School Library Journal: the magazine of children's, young adult, and school librarians* (1954, Cahners, U.S.), Cahners publishes the two top journals in these fields of librarianship. *SLJ* is number one in its coverage of school and youth services including news, information, issues, practical articles and reviews. The number one journal for school library media research, however, is *School Library Media Research* ([Online: http://www.ala.org/aasl/slmr] 1951, American Association for School Librarians, American Library Association, U.S.) and is now available only online since *School Library Media Quarterly* migrated to an electronic format. An excellent Canadian journal edited and published by Ken Haycock and essential reading for school libraries is *Teacher Librarian: the journal for school library professionals* (formerly *Emergency Librarian*, 1973, Haycock, Canada). This journal is especially noted for its theme issues and its readable feature articles and action research approach for the practicing teacher librarian.

Special Libraries (General)

The number one generic special libraries journal is *Information Outlook* (Continuation of *Special Libraries* and *SpeciaList*, 1910, Special Libraries Association, U.S.) which is the official publication of the Special Libraries Association. The name change reflects the broader outlook of the journal and incorporates information on new special library professions and information technologies. The research articles are in-depth and well documented. The only LIS journal selected that publishes proceedings is *ASLIB Proceedings* (1949, Association for Information Management, U.K.) because it is a substantial and thorough journal that also includes contributed research articles on issues of information management.

Special Libraries (Specific Type)

Unlike the other subcategories where similar journals were discussed, this subcategory represents a combined listing of unique specific types of libraries with one journal chosen to represent each type. The titles are discussed below by publisher rather than specialty.

Three special types of library journals are refereed and published by one of the leading for-profit publishers of quality LIS journals of the century, The Haworth Press, Inc. of Binghamton, New York. *Behavioral & Social Sciences Librarian* (1979, The Haworth Press, Inc., U.S.) focuses on current in-depth research in the area of social sciences information services and resources. *Journal of Business & Finance Librarianship* (1989, The Haworth Press, Inc., U.S.) serves information professionals dealing with business information resources. *Science & Technology Libraries* (1980, The Haworth Press, Inc., U.S.) includes scholarly and practical research articles in theme issues for practicing science and technology librarians.

The remaining four special library journals chosen are the best in their area and are published by their professional associations. *Art Documentation* (1972, Art Libraries Society of North America, U.S.) provides high quality substantive refereed articles in thematic issues to promote art documentation in libraries. It provides society reports and one issue each year is devoted to the annual conference. *Law Library Journal* (1908, American Association of Law Libraries, U.S.) is essential reading for any law librarian. Well documented legal research and bibliographies are presented in this esteemed journal. *Bulletin—Medical Library Association* (1911, Medical Library Association, U.S.) covers a wide range of topics in scholarly articles and is essential reading for medical librarians. *Notes—Music Library Association* (1942, Music Library Association, U.S.) offers excellent reference materials, including indexes and bibliographies as well as information and feature articles to stimulate any music librarian.

CONCLUSION AND QUESTIONS

The essential questions influencing the quality of LIS journals in the next century may well focus on where LIS professionals and educators will publish. What will be the vehicle for determining promotion and tenure for LIS faculty and academic librarians with regard to publications? How will quality journals be determined and what criteria will be used to rank them? If the prestige of journals continues to influence faculty tenure and promotion decisions, how will e-journals be ranked? Will faculty and professionals migrate to publishing in e-journals for more rapid communication to the profession? As the profession continues to specialize with emerging technologies, will more specialized journals emerge (on-line or in-print) to communicate with these newly evolving groups? How will LIS faculty and library practitioners communicate with each other? These questions may influence and create a new vehicle of communication among library faculty and practicing librarians in the next millennium.

SELECTED BIBLIOGRAPHY
FOR LIBRARY SCIENCE JOURNALS

Blake, Virgil L. P. "In the Eyes of the Beholder: Perceptions of the professional journals by library/information science educators and district school library media coordinators." *Collection Management* 14 (3/4): 101-143, 1991.

Blake, Virgil L. P. "The Perceived Prestige of Professional Journals, 1995: A replication of the Kohl-Davis study." *Education for Information* 14: 157-179, 1996.

Blake, Virgil L. P. and Renee Tjoumas. "The Role of Professional Journals in the Career Advancement of Library and Information Science Educators." *The Serials Librarian* 18 (3/4): 47-71, 1990.

Bobinski, George S. "An Analysis of 105 Major US Journals in Library and Information Science," in *Library Science Annual*. Littleton, CO: Libraries Unlimited, 1985-86, pp. 29-41.

Borgman, Christine L. and Ronald E. Rice. "The Convergence of Information Science and Communication: A bibliometric analysis." *Journal of the American Society for Information Science* 43, 397-411, 1992.

Bowman, Mary Ann. *Library and Information Science Journals and Serials.* Westport, CT: Greenwood Press, 1985.

Budd, John. "Publication in Library and Information Science: The state of the literature." *Library Journal* 113 (14): 125-131, 1988.

Buttlar, Lois. "Analyzing the Library Periodical Literature: Content and authorship." *College and Research Libraries* 52 (1): 38-53, 1991.

Dixon, Diane. "Rivals and Competitors." *The Library Association Record* 101 (1): 30-31, 1999.

Eaton, Gale and Robert Burgin. "An Analysis of Research Articles Published in the Core Library and Information Science Journals of 1983." Research Paper, School of Library Science, University of North Carolina at Chapel Hill, 1984.

Esteibar, Belen Altuna and F. W. Lancaster. "Ranking of Journals in Library and Information Science by Research and Teaching Relatedness." *The Serials Librarian* 23 (1/2): 1-10, 1992.

Fang, Min-Lin Emily. "Journal Rankings by Citation Analysis in Health Sciences Librarianship." *Bulletin of the Medical Library Association* 77 (2): 205-211, 1989.

Feehan, Patricia E., W. Lee Gragg II, W. Michael Havener, and Diane D. Kester. "Library and Information Science Research: An analysis of the 1984 journal literature." *Library and Information Science Research* 9 (3): 173-185, 1987.

Katz, William and Linda Sternberg Katz. *Magazines for Libraries,* Ninth Edition. New Providence, New Jersey: Bowker, 1997.

Kim, Mary T. "Ranking of Journals in Library and Information Science: A comparison of perceptual and citation-based measures." *College and Research Libraries* 52 (1): 24-37, 1991.

Kim, Mary T. "A Comparison of Three Measures of Journal Status: Influence weight, importance index, and measure of standing." *Library and Information Science Research* 14 (1): 75-96, 1992.

Kingsbury, Mary. "How Library Schools Evaluate Faculty Performance." *Journal of Education for Librarianship* 22: 219-238, 1982.

Kohl, David F. and Charles H. Davis. "Ratings of Journals of ARL Library Directors and Deans of Library and Information Science Schools." *College and Research Libraries* 46 (1): 40-47, 1985.

Maguire, Carmel. "Good, Bad, or Irrelevant: Quality, price and value of library journals." *IFLA Journal* 14 (4): 318-323, 1988.

McDonald, Steven and John Feather. "British Library and Information Science Journals: A study of quality control." *Journal of Information Science* 21 (5): 359-369, 1995.

Nour, Martyvonne Morton. "Research in Librarianship: An analysis of research articles in core library journals of 1980." Master's Thesis, University of North Carolina at Chapel Hill, 1983.

O'Connor, Daniel and Phyllis Van Orden. "Getting into Print." *College and Research Libraries* 39 (5): 389-396, 1978.

Rice, Ronald E. "Hierarchies and Clusters Among Communication and Library and Information Science Journals," in *Scholarly Communication and Bibliometrics.*

Edited by Christine L. Borgman. Newbury Park, CA: Sage Publications, 1990, pp. 138-153.

Thompson, Christine E. "Using Citation Analysis to Analyze Library and Information Science Journal Characteristics." *College and Research Libraries News* 52 (7): 439-441, 1991.

Tjoumas, Renee and Virgil L. P. Blake. "Faculty Perceptions of the Professional Journal Literature: Quo vadis?" *ALISE* 33 (3): 173-194, 1992.

Ulrich's International Periodical Directory, 1999. 37th edition. New Jersey: Bowker, 1999.

Van Fleet, Connie. "Evidence of Communication Among Public Librarians and Library and Information Science Educators in Public Library Journal Literature." *Library and Information Science Research* 15, 1993.

CLUSTER II:
MUSIC, MUSEUMS, AND METHODISTS

This is the cluster of special places: concert halls, galleries, churches, and philosophical vantage points. We could have called this the humanities cluster, but the anthropologists, if not necessarily the archeologists, see themselves primarily as social scientists. Historically, the humanities also did not include divinity studies (indeed that's why they are called the humanities!). But several other shared traits have proven our grouping of subjects workable:

- Journals in this cluster have many crossover interests. We have ethnomusicology, biblical archeology, semantics and semiotics, aesthetics, religious art and music, faith-healing, folklore and mythology, handicrafts and artifacts, old debates on human evolution, and new debates on the role of women.
- This cluster had the highest involvement of publications from both the romance countries, and the "Rest of the World," category, including virtually all the entries for Latin America, Africa, and the Asian Pacific rim. (Multiculturalism in the helping professions is recently fashionable, but the people in this cluster seem to have practiced more of it, and for a far longer time.)
- This cluster also contains most of the journals of the century that continue to publish in a language other than English, and doctoral candidates in at least three of the disciplines still routinely must master two foreign languages for reading purposes.

Overall, this was very much a balanced cluster in terms of publishing sectors, with the major players all within seven percentage points of one another. There was also greater variety among the publishers. No one publisher had more than ten journals across the entire cluster of almost 400. Not only did the usual university press stalwarts (Cambridge, Chicago, Columbia, and Oxford) do well, but many other famous schools not frequently listed in other clusters appeared here (Brown, Emory, Notre Dame, Rochester, and Southern California). To the shock of many, MIT Press was more prominent in this cluster than in either of the science ones. Two publishers with genuinely strong positions in the sciences do very well here: Kluwer and Blackwell. Likewise, we saw commercial continental publishers not listed elsewhere: notably Walter de Gruyter and Brill.

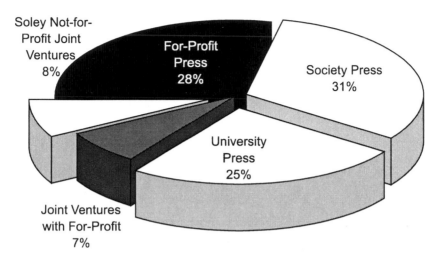

Breakdown by Publishing Sector

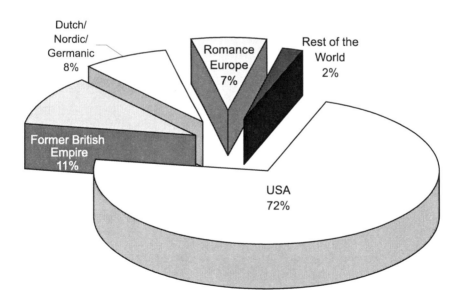

Breakdown by Region

Chapter 6

Journals of the Century in Music

Alan Karass

The extensive list of music journals published in the last century reflects the many facets of music as a discipline. These journals cover topics on musicology, music theory, ethnomusicology, music education, music therapy, popular music and jazz, music librarianship and bibliography, and performance. Some music journals cross subject boundaries or combine musical with non-musical topics. The international repertory of music journals documents musical life, music scholarship, and the state of music publishing.

Many of the important music periodicals of the twentieth century are dedicated to the broad discipline of musicology. Articles in them cover topics including composers' lives and works, compositional genres, music publication and dissemination, performance practice, aesthetics, cultural contexts of composers' works, and compositions and compositional trends. They also contain material on harmonic language, on counterpoint, and on the history, philosophy, and methodology of music scholarship. These periodicals are almost exclusively concerned with Western art music. Non-Western art music and popular music are the subject of another group of specialized publications. In the past decade, some of the musicology journals have published notable articles on the "new musicology," a term recently adopted to describe the integration of non-musical schools of thought, such as literary theory, philosophy, linguistics and gender studies, into musicology. Most of the notable musicology journals reflect the influence that German music historians and theorists have had on musicological thought for many generations, as well as the significance of the British and American schools of musicology.

This chapter originally appeared in *The Serials Librarian* 39(3): 103-132, 2001.

MUSICOLOGY

Acta Musicologia
(Basel, Switzerland: Bärenreiter, 1928-)

This journal was begun in 1928 as a publication for the members of the International Musicological Society (IMS). The IMS was founded in Basel in 1927. The early volumes predominantly consisted of membership information. With the release of volume 3 the publishers changed the journal's name from *Mitteilungen der Internationalen Gesellschaft für Musikwissenschaft* to *Acta Musicologia* and announced its first editor, Knud Jeppesen. By vol. 5, the quarterly issues consisted of four scholarly articles, several brief book reviews, a list of new publications, and IMS news.[1]

The articles reflect the broad and international scope of the Society. Topics are usually historical in nature and include musicological scholarship, research and methodology, ethnomusicology, archival studies and manuscript inventories. The official languages of the society are English, French, German, Italian, and Spanish. The current editorial board consists of scholars from Eastern and Western Europe, Great Britain, and North America. The journal prints society information in German and French. Articles are printed in the language of the contributing author and the contributorship is genuinely international.[2]

The organization and the journal were affected by the political events around World War II. The number of issues per volume and the number of contributions decreased. Book reviews were occasionally dropped. In the 1950s, the journal returned to four issues per year; however, book reviews were permanently discontinued. The postwar editors reaffirmed that the goals of the journal were to provide an international perspective on the current state of musicology and to provide a forum for the international musicology community and individual scholars. Bärenreiter became the official publisher of the journal in 1954. *Acta Musicologia* became a semiannual publication in 1972. Each issue has approximately 150 pages and an average of seven articles plus communications.[3]

Articles of the past decade include those by prominent international authors, and reflect current trends and issues and recent scholarship. Examples are Jeanne Swack's "Telemann Research Since 1975" (64.2:139-164), Helen Greenwald's "Recent Puccini Research" (65.1:23-50), Hans Tischler's "Gace Brulé and the Melodic Formulae" (67.2:164-74), David Hiley's "Writings on Western Plainchant in the 1980s and 1990s" (69.1:53-93), Amnon Shiloah's "Music and Religion in Islam" (69.2:143-155), and Elaine Sisman's "Tradition and Transformation in the Alternating Variations of Haydn and Beethoven" (62.2-3:152-182).

Archiv für Musikwissenschaft
(Stuttgart, Germany: Franz Steiner Verlag, 1918-)

Archiv für Musikwissenschaft (AMw) has been one of the most significant musicology journals since its inception in 1918. It has served as the forum for some of the most important German music scholarship of the twentieth-century. Despite a hiatus in publication from 1927 to 1952, the journal has firmly maintained continuity in title, purpose, and character. It serves as a forum for serious music scholarship. Its editors and contributors are recognized German-speaking members of the musicological community.[4]

The early volumes contained articles by important scholars, such as Curt Sachs, Egon Wellesz, and Arnold Schering. Topics included musicological methodology, iconography, ethnomusicology, and interdisciplinary inquiries. It is interesting to note that the early issues had few articles on nineteenth-century Western art music and no articles on early twentieth-century music.[5]

When *Archiv für Musikwissenschaft* resumed publication in 1952 after a twenty-five year break, its format and coverage remained the same. However, each *Jahrgang* was now divided into several issues (three or four) while the total number of pages was reduced. Although the articles were all in German and most of the contributors were German-speaking authors, the topics were not restricted to German music. The subject coverage also remained the same. Nineteenth-century music continued to be avoided and ethnomusicology excluded, but articles on twentieth-century music appeared occasionally.[6]

There have been few changes since 1952. Short biographies of contributing authors were added in the eleventh *Jahrgang*. The listing of "books received" was reinstated in 1964 after being omitted from 1952 to 1963. Since 1970, there has been a trend to include more articles on twentieth-century music, especially that of the Second Viennese School, and on ethnomusicology.[7] As of 1985, *AMw* shifted to a quarterly publication schedule. Each issue usually has four articles, and an index for each *Jahrgang* is issued at the end of the year. Advertisements for musicology-related publications are included sparingly. Since 1966, the journal has issued a series of *Beihefte,* monographs on specific topics consistent with the range of topics covered by the journal.

The editorial staff has remained constant and has included noteworthy scholars such as Carl Dahlhaus, Hans Heinrich Eggebrecht, and Kurt von

Fischer. Recent contributors are notable musicologists such as Gerhard Splitt, William Kinderman, Ulrich Siegele, Werner Breig, and Hans Tischler.

Journal of the American Musicological Society
(Chicago, IL: American Musicological Society, 1948-)

Fourteen years after the founding of the American Musicological Society in 1948, it started its official publication. The journal became the primary source of information for the society and replaced other society publications. It was quickly recognized as the foremost American musicological journal.[8] The editorial process has been consistent over the years even though it has never been clearly stated. The first two editors, Oliver Strunk and Donald Grout, emphasized the value of quality writing. A clearer policy was defined by the editor in 1978, Nicholas Temperley, and was printed in vol. 31.

Each issue has between three to six scholarly articles. Topics include Western art music from the Middle Ages through the twentieth-century, ancient music, and non-Western music. Although the majority of the articles were originally concerned with Western art music from the Middle Ages through the nineteenth-century, there is now a trend to increase coverage of twentieth-century music, popular music, jazz, and ethnomusicology. An important feature of the journal is thorough book reviews written by subject specialists. The "Communications" portion of each issue is devoted to announcements, errata, and a forum for readers to comment on articles. The "Colloquy" section was added in 1997 and contains "lengthy scholarly responses formerly printed under 'Communications.' "[9] A section on "Publications Received" began in 1954 and includes books as well as music. A list of contributors with brief biographies is included in each issue, and an index is provided at the end of each volume, in the fall issue. A moderate amount of advertisements for musicology-related publications is included. The Society also publishes a semiannual AMS Newsletter that includes general Society information and annual meeting details.

Authors of articles in the past decade include noted American scholars writing on current trends, issues, and research. Examples are "Idealism and the Aesthetics of Instrumental Music at the Turn of the Nineteenth Century" by Mark Evan Bonds (50.2-3:387-420), "Haydn's Theater Symphonies" by Elaine Sisman (43.2:292-352), "Gendering Modern Music: Thoughts on the Monteverdi-Artusi Controversy" by Suzanne Cusick (46.1:1-25), "Ruth Crawford's 'Spiritual Concept': The Sound-Ideals of an Early American

Modernist" by Judith Tick (44.2:221-261) and "Crossing Over with Rubén Blades" by Don Randel (44.2:301-323).

Journal of the Royal Musical Association
(London, England: Oxford University Press, 1874-)

In 1874, the Musical Association was started by John Stainer "for the investigation and discussion of subjects connected with the art and science of music."[10] The journal was produced to print the spoken proceedings of the society. It was not intended to be a scholarly publication and was considered entertaining reading for trained musicians.[11] By the 1930s, some scholarly articles were printed along with those for the amateur musician; however, the nature of the journal's topics was still more general than its German counterparts.[12]

The journal changed its name to *Proceedings of the Royal Musical Association* in 1944 (v.71). There had been an increase in membership and not all of the papers presented at the meetings could be printed. In the 1960s, the journal started to emulate the format of other international music journals, and scholarly essays replaced meeting papers. In 1986, the *Proceedings of the Royal Musical Association* was replaced by the semiannual publication the *Journal of the Royal Musical Association*. The new journal strives to present international scholarship covering all areas of music. Each issue contains approximately five substantial articles along with reviews and advertisements.

Recent articles by notable scholars include "Re-Reading 'Poppea': Some Thoughts on Music and Meaning in Monteverdi's Last Opera" by Tim Carter (122.2:173-204), "Vienna's Private Theatrical and Music Life, 1783-92, as Reported by Count Karl Zinzendorf" by Dorothea Link (122.2:205-257), "Palestrina as Historicist: The Two L'homme Armé Masses" by James Haar (121.2:191-205) as well as contributions by Reinhard Strohm, Jean-Jacques Nattiez, and Rob Wegman. Exceptional musicologists, such as John Butt, Richard Sherr, Mark Everist, Michael Talbot, Winton Dean, and Rose Rosengard Subotnik, have contributed the journal's reviews.

Music and Letters
(Oxford, England: Oxford University Press, 1920-)

Music and Letters began in 1920 with a specific focus. It was not conceived as a research journal, although it does contain sophisticated musicology articles. Its goal is to present well-written articles about music and about the relationship between music and other disciplines. Earlier editors, specifically A. H. Fox Strangways and Jack A. Westrup, precisely articulated the journal's purpose and dedication to exemplary writing.[13]

Articles included in the journal reflect many subjects from specific composers, genres, and instruments to ethnomusicology, and chronological periods spanning ancient to modern. There is, however, a focus on Western art music from 1500-1950. *Music and Letters* does not publish analyses. The journal is published quarterly with an occasional two issues combined. The journal includes reviews of books and music, correspondence, and a list of books received. A moderate amount of advertisements for musicology-related publications is included. The journal was under private ownership until 1955, at which point its direction was assigned to a board consisting of representatives from the Royal Music Association, the Oxford University Press, and the journal's editors.

Over the years, the journal's editors, such as Jack Westrup, Denis Arnold and Nigel Fortune, have been recognized scholars. Noteworthy recent articles include "Medieval Instrumental Dance Music" by Joan Rimmer (72.1: 61-68), "Constructing Johann Christoph Bach (1642-1703)" by Daniel Melamed (80.3:345-365), "Bartók's Last Concert?" by Malcolm Gillies (78.1: 92-100), "New Light on the Mozarts' London Visit" by Ian Woodfield (76.2:187-208), and "Donald Martino: A Survey of his Recent Music" by David Nicholls (73.1:75-79).

Musical Quarterly
(Cary, NC: Oxford University Press, 1915-)

Musical Quarterly is similar in many ways to *Music and Letters*.[14] It began in 1915 under the editorship of Oscar Sonneck. Sonneck and Rudolph Schirmer believed that a quality music journal similar to those appearing in Europe did not exist in America. The goal of the journal was and continues to be to present articles by the foremost scholars regardless of nationality.[15] Early articles were submitted by Percy Grainger, J. H. Fuller-Maitland, Camille Saint-Saëns, Egon Wellesz, Béla Bartók and Alexander Wheelock Thayer. Under the editorship of Paul Henry Lang, from 1946 to 1973, the journal became an influential forum for musicological discussion, a status which it maintains to this day.

In 1984, under the editorship of Eric Salzman, the mission of the *Musical Quarterly* shifted. In reaction to changes in music publishing and the evolution of music as a discipline, the journal now offered "a greater emphasis on contemporary and American music, on non-Western music, on the vernacular everywhere, on the vast issues of music in society, on the relationships between music and language and between music and the other arts."[16] The journal continued to publish traditional musicological articles, and encouraged authors of specialized articles and analyses to find a more appropriate forum.

Each issue contains between six and eight substantial articles along with book and recording reviews. Articles within issues are grouped by subject. Standard headings for these include "Music and Culture," "American Musics," "Institutions, Industries, Technologies," "Primary Sources," and "The Twentieth Century." Advertisements for musicology-related publications are included. Periodically, there are issues with specific themes such as "Music as Heard" (82.3-4), "75th Anniversary Issue" (75.4), and "Culture, Gender and Music: A Forum on the Mendelssohn Family" (77.4). Recent noteworthy contributions include "Film as Musicology" by Robert Marshall (81.2:173-179),[17] "Mozart and Da Ponte" by Daniel Heartz (79.4:700-718), "Music and Sociology for the 1990s: A Changing Critical Perspective" by Derek Scott (74.3:385-410), "Conversation with Nicolas Slonimsky about His Composing" by Richard Kostelanetz (74.3:458-472), "The Diatonic Looking-Glass, or an Ivesian Metamorphosis" by Allen Forte (76.3:355-382), "Irving Berlin's Early Songs as Biographical Documents" by Charles Hamm (77.1:10-34), and "Crossing Boundaries in Music and Musical Scholarship: A Perspective from Ethnomusicology" by Kay Kaufman Shelemay (80.1:13-30).

Die Musikforschung
(Kassel, Germany: Bärenreiter, 1948-)

Die Musikforschung began in 1948 under the auspices of the Gesellschaft für Musikforschung. Frederick Blume, the founding president of the Society, described it as being for all friends of musicology. The journal replaced other Society publications and provided a forum for German musicological scholarship.[18]

Each issue appears with three to four major scholarly articles, short reports, and book reviews. Articles reflect the trends and perspectives of German musicology and cover Medieval, Renaissance, Baroque, eighteenth-, nineteenth-, and twentieth-century music along with comparative musicology. Most contributors are German-speaking scholars.[19]

Valuable features of *Die Musikforschung* include a yearly compilation of all German-language dissertations completed in the previous year, a semiannual list of all music courses in German-speaking universities, and Society membership information. Also included are advertisements for books, music, and other periodicals.[20]

Editors for *Die Musikforschung* have included important musicologists, such as Hans Albrecht and Ludwig Finscher. Recent articles by notable scholars include "Neues zur Enstehungsgeschichte von Wagners 'Lohengrin': Das wiedergefundene Blatt 14 der Kompositionsskizze" (New Information about the Genesis of Wagner's 'Lohengrin': The Rediscovered Folio of Fourteen Composition Sketches) by Werner Breig (51.3:273-301), "Schumanns neuer Zugang zum Kunstlied: Das 'Liederjahr 1840' in kompositorischer Hinsicht" (Schumann's New Approach to the Art Song: The 'Liederjahr of 1840' from a Compositional Viewpoint) by Konrad Kuester (51.1:1-14), and "Johann Sebastian Bach im Urteil Moritz Hauptmanns" (Moritz Hauptmann's Opinion of Johann Sebastian Bach) by Hans-Joachim Schulze (50.1:18-23).

In addition to the titles described above, there are two noteworthy publications that focus on a specific historical period of Western Art Music: *Early Music* and *Nineteenth Century Music*.

Interest in the field of "early music" has blossomed internationally over the past twenty-five years. The term was used originally to describe the musical literature, instruments, performance practice, and a methodologies of study for music composed before 1750, the year of Johann Sebastian Bach's death. In practice, it represents music from the early Middle Ages to the end of the Baroque era. However, recent rethinking of musicology and historical performance has broadened the use of the term. Early music in contemporary musicology not only describes pre-Classical music but also the application of a new methodology to music after 1750. Therefore, the music of Haydn, Mozart, and even nineteenth-century composers such as Mendelssohn, are being reinvestigated within their historical contexts. The journal *Early Music* is an important publication for scholars and musicians.

Early Music
(London, England: Oxford University Press, 1973-)

Early Music began publication in 1973 under the editorship of J. M. Thomson. In the first issue he described the purpose of the journal:

> We want those who play or listen to early music to feel that here is an international forum where diverse issues and interests can be debated and discussed. We want to provide a link between the finest scholarship of our day and the amateur and professional listener and performer.[21]

The journal thoroughly covers all aspects of Medieval, Renaissance, and Baroque music, including instruments, performance practice, recent scholarship, notation, repertory, and composers. Articles on aspects of music from the Classical and Romantic periods are sometimes included.[22] It successfully disseminates valuable information to all members of the early music community: scholars, performers, informed amateurs, and instrument makers and collectors.

The journal's format has changed little since 1973. It is published quarterly and each issue has between 5 and 10 major articles, book, music, and recording reviews along with advertisements for related publications and recordings. Additional sections include "Reports," "Obituaries," "Salesroom," and "Correspondence." Articles are scholarly but not academic in nature.[23] Special issues are devoted to specific topics, for example, Guillaume de Machaut (5.4), Johann Sebastian Bach (13.2), The Baroque Stage (17.4 and 18.1), and Early Dance (26.2). A distinguishing feature of *Early Music* is its extraordinary visual beauty. Engravings, woodcuts, and manuscript facsimiles are generously included in each issue.[24]

Nineteenth Century Music
(Berkeley, CA: University of California Press, 1977-)

Nineteenth Century Music was founded in 1977 by a group of musicologists at the University of California who believed that recent scholarship on nineteenth-century music was not adequately represented in traditional American musicological publications.[25] The journal also wanted to present a forum for a broader approach to music scholarship, including criticism as well as historical research and analysis.[26] This is a scholarly journal intended for an educated reader, and it is the only major periodical devoted to music of the Romantic period.[27] Occasionally, articles on early twentieth-century music are also featured. The biases of American musicology are evident in the journal.[28]

The journal's format has been consistent since 1977. There are three issues a year, each issue having four or five major articles. Some issues are devoted to a specific topic or composer, such as Verdi (2.2), Schubert (17.1 and 21.2), or "Music in Its Social Contexts" (16.2). There is an unsigned "Comment and Chronicle" section at the end of each issue that announces publications and awards, and provides brief biographies for the issue's contributing authors along with other information. Some issues include reviews; all issues have advertisements for relevant publications. The last issue of each volume, which is published in the spring, contains an index for the entire volume.

Editors have included Joseph Kerman, D. Kern Holoman, Robert Winter, Walter Frisch, James Hepokoski, and Lawrence Kramer. Recent articles by important musicologists include "Schubert's 'Unfinished' Symphony" by

Maynard Solomon (22.1:11-133), "Women in Music, Feminist Criticism, and Guerilla Musicology: Reflections on Recent Polemics" by Paula Higgins (27.2:1993), "Criticism, Faith, and the *Idee:* A. B. Marx's Early Reception of Beethoven" by Scott Burnham (13.3:183-192), and "Brahms and the Variation Canon" by Elaine Sisman (14.2:132-153).

MUSIC THEORY

Music Theory has been summarized as "the abstract principles embodied in music and the sounds of which it consists."[29] In practical terms, it is a discipline closely related to musicology and music history, concentrating on music analysis and the compositional, harmonic, and formal design of musical compositions. Music theory journals include articles discussing specific genres and their harmonic and formal components, compositional techniques, broad issues of formal design, analytic techniques, and chronological aspects of compositional and analytical devices. Some recent articles discuss music theory, music analysis and their relationship to the "new musicology."

Computer Music Journal
(Cambridge, MA: MIT Press, 1977-)

Computer Music Journal was founded in September 1976 and is "devoted to high-quality musical applications of digital electronics."[30] The first publisher, John Snell, describes its goals: "To publish the results of computer music research (mostly university-based at the time), and to publish articles by composers who were making interesting use of computers."[31] The journal has successfully remained progressive and scholarly and is respected by the musical community. Much of the research and composition described in its articles has originated in prestigious research centers or academic institutions.

The journal contains articles discussing technical aspects of computer music, artificial intelligence, composition, and performance as well as interviews and conference reports. The Tenth Anniversary Issue has a complete index of contents by issue and author for vols. 1-9 by Nicola Bernardini (10.1:17-36, 37-39) and a short history of the journal. The subject index by Bernardini is included in the subsequent issue (10.2:51-55).[32] The Twentieth Anniversary Issue (20.1) includes articles on the history and current state of the art in computer music. In addition to feature articles, "Letters," "Announcements," and "News," issues regularly include "Interview," "Reviews," and "Products of Interest" departments. A limited amount of advertising appears in each issue. Sound recordings accompany some issues.

Most issues are centered on a theme. Such themes include "Recent Research at IRCAM" (23.3), "Bringing Digital Music to Life" (20.2), and "Composition and Performance in the 1990s" (18.2-3). Recent notable articles include "Recent Research and Development at IRCAM" by Hugues Vinet (23.3:9-17), "Nonlinear Dynamics in Physical Models: Simple Feedback-Loop Systems and Properties" by Xavier Rodet (23.3:18-34), "Recent Developments in Computer Sound Analysis and Synthesis" by Xavier Rodet (20.1:57-61), and "Sociological, Artistic, and Pedagogical Frameworks for Electronic Art" by Richard Povall (21.1:18-25).

Journal of Music Theory
(New Haven, CT: Yale University, 1957)

The *Journal of Music Theory* is a publication of Yale University and started under the auspices of its School of Music in 1957. The goal of the journal is to present an international forum for the exchange of ideas within the field, and to establish music theory as "a mode of creative thought" rather than a "didactic convenience, . . . a necessary discipline."[33] The range of topics covered in the journal are broad and include Western and non-Western music of all time periods, analyses of works, as well as articles on analytic techniques, the history of music theory, bibliography, and pedagogy.[34]

The *Journal of Music Theory* has been an important and influential publication for music scholarship in America. It is a serious, scholarly journal that has affected musicology and the evolution of music theory as a discipline. Many of the contributing authors are leading authorities who have investigated repertories and analytic techniques and have suggested new analytic methodologies. Landmark articles that have appeared in the journal include "Set Structure as a Compositional Determinant" by Milton Babbitt (5:72-94), "The Source Set and its Aggregate Formations" by Donald Martino (5:224-73), "Schenker's Conception of Music Structure" (3:1-30), "A Theory of Set-Complexes for Music" (8:136-83), "The Domain and Relations of Set Complex Theory" (9:173-80) by Allen Forte, and "Toward a Formal Theory of Tonal Music" by Fred Lerdahl and Ray Jackendoff (21:111-71). Many influential figures have served as editorial board members. Current board members include Sarah Fuller, Jean-Jacques Nattiez, David Lewin, and Claude Palisca.

The journal is published semiannually. Each issue has approximately four articles with additional departments, including "Reviews," "Books Received," and "Letters to the Editor." Special issues and themes appear occasionally. A modest amount of advertisement for related publications and other societies is included.

Journal of New Music Research
(Netherlands: Swets & Zeitlinger Publishers, 1972-)

This journal first appeared in 1972 as *Interface* as a result of the merger of *Jaarboek* (Seminar for Musicology in Ghent) and *Electronic Music Reports* (Institute of Sonology in Utrecht).[35] It is "devoted to discussion of all questions which fall into the borderline areas between music on the one hand, and physical and human sciences or related technologies on the other. New fields of research, as well as new methods of investigation in known fields, receive special emphasis."[36] In 1994 its name changed to *Journal of New Music Research,* and its scope was revised to represent the "growing interest of the international community in the interdisciplinary foundations of music."[37] Its contents present a "discussion of the musical and scientific issues involved in new music and new music research. These issues include the study of instrumental, electronic, and computer music; music-related work in DSP, psychoacoustics, perception, cognition, and information sciences; as well as musicological work dealing with the theoretical or historical foundations of the above topics."[38]

The *Journal of New Music Research* is scholarly and technical; its articles cover computer music technology, instrumental techniques, music cognition, music education, and music theory. The journal is published quarterly, each issue has between three and five articles and some issues include interviews, reviews, letters to the editor, or publisher's announcements. Because of the editors' language preference most of the articles are in English, but some contributions have appeared in French and German.[39] A modest amount of advertising appears in most issues.

Special topical issues are published regularly, such as "Music and Artificial Intelligence" (25.3), "Auditory Models of Music Research" (23.1-2), and "Analysis of Electroacoustic Music" (27.1-2). Recent articles include "Formalization of Generative Structures within Stravinsky's 'The Rite of Spring'" by Adriano De Matteis and Goffredo Haus (25.1: 47-76), "Formalization of Computer Music Interaction Through a Semiotic Approach" by Fernando Iazzetta (25.3:212-230), "Artificial Neural Networks Based Models for Automatic Performance of Musical Scores" by Roberto Bresin (27.3:271-292), and "Resonance in the Perception of Musical Pulse" by Leon van Noorden and Dirk Moelants (28.1:43-66).

Music Theory Spectrum
(Berkeley, CA: Society for Music Theory, Inc., 1979-)

Music Theory Spectrum is the official journal of the Society for Music Theory, founded in 1977. Scholars such as Allen Forte, Wallace Berry, Richmond Browne and Mary Wennerstrom led the amicable separation of the society from the American Musicological Society. The journal was intended as a forum for scholarly work in music theory and not as one with a specifically historical focus like the *Journal of the American Musicological Society.*[40] It is a serious, academic journal devoted to providing quality articles on a broad range of topics in music theory. Articles have appeared on Schenkerian studies, the history of theory, music analyses, speculative theory, and topics ranging from medieval to contemporary music.

The journal has been consistent in format since its inception in 1979. It is published twice a year and each issue has approximately four articles plus features such as "Reviews" and "Communications." There are ongoing series, such as "Teaching Music Theory" which appeared in vols. 2 and 3, and there have been special issues, for example vol. 7 titled "Time and Rhythm in Music." The journal's contributing authors represent the finest contemporary scholars, including Allen Forte, Edward Cone, Robert Morgan, Ethan Haimo, and Peter Westergaard. Younger scholars are also well represented. A modest amount of advertisement is included.

Noteworthy articles that have appeared in recent issues include "Symmetrical Form and Common-Practice Tonality" by Robert Morgan (20.1:1-47), "The Medial Caesura and Its Role in the Eighteenth-Century Sonata Exposition" by Warren Darcy and James Hepokoski (19.2:115-154), "Liszt's Open Structures and the Romantic Fragment" by Ramon Satyendra (19.2:184-205), and "Geometries of Sounds in Time" by Peter Westergaard (18.1:1-21). Scholars such as Nicolas Cook and William Kinderman have contributed book reviews.

Perspectives of New Music
(Seattle, WA: University of Washington Press, 1962-)

This journal was founded in 1962 with support from the Fromm Music Foundation and with the guidance of Paul Fromm, Arthur Berger, and Benjamin Boretz. In recent years, Princeton University and the University of Washington have provided financial support to the journal.[41] The purposes of *Perspectives of New Music* are to provide an American journal that concentrates on contemporary music, to provide a forum for composers, performers, and listeners, and "to probe deeply as possible into fundamental issues that by their nature must be treated concretely and analytically with sophisticated methods, and that require investigation from many different sides."[42]

The journal's articles are sophisticated and technical, and are written for an informed audience. The journal faithfully retains a forum-like approach. Although many of the articles concentrate on contemporary music or music theory, those are not the journal's exclusive topics. Young scholars as well as established ones are represented in the journal's articles. Numerous contributions have appeared by Milton Babbitt, Elaine Barkin, Arthur Berger, Benjamin Boretz, Edward Cone, David Lewin, Allen Forte, and Robert Morris. Two issues are published a year, with eight or more articles per issue. Occasionally, special double issues are published, such as "Critical Celebration of Milton Babbitt at 60" (vol. 18-19) and "A Kenneth Gaburo Memorial" (vol. 33). Interviews have featured John Adams (34.2:88-105) and Christian Wolff (32.2:54-87). Departments have varied over the years and include "Editorial Notes," "Correspondence," "Personae" and "Colloquy and Review." Sound recordings in the form of cassettes or compact discs accompany many issues in vols. 23 to 30.

Recent articles include "Electroacoustic Performance Practice" by Karlheinz Stockhausen (34.1:74-105), "Changing the Metaphor: Ratio Models of Music Pitch in the Work of Harry Partch, Ben Johnston, and James Tenney" by Bob Gilmore (33:458-503), "Fakin' It/Makin'It: Falsetto's Bid for Transcendence in the 1970s Disco Highs" by Anne-Lise François (22:442-457), and "A Conversation about Feminism and Music" by Pauline Oliveros and Fred Maus (32.2: 174-193).

ETHNOMUSICOLOGY

The field of ethnomusicology, developed in the late nineteenth-century in Europe and the United States, focuses on the cultural contexts of Western and non-Western music. Contemporary ethnomusicology includes the study of aesthetics, sociology, and anthropology of music, and musical traditions and instruments of the world.[43] General ethnomusicology journals include articles on aspects of music from specific geographic areas, chronological perspectives of specific repertories, philosophical issues and practical aspects of fieldwork, and ethical issues in ethnomusicology. Frequently, these journals contain articles that discuss specific musicological, philosophical, sociological, anthropological, psychological, and ethnographic issues.

Ethnomusicology
(Champaign, IL: Society of Ethnomusicology, 1953-)

Ethnomusicology was first published in 1953 and serves as the official organ of the Society for Ethnomusicology. It began as a newsletter called *Ethno-Musicology* and was sent to scholars interested in communicating about their research and interests. The mailing grew rapidly in the first year. The first eleven issues were later combined to constitute the first volume. The Society for Ethnomusicology was formed two years later, in 1955, at the Fifty-fourth Annual Meeting of the American Anthropological Association. The Society and the journal have had a major influence on the development of the field of ethnomusicology.[44]

The content and scope of the journal have changed over the years and reflect the evolving youthful state of ethnomusicology as a discipline.[45] Journal contents include articles on repertories, instruments, methodology, music transcriptions, dance, bibliography, and technology. Art music and popular music from all continents are discussed. In 1969, criticism of the Society and the journal prompted the editor to include more articles on music of the United States. Further concerns were voiced in a 1976 editorial regarding the lack of contributions from Latin American, African, Asian, and European scholars.

The journal is published three times a year and includes four or more feature articles, reviews and listings of current books, recordings and videos, listings of related theses and dissertations, and bibliographies. Some advertising is included in each issue. Special issues are often published. Recent examples include "Issues in Ethnomusicology" (41.2) "Music and Religion" (40.3) and "Music in Politics" (38.2). Articles are contributed by established and younger scholars alike. Recent articles of note include "The Social Meanings of Modal Practice: Status, Gender, History, and *Pathet* in Central Javanese Music" by Marc Perlman (42.1:45-80), "Pilgrimage, Politics, and the Musical Remapping of the New Europe" by Philip V. Bohlman (40.3:374-412), "Reminiscences and Exhortations: Growing up in American Folk Music" by Bess Lomax Hawes (39.2:179-192) and "Micromusics of the West: A Comparative Approach" by Mark Slobin (36.1:1-88).

World of Music
(Berlin, Germany: Verlag für Wissenschaft und Bildung, 1959-)

This journal was first published in 1959 as an update of the *Bulletin of the International Music Council* (IMC). Its purpose was to disseminate the council's action. In 1967 the International Institute for Comparative Music

Studies and Documentation (ICMSD) joined with the IMC, under new council leadership, to produce a new publication. This new publication would publish articles on the broad spectrum of the "world of music." The journal became more scholarly, and its articles increased in length. In 1978, the editor announced that format and content changes would be made; most of the journal would be devoted to world music but a portion would be used for contribution from the IMC and related organizations. Descriptive articles on musical traditions dominated the journal.[46] The numerous changes to the journal continued and, in 1997, the journal's affiliation changed once again to become the journal of the Department of Ethnomusicology of the Otto-Friedrich University of Bamberg.

World of Music is published three times a year, and most issues have a theme. Recent themes include "Hearing and Listening in Cultural Contexts" (41.1), "Music and Healing in Transcultural Perspectives" (39.1), and "Jewish Musical Culture-Past and Present" (37.1). Each issue has approximately five articles, several book and recording reviews, an article on a specific world music institution, and some advertisements. The journal's contents and the contributing authors reflect the international scope of the journal. All contributions are published in English.

Recent articles include "The Mbira, Worldbeat, and the International Imagination" by Thomas Turino (40.2:85-106), "Ritual or Imaginary Ethnography in Stravinsky's *Le sacre du printemps*" by Martin Zenk (40.1:61-78), "Cognitive and Interpersonal Dimensions of Listening in Javanese Gamelan Performance" by Ben Brinner (41.1:19-36), and "Performing the Drone in Hindustani Classical Music: What Mughal Paintings Show Us to Hear" by Bonnie Wade (38.2:41-68).

Yearbook for Traditional Music
(New York, NY: International Council of Traditional Music & UNESCO, 1981-)

The *Yearbook for Traditional Music* originated as the annual *International Folk Music Council Journal* in 1949. It featured conference papers on folksong studies and analyses, regional studies, and broad issues of folk music investigation. The council had many influential members as presidents, including Ralph Vaughan Williams, Jaap Kunst, and Zoltán Kodály.[47] There were many changes to the journal over the years. In 1969, the council decided to replace "Journal" with "Yearbook" to describe accurately the character of the publication. Also that year, the journal's numbering was reset to volume 1, and the quality and quantity of articles was increased. In 1981, the council adopted the current title, replacing "folk" with "traditional." The scope of the journal was redefined "as a vehicle for extensive studies dealing in depth with aspects of the membership's original research, presenting surveys of complete or in-progress work with specific cultural entities and or regions."[48]

The contents of the *Yearbook* reflect the themes from the conference held the preceding year. Examples include "Yugoslavfest" (4), "East Asia" (15), and "Studia Musicologia Academiae Scientarium Hungaricae" (17.2). Articles appear only in English. Included in the journal are organization proceedings, festival information, news, correspondence, and reviews. Recent articles include "Tales Tunes Tell: Deepening the Dialogue Between 'Classical' and 'Non-Classical' in the Music of India" by Matthew Allen (30:22-52), "Arrows and Circles: An Anniversary Talk About Fifty Years of ICTM and the Study of Traditional Music" by Bruno Nettl (30:1-11), "Folk Music Studies and Ethnomusicology in Spain" by Josep Marti (29:107-140), and "The Forked Shawm—An Ingenious Invention" by Jeremy Montagu (29: 74-79).

Several ethnomusicology journals concentrate on the music and traditions of specific geographic regions. Discussions of broader ethnomusicological issues are covered in relationship to these regions. Notable examples include *Asian Music* (New York, NY: Society for Asian Music, 1968-) and *Latin American Music Review* (Austin, TX: University of Texas Press, 1980-).

MUSIC EDUCATION

There are many journals dedicated to music education. Articles in these publications discuss practical and theoretical aspects of teaching music in classrooms and studios at all levels, pre-school through graduate school. Some journals concentrate on a specific instrument, population or educational philosophy, while others provide a broad perspective on teaching music.

Instrumentalist
(Northfield, IL: Instrumentalist Co., 1946-)

The first issue of *Instrumentalist* appeared in 1946, a time when school music programs were being revitalized after World War II. The journal's goal was to serve school and college band directors, instrumental teachers, and teacher-training professionals.[49] *Instrumentalist* has continued to serve these audiences. The journal has consistently published articles on standard topics, such as technique and repertory for specific instruments, arranging, fundraising, competitions, concert band, marching band, and new music. *Instrumentalist* has also reflected current trends and developments with articles on electronic music, new musical styles and instructional uses of computer technology. The journal also includes coverage of jazz bands and drum corps.

Instrumentalist has increased its frequency of publication over the decades and became a monthly journal in 1978. Each issue has approximately eight articles, and many issues have interviews with influential teachers or musicians. Regular departments include "Recent Recordings," "New Music Reviews," "Musical Stories," "Idea Exchange," "Calendar," "Job Guide," "Honors and Appointments" and "From Our Readers." Since its inception, the journal has maintained its practical perspective on instrumental music education. *Instrumentalist* has also printed directories of summer camps, clinics, and workshops. Each issue has copious advertisements for instruments, accessories, uniforms, music, and related merchandise.

Journal of Research in Music Education
(Reston, VA: MENC: The National Association for Music Education, 1953-)

During a meeting of the Music Educators National Conference (MENC) in 1952, there was a discussion of the lack of a journal devoted to publishing music education research. Articles on research in music education were printed in music, education, or general music education journals. MENC supported the publication of the *Journal of Research in Music Education* to meet the needs of the music education community.[50] The journal's mission is to publish music education research and to serve as a forum for sharing ideas, research techniques, and methodologies and for raising the standards of music education research. The journal is the oldest national music education research journal in the country. Its articles are scholarly and consistently high in quality.

The journal was published semiannually from 1953 to 1963 and has been published quarterly since 1963. Each issue has between six and nine articles along with two departments, "Forum" and "Announcements." Book reviews appeared with some regularity in early issues. There are no advertisements in the issues. The MENC "Code of Ethics" is printed regularly. The journal has occasionally published lists of completed doctoral dissertations in music and music education. Many contributors are college and university music education professors and researchers.

Recent articles include "Children's Auditory Discrimination of Simultaneous Melodies" by Helga Gudmundsdottir (47.2:101-110), "Philosophy and Advocacy: An Examination of Preservice Music Teachers' Beliefs" by James R. Austin and Deborah Reinhardt (47.1:18-30), "Senior Research Acceptance Address: Personal Perspectives on Research: Past, Present, and Future" by Rudolf E. Radocy (46.3:342-350), and "An Empirical Study Concerning Technology Relating to Aesthetic Response to Music" by John A. Lychner (46.2:303-319).

Music Educators Journal
(Reston, VA: MENC: The National Association for Music Education, 1914-)

The *Music Educators Journal* is the organ of the Music Educators National Conference (MENC). MENC is a nonprofit organization supporting all aspects of music education in schools, colleges, and universities. The journal has its origins in *School Music Magazine,* the journal of MENC's predecessor, the Music Supervisors National Conference which was founded in 1907.[51] When the organization changed its name, the journal also changed to its current title. The writing in the early issues was not sophisticated and consisted of conference news and reports and articles on practical and theoretical aspects of music education. Over the decades, the journal developed notably, and the quality of the articles increased significantly.[52] The *Music Educators Journal* is a respected music education journal with well-written, practical articles and research findings.

The journal has published nine issues a year since 1966. Each issue has approximately five articles along with regular departments, including "Music Matters," "Readers' Comment," "MENC Today," "For Your Library," "Video Views," and "Current Readings." The articles discuss teaching strategies, methodologies, repertories, results of music education studies, technology in music education, performance issues, and classroom management techniques. There are numerous book, music, recording, and video recording reviews in each issue. The abundance of advertisements in each issue is indicative of the close relationship between the music education profession and the music industry.[53]

Recent articles include "An Aural Approach to Improvisation" by Christopher Azzara (86.3:21-25), "Internet Resources for General Music" by Keith Thompson (86.3:30-36), "Stravinsky's 'Firebird' and Young Children" by Edith Roebuck (86.1:34-36, 52), and "Popular Music and the Instrumental Ensemble" by George Boespflug (85.6:33-37).

MUSIC THERAPY

The field of music therapy has grown significantly in the past two decades. Articles in music therapy journals include documentation of the clinical research and practical applications of music used to positively affect psychological and cognitive functioning and mental and physical health.

Journal of Music Therapy
(Silver Spring, MD: American Music Therapy
Association, Inc., 1964-)

The *Journal of Music Therapy* is the official publication of the American Music Therapy Association. The journal originated as the *Music Therapy Annual Books of Proceedings,* published by the National Association of Music Therapy, Inc. from 1952 to 1963. The main purpose of the *Journal of Music Therapy* is to "encourage and promote scholarly inquiry in music therapy, to disseminate results of music therapy research and innovations in clinical practice, and thus to advance knowledge of music therapy theory and practice."[54] The *Journal of Music Therapy* is a prominent publication in the field of music therapy and has published respected and influential articles.[55]

The journal has been a quarterly publication since its first issue. Each issue contains between three and five scholarly articles. Topics include theoretical and philosophical issues, research techniques, empirical studies, work with specific populations and concepts, and applications of work by psychologists and music therapists. Book reviews and guest editorials are included in current issues; however, the journal's other departments were discontinued with volume 11.

Recent articles include "Music Exposure and Criminal Behavior: Perceptions of Juvenile Offenders" by Susan Gardstrom (36.3:207-221), "Musical and Verbal Interventions in Music Therapy: A Qualitative Study" by Dorit Amir (36.2:144-175), "The Effect of Singing on Alert Responses in Persons with Late Stage Dementia" by Alicia Ann Clair (33.4:234-247), and "The Effects of Music Listening on Changes in Selected Physiological Parameters in Adult Pre-Surgical Patients" by Miroslaw Matejek, Barbara Miluk-Kolasa, and Romuald Stupnicki (33.3:208-218).

POPULAR MUSIC AND JAZZ

Journals about popular music and jazz have a lot of material to cover. Articles in these titles discuss artists, bands, concert tours, music trends, instruments, videos, the commercial world of music and concert, and recording reviews. Many of these titles also have feature articles on issues significant to popular culture, including HIV/AIDS, the effects of technology on society, and American political culture. All of these journals include coverage of American and global popular music.

Billboard
(New York, NY: Billboard Publishing Co, 1963-)

Billboard's origins go back to a publication started in 1894 titled *Billboard Advertising*. It served the music and entertainment industry, and its cover carried the slogan "A monthly resume of all that is new, bright and interesting on the boards." The first editor, William H. Donaldson, explained that it would be "devoted to the interests of the advertisers, poster printers, billposters, advertising agents, and secretaries of fairs."[56] The journal experienced many changes over the years, including two name changes: to *The Billboard* in 1897 and to *Billboard* in 1961.[57] The journal was published monthly from its inception until 1900, and weekly since May 1900. The journal assumed its current format in the 1960s and was printed on coated paper starting with the January 5, 1963 issue.[58]

An important function of *Billboard* is charting popularity of songs, recordings, and artists. Charts reflect sales, radio exposure, and consumer opinions. Its first chart, "Tunes Most Heard in Vaudeville Last Week," was printed in the early 1900s. The number of charts has expanded over the years. Current charts include "Top New Age Albums," "Hot R&B/Hip-Hop Singles & Tracks," "Hot Dance Music," "Top Country Albums," "Top Jazz Albums," "Top Classical Albums," "Top World Music Albums," "Adult Top 40," and "Top Video Rentals." Issues include news briefs, reviews, and articles on music of all genres, video and home entertainment industries, artists, technology, the concert and recording industries, promotion, marketing, sales, and the international music and entertainment market. The articles in *Billboard* reflect the developments, trends, and concerns of the recording and entertainment industries, artists, and consumers. Each issue includes plentiful advertising for recordings, record labels, playback equipment, retailers, and artist management companies.

Down Beat
(Chicago, IL: Maher Publications, 1934-)

When *down beat* was first published in 1934, it was originally intended to be "the musicians' newspaper."[59] Over the decades, its audience has grown to include professionals, amateurs, students, teachers, aficionados, and members of the music industry. The journal's goal has been to reflect the contemporary music world. Its coverage has varied somewhat over the decades but has generally focused on jazz, blues, and rock. *Down beat* has consistently been an advocate of musicians' interests.[60]

The journal was published bimonthly from 1939 to 1979 and monthly from 1934 to1938 and from 1979 to the present.[61] For many years, *down beat* issues included a city-by-city list of performances. In recent years the journal has included interviews, articles on influential musicians, performance, techniques, recording and video reviews, correspondence and music and trade news. Other features include readers polls, critics polls, and the "Blindfold Test," in which a musician listens to several tunes on a similar instrument or in a related idiom and tries to identify the players and to evaluate the performance.[62] Each issue contains many advertisements for recordings, instruments, educational materials, books, music, and equipment.

Melody Maker
(London, England: IPC Specialist & Professional Press, Ltd., 1926-)

Melody Maker's original purpose was to print lyrics for hit songs and to increase sheet music sales. Its early coverage included jazz, big band music, and music from Tin Pan Alley and musical theater. Because of the pressure of competition from other publications in the late 1950s, lyrics were replaced by coverage of the rock and popular music world. The journal's coverage, sophisticated style, and informative approach contributed to its success in the 1960s. Many of the best writers contributed to *Melody Maker.* Supposedly, many great bands, including Led Zeppelin and the Jam, formed through the magazine's classified ads.[63]

Melody Maker's editorial policies and British perspective have remained consistent. The journal's circulation has gradually decreased because other British popular music journals cover new trends more effectively and are more appealing to younger readers. Each weekly issue includes a broad coverage of the popular music world, including news briefs and articles on musicians, the music industry, sales and marketing, equipment, and domestic and international trends. Many of the journal's editors and writers have been respected figures in the popular music community. Record and concert reviews, itineraries, charts, and club calendars are also included in each issue.[64]

Rolling Stone
(New York, NY: Straight Arrow Publishers, 1967-)

The first issue of *Rolling Stone* was published on November 9, 1967 by owner and editor Jann Wenner. Wenner's journalistic style and effective distribution contributed to *Rolling Stone*'s success. It has provided important professional coverage of contemporary popular music and culture not available from fanzines and trade journals.[65] The journal's articles discuss many facets of rock and popular music and the entertainment industry, frequently with an emphasis on topics related to political, social, and cultural issues. Coverage has varied through the decades to reflect current trends and successfully target the journal's audience.[66] Recent issues have included retrospective surveys of music and popular culture and thorough articles on technology, AIDS, visual and performing artists, television, television personalities, classical music, and interviews.

Rolling Stone has been consistently published semimonthly since the first issue, with the exception of some double issues. Issues include up to ten feature articles, correspondence, charts, and reviews of recordings and movies. Each issue contains copious photographs and advertisements for a wide range of products, including recordings, clothes, computers, candy, health and beauty aids, cologne, cars, cigarettes, alcoholic beverages, and retailers. Many of the journal's covers and the photographs contain striking and provocative images.

Recent articles include "Confessions of a Virus Writer: The Terrorist Threat of the Digital Age" by Kim Neely (821:65-67, 130), "Nothing Weighs As Much As a Heartache: Thirty Years of Ups and Downs With The Allman Brothers Band" by Gavin Edwards (826:54-68, 114-119), "The Agony of the Kurds: A History of Persecution, Genocide and the Struggle to Find a Home" by David Harris, photographs by Sebastião Salgado (771:55-61, 123-124), and "Beastie Boys: The Boys are Back in Town" by Joe Levy, photographs by Mark Seliger. (792:48-53, 78, 80).

MUSIC LIBRARIANSHIP AND BIBLIOGRAPHY

Three noteworthy journals cover the field of music librarianship and bibliography. These journals include articles on music printing and publishing, specific music collections, surveys of materials on particular topics, collection development, technical and reference services in music libraries, and historical perspectives of music librarianship. An important feature of these journals is the book, score, journal, and recording review section.

Brio
(Birmingham, England: UK Branch of the International Association of Music Libraries, Archives and Documentation Centres, 1964-)

Ten years after the United Kingdom Branch of the International Association of Music Libraries, Archives and Documentation Centres was founded, its members voted to publish a journal.[67] *Brio* has been published twice a year since its first issue in 1964. Early issues included an index to current British music periodicals and articles on music libraries in the United Kingdom, aspects of music librarianship, and music bibliography. These issues also included some book reviews, reports from organizational meetings and member news. In 1973, the early editors resigned and the journal nearly ceased publication because of a lack of human resources, money, and publishable material. Clifford Bartlett and Malcolm Jones were persuaded to assume editorial responsibility for *Brio*. They were advised to reduce production costs and to include articles directly related to library activities. With these adjustments, the journal survived. Bartlett and Jones served as co-editors until 1980. Bartlett assumed sole responsibility for the journal until 1985 when Ian Ledsham succeeded him.[68]

Since 1974, the journal has endeavored to serve its readership, consisting primarily of British music librarians.[69] The journal disseminates branch information and contains articles on music librarianship and bibliography. There is coverage of IAML (International Association of Music Libraries, Archives and Documentation Centres) activities as well as developments in the library world.[70] Each issue contains approximately 5 articles, numerous book reviews, and regularly occurring departments, such as "News and Views," "List of Items Received," "Some Recent Articles on Music Librarianship," and an editorial. In recent years, *Brio* has included an annual bibliography of recently published music bibliographies and reference works. There is very little advertising in *Brio*.

Recent articles include "Bruckner's Publisher's, 1865-1938" by Nigel Simeone (36.1:19-38), "Oxford University Press and Music Publishing: A 75th Anniversary Retrospective" by Simon Wright (35.2:90-100), "The Prayer Book In Practice: Textual Anomalies and Their Implications in Tudor Musical Settings of the First Book of Common Prayer" by Stefan Scot (34.2:81-89), and "Managing for Quality Services" by David Ruse (29.2: 59-70).

Fontes Artis Musicae
(Madison, WI: A-R Editions, 1954-)

Fontes Artis Musicae is the organ of the International Association of Music Libraries, Archives and Documentation Centres (IAML). IAML's first meeting was held in 1951; its communications were published in *Bulletin d'information*. In 1954, the Executive Council announced that this informal publication would be replaced by a journal published by Bärenreiter. The journal's purposes "were both to facilitate the work of the organization by communicating with its scattered members between meetings and to reach a wider audience than just the members with information on music source materials."[71] The mission of *Fontes Artis Musicae* has remained the same since 1954. The journal publishes the organization's news and information, meeting and members' reports, along with articles on music libraries, music librarianship and bibliography, as well as musicological research. In 1993, A-R Editions assumed the role of publisher for the journal.

Fontes Artis Musicae is published quarterly. The portion of the journal with IAML reports includes "Council Minutes," "Treasurer's Report," and "IAML Outreach" along with reports on professional branches, subject commissions, working groups and publications, and national music library associations. Book reviews and articles on the state of music librarianship in a specific country appear regularly. Articles on music bibliography and music research are contributed by music librarians and music scholars. Although English is the primary language of the journal, there are some contributions in German. French and German abstracts are included for English articles.

Special issues that have appeared recently include "Music in Italian Libraries: The Last Decade" (43.1) "Archives and Music Libraries" (43.3), and "Music Libraries in Denmark" (42.1). Recent articles include "Music Cataloging and the Future" by James Cassaro (41.3:245-250), "Knowing the Score: Preserving Collections of Music" by Susan Sommer (41.3:256-260), "Down the Yellow Brick Road: What Should We Teach About Internet Resources?" by Sherry Vellucci (43.4:315-324), and "Köchel 2000: Suggestions for a New Catalogue of Mozart's Works" by Raul van Reijen (42.4:299-310).

Notes, Quarterly Journal of the Music Library Association
(Canton, MA: Music Library Association, Inc., 1934-)

The Music Library Association was founded in 1931 by librarians attending an American Library Association conference. Under the editorship of Eva O'Meara, *Notes for the Members of the MLA* was established in 1934 to address the concerns of the membership: collection development, cataloging and classification, bibliographic aids, and interlibrary communication. *Notes* is the oldest continuous periodical on music librarianship. The first series of the journal was printed in mimeographed form between 1934 and 1942. These issues were informal; they contained lists of bibliographic tools, bibliographies, descriptions of American music libraries, music checklists, articles on cataloging, indexing, and classification, and calls for cataloging codes and music subject headings. The second series, *MLA Notes 1,* began in 1943 under the editorship of Richard Hill. The aim of the publication remained the same despite several physical changes. This series appeared as a printed journal in octavo format, and its contents were divided into clearly defined sections. The departments and layout of the journal have remained constant since the second series.[72] In 1966, the journal's current title was adopted: *Notes, The Quarterly Journal of the MLA.*[73]

Each issue includes two or three significant articles, book and music reviews and lists of books and music recently published, communications, new and current publishers' catalogs, and new journals. The subject coverage of the journal's articles includes music librarianship, music bibliography, discography, the music trade, and certain aspects of music history.[74] An obituary/necrology index has been included for many years. Advertisements for books, scores, recordings, journals, and library vendors are included also. An index to recording reviews appeared until 1997. The journal regularly prints articles on price trends in music materials.[75] The Music Library Association also publishes the *MLA Newsletter* that contains articles and information on the organization, regional chapters, meetings, reports, and member news.

Over the years, *Notes* has printed several articles on music periodicals. These include "Mid-Nineteenth-Century American Periodical: A Case Study" by Mary Wallace Davidson (54.2:371-387), "The Mysterious WPA Music Periodical Index" by Dena Epstein (45.3:463-482), and "Searching and Sorting on the Slippery Slope: Periodical Publications of Victorian Music" by D. W. Krummel (46.3:593-608).

The articles and reviews in *Notes* are written by influential librarians, musicologists, composers, publishers, and critics. Recent articles include "The Uses of Existing Music: Musical Borrowing as a Field" by J. Peter Burkholder (50.3:851-870), "Information Literacy for Undergraduate Music Students: A Conceptual Framework" by Amanda Maple, Beth Christensen, and Kathleen A. Abromeit (52.3:744-753), and "Archival Guidelines for the Music Publishing Industry" by Kent Underwood et al. (52.4:1112-1118). Recent reviews have been contributed by Susan McClary, Malcolm Bilson, Richard Kostelanetz, David Locke, and Alfred Dürr.

MUSIC PERFORMANCE

There are numerous journals dedicated to music performance or a specific musical genre. These journals include articles on technique, interpretation, historical issues, significant current and historical performers, instrument making, and reviews of books, scores, videos, and performances. These journals frequently serve as forums for performers as well as musicologists, music theorists, and music educators.

Cambridge Opera Journal
(New York, NY: Cambridge University Press, 1989-)

Within its first ten years of publication, the *Cambridge Opera Journal* has become a respected and important music periodical. In the first issue, editors Arthur Groos and Roger Parker state that "initial contributions do seem to confirm that the time has come for a scholarly journal devoted exclusively to the study of opera."[76] Their goal was to provide a forum for presenting and discussing interdisciplinary discourse about opera and to cover as broad a scope as possible. The editors and the editorial and advisory board members are specialists in a variety of humanistic disciplines.[77] After ten years, Groos and Parker decided to "stand down" as editors,[78] and Mary Hunter assumed editorial responsibilities for the journal.

Since its inception, the journal has appeared consistently three times a year. Each issue includes approximately five articles and often one or two book reviews. A special issue was published in 1998 titled "A Symposium on Pellegrin and Rameaus' *Hippolyte et Aricie*" (10.3). A limited number of advertisements for related publications and organizations are included in each issue.

The journal has published works by young scholars as well as established ones. Recent articles include "Monteverdi's *Il ritorno d' Ulisse in patria* and the Power of 'Music'" by Ellen Rosand (7.3:179-184), "Debussy's Phantom Sounds" by Carolyn Abbate (10.1:67-96), and "Discourse and the Film Text: Four Readings of *Carmen*" by H. Marshall Leicester, Jr. (6.3:245-282). Reviews have been contributed by Peter Kivy, Reinhard Strohm, and Julian Budden.

Opera Quarterly
(Cary, NC: Oxford University Press, 1983-)

Opera Quarterly, first issued in the spring of 1983, was intended for a wide variety of readers: scholars, performers, and opera lovers. Sherwin and Irene Sloan were the founding editors, assisted by numerous opera scholars and professionals. University of North Carolina published the journal from 1983 to 1989. Duke University Press assumed publication from 1990 to 1998, and Oxford University Press is the current publisher. The journal's articles discuss opera and music history, libretti, stage direction, performers, composers, performance, and interpretation.[79]

Each issue has approximately five articles plus book, video, and recording reviews, lists of received books, videos and recordings, and correspondences. Issues include attractive photographic reproductions and illustrations. For many issues M. Owen Lee has contributed the "Quarterly Quiz," and, recently, "OperaKrostik" by Alan W. Agol has become a regular feature. Advertisements for related books are included in each issue. Commemorative issues have recently featured Rossini (9.4), Donizetti (14.3), and Strauss (15.3).

Recent articles include "Mary Garden: Debuts and Debussy: 1900-1903" by Michael T. R. B. Turnbull (13.4:5-18), "Donizetti: European Composer" by Philip Gossett (14.3:11-16), " 'One Priest, One Candle, One Cross': Some Thoughts on Verdi and Religion" by Roger Parker (12.1:27-34), and "Igor and Tom: History and Destiny in *The Rake's Progress*" by Mary Hunter (7.4:38-52).

Strad
(Harrow, Middlesex, England: Orpheus Publications, 1890-)

Strad was founded in 1890 by Harry Lavendar and remained in the Lavendar family until 1964, when it was bought by Novello. Family members remained involved with the publication into the 1980s. In 1988, Orpheus Publications acquired *Strad*. The monthly journal is intended for amateurs and professionals connected with any aspect of the violin family. Coverage includes instrument making, dealing, and collecting as well as repertory, performance, and teaching. Since its inception the journal has maintained high standards.[80]

Each issue of *Strad* is currently divided into five sections: "String Player" articles discuss performers, technique, repertory, and performance related issues; "String Teacher" articles cover great teachers, teaching techniques and schools; "Luthier & Trade" articles discuss important instruments, instrument makers, specific materials for instrument building, sales, and instrument collecting; "Music Matters" includes articles on competitions, festivals, orchestras, repertory, and recordings; and "Regulars" includes announcements of awards and competitions, news and reviews of recordings, videos, concerts, books, and products. Interviews and detailed articles on specific instruments and makers are regular features as well. Each issue is filled with exquisite photographs of instruments and artists, and numerous advertisements for instruments, accessories, related publications, and retailers and dealers. *Strad*'s coverage is international and reflects current trends.

Special issues appear occasionally on performers, instruments, and other topics, such as "Strings in China" (110:1312) and "Southern Climes: Exploring Strings in Latin America" (108:1281). *Strad* also publishes an international directory of dealers and makers and a guide to summer schools.

Piano & Keyboard
(San Anselmo, CA: SparrowHawk Press, 1952-)

This journal, published as *The Piano Quarterly Newsletter* from 1952 to 1958 and *The Piano Quarterly* from 1958 to 1992, was initially intended as a forum for private piano teachers in America. Many of these teachers were self-employed and worked in isolation. Early issues consisted of reviews and discussions of repertory. With the change of title in 1958, American musicologists William J. Mitchell and William S. Newman were appointed contributing editors. They wrote articles on history and interpretation as well as book reviews. As other new features were added, the journal's perspective became more scholarly.[81] Many more changes occurred over the years.

In 1993, the journal titled changed to *Piano & Keyboard*. String Letter Press assumed publication responsibility and established a bimonthly publication schedule. In August 1995, SparrowHawk Press took over as the journal's publisher. The new journal is aimed at a broader audience consisting of amateurs, professionals, scholars, students, and teachers. Each issue has approximately five feature articles covering performers, composers, teachers, pedagogy, competitions, career development, and repertory. Regular departments include "Letters," "Mind and Body," "Multimedia" and "Market Tips." Each issue includes reviews of and numerous advertisements for books, music, recordings, teaching materials, and instruments. The addition of "Keyboard" to the title in 1993 corresponds to the addition of articles on and reviews of electronic keyboards.

There are two other unique music journals that deserve consideration, *Gramophone* and *Musik und Kirche*.

Gramophone
(Harrow, Middlesex, England: General Gramophone
Publication Ltd., 1923-)

The first issue of *Gramophone* appeared at bookstands on April 23, 1923. Sir Compton Mackenzie, who wanted to initiate the first monthly journal devoted to reviewing recordings and playback equipment, inspired the journal. At the end of 1926, the journal's financial condition was poor.[82] A young accountant, Cecil Pollard, agreed to become business manager for the journal. Since then, *Gramophone* has been fiscally sound. Initially, the journal was intended for readers in the United Kingdom. Over the decades, its coverage has expanded, and *Gramophone* has become an audiophile and recording industry forum for the international English-speaking community.[83]

Each issue includes feature articles on aspects of classical music and performers, their relationship to the recording industry, recording industry, recording technology, news, and recent developments. Each issue has numerous comprehensive reviews of equipment. Many recording and equipment advertisements are printed throughout each issue as well. There are copious signed recording reviews, which are grouped by genre, and an index to the reviews is printed in each issue. Noted performers, scholars, and critics contribute *Gramophone*'s thorough and informative recording reviews. Recent contributors include Joan Chissell, David Fallows, Iain Fenlon, Tess Knighton, Julie Anne Sadie, Stanley Sadie, Robert Seeley, and John Warrack.

Musik und Kirche
(Kassel, Germany: Bärenreiter, 1929-)

The first issue of *Musik und Kirche* was issued in early 1929. It was the successor of two other related German periodicals, *Siona* and *Zeitschrift für evangelische Kirchenmusik*. The journal's goal, clearly established in the first issue, was to cover Protestant church music and, especially, German Lutheranism, with equal emphasis on "music" and "church."[84] Church music, theology, and liturgy were all represented in the early issues. From 1933 to 1938 (vols. 2-6), the journal also served as the organ of the Neue Schütz-Gesellschaft.[85]

*Musik und Kirch*e's contents and size underwent considerable change during the World War II years, and publication was suspended from 1945 to 1946. The journal was transformed after the war; it published more scholarly articles along with articles on organs, organ technology, nineteenth- and twentieth-century music, contemporary composers, and jazz.[86] The journal is printed bimonthly, and current coverage includes performance practice, composers, musicological issues, specific musical literature and genres, organs, theology, liturgy, and general church music. Reviews are included for related books and music. The journal's articles are entirely in German.

Musik und Kirche has printed numerous notable articles over the years. Representative articles include "Motivic Integration, Proportion, and Number Symbolism in Johann Sebastian Bach's Magnificat" by Wolfgang Hösch

(46.6:265-69), "Church Music in Crisis?" by Heinrich Eggebrecht (46.5:214-222), "The Passion in the 20th Century" by Kurt von Fischer (67.1: 30-40), and "Funeral Music: A Controversy" by Klaus Seidel (69.5:297-305).

NOTES

1. Linda M. Fidler and Richard S. James, Eds. *International Music Journals* (New York: Greenwood Press, 1990), 3.

2. Ibid.

3. Ibid., 4.

4. Ibid., 40.

5. Ibid., 41.

6. Ibid., 42.

7. Ibid.

8. *Notes, Quarterly Journal of the Music Library Association* 6: 240.

9. *Journal of the American Musicological Society* 50.1: 5.

10. *Proceedings of the Royal Musical Association* 100: x.

11. Linda M. Fidler and Richard S. James, Eds. *International Music Journals,* 382.

12. Ibid., 383.

13. Ibid., 244.

14. Ibid., 245.

15. Ibid., 275.

16. *Musical Quarterly* 71.1: i-ii.

17. This issue has numerous articles on film and musicology; other authors include Lewis Lockwood, Jeffrey Kallberg, and Kay Kaufman Shelemay.

18. Linda M. Fidler and Richard S. James, Eds. *International Music Journals,* 295.

19. Ibid.

20. Ibid., 296.

21. *Early Music* 1.1: 1.

22. Three issues were devoted to issues of performance practice in Mozart's music (19.4, 20.1, and 20.2).

23. Linda M. Fidler and Richard S. James, Eds. *International Music Journals,* 124.

24. Ibid.

25. Ibid., 316; and *Nineteenth Century Music* I: 90-91.

26. Linda M. Fidler and Richard S. James, Eds. *International Music Journals,* 316.

27. Ibid.

28. Ibid., 317.

29. Don Randel, Ed. *The New Harvard Dictionary of Music* (Cambridge, MA: Belknap Press, 1986), 844.

30. *Computer Music Journal* 1.1: cover.

31. Ibid., 10.1: 13.

32. Linda M. Fidler and Richard S. James, Eds. *International Music Journals*, 96.

33. Ibid., 195; and *Journal of Music Theory* 1: 1.

34. Linda M. Fidler and Richard S. James, Eds. *International Music Journals*, 195.

35. Ibid., 170.

36. *Interface* 14.1-2: inside cover.

37. *Journal of New Music Research* 23.1: 3.

38. Ibid.

39. Linda M. Fidler and Richard S. James, Eds. *International Music Journals*, 171.

40. Ibid. 259.

41. Ibid., 339.

42. *Perspectives of New Music* 1.1: 4.

43. Stanley Sadie, Ed. *The Norton/Grove Concise Encyclopedia of Music* (New York: W. W. Norton & Co., 1988), 243.

44. Linda M. Fidler and Richard S. James, Eds. *International Music Journals*, 126.

45. Ibid.

46. Ibid., 446-47.

47. Ibid., 449.

48. Ibid., 450.

49. Ibid., 166; and *Instrumentalist* 1.1: 3.

50. Linda M. Fidler and Richard S. James, Eds. *International Music Journals*, 203.

51. Ibid., 249.

52. Ibid., 250.

53. Ibid., 252.

54. Ibid., 198; and *Journal of Music Therapy* 17: 46.

55. Linda M. Fidler and Richard S. James, Eds. *International Music Journals*, 199.

56. Ibid., 51; and *Billboard Advertising* 1.1: 1.

57. Linda M. Fidler and Richard S. James, Eds. *International Music Journals*, 52.

58. Ibid.

59. Ibid., 116.

60. Ibid., 117.

61. Ibid., 119.

62. Ibid., 117.

63. Ibid., 220.

64. Ibid., 220-221.

65. Ibid., 379.

66. Ibid., 380.

67. *Brio* 1.1: 3.

68. Linda M. Fidler and Richard S. James, Eds. *International Music Journals*, 66.

69. Ibid.

70. Ibid.

71. Ibid., 138; and *Fontes Artis Musicae* (1:1)

72. Linda M. Fidler and Richard S. James, Eds. *International Music Journals,* 319.

73. Ibid., 322.

74. *Notes, Quarterly Journal of the Music Library Association* 56.1: 9.

75. The most current is "Trends in the Price of Music Monographs and Scores as Reflected in *Notes, 1992-1997*" by Calvin Elliker (55.2:341-353).

76. *Cambridge Opera Journal* 1.1: iii.

77. Ibid.

78. Ibid., 10.1: 1.

79. Linda M. Fidler and Richard S. James, Eds. *International Music Journals,* 465.

80. Ibid., 408.

81. Ibid., 344.

82. Ibid., 145.

83. Ibid., 146.

84. Ibid., 292.

85. Ibid.

86. Ibid.

Chapter 7

Journals of the Century in the Visual Arts

Alexandra de Luise

This article describes journals devoted to the field of visual arts, a term that includes painting, drawing, the graphic and media arts, sculpture, architecture, decorative arts, design, and photography. Journals devoted to the visual arts have a broad readership, including art historians, artists, museum and gallery-goers, art librarians, art dealers, curators, hobbyists, students, and the interested public. In order to address this group's diverse interests and expertise, numerous visual arts journals were launched in the twentieth century and many hundreds are presently in publication worldwide. Every country in the world publishes at least one national art journal. The United States is considered to be at the forefront of journal publishing for the visual arts.

Germany was the first country to lead in the development of art journals in the eighteenth century. Factors contributing to the growth of visual arts serials in the early twentieth century included the middle class's developing interest in art, the growth of art museums and art schools during this period, efficiencies in the processes used for reproducing images, and the public's desire to document their cultural heritage. Another strong contribution came from those important European art historians who immigrated to the United States in the 1930's and 40's to flee Nazi persecution. Their scholarly contributions at universities and museums throughout the United States had important consequences for the development of journals devoted to the visual arts.

I was invited to review this important topic with the Serials Collection Manager in mind, and in doing so, select and discuss approximately three of the most important journals for each of the major areas within the visual arts. Since my review does not include journals devoted to the processes used in making art, professional journals (journals for the professional artist, architect, photographer, etc.) are typically excluded, except when the journal's lengthy history or unique subject matter otherwise qualified it for

This chapter originally appeared in *The Serials Librarian* 39(4): 79-102, 2001.

inclusion. Journals devoted to the art market, art education, museum studies, and those for collectors and hobbyists have also been excluded. My intention for this review is to concentrate on journals that focus on the history and study of art. I have organized this broad subject area into the following categories: Institutions (museums, societies and associations, schools and universities); Methods (iconography, connoisseurship, art criticism); Styles (general art history, art periods, national/regional surveys); Special interest groups; and Ideologies. 'Art' journals are given the most thorough treatment because they typically concentrate on many different media and time periods. Following this discussion is a brief overview of journals serving other media, such as Drawing, Prints, Sculpture, Architecture, Design, Decorative Arts, Crafts, and Photography. Journals selected for review must be in print and in publication for approximately ten years. Those journals that I consider the most influential of the 20th century have been selected on the basis of their lasting research value, strong reputation, long publication history, and indexing. North American and Western European journals predominate as these geographical areas publish the majority of visual arts journals in the world. Several journals were equally suitable for inclusion into two or more categories-creative license was used in these cases. Since I was confined to the selection of the most influential journals in each category, many journals of lesser importance are not included. Due to the enormity of this topic, this review should be interpreted as a general overview of the field.

MUSEUM SERIALS

Museums are places where collections of objects are exhibited, and there are museums for art, history, science, and so on. Most art museums publish newsletters, bulletins and occasionally, annual publications, in addition to exhibition catalogs. Art museum bulletins typically review objects in their own collections, publish results of scholarly research by curators from the museum or other experts, and present news of museum activities. Museum publications are an important acquisition for art libraries and many museum libraries obtain them on exchange programs with other museum libraries.

MUSEUM SERIALS: USA

Several of the major American museums in Boston, Philadelphia, New Haven, Providence, New York City, Princeton, Baltimore, Chicago, Cincinnati, Cleveland, Detroit, St. Louis, Los Angeles, and Malibu produce excellent museum bulletins. Although many are worthy of discussion, two titles that contain scholarship of the highest standards include *The Metropolitan Museum of Art Bulletin* (United States, The Metropolitan Museum of Art, 1905-) and its sister publication, *The Metropolitan Museum Journal* (United States, The Metropolitan Museum of Art, 1968-). As the bulletin for one of the oldest, best known, and one of the largest museums in the world, *The Metropolitan Museum of Art Bulletin* enjoys a wide readership, contains descriptions of art owned by the Museum from every time period and in-depth articles written by museum curators. The *Journal* is a hardcover annual that contains more detailed studies on fields of art represented in the Museum. It replaced *Metropolitan Museum Studies,* a publication devoted to scholarly research that was discontinued in 1936.

MUSEUM SERIALS: EUROPE

European museums have a much older history and their collections were acquired over a longer period of time than museums in the United States. Two exemplary titles from European museums are *Bulletin van het Rijksmuseum* (The Netherlands, SDU Uitgeverij, 1953-), a journal devoted to this museum's splendid collection of Dutch seventeenth century art; and *La Revue du Louvre: la Revue des Musées de France* (France, Reunion des Musées Nationaux, 1950-), the official publication for the major museums of France, featuring articles on French collections, new exhibitions, and acquisitions.

ART HISTORY SOCIETIES/ASSOCIATIONS

Art history societies flourished in the late nineteenth and early twentieth centuries, particularly in Germany where the study of art history began. The development of art society journals greatly enhanced the study of art history during the twentieth century by giving scholars a forum in which to share ideas and present the results of their research.

ART HISTORY SOCIETIES AND ASSOCIATIONS: USA

In the United States two of the most influential society publications published by the same association are *The Art Bulletin* (United States, College Art Association, 1912-) and *Art Journal* (United States, College Art Association, 1941-). *The Art Bulletin* is the principal journal for scholarly art historical research in the world and features highly specialized articles on all periods and areas of art history, and has a section on scholarly book reviews. *Art Journal* emphasizes nineteenth and twentieth century art history. Until very recently, its articles were organized around a topic. It too contains scholarly articles, as well as information on art education useful to art professors teaching at the college level. Another worthy publication is *Source: Notes in the History of Art* (United States, Ars Brevis Foundation, 1981-), a small format, scholarly publication of art and archaeology with articles all under 2000 words in length to keep the publication confined to 32 pages. This publication is devoted to new discoveries, original research, and publishes occasional thematic issues.

ART HISTORY SOCIETIES AND ASSOCIATIONS: EUROPE

The tradition of art societies is older and more established in Europe than in the United States, particularly in Germany. Among the art society journals still in publication, three leading ones have been selected. *Art History* (United Kingdom, Blackwell, 1978-) is a scholarly British journal featuring well-researched, scholarly articles on art and architecture, lengthy book reviews, and topics emphasizing the social, cultural, and economic influences on art. *Histoire de l'Art*, published in collaboration with the Association des Professeurs d'Archéologie et d'Histoire de l'Art des Universités, (France, Editions C.D.U.-S.E.D.E.S., 1988-) is the society organ of the Institut National d'Histoire de l'Art and later, the APAHAU. Its goal is to feature works by young scholars and articles on all fields of art history, written primarily by French art historians. Issues are thematic and an indispensable section at the back of the journal called "Informations" covers legislative matters, conference reports, prizes, book lists, notices of new periodicals, and art history degrees awarded in France. *Konsthistorisk Tidskrift* (Norway, Scandinavian University Press, 1932-) is a major Scandinavian art history journal that is highly regarded in the United States. Founded by The Society of Art Historians, the majority of articles feature art of the past and are written in German, French, English, and Swedish. An annual bibliography of Swedish art books was published from 1960 to 1980.

UNIVERSITY PUBLICATIONS

The formal study of art history began in Germany in the nineteenth century. New research in art flourished as a result and required a forum for its publication. University-run journals in art history have always been an important arena for publication for young scholars beginning their academic careers. University-run journals may sometimes appear irregularly due to editorial, economic, or staffing shortages. Two general art history titles that have maintained a high level of excellence despite such irregularities are: *RACAR: Revue d'Art Canadienne/Canadian Art Review* (Canada, Universities Art Association of Canada, 1974-), a scholarly Canadian art journal that features articles on western, native art, and publishes occasional theme issues written in either French or English, and *Oxford Art Journal* (United Kingdom, Oxford University Press, 1978-), which operates with an independent editorial board. It is a scholarly, progressive art history journal with a British slant. Lengthy research articles examine the social and political history of art from all time periods. The journal also has an extensive book review section.

ICONOGRAPHY

Iconography is the study and interpretation of signs, symbols, objects, and themes to help explain the literal or symbolic meanings of an image. Such images can be literary, theological or historical. An understanding of iconography is necessary for the study of Medieval and Renaissance art. For example, a student of art history might be asked to trace the poses of the figures in paintings of the Madonna and Child through a period of time. Three journals specializing in the study of iconography have been selected. *Journal of the Warburg and Courtauld Institutes* (United Kingdom, Warburg Institute, University of London, 1937-) is an excellent scholarly British journal devoted primarily to Medieval and Renaissance art. This prestigious journal was started by the art historian, Ernst H. Gombrich (1909-), who, until 1976, was the Director of the Institute. *Simiolus* (The Netherlands, Stichting voor Nederlandse Kunsthistorische Publicaties, 1966/67-) is another excellent iconography journal featuring Netherlandish art of the sixteenth and seventeenth centuries. Since 1970 it has been published in English. *Studies in Iconography* (United States, Western Michigan University Press, 1975-) is a scholarly journal that focuses on the literary and pictorial uses of iconography in art and literature.

CONNOISSEURSHIP

Connoisseurship is an important concept in art history. The term defines a level of expertise in judging what is rare and valuable, attained through many years of study in a particular area, in this case art. England is the leader in connoisseurship and publishes several journals that discuss art using this approach. The "Big Three" as they are referred to, are *Connoisseur,* now ceased (United Kingdom, then United States, Hearst Corp., 1901-92), *The Burlington Magazine* and *Apollo: The International Magazine of the Arts. The Burlington Magazine* (United Kingdom, Burlington Magazine, 1903-) is a highly respected journal with authoritative articles on western art history through the early 20th century, exhibitions, book reviews, and information on museum acquisitions. Important scholars, including Roger Fry and Sir Herbert Read, have edited the journal and major art historians regularly contribute articles. It is considered to be the first English language art history journal. *Apollo* (United Kingdom, Apollo, 1925-) is a beautifully illustrated journal on art history devoted to European painting, decorative arts, and collections.

ART CRITICISM

Art criticism is the critical analysis and interpretation of art. Art critics function as interpreters of artists' works for the public. Art critics may take a strong position on the work of a particular artist, an exhibition, or artistic trend. Depending on their reputation and readership, their reviews may influence public opinion and the art market. In the area of art criticism, there are several journals worth mentioning. The first is *The New Art Examiner* (United States, Chicago New Art Association, 1973-), a tabloid committed to the presentation of diverse perspectives on all aspects of artistic practice in the United States. A section called "Art press review" is one of the few places where one may find reviews of art magazines. *The New Criterion* (United States, Foundation for Cultural Review, 1982-) is an important conservative monthly review of art criticism, architecture, photography, music, poetry, and literature whose founder and current editor is the former *The New York Times* art critic, Hilton Kramer. At least one article per issue is devoted to the theory and practice of art, architecture, and photography. *October* (United States, Institute for Architecture and Urban Studies, MIT Press, 1976-) is a politically left, avant-garde magazine featuring current trends in art criticism and theory. Former staff members of the periodical *Artforum* founded this critical journal of painting, music, photography, dance, cinema, and video. A well-regarded society publication is *The Journal of Aesthetics and Art Criticism* (United States, The American Society for Aesthetics, 1941-), which examines all the arts from a philosophical, psychological, artistic, literary, musical and scientific point of view. Lastly, a dark horse winner is the small format journal, *Art Criticism* (United States, State University of New York at Stony Brook, 1979-), a serious, non-illustrated journal, edited by art historians at the school. It features articles that explore the interrelationship of modern art, architecture, and photography with psychoanalysis and philosophy.

ART HISTORY

The following journals are organized according to their country of publication. They cover a broad area of art history as well as the art of their country. The journals published by three countries, in particular, have been selected: France, Germany, and Italy.

France

France has had a rich and long history in the field of art history. Its literary and artistic criticism and iconographic investigations date back to Diderot's eighteenth century work, the *Encyclopédie*. Early French art historians were influenced by the written works of such authors as Sartre and Malraux, philosophers who reconsidered the way art was examined. France has produced numerous excellent art journals in the twentieth century. One of the best journals that has survived more than a century of change is *Gazette des Beaux Arts* (France, Les Beaux-Arts, 1859-). As the oldest and most highly regarded publication for art historical studies, it features well-documented research articles on a variety of art topics, particularly French art of the seventeenth and eighteenth centuries. Supplements called "La Chronique des Arts et de la Curiosité" contain important information on exhibitions, books, colloquiums, news briefs, reports on museums and exhibits, recently published books, etc. *Revue de l'Art* (France, Centre National de la Recherche Scientifique, 1968-), founded by art historian André Chastal, is an important scholarly journal focusing on France and Europe, particularly art of the Neoclassical to Impressionist periods. It also contains abstracts in English and the occasional article on modern art. *L'Oeil* (France, Publications Artistiques Françaises, 1955-) examines important issues in European art history and has recently begun featuring contemporary interior design.

Germany

Germany has a long tradition in the field of art history and was one of the first countries to publish art journals. The three leading German art historical publications are: *Bruckmanns Pantheon* (Germany, Bruckmann, 1928-), an annual of art historical research that features European and some Oriental art, and contains English summaries; *Zeitschrift für Kunstgeschichte*

(Germany, Deutscher Kunstverlag, 1932-), a well-respected journal with articles on all aspects of art historical investigation and is edited by the art historians at the Art History Institute of the University of Munich, and *Kunstchronik* (Germany, Fachverlag Hans Carol GmbH & Co., 1948-), a general art serial that is particularly valuable for its information on current exhibitions, news of museums, exhibitions, institutes, congresses, research, book reviews, etc.

Italy

Italy has also enjoyed a long tradition in art historical writing and has produced many illustrious Italian scholars who followed in the tradition of the eminent art historian, Adolfo Venturi. Four Italian journals have been selected for this category. The first is *Bollettino d'Arte* (Italy, Istituto Poligrafico e Zecca dello Stato for the Ministero per i Beni Culturali e Ambientali, 1907-), which was founded as the official journal for the country's galleries and museums, and contains scholarly articles and lengthy discussions on Italian painting, sculpture, architecture, ancient art, and non-Italian art. *Critica d'Arte* (Italy, La Lettere, 1935-) is another important art journal under the directorship of art historian, Carlo Ludovico Ragghianti until his death in 1987, and features scholarly articles on ancient to modern Italian and non-Italian art. *Storia dell'Arte* (Italy, Nuova Italia, 1969-), directed by art historian, Giulio Carlo Argan, features substantial articles, mainly on Italian art. *Paragone* (Italy, Sansoni, 1950-), founded by the art historian, Roberto Longhi (1890-1970), who studied with Adolfo Venturi, is a journal devoted to the promotion and preservation of Italy's artistic heritage. It appears alternately with issues devoted to literature.

ART PERIODS

In this section I will discuss Islamic, Ancient, Medieval, Renaissance, 20th century and contemporary periods of art history. Excluded are those periods from the Baroque to the early nineteenth century, which I feel are adequately covered in more general art historical journals.

Art: Islamic

Islamic art represents the secular art produced in lands under Islamic rule or influence. It began in the seventh century, from the time of Mohamed and flourished until the sixteenth century. Each country influenced by Islamic rule developed its own regional, artistic characterizations. As a consequence of this blending of cultures, influences, and histories, Islamic art is usually studied together with Asian and Ancient art. Journals of Islamic art examine the architecture, craftsmanship, calligraphy, textiles, coins, tiles, metalwork, enamels, carpets, and illuminated manuscripts of Muslim countries. There are three important titles in this category. *Arts & the Islamic World* (United Kingdom, Islamic Arts Foundation, by New Century, 1982/83-) features both contemporary and traditional arts, museums, and collections in Middle Eastern countries, as well as the contemporary art scene. *Muqarnas: An Annual on the Visual Culture of the Islamic World* (The Netherlands, Brill, 1983-) is a hardcover scholarly annual from the prestigious Aga Khan Program for Islamic Architecture, Harvard University, that features medieval to modern art and architecture from Syria, Persia, Turkey, and Egypt. *Ars Orientalis: The Arts of Islam and the East* (United States, University of Michigan, Department of the History of Art, Ann Arbor, 1954-), contains scholarly articles on Islamic art and archeology of the Asian continent.

Art: Ancient

Ancient art is the art of the ancient cultures of Greece, Rome, Egypt, Mesopotamia, and Byzantium. The study of Ancient art, antiquities, and artifacts is often discussed within the field of archaeology, either in connection with digs, expeditions, or in the presentation of historical findings. Articles on Ancient art may also be found in art historical journals, such as *Art Bulletin, Bollettino d'Arte* and the July issue of *Apollo,* which focuses on Ancient art. For this category I selected one Ancient art journal and one archeology journal that typically features a significant number of articles on Ancient art. *Antike Kunst* (Switzerland, Vereinigung der Freunde Antiker Kunst, c/o Archäologisches Seminar der Universität, 1958-) is a scholarly journal with articles written in various languages on a wide range of classical subjects. Many of the articles describe artifacts held in private collections. Most libraries that subscribe to *Antike Kunst* will also have at least one journal from the influential German archeology institute called the Deutsches Archäologisches Institut, headquartered in Berlin. The DAI, as it is known, publishes an impressive number of series titles and periodicals, some of which are issued from the organization's regional locations in Rome, Athens, Istanbul, Damascus, Baghdad, etc. A representative, scholarly annual from this institute that is at the forefront for the study of archeology is the *Jahrbuch des Deutschen Archäologischen Instituts* (Germany, Walter De Gruter, 1886-). It focuses on the period from Early Bronze Age to Late Antiquity, with an emphasis on the Greek and Roman periods. It is written in German.

Art: Byzantine-Medieval

Art of the Middle Ages describes architecture, sculpture, painting, and the minor arts in the West after the fall of Rome and before 1200. Christianity in the West and Islamic influences in the Middle East helped to shape the art from this period. There are many important journals devoted to Medieval Art. Three of the most significant ones have been selected. *Gesta* (United States, International Center of Medieval Art, 1963-) is an important journal devoted to the investigation of medieval art and architectural history. Many of the works featured are found in The Cloisters (a branch of the Metropolitan Museum of Art) in New York. *Bulletin Monumental* (France, Société Française d'Archéologie, 1834-) is an important publication of French medieval archeology, art and architecture published for the Society. *Dumbarton Oaks Papers* (United States, Dumbarton Oaks Research Library of Harvard University, 1940-) is a scholarly, hardcover annual on late antiquity, Byzantine, Medieval art, and related fields.

Art: Renaissance

Journals on the Renaissance cover the period that began in Europe in the fifteenth century. The Renaissance refers to the rebirth of the culture and civilization of classicism, and the nucleus for this artistic creativity was Florence. Although Renaissance themes are discussed at length in general art historical journals, such as in *Art Bulletin,* three specialized journals on the subject include *Renaissance Quarterly* (United States, Renaissance Society of America, 1948-), a journal devoted to all aspects of Renaissance life, art, architecture, philosophy, and literature. *I Tatti Studies: Essays in the Renaissance* (Italy, Villa I Tatti for the Harvard University Center for Renaissance Studies, 1985-) is a scholarly, interdisciplinary journal produced by this important center for the study of the Italian Renaissance. *Mitteilungen des Kunsthistorischn Institutes in Florenz* (Italy, Kunsthistorisches Institut in Florenz, 1908-41; 1956-) is a journal devoted to promoting an understanding of the art of the Renaissance. It also discusses the works of foreign artists who were working in Italy during this period. Articles are written in German, Italian, or English.

Modern and Contemporary Art

The term "modern" in the history of art refers to the period that began in the nineteenth century and ended in the twentieth (some place it between the 1860s and the 1970s), whereas contemporary art is art produced after this period. During the twentieth century, various 'isms' were defined to describe certain art movements, such as Fauvism, Expressionism, Cubism, Dadaism, Futurism, and Surrealism. These movements spawned several important, but short-lived, art journals. In the latter half of the 20th century many modern and contemporary art journals were founded, largely as a result of postwar prosperity in Europe and the United States, and a renewed interest in modern and international art. Three influential journals include *Artforum* (United States, Artforum International Magazine, 1962-), a leading publication devoted to contemporary art, art criticism, and exhibition reviews. It began as an alternative magazine and is now a leading international journal of contemporary trends in art. *ARTnews* (United States, ARTnews Associates, 1902-) is a general interest magazine that provides reviews on major international exhibitions. Together with an annual now defunct, entitled *Art News Annual* (United States, Newsweek, 1927-73), they provide an encyclopedic compendium of information on art of the 20th century. *Flash Art: The World's Leading Art Magazine* (Italy, Giancarlo Politi, 1967-) is the confident, international journal of European and North American contemporary art, and features interesting viewpoints on American art from a European perspective.

NATIONAL/REGIONAL SURVEYS

The next set of categories are part of national or regional surveys. These journals focus on the art from individual countries or regions of the world. For brevity, only a selection of countries and regions have been considered.

Art: African

African art refers to the traditional and contemporary arts of Africa and Oceania. The study of African art as a discipline began relatively recently. Two journals that present the arts of this region with sensitivity and intelligence, although neither is published there, are *African Arts* (United States, James S. Coleman African Studies Center, University of California at Los Angeles, 1967-), the premier journal for African art, featuring articles on metal, wood, ceramic, ivory, stone, figure, architecture, personal adornment, contemporary, fine, and popular arts. Its purpose is to stimulate the creative arts in Africa by documenting art from the past and from contemporary African artists. A more contemporary journal is *Arts d'Afrique Noire* (France, Raoul Lehuard, 1972-), a publication that offers an interesting perspective in its specialization in francophone Africa. A third journal that offers promise, but is too new to be included is *NKA: Journal of Contempo-*

rary African Art (United States, The Mario Einaudi Center for International Studies & the Africana Studies and Research Center, Cornell University, 1994-), exploring new perspectives in contemporary African art and featuring profiles on Africa's leading artists.

Art: American

By the 1950's, many art journals were in publication in the United States, which helped to spread the concepts of modernism to a broader readership than ever before. The United States is rich in journals that explore themes in American art, ranging from early American portraiture to the latest gallery exhibits of American artists. One journal devoted to the early art of America is *Archives of American Art Journal* (United States, Archives of American Art, 1950-), focusing on the enormous collection at the Archives of American Art, which is part of the Smithsonian Institution. Its collection includes the personal papers and other primary source materials of every major American artist, representing every period and style. Another journal of American painting, sculpture, decorative arts, photography, and architecture from the seventeenth to the early twentieth centuries is *The American Art Journal* (United States, Kennedy Galleries & Israel Sack Inc., 1969-). Written by American art scholars, the journal is published by a prestigious New York gallery that specializes in this area. A third journal that ties in the art of the past with that of the present is *American Art* (United States, National Museum of American Art, 1987-), formerly called *Smithsonian Studies in American Art*. Published by the National Museum of American Art, Smithsonian Institution, it features painting, sculpture, graphics, decorative arts, and architecture from the seventeenth century to the present. Articles are written by art historians, essayists, and critics. Another prominent journal is *Art in America* (United States, Frederick Fairchild Sherman, 1913-). It is devoted to all aspects of the arts, with an emphasis the current American art scene. While *Art in America* began as a periodical devoted to the study of European art in American collections, over time, American artists were given more coverage in the journal. Today, it is considered to be the most comprehensive journal for the study of American contemporary art. Since 1982, a useful reference work, entitled "Guide to Galleries, Museums, Artists" has been published as its August issue.

Art: Asian

Asian art refers primarily to the art of three major civilizations: China, Japan and India. Cultural, religious, and other influences brought on by foreign invasions all served to shape the art in these regions. Religion also played a very important role in the history of Asian art. Asian art developed independently from the art of the West and has been studied by westerners for many decades. Within the field there are several excellent English language journals. The most scholarly ones include *Archives of Asian Art* (United States, The Asia Society, 1945/46-), a highly regarded journal that features all aspects of Asian art, with articles and papers, many first presented as lectures at the Society. It includes descriptions of objects acquired by American museums of Asian art. *Oriental Art* (United Kingdom, Oriental Art Magazine Ltd., 1955-) is considered to be one of the best journals for this area and contains scholarly articles on art objects with an emphasis on Far Eastern and Indian art. *Artibus Asiae* (Switzerland, Museum Rietberg in cooperation with the Arthur M. Sackler Gallery, Smithsonian Institution, 1925-) is a scholarly journal devoted to the ancient art of this region and contains articles on excavations and art objects. The best art journal from India today is *Marg: A Magazine of the Arts* (India, Marg Publications, 1946-). This journal features all periods of Indian art, including sculpture, architecture, painting, book arts, and manuscripts, as well as dance and music. Issues are beautifully illustrated and some are thematic.

Art: Canadian

Canadian art developed independently from art in the United States. It has always derived much of its artistic influence from Europe. Canada is officially a bilingual country, geographically dispersed, with a small market for art magazines. The most important journal for the study of Canadian art was *Artscanada* (Canada, Society for Art Publications, 1943-82) and it served as the national art history periodical. After many years in publication it ceased and was superseded, in part, by *Canadian Art* (Canada, Canadian Foundation in association with Key Publishers, 1984-), a journal similar to *ARTnews* in its comprehensive focus on all the visual arts, from painting to video. It features articles, profiles of emerging and established artists, and exhibition and book reviews. *The Journal of Canadian Art History/Annales d'Histoire de l'Art Canadien* (Canada, Concordia University, 1974-) is the only journal devoted to Canadian art history. It publishes scholarly articles and shorter notes on Canadian art and architectural history, decorative arts, and Inuit and Native art, and it includes lists of these topics by subject. Articles written in French have a condensed English translation. *Vie des Arts* (Canada, Société La Vie des Arts, 1956-) is a long-standing, French Canadian art journal with an international scope that also features contemporary Québec and Canadian art. During its early years of publication, it was instrumental in educating Québecers on their cultural history. It is written in French with English summaries.

Art: Dutch

Dutch art usually refers to the Golden Age of Dutch painting, a exceptional period of time in Holland during the seventeenth century, specifically between 1645 and the 1660s, when painters such as Rembrandt, Vermeer, Hals and Steen were painting their most important works. Previous to this, in the late sixteenth century, The Netherlands was artistically divided between the Protestant provinces of Holland in the north and the Catholic, Flemish speaking provinces in the south. Several Dutch periodicals are noteworthy, including *Oud Holland* (The Netherlands, Stichting tot Exploitatie van het Rijksbureau voor Kunsthistorische Documentatie Uitgeverij Nauta, 1883-), an old, well-established scholarly journal, particularly important for Dutch seventeenth century art and Flemish art. Written in Dutch and English, it has been at the forefront for Dutch art for more than 100 years. *Nederlands Kunsthistorisch Jaarboek/Netherlands Yearbook for History of Art* (The Netherlands, Waanders Uitgevers, 1947-) focuses on sixteenth and seventeenth century Dutch art and architecture. Since 1974, it consists of volumes devoted to a single theme.

Art: Latin American

Latin American art refers to the art and architecture of Central and South America, Mexico and parts of the United States. The journals presented here are mainly post-Colonial in content, after Spanish and Portuguese conquerors arrived in these areas and Pre-Columbian objects were replaced by religious ones. The study of Pre-Columbian and Meso-American art is more appropriately discussed within the context of archaeology, which can be found in journals such as *Ancient Mesoamerica* (United States, Cambridge University Press, 1990-) and *Latin American Antiquity: A Journal of the Society for American Archeology,* (United States, Society for American Archeology, 1990-). Latin American art journals can be either historical or contemporary. Historical journals are usually published by a sponsoring museum or academic institution. One of the best is *Anales del Instituto de Investigaciones Estéticas* (México, the Instituto, Universidad NA de México, 1937-), a carefully researched journal devoted to sixteenth through nineteenth century art and architecture of Latin America. Articles are written in Spanish or English. Another fine journal from Mexico is *Artes de México* (Mexico, Artes de México, 1953-

76; nueva epoca 1988-), which focuses on all of the arts, including painting, architecture, sculpture, antiques, photography, jewelry, and folk art. It is beautifully illustrated and contains English translations. In the area of contemporary art, an excellent journal is *Art Nexus: The Nexus Between Latin America and the Rest of the World* (Colombia, Arte en Colombia, 1976-), a glossy yet significant contemporary art periodical for Latin America. It provides a comprehensive review of the continent's art scene, including architecture, film and photography. Initially published as *Arte en Colombia* in 1976, it then changed its title and scope, and reappeared in 1991 with English and Spanish editions.

Art: Spanish

Spain's rich and diverse history led to a greater variety of art styles than in other European countries. The country's Islamic and French influences played an important role in shaping this diversity. The seventeenth and eighteenth centuries are considered the apex of Spanish painting, during which time master artists such as Velasquez, El Greco and Goya painted their most important works. Spanish art history established itself at the end of the nineteenth century with several important art history journals, some of which have ceased publication. One important art journal that first appeared as *Archivo Español de Arte y Archeologia* (1925-1937), discontinued during the Spanish Civil War. It reappeared later, divided into two journals, one of which is entitled *Archivo Español de Arte* (Spain, Instituto Diego Velázquez, Consejo Superior de Investigaciones Cientificas, Centro de Estudios Históricos, 1925-). It emphasizes articles on seventeenth and eighteenth century painting, sculpture, architecture, and decorative arts, written by an international group of scholars. Another important journal is *Goya: Revista de Arte* (Spain, Fundación Lázaro Galdiano, 1954-), devoted to all periods of painting, sculpture, and architecture, including some coverage of art from other parts of the world.

Art: Special Interest

There are a number of special interest groups that have developed their own journals. These journals were created to provide a forum for special interests that were not being sufficiently covered in the more mainstream journals. Many have achieved considerable success, including *Woman's Art Journal* (United States, Woman's Art Inc., 1980-), a scholarly journal on the history of women in the visual arts with a mandate to publish on neglected women artists of the past who have not been completely acknowledged for their work. It also serves as a forum for critical analysis of contemporary art issues as they relate to women. *The International Review of African American Art* (formerly *Black Art,* United States, Hampton University Museum, 1976-) is primarily Afro-American in its focus, although it also covers contemporary African art and its contributions to the New World. Thematic in nature, it features interviews with artists and biographical sketches, and is an informative journal for anyone interested in African American culture. Another special interest journal is the annual *Jewish Art* (Israel, Jerusalem Center for Jewish Art of the Hebrew University, 1974-), featuring scholarly, in-depth articles on Jewish art throughout the ages.

ARTS AND IDEOLOGIES

The following journals feature the arts in general. They do so by examining art, in addition to one or more subject areas, such as literature and the performing arts. Such publications are usually found in the NX section of the periodical collection. One such title is *Leonardo* (United States, MIT Press for the International Society for the Arts, Sciences and Technology, 1968-), a unique society publication focusing on the technology of modern art and its interrelationships with music, literature, video, performance, and science. Articles are usually written by artists and deal with the technical aspects of their work, some of which include digital imagery, multimedia performance, and computer art. A website of the journal includes sound samples and a gallery area displaying multimedia works by artists. *Artibus et Historiae: An Art Anthology* (Poland, IRSA, 1980-) is a hardcover publication that provides a scholarly outlet for research by examining nontraditional ways of looking at Western art history. Interdisciplinary and global in scope, it features all kinds of art over a wide time period. International contributors write in their own language, with English summaries provided. Although not technically a journal, *Umbrella* (United States, Umbrella Associates, 1978-) is a fascinating newsletter that focuses on artists' books and alternative media, such as mail art, copy art, etc. Produced by its founder and editor, Judith Hoffberg, it features topics usually not discussed elsewhere, profiles of art publishers, exhibition and book reviews, as well as news on the contemporary art world.

DRAWING

Drawing is art done on paper using pencil, charcoal, pastel, crayon, watercolor, pen, or ink. Numerous artists throughout history, such as Degas and Ingres, were both excellent painters and draftsmen. Journals specializing in this medium usually concentrate on drawing's history, technique and marketing aspects. In this area, several important journals have ceased publication. One that remains in publication is *Master Drawings* (United States, Master Drawing Associates, 1963-), a beautifully illustrated periodical devoted to drawings by the 'Old Masters,' primarily those artists of the Western European, post-Renaissance period. Historical and theoretical articles are written by leading scholars and curators in the field.

PRINTS

A print is a marking or shape made from a plate or block, which is then covered with wet color (usually ink) and pressed onto paper. Printmaking may be done using a variety of processes, including aquatint, engraving, etching, intaglio, lithography, mezzotint, monoprint, serigraphy, and silkscreen. It is a medium that has been practiced since the Middle Ages, and several important painters, including Dürer and Rembrandt, were also successful printmakers. Two important journals examine the history of printmaking include *Print Quarterly* (United Kingdom, Print Quarterly Ltd., 1984-), the most scholarly and elegant of all print-related publications, written for the scholar, curator, and advanced student. It fills a gap created by several discontinued print journals and contains contributions from the museum and academic print world. It features prints of all types, their history, upcoming exhibitions, and book reviews. The other journal is *Art on Paper* (United States, Fanning Pub. Co., 1970-), formerly *On Paper,* and before this, *Print Collector's Newsletter.* It is an invaluable resource of information on contemporary prints, drawings and photographs for the collector and serious student.

SCULPTURE

Sculpture is a medium that has been practiced since prehistoric times. It involves the creation of artwork in three dimensions, which is normally left either free standing or placed in relief. Sculpture materials may include wood, clay, stone, or metal. The history of sculpture, like that of painting, is usually studied and presented within the context of art history, and therefore, much of the periodical literature is found within general art historical journals. Sculpture journals that feature contemporary sculpture include *Sculpture* (United States, International Sculpture Center 1969-), a dependable publication covering contemporary American sculptors, sculpture techniques, exhibitions, competitions, and events held in the United States. Another is the society journal *Sculpture Review* (United States, National Sculpture Society, 1951-). It has a long and distinguished history, and is devoted to figurative sculpture in the United States. A third journal that takes a slightly different look at sculpture is *Public Art Review* (United States, Public Art Review, 1989-). Public art is art that is made specifically for public display. While it can include all types of art, public art usually refers to sculpture, murals, earthworks, and other forms of environmental art. Although public art is not new, its formal study began only recently, made popular with the establishment of percent-for-art programs, which assigns a certain percentage of a construction budget for a public project.

ARCHITECTURE

Architecture is the practical art of building. This medium is the most lasting and visible of the visual arts and it is important that buildings be designed to be visually appealing. The twentieth century witnessed a significant increase in public awareness of the importance of good architectural design. Architecture is a subject for which there are many excellent periodicals, both for the professional architect and layperson. Due to the enormity of this field, I have selected those journals that focus on two areas: the history of architecture and contemporary architecture.

Architectural History

The study of the history of architecture first began in Europe, particularly in France, Germany and England, in the late seventeenth century. Early historians were interested in the architecture of the past, from the Ancient world up to the time of the Baroque. The formal study of architectural history began much later in the United States, in the late nineteenth century. Three excellent journals of architectural history include *Journal of the Society of Architectural Historians* (United States, the Society, 1940-), a publication that features scholarly articles on the history of architecture, and similar to *Art Bulletin* in its scope and quality. Its coverage of architectural history is worldwide and includes all time periods. Membership in the Society includes a subscription to the *Newsletter,* which includes book lists and other information essential to the field. Another society journal for architectural history is *Architectural History* (United Kingdom, the Society of Architectural Historians of Great Britain, 1958-), an annual publication with an emphasis on British architecture from medieval through modern times. It serves as the British counterpart to the *Journal of the Society of Architec-*

tural Historians, although more limited in scope, and features scholarly articles and source material of interest to architectural historians. Another excellent journal is *Architectura, Zeitschrift für Geschichte der Baukunst/ Journal of the History of Architecture* (Germany, Deutscher Verlag, 1971-), an important, scholarly, German journal of architectural history produced by leading historians in the field. It features all periods and styles: church architecture, historic buildings, etc., and is written in German and English.

Architecture: USA

At the start of the twentieth century American architecture journals were concerned with the Beaux Arts tradition that emphasized classical shapes and forms. At that time, architecture journals were important in providing information to architects on building methods. Today, American architecture journals must attract and keep a more general readership that is both knowledgeable and sophisticated about architecture. They must present new works by leading architects in the field while still maintaining an objective and impartial critical eye. While several key architecture journals of the twentieth century ceased publication (e.g., *Architectural Forum* and *Pencil Points,* which later became *Progressive Architecture*) one journal that has been in publication throughout the century is *Architectural Record* (United States, McGraw Hill, 1891-). It is considered the most important and influential journal from the United States, devoted to current trends in commercial and residential architecture, planning, building technology, housing and urban planning. Although published for the architectural profession, *Architectural Record* is also useful to the researcher and interested layperson, and offers comprehensive information on the works and interests of professional architects from the last decade of the nineteenth century through the present. Another journal that began as the society journal of the American Institute of Architects until its recent disassociation from that organization is *Architecture* (formerly *AIA Journal,* United States, BPI Communications, 1944-). It covers recent developments in commercial and landmark architecture, design projects, competitions, and membership news. A third journal is *Assemblage: A Critical Journal of Architecture and Design Culture* (United States, MIT Press, 1986-), a distinguished and provocative publication emphasizing theories in architecture. Articles explore history, criticism, and practices, particularly as they relate to contemporary culture, by professors of architecture. Founded by Harvard professor Michael Hays, *Assemblage* will soon cease publication.

Architecture: England and France

One journal that serves the architecture of England as well as *Architectural Record* serves the architecture of the United States, is *Architectural Review* (United Kingdom, Architect Press Ltd., 1896-), an influential journal that covers recent architectural projects, urban design, theory, and publishes supplemental special issues. In its beginnings, *Architectural Review* was instrumental in emphasizing a classical view of architecture. Issues are often thematic, and contain articles, product survey sections, and advertisements. *Architectural Design* (United Kingdom, Academy Editions, 1930-), directed by Andreas Papadakis, is a high quality, provocative, internationally oriented journal with coverage of recent designs in architecture. Each issue is thematic, guest-edited, and features articles that explore architectural influences on art, urban and regional planning, and design. In 1977 a series of "Profile" issues was started, which are published concurrently with the journal. *L'Architecture d'Aujourd'hui: Recherche-Formes Interieures-Arts-Urbanisme* (France, Groupe Expansion, 1930-) is a French architectural publication featuring articles on architectural projects and theoretical issues of interest to the professional architect and researcher.

Architecture: Japan

Japan has often been receptive to foreign cultures, and many of today's leading Japanese architects began their careers in the firms of well-known American and European architects. Japan produces several stunning architecture journals, notable for their full-page color photography of new buildings designed by the foremost architects of today. The most well known journal that is part of a series of publications called "Global Architecture," is *GA Document (Global Architecture)* (Japan, Edita, 1980-). This journal features the finest in international design and residential architecture. Each issue thoroughly documents one or more buildings or projects, and features interviews and writings by architectural critics and historians. Together with other titles not mentioned here, the entire GA series of periodicals serves as an encyclopedia of modern architecture. *A & U: Architecture & Urbanism* (Japan, A & U Publishing Co., 1971-) is a visually beautiful journal with in-depth coverage of buildings, designs, and plans by the world's leading architects. *The Japan Architect* (Japan, Shinkenchiku-Sha, 1959-) is a thematic journal that features important Japanese architects, architectural firms, projects, city planning, and new trends. It contains beautiful photography, and is written in English and Japanese.

Architecture: Italy

Any discussion of architecture and its related fields of interior design and home furnishings would not be complete without a review of Italy's contribution. In the twentieth century, Italy has been at the forefront in the beautiful design of many functional objects, such as luxury cars, furniture, machinery, and kitchenware. Its manufacturing industry plays an integral role in this prolific output: Italian architects, designers, and manufacturers are all valued for their expert contribution to the design product. One of the first journals to combine architecture and home design is *Domus: Monthly Magazine of Architecture, Design and Art* (Italy, Editoriale Domus, 1928-). Conceived by architect/designer Gio Ponti, it features the latest in design for homes and commercial interiors, with articles on national and international architectural projects for the professional architect or interior designer. A journal that complements *Domus* is *Casabella: Rivista di Architettura* (Italy,, Elemond Spa, 1928-), a prestigious journal of international architecture and design that features articles and critiques on analysis, method, construction techniques, and architectural projects, in Italian with English translation. Its primary focus is on public buildings, urban design, and architectural history. Two more recent publications include *Abitare* (Italy, Abitare, 1961-), a leading international Italian/English journal of contemporary European residential and commercial architecture, interior design, furnishings, and design. Sections featuring new products and advertisements provide useful information to designers. A distinguished journal more suited for the theorist than the practitioner is *Zodiac* (Italy, Abitare Segesta, first series 1957-73; second series 1989-). A prestigious journal that recently started again under a new series, it now appears in separate Italian and English language editions. It provides thematic and in-depth coverage of architecture, urban planning, and design, with essays, projects, interviews and beautiful color plates.

INTERIOR DESIGN

Interior design journals examine the creation of objects for everyday use. As an art form, interior design journals present objects both for home and commercial environments. Periodicals, rather than books, are the principal source of current information for interior designers and students. Lavishly illustrated journals can feature information on the design of consumer products, designers, design firms, new media, furniture, packaging, equipment, product surveys, and design competitions. Three journals of contemporary interior design are *I.D. (International Design)* (United States, I.D. Magazine, 1954-), the leading publication of the art, business, and culture of design; *Interiors: For the Contract Design Professional* (United States, Billboard Publications, 1888-), oriented towards the professional engaged in designing high-end commercial and residential space and one of the oldest design journals in existence, and *Interior Design* (United States, International Design Division of Whitney Communications, 1950-), a richly illustrated journal featuring residential and commercial design. Published under the auspices of the American Institute of Decorators, it is less trade-oriented than *Interiors* and is a respected publication for interior designers.

Design: History

Design history is a discipline that began in England thirty years ago. Design history examines the history of design from its earliest origins, tracing the revival of ancient motifs during the neoclassical period through nineteenth century England, and from the Industrial Revolution to modern times. Three journals that have distinctly different approaches to design history include *Journal of Design History* (United Kingdom, Oxford University Press, 1988-), a journal published for the Design History Society, which began in 1977 to promote the study of design history. It features the design history of all periods of Western and non-Western cultures and integrates it with the study of anthropology, architectural history, economic and social history, etc. *The Journal of Decorative and Propaganda Arts* (United States, Wolfsonian Foundation of Decorative & Propaganda Arts, 1986-) publishes thematic issues to examine a single aspect of design history and propaganda arts from 1875 to 1945. *Design Issues: History/Theory/Criticism* (United States, MIT Press, 1984-) is a thought-provoking journal featuring the history, theory, and criticism of design, written by academics in the field.

DECORATIVE ARTS AND ANTIQUES

The decorative arts refers to ceramics, enamels, furniture, glass, metalwork, textiles, armor, clocks, carpets, etc., especially when discussed in reference to interior decoration and historic houses. Most journals of the decorative arts contain beautiful color photographs, articles on specific works and media, as well as information on auctions and exhibitions. Three journals of such description are *Connaissance des Arts* (France, Société Française de Promotion Artistique, 1952-), a journal featuring French decorative art and architecture; *The Magazine Antiques* (United States, F. E. Atwood, 1922-), with richly illustrated articles on international and American decorative arts, minor arts, and interiors of the seventeenth to nineteenth centuries, and the interdisciplinary *Winterthur Portfolio* (United States, University of Chicago Press for the Henry Francis du Pont Winterthur Museum, 1964-), a scholarly journal published by a museum devoted to decorative and American arts up to 1900 and their role in American life.

CRAFT

The study of craft arts, which include ceramics, glass, fiber arts, jewelry, metalwork, and woodworking, is relatively new. During most of the twentieth century, crafts were not considered an art form. They were felt to be distinct from art since these items were made and designed to be functional rather than admired. This distinction weakened over time and crafts persons are now considered artists in their own right. As the interest in crafts developed worldwide, so have the number of journals in circulation today, many of which specialize in one specific medium, such as ceramics. While each medium could not be discussed here, three exemplary journals that analyze crafts, including their technical and historical development are *American Craft* (United States, American Craft Council, 1941- , formerly *Craft Horizons*), a journal that offers authoritative coverage on all crafts, including ceramics, fiber, glass, jewelry, metalwork, and woodworking; *American Ceramics* (United States, American Ceramics, 1981-), dedicated to the critical evaluation and appreciation of contemporary ceramics, and *Ceramics Monthly* (United States, American Ceramics Society, 1953-), a sophisticated journal devoted to the interests of potters, sculptors, students, and the interested public. It features profiles of artists, as well as articles related to the making of ceramic art and craft.

PHOTOGRAPHY

Photography was invented in the nineteenth century and underwent unparalleled growth in the twentieth century. There are many journals of photography in publication today, both for the amateur, professional, and historian of photography. In the area of photography I have divided the subject into two categories: the history of photography and contemporary photography.

Photography: History

An appreciation of the history of photography is important for the understanding of this medium as an art form. Photography, which first began in

Victorian England in 1839, flourished simultaneously in France and later in the United States. Two exemplary journals with well-researched articles that feature all aspects of photographic history, including biographies of photographers, equipment, and styles are *History of Photography* (United Kingdom, Taylor Francis Ltd., 1977-), a beautifully illustrated journal with excellent research articles, and *Image* (United States, the International Museum of Photography at George Eastman House, 1952-), a journal featuring articles related to the collections and exhibitions at the Museum.

Photography: Contemporary

Journals in this category feature the works of established and emerging international photographers. Three are noteworthy: *Afterimage: The Journal of Media Arts and Cultural Criticism* (United States, Visual Studies Workshop, 1972-), a tabloid format publication featuring current trends in photography, video, film, artists books, art funding, and politics; *Aperture* (United States, Minor White, 1952-), an important journal edited by Minor White, that discusses photography as an art form, with quality reproductions, articles by scholars, and special monographic issues on major photographers, and *European Photography* (Germany, Andreas Müller-Pohle, 1981-), a beautiful, contemporary journal with portfolios, criticism, and essays by and about European photographers, written in German and English.

CONCLUSION

This review summarizes some of the most important journals in the field of visual arts. Today's visual art journals are in a process of reassessment as technology is forcing publishers to re-examine the future of their market. Electronic publishing will continue to become a more important part of art publishing, as it already has in other fields. The technology used to reproduce images electronically will undoubtedly be improved upon, as readers access journals electronically to conduct research and read articles on art. The possibility exists that it could one day become the dominant medium for periodical publishing. Those of us who prefer the visual and tactile pleasure of perusing an art journal rather than scrolling through its pages on a computer can take solace that such changes are likely to occur in stages and over time. Until then, the printed page will continue as the most important and visually satisfying medium to describe and depict the history, promotion, display, and understanding of the visual arts.

REFERENCES

Udo Kultermann, *The History of Art History.* [New York]: Abaris Books, 1993.

Stanley T. Lewis, "Periodicals in the Visual Arts," *Library Trends,* 10 (3): 330-352, January 1962.

Connie Okada, "Art Periodicals," *The Serials Librarian,* 14 (2): 129-134, 1988.

"Periodical," in: *The Dictionary of Art.* New York: Grove's Dictionaries, v. 24, 1996, 420ff.

Suzanne Stephens, "Architectural Journalism Analyzed: Reflections on a Half Century," *Progressive Architecture,* 51: 132-139, June 1970.

Edward H. Teague, "A Survey of Architecture Magazines," *Serials Review,* 7 (2): 9-25, April-June 1981.

Chapter 8

Journals of the Century
in Anthropology and Archaeology

Gregory A. Finnegan
Joyce L. Ogburn
J. Christina Smith

Closely allied with many sciences since its beginnings, anthropology developed its own identity and publications in the late 19th century. Publications with anthropological themes abounded in general scientific, medical, and natural history journals, among these *Science, Nature,* and *American Naturalist.* Anthropologists have served in the office of president of the American Association for the Advancement of Science, and Anthropology continues today as a section of that organization. Archaeology, considered part of anthropology here in the United States, has lengthy and obvious ties to history, but nevertheless has a strong scientific component that has grown over time. Anthropology in the U.S. was shaped intellectually by the fact that much early research was focused on Native Americans: Past populations were linked to living peoples, whose languages needed to be learned so that people could be interviewed and oral texts recorded. So American anthropologists tended to be trained in the four-subfield view of the discipline, in which one learned cultural, linguistic, and physical anthropology, and archaeology, as interlocking facets of an underlying discipline. The founding figures of U.S. academic anthropology (like Franz Boas and Frederic Ward Putnam) and their students (Alfred Kroeber, Alfred Tozzer and many others) made substantial contributions to all subfields. Although in recent years the centrality of the four subfields to anthropology has been challenged, recognizable specialties within anthropology are still published in the journal literature of anthropology.

Anthropology as an interdisciplinary and eclectic science has many journals of note (not included in this article) that reflect specific schools of research. Examples include applied anthropology, medical anthropology, ethnomusicology,

This chapter originally appeared in *The Serials Librarian* 39(4): 69-78, 2001.

primatology, and so on. It is also the case that much important anthropological research is published in area-studies journals like *Africa* (U.K., International African Institute, 1928), and *Oceania* (Australia, University of Sydney Press, 1930) or in interdisciplinary fields such as forensic sciences or history.

GENERAL ANTHROPOLOGY

Several outstanding journals publish in the breadth of anthropology research. In the formative period of anthropology, journals such as the *American Anthropologist* (U.S., American Anthropological Association, 1888) published work in all subfields, ensuring that the entire profession (some 80 people at the 1941 annual meeting of the journal's sponsoring American Anthropological Association) kept up with all research. Today the articles in the *American Anthropologist* continue to encompass the entire field of research. *"The Anthropologist"* (using its long-time nickname) is certainly the most important journal of the century for anthropology, from the beginning of the current series in 1899 onwards.

Current Anthropology (U.S., University of Chicago, 1960), although a relative newcomer, is a close second in importance in supporting all of anthropology. The title originated as *Yearbook of Anthropology* in 1955, but quickly moved to a journal format. Like *American Anthropologist,* its content encompasses the scholarship of the four subfields, with an emphasis on theory and method. *CA* publishes works from anthropologists located throughout the world and included articles from the USSR and China during the Cold War. It is rather unique in that it publishes articles with comments by a wide range of scholars along with the authors' replies.

Anthropology also has achieved a general popularity, primarily through coverage in journals like *National Geographic* (U.S., National Geographic Society, 1888). This journal is a publication of the National Geographic Society, which has funded anthropology research such as the search for early fossils by the Leakey family and the study of chimpanzees by Jane Goodall. The popularity of anthropology has been advanced by the thoughtful and artfully illustrated articles in *National Geographic;* it also has achieved some notoriety through its associated photographs of peoples around the world wearing various amounts of clothing.

PHYSICAL ANTHROPOLOGY

Physical anthropology grew up as a subfield devoted to the comparative study of human populations. Early research such as Samuel Morton's work

Crania Americana (1839) concentrated on measuring the skull to determine the relative "rankings" of peoples of the world. American peoples, primarily Native Americans and African Americans, were often central to this study. In the latter part of the 19th century physical anthropologists branched out to other areas of study such as human evolution and comparative primatology. Today physical anthropology broadly covers genetics, human evolution, origins of disease, forensic studies, primate behavior, and other biological aspects of anthropology. With their strong biological base, physical anthropologists are increasingly finding alternative research and teaching homes in medicine, genetics, primatology, and other areas in the sciences. By way of example, important papers are now routinely published by physical anthropologists in the *American Journal of Primatology* (U.S., Wiley for the American Society of Primatologists, 1981), the *American Journal of Human Biology* (U.S., Wiley for the Human Biology Association, 1989), and even the *Journal of Forensic Sciences* (U.S., American Academy of Forensic Sciences and the American Society for Testing and Materials, 1956). These worthwhile journals must nonetheless yield primacy of place to the following titles.

The first and most important journal, the *American Journal of Physical Anthropology* (U.S., Wiley-Liss, 1918), became the official publication of the American Association of Physical Anthropologists in 1930. The founder and first editor of *AJPA* was the formidable Aleš Hrdlička (also first president of the AAPA), who wrote many of its articles and ruled its content and philosophy (for example, he forbade the inclusion of statistics) for almost twenty-five years. Although it deserves the honor of being the preeminent journal of the field, it also carries the stigma of being far and away the most expensive journal in anthropology. The *Yearbook of Physical Anthropology* (U.S., Wiley-Liss, 1945) is an ancillary publication of the *AJPA* that publishes longer, subject review articles.

Other journals cover more specifically targeted interests of the discipline. As its title suggests, the *Journal of Human Evolution* (U.S., Academic Press, 1972) devotes its pages to the study of paleoanthropology. It was started to serve as a means to bring together disparate research with the common theme of evolution. Within its scope it covers a wide-range of topics in genetics, behavior, environment, ecology, and comparative studies of living animals. *Human Biology* (U.S., Wayne State University Press, 1929) is at present the official journal of the American Association of Anthropological Genetics, which was formed in 1994. It has a much longer history with learned societies, having previously been the publication of the Human Biology Council (now Association).

CULTURAL ANTHROPOLOGY

As the field of anthropology burgeoned demographically and intellectually in the post-World War II era, specialized journals in cultural anthropology started to develop. Among those is the *Journal of Anthropological Research* (U.S., University of New Mexico Press, 1945). This began as the *Southwestern Journal of Anthropology*, reflecting its location at the University of New Mexico. In 1973 the *SWJA* changed its name to reflect what had long been true: a worldwide rather than regional focus and an emphasis on articles that did not merely report data, but advanced the discipline's methods and theories.

As the *American Anthropologist* tried to cope with increasing numbers of submissions and increasing fragmentation of research specialization (such that keeping up with one's own niche made keeping current across the entire discipline a nostalgic fantasy), the AAA launched a new journal in 1974 for cultural and social anthropology: *American Ethnologist* (U.S., American Anthropological Association). This became a major journal in its own right.

Also important for much of the century was the *Journal of the Royal Anthropological Institute of Great Britain and Ireland* (U.K., Royal Anthropological Institute of Great Britain and Ireland). While having a somewhat narrower definition of anthropology than publications from the U.S., the *JRAI* nevertheless always carried articles of importance on both sides of the Atlantic. The *JRAI* began in 1871, merged with its companion newsletter under the latter's title, *Man,* in 1966, and reverted to the original title in a new series in 1995. Similarly, the main French anthropology journal, *L'Homme* (France, l'École des Hauts Études en Sciences Sociales), almost from its founding in 1961 was of great importance in U.S. and British anthropology as the influence of Claude Levi-Strauss and his Structuralist school spread.

LINGUISTIC ANTHROPOLOGY

Because U.S. anthropologists had to learn unwritten languages to do field research, from early in the discipline's history there was a need to develop techniques and theories for recording and understanding languages far outside the Indo-European family more familiar to U.S. and European scholars in all fields. In addition, a sense at the end of the 19th century that Native American cultures were in danger of being lost as communities were decimated by disease and significantly affected by immigrant settlement of North America led to a focus on meticulous recording of oral texts in their original languages while native speakers were still alive. The fact that most

American anthropologists had to confront language in such detail increased their appreciation of it as the largest component of cultural systems. More than their European colleagues, then, American anthropologists study languages and publish on them. The boundary between anthropological linguistics and the separate field of linguistics itself has never been clear, as anthropologists like Boas and Edward Sapir made major contributions to linguistics. The relationship is not unlike that between classical and anthropological archaeology, where a body of common techniques underlies somewhat different emphases in research.

Given the origin of anthropological linguistics in the need of anthropologists to do research in Native American cultures, the key journal has been the *International Journal of American Linguistics* (U.S., University of Chicago Press, 1917), founded by the Linguistic Society of America and the American Anthropological Association. The LSA's own journal *Language* (U.S., Linguistic Society of America, 1925) is also important, as are *Anthropological Linguistics* (U.S., Indiana University, 1959) and the more recent publication of the AAA, *Journal of Linguistic Anthropology* (U.S., American Anthropological Association, 1991). *Language in Society* (U.K., Cambridge University Press), founded in 1972 with the flowering of sociolinguistics, reflects anthropological linguists' interest not only on languages as cultural and grammatical systems, but as the means of communication between humans organized into societies whose contexts shape, and are shaped by, language.

ARCHAEOLOGY

Archaeology is defined as the scientific study of the human past through its material remains. The origins of archaeology may be traced to 15th and 16th century humanistic antiquarianism in Europe, with the excavation and collection of antiquities by wealthy patrons (dilettanti). In the 19th century, the publication of Charles Lyell's *Principles of Geology* (1830-1833); the development of the Three-Age system (Stone/Bronze/Iron); and the publication of *The Origin of Species* (1859) spurred the development of archaeology as a science. In the Old World archaeology emerged as a discipline allied to both geology and history. In the New World, archaeology grew out of sociocultural anthropology and the study of native cultures.

As noted for general anthropology, popular treatment of archaeological subjects has long been a mainstay of *National Geographic* (U.S., National Geographic Society, 1888). Notable for funding and publicizing the search for early man by the Leakey family in East Africa, *National Geographic* has reported on Society-sponsored archaeological work in Africa, the Americas, Asia, Europe, the Pacific islands, and underwater. The premier general archaeology magazine is *Archaeology* (U.S., Archaeological Institute of America, 1948). A "technical magazine" drawing upon "all the world's archaeology, using the resources of modern photography," *Archaeology* contains "valid but not exhaustive articles, written by experts for readers not technically equipped." Recent issues have highlighted early man as well as industrial archaeology at Bethlehem Steel.

The *American Journal of Archaeology* (U.S., Archaeological Institute of America, 1885) is the scholarly journal of the Archaeological Institute of America (AIA), the oldest (1879) and largest archaeological organization in North America. Originally titled *The American Journal of Archaeology for the Study of the Monuments of Antiquity and of the Middle Ages,* its scope is the art and archaeology of ancient Europe and the Mediterranean world, including the Near East and Egypt, from prehistoric to late antique times. Prior to World War I it also included some New World archaeology, but as early as 1888 a disgruntled reader complained that the journal should discard the superfluous word "American" from its title and rename itself the *Journal of Old World Archaeology.* In its 115th year of publication in 2000, the *American Journal of Archaeology* announced that it would be more responsive to its original mandate by "publishing articles, field reports, newsletters, and reviews that reflect the vast changes in the scope, diversity, and complexity of the study of art and archaeology of western Eurasia and northern Africa over the past half century." It also plans to publish articles reporting significant new work in art and archaeology beyond the geographic and chronological boundaries of the *Journal*'s original mandate. In January 2000, the electronic version of the *American Journal of Archaeology* made its appearance; by 2001, subscribers may choose to subscribe to a fully online version.

International in content and readership, *Antiquity* (U.K., Antiquity Publications, 1927) was founded as an independent, subscription-only journal by O. G. S. Crawford, whose goal was to provide a review journal of archaeology written by specialists who would contribute popular yet authoritative accounts of their research. Subject matter included ethnology, folklore, numismatics, and human evolution, as well as archaeology. To this day "its aim is to present the broad range of archaeological scholarship to a general audience interested in archaeology across the world and across the subdisciplines. *Antiquity* has a long tradition of publishing important new material, discoveries and theories." In the first six decades of the journal's existence, there were but two editors, Crawford (1927-1957) and Glyn Daniel (1958-1986). *Antiquity* debuted with a World Wide Web presence in 1996 under its third editor, Christopher Chippendale.

American Antiquity (U.S., Society for American Archaeology, 1935) is the quarterly journal of the Society for American Archaeology, which was founded in 1934 to facilitate cooperation between professional archaeologists and amateurs. From the beginning, however, *American Antiquity* has been geared more towards professional archaeologists than non-professionals, and there has been concern periodically about what some have described as mumbo-jumbo, abstruse technical language, and jargon and mathematics filling the pages of the journal. *American Antiquity* publishes papers on New World archaeology and on archaeological theory, method and practice worldwide. From modest beginnings during the Depression it has grown to be the preeminent scholarly journal of New World archaeology, renowned internationally for its presentation of methodological and theoretical advances. Of the three archaeology journals, its focus is the most anthropological in nature.

BIBLICAL, EGYPTIAN,
AND NEAR EASTERN ARCHAEOLOGY

Biblical archaeology has long had a large popular following. *Biblical Archaeologist* (U.S., American Schools of Oriental Research, 1938) was started by archaeologist G. Ernest Wright as a four-page leaflet, to meet "the need for a readable, non-technical, yet thoroughly reliable account of archaeological discoveries as they are related to the Bible." Articles are written by scholars but aimed at nonspecialists. In 1998, as the American Schools of Oriental Research changed their focus away from biblically oriented archaeology to Bible-neutral archaeology, *Biblical Archaeologist* became *Near Eastern Archaeology* (U.S., American Schools of Oriental Research, 1998), a title change opposed by eighty-three percent of the membership. *Near Eastern Archaeology* "brings to life the ancient world from Mesopotamia to the Mediterranean with vibrant images and authoritative analyses." *Biblical Archaeological Review* (U.S., Biblical Archaeology Society, 1975), or *BAR,* has similar origins. Its aim was "to make available in understandable language the current insights of professional archaeology as they relate to the Bible." Today, inclusive of both the Old and New Testaments, "*BAR* presents the latest discoveries and controversies in archaeology with breathtaking photography and informative maps and diagrams."

Scholarly journals in Near Eastern archaeology have a long and distinguished history. Interest in the ancient Near East at the University of Chicago dates back to the university's founding in 1891. William Rainey Harper, its first president, was also chair of the Department of Semitic Languages and the director of the Haskell Oriental Museum, founded in 1896.

James Henry Breasted (the first American to receive a Ph.D. in Egyptology) came to the University of Chicago in 1894 to be the first professor of Egyptology in the U.S. In 1903, the university undertook its first excavations in Mesopotamia. Breasted founded the Oriental Institute in 1919. The Institute, a pioneer in the archaeology, philology, and history of early Near Eastern civilizations, has undertaken excavations in every country of the Near East. The *Journal of Near Eastern Studies* (U.S., University of Chicago, 1884) is "devoted exclusively to an examination of the ancient and medieval civilizations of the Near East. Appearing in its pages are contributions from scholars of international reputation on archaeology, art, history, literature, linguistics, religion, law, and science. Old Testament and Islamic studies are also featured." The *Journal* traces its origins to *Hebraica,* begun in 1884 by William Rainey Harper, and renamed the *American Journal of Semitic Languages and Literatures* in 1895. When the first issue of the *Journal of Near Eastern Studies* emerged in 1942, its editors wrote that the journal now bore "a name more truly descriptive of its content," and noted that "the editors of the *American Journal of Semitic Languages and Literatures* throughout the period of its existence, have always welcomed contributions on near eastern languages outside of the Semitic family . . . as well as on archeology and history . . . "

The American Schools of Oriental Research (ASOR) was founded in 1900 "to enable properly qualified persons to pursue biblical, linguistic, archaeological, historical, and other kindred studies and researches under more favorable conditions than can be secured at a distance from the Holy Land." ASOR and its Jerusalem Institute played an important role in the discovery of the Dead Sea Scrolls. The *Bulletin of the American Schools of Oriental Research* or *BASOR* (U.S., American Schools of Oriental Research, 1919), publishes reports of original research and scholarship in the "art, archaeology, history, anthropology, literature, philology, and epigraphy of the Near East and eastern Mediterranean world from the Paleolithic period through early Islamic times."

Midway through the 20th century, the *Israel Exploration Journal* (Israel, Israel Exploration Society, 1950) emerged as an "interdisciplinary scholarly forum for current archaeological, historical and geographical research about Israel and environs."

ARCHAEOLOGY OF THE GREEK
AND ROMAN WORLD IN CLASSICAL TIMES

Hesperia (U.S., Harvard University Press, 1931) is the premier journal of the archaeology of classical Greece. A relative newcomer, the *Journal of*

Roman Archaeology (U.S., Journal of Roman Archaeology, 1988) is an annual international journal publishing articles on Roman archaeology in English, French, German, Italian, and Spanish. Mediterranean-wide in coverage, the *Journal of Roman Archaeology* is concerned with all aspects of archaeology in Italy and the Roman world from 700 B.C. to 700 A.D.

OTHER AREAS AND ERAS

Latin American Antiquity (U.S., Society for American Archaeology, 1990) publishes original papers in English and Spanish on the archaeology, prehistory, and ethnohistory of Latin America (Mesoamerica, Central America, and South America). Since the debut of *Latin American Antiquity* in 1990, *American Antiquity* coverage of Latin American archaeology has been limited to broad methodological, theoretical, or comparative issues extending beyond Latin America. The principal archaeology journal for the western rim of the Pacific, Australia, and the islands of the Pacific is *Archaeology in Oceania* (Australia, University of Sydney, 1966), formerly *Archaeology and Physical Anthropology in Oceania*. Archaeology and prehistory of Africa and neighboring islands is featured in *African Archaeological Review* (U.S., Plenum, 1983).

REFERENCES AND SUGGESTED READINGS

Barley, Nigel. "Specialist Issues: Anthropology." *Times Literary Supplement* June 12: 641, 1987.

Cameron, George G., William F. Edgerton, and Raymond A. Bowman. "Editor's Announcement." *Journal of Near Eastern Studies* 1 (1): 1-2, 1942.

Chippendale, Christopher. "Editorial." *Antiquity* 61 (231): 4-9, 1987.

Crawford, O.G.S. "Editorial Notes." *Antiquity* 1 (1): 1-4, 1927.

Daniel, Glyn E. *A Hundred and Fifty Years of Archaeology.* 2nd ed. London: Duckworth, 1975.

Donohue, A.A. "One Hundred Years of the American Journal of Archaeology: An Archival History." *American Journal of Archaeology* 89: 3-30, 1985.

Dow, Sterling. "Archaeology." *Archaeology* 1 (1): 5-6, 1948.

Garfield, Eugene. "Anthropology Journals: What They Cite and What Cites Them." *Current Anthropology* 25: 514-528, 1984.

Griffin, James B. "The Formation of the Society for American Archaeology." *American Antiquity* 50 (2): 261-271, 1985.

Guthe, Carl E. "Reflections on the Founding of the Society for American Archaeology." *American Antiquity* 32 (4): 433-440, 1967.

Hawkes, Jacquetta. "A Quarter Century of Antiquity." *Antiquity* 25: 171-173, 1951.

Hitchner, R. Bruce. "A Letter from the Editor-in-Chief." *American Journal of Archaeology* 104: 1, 2000.

Hudson, Kenneth. *A Social History of Archaeology: The British Experience.* London: Macmillan, 1981.

Malone, Caroline, Simon Stoddart, and Nicholas James. "Editorial." *Antiquity* 73 (282): 723-734, 1999.

McMillen, Liz. "A Shake-up in Anthropology: New Editors Dramatically Revise a Staid Journal." *Chronicle of Higher Education* 41(4): A10-A11, A17, 1994.

Meltzer, David J., Don D. Fowler, and Jeremy A. Sabloff, eds. *American Archaeology, Past and Future: A Celebration of the Society for American Archaeology, 1935-1985.* Washington: Published for the Society for American Archaeology by the Smithsonian Institution Press, 1986.

Meltzer, David J. "North American Archaeology and Archaeologists, 1879-1934." *American Antiquity* 50 (2): 249-260, 1985.

Sabloff, Jeremy A. "American Antiquity's First Fifty Years: An Introductory Comment." *American Antiquity* 50 (2): 228-236, 1985.

Stern, Gwen, and Paul Bohannan. "American Anthropologist: The First Eighty Years." *Anthropology Newsletter* 11 (1): 6-12, 1970.

Sterud, Eugene L. "Changing Aims of American Archaeology: A Citations Analysis of American Antiquity-1946-1975." *American Antiquity* 43 (2): 294-302, 1978.

Stewart, T. D. "Aleš Hrdlicka. Pioneer American Physical Anthropologist." In *The Czechoslovak Contribution to World Culture* (Miloslav Rechcigl, ed.) The Hague: Mouton and Co., 505-509, 1964.

Trotter, Mildred. "Notes on the History of the AAPA." *American Journal of Physical Anthropology* 14: 350-364, 1956.

Willey, Gordon R., and Jeremy A. Sabloff. *A History of American Archaeology.* 2nd ed. San Francisco: W. H. Freeman, 1980.

Chapter 9

Journals of the Century in Philosophy

John M. Cullars

I have made a number of working assumptions and exclusions in carrying out this project. Firstly, I am restricting this listing to Western philosophy. Chinese, Indian, Islamic, and African philosophies are not considered. This exclusion reflects my own lack of expertise in non-Western philosophy and should not be taken as a negative judgment on these areas. Disciplines that are covered by other essays in this series—aesthetics (as covered by literature, music, and the visual arts), law, history, politics, religion, and the social sciences—are also excluded, though certain selected journals at least tangentially deal with some of these topics. Metaphysics, for instance, does treat religious concerns but not from a theological or doctrinal perspective. Feminist philosophy can draw on all or most of the disciplines listed above but for its own autonomous purposes. In the cases of Existentialism and Phenomenology and of Idealism and Metaphysics, I have taken the liberty of combining each pair into one category for the following reasons: I feel that these movements, though no longer in the ascendant, are too important historically and intellectually to be excluded or subsumed under more general headings. On the other hand, they are not important enough to modern philosophers to justify treating them separately.

I also chose not to have separate categories for "the philosophy of XYZ" except for the philosophy of science; I feel this category is justified, indeed demanded, by the strong scientific grounding both methodologically and in terms of foundational principles of so many twentieth century schools of philosophy, particularly of Anglo-American philosophy. I have excluded Structuralism because I feel that its major contributions have been in linguistics, which is covered, and in literary and cultural studies, which is also where I would place Deconstruction. I have drawn brief expository descriptions of the chosen categories from the *Cambridge Dictionary of Philosophy,* noting the identity of the contributing scholar, except in two cases (general philosophy and the history of philosophy) which I hope are sufficiently

This chapter originally appeared in *The Serials Librarian* 39(2): 39-58, 2000.

transparent as to need no explanation even to readers with no background in or knowledge of the discipline.

My choice of three journals in each category is by necessity somewhat arbitrary. While I have considered library holdings and the citation history of the journals, such data is of uncertain value in determining these rankings. Since I am seeking to designate the three top journals in each category, the holdings of libraries that can be obtained from OCLC or RLIN means little; of course, such major journals must be held by virtually all academic libraries that support research and teaching in philosophy. If they are not widely held, I would question their presence on this list. Nor are citations to the journals an altogether reliable gauge of their value. Such lists are based on total citations to a given title in the discipline. If this list dealt only with generalist, ranking by the number of citations would be more meaningful. But such generalist philosophy journals make up only a single category here. Obviously specialist journals do not rank highly in such citation lists and just as obviously journals whose topics have an interdisciplinary appeal and are thus indexed by a variety of services are likely to be more heavily cited.

In making the choices of journals to recommend, I have relied on standard library sources listed in the bibliography and the advice of faculty in philosophy as well as of other librarians. For the reasons given above, holdings and citation information were not sufficient criteria for inclusion in the absence of further corroborating testimony, both printed and anecdotal. I gathered detailed information on 86 journals and ultimately chose 42 for inclusion. The final step was to physically examine the most recent issue of each journal to verify the accuracy of pricing, to verify editors and publishers, and frequently to quote from editorial statements. The number of articles and their length are based on these recent issues and may not hold for the complete run of older serials. In two cases (indicated in the discussion) I was unable to locate the most recent issue and thus the price, editor, and publisher may be inaccurate since the sources available for serial verification rely on self-reporting from the journals and may be out-of-date when changes are not reported.

Where different prices are quoted, unless otherwise noted, the first is the institutional price for the United States; the second is for individuals, and the third is for students. Slashes separate these prices. One interesting finding was that in virtually all cases in which comparative data on the number of subscriptions was available between sources from the mid-1980s and current subscription figures, the number of subscriptions often had fallen significantly. Six specialized journals had subscription rates drop by between 7.9 percent and 9.4 percent while two journals, one in general philosophy and the other in the philosophy of science, showed increases of between 8.6 percent and 9.3 percent between 1986 and 1998. Presumably this reflects the rising costs of the more expensive serials, which have priced themselves out of the reach of individuals. Indeed, as can be seen in the listing, many journals no longer advertise individual subscription rates, though some invite individuals to contact the publisher for information.

ANALYTIC PHILOSOPHY

(sometimes called Oxford or linguistic philosophy) has been principally the province of English-speaking philosophers drawing on Bertrand Russell, G. E. Moore, and Ludwig Wittgenstein. "Analysis, as practiced by Russell and Moore, concerned not language per se, but concepts and prepositions. In their eyes, while it did not exhaust the domain of philosophy, analysis provided a vital tool for laying bare the logical form of reality. Wittgenstein contended . . . that the structure of language reveals the structure of the world; every meaningful sentence is analyzable into atomic constituents that designate the fine-grained constituents of reality" (1, p. 22, John Heil). This was influential on the Vienna Circle in the 1920s-30s and Logical Positivism.

Analysis. 1933-. new series 1947-. 0003-2638. Quarterly. Basil Blackwell, Oxford, England. $59. Available online. Editor [henceforth "Ed."] Michael Clark as of September 1, 1999. Copyright retained by authors. This journal is "one of the few forums for active debate among scholars of modern contemporary philosophy" (3, p. 9). It largely excludes the historical or the expository in favor of critiques of concepts in semantics, physicalism, epistemology, logic, and philosophy of mind. "An attempt is made to include philosophy that is analytic without being in the established Anglo-Saxon analytic tradition. . . . Most articles are either carefully developed criticisms of arguments or positions in contemporary analytic philosophy or defenses against such criticism" (4, pp. 24-25). Each number carries 8-12 articles, generally of approximately 5-8 pages. No book reviews. Discussions of articles can extend over several numbers.

American Philosophical Quarterly. 1964-. Quarterly. 0003-0481. North American Philosophical Publications, Verona, PA, USA. $175/$40. Founding Executive Ed. Nicholas Rescher, current Ed. Robert F. Almeder. Editorial board of 25. According to the editorial statement, "the *American Philosophical Quarterly* welcomes articles in English by philosophers of any country on any aspect of philosophy apart from history." Journal holds copyright but "routinely accords contributors permission to reprint in books or anthologies authored or coauthored by themselves." Submissions should be "on modern or historical subjects reflective of an analytical orientation" (3, p. 7). The journal covers ethics, epistemology, metaphysics, philosophy of mind, action theory, and morality, among other topics. Its "Recent Work" feature appears several times each year and offers a valuable scholarly overview of topics of current interest. Its writing can be technical and demanding. Recent numbers have carried 5-7 articles of 15-25 pages but no book reviews.

Philosophical Studies: An International Journal for Philosophy in the Analytic Tradition. 1950-. 0031-8116. Monthly. Kluwer Academic Publications, Dordrecht, Netherlands. $774. Editor-in-Chief is Stewart Cohen and the Special Editions Ed. is Keith Lehrer. Editorial board of 30 prominent philosophers, including M. A. E. Dummett and Gilbert Harman. Journal holds copyright. "Founded by Herbert Fiegl and Wilfred Sellers, *Philosophical Studies* has established itself as one of the foremost journals for analytic philosophy. . . . Despite its high cost, this is a core collection journal" (2, p. 965). Its focus is on both contemporary issues and traditional problems explored from new perspectives. Issues covered include metaphysics, epistemology, philosophy of mind, logic, philosophy of science, action theory, and ethics. The journal publishes the papers of the American Philosophical Association each year as well as thematic issues with guest editors. According to its editorial statement, "the journal remains devoted to the publication of papers in exclusively analytic philosophy. . . . It is intended that readers of the journal will be kept abreast of the central issues and problems of contemporary analytic philosophy." Articles can vary greatly in length, from fewer than five to 50 pages in recent numbers. There are no book reviews.

ANCIENT PHILOSOPHY

in practice is largely limited to classical Greek philosophy though many journals also include certain Hellenistic and Roman developments as a secondary focus. Philosophers, Classicists, and historians of Greek and Roman antiquity tend to contribute to these journals.

Phronesis: A Journal for Ancient Philosophy. 1955-. Quarterly, formerly 3/yr. 0031-8868. Van Gorcum/Brill Academic, Assen, Netherlands. $105/$78. Eds. Keimpe Algra and Christopher Rowe. Editorial board of international scholars. Copyright held by journal. "A leading journal devoted exclusively to all aspects of ancient philosophy. . . . [Its] commitment to excellence in scholarly publishing . . . keeps *Phronesis* at the forefront of the field" (2, p. 967). The Hellenistic period is included, and articles may appear in English, French, German, Italian, and Latin. Plato and Aristotle are the central authors studied. According to the editorial note, this journal "has become the most authoritative scholarly journal for the study of ancient philosophy. It covers the whole range of Greek and Roman thought, including logic, physics, ethics, political philosophy, psychology, metaphysics, epistemology, and the philosophy of science and medicine from its origins down to the end of the sixth century A.D." Each issue contains 3-5 articles of approximately 15-25 pages as well as discussion notes and book reviews ("Book Notes").

Proceedings of the Aristotelian Society. (Continuation of *Proceedings of the Aristotelian Society for the Systematic Study of Philosophy*). Supplements are also published. 1877-. 3/yr. 0066-7374. Ed. Jonathan Wolff. Blackwell Publishers for the Aristotelian Society, Oxford, England. $81. Also available online. Copyright is held by the Aristotelian Society. "The Aristotelian Society is one of the oldest and most distinguished organizations for Anglo-American philosophy. The annual proceedings, published in June, contain the papers read at the annual Joint Sessions of the Aristotelian Society and the Mind Association. The publication invariably represents exemplary standards of scholarship, and it is highly recommended for all collections" (2, p. 967). Papers reflect the origins and development of Western traditions. "It is a clearly edifying portrait of theory and central perspectives in Greco-Roman culture" (3, p. 109). Each issue contains 4-5 papers of 20-30 pages followed by briefer discussion papers. The influence of classical philosophy on later philosophy, including the most modern, can be found. No book reviews.

Oxford Studies in Ancient Philosophy. 1983-. Annual. 0265-7651. Clarendon/Oxford University Press, Oxford, England. $69. Founding Ed. Julia Annas; Ed. D. N. Sedley succeeded C. C. W. Taylor in 1999. Copyright held by Oxford University Press. This journal addresses all facets of ancient philosophy and carries articles by leading philosophers and classicists. Its editorial board contains some of the most prominent philosophers of the period, among them Martha Nussbaum and Jonathan Barnes. It offers analysis of primary texts rather than exposition of themes. There are lengthy review articles rather than single book reviews. Each volume concludes with an *index locorum*. While the works of Plato and Aristotle attract the major part of the contributions, all aspects of ancient philosophy are open for examination. The 1998 volume contained 10 articles of 30-70 pages.

BEHAVIORISM

is "broadly the view that behavior is fundamental in understanding mental phenomena. The term applies both to a scientific research program in psychology and to a philosophical doctrine. . . . Philosophical behaviorism is a semantic thesis about the meaning of mentalistic expressions. . . . Statements containing mentalistic expressions have the same meaning as, and are thus translatable into, some set of publicly verifiable statements describing behavioral and bodily processes and dispositions." (1, p. 66, A. Marras)

Behavior and Philosophy (formerly *Behaviorism*). 1973-. 2/yr. 1053-8348. Cambridge Center for Behavioral Studies, Cambridge, MA, USA (founded by Dept. of Psychology, University of Nevada.) $60/$35/$13. Ed. J. E. R. Staddon. Both empirical and theoretical papers are welcomed, though there is a "bias toward the directly measurable" (4, p. 29). Topics addressed include theories of learning and of asymptotic behavior, behavioral ethology, economic behaviorism, verbal behavior, behavioral semantics, cognitive variables, rule-governed behavior, behavioral analysis of rationality, choice and moral judgments, and behavioral themes in philosophy. Starting in 1985, the journal was co-edited by philosophers and psychologists, leading to the title change in 1990 at vol. 18. Recent numbers carry 4-5 articles of 10-30 pages.

Journal of Mind and Behavior. 1980-. Quarterly. 0271-0137. Institute of Mind and Behavior, New York, NY, USA. $98/$46/$32. Ed. Raymond C. Russ. The editor strongly supports a working relationship between theory and method rather than stressing one at the expense of the other. The journal's editorial statement mentions the following philosophical topics, among others, as being appropriate for submission: "the psychology, philosophy, and sociology of experimentation and the scientific method . . . the mind/body problem in the social sciences, psychiatry, and the medical sciences . . . the philosophical impact of a mind/body epistemology upon psychology and its theories of consciousness [and] . . . phenomenological, teleological, existential, and introspective reports relevant to psychology, pyschosocial methodology, and social philosophy." Each number tends to contain 4-7 articles of 15-30 pages, book reviews, and lists of books received.

Psychological Record. 1937-. Quarterly. 0033-2933. Kenyon College, Gambier, OH, USA. $95/$45/$35. Ed. Charles E. Rice. Editorial board of over 30 prominent psychologists and philosophers. Copyright held by journal. While this journal began as an expression of behaviorism, drawing on the works of B. F. Skinner and Wilfred Sellers, it later broadened its scope to include linguistics, psychotherapy, and epistemology, among other topics. "The authors, mostly academicians, masterfully address the questions of current applied philosophy as it evolves into a multidisciplinary field" (3, p. 112). It carries 6-10 articles of 8-30 pages and many book reviews. Special thematic numbers are also published.

EPISTEMOLOGY

is "the study of the nature of knowledge and justification; specifically, the study of (a) the defining features, (b) the substantive conditions, and (c) the limits of knowledge and justification" (1, Paul K. Moser, p. 233). Subcategories of epistemology include evolutionary, moral, and naturalistic epistemologies; other topics falling under this heading include coherentism, foundationalism, justification, perception, skepticism, and truth.

Cognition. 1972-. Monthly since 1990, earlier irregular but aimed for 6/yr. 0010-0277. Elsevier Science, Amsterdam, Netherlands. $979. Copyright held by publisher. Ed. Jacques Mehler. Editorial board of over 60 international scholars and scientists, including Noam Chomsky and Jerry Fodor. Available online. The journal publishes theoretical and experimental papers covering all aspects of the mind as studied by psychology, linguistics, neurophysiology, ethology, epistemology, and such philosophical topics as the evaluation of meaning and reference. The journal also considers social and ethical questions facing scientists and philosophers. The authors tend to be philosophers or psychologists. Each number carries 3-4 papers of 10-40 pages and book reviews.

Mind: A Quarterly Review of Philosophy. 1876-. 0026-4423. Oxford University Press for the Mind Association, Oxford, England. $94/$54/$22. Ed. Mark Sainsbury. Copyright held by press "except as otherwise explicitly specified" (editorial statement). Available online. Past editors have included such famous philosophers as G. K. Stout, Moore, and Ryle. The journal publishes widely in all areas of epistemology, the philosophy of language, metaphysics, and philosophy of mind. It publishes 2-3 lengthy (up to 50 pages) articles, discussion pieces, book reviews, books received, and announcements per number. Position papers (pro or con submissions from earlier articles) are a common feature that can take up 30-40 pages.

Synthèse: An International Journal for Epistemology, Methodology and Philosophy of Science. 1936-. Monthly (originally 3/yr.) 0039-7857. Kluwer Academic Publications, Dordrecht, Netherlands. $990. Copyright held by publisher. Ed. Jaakko Hintikka. This journal addresses such epistemological topics as the theory of knowledge, mathematical, philosophical and symbolic logic, the philosophy of science, scientific reference, induction, causation, probability, and linguistics and examines them through formal methods of analysis. The editorial statement includes the information that "special attention will be paid to the role of mathematical, logical and linguistic methods in the general methodology of science and the foundations of the different sciences, be they physical, biological, behavioral or social." Philosophers, scientists, mathematicians, and economists are among the scholars who contribute to the journal. Articles tend to be highly technical and addressed to the specialist. Each issue carries 5-6 articles of 10-20 pages each.

ETHICS

is "the philosophical study of morality. The word is also commonly used interchangeably with 'morality' to mean the subject matter of this study. . . . Ethics, along with logic, metaphysics, and epistemology, is one of the main branches of philosophy." (1, p. 244, John Deigh)

Ethics: An International Journal of Social, Political, and Legal Philosophy (formerly *International Journal of Ethics*). 1890-. Quarterly. 0014-1704. University of Chicago Press, Chicago, IL, USA. $99/$35/$25. Ed. John Deigh. The 55-person editorial board contains such prominent philosophers as Gerald Dworkin, a former editor, Martha Nussbaum, Amartya Sen, and Alasdair MacIntyre. The journal considers moral concerns in the social science, politics, law, psychiatry, theology, public policy issues, normative economics, and rational choice theory. According to the editorial statement, it "publishes work arising from a variety of disciplines and intellectual perspectives, including philosophy, social and political theory, theories of individual and collective choice, social and economic policy analysis, jurisprudence and international relations. It is especially concerned to foster work that draws on more than one disciplinary approach." Ruben rates *Ethics* as "one of the leading philosophical journals in America" (3, p. 39), and Katz categorizes it as having "clearly established itself as a leading journal in the fields of social and political philosophy and ethics. . . . Highly recommended for all collections" (2, p. 959). It addresses both classical traditional theories and contemporary developments. Each issue contains 3-5 articles of 20-30 pages each, discussions of current theory, book reviews, and book notes. Symposia are also frequently discussed in depth.

Pacific Philosophical Quarterly (formerly *Personalist*). 1919-. Quarterly. 0279-0750. Blackwell Publishers for School of Philosophy, University of Southern California, Oxford, England. $92/$45. Frank A. Lewis, Chair of editorial board. Copyright held by publisher. This journal, which draws on an international editorial board and contributors, presents theoretical discussions of human character and behavior, ontology, logic, and the history of philosophy. Topics in continental philosophy are largely excluded. The journal "continues to offer theoretical essays on human character and behavior, and the circumstances inherently involved" (3, p. 94). Each issue contains 4-7 articles of up to 30 pages each but no book reviews

Hastings Center Report. 1971-. Bimonthly. 0093-0334. Hastings Center, Garrison, NY, USA. $75/$64/$48. Ed. Bette-Jane Crigger. This journal "is the premier journal of biomedical ethics. Its reputation alone is that of central organ for discussion of ethical problems associated with medicine, professionalism, and applied disciplines. . . . There is no doubt that [it] is the ideal serial for medical and university libraries" (3, p. 46). According to the editorial note, submissions are welcomed dealing with "educational and research programs or ethical issues in medicine, health care, technology, and the environment . . . " Issues of analytic philosophy and the history of philosophy are excluded. Topics of contemporary currency are stressed but not to the exclusion of historical placing of the problems considered. The editorial board draws on the expertise of lawyers, philosophers, physicians, and scholars in various relevant disciplines. Each number contains 3-5 articles of 3-12 pages and varying numbers of reviews on case studies, book reviews, books received, notes, and news items.

EXISTENTIALISM/PHENOMENOLOGY

Existentialism [is] a philosophical and literary movement that came to prominence in Europe, particularly in France, immediately after World War II, that focused on the uniqueness of each human individual as distinguished from abstract universal human qualities. (1, p. 255, William L. McBride)

Phenomenology is a principally German movement most prominently espoused by Edmund Husserl that has contributed to the existential thought of such French philosophers as Jean-Paul Sartre and Maurice Merleau-Ponty. While it cannot be succinctly defined due to the variant doctrines of its philosophers, "it has been said that phenomenology consists in an analysis and description of consciousness; it has been claimed also that phenomenology simply blends with existentialism." (1, p. 578, Joseph J. Kockelmans)

Philosophy and Phenomenological Research: A Quarterly Journal Founded by Marvin Farber. 1940-. 0031-8205. Quarterly. International

Phenomenological Society, Brown University, Providence, RI, USA. $73/$24. Ed. Ernest Sosa. Editorial board of 55 including Robert Audi, Jerry Fodor, Paul Moser, and Barry Stroud. The journal addresses a broader spectrum of issues and philosophical approaches than the title might lead one to expect; indeed, the editorial statement makes this explicit: "No specific methodology or philosophical orientation is required in submissions." Publications are as apt to be in the analytic tradition as in continental trends normally associated with Existentialism and Phenomenology, which is reflected in its subscription rate of 1800, high for a specialist interest. Katz ranks the journal "in the upper echelon of analytic philosophy journals" (2, p. 966). There are discussions of symposia and special volumes published as well as 5-8 articles of 10-25 pages, review essays, book reviews, and news features in each number.

Human Studies: A Journal for Philosophy and the Social Sciences. 1978-. 0163-8548. Quarterly. Kluwer Academic Publishers, Dordrecht, Netherlands. $270. Eds. George Psathas (founder) and Lenore Langsdorf. This journal seeks to promote the discussion between philosophy and the social sciences, stressing phenomenological and existential approaches. It presents a "clear statement of the nature and strategy underlying science, objectivism, and methodology" (3, p. 49). The editorial page states that the journal is "dedicated primarily to advancing the dialogue between philosophy and the human sciences. In particular, such issues as the logic of inquiry, methodology, epistemology and foundational issues in the human sciences exemplified by original empirical, theoretical and philosophical investigations are addressed. Phenomenological perspectives, broadly defined, are a primary, though not exclusive focus." Five to 7 papers of 10-30 pages, review essays, and a call for papers are included in each number.

Research in Phenomenology. 1973-. Annual. 0085-5553. Humanities Press, Atlantic Heights, NJ, USA. $60/$47. One reason that this is a valuable journal is that its research models differ from those typically employed by *Philosophy and Phenomenological Research,* excluding analytic philosophy and addressing the works of French and German philosophers in the continental existential and structuralist traditions. This makes it an important complement to that title. Yudkin reports that the journal is intended for "professional philosophers well conversant with the themes, problems and representative figures of continental thought" (4, p. 92). Ruben refers to the production of this journal as "valuable discourse on practical evidence in science" (3, p. 115). According to the editorial statement, "the Editorial Directors . . . welcome submission of manuscripts that deal with phenomenological philosophy in a broad sense, including original phenomenological research, critical and interpretive studies of major phenomenological thinkers, studies dealing with the relation of phenomenological philosophy to other disciplines, and historical studies that have some special importance for phenomenological philosophy." Each issue contains 5-7 articles of approximately 20 pages each, review articles of 4-5 pages, and individual book reviews [next to last vol. published examined].

FEMINIST PHILOSOPHY

is "a discussion of philosophical concerns that refuses to identify the human experience with the male experience. Writing from a variety of perspectives, feminist philosophers challenge several areas of traditional philosophy on the grounds that they fail (1) to take seriously women's interests, identities, and issues; and (2) to recognize women's ways of being, thinking, and doing as valuable as those of men." (1, p. 262, Rosemarie Tong)

Hypatia: A Journal of Feminist Philosophy. 1982-. Quarterly (originally semimonthly). 0887-5367. Indiana University Press, Bloomington, IN, USA. $75/$35. Eds. Laurie Shrage and Nancy Tuana. A part of *Women's Studies International Forum* until 1986, it "was the first journal in North America entirely devoted to the articulation and development of progress within the women's movement on such issues as ethics, aesthetics, political theory, sociobiology, and sexuality. . . . Enunciation of this seemingly 'activist' philosophy does not spare objectivity in its arguments" (3, p. 52). Its "Forum Section" publishes short papers on a given topic. There are also special issues on themes of contemporary interest in women's studies, most recently on the philosophy of Simone de Beauvoir. Each issue contains 6-10 articles of 12-20 pages and book reviews.

Signs: Journal of Women in Culture and Society. 1975-. Quarterly. 0097-9740. University of Chicago Press, Chicago, IL, USA. $127/$38/$27. Copyright held by publisher. Eds. Carolyn Allen and Judith A. Howard. This serial has been acknowledged "internationally as one of the most respectable journals devoted to the discussion of scholarship about women. Original research, contemplative essays and commentary bridge the humanities and social sciences by examining the status of women and religion, and national development and the workplace" (3, p. 125). According to the editorial note, the journal publishes "articles from a wide range of disciplines in a variety of voices—articles engaging gender, race, culture, class, nation, and/or sexuality. Essays may be discipline specific if they are framed so that they enter critical conversations of interest across disciplines, or they may be cross-disciplinary in their theorizing, their methodology, or their sources." Contributors are mainly female scholars in philosophy and the social sciences. Each number carries 4-5 articles of 25-35 pages, book reviews, and a review essay focusing on developments in a given discipline.

Feminist Studies: FS. 1972-. (Founded in 1969 by Ann Howard Calderwood.) 3/yr. 0046-3663. Women's Studies Program, University of Maryland, College Park, MD, USA. $85/$30. Ed. Claire G. Moses. According to the editorial statement, the journal publishes "serious writing of a critical, scholarly, speculative and political nature. . . . [It was founded] "to encourage analytic responses to feminist issues and to open new areas of research, criticism, and speculation. . . . We wish not just to interpret women's experiences but to change women's condition." It also publishes fiction and art, manifestos, and position papers. Professional female philosophers are often represented among the female scholars whose work is featured. Each number has 3-4 articles of 20-25 pages each, review essays, book reviews, notes, and letters.

GENERAL PHILOSOPHY

Philosophical Review. 1892-. Quarterly. 0031-8108. Sage School of Philosophy, Cornell University, Ithaca, NY, USA. $54/$33. Ed. by faculty of Sage School of Philosophy since 1938; early distinguished editors included Jacob G. Schurman, James E. Creighton, Frank Thilly, and Gustavus Watts Cunningham. John Rowehl is Managing Editor. "One of the first comprehensive treatments of analytic philosophy. . . . A professional milestone in the global picture of philosophical development" (3, p. 99). Treats metaphysics, ethics, the philosophy of science, epistemology, history of philosophy, the philosophy of mind, and philosophy of language. Recent numbers carry lengthy articles of up to 50 pages each, as well as many book reviews.

Philosophy (continues *Journal of Philosophical Studies*). 1925-. Quarterly. 0031-8191. Cambridge University Press, Cambridge, England. $230. Ed. Anthony O'Hear. Available online. The official publication of the Royal Institute of Philosophy (RIP) of Great Britain, which holds copyright. "All branches of philosophy are discussed in its pages, and no emphasis is placed on any particular school or method . . . invariably representing the highest standards of scholarship" (2, p. 965). The RIP Lectures Series is now included as a supplement in the subscription price. Nontechnical vocabulary is strongly recommended by the editor, making the journal's articles particularly accessible to students and non-specialists. Each number contains 6 articles between approximately 10-30 pages each and 3-4 discussion notes, book reviews, booknotes, and lists of books received.

Journal of Philosophy (continues *Journal of Philosophy, Psychology, and Scientific Methods*). 1904-. Monthly. 0022-362X. Columbia University, New York, NY, USA. $75/$35/$20. Managing Ed. Michael Kelly with editorial board of 15 editors and consulting editors. Copyright held by journal. The editorial statement affirms that its purpose is "to publish philosophical articles of current interest and encourage the interchange of ideas, especially the exploration of the borderline between philosophy and other disciplines." In its near century of publication, its editors have included such distinguished philosophers as John Randall, Bernard Berofsky, Arthur Danto, Charles Parsons, and James Walsh. "The *Journal of Philosophy* has been a pioneering vehicle for philosophical exchange for over [90] years. . . . [It is] "a required journal for every aspiring student and professional in the field" (3, p. 69). Topics address virtually all areas of philosophy-metaphysics, epistemology, philosophy of mind, analytic philosophy, logic, social and political philosophies, ethics, action theory, and aesthetics. Katz classifies it as a "core collection journal" (2, p. 962). Recent numbers contain 2-4 articles of 10-30 pages, and some, but not all, carry comments and criticisms, book reviews, and correspondence on prior publications.

HISTORY OF PHILOSOPHY

Journal of the History of Philosophy. 1963-. Quarterly. 0022-5053. Dept. of Philosophy, Emory University, Atlanta, GA, USA. $65/$25/$18. Ed. Gerald A. Press. Copyright held by the journal. Katz classifies this as a "leading journal for the history of Western Philosophy" (2, p. 962). It deals with historical movements and both major and minor philosophers and scientists. All periods are covered. Articles are accepted in French and German as well as English, though most are in the latter. The typical issue contains 6-7 articles of 10-30 pages each, book reviews, books received, and announcements.

Journal of the History of Ideas. 1940-. Quarterly. 0022-5037. University of Rochester, Rochester, NY, USA. $64/$26. Ed. Donald R. Kelley. Copyright held by journal. According to the editorial statement, the journal was founded "to foster studies which will examine the evolution of ideas in the development and interrelations of . . . the history of philosophy, of literature and the arts, of the natural and social sciences, of religion and of political and social movements . . . " It excludes analytic philosophy. Favored topics include the history of science, major intellectual movements, individual thinkers, and relationships between or among philosophers or schools. All authors have institutional affiliations. Each number carries 6-8 articles of 15-30 pages, a comprehensive review essay, and news, including obituaries.

Topoi: An International Review of Philosophy. 1982-. Semi-annual. 0167-7411. Kluwer Academic Publishers, Dordrecht, Netherlands. $270.

Ed. Ermanno Bencivenga. Available online. This journal is sponsored by the Department of Philosophy and the School of Humanities, University of California, Irvine. Most or all of each issue is devoted to a single topic, usually with the collaboration of a guest editor, "an expert who will identify contributors and interact with them in a constructive way" [editorial statement], but the editor does not rule out submissions outside the announced *topos*. According to Yudkin, the journal is "devoted to philosophical studies and to the history of philosophy, dedicated to illustrating the most important topics that have emerged from these disciplines in recent years . . . " (4, p. 108). The journal is not restricted to history or even the historical treatment of topics, but very frequently these have been the center of attention. Recent topics have included medieval supposition theory, Descarte's ontology, and most recently, probability, logics and exactitude. Guest editors have included Paul Draper, Georgios Anagnostopoulos, Alan Nelson, and Franz Wimmer. Recent issues have contained 6-8 articles of 5-20 large-format pages plus an introduction by the guest editor. There are no book reviews.

IDEALISM/METAPHYSICS

Idealism is "the philosophical doctrine that reality is somehow mind-correlative or mind-coordinated—that the real objects constituting the 'external world' are not independent of cognizing minds, but exist only as in some way correlative to mental operations." (1, p. 355, Nicholas Rescher)

Metaphysics, under which idealism may be subsumed for purposes of this project, is "most generally the philosophical investigation of the nature, constitution, and structure of reality. . . . Perhaps the most familiar question in metaphysics is whether there are only material entities—*materialism*—or only mental entities, i.e., minds and their states—*idealism*—or both—*dualism*." (1, p. 489, Panayot Butchvarov)

Idealistic Studies: An Interdisciplinary Journal of Philosophy. 1970-. 3/yr (formerly quarterly). 0046-8541. Dept. of Philosophy, Clark University, Worcester, MA, USA. $39.95 US institutions/$44.50 foreign institutions/$25 US individuals/$29.95 foreign individuals. Copyright held by Idealistic Studies, Inc. MA. Ed. Walter E. Wright. The philosophies of Plato, Berkeley, Hegel, Schelling, Bradley, and McTaggart, among others, are examined, as well as historical and modern analyses of idealistic methodologies applied to history, logic, ontology, and psychology. From the editorial statement: "*Idealistic Studies* is a journal which focuses on two related themes. First, are the historical and contemporary philosophical statements of idealistic argumentation, and critical studies of idealism. Second, are the implications of contemporary science and mathematics for both traditional and new idealist issues." The journal includes both positive and negative views of idealistic arguments. "The constructive criticisms in ontology, Hegelian phenomenology, and scientific progress are particularly relevant to introductory philosophy students" (3, p. 5). Each number carries 5-6 articles of 20-30 pages, survey articles, and announcements.

Monist: An International Journal of General Philosophical Inquiry. 1890 (founded 1888)-. Quarterly. 0026-9662. Hegeler Institute, La Salle, IL, USA. $48/$25. Ed. Barry Smith. Copyright is held by the Hegeler Institute. Begun by Paul Carus (1852-1919), editor of Open Court Publishing Company, in its more than century of existence this journal has moved from an idealistic to a more general orientation. Each issue is thematically conceived with topics publicized two to three years in advance and listed on the back cover. Favored topics include logic, metaphysics, and epistemology with contributions in both historical traditional philosophical figures and schools and more modern trends such as Phenomenology and Feminism equally welcomed by the editor. Opposing views are sometimes presented back-to-back. Katz classifies *The Monist* as "a very attractive publication" due to "its broad scope, high-quality scholarship, and reasonable cost . . . " (2, p. 963). Recent issues tend to include eight to ten 10-20 page articles built around a chosen theme coordinated by an advisory editor. The editor solicits some articles from renowned scholars. There are lists of recent publications but no book reviews.

Noûs. 1967-. Quarterly. 0029-4624. Blackwell Publishers, Oxford, England. $180/$67. Co-eds. Louise M. Anthony, William G. Lycan, and James E. Tomberlin. Blackwell holds copyright. It assumed the role of publisher from Indiana University Press following the retirement in 1990 of founding editor Hector-Neri Castaneda. While never strictly a vehicle for Idealism, in its first decades the editor's preference for idealistic analysis and methodologies justifies its inclusion in this section (given the fact that most of these classifications are loose and even arbitrary conveniences). While the new editors accept submissions that include much the same subject matter (metaphysics, epistemology, logic, religion, ethics, and the history of philosophy) their approaches are more eclectic. From the editorial statement: it "publishes quality essays on philosophical problems regardless of the author's school or point of view. In addition, *Noûs* will publish symposia, surveys of work on specially selected philosophical topics, and critical studies of recent publications in philosophy." Katz opines that this "is a high-quality journal that belongs in all but the smallest collections" (2, p. 963). Each number consists of 5-7 articles of 15-30 pages, book reviews, and announcements.

LANGUAGE/LINGUISTICS

is "the philosophical study of natural language and its workings, particularly of linguistic meaning and the use of language. . . . Contemporary philosophy of language centers on the theory of meaning, but also includes the theory of reference, the theory of truth, philosophical pragmatics, and philosophical linguistics" (1, p. 586, William G. Lycan). Linguistic and other language-oriented concerns have been central to many of the twentieth century Anglo-American as well as continental Structuralist schools of thought.

Semiotica. 1969-. 5 vols. of 2 double issues/yr (about 2000 pages). 0037-1998. Walter de Gruyter, Berlin, Germany. $632/$250. Ed. Thomas Sebeok. Copyright held by publisher. The journal is the organ of the International Association of Semiotic Studies, Paris. Articles are mainly in English or French, but sometimes in German. They investigate the structure of language and verbal communication, general conversation, semiosis, and meaning in general. "The essential reason for *Semiotica,* apart from disciplinary interest, is to declare independence from other synthetic treatments of linguistic behavior" (3, p. 124). The editor's increasingly central position in the field since the journal's inception has doubtless contributed to its becoming central to the discourse of aspects of the discipline. There can be special issues with guest editors, the most recent being on notational engineering, edited by Jeffrey G. Long. Each number carries 18-20 generally brief and highly technical articles.

Linguistics and Philosophy: A Journal of Natural Language Syntax, Semantics, Pragmatics, and Processing. 1977-. Bi-monthly. Kluwer Academic Publishers, Dordrecht, Netherlands. $347.50/$116. Ed. Manfred Krifka. The journal's focus is the philosophy of language, semantics, and logic with a preference for analytic philosophical approaches. Psychological and sociological trends in language are other areas of concern. According to the editorial statement, other themes that are examined in the journal are philosophical theories of truth, reference, description; linguistic theories of semantic interpretation; psycholinguistic theories of semantic interpretation; mathematical and logical properties of natural language; and philosophical questions raised by linguistics as a science. Contributions are intended to appeal to both disciplines mentioned in the title. Articles tend to be quite long (up to 70 pages) and thus limit the number of articles to 2-3 per number.

Kodikas-Code/Ars Semeiotica: International Journal of Semantics. 1975- (new series 1979; combined with *Ars Semeiotica* in 1982). 2/yr (formerly quarterly). 0171-0834. Gunter Narr Verlag, Tübingen, Germany. 148 DM/96 DM. This journal gives priority to the analysis of communication and the interchange of information among human beings and other sentient beings. Authors and intended audience are trained professionals and the language is technical and specialized, which tends to be true for this discipline. Articles are generally authored by "formidable authorities in the field" (3, p. 77) and may be in English, German, or French. At least one number per year, sometimes supplementary rather than in the sequence of four, is built around a special topic in semantics. Also publishes supplementary monographic series. (Not seen; based on Ulrich's, Ebsconet, and Ruben.)

LOGIC

or formal logic is "the science of correct reasoning, going back to Aristotle's *Prior Analytics,* based upon the premise that the validity of an argument is a function of its structure or logical form. The modern embodiment of formal logic is *symbolic (mathematical) logic."* (1, p. 274, George F. Schumm)

Journal of Philosophical Logic. 1972-. Quarterly. 0022-3611. Kluwer Academic Publishers for the Association of Symbolic Logic, Dordrecht, Netherlands. $290/$96. Eds. Vann McGee and Krister Segerberg. Despite its connection to the Association of Symbolic Logic, this journal addresses the full scope of philosophical logic. Thus authors address issues drawing on a variety of logical approaches, formal logic as applied to epistemology, and the philosophy of language, mathematics, and science. The editorial statement reveals that "the scope is limited to philosophical studies utilizing formal methods or dealing with topics in logical theory" including "inductive logic, modal logic, deontic logic, quantum logic, tense logic, free logic, logic of questions, logic of commands, logic of preference, logic of conditionals, many-valued logic, relevance logics." Ruben writes that it "is the most prestigious journal specializing in philosophical logic" (3, p. 68). The writing is technical in nature and would be beyond the scope of most non-specialists or undergraduates. The 4-7 articles per number vary greatly in length and complexity with some running up to 50 pages.

Notre Dame Journal of Formal Logic. 1960-. Quarterly. 0029-4527. University of Notre Dame, Notre Dame, IN, USA. $48/$27. Eds. Michael Detlefsen and Anand Pillay. "This journal will be of interest to specialists working in all areas of philosophical and mathematical logic, including the philosophy, history, and foundations of logic and mathematics" (2, p. 963). There is an emphasis on the philosophy of language and formal semantics for natural languages. The number and length of the articles varies greatly with some taken up by 2-3 quite long papers and others containing as many as 9-11 articles of no more than 15 pages each. [This journal has not produced an issue in 1999, but is still listed as active but delayed by Ebsco.]

Studia Logica: An International Journal for Symbolic Logic. 1953-. Bimonthly (formerly quarterly). 0039-3215. Kluwer Academic Publishers for the Institute of Philosophy and Sociology, Polish Academy of Sciences, Dordrecht, Netherlands. $450. Copyright held by publisher. Ed. Ryszard Wojcicki. The principal focus is on mathematical and philosophical logic, semantics, methodology, and logical systems with analytic analyses the preferred methodological approach. There is a further emphasis on new technical results. From the editorial statement: "The distinctive feature of *Studia Logica* is its series of monothematic numbers edited by outstanding scholars and devoted to important topics of contemporary logic, or covering significant conferences." Each issue contains 5-6 articles of 15-30 pages and book reviews.

PHILOSOPHY OF SCIENCE

is "the branch of philosophy that is centered on a critical examination of the sciences: their methods and their results. One branch of the philosophy of science, *methodology,* is closely related to the theory of knowledge. . . . Other branches of the philosophy of science are concerned with the meaning and content of the posited scientific results and are closely related to metaphysics and the philosophy of language . . . . Finally, philosophy of science explores specific foundational questions arising out of the specific results of the sciences." (1, p. 611, Lawrence Sklar)

Philosophy of Science: Official Journal of the Philosophy of Science Association. 1934-. Quarterly. 0031-8248. University of Chicago Press, Chicago, IL, USA. $89 US institution/$94 institution elsewhere/$55-$85 depending on income/$24 individual. Ed. Philip Kitcher. "This important journal publishes articles dealing with fundamental issues in the philosophy of science, such as the logic of deductive-nomological and statistical explanations, the structure of scientific laws and theories, observation, evidence, confirmation, induction, probability and causality. . . . This is an essential journal for all academic libraries" (2, p. 966). Contributors address philosophical questions arising in the framework of the sciences. Articles are generally the work of philosophers or scientists. Each number contains 7-9 articles of 8-25 pages, book reviews, and books received. Special issues are sometimes published.

British Journal for the Philosophy of Science. 1950-. Quarterly. 0007-0882. Oxford University Press, Oxford, England. $99/$35 for members. Ed. Peter Clark. The official publication of the British Society for the Philosophy of Science, the journal has a more historical orientation than the American *Philosophy of Science,* though the two journals address much the same issues. According to Katz, "this is a polished, professional, core collection journal" (2, p. 958). Its purpose, according to its editorial statement, is "to study the logic, the method and the philosophy of science as well as those of the various special sciences, including social sciences." Each issue contains 4-7 articles of 20-30 pages, discussions, a lengthy review article, many book reviews, and lists of recent publications.

Diogenes. 1953-. Quarterly. 0392-1921. Blackwell Publishers, Oxford, England. $157/$50. Ed. Paola Costa Giovangigli. This journal is published under the auspices of the International Council for Philosophy and Humanistic Studies with the support of UNESCO in parallel editions in Arabic, English, French, and Spanish. It is an international review of the human sciences. "Articles concern the broad scientific fields, cultivating a synthesis more than analysis of semantics, demography, epistemology, political economy, psychiatry, and the history of commerce. . . . Since *Diogenes* represents worldwide scientific organizations, the link it establishes between specialists and scholars is unique to most periodicals" (3, p. 33). An issue generally contains 6-9 articles of 10-20 pages and book reviews.

FOREIGN-LANGUAGE JOURNALS

This category acknowledges the fact that, with English the accepted language for most of Western society's major communications in all fields of endeavor, fewer scholars outside the disciplines of language and/or literature develop an in-depth reading knowledge of foreign languages. Many Western European scholars and academics (and even more who are not) routinely write and publish articles and books in English in countries whose native language is not English. Therefore, in seeking to designate a mere three journals in each category of philosophy, I have felt constrained to limit myself to journals whose language is at least predominantly English. In the following category, I list a single journal of exceptional quality in French, German, and Italian that in the scholarly world of 50 years ago would have each figured in the classifications above.

Revue philosophique (formerly *Revue philosophique de la France et de l'étranger*). 1876-. Quarterly. 0035-3833. Presses Universitaires de France (PUF), Paris, France. 480 FF foreign/420 FF. Ruben refers to this journal as "this unique collection of twentieth-century themes in philosophy. . . . While the French ideology narrows the vantage point, [it] is still made the centerpiece of recent trends in theoretical philosophy" (3, p. 118). It is further recommended for the historical background and analysis offered of Anglo-American schools of thought that generally neglect or explicitly reject such perspectives. Katz points out that it also offers especially valuable examinations of the thought of such continental philosophers or intellectuals as Descartes, Malebranche, Pascal, Rousseau, Diderot, and Comte (2, p. 968). The typical issue carries 5-6 articles of 10-20 pages, review articles, announcements and communications.

Zeitschrift für philosophische Forschung. 1946-. Quarterly. 0044-3301. Vittorio Klostermann, Frankfurt am Main, Germany. 178 DM/98 DM/48 DM. Eds. Otfried Höffe and H. M. Baumgartner (who died May 11, 1999. The 55(3) 99 vol. carries his obituary by his co-editor). Katz writes that "this leading German philosophy journal is a good source for historically oriented discussions, particularly on ancient philosophy and German philosophy" (2, p. 970) and that it is a prime source for discussions of the theories of Kant, Hegel, and Heidegger. Occasionally articles are in English, but most are in German. The typical number has 4-6 articles of 20-40 pages and book reviews.

Filosofia: Rivista quadrimestrale. 1950-. 3/yr. 0015-1823. Gruppo Ugo Mursia Editore, Turin, Italy. 120,000 lire outside Italy. Eds. Vittorio Mathieu and Marzio Pinottini. This journal, founded, edited and published until 1986 by the late Augusto Guzzo, "è voce della Biblioteca Filosofica di Torino, della Fondazione 'Luisa Guzzo' e dell'Istituto Italiano per gli Studi Filosofici." It accepts some contributions in languages other than Italian and "is the systematic study of philosophically-based reasons and causes of human behavior. It covers the entire corpus of philosophy topics from classicism to contemporary problems 778. . . . Philosophers of social theory are perhaps the best candidates to appreciate this journal" (3, p. 42). Specifically Italian academic viewpoints, including a religious orientation, are offered on a wide variety of philosophical questions, figures, trends, and movements. Single numbers usually have 4-7 articles of 15-40 pages and book reviews. [December 1998 most recent issue seen.]

BIBLIOGRAPHY

1. Audi, Robert, General Editor, *Cambridge Dictionary of Philosophy* (Cambridge and New York: Cambridge University Press, 1995).

2. Katz, Bill, and Linda Sternberg Katz, eds., *Magazines for Libraries* (New York: R. R. Bowker, 1997).

3. Ruben, Douglas H., *Philosophy Journals and Serials: An Analytic Guide* (Westport, CO: Greenwood Press, 1985).

4. Yudkin, Marcia and Janice M. Moulton, *Guidebook for Publishing Philosophy* (Newark, DE: American Philosophical Society, 1986).

Chapter 10

Journals of the Century in the American Religious Experience

Donna L. Gilton

INTRODUCTION: FROM A FIXED MOSAIC TO A CHANGING KALEIDOSCOPE

The United States has always had a very rich religious history, and the twentieth century saw a parallel enrichment of its journal literature. This flowering of the periodical press did not proceed on an even pace. When World War II ended, most urban and suburban Americans, particularly in the upper Midwest and on either coast, were either members of one of several well-established and somewhat distinct Protestant groups or were Roman Catholics. (Rural Americans, white Southerners, and African Americans had a somewhat greater variety of smaller Protestant denominations, in addition.) The only sizeable group of non-Christians was Jews. Publications reflected this compartmentalized social order. They concerned a specific denomination, and were written by and for its members. New, nationally circulated religious journals did arise intermittently, but not from new religions, or even from religions new to America. Rather, they tended to come from smaller religious groups long resident in the United States whose membership and finances had finally achieved sufficient critical mass to support a periodical published on a regular basis. Publications for the Greek Orthodox community were a typical example.

There were some readily understood exceptions to this veritable segregation by affiliation, even before WWII. Many scholarly journals in religion routinely crossed Protestant boundaries, reflecting changes already well underway by the late 1800s in both university-based Protestant Divinity schools (which increasingly became multi-denominational or nondenominational) and in attitudes toward Protestant intermarriage (well-accepted at least between urban and suburban couples who were members of differing

This chapter originally appeared in *The Serials Librarian* 39(4): 25-40, 2001.

mainline denominations). Although the zealous ideal of having missionaries convert "foreign pagans" had greatly diminished by mid-century, there was a kindling of academic interest in the formal study of comparative religions, including Islam in particular, but publications were more dispassionately observational than passionately testimonial. Some liberal Christian periodicals crossed sectarian boundaries because they dealt with social problems of widespread national concern. Conversely, trade magazines aimed at the clergy of one Protestant denomination often gained readership in many others because of the shared professional peculiarities of being any type of minister. But while there was a handful of politely ecumenical publications (involving only differing Christian denominations) before the 1960s, there were hardly any genuinely interfaith (Christians, Jews, Muslims, Buddhists, etc.) titles.

Since the 1960s, there has been an explosion of publications touching on religion. New American periodicals now come from more than the routine Christian, Jewish, or blended groups. While much of the credit is given to the calling of the Second Vatican Council of the Roman Catholic Church in Europe, virtually all churches in North America and the publishing industry at large were just as strongly influenced by accelerating social changes and the literally tens of millions of immigrants who were neither Christian nor Jews, nor sought to become either as part of their naturalization. Having long crossed denominational boundaries, academic journals in religion now crossed over into other disciplines and spheres entirely: into law, politics, psychology, medicine, and ecological awareness, to name a few. Where stability and demarcations were the watchwords for the first half of the century, change and fusion were the hallmarks of the second. Changes in forms of worship, in respect for hierarchical authority, in gender relations, in the permanence of marriage, in the acceptability of intermarriage, in child-rearing, religious education, and in attitudes towards using broadcast media and towards proselytism and conversion, all drove the founding of new journals. Indeed, many new journals have been founded by conservative groups in reaction to liberal successes, virtually doubling the effect.

THE PLAN OF THE PAPER

This paper will be divided into three parts. Part One will deal with journals for scholars, both the generally academic and nondenominational and now often multidisciplinary, and those that have standing as journals of record, policy-setting, or serious discussion, for major faiths and denominations, active in America. Part Two will deal with publications for clergy and particularly committed laypersons who are currently active "in the work of the faith," generally within their denomination, but sometimes ecumenically. Part Three will feature general interest journals that tend to have religious sponsorship, and usually some social commentary.

PART I:
JOURNALS FOR ACADEMICS

Scholarly religious journals have long been published by professional associations, schools of theology, universities, and religious groups. This section contains journals of general religion, as well as more specialized periodicals on the history of religion, comparative religion, ecumenical outreach among groups, and the interrelationships between the formal study of religion and other academic disciplines.

General research journals on religion have been a major part of the religious literature since the early twentieth century but have grown only slightly in number since then. Because of the massive rise of more specialized periodicals, they now represent a smaller proportion of all religious periodical publications at the end of the twentieth century.

ACADEMIC JOURNALS
COVERING ALL RELIGIONS GENERALLY

Most of the oldest U.S. scholarly publications now investigate all religions. Those produced by historically Protestant divinity schools are leaders in this genre. These include *The Journal of Religion* (U.S. University of Chicago, 1921), *The Harvard Theological Review* (1908), and *Theology Today* (Princeton Theological Seminary, 1944). The Society of Jesus ("the Jesuits") publishes *Theological Studies* (Georgetown University, 1940), which has a similar standing and also covers a wide variety of subjects, albeit with Catholic emphasis.

Other scholarly journals have their own particular slant while still covering many different religious traditions. *The Journal for the Scientific Study of Religion* (Society for the Scientific Study of Religion, Brigham Young University, 1961) publishes articles by anthropologists, psychologists, sociologists, and scholars from many other fields on religious institutions, organizations, and other phenomena. *The Journal of the American Academy of Religion* (Scholars Press, 1933) and *Horizons: The Journal of the College Theology Society* (Villanova University, 1974) are written especially for professors who teach religion to college undergraduates. Aside from publishing articles on all aspects of religion, these periodicals also publish

teaching ideas for professors. *The Religious Studies Review* (Council of Societies for the Study of Religions, Inc., Valparaiso University, 1975) specializes in publishing extensive reviews and bibliographic essays as well as
brief notes on recent publications.

HISTORY OF RELIGIONS
AND HISTORIES OF GIVEN DENOMINATIONS

There have been several scholarly periodicals focusing on the history of
all religions. The *History of Religions,* published since 1961 by the University of Chicago is the most notable. Just as *American Jewish History* (American Jewish Historical Society, 1933) covers all types of Jewish obser-
vances, *Christian History* (Christianity Today, Inc., 1982) is a more popular
publication for an informed general audience that covers all aspects of the
history of Christianity, albeit with some Protestant emphasis. *The Catholic
Historical Review* (The American Catholic Historical Association, 1915)
and *The Coptic Church Review* (Society of Coptic Church Studies, 1980)
ably handle their denominations. *Church History: Studies in Christianity
and Culture* (American Society of Church History, 1932) focuses even more
specifically on Protestant denominations. Periodicals on specific Protestant
denominations include *Historic Magazine of the Protestant Episcopal
Church* (Historical Society of the Episcopal Church, 1932), *Methodist History* (General Commission on Archives and History, United Methodist
Church, 1962), *American Presbyterians: Journal of Presbyterian History*
(Presbyterian Historical Society, 1901), *American Baptist Quarterly* (Ameri-
can Baptist Historical Association, 1958), and *Baptist History and Heritage*
(Historical Commission of the Southern Baptist Convention and Southern
Baptist Historical Society, 1965).

JOURNALS OF RECORD:
MAJOR PROTESTANT DENOMINATIONS

Many periodicals continue to be published by and for designated
Protestant, Roman Catholic, Orthodox Christian, and Jewish groups. In
many cases, they are effectively journals of record. Those by Protestant
groups include the *Lutheran Quarterly* (American Lutheran Church and
Lutheran Church in America, 1849-1977), *Concordia Journal* (Lutheran,
Missouri Synod, Concordia Seminary, 1855), the *Mennonite Quarterly Review* (Mennonite Quarterly Review Publication Committee, Goshen College, 1927), *Quaker Religious Thought* (Quaker Theological Discussion

Group, 1959), and *Adventist Review* (Review and Herald Publishing Association, 1850).

JOURNALS OF RECORD:
AFRICAN AMERICAN PROTESTANT DENOMINATIONS

A number of journals, magazines, newspapers, and newsletters have been published by African American denominations and seminaries and have achieved high standing. Scholarly journals published by seminaries include the *Journal of Religious Thought* (Howard University, 1943) and the *Journal of the Interdenominational Theological Center* (1973). Scholarly and general publications include the *African Methodist Episcopal Church Review* (1883), the *African Methodist Episcopal Zion Quarterly Review* (1890), *The Christian Index* (Christian Methodist Episcopal Church, 1870), *The Whole Truth* (Church of God in Christ, 1996), *National Baptist Voice* (National Baptist Convention, U.S.A., 1915) and *Baptist Progress* (Progressive National Baptist Church, 1966). *Visions* is a newsletter published by the Congress of National Black Churches (1990) and *Message* (Review and Herald Publishing Association, 1973), a popular publication of the Seventh Day Adventists, has been received by African Americans in a number of denominations.

JOURNALS OF RECORD:
ROMAN CATHOLIC PUBLICATIONS IN AMERICA,
NATIONAL BUT NOT OFFICIAL,
OFFICIAL BUT NOT NATIONAL

While it may seem surprising, there are no regularly issued Roman Catholic publications, published in America, that are both nationally circulated and canonically authoritative, for the whole country. There are many national publications for Catholics, but they are not published by the hierarchy (bishops, archbishops, cardinals) who alone among Americans have official teaching power, albeit as a practical matter limited to their dioceses. This leads to hundreds of official diocesan weekly newspapers (by far the favored mode of Catholic publication) and about a dozen diocesan magazines, but with none having the influence over Catholics nationally as national publications have in Protestant communities. Catholic periodicals of national interest are published either by colleges and universities, by religious orders, or by lay people. These periodicals are not considered to be canonically authoritative.

This curious publishing situation is based on three historical factors operating in the Catholic church in America.

First, although the Roman Catholic bishops within America do meet from time to time in National Conferences, these are still advisory bodies, not self-sufficient authorities: Definitive rulings must still be vetted in Rome on many matters. Hence, there is no *The Bishops Speak* magazine (although there is a supplement to the minor publication *Our Sunday Visitor* called *The Pope Speaks!*).

The second historical factor is that up until the 1950s, the Roman Catholic Church had to work rather hard to energize and involve more actively a hitherto sedate laity (much of which was historically blue collar or overwhelmed with the practical need to get ahead in their small businesses), in church affairs including supporting Catholic publications, while still insisting that the laity show deference to the will of the bishops. The bishops ironically succeeded in the first endeavor beyond their wildest expectations, but largely at the expense of the second. Today lay men and lay women publish some of the very most influential Catholic magazines and newspapers.

The third historic fact is that one of the greatest agents for intellectual growth and a natural center for publications used much more frequently in other denominations—indeed the primary engine of the transformation of American Catholics into the most highly educated religious group in America today, surpassing even Jewish Americans—the Catholic university system, has never quite been under the direct control of local bishops or under the complete control of the Vatican. This is largely because historically, most colleges and universities are managed by members of religious orders (Jesuits, Benedictines, Franciscans, Dominicans, Ursulines, etc.) who had an added line of authority that could bypass the local bishop, by appealing to the provincial superiors of their orders in America, and thence to their Superiors General in Rome. This situation has further been exacerbated in that most Catholic religious orders, long faced with declining membership, have shared extensive power with, or even turned over final legal control to, lay boards of trustees. Publications from most Catholic universities, then, are as free of expression as those run by the independent laity.

It should be noted that the current Pope, many of the hierarchy he has appointed, and a staunch core of Catholic traditionalists (including members of Opus Dei) have opposed this sort of "freedom of the Catholic Press" movement, regarding its proponents as disrespectful and undisciplined and have fielded counterpublications that have a smaller, but nonetheless nationally distributed following.

Arguably the most obviously liberal of the major Catholic national magazines is the *National Catholic Reporter* (National Catholic Reporter Publishing Company, 1964), followed by a somewhat liberal *Commonweal*

(Commonweal Foundation, 1924). *America,* a nominally lay publication (America Press, 1909), but having a very long tradition of Jesuit involvement, and the *U.S. Catholic,* published by the Claretian Order (Claretian Publications, 1963) are generally middle of the road. On the conservative side one finds the intellectually highbrow *New Oxford Review,* and the sternly plain spoken *The Wanderer* (Wanderer Printing Company, 1867).

JOURNALS OF RECORD:
EASTERN ORTHODOX AND COPTIC CHRISTIANS
IN THE UNITED STATES

Orthodox Christian and Coptic publications include the *Greek Orthodox Theological Review* (Holy Cross Greek Orthodox School of Theology, 1954), *Orthodox America* (Russian Orthodox Church Outside of Russia, Nikodemos Orthodox Publication Society, 1980), *The Armenian Church* (Armenian Church of America, 1980), *Orthodox Word* (St. Herman of Alaska Brotherhood, 1965), *Copts: Christians of Egypt* (American Copt Society, 1974), and *Diakonia: Devoted to Promoting Eastern Christianity in the West* (John XXIII Center, 1966). *Diakonia,* published by the Roman Catholic Church, is an ecumenical periodical for Eastern Rite Catholics and for members of the various national Orthodox denominations that are not in union with the Catholics but share a great many common liturgical and theological traditions.

FORMAL STUDIES OF JEWISH LIFE AND OBSERVANCE

General scholarly periodicals on Judaism include *AJS* (Association of Jewish Studies) *Review* (1995), *Judaism: A Quarterly Journal of Jewish Life and Thought* (American Jewish Congress, 1952), and *Modern Judaism* (Johns Hopkins University, 1981). Periodicals reflecting the different approaches to Jewish customs and beliefs are *Tradition: A Journal of Orthodox Jewish Thought* (Rabbinical Council of America, Human Sciences Press, 1958), *Conservative Judaism* (Rabbinical Assembly, 1945), *CCAR* (Central Conference of American Rabbis) *Journal: A Reform Jewish Quarterly* (CCAR Press, 1953), *Reconstructionist* (Reconstructionist Press, 1935), and *Humanistic Judaism* (Society for Humanistic Judaism, 1967).

JOURNALS OF RECORD:
NEW FAITHS BORN OR REESTABLISHED IN AMERICA

Several new faiths have been born and have become influential in the U.S. They include the Church of Jesus Christ of Latter-day Saints (the Mormons), the Christian Science Church, Jehovah's Witnesses, Ethical Culture and other forms of humanism, and New Age philosophies. The U.S. has also experienced the rebirth of the old faith system of European paganism in the form of Wicca and similar movements. Each of these movements has produced periodical literature and other publications and information.

Dialogue: A Journal of Mormon Thought (Dialogue Foundation, 1966) is a scholarly publication for an informed general audience that describes Mormon culture and relates Latter-day thought and doctrine to daily, secular life. The *Christian Science Journal* (1883) has been the main organ for publicizing the teachings of the Christian Science Church and its founder, Mary Baker Eddy, and it publishes articles on Christian Science theology. A more famous publication is the *Christian Science Monitor* (1908), an award-winning general newspaper read by both members and nonmembers. Both are published by the Christian Science Publishing Society. The Jehovah's Witnesses produce two general periodicals, *The Watchtower* (1879) and *Awake!* (1919). These are published by the Watchtower Bible and Tract Society of New York.

The Humanist (American Humanist Association, 1941), "a magazine of critical inquiry and social concern," according to its masthead, takes a nontheistic and secular approach to social issues and concerns. *Anima* (Conococheague Association, 1975) is a feminist periodical celebrating encounters between East and West, which includes Christian and New Age thought and theology. *Crescent Magazine: A Pagan Publication of Art, Philosophy and Belief* (http://www.crescentmagazine.com, 1977) is an online periodical for witches, wiccans, and other practitioners of European paganism.

JOURNALS OF RECORD:
THE EASTERN RELIGIONS OF THE NEW IMMIGRANTS
AND THEIR AMERICAN CONVERTS

Eastern religions have become increasingly popular and influential in the U.S. in the last decades of the twentieth century because of increased Asian immigration to the U.S. and because of western converts to these faiths and traditions. Several major periodicals on these religions have been published in the U.S. *Philosophy East and West: A Quarterly Journal of Comparative Philosophy* (University of Hawaii, 1951) includes articles on Buddhism, Shinto, Tao, and Hinduism, as well as the relationship of these religions to Christianity, Judaism, and Islam.

A major, well-established U.S. periodical on Islam and on Christian-Muslim relationships is *The Muslim World* (Duncan and Black MacDonald Center, Hartford Seminary, 1911). With the growth in the Moslem population in the U.S., this journal has been joined by the scholarly *American Journal of Islamic Social Sciences* (Association of Muslim Social Sciences, 1984), as well as the more general periodicals, *The American Muslim* (American Muslim Support Group, 1989) and *Islamic Horizons* (Islamic Society of North America, 1963).

Baha'i developed from Islam but has been influenced by all of the world's major religions. It is now a world-wide religion with many members in the U.S. and it publishes *American Baha'i* (National Spiritual Assembly of the Baha'i of the United States, 1969).

There are several influential publications on Hinduism and Buddhism that have been published in the U.S. The leading Hindu periodical is *Hinduism Today* (Himalayan Academy Publications, 1979). Buddhism is represented by a scholarly journal, the *International Association of Buddhist Studies Journal* (University of California, Berkeley, 1978), and by a more popular magazine, *Tricycle: The Buddhist Review* (Buddhist Ray, Inc., 1992).

Religious publications for and by members of other Asian religions are still in early stages of development. One such scholarly publication is the *Journal of Asian and Asian American Theology* (Center for Pacific American Ministries, School of Theology at Clairemont, 1994).

DIALOG AND CONVERSATION: ECUMENICAL OUTREACH BETWEEN GROUPS

Several U.S. journals and periodicals promote dialog and conversation among people of different faiths. *Cross Current* (Association for Religion in Intellectual Life, 1950) was originally an ecumenical journal edited by Catholic editors reaching out to other Christians. It now promotes scholarly conversation among intellectuals of all faiths. *Buddhist-Christian Studies* (University of Hawaii, 1981) reports specifically on dialog between Christians and Buddhists. Other ecumenical publications include *Journal of Ecumenical Studies* (Temple University, 1964) and *Mid-Stream: The Ecumenical Movement Today* (Council on Christian Unity of the Christian Church, Disciples of Christ, 1962).

ACADEMIC JOURNALS ON THE RELATION OF RELIGION TO OTHER SPHERES OF LIFE AND FIELDS OF STUDY

The second half of the twentieth century has seen a great growth in the literature, both on the impact of religion on society, and on the relationships between religions and other academic disciplines and professions. Journals describing the impact of religion on society include *Religion and American Culture: A Journal of Interpretation* (University of California Press, 1991), *Religion and Public Life* (Transaction Publishers, 1983), the *Journal of Church and State* (Baylor University, 1959), and the *Journal of Religious Ethics* (Georgetown University, 1973).

Periodicals that interrelate theology or religion with other subjects abound. Those in the sciences include *Zygon: Journal of Religion and Science* (Blackwell Publishers, Malden, MA, 1966) and the *Journal of Religion and Health* (Human Sciences Press, 1961). Those in the social sciences include *Sociology of Religion* (Association for the Sociology of Religion, Cambridge, IL, 1940), the *Journal of Psychology and Theology: An Evangelical Forum for the Integration of Psychology and Theology* (Rosemead School of Psychology, Biola University, 1973) and the *Journal of Feminist Studies in Religion* (Scholars Press, 1985).

The area of psychology of religion is especially rich with three noted publications, *American Journal of Theology and Philosophy* (United Theological Seminary, 1980), *Religious Studies: An International Journal for the Philosophy of Religion* (Cambridge University Press, NY, 1965) and *International Journal for Philosophy of Religion* (Kluwer Academic Publishers, 1970). Two periodicals have also attempted to combine religion with the arts, the scholarly *Religion and the Arts* (Boston College, Brill Academic Publishers, 1996), and the more popular *Christianity and the Arts* (Christianity and the Arts, 1993).

PART II:
JOURNALS TO ASSIST THE DAILY WORK
OF THE ORDAINED CLERGY AND ACTIVIST LAITY

Periodicals described in this section are resources for Christian and Jewish clergy and lay people doing the work of the church or temple. Periodicals in these areas will be briefly mentioned: Biblical study; resources for leaders; worship, praise, and music; and religious education.

STUDYING THE WORD

Scholarly publications in this field include *Interpretation: A Journal of Bible and Theology* (Union Theological Seminary, 1947), *Catholic Bible Quarterly* (Catholic Biblical Association of America, Catholic University of America, 1939), *Journal of Biblical Literature* (Scholars Press, 1881), and *Semeia* (Society of Biblical Literature, Scholars Press, 1974). *Interpretation* is written from a non-sectarian viewpoint but has been including more Evangelical perspectives in recent years. *Catholic Bible Quarterly* is written from a Catholic emphasis, but has always included perspectives of other faiths. *Journal of Biblical Literature* is written from a Protestant focus. While these three journals focus on traditional Bible study, *Semeia* uses a much more interdisciplinary approach to this field.

Less scholarly periodicals for an informed audience include *The Bible Today* (Liturgical Press, St. John's Abbey, Collegeville, MD, 1962), *Bible Review* (1985) and *Bible Archaeology Review* (1975). *The Bible Today* is the most popular in approach. Most of its subscribers are Catholic but it publishes writers from many traditions. *Bible Review* and *Bible Archaeology Review* are both published for informed, general audiences by the Bible Archaeology Society. *Bible Review* is written for audiences in Protestant, Catholic, and Jewish traditions. *Biblical Archaeology Review* was established to communicate archeological research relevant to the Bible to a general audience. This periodical is especially popular among lay people.

DELIVERING THE WORD:
RESOURCES FOR PASTORS, PRIESTS,
RABBIS, AND OTHER LEADERS

General professional periodicals for clergy include *Pastoral Life: The Magazine for Today's Ministry* (Society of St. Paul, 1952) and *Chicago Studies* (Civitas Dei Foundation, 1962) for Catholic priests; *Leadership: A Practical Journal for Church Leaders* (Christianity Today, Inc., 1980), and *Christian Ministry* (Christian Century Foundation, 1969) for Protestant clergy and leaders and *Hadorum* (Rabbinical Council of America, 1966) for rabbis.

Several periodicals specifically on preaching or homilectics also exist. *Homilectic and Pastoral Review* (Ignatius Press, 1900) and *Preaching* (Preaching Resources, Inc., 1985) publish on pastoring and preaching from Catholic and Protestant perspectives, respectively. *Homilectic: A Review of Publications in Religion* (Homilectic, 1976) and *Religious Communication Today* (Religious Speech Communications Association, 1978) have both published on religious communication in the broader sense, including the use of preaching, worship, and media. These periodicals are also published from Catholic and Protestant perspectives, respectively. Counseling periodicals for clergy include *Pastoral Psychology* (Human Science Press, 1952) and *Chaplaincy Today* (Association of Professional Chaplains, 1936).

ACCLAIMING THE WORD AND MAKING A JOYFUL NOISE: WORSHIP, PRAISE, AND MUSIC

Specialized periodicals on worship and liturgy have been published by religious bodies with formal worship traditions. This is especially true of the Roman Catholic Church and of Jewish denominations. The Catholic Church has published the most on this with *Worship* (St. John's Abbey, 1926) and *Liturgy* (Liturgy Conference, Inc., 1955) being the most important. With changes in the Catholic mass and its music since Vatican II, another periodical, *Modern Liturgy* (Resource Publications, Inc., 1973) has been added. In more recent years, the Catholic Church has produced *Gratias!*, the first U.S. periodical completely dedicated to U.S. Hispanic worship, and *Plenty Good Room* (1993), a forum on African American Catholic worship. Both of these periodicals are published by Liturgy Training Publications. The Cantorial Council of America has also produced the *Journal of Jewish Music and Liturgy* (1976).

For the most part, the few specialized periodicals on church music have focused on hymns or traditional European-based sacred music. Two important periodicals are *Hymn* (Hymn Society in the United States and Canada, Boston University, School of Theology, 1949) and *Sacred Music* (Church Music Association of America, 1874). A more recent publication is *Gospel Today Magazine: America's Leading Gospel News Magazine* (Gospel Today, 1990).

TEACHING THE WORD: RELIGIOUS EDUCATION, YOUTH GROUPS, COLLEGE MINISTRIES

Periodicals on religious education have been published in the Jewish, Catholic, and Protestant traditions. *Jewish Education* (Board of Jewish Education of Greater New York, 1929) publishes articles on the challenges of teaching Hebrew, religion, and ethics both in part-time programs and in separate Jewish schools. *Religious Education* (Religious Education Association, 1906) discusses all aspects of this subject in all Christian churches from Sunday School to the seminary. *Christian Education Journal* (Trinity International University, 1980) is a more evangelical, scholarly publication describing Christian Education from Sunday School to campus ministries. *The Journal of Christian Education of the African Methodist Episcopal Church* (Christian Education Department, AME Church, 1936) is much more denominational in focus, but still has articles on many subjects of interest to other churches or denominations, especially those working with

African American youth. There is a list of resources from the Black Christian tradition in every issue. *Human Development* (Jesuit Educational Center for Human Development, 1980) publishes information on psychology, psychiatry, medicine, and spirituality that would be relevant for people working in Christian Education. Much of this information is also useful across denominational lines.

Christian Education in Protestant churches has historically taken two forms: the Sunday School and Vacation Bible School to specifically teach about the Bible, and the youth group or youth ministry to teach the young how to apply the Bible, be ethical, and be leaders. More recently youth ministries have shifted in emphasis to deal with the developmental issues of young people. During the last generation churches have developed new programming to deal with the needs of children and teens, including after-school programs for children. They have also experimented with a variety of programs for children and teenagers, ranging from nurseries to separate youth services that function during part or all of the general service. A different group of periodicals has emerged to serve the needs of clergy and lay people who work in this area. Group Publications, Inc. publishes three magazines to serve three age groups: *Group: The Youth Ministry Magazine* (1974), *Junior High Ministry* (1985), and *Children's Ministry* (1991), which all stress practical ideas and activities for the busy youth director. They also discuss trends affecting young people. A more scholarly periodical with more analysis is *Youthworker* (Youth Specialties, Inc., 1983). Each issue looks at a specific theme in depth. For campus ministries and chaplains, the *NICM* (National Institute for Campus Ministries) *Journal* (1976) has published scholarly articles from Protestant, Catholic, Orthodox, and Jewish viewpoints.

PART III:
GENERAL INTEREST PERIODICALS

General interest religious periodicals can be divided into two groups. One set of periodicals focuses on the personal religious life and sometimes some forms of outreach. The other set deals with social issues. There are also a few periodicals that publish on both the personal and the social.

OBSERVING AND APPLYING THE FAITH

Protestant magazines on the personal Christian life that existed through most of the twentieth century included *Christian Herald* (Christian Herald

Association, 1901-1992), *Moody's Monthly* (Moody Bible Institute of Chicago), and *Guideposts: A Practical Guide to Successful Living* (Guideposts Associates, 1945). In the second half of the century these periodicals were joined by *Christianity Today: A Magazine of Evangelical Conviction* (Christianity Today, Inc., 1956) and James Dobson's *Focus on the Family* (1983). *Christianity Today* was originally a scholarly publication of Billy Graham's ministry. It is now a popular magazine on both the personal Christian life and on social issues. In addition, *Indian Life* (Indian Life Ministries, 1979), a newspaper created by missionaries and now published by Native Americans in the western U.S. and Canada contains news and testimonies of national interest. This ministry publishes and distributes a variety of other Christian materials as well. As people from ethnic minorities continue to develop materials, this is an area that should grow a great deal in library collections.

One of the most important Protestant magazines on the personal Christian life published in the late twentieth century may be *Discipleship Journal* (The Navigators, Nav Press Periodicals, 1981). It is a well-illustrated, popular periodical with Bible studies and many practical ideas on personal Christian living. It also stresses practical approaches to building churches through small groups and personal evangelism. There are Catholic counterparts to *Discipleship Journal*. *The Catholic Faith* (Ignatius Press, 1995) is a practical guide to the Christian life. *Lay Witness* (Catholics United for the Faith, 1979) has information on the Catholic Church and ideas for spreading the faith.

DEALING WITH SOCIAL ISSUES: FROM THE LIBERAL TO THE CONSERVATIVE

Liberal and conservative periodicals on social issues have emerged from Catholic, Protestant, and Jewish traditions. This author suspects that the liberal (and conservative) periodicals may be more similar to each other than all periodicals within a tradition. Most of the liberal periodicals have existed since the late nineteenth or early twentieth century, although some have been created since. Many of the conservative periodicals seem to be more recent.

To recapitulate, members of the Catholic church have published the liberal *National Catholic Reporter* (National Catholic Reporter Publishing Company, 1964), the somewhat liberal *Commonweal: A Review of Public Affairs, Literature, and the Arts* (Commonweal Foundation, 1924), and the moderate *America* (America Press, Inc., 1909), and as well as more conservative publications, such as the *New Oxford Review* (New Oxford Review

Inc., 1940) and *The Wanderer* (Wanderer Printing Company, 1867). Protestant liberal publications like *The Christian Century* (The Christian Century Foundation, 1900), *Christianity and Crisis: A Christian Journal of Opinion* (Christianity and Crisis, 1941), *Sojourners* (1971), and *The Other Side* (1965) have been joined by several very recent periodicals, such as *First Things: A Monthly Journal of Religion and Public Life* (Institute on Religion and Public Life, 1990), *Books and Culture* (Christianity Today, Inc., 1995), and the *Mars Hill Audio Journal* (Mars Hill Audio, 1992). *Tikkun: A Bi-Monthly Jewish Critique of Politics, Culture and Society* (Institute for Labor and Mental Health, 1986) is a liberal counterpart to *Commentary: Journal of Significant Thought and Opinion on Contemporary Issues* (American Jewish Committee, 1945).

Last, to show that Christians can laugh at themselves, there is even *The Door Magazine: The World's Pretty Much Only Religious Satire Magazine* (Trinity Foundation, 1991). Formerly *The Wittenburg Door,* this magazine has served as a Christian counterpart to *Mad Magazine* and especially *The National Lampoon.* However, each issue has a serious and well-conducted interview with a person active in the Christian world. Many of these interviews were published as a book, *The Door Interviews,* which was edited by Mike Yaconelli (Zondervan, 1989).

REFERENCES

1. Berndt, Judith and Kathleen Joyce Kruger. "Religion and Society: A Selected, Annotated Bibliography of U.S. Periodicals." *Serials Review.* Fall, 1987 pp. 43-49.

2. "Catholic Periodical Sampler '99" *America.* Jan. 16, 1999 pp. 16-19.

3. Cornish, Graham (ed.). *Religious Periodicals Directory.* Santa Barbara, CA: ABCCLIO, 1986.

4. Dawsey, James. *A Scholar's Guide to Academic Journals in Religion.* Metuchen, NJ: Scarecrow, 1988.

5. Fieg, Eugene C. *Religion Journals and Serials.* Westport, CT: Greenwood Press, 1988.

6. Gilton, Donna L. "This Far by Faith: Resources of the African-American Church." *RQ* v. 32 no. 4 Summer, 1993 pp. 468-484.

7. Katz, Bill and Linda Sternberg Katz. *Magazines for Libraries.* New Providence, NJ: Bowker, 1997 pp. 1130-1143.

8. Ng, Greer Anne Wenh-In. "Pacific-Asian North American Religious Education" in *Multicultural Religious Education* (edited by Barbara Wilkerson). Birmingham, AL: Religious Education Press, 1997 pp. 208.

9. Ulrich's International Periodicals Directory 2000. New Providence, NJ: Bowker, 1999.

CLUSTER III:
BUSINESS AND LAW

For all the talk of a global economy during the twentieth century, the decisions as to what products and services were available in the American marketplace were made more often than not by American businessmen. Likewise, even though there was a great deal of international law generated in the twentieth century, most American lawyers practiced in courtrooms and offices where only American codes and commentary held much sway. Business and law had a shared reliance on Anglo-American traditions concerning private property and the role of written contracts since the 1700s. Two twentieth-century trends further bound the business and legal community and their publishing patterns as seen in this cluster. The first was the propensity for most business transactions of any size to involve an ever-increasing number of lawyers for researching an ever-increasing number of government regulations concerning monopolization, taxes, environmental matters, unionization, worker safety, and product liability. Publications from official agencies in this chapter had a market share second only to those found in the military affairs chapter!) Secondly, both business and law eventually formalized their preferred method of formal training in America during the twentieth century via university-affiliated post-baccalaureate degree programs, the MBA and JD, respectively. Both were usually housed in separate buildings on campus, had their own libraries, and most important, published their own journals.

Professional-school based reviews, many of them including the results of student or joint student-faculty research, actually dominated the selections of those from Harvard and the University of Chicago, playing a particularly important role. The hegemony of these universities was restrained only by the fact that the top echelon of business and law schools is more crowded than might be first imagined, with journals from Columbia, Michigan, Pennsylvania, Virginia, and some of the California schools contending with entries of importance in both business and law. Many other schools fielded notable journals in one or the other of those fields. Even a fair number of the society presses in this cluster were strongly dependent on law and business school faculty presentations.

The authorship and sector situations changed as the content became more procedural and less theoretical. Publications from both regional and national accounting and tax law associations had many more papers from practitioners than from professors. American trade level literature in retail banking, insurance, and investing were for-profit properties and routinely generated multi-million dollar subscription revenues. Foreign-owned entries included more academic titles from Blackwell and practical publications from Commerce Clearing House, which had strong followings in both business and law and is now owned by Thomson.

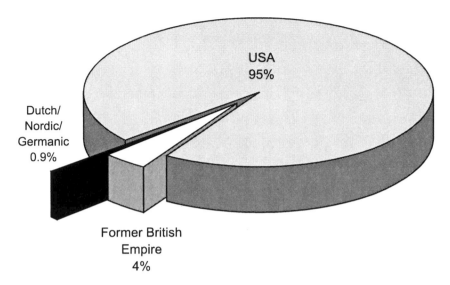

Breakdown by Region

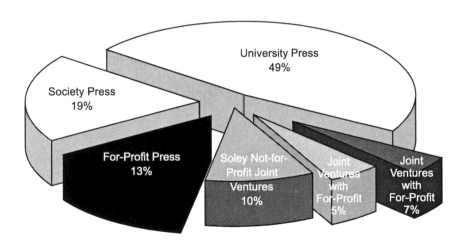

Breakdown by Publishing Section

Chapter 11

Journals of the Century
in Business and Economics

Colleen Anderson

INTRODUCTION

Academic business librarians spend much of their time linking to journals that will supply them with a critical article needed for a student's paper or a faculty member's research. Through this activity we become familiar with, and learn to depend on, a core of journals whose usefulness has been proven over time. Andreas Werner accurately describes such journals as " . . . [those] that thoroughly cover an area of study and are of fundamental importance . . . those which are used regularly by all who are studying in the field."[1] These are the titles resting on the shelves of every top academic business library across the country; the ones we would never cut. Some of them fit as comfortably in the library of a practitioner as of a researcher, but the magnitude of their contribution to a particular business discipline cannot be argued. This paper is an attempt to give formal recognition to these valuable journals.

SELECTION CRITERIA

Selecting journals to include in a list of top business journals of this century is both a science and an art. The science of the task involves reviewing numerous empirical studies conducted in an attempt to measure a journal's "value" by citation analysis and other objective methodologies. Citation analysis involves analyzing the importance of a journal by determining the number of times journal articles from a particular year cite articles from the journal being measured. Though it sounds like a logical method for measuring journal value, researchers such as John B. Davis in his article "Problems in Using the Social Sciences Index to Rank Economics Journals"[2] and

This chapter originally appeared in *The Serials Librarian* 39(2): 59-85, 2000.

Liebowitz and Palmer in their article "Assessing the Relative Impacts of Economics Journals,"[3] discuss problems that arise from measuring journal value in such a manner. To use citation analysis effectively one has to know exactly what kind of value one wants to measure and then adjust for numerous variables (e.g., length of time journals have been in publication, number of regular articles published in each journal title, etc.). Other objective means for measuring journal value such as survey questionnaires and consideration of a journal's association with a leading academic institution also fail as "scientific" measures for obvious reasons—survey respondents may have biases toward journals they publish in, and determining which departments of academic institutions are "leading" can prove more controversial and perplexing than ranking the journals they generate. Despite the fact that complete objectivity in journal selecting does not exist, the available research using the methods mentioned above proved useful for validating my selections. After choosing a particular journal, I checked to see if the journal I had chosen was consistently listed as a top selection in articles that have been written on ranking business and economic journals (see *Other Sources Consulted*). The "art" to my journal selection consisted of using my experience and expertise in business collection development to select those journals I have come to value and rely on as sources of research and news articles.

One distinction must be mentioned. There is a peculiarity about business and economics that affects any selection of top journals within the unique disciplines associated with the fields. Citation analysis and other objective measures used to value a journal examine academic journals; however business, and to a lesser extent, economics are both practical fields. There is continual interplay in the literature between practitioners and researchers, and because of this interplay, many times the journals considered the most valuable are trade publications (e.g., *Advertising Age* and *ABA Banking Journal*). These respected journals are almost exclusively generated from the leading trade association within a particular discipline and often were born in the first few years of the association's formation and have remained influential over time.

Finally, when selecting journals to be included for each category, I used as my general guideline Werner's three measures for valuing a serials collection overall; i.e., continuity, consistency, and current relevance.[4] Each journal selected for inclusion in this article has been around for more than 20 years (with the exception of those listed in the relatively new fields of Strategy and Business Ethics), and since its inception, has been ranked consistently as a top journal in its particular subject area. Each is also making a critical contribution today and is indexed in the leading subject index for its discipline and in the leading general business indexes (e.g., *ABI Inform,*

General BusinessFile ASAP). In a tie between two journals, both of which seem equal in value, I have decided to choose and include that journal which has been around the longest. These are the journals I would recommend to other business librarians attempting to make selections on a limited budget, though this article is meant only as a guide for reviewing some of the top business and economics journals, and not as a comprehensive list.

ACCOUNTING—GENERAL

Accountants are professionals who, as do librarians, provide needed information to their clients. Public accountants (licensed CPAs) perform accounting and tax analysis for individuals, companies and/or the government. The Certified Public Accountant has proven his/her ability by passing one of the most rigorous professional licensing exams on record—the notorious CPA Exam. Management accountants focus on the internal financial status of the particular organization they work for and often play a key role in the development of that organization's strategy. Internal auditors check and verify a company's financial reporting and records to ensure that it conforms with Generally Accepted Accounting Principles. Government accountants handle the daily financial transactions involved with running the government and audit the records of the government and the many businesses and individuals who are required to pay taxes. Accounting professionals need information that will help them keep current on the accounting literature promulgated by the FASB (Financial Accounting Standards Board); on new technologies that make their jobs easier; and on the general economic, financial, and tax environment within which they are attempting to perform their duties.

The Accounting Review

United States. (Sarasota, FL: American Accounting Association) March 1926- Quarterly. ISSN: 0001-4826.

The editors of *The Accounting Review* state that the journal " . . . should be viewed as the premier journal for publishing articles reporting the results of accounting research and explaining and illustrating related research methodology."[5] Journal contents include approximately five research articles followed by several book reviews and postings of job openings in accounting departments at colleges and universities across the country. *The Accounting Review* continues to be a premier source for accounting faculty and students to become informed about the cutting edge in academic accounting research.

Journal of Accounting, Auditing and Finance

United States. (Westport, CT: Greenwood Publishing Group, Inc.) Fall 1977- new series, v. 1-winter 1986- Quarterly. ISSN: 0148-558X.

The *JAAF* is sponsored by the Vincent C. Ross Institute of Accounting Research at the prestigious Leonard N. Stern School of Business at New York University. The journal promotes the advancement of knowledge in accounting and finance by publishing empirical, theoretical and experimental research in the many areas of these disciplines. Many of the articles discuss how accounting interacts with other disciplines such as economics, public administration, political science, etc.

Journal of Accounting Research

United States. (Chicago, IL: Institute of Professional Accounting, Graduate School of Business, University of Chicago). Spring 1963- Semi-annual with annual supplement. ISSN: 0021-8456.

The University of Chicago houses the Institute of Professional Accounting, an association responsible for coordinating the accounting activities in the Graduate School of Business. This body also publishes the semi-annual *Journal of Accounting Research* and each year sponsors a conference on research in accounting resulting in an annual supplemental issue containing the conference papers and proceedings. Both the journal and its supplement publish original research " . . . using analytical, empirical-archival, empirical-experimental and field study methods in all areas of accounting research."[6]

ACCOUNTING—AUDITING

The Internal Auditor

United States. (Altamonte Springs, FL: Institute of Internal Auditors) 1944- Bimonthly. ISSN: 0020-5745.

The founder's stated objectives for the Institute of Internal Auditors included the need to educate corporate officers and businesspeople in understanding the scope and potentialities of internal auditing, and the desire to study the problems of internal auditing and to provide the needed professional literature in this field.[7] The latter objective was partially fulfilled upon the publication in 1944 of the association's periodical entitled *The Internal Auditor*. Current issues of *The Internal Auditor* contain practical, timely articles and recurring departments such as "Computers & Auditing," "Fraud Finds," and "Round Table."

ACCOUNTING—COST/MANAGERIAL

Strategic Finance

United States. (Montvale, NJ: Institute of Management Accountants) v. 80-, no. 9- March 1999- Monthly. (Formerly titled: *Management Accounting*-Feb. 1999) Monthly. ISSN: 1524-833X.

This journal's new title reflects the expansion of the profession of management accounting from an occupation focused solely on internal accounting functions into a profession whose members make a significant contribution to the strategic planning process within organizations. Subtitled "Leadership Strategies in Accounting, Finance, and Information Management," this publication has short (5-6 pages), practical articles that deal with issues from the "real world" of accounting and finance.

ACCOUNTING—PUBLIC

The CPA Journal

United States. (New York: New York State Society of Certified Public Accountants) 1930- (Formerly titled: *New York Certified Public Accountant*-1972) Monthly. ISSN: 0732-8435.

The CPA Journal is a broad-based journal that can be appreciated by any person associated with the accounting profession. Feature articles cover a range of accounting issues: tax developments, issues and interpretations, accounting and auditing standards, and technology related topics, among others. In addition to the five to six feature articles published each month, the journal content also includes numerous regular departments such as "Auditing," "Estates and Trusts," and "The CPA Manager."

Journal of Accountancy

United States. (Jersey City, NJ: American Institute of Certified Public Accountants) Nov. 1905- Monthly. ISSN: 0021-8448.

Since the beginning of the century, this monthly publication of the AICPA has been a "must read" for practicing Certified Public Accountants. Focusing on the latest news and developments related to accounting, the journal is an indispensable source for learning about technological and other trends affecting CPAs in public and private practice.

ACCOUNTING—TAXATION

Tax practitioners and scholars need timely information to help them keep current on the rapidly changing and evolving regulatory, legislative and case law that constitutes our federal tax system. Many times they also need to find the current tax environment of another country. While the study and debate of tax issues demands a knowledge and understanding of the current issues of the day, the practice of taxation demands the knowledge and availability of established tax rules and regulations.

The Journal of Taxation

United States. (Boston: RIA Group) June 1954- Monthly. ISSN: 0022-4863.

This key tax journal reports on tax developments and trends and serves as an essential tool to help tax practitioners stay current in this rapidly changing field. Issues provide analysis of court and revenue rulings, report on tax law changes and administrative actions, and provide advice on solving daily tax problems.

The National Tax Journal

United States. (Washington, DC: National Tax Association) 1916- (Formerly titled: *Bulletin of the National Tax Association*-1947) Quarterly. ISSN: 0028-0283.

The National Tax Association is a multinational association that "promotes scientific, nonpolitical study of taxation; collects tax information and encourages better understanding of the common interests of national, state, and local governments in matters of taxation and public finance."[8] The Association's journal, *The National Tax Journal,* is a scholarly publication containing articles written by researchers in academics, government and nonprofit organizations. Article content deals with federal, state and local public finance as well as taxation.

Taxes: The Tax Magazine

United States. (Chicago: CCH, Inc.) 1923- (formerly titled: *Tax Magazine-*1939). Monthly. ISSN: 0040-0181.

A long-standing, reliable practitioner's guide to current tax developments published by a leading tax publisher. *Taxes: The Tax Magazine* provides " . . . cogent, innovative, and practice-oriented analyses of federal, state, and international tax issues."[9] This journal is a good resource for keeping informed about tax court decisions. Its authoritative articles are signed by CCH tax analysts, tax professors, and tax lawyers. Recurring columns in each issue report on tax trends, technology, business taxes, and international taxes.

BUSINESS ETHICS

The expectation that business transactions will be conducted within an appropriate ethical framework has existed since the beginning of what we know as commerce; however, there are several reasons for the growth of business ethics as a serious field of study within business programs in colleges and universities. First, the growth of media such as TV and newspapers as an impressionable influence in everyday life has provided knowledge to the general public of the abuse of a breach of trust with consumers. The publicizing of cases such as the Dow Corning silicon breast implants and the Ford Pinto have made consumers demand retribution for a corporation's unethical practices and breach of trust. Second, the exponential growth of the "global economy" has made business men and women aware of the problem of foreign ethical standards that may not coincide with our domestic standards and begs the question of how one acts when conducting business under conflicting ethical outlooks.

Business and Society Review

United States. (Malden, MA: Blackwell Publishers, Inc.) 1972- Quarterly. ISSN: 0045-3609.

This journal, edited at the Center for Business Ethics at Bentley College in association with Blackwell Publishers, explores the dynamic relationship between business, society, and the public good. Articles concerned with ethical problems in business, government and professions, and society are predominant in the journal content. Recent article titles include: "Ethics and Values in Advertising: Two Case Studies," "Business Ethics and Compliance: What Management is Doing and Why," and "The Ethics of Arbitration in the Securities Industry."

Journal of Business Ethics

The Netherlands. (Dordrecht; Norwell, MA: Kluwer Academic Publishers) Feb. 1982- Semi-monthly. ISSN: 0167-4544.

The *Journal of Business Ethics* publishes original research on the many moral and ethical issues that arise during the course of conducting business. The editors encourage articles covering a broad range of business disciplines such as marketing, advertising, labor relations, public relations, and organizational behavior. They define the term "business" to include all systems involved in the exchange of goods and services, and "ethics" as all human action aimed at securing a good life.[10] Book reviews are a regular feature of the journal along with the 7-8 feature articles.

COMPUTER INFORMATION SYSTEMS/MANAGEMENT INFORMATION SYSTEMS

Information technology serves all areas of business, and the quality of the work performed by a company's Information Technology department can determine how well a company competes. The quick and unceasing introduction of new technologies demands that practitioners have constant awareness of new product developments as well as an understanding of new research being done that may have a practical application. CIS/MIS is a field where there is an urgent need for ongoing dialogue between practitioners, academicians and researchers.

Computerworld

United States. (Framingham, MA: IDG Communications, Inc.) 1967- Weekly. ISSN: 0010-4841.

For several decades *Computerworld* has been an excellent resource for keeping current on companies, people, and events within the computer industry. Issue content consists of news and opinion articles categorized under the headings of "News," "Business," and "Technology." The journal is known for its valuable supplements and special issues. Professionals in the Information Technology field look for the publication of the annual salary survey published in September of each year which reports on average salaries for jobs.

MIS Quarterly: *Management Information Systems*

United States. (Minneapolis, MN: Society for Information Management (SIM) and the Management Information Systems Research Center (MISRC) at the Univ. of Minnesota) March 1977- Quarterly. ISSN: 0276-7783.

MIS Quarterly serves as a forum for high-quality articles addressing the management systems field and has as its goal "to bridge the gap between academics doing research in the field and practitioners managing the information function in the corporation."[11] For the convenience of busy executives, the editor-in-chief or senior editor annotates articles from a particular issue and provides these overviews of the articles at the beginning of the issue in a section entitled "Executive Overviews." The journal also publishes an annual index to doctoral dissertations which includes 500 to 1,000 word abstracts providing a short description of the research topic, methodology, and finds. Dissertations can be ordered through University Microfilms International.

ECONOMICS—ECONOMIC INDICATORS AND STATISTICAL INFORMATION

Businessmen look to economists for their ability to help predict the future. One only has to watch the market response to a few words from Alan Greenspan to understand the profound impact a small change in the economic environment (e.g., interest rates) can have on business. People reading economic publications are usually looking for data, economic forecasts and/or arguments or theories on why and how the economy works the way that it does. The U.S. government and its many bureaus, councils, and agencies (e.g., Federal Reserve Board, Council of Economic Advisors) gather data and disseminate many of the statistical publications used by economists and businesspeople.

Economic Indicators

United States. (Washington, DC: U.S. G.P.O. Prepared for the Joint Economic Committee by the Council of Economic Advisers). May 1948- Monthly. ISSN: 0013-0125.

Economic Indicators, the well-known monthly publication produced by the Council of Economic Advisers, is a gold mine of economic data researchers can use to analyze the current domestic economic environment. Data is arranged into the following aggregate categories: Total Output, Income, and Spending; Employment, Unemployment, and Wages; Production and Business Activity; Prices; Money, Credit, and Security Markets; Federal Finance; and International Statistics. Most of the data is given for a total of ten years with monthly or quarterly tabular data presented for the past 2-4 years and annual data for the historical figures.

Survey of Current Business

United States. (Washington, DC: Bureau of Economic Analysis of the U.S. Department of Commerce) August 1, 1921- Monthly. ISSN: 0039-6222.

The Bureau of Economic Analysis is an agency in the Economics and Statistics Administration of the Department of Commerce. The mission of the BEA is to " . . . produce and disseminate accurate, timely, relevant, and cost-effective accounts statistics that provide government, businesses, households, and individuals with a comprehensive, up-to-date picture of economic activity."[12] The *Survey of Current Business* gathers BEA estimates, analysis, research and methodology into one monthly publication. Content of the journal includes regular features on the "Business Situation" and "Personal Income by State and Region (quarterly)." Current data is usually presented as quarterly data with annual figures included for the past 2-3 years.

ECONOMICS—GENERAL

American Economic Review

United States. (Nashville, TN: American Economic Association) 1911- Published five times a year; every fourth year is published six times a year. ISSN: 0002-8282.

The American Economic Association (AEA) was formed in 1885 at Saratoga, N.Y. and today includes a membership of approximately 22,000 economists and 5,500 institutes, over 50 percent of which are academic institutions. Its mission is to encourage economic research, to issue publications on economic subjects, and to encourage the freedom of economic discussion.[13] The *American Economic Review,* an AEA journal, is a broad publication covering articles and short papers on all aspects of economics.

Quarterly Journal of Economics

United States. (Cambridge, MA: Published for Harvard University by the MIT Press) Oct. 1886- Quarterly. ISSN: 0033-5533.

A proven classic, the *Quarterly Journal of Economics* is edited at the Department of Economics at Harvard University and is the oldest professional journal of economics in the English language. Though the journal once had an emphasis on microtheory, its article coverage has expanded to include empirical and theoretical macroeconomics. The journal's lengthy, academic articles run from thirty to fifty pages.

Journal of Political Economy

United States. (Chicago, IL: University of Chicago Press) Dec. 1892- Bi-monthly. ISSN: 0022-3808.

Since 1892 this prestigious journal has been publishing critical scholarship in economic theory and practice. Research published in the journal must be of interest to a wide, general audience interested in economics. Articles accepted for publication cover all the traditional areas of economics-monetary theory, fiscal policy, labor economics, planning and development, micro- and macroeconomic theory, international trade and finance, and industrial organization. Some papers written on interdisciplinary topics such as the history of economic thought and social economics are also accepted.

ECONOMICS—ECONOMETRICS

Econometrica

United States. (Evanston, IL: Econometric Society, Dept. of Economics, Northwestern University) Jan. 1933- Bi-monthly. ISSN: 0012-9682.

The Econometric Society, publishers of *Econometrica,* has as its objective ". . . to promote studies that aim at the unification of the theoretical-quantitative and the empirical-quantitative approach to economic problems and that are penetrated by constructive and rigorous thinking."[14] The journal publishes original research in all branches of economics and attracts high quality research in applied economics by awarding the biennial Frisch medal for the best applied paper published in the journal during the previous five years. Along with the feature articles, each issue also contains a "Notes and Comments" section and communications among the membership of the Society.

ECONOMICS—INTERNATIONAL

The Economist

United Kingdom. (London: The Economist Newspaper, NA, Inc.) Sept. 2, 1843- Weekly. ISSN: 0013-0613.

An essential read for keeping up on the economic, financial, and political situation around the world. All articles in *The Economist* are written by anonymous authors in plain language and with what the editors claim is a "radical, extreme centre position."[15] Recurring coverage in each issue now includes segments on the United States, Britain, the Americas, Europe, Asia, and an International segment. The remainder of the journal includes business, finance and economics, science and technology new coverage, and an "indicators" section that provides economic and financial statistics from around the world. Lastly, *The Economist* is known for the scope and quality of its book reviews published in a literary supplement entitled "Review of Books" (latest in the July 17, 1999 issue) and available through the journal Web site.

Far Eastern Economic Review

China. (Hong Kong: Review Publishing Co. Ltd.) Oct. 16, 1946- Weekly. ISSN: 0014-7591.

The journal to read for comprehensive coverage of the political, business, and economic situation in the far east. This news weekly carries a feature cover story and segments on "Politics and Policy," "Arts & Society," and "Business." There are also regular features that include an index to companies, a technology update, a regional briefing, and an economic monitor.

The glossy cover and pictures give the look and feel of a *Business Week* with all the news you need to understand and keep current on far eastern economics and business.

International Economic Review

United States. (Philadelphia: Economics Dept. of the University of Pennsylvania and the Osaka University Institute of Social and Economic Research Association) 1960- ISSN: 0020-6598.

A scholarly journal published as a joint academic venture between Osaka University's Institute of Social and Economic Research and the University of Pennsylvania's Department of Economics. Subject matter of the journal articles includes econometrics, international and economic development, international finance, public policy economics and other related topics. The Osaka Office of *IER* occasionally sponsors or co-sponsors international conferences and later publishes some of the conference papers in the journal. The journal also publishes lectures from its annual Klein Lecture series, a series begun in 1997 that features lectures given by some of the most prominent economists in the world.

ENTREPRENEURSHIP

Those adventuresome individuals who take an idea and turn it into a profitable business are collectively much more influential in our individual lives than huge corporations we hear about daily in the news. According to *The State of Small Business: A Report of the President* (1997), 23.2 million small business tax returns were filed in 1996 providing 53 percent of employment and 51 percent of private sector output.[16] Ask any international student why he values the business climate in our country, and he will respond that it is the opportunity and freedom given to individuals to develop their creativity and new ideas without the hindrance of overbearing traditions and government. The United States is still admired for its pioneering spirit.

Inc.

United States. (Boston: Goldhirsh Group Inc.) 1979- Monthly, except twice monthly in March, May, June, Sept., Oct., and Nov. ISSN: 0162- 8968.

Inc. has been helping small businessmen and women create and sustain the company of their dreams since its inception in 1979. The publishers had 4 goals for the magazine when it was established: (1) to publish experiences of smaller-company managers, (2) to report on events affecting small to midsize companies, (3) to provide practical "how-to" columns on all aspects of small company management, and (4) to be a platform fighting against legislation and regulation adversely affecting small business. Each year the journal publishes its Inc. 500 list of the fastest-growing privately held companies in the United States (see v. 21, issue 15, October 1999).

Journal of Small Business Management

United States. (Morgantown, WV: Published by the Bureau of Business and Economic Research at the West Virginia University College of Business and Economics and the International Council for Small Business) 1963- Quarterly. ISSN: 0047-2778.

Winner of the 1997 award for Best Continuous Publication from the Association for University Business and Economic Research (AUBER) and the 1999 Anbar Golden Page Award for Originality. International in scope, *JSBM* publishes articles on small business research from around the world. The journal includes refereed articles on a variety of topics of interest to small businessmen and women (e.g., new venture creation, small enterprise finance, family enterprises, legal issues and small enterprises, etc.). Each issue contains a "global perspectives" section.

FINANCE

No matter how sophisticated the financial instruments, the goal of the study and practice of finance is to make money for an individual or an institution. Investment managers and corporate finance officers need to have a handle on day-by-day market activity as well as insight into how well their company or companies are performing within their respective industries. Again, wise investment decisions depend on an understanding of the bigger picture of domestic and international economics.

FINANCE—BANKING

ABA Banking Journal

United States. (New York: Published for the American Bankers Association by Simmons-Boardman Pub. Co.) 1908- (Formerly titled: *Banking, Journal of the American Bankers Association*-Dec. 1978) Monthly. ISSN: 0194-5947.

Founded in 1875, The American Bankers Association (ABA), is one of the oldest and most powerful of professional associations. Its 8,000 member commercial banks and trust companies hold assets that make up approximately 90 percent of the U.S. banking industry.[17] Its journal, The *ABA Banking Journal,* was first published in 1908 and has always been attentive to regulatory and legislative activities affecting the banking industry.[18] Current issues of the journal consist of feature articles on banking and bank-related topics; ABA member news; opinion columns; and recurring departments with topics such as "Community Banking," "Technology Topics," and "Web Notes." It would be impossible to function as a banking executive and not have a copy of this key publication on your desk or desktop each week.

Banking Strategies

United States. (Chicago, IL: Bank Administration Institute) 1927- (Formerly titled: *Bank Management*-1996) Bimonthly. ISSN: 1091-6385.

The Bank Administration Institute began in 1927 as the Associated Conferences of Bank Auditors and Controllers[19] and is today a leading association dedicated to helping such executives improve their performance through research and education.[20] The mission of the BAI's journal, *Banking Strategies,* is to ". . . provide high-quality editorial coverage of strategic and management issues in today's dynamic financial services industry."[21] Each issue includes interviews with leading financial services executives and articles on trends and strategic planning within the financial services industry.

Federal Reserve Bulletin

United States. (Washington, DC: Board of Governors of the Federal Reserve System) 1915- Monthly. ISSN: 0014-9209.

Invaluable to any business librarian for its statistics on interest rates and the money supply, the *Federal Reserve Bulletin* consists of articles on economic development and bank regulation as well as tabular data. The "Financial and Business Statistics" take up more than half of the journal and include domestic financial statistics, domestic nonfinancial statistics (labor force, personal income, industrial production, etc.), and international statistics. The *Federal Reserve Bulletin* also publishes the *Minutes of the Federal Open Market Committee Meetings*.

U.S. Banker

United States. (New York: Thomson Financial Media) 1891- (Formerly titled: *United States Banker*-1994) Monthly. ISSN: 0148-8848.

Known as *Bankers Magazine* until 1994, the *U.S. Banker* is a leading trade journal in the banking industry. Each issue reports on news, opinions and statistical information covering banking, savings institutions, insurance, mortgage and real estate, credit unions, and more.

FINANCE—GENERAL

FM (Financial Management)

United States. (Tampa, FL: Financial Management Association International) Spring 1972- (Formerly titled: *Financial Management*-1998, ISSN). Quarterly. ISSN: 1087-7827.

The Financial Management Association International serves academics and practitioners concerned with financial management in both the corporate and non-profit world. Its official journal, *FM*, offers research articles and analysis on the economic and financial aspects of operating a firm. Topics covered include capital budgeting, portfolio and security analysis, and corporate finance. Issues also include news briefs on the latest developments in the field of finance.

Financial Analysts Journal

United States. (Charlottesville, VA: Association for Investment Management and Research) 1945- Bimonthly. ISSN: 0015-198X.

The Association for Investment Management and Research (AIMR) is devoted to the advancement of investment management and security analysis. The editors of the *Financial Analysts Journal* seek articles that are "practitioner-oriented, forward-looking, and rigorous" that will interest their primary audience of investment practitioners who are members of the AIMR.[22] Topics covered in a recent issue included valuation, portfolio management, mutual fund performance, and behavioral finance. Each issue concludes with one or two book reviews of new finance/investment titles.

The Journal of Finance

United States. (Malden, MA: Blackwell Publishers, Inc. for the American Finance Association) Aug. 1946- Bimonthly. ISSN: 0022-1082.

The Journal of Finance is a scholarly journal which publishes original research across all the major fields of finance. Journal contents include 7-8 lengthy, academic articles written by finance professors; several shorter papers; and a couple of book reviews. The best journal for keeping current on the most important research being done in finance and financial economics.

FINANCE—INVESTMENT MANAGEMENT

Barron's, *The Dow Jones Business and Financial Weekly*

United States. (Chicopee, MA: Barron's) 1921- (Formerly titled: *Barron's National Business and Financial Weekly*-1994). Weekly. ISSN: 1077-8039.

Barron's goes beyond financial reporting of numbers to provide investment analysis on companies, industries, and topics of interest to investors. Content includes several feature articles, commentaries in recurring sections such as: "Up and Down Wall Street," and the "Market Week" section with its financial tables providing extensive statistics for the markets (stocks, bonds, mutual funds, commodities, etc.), the indicators (federal reserves statistics, money supply, IPOs, bond redemptions, etc.) and the indexes (Dow Jones Averages, key foreign market indexes, Russell indexes, Standard & Poor's, etc.). "Must read" sections in the "Departments" include the advisory opinions found in the "Market Watch" and the "Research Reports" which reprint samplings from company research reports issued recently by investment firms. A quarterly survey of mutual fund performance is issued by the paper under the title: "Barron's Mutual Funds: Special Lipper Report on . . . Quarter Performance."

Institutional Investor

United States. (New York: Institutional Investor, Inc.) Mar. 1967- Monthly. ISSN: 0020-3580.

A British journal with an international edition available, *Institutional Investor* publishes practical articles of interest to money managers on such topics as pensions, mergers and acquisitions, emerging markets, foreign exchanges and currencies, etc. In each monthly issue "The Corporation" section includes a CEO interview, and the "Investing" section includes articles on Portfolio Strategy, Money Management and other investment subjects. *Institutional Investor* is especially valued for its useful special features published in various issues throughout the year. Probably the most well-known section, the October issue prints the "All-America Research Team," the magazine's selection of the brokerage analysts who have done outstanding work during the past year.

MANAGEMENT

What any wise leader values most is an effective manager. Management fads come and go, but individual managers—those who can motivate workers to get the job done—are a character mix of intelligence, enthusiasm and humility. Regardless of whether great managers are born or made, they can always learn from the tremendous amount of research done within every field of management. In the end, however, as one of the most respected and prolific of writers on the art of management, Peter Drucker, has said: "Management is doing a very few simple things and doing them well."

The Academy of Management Journal

United States. (Mississippi State: Academy of Management). 1958- (formerly titled: *Journal of the Academy of Management*-1962) Quarterly. ISSN: 0001-4273.

The Academy of Management, founded in 1936 by Charles Laselle Jamison,[23] is the premier professional association for professors who teach management in business programs at accredited colleges and universities. *The Academy of Management Journal* publishes original, empirical research; purely theoretical articles are published in the Academy's other journal, *The Academy of Management Review* (v. 1-, 1976-). The journal contains articles of interest to its members involved in the various interest groups and divisions, including groups ranging from human resources to management history to gender and diversity in organizations. The first part of the journal consists of research articles and the second part the shorter commentaries in the form of research notes.

Administrative Science Quarterly

United States. (Ithaca, NY: Johnson Graduate School of Management, Cornell University). June 1956- Quarterly. ISSN: 0001-8392.

Read any article evaluating top management journals and you will be sure to find *ASQ*, the *Administrative Science Quarterly*, ranked among the top five best. The journal motto reads: "Dedicated to advancing the understanding of administration through empirical investigation and theoretical analysis."[24] The *ASQ* Web site boasts that the journal presents the best dissertation research in organization studies and notes that papers published in *ASQ* have won the "Best Paper Award" from the Academy of Management's Organizational Behavior Division for the past three consecutive years.[25] The second half of the journal provides new book information in the form of thoughtful book reviews and new books received. For over 40 years this outstanding journal has been contributing new ideas to the practice of administration.

Harvard Business Review

United States. (Boston: Harvard Business School Publishing Corporation). Oct. 1922- Bi-monthly. ISSN: 0017-8012.

The *Harvard Business Review* must be included as a top ranked business journal for two reasons: (1) its been around so long, and (2) so many people like to read it. You don't have to be a top executive, a business professor, or even a business student to read, enjoy, and learn from this inestimable journal. The journal serves as a practitioner's tool in that it offers articles that address contemporary business problems and their solutions. The *Harvard Business Review* offers continuing features along with its informative articles. The Briefings from the Editors include reports on "new and notable management research from academia and the field." Other features include: The Manager's Tool Kit, Books in Review, and Executive Summaries which summarize each article in the issue and provide a reprint number executives can use to order reprints.

Sloan Management Review

United States. (Cambridge, MA: Sloan Management Review Association, MIT Sloan School of Management) 1959- (formerly titled: *IMR*-1970). Quarterly. ISSN: 0019-848X.

This journal's strength lies in its ability to present complex, theoretical articles in straightforward, non-technical language. The journal editors state that the *SMR* ". . . provides senior managers with the best current management theory and practice" and state that the journal's mission is "to provide practicing managers with thought-provoking strategies that offer real-world solutions to today's and tomorrow's challenges."[26] Each issue contains approximately seven feature articles, one or two book reviews, a listing of recent management publications, and "Executive Briefings"—a summary of each article in the perspective issue with reprint ordering information included. An author and subject index for a previous volume is published in the back of the first issue of a succeeding volume.

MANAGEMENT—LABOR RELATIONS

The Industrial and Labor Relations Review

United States. (Ithaca, NY: New York State School of Industrial and Labor Relations, Cornell University). Oct. 1947- Quarterly. ISSN: 0019-7939.

The IRL school at Cornell is the only institution of higher education offering a full four-year undergraduate program in industrial and labor relations, and the school's faculty consists of the largest concentration of scholars in the field.[27] Its not surprising that one of the most consulted journals in the area of labor relations, *The Industrial and Labor Relations Review,* began being published at the ILR school in 1947 and has remained an important source for scholarly research on all issues impacting labor. The journal consists of 6-7 medium-length (15-20 pages) research articles, book reviews on recent books on labor topics, and "Research in Progress" arranged by subject specialties such as labor and employment law; labor economics; human resources, management, and personnel.

Monthly Labor Review

United States. (Washington, DC: Bureau of Labor Statistics of the U.S. Department of Labor) July 1915- (formerly titled: *Monthly Review of the Bureau of Labor Statistics*-1918) Monthly. ISSN: 0098-1818.

Acclamation must go to the U.S. government for certain statistical publications it produces that librarians can't live without. The *Monthly Labor Review* is one of these publications. The 4-5 feature articles in each issue are written by statisticians and economists from the Bureau of Labor Statistics as well as by private sector professionals and experts from state and local government. The focus of many articles is on statistical and trend analysis which provides insight into the state of the economy and the outlook for the labor force. Book reviews and current labor statistics are included in each issue. The statistics presented each month take up approximately half of the journal and are comprised of the principal statistical series collected and calculated by the Bureau of Labor Statistics. This is one of the best sources for obtaining statistical data profiling the global employment situation and discussing current labor issues.

Dispute Resolution Journal

United States. (New York: American Arbitration Association). 1937- (formerly titled: *Arbitration Journal*-1993) Monthly. ISSN: 1074-8105.

The American Arbitration Association is well-known for its Panel of Arbitrators and Mediators whom they refer to parties involved in disputes. As such, the award-winning publication of the Association, the *Dispute Resolution Journal,* is a journal written and read by leading practitioners and scholars who wish to keep up on Alternative Dispute Resolution issues, emerging techniques, and new applications of ADR processes. The *Journal* also contains the latest ADR news, court decisions and book reviews.

MANAGEMENT—HUMAN RESOURCE MANAGEMENT

HR Magazine

United States. (Alexandria, VA: Society for Human Resource Management). 1950- (formerly titled: *Personnel Administrator*-1989). Monthly. ISSN: 1047-3149.

The Society for Human Resource Management is the leading professional organization for human resource personnel executives. *HR Magazine* their flagship publication, is *the* resource for practitioners who wish to keep up on new ideas, leading trends, and legal issues in the field of human resources, personnel and industrial relations. The journal articles are precise and to the point and fall in the areas of compensation, benefits, labor relations, employer/employee rights, work and family, training, organizational development and management. Each issue also includes a column with technology solutions and updates, and book reviews.

Human Resource Management

United States. (Ann Arbor, MI: John Wiley & Sons for the University of Michigan Business School in alliance with the Society for Human Resource Management) 1948- (formerly titled: *Management of Personnel Quarterly*-1972). Quarterly. ISSN: 0090-4848.

Human Resource Management acts as a bridge journal which provides both practicing managers and academics with the latest information for problem solving in the field of HRM. Articles consist of new theories, new techniques, case studies, models, and research trends of significance to practicing managers. The journal has a practice of, at irregular intervals, designating special issues on a particular topic; e.g., "Special Issue: The 'New' HR: A Supply Side Perspective with Robert L. Heneman as guest editor" (Summer 1999, v. 38, n. 2). Most issues contain a review of a featured book and the "Bookshelf" consisting of book reviews of additional books at the end of each journal issue.

Workforce

United States. (Costa Mesa, CA: ACC Communications Inc.) 1922- (formerly titled: *Personnel Journal*-1996) Monthly. ISSN: 1092-8332.

Penned as "the business magazine for leaders in human resources," the journal consists of short, informative articles that HR executives can read to stay informed about contemporary HR issues and to find solutions to real life problems and conflicts that arise within the workplace setting. A typical feature article is the June 1999 article by Marcus Buckingham and Curt Coffman entitled "How Great Managers Develop Top People."

MANAGEMENT—STRATEGY

Journal of Business Strategy

United States. (New York: Faulkner & Gray, Inc.) 1980- Bi-monthly. ISSN: 0275-6668.

The *Journal of Business Strategy* informs CEOs, members of the board, and other senior executives responsible for strategic planning within multinational companies about current theories, trends, developments, techniques, and case studies in formulating and implementing business strategy.[28] Articles are written by both reporters and professionals who have "hands on" experience in the strategic planning process. Issue contents include 4-5 feature articles, interviews with prominent executives and experts, and regular columns on timely topics (e.g., "real time strategy," "outsourcing," "turnarounds," and "strategic planning").

Long Range Planning

United Kingdom. (London: Elsevier Science Ltd., Published in association with The Strategic Planning Society and The European Strategic Planning Federation) 1968- Bi-monthly. ISSN: 0024-6301.

The Strategic Planning Society and The European Strategic Planning Federation are both multinational associations based in London, England. Both groups have a common mission of improving strategic planning techniques for corporations and organizations through providing knowledge, resources and the exchange of ideas to business planners.[29] *Long Range Planning,* the journal common to both associations, claims to be the leading international journal in the field of strategic management. Articles published in the journal, though scholarly and contributed by consultants and practitioners as well as researchers, offer current and practical information on developing and implementing strategy. The audience for the journal includes senior managers in industry and government as well as consultants and academics and researchers.

Strategic Management Journal

United Kingdom. (Cichester, UK: John Wiley & Sons) Jan/Mar 1980- Monthly. ISSN: 0143-2095.

Strategic Management Journal is a scholarly journal containing articles on all aspects of strategic management and focusing on the improvement of both theory and practice. Topics discussed include, but are not limited to, strategic resource allocation; organization structure; methods and techniques for evaluating and understanding competitive, technological, social, and political environments; and planning processes. Each issue contains approximately four feature articles and "Research Notes and Communications" from readers on published papers or current issues.

MARKETING—ADVERTISING

Advertising Age

United States. (Chicago, IL: Crain Communications). 1930- Weekly. ISSN: 0001-8899.

This journal, which has always been known for its superb news coverage of all aspects of advertising from new brands to notable people, is also one of the best sources to go to for current statistics on the advertising industry. *Ad Age's* annual and special issues include: *100 Leading National Advertisers* (last September issue), *100 Leading Media Companies* (last June issue), *Agency Report* (last March issue), *Research Business Review* (first June issue), *The Top 200 Brands* (quarterly, usually in mid-February, May, August, November issues), and *The Advertising Fact Book* (a special issue in January that collects and updates the more important ranked lists).

Adweek

United States. (New York: ASM Communications, Inc.) Various regional editions. Weekly, except the last week in December.

> Eastern Edition. 1960- ISSN: 0199-2864
> Western Edition. 1919- ISSN: 0199-4743
> Midwest Edition. 1963-
> New England Edition. 1964- ISSN: 0888-0840
> Southeast Edition. 1980- ISSN: 8756-6389
> Southwest Edition. 1979- ISSN: 0746-892x

A trade weekly with each regional edition covering the marketing and advertising news for that particular area. Among the special features included in each issue are: "AIR" (Accounts in Review), "Art & Commerce," "News Analysis," "IQ News," covering internet advertising news, and "Creative," reporting on the latest in popular ads. *Adweek* also publishes an annual *Adweek Agency Directory* and *Adweek New England* reports on that region's media in a guide entitled: *Adweek's Guide to New England Markets & Media.*

Journal of Advertising

United States. (Clemson, SC: CtC Press for the American Academy of Advertising) 1972- Quarterly. ISSN: 0091-3367.

The AAA disseminates research and scholarly contributions to the field of advertising through *The Journal of Advertising,* an academic/scholarly advertising journal with a mission ". . . to contribute to the development of advertising theory and its relationship to advertising practices and processes."[30] The editors welcome theoretical, empirical and practical research articles that encourage the development of the psychological and philosophical aspects of communication and the practical application of this and other research on the advertising process.

MARKETING—GENERAL

Getting the finished product into the hands of a consumer involves much more than selling. Marketing draws upon psychology and the latest marketing research methods to both tap into what consumers want and also to create wants in consumers. Though much is written about the individual consumer, the field of industrial or business-to-business marketing is a booming field being transformed by the internet with its capacity to advertise and market at a reasonable rate to a large number of industrial customers.

Business Marketing

United States. (Chicago, IL: Crain Communications) 1916- (Formerly titled: *Industrial Marketing*-1983). Monthly. ISSN: 1087-948X.

Subtitled "The Newspaper of Business-to-Business Marketing," this long-standing trade journal carries news and information on happenings within the world of business-to-business marketing. *Business Marketing*'s primary audience is industrial advertising managers and other executives responsible for advertising and sales of products and services to businesses. Contents of each issue include news on people and companies involved in business-to-business marketing, advertising strategies for such companies, "how-to" articles, and trade show information. Issues also carry articles with rankings and ratings such as the "1999 Business-to-Business Agency Ranking" published in the July 1999 issue.

JMR: Journal of Marketing Research

United States. (Chicago, IL: American Marketing Association) Feb. 1964-
Quarterly. ISSN: 0022-2437.

As this publication's sister journal, *The Journal of Marketing,* expanded
and began publishing a wider variety of articles, the Association saw a need
for a journal devoted exclusively to cutting-edge research. *The JMR,* first
published in 1964, fills this need by publishing articles exclusively on research techniques, methods and applications. Articles published present
new techniques for solving marketing problems; contribute to marketing
knowledge based on experimental, descriptive, or analytical techniques;
and review and comment on the developments in related fields that have a
bearing on marketing research.[31]

The Journal of Marketing

United States. (New York: American Marketing Association). 1936- Quarterly. ISSN: 0022-2429.

The American Marketing Association's official journal, *The Journal of
Marketing,* has become, along with the *Journal of Marketing Research,* a
premier research publication for marketing. Its stated mission is to bridge
the gap between theory and application,[32] a very appropriate task for a journal which has always had an academic/practitioner split among its readers.
A series of editors over the years have taken the journal through many
changes beginning with its early focus on marketing education and broad-
ening out into other topics as the field of marketing has become more sophisticated.[33] The journal editors have had a continuing interest in alerting
AMA members to current marketing literature and research, and this interest is reflected in a special section of each issue entitled: "Marketing Literature Review." This feature includes a selection of marketing-related abstracts taken from UMI's ABI/INFORM business database and reviewed by
JM staff.

NOTES

   1. Andreas Werner. "Serials Acquisition: Selection—An Overview of Criteria,"
part III of "Serials Librarianship in Germany," Edited by Hartmut Walravens. *The
Serials Librarian* 29 (1/2): 159, 1996.

2. Davis, John B. "Problems in Using the Social Sciences Index to Rank Economics Journals," *American Economist* 42 (2): 59-64, Fall 1998.

3. Liebowitz, S. J. and J. P. Palmer. "Assessing the Relative Impacts of Economics Journals," *Journal of Economic Literature* XXII: 77-88, March 1984.

4. Werner, 144-145.

5. See The American Accounting Association Web site for *The Accounting Review,* Available: http://www.rutgers.edu/Accounting/raw/aaa/pubs.htm/. Viewed 11/1/99.

6. See *The Journal of Accounting Research* Web site, Available: http://gsbwww.uchicgo.edu/research/journals/jar.

7. *Business Journals of the United States.* Ed. William Fisher (Westport, CT.: Greenwood Press, 1991): 133.

8. *Encyclopedia of Associations,* Eds. Christine Mauere and Tara E. Sheets. (Detroit: Gale Research Co., 1998) 33rd ed., vol. 1: 592.

9. *Taxes: The Tax Magazine,* 77 (7): 2, July 1999.

10. See *The Journal of Business Ethics* Web site, Available: http://kapis.www.wkap.nl/aims_scope.htm/0167-4544. Viewed 11/1/99.

11. See *MIS Quarterly* Web site, Available: http://www.allenpress.com/cgi-bin/test-cat.cgi?journal=mis_q. Viewed 11/1/99.

12. "BEA's Mission," Bureau of Economic Analysis Web site, Available: http://www.bea.doc.gov/bea/role.htm. Viewed 11/1/99.

13. "Organization Information," American Economic Association (AEA) Web site, Available: http://www.vanderbilt.edu/AEA/. Viewed 11/1/99.

14. *Cabell's Directory of Publishing Opportunities in Accounting, Economics and Finance.* David W. E. Cabell, Ed. and Deborah L. English, Assoc. Ed. (Beaumont, Texas: Cabell Publishing Co, 1997-98) 7th edition, vol. 1: 241.

15. "About Us," *The Economist* Web site, Available: http://www.economist.com/help/about_logo_history.html. Viewed 11/1/99.

16. *The State of Small Business: A Report of the President* (1997). Written together with the Office of Advocacy's Annual Report on Small Business and Competition. (Washington: U.S. Government Printing Office): 3.

17. *Encyclopedia of Associations,* vol. 1: 48.

18. *Business Journals of the United States,* 3.

19. *Business Journals of the United States,* 31

20. *Encyclopedia of Associations,* Vol. 1: 49.

21. *Banking Strategies* Web site, Available: http://www.bai.org/ banking strategies/index.html. Viewed 11/1/99.

22. *Cabell's Directory of Publishing Opportunities in Accounting, Economics and Finance,* Edited by David W. E. Cabell. (Beaumont, Texas: Cabell Publishing Co., 1997-98) 7th ed., vol. 1: 348.

23. *Business Journals of the United States,* 5.

24. Title page, *Administrative Science Quarterly,* 44 (3) September 1999.

25. *Administrative Science Quarterly* Web site, Available: http://www.gsm.cornell.edu/ASQ/. Viewed 11/1/99.

26. "Who We Are," *Sloan Management Review* Web site, Available: http://mitsloan.mit.edu/smr/whoweare.html. Viewed 11/1/99.

27. "History of the ILR School," New York State School of Industrial and Labor Relations, Cornell University Web site, Available: http://www.ilr.cornell.edu/general_ ilr_info/aboutilr.html. Viewed 11/1/99.

28. *Cabell's Directory of Publishing Opportunities in Management and Marketing,* Ed. David W. E. Cabell, Assoc. ed. Debroah L. English (Beaumont, Texas: Cabell Publishing Co., 1997-98), vol. II: 795.

29. *Encyclopedia of Associations: International Organizations* (Detroit: Gale Research Inc., 1994) 28th edition, Part 1: 153-154.

30. "About the Academy," American Academy of Advertising web site, Available: http://advertising.utexas.edu/AAA/About.html. Viewed 11/2/99.

31. *JMR: Journal of Marketing Research* Web site, Available: http://www.ama.org/pubs/jmr/info/. Viewed 11/2/99.

32. *Journal of Marketing* web site, Available: http://www.ama.org/pubs/jm/info. Viewed 11/2/99.

33. *Business Journals of the Untied States,* 162.

OTHER SOURCES CONSULTED

Coe, Robert and Irwin Weinstock. "Evaluating the Management Journals: A Second Look." *Academy of Management Journal* 27 (3): 660-666, September 1984.

Daniells, Lorna M. *Business Information Sources.* Los Angeles, CA.: University of California Press, 1993. 3rd edition.

Extejt, Marian M. and Jonathan E. Smith. "The Behavioral Sciences and Management: An Evaluation of Relevant Journals." *Journal of Management* 16 (3): 539-551, 1990.

Johnson, Jonathan L. "Journal Influence in the Field of Management: An Analysis Using Salanick's Index in a Dependency Network." *Academy of Management Journal* 37 (5): 1392-1407, 1994.

Lab, David N. and John M. Wells. "The Scholarly Journal Literature of Economics." *American Economist* 42 (2): 47-58, Fall 1998.

Sharplin, Arthur D. and Rodney H. Mabry. "The Relative Importance of Journals Used in Management Research: An Alternative Ranking." *Human Relations* 38 (2): 139-149, February 1985.

Tahai, Alireza and Michael J. Meyer. "A Revealed Preference Study of Management Journals' Direct Influences." *Strategic Management Journal* 20 (3): 279-296.

Tega, Vasile G. *Management and Economic Journals: A Guide to Information Sources.* Detroit: Gale Research Co., 1977. (Management Information Guide; 3).

Chapter 12

Journals of the Century in Law

Christopher D. Byrne

Ranking things is an inherently human behavior that never ceases to either gratify or antagonize. Rankings create order where none existed. They convey information quickly and eliminate grey areas by simplifying the complex. That simplification can illuminate or mislead, especially if the reader is unaware of the methodology used in the ranking process.

No one can deny the appeal of lists, however. I remember reading the *Book of Lists* as a child and being entertained for hours by the rankings of the banal and the bizarre. Today, on the Internet, one can find an almost inconceivable number of lists on a multitude of topics. Rankings are interesting, fun, and conversation starters.

In this essay I will humbly add my contribution to this vast literature by ranking the twentieth century's best law journals. I am not treading upon virgin ground. Over the past twenty years a number of scholars have ranked law reviews and journals using a variety of methodologies.

Studies have ranked by the number of citations to them in law reviews and court cases, the prestige of the authors of the articles published in them, and library usage.[1] I reviewed these studies and performed a rough citation analysis using Westlaw (JLR database) and Lexis (LAWREV;ALLREV database) to derive my own rankings. My analysis covers citations of journals from 1985 to mid-1999. I compared general law reviews with other general law reviews and specialized journals in a given discipline with the other journals in the field. I do not desire to gloss my results with a scientific veneer of respectability. The rankings are subjective based upon my citation analysis, interpretation of other studies, and experience as a lawyer and law librarian.

Before delving into the results, an overview of what law reviews are and why they are worthy of ranking will be useful to those unfamiliar with the law as an academic discipline. Law reviews contain articles written by law professors, students, practitioners, and other scholars. The articles explore

This chapter originally appeared in *The Serials Librarian* 39(2): 87-103, 2000.

legal topics in-depth. Reviews also can contain brief commentaries on recent cases or current topics, the writings from legal symposiums, and book reviews. The format of law reviews has changed little since the publication of the *Harvard Law Review* in 1887.

Law students edit and publish most law reviews in contrast to the peer edited journals in other academic disciplines. Most students strive to be on the staff of their law school's main law review publication. The law students on journals usually have either "written on," i.e., passed a test, and/or "graded on," i.e., had a sufficient grade point average to warrant recognition.

Like any professional literature, law reviews are useful sources of scholarly discussion and relevant citations. Articles are heavily footnoted with references to cases, statutes, regulations, and secondary sources. Some articles have influenced court decisions including those of the United States Supreme Court.

Law reviews provide legal scholars with a forum for their ideas and with a rough tool to measure the contributions of their colleagues. Scholars that are published in the more prestigious law reviews have better opportunity to work and obtain tenure at a top law school. Law review prestige is usually pegged to the prestige of the law school associated with its publication.

Law reviews in the United States are a relatively recent phenomenon, originating at the end of the nineteenth century. Initially, most law reviews covered all areas of the law. Over the past fifty years the number of subject-specific law reviews has exploded. They now far outnumber the general reviews. Their growth reflects increasing specialization in the law and a desire of law students to participate in the law review experience.

Most law schools accredited by the American Bar Association produce a general law review. The number of law reviews covering a certain topic varies with the topic, but some topics, such as administrative law, may only be covered by a few reviews. That is not to say that general law reviews do not cover administrative law issues, they do, but to compare a law review on administrative law with a general law review is to compare an apple to an orange. They serve different functions. While general law reviews cover major areas of law, subject-specific journals can publish articles that are much more technical in nature and of primary interest only to people involved in the field.

General law reviews from top law schools are more prestigious than specialized journals from the same top schools. In law review rankings, specialized journals do not rank as highly as the top general law reviews. In a fairly recent ranking of the top law reviews based on frequency of citation in other reviews, only the *Journal of Legal Studies* and *Harvard Civil Rights-Civil Liberties Law Review* broke the top twenty.[2]

I have ranked general and subject-specific law reviews separately because of their differing purposes and prestige. Most of the specialized journals listed below as the best in their categories would not be considered more prestigious than the top twenty or so general law reviews. Therefore, journals listed in the specialized journals section cannot automatically be presumed better than law reviews not listed in the general law review section.

A final word of caution before the rankings. Librarians should view these law review rankings with circumspection. Attorneys and pro se litigants are bound by the law of their jurisdiction. An attorney or lay patron only cares about finding articles that further their understanding of a particular topic, not about the relative merits of a particular journal. For example, a practitioner in Virginia, researching a state law issue, often will find that only law journals published in Virginia will cover the Virginia law on the topic. The same is true for practitioners in other states. A local law review can be more valuable to attorneys and lay patrons than a prestigious, out-of-state review.

No more than 3 or 4 journals are ranked in each category because of the editorial rules governing the Journals of the Century Project. A number of top notch law reviews could not be included. The absence of a particular law review is not a negative comment on its overall merit.

The law reviews are listed by name with the country of publication, publisher, and date of first issue in parentheses. The subject categories used for specialized law reviews are from *Anderson's 1997 Directory of Law Reviews and Scholarly Legal Periodicals.*[3] The subject areas reviewed include business law, constitutional and public law, criminal law, environmental law, human rights law, intellectual property and entertainment law, international law, medicine and health law, public policy, taxation, and women's issues. With those explanations, let's go to the rankings!

GENERAL LAW REVIEWS

Harvard Law Review
(USA, Harvard Law Review Association, 1887)

In 1886 members of the Langdell Society, a student organization devoted to the discussion of legal topics, decided to create a law journal after becoming aware of the *Columbia Jurist,* a short-lived law review produced by Columbia Law School students. Their creation, the student-edited *Harvard Law Review,* set a standard of success that other journals strive to achieve.

Initially, financial problems beset the law review. Harvard Law School professors refused to participate in the journal, which received no funding from the law school. Fortunately, the Harvard Law School Association's decision to purchase subscriptions for its members removed the journal's financial difficulties.[4] The eventual success of the *Harvard Law Review* led other law schools to develop law reviews based upon the Harvard model, including Yale and Columbia among others.[5]

In the various studies I reviewed, the *Harvard Law Review* consistently ranked first in terms of library usage and frequency of citation in other journals and by the courts.[6] My own citation analysis confirmed the previous authors' findings. Law reviews and the United States Supreme Court have cited the *Harvard Law Review* more times than any other review. By 1995 the *Harvard Law Review* had published 42 of the 102 most cited law review articles of all-time and 30 of the 103 most cited articles published between 1982 and 1991.[7] By all measures the *Harvard Law Review* has been and continues to be a heavily influential law review.

Yale Law Journal
(The Yale Law Journal Company, Inc., 1891)

Unlike the students at Harvard, the students starting the *Yale Law Journal* had the support of the law school and the faculty. A Quiz Club conceived of the new journal in 1890 and a student committee was formed, which recommended that the project be commenced the following year. The dean of the law school and several professors guaranteed the financial stability of the enterprise, but the guarantee was not needed. From its beginning, the *Yale Law Journal* succeeded financially and academically.[8]

A law review in the same mode as the *Harvard Law Review,* the *Yale Law Journal,* like its counterpart, consistently ranks in the top two or three law reviews in studies using citation and other analyses. In my citation analysis the *Law Journal* is the second most cited law review by the United States Supreme Court and other law reviews. In only one study did the *Yale Law Journal* fail to rank in the top 3.[9] It ranks second to only the *Harvard Law Review* in the number of articles published that are listed as the most frequently cited law review articles.[10] The *Yale Law Journal* continues to be considered one of the premier law reviews published in the United States.

Columbia Law Review
(USA, Columbia Law students, 1901)

As mentioned above, Columbia law students published the *Columbia Jurist* for two years before the first issue of the *Harvard Law Review.* The *Columbia Jurist* lasted just one more year before being discontinued and replaced by the *Columbia Law Times,* which ran until 1893. The hiring of a professional law librarian and an improving law library helped renew student interest in publishing a law review, and in 1901 they established the *Columbia Law Review.* Columbia's dean told the law review members to seek the advice of the *Harvard Law Review*'s editors and to emulate its format.[11]

In the studies reviewed, the *Columbia Law Review* most often ranked third behind Harvard and Yale's law reviews. My citation analysis confirmed those results in terms of citations to its law review by the Supreme Court and other law reviews. The *Columbia Law Review* can rightfully take its place in the pantheon of great law reviews of the twentieth century.

Three of the oldest law reviews are among the top law reviews in the nation. The explanation lies in Harvard, Yale, and Columbia law schools' continuing reputation for excellence. First rate facilities attract similarly first rate faculty and students. Therefore, the regard in which the law reviews at those schools are held is not surprising.

Honorable Mention: I easily could have included the *Stanford Law Review* as one of the top three general law reviews. Established in 1948, it consistently ranks among the top three or four law reviews in recent citation studies. Other notable reviews are the *California Law Review, Michigan Law Review, University of Chicago Law Review, University of Pennsylvania Law Review,* and *University of Virginia Law Review.*

SPECIALIZED LAW REVIEWS

Law school admissions enjoyed a marked increase after World War II. The growth of existing law schools and the creation of new institutions helped spur the creation of general and specialized law reviews. Criticism of the proliferation and uniformity of general law reviews fueled the rise in the number of specialized journals as did the needs of students and faculty.[12] From 1950 through the 1990s law students and law schools created 324 specialized journals. The 1990s alone saw the creation of 137 titles.[13]

The boom in subject-specific law reviews reflects the increasing complexity and specialization of legal practice and disciplines. Disciplines such as environmental law, employment discrimination, and entertainment law, to name only a few, did not exist over thirty years ago. Specialized reviews provide an outlet for scholarship in these relatively new areas of law.

The top law schools often publish several subject-specific law reviews. Some law schools form a subject-specific law journal to signify a specialty in a given area of law.[14] As a practical matter, more journals allow more students to have the law review experience and offer more publishing opportunities for legal scholars.

I have only analyzed special journals that have a significant number of competitors in their subject area as listed in *Anderson's 1997 Directory of Law Reviews and Scholarly Legal Periodicals*. I did not analyze journals that have no or only a few direct competitors. If the top three journals are the only journals on the subject, the ranking of such journals becomes relatively meaningless.[15] The end result is that some excellent journals were not evaluated in this article because there were not enough direct comparisons available to make a ranking meaningful. I do include a list of the more notable omissions at the end of the article.

With that caveat, the following are the rankings for specialized journals:

BUSINESS LAW REVIEWS

Business Lawyer
(USA, Section of Business Law of the American Bar Association, 1946)

The *Business Lawyer* is published jointly by the American Bar Association's Business Law and students at the University of Maryland Law School. A quarterly publication, the journal contains case law, analysis, developing trends, book reviews, and annotated listings of recent literature. The ABA claims on its Web site that only the *Harvard Law Review* is cited more in other law reviews.[16] In my citation analysis the *Business Lawyer* is the most cited business law review over the past 14 years by a wide margin. Using a citation analysis derived from *Shepard's Law Review Citations*, Lindgren and Seltzer rank the *Business Lawyer* 15th in a list of the top 40 law reviews. It is also the only specialized journal listed in that ranking. Using the *Social Sciences Index* instead of *Shepard's*, Lindgren and Seltzer found that the *Business Lawyer* is the 27th most frequently cited journal.[17]

The Journal of Corporation Law
(USA, The Journal of Corporation Law, 1975)

The *Journal of Corporation Law* is the nation's oldest student-published periodical specializing in corporate law.[18] Professors George and Guthrie listed *The Journal of Corporation Law* 7th in their ranking of the top 100 specialized journals based upon author prominence.[19] My citation analysis ranked them second only to the *Business Lawyer.*

(Tie) Delaware Journal of Corporate Law
(USA, Students of Widener University School of Law, 1976)
and Columbia Business Law Review
(USA, Columbia Business Law Review, 1986)

Widener's primary law review, the *Delaware Journal of Corporate Law,* ranks 18th in the George and Guthrie study. The *Columbia Business Law Review* ranks 19th in the same study. My citation analysis ranked both journals closely, especially over the last five years, but clearly behind the *Business Lawyer* and *The Journal of Corporation Law.*

CONSTITUTIONAL AND PUBLIC LAW JOURNALS

Supreme Court Review
(USA, The University of Chicago Press, 1960)

The *Supreme Court Review* is the preeminent publication of its kind in the United States. Edited by University of Chicago Law School faculty members, the *Supreme Court Review* contains articles written by legal scholars, attorneys, judges, and other experts. The articles analyze the important cases decided during the most recently completed Supreme Court term. The review is published once a year as a book. It really is not a true law review in its traditional form. Nevertheless, the *Supreme Court Review* is a very influential resource. It ranks first in the George and Guthrie study.

Hastings Constitutional Law Quarterly
(USA, Students of the University of California,
Hastings College of Law, 1974)

The *Hastings Constitutional Law Quarterly* is a heavily cited law review focusing on constitutional issues.

William & Mary Bill of Rights Journal
(USA, students of the Marshall-Wythe School of Law
of the College of William & Mary, 1992)

The *William & Mary Bill of Rights Journal* focuses on constitutional issues involving civil and individual liberties. In a very short period of time the journal has become one of the most well regarded constitutional law journals. George and Guthrie ranks the journal as the 7th best specialized journal based upon author prominence. *Hastings Constitutional Law Quarterly* ranks 64th.

Honorable Mention: *Constitutional Commentary* ranks 3rd in the George and Guthrie study. It is one of the country's few faculty-edited law reviews. Founded in 1984 by faculty at the University of Minnesota Law School, it contains shorter articles than the articles in traditional law reviews and features review essays, book reviews, and a popular commentary.

CRIMINAL LAW JOURNALS

American Criminal Law Review
(USA, Georgetown University Law Center, 1963)

Originally titled the *American Criminal Law Quarterly,* the *American Criminal Law Review* is published by students at Georgetown University Law Center. One of the most cited criminal law reviews in the country, it ranks as the 30th most cited law review in the Lindgren and Seltzer survey. The study by George and Guthrie lists it as the 12th best specialized review. The journal is particularly known for its White Collar Crime Project, a comprehensive guide to developments in the field of white collar crime published each Spring.

Journal of Criminal Law and Criminology
(USA, Northwestern University School of Law, 1910)

The *Journal of Criminal Law and Criminology* is published by students at Northwestern University School of Law. It and the *American Criminal Law Review* are the only criminal law reviews listed in the Lindgren and Seltzer study.[20] The journal is one of only four criminal law journals ranked in the top 100 specialized journals by George and Guthrie.

Honorable Mention: *American Journal of Criminal Law* is published by students at the University of Texas Law School and is ranked 68th by George and Guthrie. According to my citation analysis, it is the 3rd most cited criminal law journal over the past five years, but the number of citations does not approach those to the *American Criminal Law Review* and the *Journal of Criminal Law and Criminology.*

ENVIRONMENTAL LAW

Ecology Law Quarterly
(USA, University of California Press, 1971)

Students at Boalt Hall School of Law, University of California produce the *Ecology Law Quarterly*. The journal published its first issue in 1971. A sizable grant from the Ford Foundation helped secure the financial footing of the quarterly. In 1990 the United Nations Environmental Programme awarded the *Ecology Law Quarterly* its global 500 award, a recognition of the journal's outstanding achievements in the protection and improvement of the environment. The quarterly ranks as the most cited environmental law review in my citation analysis and 1st in Professor Scott Crespi's survey of environmental law professors asked to name the top law reviews in the field.[21]

Harvard Environmental Law Review
(USA, Harvard Environmental Law Review, 1976)

The *Harvard Environmental Law Review* has earned a reputation as one of the top environmental law reviews. It ranks 2nd in my citation analysis and second in Crespi's faculty survey.[22]

Columbia Journal of Environmental Law
(USA, Columbia Journal of Environmental Law, Inc., 1974)

Columbia law students founded the journal in 1973 with a grant from the Ford Foundation. It is one of the most frequently cited environmental law reviews and is one of the few environmental law reviews ranked in the George and Guthrie study.

Honorable Mention: *Environmental Law*, a publication of the students of Northwestern School of Law of Lewis & Clark College, is the nation's oldest environmental law review.[23] It ranks 3rd in Crespi's study. *Boston College Environmental Affairs Law Review* claims, as does the *Columbia Journal of Environmental Law,* to be the second oldest environmental law review.[24] In my citation analysis it ranked ahead of the *Columbia Journal of Environmental Law* for the last five years and was ranked 7th by Crespi.

HUMAN RIGHTS JOURNALS

Harvard Civil Rights-Civil Liberties Law Review
(USA, students of Harvard Law School, 1966)

This law review publishes articles analyzing individual civil rights and civil liberties. In my citation analysis it has nearly twice the number of citations than the next leading human rights journal. It ranks as the 17th most cited law review and the 14th best specialized review in terms of author prominence.[25]

New York University Review of Law & Social Change
(USA, New York University Review of Law & Social Change, 1971)

Established three years after the *Harvard Civil Rights-Civil Liberties Law Review*, the *Review of Law & Social Change* publishes articles that provide innovative solutions to social, economic, and political injustice. Managed by students at the New York University School of Law, it is the 2nd most cited human rights journal in my citation analysis.

Columbia Human Rights Law Review
(USA, Columbia Human Rights Law Review, 1968)

Columbia law students publish this review which contains articles that discuss and analyze human rights and civil liberties under both domestic and international law. Over the past five years, the *Columbia Human Rights Law Review* ranked 3rd in my citation analysis.

Honorable Mention: The *Journal of Law Reform*, published by University of Michigan law students beginning in 1968, ranks 31st in the George and Guthrie study and was cited almost as much as the *Columbia Human Rights Law Review* over the past five years according to my citation analysis.

INTELLECTUAL PROPERTY AND ENTERTAINMENT LAW JOURNALS

Cardozo Arts & Entertainment Law Journal
(USA, Students of the Benjamin N. Cardozo School of Law, 1982)

Founded in 1982 as the first student-edited law review focused on entertainment law, sports, telecommunications, and intellectual property law, the *Cardozo Arts & Entertainment Law Journal* ranks 1st in my citation analysis.[26]

Hastings Communications and Entertainment Law Journal
(USA, Students of the University of California, Hastings College of the Law, 1977)

Hastings Communications and Entertainment Law Journal covers communications, entertainment, and intellectual property law. It ranks 2nd in my citation analysis.

Columbia-VLA Journal of the Law and the Arts
(USA, Students of the Columbia University School of Law, 1974)

This journal ranks 3rd in my citation analysis. It explores the national and international aspects of law and the arts, entertainment, media, and intellectual property.

Honorable Mention: The Copyright Society of the U.S.A. has published the *Journal of the Copyright Society of the U.S.A.*, formerly the *Bulletin of the Copyright Society*, since 1953. The goal of the organization is to gather and disseminate information concerning protection and use of rights in intellectual property. It was one of the first journals to specialize in copyright law. The *Journal of Intellectual Property*, published by students at the University of Georgia Law School, ranks 17th in the George and Guthrie study.

INTERNATIONAL LAW JOURNALS

American Journal of International Law
(USA, The American Society of International Law, 1907)

This is one of the nation's preeminent journals in international law. Published quarterly since 1907 by the American Society of International Law, the journal contains commentaries, articles, editorials, and summaries of decisions of national and international courts and tribunals. Professor Crespi ranks the *American Journal of International Law* first in his survey of law school professors specializing in international law.[27] According to Lindgren and Seltzer, it is the 23rd most cited law review.

American Journal of Comparative Law
(USA, The American Society of Comparative Law, 1952)

The American Society of Comparative Law is an organization of institutional members (including universities) devoted to study, research, and writing on foreign and comparative law in the United States. The journal combines scholarly writing of both a theoretical and practical nature. The journal ranks 2nd in Crespi's study.[28]

Virginia Journal of International Law
(USA, Virginia Journal of International Law Association, 1960)

The *Virginia Journal of International Law* is the oldest continuously-published, student-edited international law journal in the United States.[29] The journal continues to rank highly, especially vis-à-vis its student-edited peers, the *Harvard International Law Journal, Columbia Journal of Transnational Law,* and the *Yale Journal of International Law.* In my citation analysis of international law reviews, the *Virginia Journal of International Law* is the most cited student edited review. It is the highest ranked international law journal in the George and Guthrie study and the 6th ranked journal in the Crespi survey.

Honorable Mention: The *Columbia Journal of Transnational Law, Harvard International Law Journal,* and the *Yale Journal of International Law* are all highly regarded international law journals that easily could have taken a place among the top three without any strenuous objections being made on my part. The *Harvard International Law Journal* ranks 39th in the Lindgren and Seltzer study.

MEDICINE, HEALTH, PSYCHIATRY, PSYCHOLOGY AND LAW

American Journal of Law & Medicine
(USA, American Society of Law, Medicine & Ethics and Boston University School of Law, 1975)

This journal is one the premier journals focused upon the nexus between law and medicine. It ranked first in my citation analysis.

Law and Human Behavior
(USA, Kluwer Academic/Plenum Publishers, 1977)

Law and Human Behavior is the official journal of the American Psychology-Law Society division of the American Psychological Association. It discusses issues arising out of the relationship between human behavior and the law, legal system, and legal process. In addition to articles, comments and book reviews, the journal contains sections on research issues in practice and an adversary forum for debates. Lindgren and Seltzer list it as the 29th most frequently cited law review.

Journal of Contemporary Health Law & Policy
(USA, a Student Editorial Board Drawn
from the Columbus School of Law
of The Catholic University of America, 1985)

Founded in 1984, the *Journal of Contemporary Health Law & Policy* is dedicated to the in-depth legal analysis of the recent trends in modern health care. It ranks 3rd in my citation analysis.

PUBLIC POLICY JOURNALS

Law & Contemporary Problems
(USA, Duke University School of Law, 1933)

Established by the faculty of the Duke Law School in 1933, this journal remained exclusively faculty edited and managed until a student editorial review board was established in the 1970s.[30] The articles published usually take an interdisciplinary approach to contemporary problems. It easily outpaced the competition in my citation analysis of comparable journals and ranked 13th out of 161 journals surveyed in Richard Mann's citation analysis of law reviews.[31] *Law & Contemporary Problems* also placed 32nd in the Lindgren and Seltzer study.

Harvard Journal of Law & Public Policy
(USA, Harvard Society for Law & Public Policy, Inc., 1978)

Students at Harvard Law School publish this journal on law and public policy. It ranks 28th in the George and Guthrie survey and second in my citation analysis.

Yale Law and Policy Review
(USA, Students of the Yale Law School, 1982)

This review focuses on American domestic policy. It ranks 44th in the George and Guthrie survey and third in my citation analysis.

TAX JOURNALS

Tax Law Review
(USA, Warren, Gorham & Lamont, 1945)

The *Tax Law Review* is managed and edited by faculty at the New York University School of Law. Each issue contains articles and essays by legal academics, practitioners, and economists. It ranks 1st in my citation analysis and 2nd in George and Guthrie's ranking of the top 100 specialized law journals.

Journal of Taxation
(USA, RIA Group, 1954)

This monthly journal is devoted to in-depth articles, written by scholars and practitioners, that provide planning and suggest solutions to problems faced by tax lawyers and accountants. It ranks 2nd in my citation analysis.

National Tax Journal
(USA, National Tax Association, 1948)

The National Tax Association is an educational association founded in 1907 that fosters the study and discussion of complex and controversial issues in tax theory, practice and policy, and other aspects of public finance. The *National Tax Journal*'s audience is mainly practitioners, scholars, and administrators. It ranks 3rd in my citation analysis.

Honorable Mention: The *Virginia Tax Review*, a student-edited journal at the University of Virginia Law School, ranked 2nd in my citation analysis over the last five years and was listed 24th in the George and Guthrie study.

WOMEN'S ISSUES

Harvard Women's Law Journal
(USA, Harvard Women's Law Journal, 1978)

The *Harvard Women's Law Journal* is devoted to developing and advancing feminist jurisprudence. This student-edited journal ranks 89th in the George and Guthrie survey and 1st in my citation analysis.

Berkeley Women's Law Journal
(USA, University of California Press, 1985)

Founded in 1984, this student-edited journal takes a multi-disciplinary approach to critical legal issues affecting women, particularly under-represented women: women of color, poor women, lesbians, and disabled women. The journal ranks 3rd in my citation analysis. It is the first women's law journal listed in the George and Guthrie survey and 27th overall.

Women's Rights Law Reporter
(USA, Women's Rights Law Reporter, 1971)

Feminist activists, legal workers, and law students founded the *Women's Rights Law Reporter* in 1970 and published it independently until it affiliated formally with Rutgers School of Law at Newark in 1974. Now entirely managed and edited by law students, it is the oldest law review devoted to women's rights law.[32] It ranks 2nd in my citation analysis.

OTHER SPECIALIZED JOURNALS OF NOTE

Not all of the significant law journals fit neatly into subject categories or can be compared to rival publications, especially if there are none. Nevertheless, these journals deserve recognition because of their continued excellence and contribution to legal scholarship. They are listed here in alphabetical order.

Journal of Law & Economics
(USA, The University of Chicago Press, 1958)

The *Journal of Law & Economics* explores the complex relationships between law and economics, focusing on the influence of regulation and legal institutions on the operation of economic systems. It is published semiannually by the University of Chicago. It ranks 15th in the Lindgren and Seltzer study.

Journal of Legal Education
(USA, Association of American Law Schools, 1948)

The *Journal of Legal Education* fosters an interchange of ideas and information about legal education. Lindgren and Seltzer rank it 30th.

Journal of Legal Studies
(USA, University of Chicago Press, 1972)

The *Journal of Legal Studies* is an interdisciplinary journal of theoretical and empirical research on law and legal institutions. It is published semi-annually. The journal ranks as the top specialized journal in the Lindgren and Seltzer's citation study based upon the *Social Sciences Citation Index* and 10th overall.

Law and History Review
(USA, University of Illinois Press for the American Society for Legal History, 1983)

The American Society for Legal History sponsors the *Law and History Review.* Founded in 1956, the society fosters scholarship, teaching, and study concerning the law and institutions of all legal systems, both Anglo-American and international. Articles in the *Law and History Review* focus on the social history of law and the history of legal ideas and institutions. *The American Journal of Legal History,* the former official publication of the American Society for Legal History established in 1957, is currently published by Temple University School of Law.

Law & Social Inquiry
(USA, University of Chicago Press, 1976)

Law & Social Inquiry is a multi-disciplinary quarterly that features both empirical and theoretical studies of socio-legal processes. The American Bar Foundation sponsors this peer-reviewed journal, hence its former title, the *American Bar Foundation Research Journal.* It ranks 37th in the Lindgren and Seltzer survey of the most frequently cited law reviews.

Law & Society Review
(USA, Law and Society Association, 1966)

Law & Society Review publishes articles exploring the relationship between the legal process and society. The review focuses on the cultural, economic, political, psychological, or social aspects of law and legal systems. Lindgren and Seltzer rank it as the 20th most cited law review.

NOTES

1. Here is a listing of the studies I reviewed in reverse chronological order. Tracey E. George and Chris Guthrie, *Symposium: An Empirical Evaluation of Specialized Law Reviews*, 26 Fla. St. U. L. Rev. 813 (1999); Gregory Scott Crespi, *Ranking Environmental Law, Natural Resources Law, and Land Use Planning Journals: A Survey of Expert Opinion*, 23 Wm. & Mary Envtl. L. Pol'y Rev. 273 (1998); Gregory Scott Crespi, *Ranking International and Comparative Law Journals: A Survey of Expert Opinion*, 31 Int'l Law. 869 (1997); Robert M. Jarvis and Phyllis G. Coleman, *Ranking Law Reviews: An Empirical Analysis Based on Author Prominence*, 39 Ariz. L. Rev. 15 (1997); Fred R. Shapiro, *The Most-Cited Law Review Articles Revisited*, 71 Chi-Kent L. Rev. 751 (1996); James Lindgren and Daniel Seltzer, *The Most Prolific Law Professors and Faculties*, 71 Chi.-Kent L. Rev. 781 (1996); Colleen M. Cullen and S. Randall Kalberg, *Chicago-Kent Law Review Faculty Scholarship Survey*, 70 Chi.-Kent L. Rev. 1445 (1995); Janet M. Gumm ed., *Chicago-Kent Law Review Faculty Scholarship Survey*, 66 Chi-Kent L. Rev. 509 (1990); James Leonard, *Seein' the Cites: A Guided Tour of Citation Patterns in Recent American Law Review Articles*, 34 St. Louis U. L. J. 181 (1990); The Executive Board, *Chicago-Kent Law Review Faculty Scholarship Survey*, 65 Chi-Kent L. Rev. 195 (1989); Margaret A. Goldblatt, *Current Legal Periodicals: A Use Study*, 78 L. Libr. J. 55 (1986); Richard A. Mann, *The Use of Legal Periodicals by Courts and Journals*, 26 Jurimetrics J. 400 (1986); Louis J. Sirico, Jr. and Jeffrey B. Margulies, *The Citing of Law Reviews By the Supreme Court: An Empirical Study*, 34 UCLA L. Rev. 131 (1986); Fred R. Shapiro, *The Most-Cited Law Reviews*, 73 Cal. L. Rev. 1540 (1985); Olavi Maru, *Measuring the Impact of Legal Periodicals*, 1976 Am. B. Found. Res. J. 227.

2. James Lindgren and Daniel Seltzer, *The Most Prolific Law Professors and Faculties*, 71 Chi.Kent L. Rev. 781, 791 (1996). They based their citation analysis on the *Social Sciences Citation Index* and *Shepard's Law Review Citations*. More specialized journals made the top twenty when they used data from only the *Social Sciences Citation Index*.

3. *Anderson's 1997 Directory of Law Reviews and Scholarly Legal Periodicals* (Michael H. Hoffheimer compiler, 3d ed. 1997).

4. The Harvard Law School Association, *The Centennial History of the Harvard Law School 1817-1917*, 139-140 (The Harvard Law School Association 1918)

5. Michael L. Closen and Robert J. Dzielak, *The History and Influence of the Law Review Institution*, 30 Akron L. Rev. 15, 35. (1996)

6. See footnote 1 for a list of studies reviewed.

7. Fred R. Shapiro, *The Most-Cited Law Review Articles Revisited*, 71 Chi.-Kent L. Rev. 751, 763. (1996)

8. Fred C. Hicks, *Yale Law School: 1869-1894 Including the County Court House Period* 65-70 (Yale University Press 1937).

9. Robert M. Jarvis and Phyllis G. Coleman, *Ranking the Law Reviews: An Empirical Analysis Based on Author Prominence*, 39 Ariz. L. Rev. 15, 19 (1997). Jarvis and Coleman ranked Yale ninth out of 161 law reviews in terms of the prominence of its authors.

10. Shapiro, *supra* note 7, at 763.

11. Michael I. Swygert and Jon W. Bruce, *The Historical Origins, Founding, and Early Development of Student-Edited Law Reviews*, 36 Hastings L. J. 739, 782-783 (1985); Garrard Glen, *Law Reviews—Notes of an Antediluvian*, 23 Va. L. Rev. 46 (1936).

12. Jean Sefanck, *The Law Review Symposium Issue: Community of Meaning or Reinscription of Hierarchy?* 63 U. Colo. L. Rev. 651, 655 (1992); Tracey E. George and Chris Guthrie, *Symposium: An Empirical Evaluation of Specialized Law Reviews*, 26 Fla. St. U.L. Rev. 813, 817-818 (1999).

13. George and Guthrie, *supra* note 12, at 818.

14. Id.

15. That does not mean that all the specialized journals cannot be generally compared to each other regardless of subject area. One interesting study that I have used in my analysis evaluates and ranks all specialized journals on the basis of author prominence. See George and Guthrie, *supra*, note 12.

16. American Bar Association Web page (visited Dec. 12, 1999) <http://www.abanet.org/buslaw/buslawyer.html>

17. Lindgren and Seltzer, *supra*, note 2, at 787, 789. Hereafter referred to in the text as Lindgren and Seltzer.

18. The University of Iowa College of Law, Journal of Corporation Law Web page (visited Dec. 3, 1999) <http://www.uiowa.edu/~lawcoll/journals/jcl.shtml>

19. George and Guthrie, *supra*, note 12. Hereafter referred to in the text as George and Guthrie.

20. The Journal of Criminal Law & Criminology ranked 39th.

21. Scott Gregory Crespi, *Ranking the Environmental Law, Natural Resources Law, and Land Use Planning Journals: A Survey of Expert Opinions*, 23 Wm. & Mary Envtl. L. & Pol'y Rev 273, 280 (1998).

22. Id.

23. Northwestern School of Law, Environmental Law Web page (visited Dec. 5, 1999) <http://www.lclark.edu/~envtl/home_ndx.html>

24. *See* Columbia Journal of Environmental Law web page (visited Dec. 13, 1999) <http://www.columbia.edu/cu/cjel/>; Boston College Law School, Boston College Environmental Affairs Law Review (visited Dec. 13, 1999) <http://www.bc.edu/bc_org/avp/law/lwsch/envirrev.html>

25. Lindgren and Seltzer, supra note, 2, at 787; George and Guthrie, *supra*, note 12.

26. Benjamin N. Cardozo Law School, Cardozo Arts & Entertainment Law Journal Web page (visited Dec. 13, 1999) <http://www.cardozo.yu.edu/aelj/index.html#introduction>

27. Gregory Scott Crespi, *Ranking International and Comparative Law Journals: A Survey of Expert Opinion,* 31 Int'l Law. 869, 874 (1997).

28. *Id.*

29. Virginia Journal of International Law Web page (visited Dec. 13, 1999) <http://www.student.Virginia.EDU/~vjil/>

30. Duke University School of Law, Law and Contemporary Problems Web page (visited Dec. 14, 1999) <http://www.law.duke.edu/journals/lcp/>

31. Richard Mann, *The Use of Legal Periodicals by Courts and Journals,* 26 Jurimetrics J. 400, 407 (1986).

32. Rutgers School of Law at Newark Web page (visited Dec. 13, 1999) <http://info.rutgers.edu/RUSLN/stupubs.html>

CLUSTER IV:
WAR AND PEACE

This century had more than its share of conflicts, some rooted in old geopolitical rivalries, some based on economic or ideological tensions. This is a cluster of the causes of war, the stories of the warriors and their peacetime bosses, and the chroniclers of it all: the historians.

Official journals from branches of the military were classified as government publications, because of the policy of military subordination to the civilian government in most of the Western world. This ruling affects both domestic and international publications from service academies, and from advanced training centers for the senior ranks of the military, the latter of which multiplied over the course of the century. This classification explains the best showing of the governmental sector of publishing in this cluster when compared to all the others. A surprise to many non-veterans will be the presence of many voluntary associations of ex-military, and even some foreign service, officers. (Once a marine, always a marine!) Their journals are treated as not-for-profit society entries.

This is not to say that day-to-day local, state, and federal government, the rise of political parties, elections, and social history were neglected by authors in this cluster. One of the major developments of the twentieth century was the blossoming of the academic discipline of political science and the professional schools of public administration. They effectively joined history as recognized departments and university presses published much of their work. Both national and regional associations became significant publishers in the course of the century as well, sometimes in concert with the universities that employed most of their members. But in one somewhat ironic sense, the War and Peace cluster is more like the laboratory sciences than the social sciences: the majority of the most important for-profit publishers are foreign. Jane's and Blackwell are British, and Monch is German.

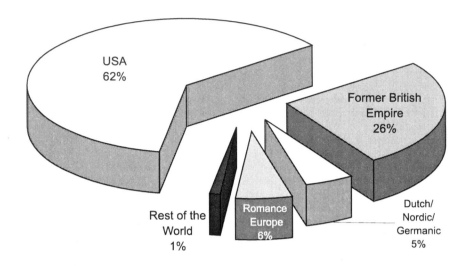

Breakdown by Region

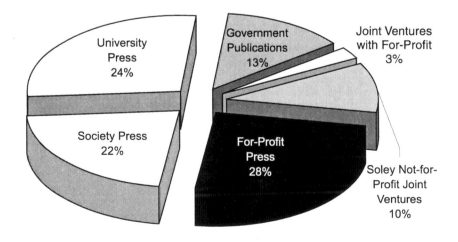

Breakdown by Publishing Sector

Chapter 13

Journals of the Century in Modern History

Edward A. Goedeken

INTRODUCTION

Serials as a form of communication have a long history, dating back per-haps as far as the ancient Egyptians who inscribed annals on the tombs of honored kings. A form more recognizable to contemporary readers devel-oped in the mid-seventeenth century almost simultaneously in England and in France as a result of efforts by their respective scientific societies to pro-mote scientific discoveries.[1] It would take two more centuries before the first journal devoted strictly to historical scholarship appeared in Germany. From that simple beginning historical journals have proliferated remark-ably. Indeed, a look at the 2000 edition of *Ulrich's International Periodical Directory* yields an estimated 3500 titles that treat some manner of history.[2]

The task before me is to sift through this mass of literature and identify the most important journals relating to modern history published in the twentieth century. Although chronological periodization is a matter of de-bate, for my purposes, modern history will be considered the period since 1500.[3] Unfortunately, so far little has been done to create a core list of Euro-pean history journals. Janet Fyfe's *History Journals and Serials: An Analyt-ical Guide* is quite useful, but she was not selective nor did she include for-eign language journals.[4] Goedeken and Hérubel used citation analysis to compile a core list of American history journals, but a similar effort has so far not appeared for European history.[5] Simply winnowing down the vast number of history titles was a challenge in itself. The CD-ROM *Historical Abstracts* indexes over 2,000 titles, many of which, however, do not deal with European history. Similarly H. W. Wilson's *Humanities Index* indexes over 400 titles, but again, many of these journals cover non-historical topics. Happily, the venerable American Historical Association came to my rescue with its recently published third edition of the *AHA Guide to Historical Lit-erature,* wherein is found a chapter listing approximately 450 journals that

This chapter originally appeared in *The Serials Librarian* 39(4): 41-68, 2001.

the editors considered important for historical scholarship.[6] Cross-checking these titles with those identified in *Historical Abstracts* and Wilson's *Humanities Index* that pertain specifically to aspects of modern European history netted me 78 titles worthy of inclusion in my list of prominent modern history journals.

This chapter will be divided into three major sections: The first discusses the earliest major journals that established the format for most of the succeeding historical serial literature. This section is followed by two others that separate the remainder of the journals by geographical and topical areas. Each title will be in bold italics at first mention, and in italics-only for any subsequent reference.

FOUR JOURNALS THAT STARTED IT ALL

In her magisterial study of history journals, Margaret Stieg identifies four publications, all of which began in the nineteenth century, that should be considered the founding fathers of all modern historical journals.[7] As writing in history matured during the years after Napoleon, the Germans—who were first to contribute in many areas of the scholarly enterprise—were the first to create a specific organ devoted solely to historical research.[8] Heinrich von Sybel, a student like so many others of the great German historian Leopold von Ranke, gained support of the Bavarian King Maximilian II, who had a personal interest in history and was willing to underwrite this new venture, and the **Historische Zeitschrift** (Germany, R. Oldenbourg Verlag, 1859) was born in Munich in 1859.[9] Von Sybel had the advantage of launching his new journal within the vibrant intellectual climate of mid-nineteenth century Germany, and the *Historische Zeitschrift* has survived to the present day as one of the most important German language journals. The German historians believed that history was not a remote academic subject, but a discipline whose writings were highly relevant to solving the problems of the day. Thus historical knowledge could be applied more broadly when encompassed within the covers a single journal that existed for the promotion of historical research and could be used to measure the quality of professional scholarship.[10]

The *Historische Zeitschrift* also established the general framework of historical journals, which included several article-length contributions followed by reports on newly discovered primary resources. Each issue concluded with a section, highly valued by historians both then and now, devoted to reviews of new books. Even a century and a half later, historical scholarship is best represented by the book-length study, and reviews remain a valuable component of most history journals. Von Sybel also initiated the concept of peer-review, wherein manuscripts would be scrutinized by scholars in the field to maintain a certain level of quality in the final published product. The editor as gatekeeper also remains a feature of contemporary journal publishing, and acceptance in a respected journal is a key component of establishing an academic reputation.[11]

What began in Germany was quickly copied by the other major European countries and the United States. The ***Revue Historique*** (France, Presses Universitaires de France, 1876) was started by Gabriel Monod, who had been trained in Germany and was a leading young French historian. Monod hoped, through the pages of his new journal, to be able to create a community of scholars similar to what existed in Germany. Although initially devoted to the period from 395 to 1815, the *Revue Historique* has over the years extended its scope to include twentieth century topics.

In England the two major universities, Oxford and Cambridge, had by the 1700s established Regius Professors of Modern History, but only in the nineteenth century did practicing historians occupy those positions. Like the French, the British had a poorly organized historical community that only late in the century began to coalesce around a specific journal. In 1886 a group of British historians established the ***English Historical Review*** (UK, Oxford University Press, 1886). The broad canvas of European history fell within the declared purview of the *English Historical Review,* and most articles were kept around twenty pages in length. (In contrast the *Revue Historique* allowed articles to run to nearly fifty pages in some cases.) The rest of each issue consisted of book reviews, and bibliographical and news notes.[12]

Finally, the Americans came along with their own contribution in 1895, when the American Historical Association sponsored the founding of its own journal, the ***American Historical Review*** (US, American Historical Association, 1895). Of the four prototype historical journals, the *AHR* was the only one issued by a organization of professional historians.[13] Also of the four, the *AHR* divided the focus of its articles fairly evenly between the United States and Europe, while the others devoted much of their early volumes to national histories. Thus by the end of the nineteenth century the major countries in Europe, along with the United States, had in place established historical journals. But there would always be room for more. The remainder of this essay will treat the most significant of these publications.

Today each of the major European countries (and the United States) is the site for one or more prominent scholarly historical journals that are general in approach, meaning they do not concentrate solely on a single country's history. For the purposes of this essay, the next section will be devoted to this type of publication arranged by country of publication. It will soon become apparent as the reader progresses through this essay that on several occasions the British and Americans established competing (or complementary, depending on your part of view) journals for the same specialized area. Historians in the English-speaking world are the richer for this seeming redundancy. Following the country of publication section, the rest of the journals under consideration will be viewed within either a chronological or a topical framework.

GENERAL STUDIES BY COUNTRY OF PUBLICATION

United States

On par with the *American Historical Review* for the quality of its articles, **The Journal of Modern History** (US, University of Chicago, 1929) was founded by a group of American historians who believed a journal devoted to modern European history was necessary. Sponsored by the Modern European History section of the American Historical Association, the *Journal of Modern History* must be considered one of the major English language journals published in the United States that focuses on European history since the Renaissance. From the outset the editors have sought a blend of articles that treat intellectual and fine arts history with the same attention that the more traditional areas such as political, religious, social, and economic history often receive. In addition to the two or three articles that appear in each quarterly issue, the *Journal of Modern History* also assigns space for significant review essays that explore the recent literature on a given topic. The rest of each issue contains usually around fifty signed book reviews.

Phi Alpha Theta International Honor Society in History sponsors **The Historian: A Journal of History** (US, the Society, 1938), which covers the entire spectrum of history, both geographically and chronologically. The majority of articles deal with American topics, but the journal remains an important and widely distributed vehicle for European history as well. Each issue contains five to seven articles accompanied by fifty to sixty signed reviews.

Many historical journals have less than 1500 subscribers who are typically only libraries and professional historians. **Current History** (US, Current History, Inc., 1914) reports a circulation of over 22,000, which makes it one of the most readily available general history periodicals in the world. Each issue concentrates on a specific country or region, with attention to current events its primary goal. But often the articles contain historical aspects, sometimes covering decades or centuries. The authors are recognized authorities on the topic, and usually six to eight articles appear in each issue.

For nearly a century *Current History* has provided the general public with authoritative and readable syntheses of historical topics.

Originally published at the University of Waterloo, Ontario (thus the reason for its bilingual title), **Historical Reflections/Reflexions Historique** (US, Alfred University Division of Human Studies, 1974) takes a broad view of the historical landscape with an emphasis on intellectual and cultural topics. Early members on its board of consulting editors included such major scholars as Paul Ricoeur, G. R. Elton, Russell B. Nye, and Kenneth Stampp. The period since 1700 receives the most attention and thematic issues appear sporadically. Each issue contains from three to six articles, either in French or English. There are no book reviews.

Although not technically published in the United States, I will nonetheless include in this section Canada's major journal, the **Canadian Journal of History/Annales Canadienne d'Histoire** (Canada, University of Saskatchewan, Department of History, 1966). In contrast to the *Canadian Historical Review,* the *Canadian Journal of History* takes as its purview all non-Canadian history in all periods. The authors are usually from Canadian universities, but not exclusively. Each issue consists of four to five articles, and, often, a section of extended reviews, followed by signed book reviews organized by geographical region.

United Kingdom

The British have produced more significant journals that take a general approach than those produced in the United States. Thus this section is rather larger than the one for the United States. After World War II a group of British historians with Marxist leanings endeavored to reignite the intellectual vigor of the 1930s progressive historians and created **Past and Present** (UK, Oxford University Press, 1952). The new journal sought to break from the traditional historiography represented by the long-established *English Historical Review,* and over the years has become a worthy competitor. The new editors wished to incorporate more sociological and economic methodologies in the writings they published. In this way, *Past and Present* reflected the approach taken by the French journal *Annales,* which will be discussed below.[14] It has championed a wide range of approaches, both in cultural and social history and in broad interdisciplinary study. Empirical and broadly Marxist, linked to the ideals of Marc Bloch and Lucien Febvre, as well as those of the radical-liberal historians, *Past and Present* willingly publishes manuscripts dealing with all parts of the world, but its emphasis from the beginning has been on modern British and European history. Unlike most history journals, *Past and Present* seldom publishes book reviews, although it has over the years served as a forum for spirited historiographical debates.

In the 1920s historians at Cambridge University believed their counterparts at Oxford University should not be the only ones with a journal, so they created the **Cambridge Historical Journal** (UK, Cambridge University Press, 1923) to complement the *English Historical Review.* The editorial board of this new historical publication would represent the liberal historical viewpoint of the post World War I historiography and contain such outstanding historians as John Bagnell Bury, the famous Egyptologist, and European historians such as John Harold Clapham and Harold Temperley.[15] Later prominent board members included Herbert Butterfield and John Harold Clapham, both eminent scholars of the eighteenth century. The *Cambridge Historical Journal* published four to five articles each issue with additional information on important primary sources that had recently surfaced. In 1958 it dropped *Cambridge* from its title to become the **Historical Journal** and started over with a new volume 1. Over the years, the journal's focus has been broadly European, with rather more emphasis on British and Commonwealth subjects.

Another significant general history journal is **Historical Research: The Bulletin of the Institute of Historical Research** (UK, Blackwell, 1923). The journal is sponsored by the Institute of Historical Research, the University of London's center for postgraduate studies in history and an important meeting ground for historians from all over the world. Similar to the *Historical Journal,* which was founded the same year, *Historical Research* reflects a wide-ranging scholarship, with much of its contents reflecting explorations into the vast expanse of British history. Each issue contains five to six articles with additional comments on primary documents.

In 1903 the Librarian of John Rylands University began a small publication to publicize recent library acquisitions and news. Within a few years the **Bulletin of the John Rylands University Library** (UK, John Rylands University Library, 1903) was the source for writings from historians all over England on a wide range of topics in British and European history. The *Bulletin* appears three times a year and often has thematic issues guided by a guest editor that contain as many as fifteen articles.

With arguably the greatest circulation of any current historical periodical **History Today** (UK, History Today Ltd., 1951) boasts over 35,000 subscribers, easily dwarfing all fellow publications. Profusely illustrated, it knows no bounds in its chronological and topical coverage, but does favor British and modern European themes. Each issue contains from eight to ten articles and there are also special sections devoted to selected historiographical debates. Rather lengthy book reviews help supplement the well-written text.

Finally, last but certainly not least, is the impressive *Journal of Contemporary History* (UK, Sage, 1966) co-edited for years by Walter Laqueur and George L. Mosse, two of the most renowned historians of the post-World War II era. Its focus is somewhat narrower than the *Journal of Modern History* noted above, concentrating more on the nineteenth and twentieth centuries than earlier eras. Moreover, the *Journal of Contemporary History* emphasizes political and military history over social and economic subjects, which makes it a more traditional journal than others of similar vintage. The format is straight-forward with seven or eight well-written and impressively researched articles—sometimes based on a specific theme, but more often not—and nothing else.

France

Of all the journals under review in this paper, probably none have had a more significant impact on the historiography of the twentieth century than the famous *Annales, Histoire, Sciences Sociales* (France, Armand Colin, 1929). Reflecting the name of the Annales School, whose founders were the incomparable French historians Lucien Febvre and Marc Bloch, the *Annales* provided these intellectual giants with ready forum for their explorations of non-traditional historical topics that moved away from great men and great events to the consideration of the daily human concerns of love, sex, and death. Later in the century Fernand Braudel joined Febvre and Bloch and added geography as another rich methodological vein to investigate. The combination of these approaches inspired numerous other journals to imitate, but seldom exceed, the rich and nuanced writings of the original. The four methodological pillars that uphold the edifice of the Annales School—geography, demography, sociology, and economics—have remained strong into the new century.[16] As for the journal and its construction, the *Annales* has a couple of features unique to it. Usually one or two essays are grouped together beneath specific topics. Thus within a single issue four different topical areas will receive attention. Also—and this is not duplicated anywhere else among the journals listed in this paper—the *Annales* will feature a set of ten to fifteen book reviews all relating to one of the subjects being treated in the issue. Thus for a particular subject the reader can examine one or two specialized essays augmented by several reviews of related new books on that topic. The *Annales* would easily justify selection as the journal of the century for modern European history.

Another important journal that takes a large view of the historical landscape is *Revue d'Histoire Moderne et Contemporaine* (France, Société de Moderne et Contemporaine, 1954), which appears quarterly out of the Sorbonne. Its purview is primarily from the 1750s onward, although articles treating the Middle Ages do appear now and then, and the text is entirely in French. French history receives its due, yet the rest of Europe and the Americas are included to balance out the coverage. Three to four articles begin each issue and 20 or more book reviews conclude it, with space allocated in between for comments on important primary sources or debates on their interpretation.

Similar in focus, but sponsored by universities outside of Paris, *Cahiers d'Histoire* (France, Comite Historique du Centre-Est, 1956) covers the last 500 years of European history with a slight preponderance of articles dealing with France as opposed to the rest of Europe. The journal publishes conference proceedings as well as occasional thematic issues—especially in the last ten to fifteen years. Normally three to four articles lead each issue plus about ten book reviews.

Germany

German historians have established two major journals to complement the venerable *Historische Zeitschrift,* all created since World War II. The first is the *Zeitschrift für Geschichtwissenschaft* (Germany, Friedrich Veitl, Metropol-Verlag, 1953), which covers European history since the Middle Ages, with the bulk of its articles dealing with the period since 1750. The journal's early years reflected the influence of Marxist historiography, but in the past decade this approach has mellowed into a more mainstream approach. The articles are in German and number from two to four each issue. There are always book reviews, sometimes as many as thirty, joined occasionally by a review essay, and some issues concentrate on a specific theme.

The other prominent German historical journal is *Geschichte und Gesellschaft: Zeitschrift für Historische Sozialwissenschaft* (Germany, Vandenhoeck und Ruprecht, 1975), which, as its name implies, focuses on the intersection of history and society. Although somewhat young as history journals go, *Geschichte und Gesellschaft* has quickly established itself as an important source for historical scholarship on Germany and the greater European countryside. Most essays treat the period since 1600, although earlier centuries are ripe for explication as well. The issues are often thematic, containing three to four lengthy articles buttressed with periodic discussion forums. There are no book reviews.

Italy

The Italians have a long tradition of historical scholarship represented in this section by one very old journal and one much newer. Similar to the

American Historical Review in approach and format, **Rivista Storica Italiana** (Italy, Edizioni Scientifiche Italiane, 1884) is the grand old man of Italian history journals. Wide-ranging in topic and chronology, the *Rivista Storica Italiana* usually has only one or two long articles—sometimes over fifty pages in length. This length is mirrored by equally lengthy book reviews, many over 1,000 words. Thematic issues appear now and then along with discussion forums.

Although a younger publication, yet clearly established as a worthy companion to *Rivista Storica Italiana* is **Studi Storici** (Italy, Instituto Gramsci, 1959). With emphasis on modern Italy, as well as modern Europe—although it also treats ancient and Medieval topics—*Studi Storici* reflects a Marxist approach to historical inquiry, especially in its early years. Each issue contains from three to five articles, discussion essays, one or more research notes, and several book reviews.

CHRONOLOGICAL PERIODS

Renaissance and Reformation

For our purposes this rather lengthy period of remarkable change in the fifteenth and sixteenth centuries will be combined into one section that considers both periods. The Reformation era is aptly treated by **Archiv für Reformationsgschichte/Archive for Reformation History** (Germany, Guetersloher Verlagshaus Gerd Mohn, 1904), which publishes articles in German and English, as well as French and Italian. Since 1951 it has been issued jointly by the Verein für Reformationsgeschichte and the American Society for Reformation Research. Most issues contain 12-15 articles accompanied by several book reviews. Of particular usefulness is an annual supplement, or *Beiheft,* that surveys the past year's literature on Reformation history.

The rich tapestry of the Renaissance is the subject of two journals, one from America and the other from Great Britain, with nearly similar titles. The older of the two, and the one considered the most prominent, is **Renaissance Quarterly** (US, Renaissance Society of America, 1954), sponsored by the major scholarly society with an interest in the period. With usually no more than three moderately lengthy articles, *Renaissance Quarterly* scans the vast stage of the fifteenth and sixteenth centuries incorporating all manner of topics and methodologies within its pages. Of special value are the 25-30 signed reviews as well as an extensive listing of books received. The proceedings of the Society also appear annually.

The British counterpart, the Society for Renaissance Studies, was founded in 1967, but not until 1987 did it start *Renaissance Studies* (UK, Oxford University Press, 1987). Each issue contains five to six articles covering the historiographical spectrum of the Renaissance with occasional thematic issues. In contrast with its American equivalent, *Renaissance Studies* has far fewer book reviews, but each is between 1000 and 1500 words.

Finally, this section would not be complete without reference to *Studies in Medieval and Renaissance History* (US, AMS Press, 1964), which appears annually. Its original purpose was to provide a forum for scholarly essays that would be too lengthy for regular articles, but still not sufficient in size to warrant being captured in a book. Each essay is between 40 and 60 pages long, and there are usually four to six of these. Some issues contain review essays, and the later volumes began including signed reviews for as many as 20-25 recent books.

Sixteenth and Seventeenth Centuries

Sandwiched between the Renaissance and Reformation and the modern era are two centuries that generate their own level of excitement with scholars. By the end middle of the sixteenth century the European world was already moving beyond the Reformation toward the post-Medieval era with the concomitant challenges modernization would bring. One of the best journals devoted to this period is *Sixteenth Century Journal: The Journal of Early Modern Studies* (US, Sixteenth Century Journal Publishers, Inc., 1970) published at Truman State University (formerly Northeastern Missouri State University). All aspects of the 1500s are fair game for this outstanding publication. Beginning with six to seven articles, the editors supplement these with a listing of a greater than usual number of new books recently published followed by over 60 signed book reviews.

The seventeenth century is well described in the long-standing French journal *Dix-Septieme Siecle* (France, Societe d'Etude du Dix-Septieme Siecle, 1948). Sponsored by the society by the same name, the journal focuses on wide-ranging topics relating to the 1600s. Each issue is comprised of from six to twelve articles, many times according to a specific theme, followed by 15-20 signed book reviews and a section recounting newly discovered primary documents.

Eighteenth Century

The years encompassed within the confines of this century were packed with remarkable change; change that has generated a plethora of solid journals seeking to explain the who, what, why, and how it all happened. Two English-language journals provide excellent coverage and are of equal quality. *Eighteenth Century Studies* (US, Johns Hopkins University Press, 1967) is the younger of the two and may be a little more oriented towards literary than historical topics. Sponsored by the American Society for Eighteenth Century Studies, *Eighteenth Century Studies* usually publishes four to five articles dealing with all aspects of the century, but especially those that reflect an interdisciplinary approach. Also of value are the forums that represent the divergent views of two to three scholars on a current controversial topic. This is augmented with a review essay and five to ten signed book reviews.

The other prominent American journal examining this dynamic century is *Eighteenth Century: Theory and Interpretation* (US, Texas Tech University, 1959). Its original title was *Studies in Burke and His Times,* but changed its moniker in 1979 to reflect a broadened chronological purview: from 1660-1880. The editors are interested in scholarship that treats British, Continental, and even American culture of the period through an array of disciplinary lenses including literary, historical, fine arts, science, the history of ideas, and even sociological. They are especially receptive to methodological approaches that reflect the most current theoretical constructs. Most issues include five to eight articles, with an occasional thematic issue sprinkled among the volumes. Many times the articles are supplemented by a review essay, but there are no book reviews.

A distinguished annual that collects solid scholarship on the period between 1750 and 1850 is the *Consortium on Revolutionary Europe, 1750-1850: Selected Papers* (US, Consortium on Revolutionary Europe, 1972). Sponsored by the Institute on Napoleon and the French Revolution, this journal—as its title suggests—wanders deep into the nineteenth century. Nevertheless, its focus is for the most part on the Napoleonic Era that wraps across the turn of the nineteenth century. Each volume reproduces much of the Institute's annual conference, which began in 1972 with six papers and within 25 years had blossomed to an annual outpouring of more than 50 papers. The proceedings contain articles in both French and English on all aspects of the period under the journal's purview.

In addition to the English-language *Consortium on Revolutionary Europe* noted above, the French produce their own impressive journal entitled *Annales Historique de la Révolution Française* (France, Institute d'Histoire de la Révolution Française, 1908). The official publication of the Société des Études Robespierristes, the *Annales Historique de la Révolution Française* offers a specialized look at the Revolutionary Era. Many issues are thematic with as many as 10 articles accompanied by 10-15 book reviews. A rather unique feature of the journal is its periodic inclusion of three to four page summaries of recent dissertation research on the Revolution. Another aspect—uncommon in the journals surveyed here—is the inclusion of abstracts of the major articles in a host of languages including French, German, English, Italian, and even Russian.

Nineteenth Century

The nineteenth century can easily be considered simply the Victorian Era in honor of the long-reigning Queen of England, who dominated British culture and society from 1837 to 1901. The major journal devoted to the period is the aptly named *Victorian Studies* (US, Indiana University Press, 1957) and one of the early journals to promote an interdisciplinary strategy for the scholarly investigation of the entire century. From the outset its subtitle referred to its desire to be "a quarterly journal of the Humanities, Arts, and Sciences," thus blending all appropriate disciplines in its pages. Three or four articles often introduce each issue, followed by a review essay and 30-40 signed book reviews. Occasional thematic issues will also appear.

The other journal assigned to this section probably would also fit in the next chronological period as well: *Journal of Imperial and Commonwealth History* (UK, Frank Cass, 1972). Reflecting the growth of interest in Britain's imperial past that developed in the 1960s, this is the premier publication in its area. Four to six articles introduce each number with occasional review essays. Some issues focus on specific topics, but for the most part thematic issues are relatively rare. From the outset the journal has reserved a section in one issue each year to describe important archival collections pertinent to the understanding of the development of Britain's colonial empire. Additionally about 30 signed book reviews appear each time.

Twentieth Century

The French seem to have laid claim to producing specialized journals devoted to the twentieth century. *Vingtième Siecle: Revue d'Histoire* (France, Presses de Sciences, 1984) trains its sights on Europe and the West with seven to eight articles, in French, accompanied by a section of short book reviews and a section that looks at recently discovered primary documents. Most of the authors come from French universities.

The warlike nature of the century just past is well reflected in another major French journal that has as its charge the explication of the wars of the past 100 years. *Guerres Mondiales et Conflits Contemporaines* (France, Presses Universitaires de France, 1951) is the official organ of the Institute d'Histoire de Conflits Contemporaines and succeeded the earlier *Revue d'Histoire de la Deuxième Guerre Mondiale* and broadened its coverage to include all wars (mostly European) between 1914 and 1962, which thus includes the Algerian conflict. More often than not the issues are thematic with four to five articles devoted to the designated theme plus another four to five articles on other topics. A nice feature is the inclusion of abstracts in both English and French, although the articles are in French. Commonly, the issue will conclude with seven to ten book reviews.

SPECIFIC GEOGRAPHICAL AREAS

Great Britain

Of the journals mentioned in the United Kingdom section above, most treat various historical aspects of Great Britain as well as Continental Europe. Nevertheless, one publication has as its entire focus the British Isles and it deserves placement here. *Journal of British Studies* (US, University of Chicago Press, 1961) is—ironically or not—published in the middle of the United States under the auspices of the North American Conference on British Studies. This gives the journal an admittedly "American" viewpoint, which can serve as a useful corrective to the perspective of the extensive batch of British historical journals that appear regularly from across the pond. Unabashedly, the *Journal of British Studies* adopts an interdisciplinary attitude in exploring the history of Albion, primarily since 1500, from a variety of angles: historical, archeological, literary, artistic, political, and sociological. Review essays often follow the major four to six articles. There are a limited number of book reviews.

France

Although there are numerous French-language historical journals treating various aspects of French history, two English-language publications represent some of the best scholarship on this region. The award for the longest title should easily go to the *Proceedings of the Western Society for French History: Selected Papers of the Annual Meeting* (US, University Press of Colorado, 1974), an annual publication that publishes the proceedings of this group dedicated to French history. The conference moves around each year and the *Proceedings* publish the editors' choices as best papers. Usually 20-25 articles appear each year, mostly in English with a sprinkling of ones in French.

Equally valuable is **French Historical Studies** (US, Duke University Press, 1958) sponsored by the Society for French Historical Studies, which is edited at Purdue University and appears twice yearly. Emphasizing all aspects of French history from all methodologies and eras since the Early Middle Ages, *French Historical Studies* prints three to five major articles, but of special importance is the inclusion of a forum in nearly every issue that contains differing scholarly viewpoints on the burning historiographical topic of the day. Also of significance for historians are the journal's annual bibliographies of articles, books, and dissertations on French history.

Central Europe

The major journal in English devoted to this essential region of Europe is **Central European History** (US, Humanities Press, 1968). Sponsored by the American Historical Association's Conference Group for Central European History this well-edited publication focuses—not surprisingly, given its title—on historical questions relating to the German-speaking parts of Central Europe for all periods since 1500. A review essay usually follows the three to four major articles, all of which are in English. But the book review section considers German language monographs for a hefty portion of its content, which can easily number between 20 and 25.

Also of significance is **Vierteljahrshefte für Zeitgeschichte** (Germany, R. Oldenbourg Verlag, 1953), which is sponsored by the Institut für Zeitgeschichte in Munich and contains essays on contemporary German history since World War II. This journal casts a wide net displaying an interest in political, economic, technical, and social history. Usually issues contain four to six articles, always in German, but the editors have thoughtfully included abstracts in English. The articles are supplemented with a section devoted to exploring important primary documents. With over 4,500 subscribers the *Vierteljahrshefte für Zeitgeschichte* has a wide readership in Germany and in the other parts of the western world.

Eastern Europe

With a title and subtitle representing three languages, the relatively young **East Central Europe/L'Europe du Centre Est: Eine wissenschaftliche Zeitschrift** (US, Charles Schlacks, Jr., Publisher, 1974) also has the distinction of being edited and published by a single individual. Schlacks decided the historical profession needed a journal that would publish research from the international community of scholars on East Central Europe, so he established one himself! And since its inception, Schlacks has been both editor and publisher. The focus is on the region between the Baltic and the Adriatic with most articles in English, although now and then ones appear in French and German. *East Central Europe* investigates primarily the period since 1700 with usually three to six articles per issue. Occasionally an issue is thematic in nature. One of the journal's best features is an extensive book review section that includes upwards of 50 reviews each issue.

Begun in response to the 1964 demise of the *Journal of Central European Affairs*, **East European Quarterly** (US, East European Quarterly, 1967) is disarmingly simple in format and layout (it takes no advertising, for example). But it has carved out a niche as one of the more important journals in its area. Usually six to eight articles leadoff each issue, with the majority of them in English and an occasional piece in German or French. Much of the emphasis is on the period since the middle of the nineteenth century. A limited book review section appears in most, but not all, issues.

Another journal with articles primarily in English (although the title seems to indicate otherwise) is **Acta Poloniae Historica** (Poland, Polish Academy of Sciences, Institute of History, 1958). Actually in its first two decades the table of contents was in French, while the articles were in French, German or English. The past twenty years or so, the table of contents has been in English. *Acta Poloniae Historica* concentrates for the most part on Polish history, with attention also devoted to the region of East and Central Europe, from the early Middle Ages to the present. Appearing twice yearly, the journal usually contains between five and ten articles along with a discussion section and book reviews. A nice feature, not overly common among the journals under review, is the inclusion of information on historical research in progress.

The major German language publication for this region is **Jahrbücher für Geschichte Osteuropas** (Germany, Franz Steiner Verlag, 1936). Like its counterparts from other countries, the *Jahrbücher für Geschichte Osteuropas* covers the region plus Russia since the 1500s. Most articles, of which there are usually three to five per issue, are in German, with an occasional outing in English. Book reviews conclude each number.

Also of importance is **Osteuropa: Zeitschrift für Gegenwartsfragen** (Germany, Deutsche Verlags-Anstalt, 1950), which as its subtitle indicates is primarily concerned with contemporary issues. The twentieth century receives the bulk of the attention with articles looking at developments in Russia, but especially the areas of eastern, central, and southern Europe. Social and political events loom large in its offerings, which usually consist of 5-10 major articles, an occasional discussion forum, and 20-25 book reviews.

Nearly every issue has a section that explicates recent archival discoveries to support future research.

Russia and the Soviet Union

The geographical significance of Russia as a major player in European history over the centuries has generated a solid core of important journals dedicated to this topic. As has been the case in other sections of this essay, the Americans and the British produce complementary journals that nearly mirror each other in format and approach. Of the two, the oldest is **Slavonic and East European Review** (UK, W. S. Maney & Son, Ltd., 1922), which started soon after the Russian Revolution. Sponsored by the Modern Humanities Research Association and the School of Slavonic and East European Studies, University of London, this is an exceedingly well-done publication devoted to the study of the entire history of Russian culture. The major articles, of which there are usually six to nine, are divided into three sections: language, literature, and history. There are not always language and literature sections, but there is always one devoted to history. Thus nonhistorical topics can be the dominant feature in many issues. Of particular value are the review essays that feature collective reviews of books on a specific theme. The 50-60 signed book reviews in each number cover publications in various European languages.

Begun when the Second World War was already underway, **Slavic Review** (US, American Association for the Advancement of Slavic Studies, 1941) has a focus similar to its British counterpart. On the whole, however, *Slavic Review* publishes a greater percentage of articles on historical topics, although literature and fine arts are fair game, too. One interesting aspect of this journal is that all authors who publish in it are expected to become members of the Association. Five to seven articles, review essays and/or discussion forums, and 50-60 signed book reviews comprise an average issue.

TOPICAL AREAS

Agriculture

As one of humankind's most ancient endeavors, agricultural history is well represented by two excellent journals—one American and one British. The senior publication is sponsored by the Agricultural History Society and edited at Iowa State University, an obvious place for agricultural topics to be researched. **Agricultural History: The Quarterly Journal of the Agricultural History Society** (US, University of California Press, 1927) is the official publication of the Society, which was founded in 1919. Its interest is in the broad canvas of agricultural and rural history in all countries, although most articles focus on agricultural themes in the United States, Canada, and other parts of the Western Hemisphere. Europe and other parts of the world do receive limited attention. Most issues have three to four articles, and there are occasional thematic issues where the number of essays can easily quadruple. Signed reviews of books and films appear, and of particular usefulness is an annual listing of new books on agricultural history.

The British peer of *Agricultural History* has a similar title, but is nearly thirty years younger. Sponsored by the British Agricultural History Society, which was established in 1952, ***Agricultural History Review*** (UK, University of Exeter, 1953) has a strong emphasis on British agricultural history. The majority of the five to six articles published in each issue deal with rural and agricultural questions in either Great Britain or the Commonwealth. Other parts of the world receive limited consideration, and the United States almost never. In addition to the 15-20 signed book reviews, the *Agricultural History Review* includes now and then a review essay, and also an annual listing of periodical articles relating to matters of agricultural history—something few other journals include.

Economics

The economic lives of peoples and countries have fascinated historians for many decades, and two very significant journals appeared in the first half of the twentieth century to document this interest. The older of the two, ***Economic History Review: A Journal of Economic and Social History*** (UK, Blackwell, 1927), is published on behalf of the British Economic History Society and, as its subtitle suggests, originally contained research on both economic and social history. Over the decades, the journal has increasingly focused on the economics and less on social questions (leaving this task up to the social history journals, of which there are plenty). Four to six articles lead each issue, with the majority looking at British and European economies since 1500, although there are occasional papers on American topics. These are supplemented with special review essays, usually historiographical in approach. Rounding out each issue are 40-50 signed book reviews.

The *Economic History Review* is joined by another publication nominally produced in England, but actually more American in emphasis. ***Journal of Economic History*** (UK, Cambridge University Press, 1941) has a British publisher, but its editorial offices are at Northwestern University and most its editorial board is made up of faculty from American universities.

Published for the Economic History Association in cooperation with Northwestern University, the *Journal of Economic History* is produced in the New York offices of Cambridge University Press. Not surprising, the journal has more articles on United States topics, although there remains a healthy percentage of essays devoted to European and international topics. With an average of six to eight major contributions in each number, there is also room for a notes and discussion section plus a review essay. The book reviews, of which there may be as many as 50, are arranged geographically and are mostly of English language titles.

Younger than the others in this section, but valuable nonetheless because of its focus specifically on Europe is *Journal of European Economic History* (Italy, Banca di Roma, 1972). Edited for over twenty years by Luigi de Rosa, who is joined by an editorial board with broadly international representation, the *Journal of European Economic History* is concerned with not only European economic events, but also how the economies of other continents affected Europe, primarily after 1500. Thus an article on the trade policies of eighteenth century Mexico and their impact on Spain would find a ready audience in this journal. Published thrice yearly, each issue begins with three major articles followed usually by a review essay or debate section where historiographical opinions are aired. Ten to fifteen book reviews occupy the last part accompanied by a rather large listing of recently received books. Of special note is the journal's willingness to publish research in progress under a section entitled "problems."

Interdisciplinary

It could be easily argued that historical writing is by its very nature interdisciplinary with borrowings from various other disciplines. Furthermore, many of the journals described in this essay accept, and indeed welcome, research that exemplifies interdisciplinary methodologies. As the flurry of new historical work began to crest in the 1960s a new journal was founded to promote the cross-fertilization of methodologies, *The Journal of Interdisciplinary History* (US, MIT Press, 1969). With an eye to being catholic both conceptually and geographically, the editors seek to publish articles that reflect the research coming from a multitude of non-historical disciplines such as anthropology, psychology, art criticism, or even numismatics, and of course the impact of the computer on research methodologies. They hope to blend these approaches, *pace* the more famous French journal *Annales,* and create a "new history" synthesis. Typical issues will include one or two articles, a research note, one or two review essays that summarize recent literature on a topic, and a section containing debate on a recent article. Finally, each issue contains 25-30 signed book reviews.

A little older than the *Journal of Interdisciplinary History,* but still avowedly interdisciplinary in approach is **Comparative Studies in Society and History: An International Quarterly** (UK, Cambridge University Press, 1959). One of the more broadly international in scope, this journal takes a comparative approach to its historiography and groups its main articles (of which there are often two or three) under specific topics in an obviously comparative sense. Thus, for example, a subject such as poverty will be treated historically from the standpoint of British, France, and Algeria experiences. By blending disciplinary approaches ranging from anthropology to political science to cultural studies theory scholars are able to create new interpretations of historical events. Each issue often includes a discussion section or review essay on a current historiographical problem. There are no book reviews.

Labor

In an attempt to fill in gaps that were perceived as appearing in the historical corpus vis-à-vis the laboring man the Society for the Study of Labour History created a bulletin to publish their own scholarly efforts in 1960. Thirty years later its title was changed to **Labour History Review** (UK, Edinburgh University Press, 1960) and has by now become the major publication devoted to exploring the lives of the "ordinary" workingman in Great Britain and the Commonwealth. Usually four to six major articles introduce each issue along with periodic review essays and book reviews. Now and then an entire issue will be devoted to a specific problem. It should be noted that the Australian counterpart, entitled **Labour History** (Australia, University of Sydney, 1962) also publishes well-written scholarship on labor topics, but its focus is primarily on Australia with occasional pieces on other Commonwealth countries.

Philosophy

The examination of the philosophy of history has a deep and distinguished lineage characterized by the two manners in which the topic is approached: (1) the philosophical examination of human history as invented mostly by Hegel, or (2) the attempt to explain what historical understanding is or ought to be, which may be more accurately called historiography.[17]

There can be little argument that the most important journal is this area is **History and Theory** (US, Wesleyan University/Blackwell, 1960). With its initial editorial committee consisting of such outstanding historians as Sir Isaiah Berlin, Raymond Aron, Crane Brinton, Pieter Geyl, and Sidney Hook, *History and Theory* quickly became the premier journal of its kind. Its focus has been broadly conceived to comprise of studies that investigate speculative and critical philosophies of history, as well as all aspects of historiography and the history of historiography. Critical theory and the always intriguing questions of time and culture also fall within the journal's purview. For forty years each issue has been consistently constructed to include a section of four to six articles (sometimes on a specific topic) and review essays, which are actually extended book reviews. *History and Theory* really has no peer in the field.

Although younger than the two titles mentioned previously, the **History of Political Thought** (UK, Imprint Academic, 1980) has a somewhat narrower focus, but still worthy of inclusion here because it treats exceptionally well the thorny topic of political philosophy. *History of Political Thought* uses a variety of methodologies from non-historical disciplines—especially philosophy and political science—to explore thinkers ranging from Locke to Hobbes to Machiavelli to Marx. Sir Isaiah Berlin was a long-term editorial board member. Six to ten articles often comprise the bulk of each issue, with review essays and book reviews filling out the rest of the text.

Finally, this section would not be complete without acknowledgment of another superb title, **Journal of the History of Ideas** (US, Johns Hopkins University Press, 1940). Affiliated with the Society for the History of Ideas, the *Journal of the History of Ideas* has as its goal the examination of the evolution of ideas and their influence on historical development. With a broad charge both conceptually and chronologically, it is also interested in the intersection of history with other disciplines both in the sciences and non-sciences. Seven to nine articles usually comprise an average issue with often one review essay. Although each journal number usually has no book reviews, it does sport an extensive list of books received in the area of intellectual history, which provides at least notification of recent important literature.

Politics

In the English-speaking world during much of the period under consideration, the major European political entity was the British Parliament—the oldest deliberative body in the world. Two basic publications cover historical aspects of parliamentary bodies in Europe. The most important of these is **Parliamentary History** (UK, Edinburgh University Press, 1982), which began publication as an annual of the Parliamentary History Yearbook Trust, but in recent years has begun appearing thrice yearly. It seeks to provide a forum for research covering the history of parliaments in the British Isles (including Scotland and Ireland) and also legislatures of both current and former British colonies. Usually five to seven articles dominate each issue along with one or two review essays and ten to fifteen book reviews.

Not quite as historically oriented, but still a significant source of historical information on both British and European parliamentary systems, ***Parliamentary Affairs*** (UK, Oxford University Press, 1947) is directed more toward teachers and students of British and Comparative Government than specialists or scholars of parliamentary government. Nevertheless, the scholarship is worthwhile and informative and consists of eight to ten articles followed by a book review section. Occasionally an issue will focus on a single topic, but this is relatively rare.

Religion

Scholarship on religion knows few limits, but we are fortunate that in the area of religious history two journals readily rise to the top. The first addresses itself to a sweeping view of all matters Christian regardless of denomination. Sponsored by the American Society of Church History, ***Church History: Studies in Christianity and Culture*** (US, the Society, 1932) takes as its responsibility the examination of the development of the Christian church since its inception in the first century A.D. The authors of the five to six articles that lead each issue are predominantly from universities and seminaries, although some practicing ministers do contribute on occasion. The major articles are joined by one or two review essays, and all of this is supplemented by an extensive number—as many as 70 in some instances—of signed book reviews. European religious history dominates this journal, with only a smattering of articles on American religious topics.

Begun eighty-five years ago, the ***Catholic Historical Review*** (US, Catholic University of America Press, 1915) is the premier historical journal of Catholicism. The official organ of the American Catholic Historical Association, the *Catholic Historical Review* not surprisingly devotes most of its attention to historical aspects of the Catholic Church and its development throughout the world. Non-Catholic history is not ignored, however, which makes this important journal a worthy companion to *Church History*. Catholic scholars dominate the author ranks for this, which is also not surprising. With three to four major articles accompanied by a review essay, each issue also produces between 60 and 70 signed reviews. A useful feature for scholars is the inclusion each year of a section noting recent pertinent periodicals arranged chronologically.

Science

The earliest scholarly periodicals from the seventeenth century reported scientific research from the British Royal Society, and this continued interest in scientific developments has created an impressive group of journals devoted to telling the story. Without a doubt, the foremost of these—and probably the oldest—is *Isis* (US, University of Chicago Press, 1912), which was edited for many years by George Sarton, a Frenchman, who was one of the leading early historians of science and who taught at Harvard from 1920 to 1951. The initial issues were in French, but soon changed to English. *Isis* became the official journal of the History of Science Society in 1924 and has been the Society's principal organ ever since. Interested in investigating the history of science and its cultural influences without restriction to region or era, the journal leads off with four to five articles supplemented by over 50 book reviews divided into sections chronologically and by subject. Moreover, each year *Isis* publishes an annual critical bibliography that is exceptionally valuable.

Several decades after the inception of *Isis,* the British Society for the History of Science, founded in 1947, launched its own publication, ***British Journal for the History of Science*** (UK, Cambridge University Press, 1962), with a *weltanschauung* similar to its American counterpart. Each issue has three to five solid scholarly articles, a review essay, and 15-25 book reviews. Its coverage is primarily European in emphasis, with a good percentage devoted to British or Commonwealth topics.

Closely allied to the history of science is its intellectual soul mate—medicine. Here the major journal is the venerable ***Bulletin of the History of Medicine*** (US, Johns Hopkins University Press, 1933). Sponsored by the American Association for the History of Medicine and the Johns Hopkins Institute of the History of Medicine, the *Bulletin* publishes articles on all aspects of the history of medicine, especially in the West. Five to eight articles initiate each number accompanied by a review essay and 30-40 signed book reviews.

Sociology

Probably more than other topical areas, this section refers to methodological approaches as much as it does to actually examining historically social issues. The Americans and the British each produced journals within a few years of each other that have social history in their titles and are, for that matter, quite similar in approach and focus.

First on the scene was ***Journal of Social History*** (US, Carnegie-Mellon University Press, 1967). Reflecting the burgeoning specialization of historical journals and influenced by the social upheavals of the decade, the *Journal of Social History* wished to provide a forum for broad-based inquiry into all aspects of social history restricted neither by chronology nor geography. Usually seven to ten articles anchor each issue, with the subject matter fairly evenly divided between Great Britain and Europe, with a smattering of United States topics. These are joined at times by a review essay and always by 25-30 signed book reviews.

A few years later, the British added their own version with ***Social History*** (UK, Routledge, 1976) with a concomitant interest in exploring events using methodologies from the social sciences. Acknowledging the influence of both the British Marxist historians and those who guide the *Annales,* the editors of *Social History* caution that historians must use sociological and other social science methodologies carefully, since these approaches in and of themselves are not necessarily sympathetic to the constraints of historical inquiry. Fewer articles appear than in its American counterpart, usually only three. These are augmented by a section that sponsors historiographical debates and also a review essay. Fewer book reviews are published as well, often no more than ten.

Another contribution from the British Isles is a relatively new journal, ***History Workshop Journal*** (UK, Oxford University Press, 1976), which has quickly established itself as a prominent publication in the field. It was initiated to report the results of social historians from Ruskin College, Oxford, but quickly branched out to include research from around the world. The editors vowed to address the fundamental elements of social life: work and material culture, class relations and politics, sex divisions and marriage, family, school and home. At first the journal added as a subtitle "A Journal of Socialist and Feminist Historians," but in 1995 they dropped the subtitle believing some scholars were uncomfortable labeling their scholarship in that way. Each issue contains two to three articles followed by critical essays. Especially interesting are reviews of popular media such as television or theater, as well as limited book reviews.

Finally, we can not leave the British part of this section without acknowledging another fine journal that has been around for quite some time. ***International Review of Social History*** (UK, Cambridge University Press, 1937) is one of the oldest of the social history journals and is affiliated with the Internationaal Instutuut voor Sociale Geschiedenis based in Amsterdam, although the journal is now published by Cambridge University Press. Focused on the period since 1800 and decidedly European in its subject matter, the *International Review of Social History* often has only three main articles each time. An annual supplement of special essays on a specific topic helps strengthen its already well-regarded historiographical coverage. What is especially noteworthy is its inclusion in every issue of an extensive annotated bibliography of recent books—in a variety of European languages—arranged geographically and thematically.

The French have chimed in with their own important journal in this area, *Mouvement Social* (France, Editions de l'Atelier, 1961). Broad-based in its approach to social history, with obvious influences from the more prominent *Annales, Mouvement Social* publishes sophisticated scholarship in French on various aspects of the social history of France and other European countries. Perhaps not as well known as other journals mentioned in this section, *Mouvement Social* is one of the top sixteen most heavily cited historical journals as reported in ISI's *Journal Citation Reports.*[18]

German historians have also produced an important journal devoted to social history. *Vierteljahrsschrift für Sozial- und Wirtschaftsgeschichte* (Germany, Franz Steiner Verlag, 1903) has for nearly a century been publishing solid research on German and European social and economic history (long before more specialized journals began appearing). Although most of the articles direct their attention to problems primarily in Germany, there is room for non-German investigations as well. Most issues have three to four articles, usually in German, but also in French and English. One nice touch is the inclusion in the 1970s of English parallel titles for German articles. Each issue also contains a primary documents section and book reviews.

Teaching

Historians take their subject quite seriously and have always been interested in guiding their young acolytes toward the goal of excellence in teaching. Two journals—one from the United States and one from Great Britain—serve the English-speaking world quite well. The older of the two, the *History Teacher* (US, Society for History Education, Inc., 1967), comes out of California State University-Long Beach and has the look and feel of a traditional history journal. The journal's goal is to provide a forum for improving history instruction for secondary, community college, and four-year college/university instructors. Each issue is divided into more sections than is usual for the subject-based publications. These sections include a general section for topically oriented articles followed by essays on the craft of teaching, the state of the historical profession, historiography, and reviews of both books and non-book materials. Textbooks are also reviewed.

Two years later the British produced their version with *Teaching History* (UK, The Historical Association, 1969). The British variant differs especially in its expanded focus to include primary history education. It is also more closely tied to the British school curriculum than the American one. With a slick appearance that is reminiscent of *History Today, Teaching History* usually has between eight and ten articles on historical topics as well as discussions of teaching techniques.

Not to be outdone by their English-speaking colleagues, the Germans have their own reputable journal devoted to the teaching of history. Although it has a jaw-breaking title—***Geschichte in Wissenschaft und Unterricht: Zeitschrift des Verbands der Geschichtslehrer Deutschlands*** (Germany, Erhard Friedrich Verlag, 1950)—the journal toils pridefully in the vineyard of both the teaching and the writing of history. The bulk of each issue focuses on teaching methods, although there also appear finely wrought historiographical essays as well as solid research articles on a variety of historical topics—mostly on Germany or Europe—with attention paid most often to the nineteenth and twentieth centuries. Each issue contains three to six articles accompanied by notes about primary documents and news of the profession.

CONCLUSION

From this survey it is readily apparent that the historical literature on modern Europe is well represented by an extensive array of excellent publications. Even if on more than one occasion the same area receives treatment from both British and American journals, there is still much to be gained by this seeming redundancy. Also, in many instances the journals serve as the official voice of an historical association. Overall the format is relatively consistent: several opening major articles followed by either a section for historiographical debate or a review essay where several recent monographs are evaluated. Since the book remains the primary and most honored vehicle for historical expression, almost always there is a book review section with signed reviews bringing up the rear.

For the past 150 years, the journal has served admirably as an effective medium for dispensing historical writings to scholars providing a sturdy methodological foundation for larger historical works. In addition, the shorter format lends itself readily as a place where focused historiographical discussions can occur within the limited confines of several pages. Moreover, the humble journal provides a place for news of the profession as well as where new book-length publications can be announced or analyzed. The mansion of history has many rooms, and for nearly every room—as the foregoing has shown—there is a journal dedicated to exploring its contents.

ENDNOTES

1. Andrew D. Osborn, *Serial Publications: Their Place and Treatment in Libraries* 3rd ed. (Chicago: American Library Association, 1980), pp. 24-30; and Donald Davinson, *The Periodicals Collection* Rev. and enlarged ed. (London: André Deutsch Ltd., 1978), pp. 19-22. For an historical overview of how libraries have sought to cope with the growth of serials, see Wayne A. Wiegand, "Research Libraries, the Ideology of Reading, and Scholarly Communication, 1876-1900," in Phyllis Dain and John Y. Cole, ed., *Libraries and Scholarly Communication in the United States: The Historical Dimension* (Westport, CT: Greenwood Press, 1990), pp. 71-87. Older, but still useful is Charles B. Osburn, "The Place of the Journal in the Scholarly Communications System," *Library Resources & Technical Services* 28 (October/December 1984): 315-24.

2. *Ulrich's International Periodical Directory 2000* 38th ed. (New Providence, NJ: R. R. Bowker, 1999). The section on history journals is found in volume 2, pp. 3552- 3720, but historically oriented publications are also found listed with subjects they treat throughout the *Ulrich's* volumes.

3. An excellent summary of the debate surrounding periodization can be found in, William A. Green, "Periodization in European and World History," *Journal of World History* 3 (Spring 1992): 13-53. See also, Florike Egmond and Peter Mason, *The Mammoth and the Mouse: Microhistory and Morphology* (Baltimore: The Johns Hopkins University Press, 1997), especially chapter three; and Donald J. Wilcox, *The Measure of the Times Past: Pre-Newtonian Chronologies and the Rhetoric of Relative Time* (Chicago: University of Chicago Press, 1987). Finally, two recent articles in the *American Historical Review* summarize some recent opinions on the topic of periodization: Charles S. Maier, "Consigning the Twentieth Century to History: Alternative Narratives for the Modern Era," *American Historical Review* 105 (June 2000): 807-31, and Daniel A. Segal, "*Western Civ* and the Staging of History in American Higher Education," *American Historical Review* 105 (June 2000): 770-805.

4. Janet Fyfe, comp., *History Journals and Serials: An Analytical Guide* (Westport, CT: Greenwood Press, 1986). See also Fyfe's shorter article directed at public library collections, Janet Fyfe, "History Journals for a Public Library," *Serials Librarian* 13 (December 1987): 69-75.

5. Edward A. Goedeken and Jean-Pierre V. M. Hérubel, "Periodical Dispersion in American History: Observations on Article Bibliographies from the *Journal of American History,*" *Serials Librarian* v. 27, no. 1 (1995): 59-74. For more on the issue of determining core periodical lists, see Kathleen E. Joswick and Jeanne Koekkoek Stierman, "The Core List Mirage: A Comparison of the Journals Frequently Consulted by Faculty and Students," *College & Research Libraries* 58 (January 1997): 48-55. An extensive listing of articles relating to citation studies in the social sciences and humanities, see Jean-Pierre V. M. Hérubel and Anne L. Buchanan, "Citation Studies in the Humanities and Social Sciences: A Selective and Annotated Bibliography," *Collection Management* v. 18, nos. 3-4 (1994): 89-137. Finally, for an insightful explanation of historical bibliometrics, see Jean-Pierre

V. M. Hérubel, "Historical Bibliometrics: Its Purpose and Significance to the History of Disciplines," *Libraries & Culture* 34 (Fall 1999): 380-88.

6. Mary Beth Norton, ed. *The American Historical Association's Guide to Historical Literature* 3rd ed. (New York: Oxford University Press, 1995). The list of journals is found in volume 2, pp. 1613-21. For an older listing of history journals, see Eric H. Boehm and Lalit Adolphus, eds., *Historical Periodicals: An Annotated World List of Historical and Related Serial Publications* (Santa Barbara, CA: Clio Press, 1961).

7. Margaret F. Stieg, *The Origin and Development of Scholarly Historical Periodicals* (University, AL: University of Alabama Press, 1986). Hereafter cited as Stieg, *Origin and Development*. This is by far the best study of its kind.

8. More on the development of the historical profession in Europe can be found in: Hans A. Schmitt, ed., *Historians of Modern Europe* (Baton Rouge, LA: Louisiana State University Press, 1971); and S. William Halperin, ed., *Some 20th Century Historians: Essays on Eminent Europeans* (Chicago: University of Chicago Press, 1961). An important synthesis of mid-twentieth European historiography by one of the century's most prominent historians is William H. McNeill, "Modern European History," in Michael Kammen, ed., *The Past Before Us: Contemporary Historical Writing in the United States* (Ithaca, NY: Cornell University Press, 1980), pp. 95-112. Finally, an excellent two-volume encyclopedia on the general subject of history and its scholarship is Kelly Boyd, ed., *Encyclopedia of Historians and Historical Writing* 2 vols. (London: Fitzroy Dearborn Publishers, 1999).

9. Although the literature on von Ranke is large, the best study remains Leonard Krieger's *Ranke: The Meaning of History* (Chicago: University of Chicago Press, 1977). Also valuable is a recent collection of essays edited by Georg G. Iggers and James M. Powell, *Leopold von Ranke and the Shaping of the Historical Discipline* (Syracuse, NY: Syracuse University Press, 1990).

10. On German historiography the standard work remains Georg G. Iggers, *The German Conception of History: The National Tradition of Historical Thought from Herder to the Present* Rev. ed. (Middletown, CT: Wesleyan University Press, 1983). A more narrow focus on the topic is found in Hartmut Lehmann and James Van Horn Melton, eds., *Paths of Continuity: Central European Historiography from the 1930s to the 1950s* (New York: Cambridge University Press, 1994).

11. Brett Fairbairn, "The Present and Future of Historical Journals," *Journal of Scholarly Publishing* 27 (January 1996): 61. For more on the journal editor as gatekeeper, see Stephen McGinty, *Gatekeepers of Knowledge: Journal Editors in the Sciences and the Social Sciences* (Westport, CT: Bergin & Garvey, 1999).

12. Stieg, *Origin and Development*, pp. 39-81 is the primary source for much of the information in this section. For French developments, see William R. Keylor, *Academy and Community: The Foundation of the French Historical Profession* (Cambridge, MA: Harvard University Press, 1975). An excellent overview is by Christopher Parker, *The English Historical Tradition Since 1850* (Edinburgh: John Donald Publishers, Ltd., 1990). Hereafter cited as Parker, *English Historical Tradition*. Another more recent book by Parker is also valuable, Christopher Parker, *The English Idea of History from Coleridge to Collingwood* (Aldershot, Hampshire: Ashgate Publishing, Ltd., 2000). For a more detailed examination of the early

growth and maturation of English historiography, see Doris S. Goldstein, "The Organizational Development of the British Historical Profession, 1884-1921," *Bulletin of the Institute for Historical Research* 55 (November 1982): 180-93. The origins of the *English Historical Review* are traced in Alon Kadish, "Scholarly Exclusiveness and the Foundation of the *English Historical Review*," *Historical Research: The Bulletin of the Institute of Historical Research* 61 (June 1988): 183-98. [The *Bulletin* changed its title in 1987.] For a general treatment of British and American- but especially British-historical periodicals in mid-century, see Esmond Wright, "Historical Periodicals in Britain and the United States," *Library Review* no. 130 (Summer 1959): 106-110.

13. The single best source for understanding the background and development of the AHA is Peter Novick, *That Noble Dream: The* Objectivity Question *and the American Historical Profession* (Cambridge: Cambridge University Press, 1988). For an interesting examination of origin of the AHA set within the framework of other professional organizations of the time, see Philip J. Giammatteo, "The Birth of American Social Science: An Archaeology of Power/Knowledge," (Unpublished Ph.D. Dissertation, University of Hawaii, 1998).

14. Stieg, *Origin and Development*, pp. 68-69. See also, Lee Beier, "Innovation and Tradition on the Cutting Edge: *Past and Present*, 1952-1994," *Historical Reflections/Reflexions Historiques* 24 (Summer 1998): 329-50.

15. Parker, *English Historical Tradition*, pp. 131-32, 148-49.

16. Writings on the Annales School is enormous. A good starting point for any serious investigation of the School and its members is Peter Burke, *The French Historical Revolution, The* Annales *School, 1929-89* (Cambridge: Polity Press, 1990). A shorter analysis, but still quite good, is Stuart Clark, "The *Annales* Historians," in Quentin Skinner, ed., *The Return of Grand Theory in the Human Sciences* (Cambridge: Cambridge University Press, 1985), pp. 177-98. More recently Clark has edited *The Annales School* 4 vols. (London: Routledge, 1999). For an extensive recent bibliography, see Jean-Pierre V. M. Hérubel, comp., *Annales Historiography and Theory: A Selective and Annotated Bibliography* (Westport, CT: Greenwood Press, 1994).

17. Roger Scruton, *An Intelligent Person's Guide to Philosophy* (London: Duckworth, 1996), p. 153.

18. Journal Citation Reports on Microfiche, Social Sciences Edition. Guide 1998: 44.

Chapter 14

Journals of the Century in Political Science and International Relations

Thomas E. Nisonger

INTRODUCTION

Politics as a topic of intellectual inquiry can be traced to Aristotle and Plato. Yet political science as an academic discipline did not emerge until the last quarter of the 19th century, when what had previously been termed "social science" or "political economy" divided into separate disciplines. The first political science graduate program in the United States was established at Columbia University in 1880 by John W. Burgess. The American Academy of Political and Social Science was founded in 1889 and the American Political Science Association in 1903.[1]

Most authorities agree the first two scholarly journals originated in 1665: the *Journal des sjavans,* published in Paris, and the *Philosophical Transactions* of the Royal Society of London—both general science journals.[2] Inevitably, journals devoted to specific disciplines began appearing during the following century and a half.[3] Regarding political science, two volumes of the "short-lived" *American Review of History and Politics* were published in Philadelphia during 1811-1812.[4] *Political Science Quarterly,* founded in 1886,[5] and the *Annals of the American Academy of Political and Social Science,* originating in 1891, have been continuously published ever since. As of 1999 more than 4,000 titles are listed under the heading "political science" in *Ulrich's.*[6]

This article's objective is to identify the leading political science and international relations journals of the twentieth century. (Whether international relations is a subarea of political science or a separate discipline is irrelevant for this essay's purpose.) The remaining sections will review political science journal rankings and the criteria used in selecting journals for this project. The selected journals will then be listed and described. A few analytical observations will then conclude the paper.

This chapter originally appeared in *The Serials Librarian* 39(3): 79-94, 2001.

POLITICAL SCIENCE JOURNAL RANKINGS

A formal journal ranking places a set of journals—typically those within a specific discipline or subject area—in hierarchical order according to some criteria for estimating journal worth. Most journal rankings have been based on citation data or the subjective judgment of experts, variously termed "subjective," "perception," or "quality" studies. Other ranking criteria are occasionally used. This section will review the major political science journal rankings, all published during the second half of the twentieth century, that were identified for this essay.

A convenient source for citation-based journal rankings is the *Journal Citation Reports* (abbreviated *JCR*). published annually by the Institute for Scientific Information in Philadelphia. This tool is organized into two parts: the *Science Citation Index Journal Citation Reports* (abbreviated *SCI JCR*) and, of major concern in this essay because it contains political science journals, the *Social Sciences Citation Index Journal Citation Reports* (abbreviated *SSCI JCR*). Various types of citation data are presented for thousands of scholarly journals, including total citations received and "impact factor"—considered by many the most valid citation indicator because it normalizes for journal age and size. For further details concerning the *JCR*'s citation data and journal ranking in general, see Nisonger's[7] text on serials management. In 1979, the *SSCI JCR* began a section entitled "Journals Ranked by Impact Factor Within Category" in which impact factor rankings are presented for approximately 50 subject areas. In the CD-ROM version first issued in 1994, one can "filter" by category and "sort" by impact factor to create impact factor rankings by subject. For this project, the impact factor rankings in the subject categories "political science" and "international relations" were reviewed from 1979 through 1998. (Note that 1998, released in the fall of 1999, was the most current edition when this article was submitted.) The number of journals in the political science category ranged from 92 in 1980 to 67 in 1995, although for most years it was in the 70s. The number of international relations journals ranged from 38 in 1979 and 1980 to 52 in 1989, 1990, 1991, and 1998, with the figure in the high 40s or low 50s during most years.

Table 14.1 tabulates every journal that has ever placed in the top 10 in the *JCR* political science impact factor rankings from 1979 to 1998 (a total of 40 different titles), while also indicating the number of times each title placed in the top 10, the top 5, and in first position. Table 14.2 presents corresponding data for the 28 international relations journals that placed in the top 10 in their category at least once during the 1979-1998 time span.

TABLE 14.1. High-Ranking Political Science Journals by Impact Factor in the *Journal Citation Reports*, 1979-1998

Title	Times Ranked Number 1	Times in Top 5	Times in Top 10
American Journal of Political Science	0	20	20
American Politics Quarterly	0	0	3
American Political Science Review	19	20	20
Annals of the American Academy of Political and Social Science	0	1	1
Armed Forces and Society	0	0	1
British Journal of Political Science	0	3	14
Comparative Politics	0	2	5
Comparative Political Studies	0	3	11
East European Politics and Society	0	2	2
Ethics	0	1	1
Europa Archive	0	0	1
Europe-Asia Studies	0	0	1
Foreign Affairs	0	1	2
Foreign Policy	0	1	1
Human Rights Quarterly	0	0	1
International Affairs	0	0	1
IPW Berichte	0	5	9
Journal of Conflict Resolution	0	7	16
Journal of Democracy	0	1	1
Journal of Politics	0	2	13
Legislative Studies Quarterly	0	1	4
New Left Review	0	9	12
PS: Politics and Society	0	0	1
Party Politics	0	1	2
Policy and Politics	0	0	4
Politicka Ekonomie	0	0	1
Political Geography	0	5	7
Political Psychology	0	0	2
Political Quarterly	0	0	1

Political Science Quarterly	0	1	4
Politics and Society	1	3	10
Political Studies-London	0	0	2
Political Theory	0	0	1
Problems of Communism	0	10	12
Public Choice	0	0	4
Public Opinion Quarterly	0	0	1
Radical Science	0	0	1
Scottish Journal of Political Economy	0	0	2
Socialist Review	0	0	3
World Politics	0	1	2

TABLE 14.2. High-Ranking International Relations Journals by Impact Factor in the *Journal Citation Reports,* 1979-1998

Title	Times Ranked Number 1	Times in Top 5	Times in Top 10
American Journal of Comparative Law	0	1	2
American Journal of International Law	4	18	20
Columbia Journal of Transnational Law	0	0	2
Common Market Law Review	0	0	1
Comparative Strategy	0	0	1
Cornell International Law Journal	0	0	1
Europa Archive	0	0	1
Foreign Affairs	4	17	20
Foreign Policy	0	1	16
International Affairs	0	0	11
International Interactions	0	0	4
International Journal of Geographical Information Systems	0	0	1
International Organization	3	18	20
International Security	4	16	16
International Studies Quarterly	0	4	18
Journal of Common Market Studies	0	0	3

Journal of Conflict Resolution	0	3	17
Journal of International Affairs	0	0	1
Journal of International Economics	0	2	5
Journal of Peace Research	0	0	4
Ocean Development and International Law	0	0	4
Orbis	0	0	1
Security Studies	0	1	1
Stanford Journal of International Law	0	0	1
Virginia Journal of International Law	0	0	5
World Policy Journal	0	0	2
World Politics	5	19	20
World Today	0	0	2

A number of methods were used to identify additional political science journal rankings based on criteria other than *JCR* citation data. The following online databases were searched: *Library Literature, Library and Information Science Abstracts, Information Science Abstracts, International Political Science Abstracts, PAIS (Public Affairs Information Service), Web of Science, Academic Search Elite, CARL UnCover,* and *Periodicals Contents Index.* The author also drew on his own previous research concerning political science journal rankings. Ten studies containing no less than 12 rankings were identified. Table 14.3 lists the top 10 journals in each of these rankings. In a strict methodological sense, one might argue these rankings are not comparable with each other because they contain different sets of journals and use different ranking criteria. Nevertheless, the rankings provide compelling evidence concerning the discipline's leading journals.

The earliest political science journal ranking identified for this review was a perception study published by Somit and Tanenhaus[8] in 1964. Every fifth member, with the exception of students, listed in the 1961 American Political Science Association *Directory* was mailed a questionnaire in 1963 asking them to rate the "prestige" of 10 journals (presumably representing the discipline's best titles) on a 0-3 scale. This method was replicated by Roettger, who asked individuals listed in the 1976 American Political Science Association *Directory* to rank the same 10 journals on an identical 0-3 scale. Roettger's ranking was presented at the 1978 Annual Meeting of the American Political Science Association and published by Lynn in 1983.[9]

One of the best-known political science journal rankings was published by Giles and Wright[10] in 1975. In a subjective approach, 63 journals were

TABLE 14.3. Top Ten Journals in Selected Political Science Journal Rankings

Somit & Tanenhaus-196[1]
American Political Science Review
World Politics
Journal of Politics
Political Science Quarterly
Administrative Science Quarterly
Western Political Quarterly
Public Administration Review
Public Opinion Quarterly
Midwest Journal of Politics
American Behavioral Scientist

Giles & Wright-1975
World Politics
American Sociological Review
American Journal of International Law[2]
American Journal of Sociology
American Political Science Review
Journal of Politics
Comparative Politics[3]
American Journal of Political Science
Administrative Science Quarterly[4]
Public Opinion Quarterly
Daedalus

Roettger-1978
American Political Science Review
Journal of Politics
World Politics
American Journal of Political Science
Public Administration Review
Political Science Quarterly
Public Opinion Quarterly
Administrative Science Quarterly
American Behavioral Scientist
Western Political Quarterly

Christenson & Sigelman-1985
American Sociological Review
Administrative Science Quarterly
Public Interest
Foreign Affairs
American Journal of Sociology
American Political Science Review
Law and Society Review
American Journal of International Law
Administrative Law Review
American Journal of Political Science

Giles, Mizell, & Patterson-1989
World Politics
American Sociological Review[5]
American Political Science Review

American Journal of Sociology[6]
American Journal of Political Science
Journal of Politics
American Journal of International Law
Soviet Studies
International Organization
Comparative Politics[7]
Slavic Review

Garand-1990
American Political Science Review
Journal of Politics
American Journal of Political Science
World Politics
American Sociological Review
American Journal of Sociology
Foreign Affairs
Comparative Politics
British Journal of Political Science
Western Political Quarterly

Crewe & Norris-1991 (Subjective Quality)
International Organization
World Politics
Soviet Studies
Journal of Latin American Studies
Political Theory
China Quarterly
Slavic Review
British Journal of Political Science
American Political Science Review
Political Studies

Crewe & Norris-1991 (Impact)
Political Studies
British Journal of Political Science
American Political Science Review
Government and Opposition
World Politics
International Organization
Comparative Politics
Political Theory

Norris & Crewe-1993 (Subjective Quality)
Ethics
Historical Journal[8]
International Organization
Journal of Modern History
Past & Present[9]
History of Political Thought
World Politics[10]
Soviet Studies
Journal of the History of Ideas

Political Theory[11]
Archives Europeennes de Sociologie
Review of International Studies

Norris & Crewe-1993 (Impact)
Political Studies
British Journal of Political Science
American Political Science Review
Government & Opposition
Public Administration
Parliamentary Affairs
World Politics
West European Politics
International Affairs
American Journal of Political Science

Nisonger-1993
American Sociological Review
American Political Science Review
Administrative Science Quarterly

Journal of Political Economy
American Journal of Sociology
International Organization
World Politics
Law and Society Review
Foreign Affairs
American Journal of Political Science

Buchanan & Herubel-1994
American Political Science Review
Journal of Politics
American Journal of Political Science [12]
World Politics
Journal of Peace Research
International Organization
Western Political Quarterly
Public Opinion Quarterly
Public Administration Review
American Sociological Review

---

[1]Table 3 indicates the publication or presentation date for each ranking, although the date was usually gathered one or more years previously.

[2]*American Journal of International Law, American Journal of Sociology,* and *American Political Science Review* tied for 3rd, 4th, and 5th.

[3]*Comparative Politics* and *American Journal of Political Science* tied for 7th and 8th.

[4]*Administrative Science Quarterly, Public Opinion Quarterly,* and *Daedalus* tied for 9th, 10th, and 11th.

[5]*American Sociological Review* and *American Political Science Review* tied for 2nd and 3rd.

[6]*American Journal of Sociology* and *American Journal of Political Science* tied for 4th and 5th.

[7]*Comparative Politics* and *Slavic Review* tied for 10th and 11th.

[8]*Historical Journal* and *International Organization* tied for 2nd and 3rd.

[9]*Past & Present* and *History of Political Thought* tied for 5th and 6th.

[10]*World Politics & Soviet Studies* tied for 7th and 8th.

[11]*Political Theory, Archives Europeenes de Sociologie,* and *Review of International Studies* tied for 10th, 11th, and 12th.

[12]*American Journal of Political Science* and *World Politics* tied for 3rd and 4th.

---

ranked according to their mean rating on a 0-10 quality scale, based on a survey mailed in April 1974 to 255 political scientists affiliated with Ph.D. granting universities. Giles and Wright also presented data on "familiarity," i.e., the number of respondents familiar enough with a title to rate it.

A citation-based alternative to the Giles and Wright ranking was published by Christenson and Sigelman[11] in 1985. The mean 1977, 1978, and 1979 *SSCI JCR* impact factor was calculated for 56 of the 63 Giles and Wright journals covered in the *JCR*. Technically, Christenson and Sigelman's study was a "rating," which presents a score for each journal, rather than a "ranking" which lists the titles in hierarchical order. Obviously, a ranking can be created from the rating scores.

In 1989 Giles, Mizell, and Patterson[12] repeated Giles and Wright's previous study. They ranked 78 journals (56 from the earlier study plus 22 new ones) using the mean quality rating from a 0-10 scale on 215 responses from a summer 1988 survey of randomly selected political scientists. The percentage of respondents familiar enough with a journal to evaluate the title was also indicated. Testifying to its influence, this study inspired several additional rankings.

The next year, Garand[13] reworked Giles, Mizell, and Patterson's data in order to present a different ranking of the same set of 78 journals. Garand ranked these titles according to what he termed "impact" (not to be confused with the *JCR*'s impact factor). A journal's "impact" was calculated by adding the mean rating on the 0-10 scale, i.e., evaluation, to the mean rating multiplied by the proportion of respondents who were familiar with the journal, termed "familiarity." This calculation is illustrated by the formula: IMPACT = EVALUATION + (EVALUATION*FAMILIARITY).

Offering a British perspective, Crewe and Norris[14] and Norris and Crewe,[15] published two different studies, in 1991 and 1993, each containing two noteworthy rankings (one replicating the subjective quality evaluation of Giles, Mizell, and Patterson, the other the impact methodology of Garand). The data for both studies was based on an October 1990 survey of more than 1,000 U.K. political scientists listed in the *PSA*[16] *Staff Directory, 1989,* to which 312 usable responses were received. In the 1991 study, 74 of the 78 journals from Giles, Mizell, and Patterson were included in the analysis. Crewe and Norris listed the top 20 journals based on evaluation of quality on a 0-10 scale (the Giles, Mizell, and Patterson approach) and the leading 20 according to "impact" (Garand's method of combining subjective evaluation and familiarity). In their 1993 study, Norris and Crewe presented rankings by both subjective evaluation of quality and by impact for a different (but overlapping) set of 90 journals.

Nisonger,[17] in 1993, published a citation-based alternative to the Giles, Mizell, and Patterson study. The 65 journals from Giles, Mizell, and Patterson for which data was available in the *JCR* were ranked according to the mean "adjusted impact factor" for the years 1987, 1988, 1989. (For details concerning the "adjusted impact factor," which addresses a technical issue in the *JCR*'s use that is not of concern for this essay, see Nisonger.[18])

In 1994, Buchanan and Herubel[19] compiled a ranking based on local citation data. Ninety-eight journals were ranked according to the number of times they were cited in the 32 doctoral dissertations completed in Purdue University's Department of Political Science from 1970 to 1989.

It is no surprise that these rankings have engendered considerable controversy. Moreover, they have resulted in debate over numerous issues beyond the scope of this essay: what do the various ranking methods really measure? What is the correlation between citation and perception-based rankings? How stable are rankings over time? To what extent are the rankings biased in favor of North American journals?

THE PROCESS OF IDENTIFYING THE CENTURY'S LEADING POLITICAL SCIENCE JOURNALS

Identifying the "journals of the century" is a daunting task. Since political science as a formal discipline barely predates the twentieth century, the titles selected here could just as well be viewed as "journals of the millennium."

To be eligible for inclusion a title must be a scholarly journal from the political science discipline. Accordingly, high-ranking journals (in some studies) from other disciplines, e.g., the *American Sociological Review* or the *American Journal of Sociology,* have been excluded from consideration as have political magazines, newsletters, newspapers, and yearbooks. Likewise, area studies journals such as *Slavic Review* or *China Quarterly* have been excluded because they are essentially interdisciplinary.

Criteria for selection of leading journals include durability, scholarly quality, impact, prestige, and position in both citation and perception rankings. The following methods were used in the evaluation and selection process: review of published political science journal rankings, core lists, e.g., Katz and Katz,[20] and guides, e.g., Martin and Goehlert;[21] inspection of journal Web sites; direct examination of journals (current issues in all cases, backruns for many titles); and the author's own knowledge plus subjective judgment. One should note that some traditional journal evaluation criteria, such as circulation, indexing coverage and refereeing status, have not been weighed heavily in the decision-making process, especially since all journals under consideration were refereed and heavily indexed.

The top three journals are identified for five categories: general political science journals, and four major subdivisions of the discipline—American politics, comparative politics, international relations, and political theory. Due to space limitations, top journals have not been indicated for other areas sometimes considered subdivisions of political science, e.g., political behavior, or related areas, such as administrative studies, public law, and international law.

THE JOURNALS

The leading journals in each category are listed and briefly described below. The descriptions depict each journal's focus and implicitly explain why they were selected. The founding date and current publisher are always noted, but previous publishers are not necessarily mentioned. The titles in each category are presented in alphabetical rather than hierarchical order.

General Political Science Journals

American Political Science Review. Published since 1906 in the United States as the American Political Science Association's primary scholarly journal, this title is, without doubt, the profession's premier journal. Its preeminent status is indicated by the fact that for 19 of the 20 years between 1979 and 1998, it ranked in first place by impact factor among the political science journals covered in the *Journal Citation Reports* as well as first in the rankings of Somit and Tanenhaus in 1964, Roettger in 1981, Garand in 1990, and Buchanan and Herubel in 1994. *American Political Science Review* (abbreviated *APSR*) covers all major areas of political science and contains extensive book reviewed. In 1997, Martin and Goehlert reported that *APSR* reviews approximately 400 books per year out of 1,200 to 2,000 submitted for review.[22] Parenthetically, when the author was a political science bibliographer at the University of Manitoba, he used this journal as a selection tool because of its book reviews. As of 1997, *APSR* was accepting for publication only 8 percent of submitted manuscripts.[23] A complete run of *APSR's* back issues are included in *JSTOR* with the exception of a three-year "moving wall," i.e., the most recent three years are not digitized.

British Journal of Political Science. Although published since 1971 in the United Kingdom by Cambridge University Press, this journal covers all aspects of the discipline and displays an international perspective. For illustration, the July 1999 issue asserts, "Contributions are invited in all fields of political science." Only 12 of the 23 Editorial Board members listed in that issue had institutional affiliations in the U.K., with six other countries represented on the Board, e.g., the U.S., France, Australia, Germany, Japan, and Norway. A similar international orientation is evident among the authors and in the topical coverage. *British Journal of Political Science* ranked among the *JCR's* top 10 political science journals for 14 of the 20 years between 1979 and 1998 and among the top 5 in three years, while ranking number two by impact in the 1991 study of Crewe and Norris and the 1993 study by Norris and Crewe. The title is available electronically through Cambridge Journals Online. The 1997 acceptance rate fell in the 10 percent to 15 percent range.

Political Science Quarterly: The Journal of Public and International Affairs. This is one of the most venerable political science journals, having been continuously published in the U.S. since 1886 by the Academy of Political Science, located near Columbia University in New York City. One of the original editors was John W. Burgess. While the content has obviously evolved during the last century, this journal combines a historical emphasis on public policy with coverage of all the discipline's major fields. The title contains a large number of book reviews. *Political Science Quarterly* ranked among the *JCR*'s highest 10 political science journals 4 times between 1979 and 1998 and in the top 5 once, while it was among the 10 journals included in the perception studies of Somit and Tanenhaus (1964) and Roettger (1978). This journal's acceptance rate was reported at 16 percent in 1997. All the backruns are in *JSTOR* with the exception of a five-year moving wall.

American Politics

American Journal of Political Science. This journal has been published in the U.S. since 1957 as the official publication of the Midwest Political Science Association. In fact, the first 16 volumes (1957 to 1972) bore the title *Midwest Journal of Political Science*. It is currently published on the Association's behalf by the University of Wisconsin Press. This title ranked within the top 5 in the *JCR* impact factor ranking every year from 1979 to 1998 as well as in the rankings by Roettger (1978), Giles, Mizell, and Patterson (1989), Garand (1990), and Buchanan and Herubel (1994). The masthead terms itself ". . . a general journal of political science . . . open to . . . all areas of the discipline," although the primary focus falls on American politics. In the past, the masthead stated "our greatest strength has generally been in American politics." The acceptance rate in 1997 was 12 percent. The backruns are included in *JSTOR* with a one-year moving wall.

Presidential Studies Quarterly. This journal has been published in the United States since 1972 under the auspices of the Center for the Study of the Presidency (originally located in New York City, now in Washington, D.C.), although Sage currently publishes it on the Center's behalf. The first three volumes were entitled *Center House Bulletin*. All living ex-U.S. presidents serve as honorary co-chairs of the Center's Board of Trustees, which also includes other important political figures, but the overwhelming majority of contributors are academics. The masthead proclaims this a "journal of theory and research focusing on the American presidency," but some articles take a historical or comparative perspective. Even though *Presidential Studies Quarterly* is not a highly-ranked journal within the entire discipline, this title was chosen because of the importance of its subject matter in twentieth century politics.

Public Opinion Quarterly. The official journal of the American Association for Public Opinion Research, founded in 1937, is published by the University of Chicago Press. Its Web site[24] proclaims this a journal "for practitioners and academicians studying . . . current public opinion, as well as theories and methods underlying opinion research." This journal is important to the study of American politics because of its coverage of public opinion regarding campaigns and elections. But, as the Web site notes, it also covers such issues as political tolerance, public policy, and political rhetoric. Some articles deal with public opinion in other countries. *Public Opinion Quarterly* was among the 10 journals used in the perception studies of Somit and Tannenhaus (1964) and Roettger (1978) and ranked or tied in the top 10 in Giles and Wright (1975), Buchanan and Herubel (1994), and in the *JCR* in 1998. The 1997 acceptance rate was 15 percent. *Public Opinion Quarterly* is covered in *JSTOR* with a five-year moving wall.

Comparative Politics

Comparative Political Studies. This title, along with *Comparative Politics* (see next entry), rapidly comes to mind as one of the two premier journals in comparative politics. Published in the U.S. since 1968 by Sage, this journal offers "theoretical and empirical research articles by scholars engaged in cross-national comparative study." *Comparative Political Studies* ranked among the *JCR*'s top 10 political science journals 11 times between 1979 and 1998 and in the top 5 on three occasions. Libraries with a current print subscription can access this title electronically through *Sage Journals Online.* The acceptance rate was reported in 1997 as between 17 percent and 25 percent.

Comparative Politics. Also published in the U.S. since 1968, this journal is "sponsored, edited, and published by the Ph.D. program in Political Science of the City University of New York." However, three of the five Editorial Committee members listed in the most recent issue are affiliated with Columbia University. The masthead states, "The editors welcome manuscripts devoted to comparative analysis of political institutions and behavior." From 1979 to 1998, *Comparative Politics* ranked in the *JCR*'s top 10 political science journals five times and in the top 5 twice. The title also placed among the top 10 in Giles and Wright (1975), Giles, Mizell, and Patterson (1989), Crewe and Norris's impact ranking (1991), and Garand (1990). The 1997 acceptance rate stood at 12 percent.

European Journal of Political Research. Launched in 1973, the "official organ" of the European Consortium for Political Research is now published by Kluwer Academic Publishers in Dordrecht, The Netherlands. The primary focus, as suggested by the title, falls on European politics. Considerable coverage is given to political parties and electoral behavior. Although not as highly ranked as the two titles noted above, *European Journal of Political Research* has frequently ranked in the top third of all political science journals in the *JCR* during recent years. Articles published since January 1997 are available through *Kluwer Online*. In 1997, this title's acceptance rate was 30 percent.

Political Theory

History of Political Thought. Founded in 1980, *History of Political Thought* is published in the United Kingdom by Imprint Academic. Its Web page[25] states, "The journal is devoted exclusively to the historical study of political ideas and associated methodological problems." Its Web site also reports that a plurality of articles published during the last decade dealt with the twentieth century, but Ancient Greece, Ancient Rome, the Middle Ages, the Renaissance and Reformation, and the seventeenth through nineteenth centuries were well-represented. The articles cover such political thinkers as Plato, Hobbes, Marx, Rousseau, Aristotle, Hegel, Machiavelli, and Mill. This journal tied for fifth place in Norris and Crewe's 1993 ranking by subjective evaluation of quality. The 1997 acceptance rate was reported as "about 25 percent."

Political Theory: An International Journal of Political Philosophy. Published in the U.S. since 1973 by Sage, *Political Theory* is obviously a leading journal in its area. This journal, according to its masthead, offers "essays in historical political thought and modern political theory, normative and analytic philosophy, history of ideas, and assessment of current work." It's Web page[26] indicates it covers Aristotle, Marx, Hobbes, Locke, Foucault, justice, liberalism, political order, modernism, feminism, etc. *Political Theory* placed among the highest 10 in both of Crewe and Norris's 1991 rankings and tied for 10th in Norris and Crewe's 1993 quality ranking. *Political Theory* is available electronically through *Sage Journals Online* to libraries with a current print subscription. The acceptance rate was reported in 1997 as in the 5 to 10 percent range.

Review of Politics. Founded in 1939, *Review of Politics* is published in the U.S. by the University of Notre Dame. The masthead states, "*Review of Politics . . .* is primarily interested in the philosophical and historical approach to politics." Its traditional strength lies within political theory. Scanning back issues reveals coverage of classic theorists, e.g., Plato, Rousseau, Burke, Aquinas, as well as contemporary thinkers, such as Isaiah Berlin and Eric Voegelin. Typical topics include democracy, communism, political ethics, freedom and authority, etc. Even though this title has apparently never appeared on a list of the discipline's top ten journals, it was selected because it is a well-established, venerable journal published for nearly two-thirds of a century by a major American university. The acceptance rate was 16 percent in 1997.

International Relations

Foreign Affairs. This journal has been published since 1922 by the Council on Foreign Relations, often considered the U.S. foreign policy establishment's elite club. Consistently high-ranking in the *JCR*'s international relations category, *Foreign Affairs* ranked in the top 10 each year from 1979 to 1998, in the top 5 during 17 years, and first 4 times. Among all political science journals, it ranked in the *JCR*'s top 10 twice and top 5 once as well as in the leading 5 in the study of Christenson and Sigelman (1985) and in the top 10 in Garand (1990), and Nisonger (1993). *Foreign Affairs* contributors include many illustrious academic, political, or governmental figures. In 1999 articles were published by Henry Kissinger, Theodore Sorensen, Richard Lugar, Strobe Talbot, and Lee Teng-Hui (President of Taiwan and the only world leader George W. Bush could name in the notorious pop quiz he failed), while Jimmy Carter and Zbigniew Brzezinski wrote letters to the editor. *Foreign Affairs* articles have actually influenced the course of U.S. foreign policy. Perhaps the best-known is the so-called X article (the pseudonym used by its author, George Kennan, who once served as ambassador to Russia) published at the beginning of the Cold War in 1947 advocating the "containment" of the Soviet Union.[27] This journal's acceptance rate was an exceedingly low 3.3 percent in 1997.

International Organization: A Journal of Political and Economic Affairs. Founded in the U.S. in 1947 by the World Peace Foundation, this journal is now published by MIT Press on behalf of the Foundation. *International Organization* ranked among the JCR's top 10 international relations journals every year from 1979 to 1998, in the top 5 during 18 years, and first 3 times. Among all political science journals, *International Organization* placed first in the 1991 Crewe and Norris ranking based on the perception of quality by British political scientists as well as in the top 10 in the rankings of Giles, Mizell, and Patterson (1989), Nisonger (1993), Crewe and Norris's 1991 ranking by impact, and Norris and Crewe's 1993 quality ranking. This title's focus has shifted during its existence from international organizations per se to the full dimensions of international relations. The journal now covers economic policy, security issues, foreign policy, and international cooperation, among other topics. During the journal's early years, substantial portions of each issue contained documents from the United Nations, its specialized agencies, and other international organizations. In recent years, issues are entirely composed of refereed articles. The 1997 acceptance rate was reported as "10 percent, almost always after revision." This title is in *JSTOR* with a five-year moving wall.

World Politics: A Quarterly Journal of International Relations. Published in the U.S. since 1948, this title is arguably the top international relations journal of the twentieth century. *World Politics* ranked among the top 10 international relations journals in the *JCR* every year from 1979 to 1998, in the top 5 every year but one, and first 5 times—more than any other title. Turning to rankings of all political science journals, *World Politics* placed in the *JCR*'s top 10 twice and top 5 once. Moreover, *World Politics* placed first in the rankings of Giles and Wright (1975) and Giles, Mizell, and Patterson (1989); in the leading 5 in Somit and Tanenhaus (1964), Roettger (1978) Garand (1990), the two 1991 rankings of Crewe and Norris, and Buchanan and Herubel (1994); and in the top 10 in Nisonger (1993) and the two Norris and Crewe rankings (1993). The journal is published by Johns Hopkins University Press under the editorial auspices of Princeton University's Center of International Studies. According to its masthead, *World Politics* publishes research, review, theoretical, and analytical items concerning such areas as international relations, foreign policy, and modernization. The backruns through vol. 47, 1995 are available in *JSTOR,* while the issues from vol. 48, no. 1 appear in *Project Muse.* The 1997 acceptance rate was 10 percent.

SUMMARY AND FINAL THOUGHTS

The 15 titles selected for this project are not necessarily the century's 15 "best" political science journals. Because three journals were selected in each of five categories, it is conceivable that an unselected fourth-ranked journal in one category could be of better overall quality than a third-ranked journal selected in another category. Indeed, one should mention the journals that "didn't make the cut." *Journal of Politics* was seriously considered for the general political science category, while *Congress and the Presidency* was under consideration for American politics. *Government and Opposition* and *Journal of Commonwealth and Comparative Politics* were considered for comparative politics, while *Journal of Theoretical Politics, Canadian Journal of Political and Social Theory, Politics and Society, Review of Radical Political Economics,* and *Journal of Political Philosophy* were examined for political theory. Unsuccessful candidate titles in international relations included: *Foreign Policy, International Security, International Studies Quarterly,* and *Journal of Conflict Resolution.*

Some basic statistical analysis of the 15 selected journals would be instructive. These titles are highly skewed towards the United States and, to a lesser extent, Western Europe. Twelve are published in the United States, while two are from the United Kingdom and one the Netherlands. It is unclear to what extent this reflects the author's own bias, a bias in the journal rankings, or a domination of contemporary political science by the U.S. and Western Europe. Analysis by date of origin reveals the 15 journals ranged from 1886 to 1980, with 7 originating prior to 1950. The fact that top political science journals tend to be of considerable age is consistent with one's expectations. Ten of the 15 are published by universities, university presses, or scholarly societies; four by commercial publishers, and one is jointly published by a commercial publisher and a society—a finding that might support those who argue non-commercial publishers offer greater journal value. Ironically, in light of the well-known penchant of journals to change titles, only 2 of the 15 have undergone a title change. One is tempted to speculate that top-ranked political science journals recognize the value of keeping a respected "brand name."

This article has discussed the political science journals of the twentieth century. However, the truly exciting question—to which the answer is presently unknown—concerns what political science journals will be like in the twenty-first century.

NOTES AND REFERENCES

1. Albert Somit and Joseph Tanenhaus, *The Development of Political Science: From Burgess to Behavioralism.* Boston: Allyn and Bacon, 1967, 18, 22-23.

2. Donald Davinson, *The Periodicals Collection.* rev. and enl. ed. Boulder, CO: Westview Press, 1978, 20.

3. Allen B. Veaner, "Into the Fourth Century," *Drexel Library Quarterly* 21 (Winter 1985): 12.

4. Bernard Crick, *The American Science of Politics: Its Origins and Conditions.* Berkeley, CA: University of California Press, 1959, 5.

5. Ibid. 28. *American Review of History and Politics* and *Political Science Quarterly* are the first two journals mentioned in Crick's detailed review of the discipline's origins during the nineteenth century, although he does not explicitly label them as the first founded and longest continuously published political science titles. As would be expected, the earliest scholarly political science publications were monographs.

6. *Ulrich's International Periodicals Directory,* 1999, 37th ed. Vol. 3. New Providence, NJ: Bowker, 1999, 5569-5719.

7. Thomas E. Nisonger, *Management of Serials in Libraries* (Englewood, CO: Libraries Unlimited, 1998), 124-34, 189-213.

8. Albert Somit and Joseph Tanenhaus, *American Political Science: A Profile of a Discipline* (New York: Atherton Press, 1964), 86-98.

9. Walter B. Roettger, "The Discipline: What's Right, What's Wrong, and Who Cares," paper presented at the 1978 Annual Meeting of the American Political Science Association in New York, NY. Cited by Naomi B. Lynn, "Self-Portrait: Profile of Political Scientists," in *Political Science: The State of the Discipline,* edited by Ada W. Finifter. Washington, DC: American Political Science Association, 1983, 95-123.

10. Michael W. Giles and Gerald C. Wright, Jr., "Political Scientists' Evaluations of Sixty-three Journals," *PS: Political Science and Politics* 8 (Summer 1975): 254-56.

11. James A. Christenson and Lee Sigelman, "Accrediting Knowledge: Journal Stature and Citation Impact in Social Science," *Social Science Quarterly* 66 (December 1985): 964-75.

12. Michael W. Giles, Francie Mizell, and David Patterson, "Political Scientists' Journal Evaluations Revisited," *PS: Political Science and Politics* 22 (September 1989): 613-17.

13. James C. Garand, "An Alternative Interpretation of Recent Political Science Journal Evaluations," *PS: Political Science and Politics* 23 (September 1990): 448-51.

14. Ivor Crewe and Pippa Norris, "British and American Journal Evaluation: Divergence or Convergence?" *PS: Political Science and Politics* 24 (September 1991): 524-31.

15. Pippa Norris and Ivor Crewe, "The Reputation of Political Science Journals: Pluralist and Consensus Views," *Political Studies* 46 (March 1993): 5-23.

16. The Political Studies Association, the United Kingdom equivalent of the American Political Science Association.

17. Thomas E. Nisonger, "A Ranking of Political Science Journals Based on Citation Data," *Serials Review* 19, no. 4 (1993), 7-14.

18. Thomas E. Nisonger, "A Methodological Issue Concerning Use of *Social Sciences Citation Index Journal Citation Reports* Impact Factor Data for Journal Ranking," *Library Acquisitions: Practice & Theory* 18 (Winter 1994): 447-58.

19. Anne L. Buchanan and Jean-Pierre V. M. Herubel, "Profiling Ph. D. Dissertation Bibliographies: Serials and Collection Development in Political Science," *Behavioral & Social Sciences Librarian* 13, no. 1 (1994): 1-10.

20. "Political Science," in Bill Katz and Linda Sternberg Katz (Eds.), *Magazines for Libraries.* 9th ed. New Providence, NJ: Bowker, 1997, 1077-1090.

21. Fenton Martin and Robert Goehlert, *Getting Published in Political Science Journals: A Guide for Authors, Editors, and Librarians.* 4th ed. Washington, DC: American Political Science Association, 1997.

22. Ibid., p. 6.

23. Ibid. All 1997 acceptance rates reported for other journals are taken from this source.

24. <http://www.journals.uchicago.edu/POQ/brief.html>.

25. <http://www.zynet.co.uk/imprint/hpt_intro.html>.

26. <http://www.sagepub.co.uk/frame.html?http%3A//www.sagepub.co.uk/journals/details/j0026.html>.

27. X, "The Sources of Soviet Conduct," *Foreign Affairs* 25 (July 1947): 566-82.

Chapter 15

Journals of the Century in Military Affairs

Robert E. Schnare
Alice Juda
Lorna Dodt
Pam Kontowicz
Carol Ramkey
Ron Dial

INTRODUCTION

The wealth of journal literature on military affairs is enormous, espe-cially in the United States. Military related journals have been published for many years and represent the thinking of military professionals and scholars on military strategy, policy, campaigns, personalities, and history. The in-formation contained in these journals is crucial to the study of military af-fairs and the history of the military services in the United States and other countries. This literature also provides individuals with a means to keep cur-rent and help in their self-development. The onslaught of the Internet has revolutionized how information is disseminated. Information is now glob-ally available from a wide variety of sources in print and online. Wherever possible, the web site for a journal has been listed so if one does not have ac-cess to the print copy, one can perhaps read the text of the journal article on-line.

My colleagues and I have selected a representative sample of what we consider critical journals for the study of military affairs. The mix is a blend of scholarly and service publications. In some cases we have not listed all the journals of a similar nature but only representative ones.

Journal selection was limited to those published in English; newspapers were not included. This meant leaving out such items as *Army Times, Navy Times, Air Force Times, Marine Corps Times, Early Bird,* and *Stars and Stripes.* Note that many of the U.S. military publications are available through the Government Printing Office. The authors labored over the

This chapter originally appeared in *The Serials Librarian* 39(4): 133-163, 2001.

choices and have arrived at a consensus of the journals that they feel have had the greatest impact in the field of military affairs over the past one hundred years.

A source that was of invaluable help in this research effort was the book, *Military Periodicals: United States and Selected International Journals and Newspapers* edited by Michael E. Unsworth, New York, Greenwood Press, 1990. The work of the editor and his colleagues in defining the numerous name changes and the mission and scope of military journals has been an immense help in compiling aspects of this article. Other information was gleaned from the journals themselves and from their web sites.

DEFENSE PERIODICALS

The following titles represent the defense periodicals that are the most significant journals covering the defense community as a whole. The titles address military history, strategy, the defense industry, weapons systems, acquisition, military law, international security, procurement, defense policy, intelligence activities, communications, and issues of interest to senior military leadership and governmental leaders.

Armed Forces & Society

Transaction Periodicals Consortium (U.S.)
http://www.transactionpub.com

This quarterly publication began in 1972 and is the definitive journal of the social sciences and the military. *Armed Forces & Society,* published at Rutgers University, is the leading interdisciplinary publication devoted to examining the military establishment and civil-military relations in all parts of the world. It is international in scope and publishes articles on military institutions, civil-military relations, arms control, and peacemaking. The editors and contributors include political scientists, sociologists, historians, psychologists, legal scholars, and economists, as well as specialists in military organization, strategy, and arms control. A distinguished list of editors includes John Keegan, Charles C. Moskos, and Allan R. Millet. There are numerous lengthy articles and reviews of professional books. The articles are scholarly and directed toward an academic audience.

Armed Forces Journal International

Armed Forces Journal International (U.S.)
http://www.afji.com/

This periodical, which concentrates on defense affairs, is the oldest of the U.S. military journals and has been published since 1863. It has a complicated history. The original title was *Army & Navy Journal,* but in 1950 it became the *Army, Navy, Air Force Journal.* In 1962 it combined with *Army-Navy-Air Force Register* to become the *Army Navy Air Force Journal & Register* and in 1964 it became the *Journal of the Armed Forces. Armed Forces Journal International* adopted its present name in February 1973.

The original purpose of the journal was to "provide accurate information to military and civilian policymakers during a period of notorious unreliability on the part of a partisan, sensationalistic press in the period following the Civil War." The magazine originally was a weekly publication that reflected the life and interests of the military community. It had national political-military news, as well as lists of transfers, births, deaths, and marriage announcements. The magazine also covered pensions, pay raises, housing, and other topics relating to quality of life issues.

As the years passed, the magazine's emphasis shifted to one reporting more political, technological and strategic issues. The magazine ceased weekly publication in August 1970 and became a monthly publication in 1971. A complete shift in focus occurred in 1973 when the magazine began to address issues of international military concern. The quality of life issues were left to publications such as *Army Times.*

In its original weekly format, the magazine gave an unrivaled picture of military life, concerns and issues for the first 70 years of the century. The magazine is still read today to keep up to date on technology and political-military issues. An independently owned publication, its current focus is to provide accurate, analytical, investigative reporting on defense affairs.

Defense

Armed Forces Information Service (U.S.)
http://www.defenselink.mil/pubs/almanac/

Published by the Armed Forces Information Service, *Defense* was first issued as the *Command Magazine* in 1978 but changed its name the same year to *Command Policy* to avoid confusion with another journal by the same name. In 1980 its name was changed to *Defense.* It is an official bimonthly publication of the Department of Defense (DoD). *Defense* ceased publication in hard copy format in 1998. Each year the title changed to reflect the new year, i.e., *Defense '96, Defense '97, Defense '98.* The purpose was to provide an overview of DoD issues to key military personnel. Each year the September/October issue was the "almanac" issue. It was an invaluable, must-have for every reference librarian. It was a compendium of important information on personnel, budget, and installations. There were charts, statistics, figures, and lists of defense-related information compiled from various official sources. The periodical has been revived in an online format at the URL shown above.

Defense & Foreign Affairs Strategic Policy

International Strategic Studies Association (U.S.)
http://www.StrategicStudies.org

This monthly journal was founded in 1973 as the *Defense & Foreign Affairs Digest,* and in 1979 changed its name to *Defense & Foreign Affairs.* In 1990 it became the *Defense & Foreign Affairs Strategic Policy.* The journal makes the statement that it is the only international, unclassified report dealing with global strategic issues from the perspective of "Grand Strategy." It is aimed at the senior national security professional involved in international security studies. Each issue contains articles on international security policy, information on significant elections and changes in governments around the world, key political transitions, tables of arms transfers, and several book reviews.

Jane's Defence Weekly
Jane's Intelligence Review
Jane's International Defence Review

Jane's Information Group (U.K.)
http://jdw.janes.com/
http://jir.janes.com/
http://idr.janes.com/

Jane's is a company that has instant name recognition. Jane's Information Group, based in the United Kingdom, is a prolific publisher of defense-related titles. In addition to several journals, it also publishes the popular annual yearbooks, such as *All the World's Aircraft* and *Fighting Ships. Jane's International Defence Review* and *Jane's Defence Weekly* provide accurate, timely information on the defense industry from an international perspective. Both titles consist of very short articles geared toward military professionals and others who are interested in the international military environment. *Jane's International Defence Review,* begun in 1968, is a monthly publication and is heavily oriented toward weapons, equipment, technology, and international security issues. *Jane's Defence Weekly,* formerly *Jane's Defence Review,* first published in 1984, has articles on various countries' armed forces, technology and industry issues. *Jane's Intelligence Review,* a monthly, was first published in 1989 as *Jane's Soviet Intelligence Review* and in 1991 assumed its present title. It is an international journal for threat analysis, and provides insights on events in the world's trouble spots.

Joint Force Quarterly: A Professional Military Journal

Institute for National Strategic Studies at National Defense University (U.S.)
http://www.dtic.mil/doctrine/jel/jfq_pubs/index.htm

Joint Force Quarterly is published for the Chairman of the Joint Chiefs of Staff by the Institute for National Strategic Studies at National Defense University. Even though this title is new to the list of military journals (it was first published in summer 1993), it is important for its macro look at the Department of Defense community and has gained the respect of military professionals. The purpose, according to the editor, is to promote understanding of the integrated employment of land, sea, air, space, and special operations forces. It focuses on joint doctrine, coalition warfare, contingency planning, combat operations conducted by unified commands, and joint force deployments. The lengthy articles are written by a distinguished group of senior military officials and academics. The journal is a well-done colorful and glossy publication.

Journal of Electronic Defense

Association of Old Crows (U.S.)
http://www.jedonline.com

The *Journal of Electronic Defense,* issued monthly, has been published since 1977 by the Association of Old Crows, Alexandria, VA. It is primarily intended for professionals in military electronics and includes articles on such topics as electronic warfare, command and control warfare, information warfare, intelligence, C^4I and related areas.

Journal of Military History

Society for Military History (U.S.)
http://www.smh-hq.org/jmh/index.html

Published by the Society for Military History at the George C. Marshall Library of the Virginia Military Institute, the *Journal of Military History* is a refereed quarterly publication. The organization (formerly the American Military Institute) was established in 1937, and has published a quarterly journal since that date. The *Journal of Military History* has undergone several name changes. It began publication in 1937 as the *Journal of the American Military History Foundation,* and became the *Journal of the American Military Institute* in 1939. In 1941 the title was changed to *Military Affairs,* and in 1989 it became the *Journal of Military History.*

The *Journal of Military History* includes scholarly articles and book reviews on topics in military history from all chronological periods and geographical areas. An annual list of completed military history doctoral dissertations is also published. Although the articles are not limited in focus to the Army, the majority of articles contained in the *Journal* deal with the Army and, for this reason, the magazine is widely read by those with an interest in the study of the Army's history.

Journal of Strategic Studies

Frank Cass & Co., Ltd. (U.K.)
http://www.frankcass.com

Journal of Strategic Studies began publication in 1987 and is a quarterly journal. Its goal is to examine strategy from scholarly, historical, and social perspectives. The publication has a broad approach and provides coverage of both contemporary and historical issues with a concentration on twentieth century western developments. It provides a scholarly look at the complicated strategic issues of the late-modern period with emphasis on military topics.

MHQ: The Quarterly Journal of Military History

MHQ, Inc. (U.S.)
http://www.thehistorynet.com

MHQ was first published in 1988 and is composed of scholarly articles on military history and military campaigns, with an emphasis on battles and personalities. Its aim is to promote popular appreciation of military history. It has an eight-page supplement entitled *MHQ: The Journal of Military History Review,* a newsletter of short articles on military history, news, and book reviews. *MHQ* is published in Mt. Morris, IL.

Military Law Review

The Judge Advocate General's School (U.S.)
http://www.jagcnet.army.mil/TJAGSA
(Click *enter here* on this screen, and, on the next screen, click *publications)*

Military Law Review has been published since 1958. It provides a forum for those interested in military law to share the products of their experience and research. The publication is designed for use by military attorneys in connection with their official duties. The journal encourages frank discussion of relevant legislative, administrative and judicial developments.

Military Technology

Mönch Central Marketing (Germany)
http://www.monch.com

Military Technology began in 1977 as *Military Technology and Economics.* In 1981 the title changed to *Military Technology.* This is a colorful, glossy, monthly publication that is focused on matters concerning defense on land, at sea, and in the air. The journal has a mix of articles on political issues, defense programs, industrial and economic aspects and the international military technology arena and includes interviews with senior defense leaders from various countries. It is similar in scope to *Jane's International Defence Review.*

MINERVA: Quarterly Report on Women and the Military

The MINERVA Center, Inc. (U.S.)
http://www.minervacenter.com

MINERVA, published since 1983, is the creation of Linda Grant De Pauw, Professor Emeritus of History at George Washington University. She created the journal as a forum to support the interdisciplinary study of women in war and women in the military. The journal presents cutting edge research done by independent scholars. It also serves as a source of information and networking tool for many organizations, and offers a wide spectrum of political and organizational views. Its strengths lie in the diversity of its editorial policies and the variety of materials it publishes: news, book reviews, fiction, poetry, oral history, and scholarly analysis.

National Defense

National Defense Industrial Association (U.S.)
http://www.ndia.org

National Defense, published 10 times a year with combined May-June and July-August issues, is a publication of the National Defense Industrial Association (NDIA). The publication first appeared as *Army Ordnance* in 1920 and was published by the Army Ordnance Association. In 1973 the Association and the journal changed their names respectively to American Defense Preparedness Association (ADPA) and *National Defense.* NDIA was formed in 1997 by the merger of the National Security Industrial Association and the ADPA. NDIA is a nonpartisan, nonprofit international association. The journal is dedicated to defense industry professionals whose interests include hardware, personnel, acquisition, and procurement. Articles are short and easy to read. Each issue includes a calendar of current exhibits, conferences, and symposiums of interest to the defense community.

NATO's Nations and Partners for Peace

Mönch Central Marketing (Germany)
http://www.monch.com

This journal has been evolving as NATO has grown. It started out in 1955 as *Fifteen Nations* and in 1961 was renamed *NATO's Fifteen Nations.* The journal became *NATO's Sixteen Nations* in 1983 and in 1998 it became *NATO's Sixteen Nations & Partners for Peace.* The current title was adopted in 1999. It presents a forum for in-depth discussion of topics of concern to the NATO nations and contains articles on the countries in NATO, NATO's defense structure, and the administration of military elements of younger transnational alliances around the world.

RUSI Journal

Royal United Services Institute for Defence Studies (U.K.)
http://www.rusi.org/

RUSI is a British professional association of the armed services and the defense community. Its purpose is to "study, analyze and debate the issues affecting defence and international security." The association is independent, but maintains close ties with the U.K. Ministry of Defence. The magazine was first published as the *Journal of the Royal United Services Institute for Defence Studies* in 1857. In 1972 the title was shortened to *RUSI* and in 1980 it became *RUSI Journal.* The publication has a worldwide perspective with medium length articles that are well-researched and has minimal advertising. For an international point of view, this is one of the best defense journals.

Signal

Armed Forces Communications and Electronics Association (U.S.)
http://www.afcea.org/signal

Signal, a monthly four-color journal, is one of the true pioneers in covering the growth and development of electronic communications and warfare. Its focus is on electronics, computers, communications, intelligence, and on imaging and information systems. The journal stresses accuracy, clarity and factual reporting on science and technology issues. It began in 1947 as *Signals,* the official journal of the Army Signal Association. That same year the association changed its name to Armed Forces Communication Association and in 1958 changed its name to Armed Forces Communication and Electronics Association. In 1948 the journal changed its name to *Military Signals* and became *Signals* once again in 1950, but reverted to *Signal* the same year. *Signal* has published articles on the concept of Command, Control, and Communication (C^3) and on artificial intelligence and continues to publish articles on the impact of technology on electronic communications and warfare.

Survival

International Institute for Strategic Studies (U.K.)
http://www.isn.ethz.ch/iiss/survival.htm

Survival began publication in 1959 and is a quarterly journal. Each issue covers a range of strategic studies issues: case studies set in a wider context. It presents the complexities, contradictions, and contentions of the post-Cold War international political system with emphasis on military and security issues, and contains book reviews of publications on international politics and security.

War & Society

University of New South Wales at Australian
Defence Force Academy (Australia)
http://www.adfa.edu.au/ajax

War & Society, a journal of the history of warfare and its impact on society, was first published in 1983 and is published twice each year by the School of History, University College, The University of New South Wales at the Australian Defence Force Academy. The journal publishes scholarly articles on the causes, experience, and impact of war in all periods of history. The journal's main emphasis is on the broader relationships between warfare and society, but it does include articles on the technical and operational aspects of warfare.

War in History

Turpin Distribution Services Ltd. (U.K.)
http://www.arnoldpublishers.com/journals/journtitles.htm

War in History began publication in 1994 and is a quarterly journal published in Letchworth, Hertfordshire, U.K. The journal accepts as a guiding premise that military history should be integrated into a broader definition of history. Recognizing that the study of war is more than simply the study of conflict, the journal embraces war in all its aspects: economic, social, and political as well as purely military. Its articles have centered on the study of navies, maritime power, and air forces, and also on military matters more narrowly defined.

ARMY PERIODICALS

The United States Army did not begin publishing its own magazines until the middle of the twentieth century. Prior to that, magazines directed to the Army audience were published by independent publishers or associations of officers and retired officers. The earliest Army-related publications began shortly after the Civil War.

In the 1880s the first of the "branch" journals appeared. These are a class of magazine directed at a group of specialists within the Army, such as the Infantry, Cavalry, and Field Artillery. Today, there are many of these journals that are official publications, issued by the different branches of the

Army and aimed primarily at informing and educating active duty personnel of those branches.

This list contains a mixture of official and independent publications from both the United States and Great Britain. Some of these magazines are distributed only within the Army; others are found in many college and university libraries. Some are historical in nature, while others focus on current developments and events. Taken together, the journals give an unparalleled view of the concerns, thinking, and military developments of the twentieth century.

Armor

U.S. Army
http://knox-www.army.mil/dtdd/armormag/

Armor represents one of the leading "branch" journals; that is, a publication that is primarily aimed at one of the professional specialties within the Army. *Armor* is the official journal of the U.S. Army's Armor Branch, published by the Chief of Armor at Fort Knox, Kentucky Training Center for the Army's tank and cavalry forces. It is also one of the oldest publications in the U.S., founded in 1888 by cavalry officers on the American frontier. The journal served as a means of communicating ideas on doctrine, tactics, and equipment to soldiers geographically separated by the great distances of the American West.

Originally titled the *Journal of the U.S. Cavalry Association,* the magazine changed its name to *Cavalry Journal* in 1922. As horse cavalry gave way to tanks, the title changed to *Armored Cavalry Journal* in 1946. In 1950, the magazine became *Armor.* In 1974, publication shifted from the U.S. Armor Association to the Armor Center.

Currently, the magazine's stated purpose is to "surface controversy and debate among professionals in the force. *Armor* authors frequently deal with problems they have encountered while attempting to implement official doctrine, concerns about the wisdom of particular tactics, useful discoveries they have made within their own units, and techniques that need to be shared with others. These articles have, in turn, stirred readers to reply, and the resulting debate has enlivened many of the journal's letters to the editor."

Today, *Armor* is a bimonthly publication sent to Armor officers and units worldwide. It contains articles on current and historical topics of interest to the Armor community, as well as reviews of publications of interest to the modern cavalry officer. The magazine gives an unparalleled look at the evolution of the Army from a horse-driven to a vehicle-driven service.

Army

Association of the U.S. Army
http://www.ausa.org/armyzine/Welcome.html

Army magazine has a long and varied history. In its current incarnation, which began in 1956, it is a monthly magazine focusing on the activities and interests of the U.S. Army worldwide. The magazine originated in 1904 as the *Journal of the U.S. Infantry Association;* in 1910, the magazine became the *Infantry Journal.* In 1950, this magazine was combined with the magazines *Antiaircraft Artillery* and *Field Artillery Journal* to become the *United States Army Combat Forces Journal.* The title was shortened to *Army Combat Forces Journal* in 1954 and renamed *Army* in 1956 to reflect the "whole Army" focus of the periodical.

A monthly four-color magazine, *Army* serves a readership interested in issues of national security, past and present issues involving land power, and future trends in the military arts and sciences. The magazine focuses on developing and presenting thought-provoking articles and analyses for a professionally oriented audience.

The organization that publishes *Army,* the Association of the U.S. Army, is a powerful group that lobbies for the interests of the U.S. Army. Many of the articles written in the magazine challenge the doctrinal thinking of current military leadership. As such, the magazine is widely read by the upper echelons of the service.

Army Quarterly and Defence Journal

Army Quarterly and Defence Journal, Ltd. (U.K.)

A British publication, *Army Quarterly and Defence Journal* is one of the oldest military magazines in the English language. It began publication as *Naval and Military Magazine* in 1827 and was renamed *United Services Journal* in 1829. The name was changed to *United Services Magazine* in 1842. Between 1842 and 1920, the journal had several other name changes before becoming *Army Quarterly* and finally, in 1958, was retitled *Army Quarterly and Defence Journal.*

This quarterly is an independent magazine published in Tavistock, Devon, U.K. that has always covered a wide range of current and historical military topics. As a source of information on British military actions, the magazine is unequaled.

The magazine continues to operate in the wide-ranging spirit of the early issues. A recent issue contains articles on the actions of NATO in Kosovo, on the German Army's plans for using information technology, and on the poets of the World War I Gallipoli campaign. It also contains book reviews, short items on international defense developments, and even a listing of contracts let by various countries for military equipment.

Field Artillery

U.S. Army
http://sill-www.army.mil/FAMAG/

This bimonthly magazine has had a complicated history. Originally published as *Field Artillery Journal* from 1911-1950, the magazine evolved into *United States Army Combat Forces Journal* with the merger of the Field Artillery and Infantry Associations in 1950. In 1954 this magazine shortened its name to *Army Combat Forces Journal* and in 1956 to *Army,* a magazine still being published. Then in 1974 the Field Artillery branch decided a separate magazine devoted to the field was needed, and *Field Artillery Journal* was reborn. The name was changed to *Field Artillery* in 1987. It has a subtitle: *A Professional Bulletin for Redlegs.*

The magazine is another of the "branch" magazines, similar to *Armor* and *Infantry,* as it is an official publication of the Field Artillery Branch at Fort Sill, OK. The articles are aimed at, and read by, specialists in Field Artillery. The stated purpose of the magazine is "to disseminate professional knowledge and furnishing information as to the artillery's progress, development and best use in campaign; to cultivate with the other arms a common understanding of the power and limitations of each; to foster a feeling of interdependence among the different arms and of hearty cooperation by all; and to promote understanding between the regular and militia forces by forging a close bond—all of which objects are worthy and contribute to the good of our country."

Field Artillery Professional Bulletin magazine is similar to *Armor* magazine in that it gives a good view of the issues considered important by the one of the Army's special branches.

Infantry

U.S. Army
http://www-benning.army.mil/dot/magazine/magazine.htm

Another of the branch specific magazines, *Infantry* began in 1910 as *Infantry Journal*. In 1930 it was renamed *Infantry School Mailing List,* when the magazine listed current books and articles thought to be of interest to the Infantry. In 1947 it was renamed the *Infantry School Quarterly* and in 1958 was renamed *Infantry*.

Infantry is a quarterly publication of the Army's Infantry School at Fort Benning, Georgia. Although the magazine is an official publication, the content of the magazine does not necessarily reflect the official Army position on issues.

Like the other branch journals, *Infantry* has articles of historical and current interest. Included are book reviews and articles on infantry trends, training methods, tactics, and operational art.

Journal of the Society for Army Historical Research

Society for Army Historical Research (U.K.)

The *Journal of the Society for Army Historical Research* was first published in 1921. It recently circulated its 300th issue. The Society's charge covers the land forces of the United Kingdom and of the Commonwealth and the former Empire, from their earliest origins. The *Journal,* located at the National Army Museum, London, publishes articles on medieval warfare and twentieth-century counterinsurgency strategy, with everything in between. There is a Notes and Documents section, which allows readers to raise questions and air new discoveries. A number of book reviews appear in each issue.

Military Review

U.S. Army
http://www-cgsc.army.mil/milrev/index.htm

Since 1922, *Military Review* has provided a forum for the open exchange of ideas on military affairs. The original publication, which began in 1923, contained a listing of articles and books on military subjects. Originally titled *Review of Current Military Writings,* it was renamed *Review of Military Literature* in 1931. In 1938 the title again changed and it became *Command & General Staff School Quarterly.* In 1939 the name changed to the current title, *Military Review.*

Over the years, the magazine evolved from just a listing of current military writings to one containing in-depth articles on Army issues. The focus is on concepts, doctrine, and warfighting at the tactical and operational levels of war. The magazine is published by the Army's Command and General

Staff College (a school for mid-career officers) and supports the education, training, doctrine development, and integration missions of the school.

Military Review is printed bimonthly in English and Spanish and quarterly in Portuguese and enjoys a wide readership both inside the Army and among military scholars. The magazine contains articles written on current and historical Army issues, as well as book reviews. A widely respected publication, *Military Review* is readily available for reference at most military libraries, research agencies, and civilian university libraries.

Parameters

U.S. Army War College
http://carlisle-www.army.mil/usawc/Parameters/

Begun in 1971, *Parameters* is a refereed journal published by the U.S. Army War College, a school for senior officers. The journal provides a forum for mature professional thought. The topics covered include the art and science of land warfare, joint and combined issues, national and international security affairs, military strategy, military leadership and management, military history, military ethics, and other topics of significant and current interest to the U.S. Army and the Department of Defense. *Parameters* serves as a vehicle for continuing the education and professional development of U.S. Army War College graduates and other senior military officers, as well as members of government and academia concerned with national security affairs.

Articles in *Parameters* tend to be thought provoking, challenging pieces aimed at the highest leadership levels of the U.S. Army and government. The magazine is highly regarded by military scholars and is widely available in many colleges and universities.

Soldiers

U.S. Army
http://www.dtic.mil/soldiers/

This is the official magazine of the U.S. Army and is published at Fort Belvoir, VA. It began publication as the *Army Information Digest* in 1946. The title was changed to *Soldiers* in 1970. This glossy, highly illustrated monthly is published under the supervision of the Army Chief of Public Affairs to provide the Army with information on people, policies, operations, technical developments, trends, and ideas. Although an official publication, not all of the views expressed are official.

The magazine covers stories on the active forces, reserve, and Army National Guard. It is widely distributed and widely read. An annual issue in January gives a review of the previous year and information on the size, structure, and bases of the Total Army.

NAVAL PERIODICALS

Early publishing efforts date back to the mid -nineteenth century, but it was not until after the Civil War that serious initiatives were undertaken to publish and circulate a growing number of naval periodicals. Some titles suffered an early demise, while others were successful over time and still enjoy a significant audience and popularity. In general terms, the periodicals sought to impart knowledge and disseminate information and provide insight into both the practical and theoretical aspects of naval service. A number among them endeavored to improve morale among the ranks and provide career-enhancing information; others focused on encouraging and advancing discussion, debate, innovation, and critical thinking on doctrine, strategy, and tactics. From a review of the periodical literature, much can be learned about the Navy as well as about its relationship to society at large.

Periodicals included here may be official publications of the U.S. Navy, or one of its service schools, a product of a broadly based or narrowly conceived naval association or interest group, or a commercial publishing venture. They may be directed to "all hands," or aimed specifically at the enlisted or officer ranks. Further, the periodical may be intended for a specific community within the naval service.

The following naval periodicals represent some of the most significant and influential publishing initiatives of the last hundred years. The list is neither exhaustive nor comprehensive. It includes several non-U.S. publications and one periodical that is no longer in existence. Each, however, has made a unique contribution to the naval literature and represents a source of important information about naval affairs and personnel over the course of the twentieth century.

All Hands

U.S. Navy
http://www.navy.mil/navpalib/allhands/ah-top.html

All Hands has undergone a series of name changes over the course of its publishing history. Originally published by the Navy as the *Bureau of Navigation News Bulletin,* it first appeared on August 30, 1922 and twenty years later evolved into the *Bureau of Naval Personnel Information Bulletin.* In June 1945, the magazine adopted its present name, first suggested by the appearance of the blue box indicating "This magazine is for ALL HANDS" that appeared on the magazine's cover in September 1943.

An official Navy publication, *All Hands,* published by the Naval Media Center in Washington, DC, is a source of news and information on Navy missions, operations, and personnel issues. Each issue presents a number of feature stories and department columns such as *Around the Fleet, Cyber-Sailor, Eye on the Fleet,* and *Shipmates.* The January issue is the almanac edition and appears as the *Owner's and Operator's Manual.* It provides an overview of the Navy and its activities and contains much valuable, practical information about ships, aircraft, and operations; it also includes information on such topics as recommended reading, useful web sites, ranks, ratings, monthly pay schedules, and pins and badges in easy to read format. With glossy covers front and back, it is rich in photographs and illustrations and totally devoid of advertising. This periodical is published monthly and enjoys wide readership in the fleet. It is truly an informative source of news and data for "all hands." The Marine counterpart is called *Marines* and began publishing in 1983.

The American Neptune

Peabody Museum (U.S.)
http://www.pem.org/neptune

The American Neptune, first published in 1941, is a quarterly journal of maritime history and arts. The articles, written with clarity and scholarly substance, are of interest to all who enjoy accounts of ships and the sea, and those who have sailed the seas for mercantile gain, in defense of the national interest, or for the love of voyaging and exploration. The articles, many of which have a naval focus, are for scholars, professionals, and enthusiasts.

The Mariner's Mirror: The Journal of the Society for Nautical Research

Society for Nautical Research (U.K.)

The Mariner's Mirror, a quarterly, has been published since 1911. The Society was founded in 1910 and sought to encourage research into matters relating to seafaring and shipbuilding in all ages and among all nations, into the language and customs of the sea and into other subjects of nautical interest. The emphasis is British but all aspects of naval history are covered. An excellent section of book reviews is in every issue. The membership secretary is M. P. J. Garvey, FCA, Stowell House, New Pond Hill, Cross in Hand, Heathfield, East Sussex TN21 OLX, United Kingdom.

Naval Aviation News

U.S. Navy
http://www.history.navy.mil/branches/nhcorg5.htm

Naval Aviation News, whose present title was adopted in 1943, first appeared in 1919 as *Daily Aviation News Bulletin.* Having undergone numerous changes in title, format, and publication schedule, it is now a bimonthly publication and is produced as a joint effort by the Naval Air Systems Command and the Naval Historical Center, Washington, DC. The focus has remained on the operational side of naval aviation and the magazine serves as a conduit of important information to the naval aviation community.

The publication contains short, easily read articles and boasts first-rate color photography and an abundance of sketches and artwork. The column *Flightbag* reproduces letters to the editor and there are feature articles as well as interviews, professional reading, and news about *People-Planes-Places.* A popular and long-running column, *Grampaw Pettibone* highlights real or potential flight disaster scenarios in the hope of increasing the level of pilot awareness and interest in safety concerns. *Naval Aviation News* speaks directly to the naval aviator and addresses events and issues of importance within the community.

Naval Engineers Journal

American Society of Naval Engineers (ASNE)
http://www.navalengineers.org

The *Journal of the American Society of Naval Engineers,* established as a monthly publication in the late nineteenth century, is the forerunner of today's bimonthly *Naval Engineers Journal.* Published continuously since 1889, it is academic and scholarly in content and focus and speaks to a technically sophisticated readership. The researcher benefits from use of the *Cumulative Index of the Naval Engineers Journal Covering 91 Years: 1889 Through 1979.*

A publication of ASNE, based in Alexandria, VA, it includes information and news of that Society, its meetings, symposia, and special events: The

May issue, in fact, is devoted to chronicling ASNE's annual meeting and exposition. The *Journal* publishes articles and technical papers on all subjects related to naval engineering. Despite the glossy color drawing or photo on the cover, however, each issue is printed strictly in black and white. It is clearly informational in intent and takes itself seriously: diagrams, charts, and tables abound. It speaks to naval engineers in their own language and is intended for that specialized segment of the naval service.

Naval Forces: International Forum for Maritime Power

Mönch Central Marketing (Germany)
http://www.monch.com

Naval Forces is a relative newcomer to the field of naval periodicals, having been published for the first time in 1980. It is a bimonthly publication whose scope is international. Its intended audience are those individuals both within and outside government "who bear the responsibility for the formulation and execution of naval and maritime policy." Maritime issues are presented and discussed in a global context in light of considerations that are political, economic, social, strategic, and technical in nature. Naval reports and features are written by specialists in their area of expertise.

Issues include signed articles and *Weyer's Warship Documentation* for a particular nation, or, regionally, for a group of nations. Issues also include articles on warfare concepts, naval programs, technology, industry, and exhibitions, notices of conferences and special events, and an abundance of defense industry advertising. *Naval Forces* is written for the naval professional and provides a perspective on naval affairs that is international in reach and outlook.

Naval History

U.S. Naval Institute
http://www.navalhistory.org/Naval_History/NH.html

The inaugural issue of *Naval History* appeared in April 1987 as a response to a burgeoning interest in the historical maritime record. The periodical was first issued quarterly, but now appears bimonthly and is published by the U.S. Naval Institute, Annapolis, MD. The Institute is a private nonprofit professional society, the same body that publishes *U.S. Naval Institute Proceedings*. Whereas the focus of *Proceedings* is clearly on the Navy of today and tomorrow, the focus of *Naval History* is decidedly historical. *Naval History* is visually attractive and contains many color photographs from the Naval Institute photo archives.

In addition to having feature articles, the publication highlights maritime museums and signals new exhibits. It presents naval history news capsules, reunion and pass-down-the-line notices, and book reviews. Advertisements abound for such items as videos, cassettes, films, books, art prints, antique maps and charts, pins, buckles, ships' ball caps, ship replicas, modeling kits, photos, and memorabilia of all kinds and readers are invited to make purchases or request merchandise catalogs. *Naval History* has wide appeal for the history buffs in both the enlisted and officer ranks, as well as for civilians with an abiding interest in maritime history.

Naval Law Review

Naval Justice School (U.S.)

Formerly a publication of the Judge Advocate General of the Navy, the monthly *JAG Journal* began its publishing history in 1947 "in the interest of true justice" and "to promote legal forehandedness among naval personnel charged with the administration of naval law." Now an annual publication issued by the Naval Justice School, Newport, RI, it "encourages frank discussion of relevant legislative, administrative, and judicial developments in military and related fields of law." The publication is academic in scope and educational in intent. Both professional and scholarly, it presents a handful of well-researched articles and, often, but not consistently, comments and book reviews, as well. Because of its narrow focus, the readership is limited, for the most part, to the naval legal community.

Naval Research Logistics: An International Journal

John Wiley & Sons (U.S.)
http://www.interscience.wiley.com

Naval Research Logistics continues *Naval Research Logistics Quarterly*, a journal whose publication dates back to the post-World War II and Korean War eras. It is published eight times each year in cooperation with the Office of Naval Research. A peer-reviewed operations research journal, the focus is on mathematical modeling and problem analysis in the areas of decision making, simulation, game theory, and probability and statistics and their applications to a broad range of military and civilian problem solving situations. About a half dozen articles are presented in each issue, and they include appropriate scholarly references and appendices. Abstracts precede the text of each article, and the presentation invariably includes an introduction and conclusion section. On occasion, a theme issue is published.

Authors of articles in *Naval Research Logistics* are drawn from the academic and defense industry communities and individuals serving on the Editorial Advisory Board and on the Board of Associate Editors are listed with their academic, think tank, or research facility affiliation. The journal is clearly scholarly and not intended for the rank and file.

Naval Review

Naval Society (U.K.)

Volume number 1 of the *Naval Review* was published at a time when the Royal Navy was without a professional journal. The *Naval Review* was issued in 1913 by the Naval Society "For Private Circulation among its Members." Those eligible for Society membership included officers who had attained the rank of lieutenant in the Royal Navy, Royal Marines, Royal Australian Navy or the Naval Service of Canada as well as the Minister in charge of the Naval Service of Canada, the Minister for Defence of Australia, and the First Lord and Civil Members of the Board of Admiralty. The purpose of the *Naval Review* was to provoke and promote discussion on such subjects as operations, tactics, strategy, administration, organization, education, morale, and other topics that had relevance to the Naval Service. The articles were unsigned so as to encourage the free exchange of ideas among officers, without regard to their rank. Today, the journal remains for Society members only, though membership has been somewhat expanded to include persons with a significant interest in the Royal Navy. It retains in part the factor of anonymity that characterized the earliest published issues. Tables of contents indicate the title of the article, but not the author. Whereas some articles are signed, others are unsigned or use initials only to identify the author.

As stated on the title page, the *Naval Review* seeks "to promote the advancement and spreading within the Service of knowledge relevant to the higher aspects of the Naval Profession." Each issue of the *Naval Review* displays its contents list on the front cover. Organization is generally consistent from one quarterly issue to the next; the publication consists of an editorial, articles, correspondence, book reviews, obituary notices, and new member and accounts lists. There are virtually no advertisements, the major exception being those soliciting Society membership. The Secretary-Treasurer for membership is Commander A. J. W. Wilson, RN, Jolyon, Salthill Road,

Fishbourne, Chichester, West Sussex PO19 3PY United Kingdom. Perusal of the *Naval Review* allows U.S. readers to broaden their outlook on naval affairs beyond that of the United States.

Naval War College Review

Naval War College (U.S.)
http://www.nwc.navy.mil/press/Review/review.htm

A professional journal published quarterly at the Naval War College in Newport, Rhode Island, the *Naval War College Review* is directed toward U.S. senior uniformed and civilian military leaders and is intended to "inform, stimulate and challenge readers, and to serve as a catalyst for new ideas." The focus is on matters of public policy as they relate to the maritime services and on global issues relevant to national defense and security policy. Each issue includes remarks by the President of the Naval War College, *President's Notes,* a number of scholarly articles, most of which are generously footnoted, several pages devoted to editorial correspondence, *In My View,* and a section called *Book Reviews,* often followed by a column called *Recent Books.* Articles are selected on the basis of their timeliness as well as on their intellectual and literary merit.

Initially called *Information Service for Officers,* the *Naval War College Review* was first published in 1948 and adopted its present name beginning with the September 1952 issue. Early issues were "restricted" and "for official use only," but today the publication is widely distributed and recent issues, as well as an index, 1991-present, may be accessed electronically on the Internet. A glossy picture or portrait adorns the front cover of the printed edition of this academic and scholarly periodical.

Our Navy

Our Navy enjoyed significant readership in its heyday that spanned the years 1907 through the early 1970s. Publication ceased, however, with the December 1972 issue, a consequence of declining circulation and advertising revenues and increasing competition from such titles as *All Hands* and *Navy Times.*

The concerns and interests of the enlisted sailor were addressed in *Our Navy,* a periodical whose early emphasis was on naval activities on the west coast but whose focus evolved into one having a broad scope. In magazine format, *Our Navy* was for many years published biweekly, but later was issued on a monthly basis. Content included human-interest stories, port of call articles, and, on occasion, serialized novels. There were book reviews, lists for promotions, transfers, and retirements, and articles on hobbies, such as photography and stamp collecting, sports, and entertainment. Personnel subjects were also included: living conditions on shore and afloat, reenlistment issues, and naval policies. Particularly helpful to new recruits were articles on naval practice and tradition. Though no longer in existence, this periodical made an important contribution to the naval literature of the twentieth century.

Sea Power

Navy League of the United States
http://www.navyleague.org/Seapower.htm

Published beginning in 1971 by the Navy League, *Sea Power* is the successor to such titles as *Navy: The Magazine of Sea Power, Now Hear This,* and an earlier version of a publication also called *Sea Power* that was first published in 1916. *Sea Power* is a monthly magazine intended to be "educational and motivational" in support of the mission of the Navy League of the United States (located in Arlington, VA) and its roughly 70,000 active members. It seeks to influence policy and legislation and to promote U.S. maritime defense interests. The focus of *Sea Power* is on contemporary naval issues and that focus is reflected in the various news columns, features, interviews, advertisements, illustrations, notices, and book reviews.

The January issue of *Sea Power* is the *Almanac* and it is a comprehensive source of information and current data on ships, aircraft, weapons, communications systems, and support equipment. A compendium of facts and figures, it provides statistics, addresses, acronyms, lists of flag officers, Navy League news, and lengthy survey articles and authoritative commentary on the Navy, Marine Corps, and Coast Guard. It is essential reading for Navy League members and for serious readers with an interest in the maritime services.

Submarine Review

Naval Submarine League (U.S.)
http://www.navalsubleague.com

The official journal of the Naval Submarine League located in Annandale, VA, this publication is issued quarterly and provides a forum for discussion of matters of interest to the submarine community. The emphasis is on policy, strategy, and tactical concerns as they relate to the "silent service," but some attention is given to historical events and current technological developments. Articles sometimes espouse ideas that are not in accord with official Navy doctrine and issues are often raised to counter arguments made in previously published articles.

A table of contents is easily browsed as it appears on the front cover of each issue of *Submarine Review*. Major divisions include features, articles, discussions, reflections, letters, and book reviews. Other columns include reunion announcements, e-mail address lists, Naval Submarine League news, obituary notices, and a limited number of advertisements. Though issues of the *Submarine Review* are not based on a unifying theme, the July edition invariably reports on the Submarine Technology Symposium and the Naval Submarine League's Annual Symposium and texts of speeches by COMSUBLANT, COMSUBPAC, and the OPNAV Director of Submarine Warfare are often reproduced in that issue. *Submarine Review* readership is drawn primarily from within the submarine community.

Surface Warfare

U.S. Navy
http://surfacewarfare.nswc.navy.mil/magazine
http://navy.mil and click on Navy Web Sites (alternative method)

A publication sporting a glossy cover, *Surface Warfare* first appeared in September 1975 under the direction of the Chief of Naval Operations, soon after the reorganization of the surface forces. Its stated mission is to disseminate information and "increase professionalism, improve readiness, and enhance a sense of common identity and esprit" within the surface warfare community. In its relatively short history, it has become a source of valuable information for its targeted audience. Features and columns highlight achievements and accomplishments of the community and articles touch on current events, as well as on historical and biographical subjects.

Recent issues provide a topical focus in such areas as expeditionary warfare, training, mine warfare, force protection, and maneuver warfare and each bimonthly issue concludes with a "SITREP" section. The publication offices are in Arlington, VA.

U.S. Naval Institute Proceedings

U.S. Naval Institute
http://www.proceedings.org/Proceedings/PRO.htm

Proceedings is a publication of the U.S. Naval Institute, Annapolis, MD, a not-for-profit professional society unaffiliated with the U.S. government.

The premier journal of the naval profession, its first issue dates back to 1874 and it has been published monthly since 1917. It has helped to shape modern naval thought and has provided an open forum for lively and spirited discussion and debate of significant and often controversial issues. Theme issues focus on such topics as international navies; the May issue, *Naval Review*, is the reference and almanac issue. *Proceedings* contains articles by naval officers, naval theorists, and civilian experts on new technologies, weapons systems, naval reforms, inspirational naval personalities, historical maritime events, and joint doctrine. Issues include columns or departments that provide book reviews, photographic essays, cartoons, essay contest solicitations and prize essays, a chronicle of world naval developments, advertisements of naval memorabilia, and notices of ship reunions and *pass-down-the-line* notices.

Comments and discussion are invited and encouraged and allow for often long-running debate on articles that have appeared in previous issues or on matters of interest to the naval community. The publication provides an intellectual forum for the exchange of ideas and a vehicle for the dissemination of naval thought and the advancement of naval interests. It is perhaps the most highly regarded naval publication of the twentieth century and enjoys a worldwide reputation for breadth of coverage and quality of its presentation.

MARINE CORPS PERIODICALS

In 1913, at Guantanamo Bay, Cuba, the Marine Corps Association was founded, with the mission of disseminating knowledge of military art and science among members, providing for professional advancement, and fostering and preserving the spirit, traditions and efficiency of the Marine Corps. Over the years the Marine Corps Association has played a vital and effective role in increasing knowledge, professionalism and esprit de corps among all Marines, not least by publishing the premier professional journals of the Marine Corps.

Fortitudine

U.S. Marine Corps Historical Center

This quarterly bulletin which began in 1972 takes its name from the motto of the Marine Corps during the War of 1812. Published at the rate of one copy for every nine Marines on active duty, it contains articles on Marine Corps history and traditions as well as news about the Historical Division, located in the Washington Naval Yard, Washington, DC. It also contains lists of new books in the Historical Division Library, and an historical quiz.

Leatherneck

Marine Corps Association (U.S.)
http://www.mca-marines.org/Leatherneck/lneck.html

In production since 1917, *Leatherneck* is the longest-running "all ranks" military magazine in the United States. For most of this century, monthly editions of *Leatherneck* have been an important part of the esprit that binds all Marines, past and present, in a common bond. The magazine's mission is "to inform, educate, benefit and raise the morale of all Marines, regular and Reserve, past, present, and future, members of their families and the public in general." With some 90,000 subscribers, including 17,000 high school libraries, *Leatherneck,* published in Quantico, VA, tells the Marine Corps story with news and information on worldwide Marine Corps activities, descriptions of bases and installations, news of the Marine Corps Reserve. It also contains articles on the history and tradition of the Corps, interviews with senior leaders, stories of successful active and retired Marines, and a letters section entitled *Sound Off,* which allows Marines to reminisce, ask questions, and voice issues of concern.

Marine Corps Gazette

Marine Corps Association (U.S.)
http://www.mca-marines.org/gazette/gaz.html

First published by the Marine Corps Association in 1916, the *Marine Corps Gazette,* published in Quantico, VA, is a monthly magazine developed primarily for commissioned and noncommissioned officers of the Corps. Its mission is "to provide a forum for the exchange of ideas that will advance knowledge, interest, and esprit in the Marine Corps." Above all, it provides for the exchange of ideas to improve the combat effectiveness of the Marine Corps. Although the *Marine Corps Gazette* provides some news and news updates, a monthly book review section, and a tactical decision game, its main focus is on articles submitted primarily by active duty, Marine Reserve, and retired Marine Corps officers. These articles address all aspects of Marine Corps life, including doctrine, history, biography, military education, joint operations, field operations, exercises, tactics, and weapons systems. Articles often result in lively exchanges of opinion, sometimes over a period of months, in the popular *Letters* section. These letters and the articles that provoked them provide an historical record of debate on issues affecting the Marine Corps.

Marines

U.S. Marine Corps
http://www.usmc.mil/marines.nsf

Marines, which began publication in 1971, is the official magazine of the U.S. Marine Corps. Formerly a monthly, *Marines* began quarterly publication in 2000. This glossy, highly illustrated journal is published by the Division of Public Affairs, Marine Corps News Branch, Washington, DC, to keep Marines informed about current Marine Corps plans, policies, operations, technical developments, trends, activities, and ideas. It is distributed at a rate of one for every five Marines. Each year the final issue includes an Almanac with information on Marine Corps organization and units worldwide.

AIR FORCE AND AVIATION PERIODICALS

The United States Air Force (USAF) commemorated its 50th anniversary in 1997. However, long before the USAF existed as a separate service, its noble lineage began in the Army. The Aeronautical Division of the U.S. Army Signal Corps, forerunner of the U.S. Air Force, was established August 1, 1907. By August 2, 1909, the Army had purchased its first airplane from the Wright Brothers for $25,000, plus a $5,000 bonus because the machine exceeded the speed requirement of 40 mph.

The Army Air Service (1907) was the progenitor of the Army Air Corps (1926). In turn, the Army Air Corps gave way to the Army Air Force (1941). Air strategy and air power had advanced significantly by the end of World War II. On September 18, 1947, the U.S. Air Force was established as a separate service.

Historically, the body of publishing in periodicals about aeronautics, astronautics, and space exploration can be considered a twentieth century phenomenon. From the most technical journals on air power usage to general aviation enthusiast magazines, a legacy of publishing longevity is found throughout the last century. One can witness among these periodicals the development of the "world's greatest aerospace power" through the people, words, doctrine, dissertations and human fact, as well as fiction, on the subject of aviation.

Many periodicals found here represent the official position of the U.S. Air Force or its attendant organizations. Basically, there are air associations, corporations, and government/military agencies that, as a result of air power development, grew up with the USAF. Their contributions document and lend support to air services that have enhanced the world in peace and war.

Aerospace Power Journal

Air University (U.S.)
http://www.airpower.maxwell.af.mil

Aerospace Power Journal, published quarterly, is the professional flagship publication of the United States Air Force. It is designed to serve as an open forum for the presentation and stimulation of innovative thinking on military doctrine, strategy, tactics, force structure, readiness, and other matters of national defense.

General Muir S. Fairchild's wish for a journal to underpin air power doctrine studied at Air University was realized with the publication of *Air University Quarterly Review* in 1947. Initially, AU faculty members were required to submit one article each year to the new journal. Contributors to the journal had broad discretion on subject matter and quality increased exponentially.

Air University Review was the title change made in 1963. The publishing schedule also changed to six times per year. *Air University Review* ceased publication in 1985, but reappeared in 1987 as *Airpower Journal.* The idea behind starting anew was to reclaim the doctrinal high ground in the discussion on aerospace power. Space assets and their use in the last few conflicts warranted a new title change and *Aerospace Power Journal* appeared with the Winter 1999 issue.

The main emphasis is on feature articles. *Vortices* provides a forum for short essays. *Net Assessment* is the name for the book review section. *Aerospace Power Journal* also publishes an international edition. Printed in both Spanish and Portuguese, these journals are not identical to the English edition. Their focus is Latin America and Brazil, respectively.

Air Force Journal of Logistics

U.S. Air Force
http://www.il.hq.af.mil/aflma/lgj/Afjlhome.html

Air Force Journal of Logistics (AFJL), published at Maxwell AFB, AL, is the Air Force's only professional journal for logistics and engineering. It provides an open forum for presenting research, innovative thinking, ideas, and issues of concern to the entire Air Force logistics community.

AFJL prints a mix of features on logistical history, current policy, activity coordination, lessons learned and studies on logistical programs. Articles are contributed by the general DoD populace and by individuals doing research in logistics. Footnotes normally accompany each major article. Several departments add to the magazine article content. *Candid Voices* taps high-ranking logistics specialists. The *Inside Logistics* department explores current software technology. *Personnel Career Information* talks briefly of the skills and criteria necessary for the logistics world. *Logistics Research* updates airmen on recent research efforts and breakthroughs.

AFJL has seen only one title name change. In 1977, the galley print produced the first issues as *Pipeline,* but *AFJL* has been the title since 1980. This is a serious and polished quarterly periodical on logistics.

Air Force Law Review

U.S. Air Force Judge Advocate General School (CPD/JA)
http://aflsa.jag.af.mil/jagschool/pubs

The Air Force Judge Advocate General publishes this military law journal semiannually. Sponsored by the Air Force Judge Advocate General School, located at Maxwell AFB, AL, *Air Force Law Review* provides a forum for the exchange of legal ideas, experiences, and information. It surveys legislative, administrative, and judicial developments for military and defense related fields. While the publication is officially sanctioned, the magazine disclaims any opinions, policies, or views that purport to represent the Air Force or U.S. government.

Articles are presented exhaustively on a myriad of legal subjects in a hornbook or treatise-like manner. The *Notes and Comments* section does not require a lengthy manuscript, but this section is subjected to the same review process as is the article section. This is a professional journal. Most, if not all, contributions emanate from attorneys or judge advocates.

The publishing effort was launched as the *United States Air Force JAG Law Bulletin* in 1959. In 1964 its title changed to *United States Air Force JAG Law Review.* After a decade, it was renamed *Air Force Law Review.*

Air Force Magazine

Air Force Association (U.S.)
http://www.afa.org

Air Force Magazine, a monthly publication, is easily considered one of the leading voices of defense magazines. From its early beginnings as a newsletter issued by the Army Air Service in 1918, *Air Force Magazine* has survived several title changes. Emerging as *Air Corps News Letter (ACNL)* in 1927, articles stressed the role of the Air Force to support land-based forces. *Air Force News Letter* became the title in 1941 as the publication migrated from a newsletter to magazine format. Still another title change occurred in 1942, when the journal became *Air Force: Official Service Journal of the U.S. Army Forces*. In 1946 the Air Force Association (AFA) was founded in Arlington, VA, and eventually assumed publishing responsibility and editorial control of *Air Force Magazine*. The AFA had a membership well over 100,000 around 1950. This group, along with the general Air Force community, swelled circulation and readership significantly.

Special issues and supplements to *Air Force Magazine* have been introduced over the years and these have included the still popular *Air Force Almanac*, supplements to *Jane's All the World's Aircraft*, and *Space Almanac*. Today, *Air Force Magazine* includes features such as *Aerospace World, Unit Histories*, and *Pieces of History* and *Valor*. Major articles run the gamut of aerospace and aviation topics. The almanac issue is published in May.

Air Power History

Air Force Historical Foundation (U.S.)
http://www.andrews.af.mil/tenants/historic/historic.htm

The primary focus of this scholarly quarterly periodical is the preservation and perpetuation of aerospace, aviation, and space science history. The majority of articles focus on military aviation. The Air Force Historical Foundation located at Andrews AFB, MD issued the first copy as *Air Power Historian* in 1954. In 1989 the title was changed to *Air Power History*. The *History Mystery* section, which challenges one to identify historic aircraft, is a readership favorite. Other sections include book reviews, news, reunions, notices, and the readers' forum.

Airman

U.S. Air Force
http://www.af.mil/news/airman

Airman, established in 1951, is an official monthly magazine of the U.S. Air Force and is sponsored by the Secretary of the Air Force, Office of Public Affairs, Kelly AFB, TX. It is targeted at Air Force enlisted personnel. Building morale and offering airmen human interest stories are two key ingredients of this publication. *Airman* coverage places special focus on people, operations, and equipment.

Airman conveys the "Team Air Force" message. Whether it is one's physical health, job growth or status, or recreation pleasures, the magazine tries to reach every member. *Airman* uses a glossy publication format with lots of color photography. Articles rarely stretch beyond two pages and the magazine averages around fifty pages in length.

Aviation Week & Space Technology

McGraw-Hill Companies (U.S.)
http://www.aviationnow.com/

Aviation Week & Space Technology, a weekly, is the world's leading trade publication for the aerospace industry. The publication started in 1916 as *Aviation and Aeronautical Engineering,* and in 1920 changed its name to *Aviation and Aircraft Journal.* In 1922 it changed to *Aviation* and in 1947 it became *Aviation Week.* In the space era, in 1960, it became *Aviation Week & Space Technology.* Its coverage of military aviation and space technology of all nations is primarily from an industrial point of view. The journal provides indispensable coverage of the continually evolving field of aeronautics.

USAF Weapons Review

U.S. Air Force
http://www.nellis.af.mil/usafws/

The USAF Weapons School, headquartered at Nellis AFB, Nevada, teaches graduate level instructor courses that provide the world's most advanced training in weapons and tactics to officers of the combat air forces. The *USAF Weapons Review,* sponsored by the Weapons School, provides a forum for the exchange of fact and opinion on weaponry and tactics.

The *Weapons Review* spans the entire history of the USAF Weapons School. Begun in 1951 as the *Fighter Gunnery Newsletter,* it has been in continuous publication, except during 1952 and 1953 when the entire Nellis organization focused on training fighter crews in support of the Korean War effort. In 1972 the *Fighter Gunnery Newsletter* changed from a command publication, with limited assets and distribution, to a Department of the Air Force recurring publication. Consequently, the name changed to the *USAF Fighter Weapons Review.* In 1992 the name was changed to the *USAF Weapons Review* as a result of the addition of two bomber divisions to the Weapons School.

The quarterly magazine supplies up-to-date information on procedures, tactics, weapons, and more. It provides the latest information on combat capabilities within Air Combat Command and serves as a forum for new ideas by writers throughout the Air Force. Students and instructors at the Weapons School write the majority of the articles.

World-class artwork, drawings, and graphics package this sophisticated review. The publication offers both practical and theoretical articles, replete with charts and diagrams, to inform aircrews about changing tactics and weapons.

World Air Power Journal

Aerospace Publishing Ltd. (U.K.)
http://www.airpower.co.uk

World Air Power Journal was established in 1990 and is published quarterly. It deals exclusively with contemporary military aviation. Each issue covers aircraft, weapons and systems, and air arms and operations, worldwide. It carries no advertisements and the articles are in-depth and in full color. The *Journal* serves as a constantly updated reference source for anyone interested in military aviation.

CLUSTER V:
PHYSICAL SCIENCES
AND ENGINEERING

Today, mathematical formulas, computer algorithms, and the shared use of English in written communication bind the communities of this cluster together, much more than disparate ideologies and differing languages divided it before World War II. Even though the technical organizations and publications of all the Allies certainly contributed to victory over the former world scientific leader, German, British, and American groups got to reap most of the benefits during the first two decades after the war. Both the U.K. and the United States featured a single dominant national research or professional body for each of the major physical sciences and engineering disciplines. Each of these societies had an equally impressive publishing arm, and these were not successfully challenged until the explosion of subspecialty publishing in the 1970s. Even after, Anglo-American engineering societies lost little ground because the rate of new births in engineering specialties was more gradual, except in electrical and electronics engineering. There, the U.S.-based Institute of Electrical & Electronics Engineers took no chances and became the poster child of pre-emptive launching of new subspecialty titles.

But in the basic sciences, most revisions to journal line-ups came from the Dutch-Nordic-German for-profit sector, which had both its best geographic and best sector-of-publishing representation in this physical sciences and engineering cluster. It should be noted that even the Jewish refugees from North and Central Europe played a particularly crucial role in for-profit publishing in both the United States (the Johnsons of Academic Press, originally from Germany) and the U.K. (Robert Maxwell of Pergamon, originally from what is now the Czech Republic). By century's end, American society titles still won most of the gold medals, but continental "Euro" for-profits like Elsevier and Springer actually took many more of the silver and bronzes, giving the official British journals a run for their money.

The continental for-profits also forged transnational European alliance journals which they co-published in English, with coalitions of non-English-speaking national societies. This joint venture approach was also embraced by Wiley, an old-line American firm that took an interest in some economically faltering if still prestigious German organizations. Blackwell and Taylor & Francis succeeded on a somewhat smaller scale, but often with similar strategies.

Despite the fact that university libraries complained loudly and bitterly about the numbers and costs of journals in this cluster, university presses, by and large, were not significant contributors of physical science and engineering journals. Nonetheless, Oxford, Cambridge, and Chicago published multiple notable entries in mathematics, astrophysics, and geology, sometimes in cooperation with societies.

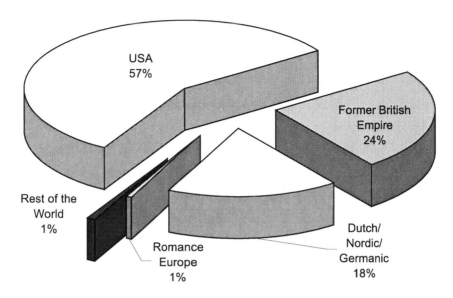

Breakdown by Region

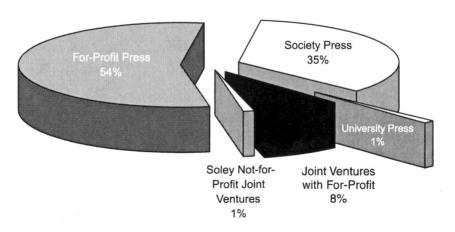

Breakdown by Publishing Sector

Chapter 16

Journals of the Century in the Basic Sciences, Part I: Mathematics and the Physical Sciences

Tony Stankus

THE PLAN OF THE CHAPTER

I propose to nominate, with a few exceptions, no more than three titles as most influential journals of the century in each of the major scientific disciplines and their most important specialties and subspecialties. I regard a science journal as having become genuinely influential when, over the course of decades within this century, and in a geographic area spanning several countries or a continent, the best authors with a journal manuscript on a topic, and the most motivated readers in search of journal information on the topic, consistently went to the same journal as their first choice to satisfy their needs.

WHY MORE THAN ONE JOURNAL AS BEST?

Now that this century is coming to an end, would it not be possible to name only the single best journal worldwide in each field? It is arguably possible, but no matter how many fields were covered, or how long such a list was, it would be strangely incomplete and biased unduly to the last decade or two. Any such list would be lacking in important nuances that reflect the history and geography of science that unfolded over the whole of these last one hundred years. Few if any of today's leading science journals got to be great without predecessors who carved out a niche for them, or ongoing competitors, who tested and sometimes bested them for sustained periods in scientifically active regions apart from their home base.

This chapter originally appeared in *The Serials Librarian* 39(1): 81-122, 2000.

HOW AND WHY REGIONAL
AND NATIONAL SCIENCE JOURNALS
SOMETIMES BECAME INTERNATIONAL LEADERS

Up to the mid-19th century, most scientific journals made their reputations primarily within their own country of publication. Many were founded by regional societies of science located in university towns or provincial cities. Others were organs of royal academies based in the national capital. Many of these groups were relatively unspecialized, covering all types of science. It may seem surprising, but relatively unschooled representatives of the prosperous merchant and industrial classes, and government officials or the old nobility were allowed to join the regional societies as financial patrons or political protectors. Royals and bureaucrats had particular influence over the national academies, particularly in Continental Europe. (Colbert, Louis XIV's finance minister, was the founder of the French Academy of Sciences.) Indeed, elevation to most national academies was akin to being awarded a knighthood by the king. Inaugurations of new members were court ceremonies. New academicians were indeed often well qualified, but also tended to be chosen from among the oldest and least controversial professors. They tended to be scientists who had advised the government, or headed up an education or health ministry. Academy membership often included a generous royal pension, a medallion on a sash, and access to academy headquarters with an excellent library. Most importantly for journal history, academicians were also generally given the exclusive right to publish their papers in the national academy's periodical.

Young foreign scientists, or scientists of any age from a scientifically young country, could of course, read notable foreign journals whenever they could get their hands on them. But a lively engagement as article authors and contributing editors was limited to the few financially well heeled and sometimes politically connected senior scientists who traveled across borders frequently to attend meetings. (Benjamin Franklin, for example, was a famous foreign member of the French Academy, during his term as ambassador to that country.) Reading the 18th-early 19th century journal for most scientists was often an after-the-fact substitute for being able to attend the oral presentations at the meetings. This meetings-based heritage is why so many older science journals have titles including words like *Accounts*, *Proceedings* or *Transactions*. The many journals for the rapid communication of brief scientific papers—those whose titles include *Letters* or *Communications*—are a much later development in publishing, but have roots in the correspondence of distant members of a society or academy. These "letters" were sometimes read aloud at meetings in their absence, generally updating the membership on new developments or disputing some findings published in a recent *Proceedings*.

Before the late-19th century, arguments over which scientist from what country deserved credit for a given discovery were understandably common in regional or national journals, because there remained a surprising amount of delay and disconnection in the timely flow of information. Apart from displaying some very large egos and xenophobia, published accounts of these disputes, and other scientific controversies of the time, disclosed a great deal of wasteful duplication of time, scarce equipment, and even scarcer samples and materials, in the search for answers in one country to scientific questions that that had actually been resolved earlier in another. The progress of science in some areas stalled because no one seemed ready to yield the floor or get on to other business. Initially, this rancorous scientific nationalism seemed in tune with the times because, in a larger context, many of the scientifically most advanced countries were also open rivals in commercial, industrial, military, and colonial contests.

But as the 19th century progressed, a freer exchange of scientific information and a more honest accounting of credit for scientific discoveries were encouraged by a developing sense of scientific professionalism and empowerment. Newer, more democratic organizations for scientists, more akin to the British Association for the Advancement of Science (1831), and a speed up of industrialization and transportation played significant roles. A growing number of organized scientists began more actively leveraging their considerable usefulness in matters of public health, agriculture, industry, and the military. Governmental tolerance and sometimes subsidies to these newer scientific organizations, sometimes including their publications, came to be seen as much in the best interest of the ruling class, as their patronage of the traditional, more exclusive royal academy and its journal had been. In more and more of the Western and Central European countries, authorities gradually reduced interference in matters of recruitment, publication policy, and liberty to travel abroad for members. Ironically, by pursuing a seemingly apolitical, strictly credentials-based membership policy, scientists in these organizations cleverly eased political and police operatives out of their meetings, and their journals, without getting into too much trouble. This did not prevent scientists from getting into plenty of trouble, however, if they put politics back into their scientific journals, or tried to become politicians themselves. Rudolph Virchow, Germany's most famous medical scientist of the latter 19th century, managed to get two research hospitals, a nursing school, and several university laboratories built via the Kaiser and patrons in the business community, despite his career as an agitator. But he was careful not to write editorials in his journal of pathology and experimental medicine, but rather in his more frankly political magazine. He balanced his criticisms and political career with notable service as a battlefield doctor, as overseer of the Berlin sewer system, a meat inspector, and ironically, as the man who convinced businessman-explorer Heinrich Schliemann, who shared his interest in anthropology and archeology, and was discoverer of the putative site of Troy, to donate his artifacts to the Kaiser's favorite museums.

The increasing availability of rail travel to the capital city, and improvements in postal delivery favored national organizations over regional ones. It was getting easier not only to get the scientist from Marseille to Paris, but also to get the journal from Paris to Marseille, Lyon, Toulouse, Strasbourg, and Bordeaux. Regional groups had difficulties matching the national groups in funding well-attended meetings. Their comparatively reduced professional visibility attracted fewer papers to their journals. Those journals grew smaller by comparison, and were often less frequently issued.

Over time, national scientific societies which focused on a specific major discipline (chemistry, physics, math, etc.) also gained enough membership to fund attractive meetings and field sustainable journals. Indeed the criteria for being elevated to the still attractive national general science academy went from providing notable scientific services to the crown, to publishing a long string of notable papers in the journal of a specific scientific discipline deemed essential to the long term progress of the nation. Increasingly, the old pattern of dual affiliation with one's regional general science society as well as with the national general science society was replaced. The new pattern became dual affiliation with the national general scientific society and with the national society devoted to a specific scientific discipline. Scientists began to enjoy the option of attending either or both types of meeting, and reading and contributing to either or both of their journals. It was but a small step from that situation to one where scientists of different nationalities, but of similar disciplinary backgrounds, began to perceive mutual interests that bridged international borders, including the right not only to read, but to contribute to foreign journals in their disciplines.

A scientific gentleman's agreement evolved and was enforced by informal but effective consequences. Being the first to publish one's results in detail in any reputable scientific journal of reasonably widespread circulation—effectively a canonization of the long known but often honored-in-the-breach priority principle—became the only contest that mattered among the increasingly urbane and sophisticated scientific community. Date stamps replaced debating trophies when dealing with bragging rights to new discoveries, and there was to be no prize for coming in second. Indeed the turn of the century became particularly notable for international scientific prizes that tended to bring great acclaim to the national scientific establishments of the prizewinners. The Nobel Prizes (beginning in 1901) represented the most notable example of the new culture of international meritocracy in science and science publishing.

Under this new ethos, persons submitting manuscripts that duplicated previously published results, or who disputed reputably published findings without clear-cut evidence of fraud on the part of the' original claimants, would find their own paper summarily rejected. Their fitness as scientists, who paid attention to the journal record, would be seriously questioned. They would no longer be considered as patriotic defenders of regional or national honor, but rather as provincial bumpkins who were out of touch. Unfortunately, in times of war, everyone was allowed to become rude, petty, suspicious, and bigoted, and scientific civility intermittently suffered notable lapses.

More and more scientific journals, therefore, began speeding up journal issuance as a competitive tactic. They sought more foreign circulation, and opened up to foreign authors. Where before, one had to be famous foreign visitor just to get into another's national science journal, that journal could now make a foreigner famous nationally and make the national journal famous internationally. In fact, it was a dubiously logical but genuine advance when a Frenchman could argue that having a German scientist publish the first paper on an important discovery in a French journal was a clear indication of the superiority of France. (Well, the discoverers of the laws of nature did not entirely change human nature.)

But a journal's very fame and success, in many cases, ironically inspired its own best competitors, some of whom could go on to surpass it. This paper aims to note both those first significant national journals in a field, and a selection of the field's current leaders, including international journals, that overtook, some, but by no means all of those 19th century national pioneers.

THE RISE OF THE MAJOR EUROPEAN SCIENTIFIC AND PUBLISHING EMPIRES: 1870-1917

While no single country had an absolute monopoly on native scientific talent in either the late 19th or early 20th centuries, it was pretty clear that some countries—England, France, and the newly consolidated German state—had evolved significantly more financial capital to fund academic and industrial infrastructure. They had a more sizeable and robust mix of universities, more governmentally sponsored labs, and more industrial research centers than others did. They had developed a successful sci-tech-med publishing capacity to service their robust clientele, based on some mix of generally not-for-profit scientific societies, for-profit publishers, and university presses. The relative size and influence of each of these sectors of publishing varied in each country. Joint ventures of two or more sectors within a country were not uncommon. (Indeed, joint ventures of not-for-profit societies and for-profit publishers were more common than not in the Continental European countries.) A key factor in the long term success of British, French and German publishers was their growing ability to market their journals across borders, once national sales proved insufficient to sustain reputational leadership under the new regime of open and competitive science journal publishing.

These countries particularly benefited from an international consensus on what would be acceptable scientific languages. At the turn of the last century, virtually anyone claiming to be a scientist was expected to read and write scientific prose in English, French and German (as opposed to Italian, Spanish, Dutch, or one of the Scandinavian or Slavic languages). This trilingual imperative was not necessarily due to any innate intellectual superiority on the part of the Big Three, nor disregard for higher education or scholarly publishing in other European countries. There were fine but generally fewer universities and smaller publishing firms in virtually all of the other European countries. It was as much a matter of cumulative advantage in numbers and size at a crucial time when science and science publishing were going international.

Not coincidentally, the Big Three had a built-in mechanism for sustaining their linguistic leads for decades. They provided most of the opportunities for doctoral or postdoctoral training for foreigners (both those arriving from other countries within Europe, and those coming in from the Americas and the Far East). While it is impressive that 33 of the first 52 winners of the Nobel Prize in Chemistry, Physics and Physiology or Medicine, were British, French, or German, it is just as telling to note that 10 of the remaining 19 had advanced training in the universities of one or more of the Big Three before winning their prize.

1917-1945

In the era between the First and Second World Wars, the United States, the Soviet Union and Japan also became first-rank international players in science.

The American experience is perhaps most readily understood. Growth in the more sophisticated manufacturing industries, ongoing agricultural abundance, the completion of a vast rail network, and plentiful fuel and raw minerals financially underwrote a growing educational infrastructure. The early 19th century spread of public and parochial school education prepared the way for the later 19th century's development of competing networks of state and private institutions of higher academia to the point of homegrown PhD programs in the early 20th century. Those programs were initially buttressed by recruited foreign scientists and later by over ten current or future Nobel Prize winners who were refugees from totalitarianism. American journals, having the additional advantage of being written in English, began appearing routinely in foreign collections, but Russian and Japanese titles, which featured a mix of native and Western languages, remained available only in the largest foreign research collections.

Some of the reasons for the less successful distribution of Russian journals internationally were political. It wasn't only a case of rabid western anti-communism (of which there admittedly was a great deal), but also some traits that were surprisingly backward for a state that advertised itself as the vanguard of progressivism. Among these were an annoying tendency to revive priority wars, often claiming for Russians credit for discoveries and inventions that clearly had not been reputably published in any major journals, even assuming they had been independently uncovered by the Russians first. Additionally it eventually became obvious that, as was the case with the Nazis in Germany, only politically reliable Russian scientists were given permission by the Soviets to publish in journals that had an international following. This exacerbated linguistic barriers as well. For although many older Russian scientists routinely published in French or German in czarist times, by Stalin's time, continued use of these Western languages, while still allowed in some publications, was nonetheless regarded by the Soviets as evidence of a dangerous tendency towards "cosmopolitanism." This charge was particularly levied against the rather large number of Jews within early Soviet science who, like Stalin's subsequently vanquished political rival Trotsky (born Bronshtein), had academic or professional connections with foreigners, or had traveled abroad unsupervised extensively. Somewhat hypocritically, the Soviets nonetheless fielded a great many low cost journals with self-serving titles like the *Uspekhi (The Successes)* review series (some translated into Western languages for export) largely with the goal of gaining international prestige. In addition to some genuinely good scientific content—the vast improvements wrought by the communists in Russian scientific education and research were remarkable—there were profiles of leading scientists with their Party memberships and Heroes of Socialist Labor medals conspicuously noted. But the international market resistance encountered because of language difficulties for many other Russian titles was only partly offset by the lure of their low prices. There were only a few hundred scientists abroad who could serve as *ad hoc* translators for their new colleagues in Western countries, and the bulk of these were ironically Jewish or political refugees from the Soviet Union who had not emigrated happily.

Japanese science and technology publications also had some linguistic disadvantages in the world market, although a substantial number of Japanese scientists, and a good percentage of affluent college students, diligently learned the major Western scientific languages, and studies abroad up through the 1920s. These emissaries had notable academic success in the old Big Three science powers and the U.S., despite facing suspicion and hostility. They effectively transferred a great deal of the science and technology they learned abroad back home, strengthening the Japanese university system, which had been deliberately remodeled along old German lines. University instruction and research were overwhelmingly slanted toward science and technology, which were seen as necessary for military and economic strength, while being less threatening to the social order and traditional cultural institutions than most Western humanities and social studies. In medicine and biology, a substantial effort was made in pharmaceuticals and in microbiology (particularly antibiotics), and in fermentation technologies that are in many respects the forerunners of today's biotechnology. Japanese scientists often greatly improved on the economy or efficiency of output of agricultural and industrial production. This was driven by a chronic fear of fuel and raw materials shortages that threatened to interrupt an economy that was straining to provide food, manufactured goods and steady employment for a burgeoning population. Despite these persistent worries, the Japanese economy was among the world's top 10 before the start of World War II.

But this success through controlled internationalism was subverted by two trends affecting Japanese science and scientific publishing. The first obstacle was administrative. The number and types of Japanese serial publications were bewilderingly complex, and not under any kind of central control. (This was partly because they adopted an early 19th century German model, with every local society, school, industrial complex, etc. having its own journal. It would surprise many scientists that the late Emperor Hirohito actually had several papers in marine biology, largely because they appeared in just these kinds of publications.) Only a handful of journals were national in scope (later 19th century German models), and even fewer saw international distribution (and not all of their content was in Western languages).

The second obstacle was ideological. By the 1930s, the Japanese government, business elite, and military switched strategy towards an anti-Western Asian Co-Prosperity Sphere whereby American and European influences in Asia and the Pacific Rim would be rooted out, and presumably replaced by those of Japan and any willing Asian allies they could prop up in conquered territories. But even though Japanese military and industrial successes in Asia went unchecked until the early 1940s, their goal of pan-Asian unity failed. The havoc wrought on their enemies in war, the looting of raw materials, and the reported cruelty of their military occupation destroyed most of the little scientific infrastructure in Asia outside of Japan. It undercut any goodwill to Japan, its science, or its journals within the conquered countries, and in much of the West. Apart from rather meager contacts with their German allies—and ironically also with the Russians (who, having been decisively beaten by the Japanese at the turn of the century, joined the Allies against Japan only in WWII's last few weeks)—Japan, and its publications, were increasingly isolated from the outside scientific world for years. Those student scientists who had not been killed in the war were nonetheless still substantially damaged in terms of scientific infrastructure, western language fluency and awareness of scientific developments.

Intriguingly, the War Department in the U.S. actually pirated and distributed German scientific journals throughout the war, although it did not translate them, presumably because most American scientists still read German freely. This appeared not to be the case with Japanese journals, although Japanese maps and oceanic charts, however, were distributed after translation.

1945-1975

In the early Cold War years, the American share of both scientific discoveries and the international journal market, increased substantially. This was driven largely by American success in the war, the lack of damage to American scientific infrastructure, America's absorption of refugee and former enemy scientific talent, freer contacts of allied foreign scientists with American universities than was seen in the Warsaw Pact, and the relatively low cost of American not-for-profit society publications on the international market.

Russian science and Russian journals also gained in international visibility and distribution ironically enhanced by Western Cold War era fears of Russian prowess in nuclear physics and weapons technology. It is important to note that while Russian-language studies were heavily subsidized within the United States—I was a Russian major on a National Defense scholarship in the late sixties and early seventies—the general level of fluency and ease of reading Russian never increased appreciably among Western scientists. Rather, a host of Western scientific societies, for-profit publishers, and some university presses signed exclusive contracts for English translations of official journals with Soviet authorities at government research institutes, universities, and research society headquarters. The Russians allowed this for reasons of gaining hard currency and prestige, confident that the political officers in every laboratory and attached to each journal staff would watch out for any real security leaks. The translation journals appeared from 18 months to two years after the original Russian language version had been printed. Translation journal prices were about triple per page of the going rate for comparable Western journals. The easy-to-read feature pleased Western scientists, but did not exactly thrill their librarians, who often had to realign their budgets to include them.

The British, French, German, and Japanese rates of success in scientific discoveries recovered quickly after the war. The British journal market share continued to grow, but much of that growth came via expansion of the pools of authors and readers in the former British Commonwealth. While these former colonies had somewhat less sophisticated scientific infrastructure, their language of instruction was British English, and the UK remained a popular spot for post-doctoral studies, even after Commonwealth countries gained national independence. (It is notable that in this era India, for example, became the world's third largest producer of M.D.s and science Ph.D.s, and the largest exporter.)

The French situation was similar, but their smaller and more rapidly diminishing empire had even less scientific infrastructure. Fewer of their colonial scholars were as technically prepared or financially capable of studying abroad, and their reliance on French as a second language proved to be less advantageous if they sought training in the larger university systems of the U.S. or the British Commonwealth.

The quick rebuilding of West German and Japanese scientific enterprises, aided by American foreign aid (and the development of the Common Market in Europe), was particularly astonishing. The resulting modernity of their labs, and the channeling of their native high energy into now largely civilian and industrial uses of science, actually gave them a competitive boost. While both Japanese and German school children were once again exposed to English via GIs, American consumer products, and TV and radio culture, systematic instruction in English was far more successful in West Germany. Part of this may have had to do with the linguistic affinity between German and English, but the Germans may have also had a greater sense of urgency in a politically and militarily divided Germany with the Red Army at their door. This seemingly small advantage in English language ability was to have a telling effect on scientific journal publication history in the years to come.

It was already clear by the 1960s that despite their rebound in terms of scientific infrastructure and article output, journals published in German and French were nonetheless declining in international market share. (Recall that Japanese sales were meager anyway.) Part of the blame rested with changes in the biggest market for science journals at the time, the U.S. There was certainly an erosion of the requirement that American science students learn foreign languages as part of their university training. Apart from a general trend towards catering to American baby-boomers disinclined towards learning any foreign language, it was felt that science curricula had to be altered to allow for more time for learning computer programming languages, which at the time, seemed key to future technical advancement in any science. FORTRAN, in a sense, replaced French, German, Russian or Japanese.

The whole university system in the U.S. was also undergoing a remarkable expansion in other ways that had very mixed effects on American science and American university presses. Scientific output from universities exploded, even as the science journal output from the university press sector within American publishing actually began shrinking relative to the scientific output of both the American not-for-profit societies and the American for-profit publishers. With a few notable exceptions university presses began to get less overall support from their universities for their operations, and began cutting back on their journals and on science in general. This may seem surprising, because journals still had the advantage of up-front payment of subscription monies. But the continuous costs of journal publishing have always been less amenable to downward adjustment during university budgetary squeezes or any downward spiral in subscriptions. The larger scientific societies and for-profit presses could, and did, offset a poor subscription performance for one or two of their journals by membership dues or indirect subsidies via their better-selling journals. But since few universities published more than a handful of science journals, that option was generally not open. By contrast, losses on book publishing were, and are, generally self-limiting. (You "remaindered" poor selling titles, and were more careful with your next few book projects.) Moreover, as science journals grew larger and larger, they required greater full-time technical expertise, more attention to deadlines, and could no longer depend on part-time, and often unpaid faculty service. Scientists, never heavily represented in university press operations (or in library administrations), began to disappear from them altogether. Humanists, who were naturally partial to the book as their primary vehicle, and business types who would watch the bottom line at the behest of the university's top management, picked up the slack in both university press and library leadership.

By contrast, not-for-profit professional societies found themselves in a better position to maintain science faculty loyalties than university presses, because society affiliation traveled along with the highly mobile faculty in the hot market for scientists in America. This demand was caused by the multiplication of new schools in the post WWII era, driven partly by the baby boom, and partly by the build up in university research projects funded by the military in the face of the perceived Russian threat. Likewise, American for-profit publishers began offering better deals, including cash and secretarial help, to some of the best remaining scientific editors among the faculty, without the annoyance of administrative paperwork, budget hearings or faculty senate votes. Just as importantly, for-profit publishers could afford to take long-term gambles on some of the newer, more specialized, smaller not-for-profit societies, offering better co-publishing deals than could be had from the financially stressed, increasingly book-oriented, humanities-inclined university presses.

All this had a hidden cost to university libraries. One of their lowest-cost sources of journals dropped out just as a host of new scientific disciplines was beginning to explode on the scene, and at a time when science faculty could make more and more demands of the university administration. Not too surprisingly, relationships between scientists put on a recruitment pedestal and librarians under the budgetary gun were beginning to go from bad to worse.

1975-2000

The closing decades of this century have seen the sustained rise of both American and foreign authorship in American society journals. (On average, better than thirty percent of U.S. not-for-profit journal content comes from abroad.) This would seem to be good news for America's cash-strapped libraries, but this was not the case. The "big readership" journals got even bigger. The relatively low per-article costs of the not-for-profit American titles were offset by the fact that the number of articles published continued to explode on an annual basis, with price rises to match. Likewise, many of the larger American societies (some now with memberships over 100,000, and with members paying much less than libraries for the same journals), took a second look at some of the small specialty titles that were particularly favored by some of the American for-profit sector, and by virtually all of the European for-profits as well. They found them thriving, and determined to share in that growth by floating a raft of specialty competitors. Librarians found themselves having to add more titles all the time for their scientists, without having proportionally more money provided by the university administration.

European publishers did not take well to this American poaching in their pool of authors and copying of marketing strategy. They were determined to fight back, ironically using some of the other features that had made American journals so successful: one common language and a giant home market.

Corporate publishers based in the Netherlands, Germany, Switzerland, and the Scandinavian countries, but owing allegiance to no particular country, began to insist on all-American-English language manuscripts from their European authors. They did not do this to insult their fellow Europeans so much as to remove lingering linguistic barriers to sales in America and the rest of the world. Most of the scientific world, apart from the French, finally acknowledged that American English had become de facto the *lingua franca* of science, and were in a position to comply because they had raised up a new generation of English-language-capable scientists by this time. These publishers then aggressively promoted international authorship and sales, rapidly increasing the number of sales and editorial branch offices in the U.S., Japan, and the newly industrialized countries of Asia. The European-for-profit sector eventually dwarfed the for-profit sector of American publishing even in the American market, garnering about 30 percent of the total manuscript output of American authors, and better than 30 percent of the typical university library budget. Some Europublishers pushed even farther, buying out their American counterparts (Lippincott, Raven, Plenum, Waverly, Cell Press). Part of their ability to accomplish this was created by currency fluctuations that gave their European monies more bang than the buck. All this further infuriated American librarians who had to pay more bucks to get these resurgent European journals, with the feeling that this would only further embolden the Europeans to buy more of the lower-cost American publishers, and field more publications that their own science faculty would want.

Despite their "American-English-only" demands, these for-profit Europublishers simultaneously cultivated a kind of *Kulturkampf* appeal to subscribers and authors from their home market, with a major redefinition of what "home" was. "Home" wasn't to be France or Germany or Italy for scientists anymore, "home" was now to be a scientifically united Europe. When some of these Europublishers renewed their contracts with the scientific societies of individual European countries, they often insisted on melding their individual national journals into pan-European journals willing and able to compete for international sales and prestige with American publications. (It still surprises many Americans that there are at least as many scientists, and as much money, in Europe as there is in the U.S.) They argued that the best European work really ought to be published in European journals, and got a positive, if not unanimous response. While American authorship in official Eurojournals has been actually lower proportionally than in other international journals published in Europe and sold in America, sales remain quite healthy in an otherwise financially strained U.S. library market, because the quality of the content was very often quite high, and American scientists demanded access.

But not all scientifically competitive countries are European, even some that are found in Europe! Britain, for example, remained prominent scientifically, but ambivalent in science journal publishing strategy. It remained partly committed to joint European ventures, and partly committed to the poetic idea that "there'll always be an England," whose publications will remain distinctly British.

In the 1990s, the production and distribution of publications from the former Soviet Union had fallen into disarray, as the old Soviet hierarchical bureaucracies fragmented. While the old *appartchiks* were often inefficient, at least the west knew with whom they had to deal. There is an ongoing debate as to whether to continue to shore up these declining Russian-language journal reputations by continuing to market them as reformed journals from reformed scientific institutions. (It's true that the translation time lag problem has almost disappeared, but it is not clear that is to the credit of the Russians. It's not uncommon for some Western organizations, working with the Russian-language manuscripts, to actually publish the English language translations before the Russians manage to get the original-language version distributed in their own country.) The alternative would be for Russian scientists to write in English in the first place, much as do the Germans and Japanese, and send their papers to the rising Eurojournals. The latter option would appear to be a better prospect for Russian authors, and further their integration into the European scientific community. But such a policy may not be sustainable in terms of subscriptions by their own impoverished libraries, as the best pan-European journals are also among the world's most expensive.

Given the failure of their WWII experience, the Japanese and most of the Eastern and Southern Asian nations, decided not to attempt to construct a pan-Asian journal network once again (or at least one dominated by the Japanese). Singapore has done fairly well lately as an international publisher in math and physics. The Australians and New Zealanders increasingly see themselves as full scientific partners in a more modest attempt to organize a Pacific Rim journal market, as opposed to an ongoing role as junior members of the old Commonwealth. But overall, most East Asian and Pacific powers have continued to export most of their best manuscripts to American and European journals, buying and reading mostly the same materials as do American and European scientists, and publishing overwhelmingly in English.

Canada fields a few dozen journals of sound, intermediate status, except for a few in natural resources which are world class. Journal collections and manuscript submission patterns in the urban scientific centers of Latin America are now essentially First World, with some local flavor.

Paying for subscriptions and building up scientific infrastructure remains extremely problematic for much of the rest of the world, including more rural portions of Latin America, most of Africa, and in politically and economically unstable parts of the Middle East and Central Asia. India is a South Asian exception, developing a stable assortment of indigenous journals that have modest amount of international sales. In any case, the best papers from all these regions (and often the best scientists) still tend to migrate to Western venues whenever possible, for post-doctoral training, if not always automatically for permanent residence.

In a particularly intriguing development in the last few years, some publishers from among the diminishing number of surviving American forprofits (most notably Wiley) have finally begun to buy out or merge with some of the remaining independent European publishers (for example, VCH, the publishing arm of the German Chemical Society) who have not been gobbled up by the European giants (Elsevier, Wolters-Kluwer, Springer, or Thomson) and thereby create, somewhat ironically, Eurojournals co-published with Americans.

American librarians may even be belatedly making their peace with American not-for-profit society presses, in ventures like the SPARC coalition. The idea is for libraries to pledge support for lower-cost domestic journals that quite frankly attempt to undercut American demand for expensive for-profit Eurojournals.

To add to the complexity, e-journals have become a wild card in a very high stakes game, with libraries betting that somehow e-journals will be an effective means to control costs from whatever country or category of publisher. While a great many low-cost e-journals that have no print predecessors have risen, it is fairly clear already that the e-journals in greatest demand are not new, but are the electronic versions of the existing, expensive, elite journals of science. But in a throwback to the days when universities were major players in science journal publishing, the early electronic efforts of Johns Hopkins (Project Muse) and Stanford (Highwire Press), deserve special mention for handling matters in a cost-conscious way that does not demonize scientists or their organizations.

HOW EXPANDING CHOICES FOR SCIENTISTS FORCED LIBRARIANS TO BECOME BUDGETARY JUGGLERS

The preceding history shows that librarians, for better or for worse, have found themselves having to cover all serious journal manuscript and reading bets made by their institution's scientists, with whatever funds were available. This assumption of responsibility devolved in three steps.

- First, as early as the turn of the century, it became certain that the liberalization of circulation and contribution to scientific journals across borders was turning the heady freedom of scientists to read formerly scarce and restricted material into the sometimes onerous duty to read as much journal literature as possible. This became the almost Faustian price a scientist paid in order to maintain his or her legitimacy as an informed professional who respected the "priority of publication" principle. Excuses of economic deprivation, geographic isolation or ethnic marginalization were no longer acceptable, even if these factors still operated to a substantial degree. Since article alerting and finding aids such as indexing and abstracting services were just getting started in the 1910s-20s, and were six months to two years behind in reporting new findings, keeping up with the journals themselves was essential. This was becoming increasingly problematic as a personal responsibility to be carried out without substantial institutional support. Science journals were growing in number, bulk, and frequency, beyond the capacity of individual scientists to archive and manage them in their own offices, or in informally run departmental collections. Real librarians would have to do that job.
- Second, despite recognizing that hiring productive scientists meant having to buy into growing and complicated science journal collections, most institutions of higher education hired them anyway. They did this both for sound educational reasons, and because they did not wish miss out on the jackpots of prestige, grant funding, and endowments that were often paid out for institutional success in science in this century. The genie was out of the bottle: Scientists realized that their undeniable contributions to the real world and to university coffers could be leveraged into better-than-average library perquisites.
- Third, despite their competing for and sometimes winning many of these institutional jackpots, schools rarely gave enough money directly to their librarians to buy all the journals that could conceivably be useful for all the scientists on campus at any given time. But because the largely humanities-backgrounded librarians, being the day-to-day administrators of library funds, were the most visible target of complaints from scientists concerning any perceived inadequacy of service or holdings, the top level of university administrations have often avoided direct criticism. Frustrated librarians often turned to criticizing publishers across the ocean rather than the financial administrators across campus, because they felt they could more readily cancel

publications with which they didn't empathize anyway, than speak out against the administrators who could cancel their jobs.

But to their credit these same schools were smart enough to hire even smarter librarians who learned to discern trends, upwards and downwards, between competing journals and among rival scientific fields. These librarians, as much as anyone else, kept the whole scientific journal enterprise from collapsing of its own weight. While this article is certainly about the most successful science journals of the century, it is also a tribute to the guts and judgment of these hard-pressed but brilliantly performing librarians who made the century a scientific success for everyone. What Winston Churchill said about RAF fighter pilots who beat back the Luftwaffe in the Battle of Britain, "Never in the field of human conflict was so much owed by so many to so few," ought to be said about this century's intrepid serials librarians.

FACTORS FAVORING SELECTION OF A SERIAL AS A JOURNAL OF THE CENTURY

I have been greatly guided by citation data in making my designations, favoring the use of total citations accrued to a journal over the last 10 or more years when sorting out enduring historical pioneers, and opting for impact-factor dominance in the last three to five years for determinations of current leaders. Nonetheless my own sense of the histories of scientific disciplines, my observation of the highly competitive world of science publishing, and my informal tracking of the collections at the libraries at global scientific centers over the years through OCLC holdings records, have also played a significant role in my designations of these journals of the century.

It is frankly admitted that some of these added procedures of mine could be regarded as eccentric, less systematic and less reproducible by other researchers than a straightforward compilation and comparison of published citation data, verifiable by anyone else independently. That approach, however, would suggest that bibliometric data alone have accounted for the hierarchy of journals in the real world over time, arguing in a sense that an indicator of the status of a journal is the root cause of that status, and that bibliometric leadership is self-sustaining. (Once on top, always on top.) Rather, in my world view of science journals and their history, a host of economic, geographic, linguistic, and cultural influences, as well as factors idiosyncratic to given disciplines, play roles in ways that may or may not show up in bibliometric data. Bibliometric data can tell us a great deal about a journal and its interactions with its competitors, but it does not tell us everything we should know in order to make sense of a journal and its times, any more than reading the accurately recorded league standings at the end of the baseball season gives us quite as much insight as having watched a lot of ball games during the season. Moreover, such a singular reliance on bibliometric data does not explain why many journals can endure despite not winning the bibliometric contest in their field, and why new journals, which have no bibliometric track record to start with, can overthrow established leaders.

With each title selected, I will indicate the following within the text of this article and in the assorted tables and indices at the end of the book version of the Journals of the Century Project:

- The current country of publication (ISSN prefixes will be used as an authority to sort out journals with multinational sponsorship, or journals published in one country whose publisher's headquarters are in another).
- The name of its current publisher, or co-publishers, up to a total of three (I will use the name as listed, for example Pergamon, even though I well realize that Reed-Elsevier owns Pergamon).
- The first year of issuance of the journal under any title that covered the topic at hand.

Sometimes I had to deal with a fairly straightforward title change, often from its original foreign language (usually German, but sometimes Russian, French, Dutch or Swedish). This was a part of a mass movement to overall publication in American English begun in the 1960s, and was easily accounted for. Therefore, I give 1924 as the year for the founding of *Cell and Tissue Research,* not 1974 when it simply changed from the *Zeitschrift fur Zellforschung und Mikroskopische Anatomie.*

In a more dramatic but still valid case, a journal may have reorganized to accommodate new emphases, while continuing its classical core. In these cases, I had to make a judgment as to whether or not I was dealing with a fundamentally new journal, or one that retained much of the spirit of its putative predecessor, even if it had added some nuances. For example, what was founded in 1890 as *Wilhelm Roux' Archiv fuer Entwicklungsmechnik der Organismen* became, in 1998, *Development, Genes, and Evolution,* which is scarcely even a loose translation of the former German title. Direct examination indicated that the journal still deals with experimental embryology, even though genes as physical objects composed of DNA, per se, were, naturally enough, not well understood in 1890. Furthermore, the meteoric rise in 1987 of a competing journal, blending genetics and molecular biology with embryology (*Genes and Development* from the Cold Spring Harbor Laboratories

Press for the Genetical Society of Great Britain) offered additional marketing motivation for the name change of the historically German publication.

Finally, in the increasing number of cases where several older journals from differing countries merged to form a new journal (particularly in the tables at the end of the finished Journal of the Century Project), I use a two-step procedure. I first determine the country of actual publication of the newly merged journal. I then credit the date of the founding only of the predecessor journal that shares the same country. Consider the *European Physical Journal,* which has four journals distinguished by the letters *A* through *D*. It has Italian, French, and German predecessors, also with assorted alphabetically or Roman numerically distinguished sections, but is now published in Germany. Therefore I give the date of the founding of the appropriate section of *Zeitschrift fuer Physik,* not that of *Nuovo Cimento* or the *Journal de Physique* for any section now published in Germany, even though the other sponsoring societies continue to play an important role. Partly because of this concern for historical perspective, however, no journal that began after 1992 is included unless it is a reasonably direct descendant of a significant title of substantially greater age and reputation.

Since this article accords roughly equal weight to historical influence and current dominance, this is not necessarily a list of the top three journals at this instant in any given specialty, a compilation recently reported elsewhere, although many of this paper's selections are indeed numbered among the best current titles, and all are currently being published. Likewise, because they have been recently exhaustively surveyed only three years ago, most review, symposium and methods journals will not be included unless the methodology of a discipline has evolved into something of a major specialty in itself.

I have deliberately omitted some subject fields that could readily qualify as sciences so as to avoid duplicating the efforts of other contributors to this project in the areas of clinical medicine, computer science, engineering, agriculture, psychology, and anthropology. I have also condensed some descriptions of scientific specialties, and compressed or suppressed some details of my decision-making processes for ranking individual journals competing within them. All this was done to allow librarians serving other disciplines space to tell their stories to their own valued audiences and to explain their journal choices more fully.

GENERAL SCIENCE

Nature (U.K., Macmillan, 1869) and *Science* (American Association for the Advancement of Science, 1896) continued to be required reading for virtually all scientists for the entire century. A third choice in this general science category is the *Proceedings of the National Academy of Sciences of the USA* (1915). While currently very heavily biological, it is a worthy representative of the many historic academy journals found in most major scientific countries that are primarily restricted in authorship to academicians and protégés whose papers the academicians endorse. Given that a significant percentage of the American National Academy's members over time have become Nobel Prizewinners, many of whom have also gone on to foster the careers of future Nobelists, this restricted authorship has scarcely proven to be a drawback.

GENERAL PURE MATHEMATICS

Many nominally general math journals developed a pattern of quasi-specialization, made possible by several historically based peculiarities of math journal publishing. First, there are many more internationally competitive general math journals than is the case with general chemistry, general biology, or general physics journals today. While these other fields typically have only a single leading national general journal (sponsored by the national society or by a for-profit publisher in cooperation with the national society), and many of these national titles have begun merging into multinational general journals, it is still common within math journal publishing in a given country to have general math titles from not only the national society, but also from regional societies and local university presses as well, (an early 19th century behavior). Second, most general math journals have remained comparatively slow growing in numbers of pages and papers published annually, leading to infamously long backlogs of accepted manuscripts awaiting appearance. Third, rather than having each general math journal balloon out to accommodate all the new specialties, editors have often informally conceded or parceled out some specialty strengths to their editorial colleagues at other general math journals, in what began as discreet gentlemen's agreements that have long endured. Even when an entire editorial board has finally been replaced through attrition, the backlog of papers awaiting publication has typically reflected years of prior subject emphases. Fourth, it has generally been easier for new editors to stay the topical course rather than attempt to change it. Consequently, designations in this Math section will justifiably include places of historical honor in specialized areas for seemingly general journals that influenced later specialty journal development; indeed, many general journals continue to have strong quasi-specialization and to compete with more frankly specialized journals.

Nonetheless, three general journals clearly deserve mention for contributions of pan-mathematical importance. These are the *Annals of Mathematics* (U.S., Princeton University Press, 1884); *Acta Mathematica* (Sweden, Almqvist & Wiksell, 1882) and *Inventiones Mathematicae* (Germany, Springer Verlag, 1966). This last title is most likely to lead the twenty first century.

GENERAL APPLIED MATHEMATICS

Three journals share this platform. Despite its seemingly generic name, *Communications on Pure and Applied Mathematics* (New York University's Courant Institute and Wiley, 1949) has been one of the two greatest American entries in applied math since its founding. The other has been the *SIAM Journal on Applied Mathematics* (U.S., Society for Industrial and Applied Mathematics, 1966). While the French, Germans and Swiss have each fielded historically important journals, the *IMA Journal on Applied Mathematics* (Institute of Mathematics & Its Applications and Academic Press, 1965) from the U.K. probably has the broadest reach and has spawned the most formidable specialized offspring without diminishing its own reputation.

MATHEMATICAL LOGIC AND FOUNDATIONS

A small priesthood of mathematical philosophers have demonstrated that many seemingly self-evident equations or laws are actually matters of ad hoc consensus rather than internally consistent logic. These specialists work to tighten up rules for reasoning and standards of proof. They foster the admission that some matters are fundamentally undecideable. Yet they have also proven that some counter-intuitive symbolic and computer logic is, in fact, provable by classical means, and that seemingly odd sets of data do exhibit certain shared characteristics. The *Journal of Symbolic Logic* (U.S., Association for Symbolic Logic, 1930) has been their leading vehicle for most of this century. The *Annals of Pure and Applied Logic* (Netherlands, North Holland, 1970) surpasses it for manuscript capacity, but has remained second in influence. While overshadowed in recent decades, the historically strong Polish contribution to the field deserves special notice, particularly *Fundamenta Mathematicae* (Polish Academy of Sciences Press, 1920).

COMBINATORICS, GRAPH THEORY, AND DISCRETE MATHEMATICS

Combinatorics is the characterization of subsets having some desired property within a larger, but nonetheless limited and well-defined set. It was born as an academic discipline largely from logic, foundations, and number theory. Graph theory is the study of network problems, also within a finite framework, with optimization of routing as a goal. It was born via electrical engineering and transportation research problems. While each of these fields retains some identity as mathematical subspecialties on their own, both are now more often seen as major contributors to the theory underlying computer science, under the more encompassing term of Discrete Mathematics (discrete largely because both fields involve finite, countable, entities or pathways, rather than indeterminate, continuous ranges). The *Journal of Combinatorial Theory* (U.S., Academic Press, 1968), the *Journal of Graph Theory* (U.S., Wiley, 1977) and *Discrete Mathematics* (North Holland, 1971) all share the distinction of being both pioneers and current leaders in this niche of interlocking fields.

HIGHER ALGEBRA

Algebra has its basis in arithmetic, and its characteristic substitutions of letters for sets of numbers has served as an aid, not only in calculation, but in an ongoing discovery process that has led to powerful generalized procedures. (In math, generalization is a good thing that implies greater ability to handle more kinds of problems.) The *Journal of Algebra* (U.S., Academic Press, 1964) has defined its field for generations, although the *Quarterly Journal of Mathematics* (U.K., The Clarendon Press of Oxford University, 1930) and *Mathematische Zeitschrift* (Germany, Springer Verlag, 1918), more general journals, have also historically contributed a significant number of key papers.

GEOMETRY

Geometry focuses on the mathematical study of points, lines, areas and shapes in two, three or more dimensions of space. While arithmetic and trigonometry were initially sufficient tools for its study, higher algebra and analysis are now far more common. The *Journal of Differential Geometry* (U.S., Lehigh University, 1967) has always published more inclusively, and influentially, than its title might suggest, and is arguably the world's current leader. The *Bulletin de la Societe Mathematique de France* (1873) and the *Duke Mathematical Journal* (U.S., 1935) are key among generalist journals making important contributions to the field on a recurring basis.

TOPOLOGY

Topology had its origin in geometry, but it has since become a major specialty in its own right. In one of its major forms, topology is focused on the mapping of points or sets of points sharing some mathematical property on surfaces. These surfaces can be changed dramatically through various mathematical contortions, without necessarily changing the inter-relations of the original points or sets of points. While there are now a number of competitors, few mathematical fields have been so well served as this one is by its leading journal, *Topology* (U.K., Pergamon, 1962). More general journals of great historical distinction include *Commentarii Mathematici Helvetici* (Switzerland, Birkhauser, 1929) and the *Proceedings of the American Mathematical Society* (1950).

ANALYSIS

Analysis, the largest general area of math by far, is the study of continuous equations pitted against each other, with the underlying idea that one can sort out the relative contribution of one portion of an equation or set of interacting equations, and see how it relates to the rest. If you've taken calculus, you've done some analysis. Most mathematical relationships discovered in science or engineering are amenable to characterization via analysis, and general mathematical analysis has spawned many specialties driven by special problems in science. Three journals share honor as leaders in general mathematical analysis. They are the academically formalistic *Archives of Rational Mechanics and Analysis* (Germany, Springer Verlag, 1957), the voluminous and workman-like *Journal of Mathematical Analysis and Its Applications* (U.S., Academic Press, 1960), and the best bridge between the academic and applied worlds, the *SIAM Journal on Mathematical Analysis* (U.S., Society for Industrial and Applied Mathematics, 1970).

DIFFERENTIAL EQUATIONS

Differential equations are that part of mathematical analysis that is most commonly used in engineering, and might be best explained to young laypersons as turbo-calculus. The *Journal of Differential Equations* (U.S., Academic Press, 1965) was the first journal exclusively dedicated to this kind of mathematics, and has remained the best by a substantial margin. It has been followed by *Communications on Partial Differential Equations*

(U.S., Marcel Dekker, 1976). The way for both was paved by more general journals like the *Indiana University Mathematics Journal* (1952).

CONTROL AND OPTIMIZATION THEORY

Control theory is a mathematical approach to analyzing fluctuations over time with an eye to optimizing the predictability, speed, smoothness, or uniformity of a continuous process, usually one that has the potential for adverse outcomes if unwatched. Control and optimization can be involved in something as simple as monitoring the assortment of given nuts going into a mixed-nuts tin, or as complex as air traffic control at a busy airport, or even predicting the spread of an epidemic. The *International Journal on Control* (U.K., Taylor and Francis, 1965) and *Automatica* (U.K., Pergamon for the International Federation of Automatic Control, 1963) have been the most historically important entries in the field, and remain the archive of many important papers. These have arguably been overtaken, among mathematicians at least, by the *SIAM Journal on Control and Optimization* (U.S., Society for Industrial and Applied Mathematics, 1966).

NUMERICAL ANALYSIS

Numerical analysis bridges algebra and general mathematical analysis. It has had an extraordinary impact on the modeling of real-life phenomena by subdividing complex continuous equations into simpler arithmetic steps which can then be more readily computed. *Numerische Mathematik* (Germany, Springer Verlag, 1959) pioneered the field. Two other journals have since joined it at the top: the *SIAM Journal on Numerical Analysis* (U.S., Society for Industrial and Applied Mathematics, 1966) and the *IMA Journal of Numerical Mathematics* (U.K., Academic Press for the Institute of Mathematics and its Applications, 1981).

STATISTICS AND PROBABILITY

Probability determines the chances of a specific outcome based on knowledge of the whole set of possible outcomes. Statistics is the development and application of rules for taking samples from larger sets where a complete counting is not feasible, and calculating with them systematically, so as to allow for a reliable estimation of outcomes. Nowadays, the terms are used almost interchangeably, and the fields have many practitioners in the social sciences and in business, although the theory remains mathematical.

Ever since its founding, the *Journal of the Royal Statistical Society* (U.K., 1938) has enjoyed a persistent edge over the *Journal of the American Statistical Association* (1888). Both, however, cite another important journal in the field, *Biometrika* (U.K., Macmillan, 1901), so that the three seem inextricably joined at the forefront of the their field.

ASTRONOMY AND ASTROPHYSICS OF DEEP SPACE

It has often been said that the number of astronomers interested in a region of space increases with its distance from earth. Three journals that focused for the most part on objects and phenomena beyond our own solar system have dominated this century. They include *Astrophysical Journal* (U.S., University of Chicago Press for the American Astronomical Society, 1895), the *Monthly Notices of the Royal Astronomical Society* (Blackwell, 1833) and *Astronomy and Astrophysics* (Germany, Springer Verlag for a consortium of largely European astronomical societies that merged their journals with the *Zeitschrift fuer Astrophysik, 1930*). They represent the greatest concentration of coverage and quality of any troika in any sizeable physical science.

SOLAR SYSTEM AND PLANETARY SCIENCE

The sun, the moon, and our local community of planets represent one of the biggest subspecialties within astronomy. *Solar Physics* (Netherlands, Kluwer) has been a center of library attention since 1967. *Icarus* (U.S., Academic Press for the Division of Planetary Sciences of the American Astronomical Society, 1962) has represented the best findings from the community of scientists who look at planets other than earth and see relevance for earth science. *Meteoritics and Planetary Science* (U.S., Meteortical Society, 1953) established itself as the journal of choice for the only reliably known interplanetary commuters in our solar system-asteroids, comets and meteorites.

MODERN GENERAL PHYSICS

Perhaps more than in any other field, the contributions of Continental scientists dominated early modern physics, with its emphasis on exploring the atom and quantum mechanics. This historical fact would make it rather difficult to single out journals. It would be hard to choose a leading German journal like the *Zeitschrift fuer Physik* without mentioning perhaps either the French *Journal de Physique* or the Italian *Nuovo Cimento*. This is further complicated by the fact that each of these journals subsequently divided into several alphabetically distinguished specialty journals over the course of the century. Fortunately, the *European Physical Journal* collaboration has resolved this dilemma by representing a consolidation of some of the best parts of all three of these families. Their most general journal, *Europhysics Letters* (France, EDP Sciences and the Italian Society of Physics) represents a 1986 merger of *Lettere al Nuovo Cimento* and the *Journal de Physique Lettres* (1974), and is a worthy choice. The choice of American general physics journal is easier: *Physical Review Letters* (U.S., American Institute of Physics for the American Physical Society, 1958). Among the remaining general physics titles, it is arguable that the British and the Russians both have claims, but frankly, the *Journal of Experimental and Theoretical Physics* (American Institute of Physics for the Russian Academy of Sciences, 1931) was probably more earnestly scanned for almost 50 years.

MATHEMATICAL METHODS IN PHYSICS

Some would say that German or perhaps French was the dominant language of physics for the first half of the century, with English the clear winner in the second half. Perhaps more accurately, mathematics has remained the dominant language for the entire century, although the topics for discussion have certainly changed. When classical, fluid, and statistical mechanics, dependent largely on differential equations, were the rage, the *Zeitschrift fuer Angewandte Mathematik und Mechanik* (Germany, Teubner, 1856) was an important leader. As the number of those who identified themselves as mathematical physicists grew internationally, and other methods (including group theory, symmetry, matrix algebra and renormalization) for quantum mechanics and particle physics entered the discussion, the more encompassing *Journal of Mathematical Physics* (American Institute of Physics for the American Physical Society, 1960) became the first among equals. Now there are a great many subspecialized journals dealing with geometry, topology, chaos, nonlinearity, superstrings and wavelets in relation to theoretical physics. But all in all, the leader going into the next century in introducing new math in new physics, without abandoning improvements in old methods or topics, is *Communications in Mathematical Physics* (Germany, Springer Verlag, 1966).

THERMODYNAMICS

Thermodynamics was developed largely via studies of heat and energy flow in liquids and gases, but its laws clearly operate in solids as well. It found welcome homes in the *Journal of Chemical Thermodynamics* (U.K., Academic Press, 1969), and the *International Journal of Thermophysics* (U.S., Plenum, 1980) but it resides most grandly in the *Journal of Statistical Physics* (U.S., Plenum, 1969).

FLUID MECHANICS

Fluid mechanics studies flow and energy transfer in liquids and gases, with greater concern about resistance, turbulence, convection, and percolation, rather than with the simple notion of heat. While the field has other leaders in its aeronautical engineering aspects, the *Journal of Fluid Mechanics* (U.K., Cambridge University Press, 1956) has been pre-eminent in the latter part of this century particularly in basic science modeling. The closest American rival has been the *Physics of Fluids* (American Institute of Physics for the American Physical Society, 1958). This title has been somewhat undercut by the prominence of *Physical Review E* (American Institute of Physics for the American Physical Society, 1990).

PLASMA PHYSICS

Plasmas are superhot fluids that generally have had their electrons greatly reduced and their unpredictability vastly increased. While previously primarily the concern of the disparate priesthoods of astrophysicists and hydrogen bomb weapons scientists, plasmas have enjoyed a renaissance of studies since the 1970s. Although the highly attractive goal of economical fusion energy is still along way off, a surprising number of currently practical applications have sustained a growing assortment of plasma journals. *Nuclear Fusion* (Austria, International Atomic Energy Agency, 1960) has led in the future energy utility race, while *Plasma Physics and Controlled Fusion* (U.K., Institute of Physics, 1984) and the *Physics of Plasma* (a 1994 scion of the above-mentioned American Institute of Physics-American Physical Society, *Physics of Fluids*) have a broader mix of papers and greater overall appeal.

ATOMIC AND MOLECULAR PHYSICS

Chemists are generally more interested in molecules than in atoms, and physicists tend to the opposite. Some physical chemists and chemical physicists are interested in both equally and would say any distinction is moot nowadays: scientists of either persuasion submit and read manuscripts of both types. I would say these fields are certainly flip sides of the same coin, but that you can still tell heads from tails upon inspection. Physical societies mint atomic and molecular journals, while chemical societies traffic largely in physical chemistry journals. The *Journal of Physics B: Atomic, Molecular and Optical Physics* (U.K., Institute of Physics, 1969) has traded internationally at the highest rate of exchange in atomic and molecular physics for decades. Its American counterparts, *Physical Review A: Atomic, Molecular and Optical* (American Institute of Physics for the American Physical Society, 1990) and the *Journal of Chemical Physics* (American Institute of Physics for the American Physical Society, 1933), while still very sound, come in second and third. All three have markedly more physicists than chemists among their contributors and readers.

ION PHYSICS, NUCLEAR PHYSICS, AND RADIOACTIVITY

We have been routinely watching the natural decay of atoms and causing their artificial smash-ups for almost a hundred years, observing or employing what was then thought to be as enormous amounts of energy. But familiarity with now routine accelerator energies has not entirely brought contempt; instead it has allowed for manageable energy beams of use in medicine and industry. *Nuclear Physics A* (North Holland, 1956) has been the persistent leader in this area for the longest time, followed by the earnest but clearly second tier *Physical Review C*—Nuclear Physics (American Institute of Physics for the American Physical Society, 1970) and the *European Physical Journal A* (Germany, EDP Sciences and Springer Verlag for the consolidating European Physical Society), a journal whose principal ancestor was the *Zeitschrift fuer Physik C* (1979).

HIGH ENERGY PARTICLES AND FIELDS

Imagine hundreds of scientists working in underground laboratories having tunnels encircling dozens of acres, with trillions of electronvolts of electrical charges coursing by—all this infrastructure and coordinated talent in the hunt for tiny and exotically strange particles and quarks, as well as for that sizeable and familiar lump of gold that makes up the Nobel Prize medal. *Nuclear Physics B* (North Holland, 1956) and its companion *Physics Letters B* (North Holland, 1962) have dominated the field. *Physical Review D*—Particles and Fields (American Institute of Physics for the American Physical Society, 1970) has made strides at catching up.

RELATIVITY AND GRAVITATION

Our grandparents' lives were governed by laws of gravity pretty adequately exemplified by that mythic apple falling down on Newton's head. Then, Einstein switched mankind's frame of reference. He got us thinking about problems of people walking within moving trains and falling in elevators that were themselves falling. After that, we actually began to worry about the nature of time and light. While the apple actually still explains most of what we actually need to know, explaining relativity at subatomic and galactic scales has continued to be an academic growth story. The *GRG Journal* (U.S., Plenum for the International Committee on General Relativity and Gravitation, 1970) was the first specialist journal, picking up from the more generalist pioneer *Annalen der Physik* (Germany, Barth, 1824). Nonetheless, in closing decades of the century *Classical and Quantum Gravity* (U.K., Institute of Physics, 1984, has established itself as the leader for the next century.

GENERAL APPLIED PHYSICS

Before the engineers can go to work on a product, someone has to figure out the underlying physics and fine tune it for practicality. The world leaders in this endeavor are the *Journal of Applied Physics* (American Institute of Phyiscs for the American Physical Society, 1937) and its companion, *Applied Physics Letters* (American Institute of Physics for the American Physical Society, 1962). There are several competitors for the final place of honor, but *Applied Physics A: Materials Science and Processing* (Germany, Springer, 1948) has focused most and best on the biggest technology of the latter half of the century, solid-state physics.

SOLID-STATE PHYSICS

While the field of solid state physics has undergone a politically correct renaming as "Condensed Matter" physics, nominally incorporating liquids, the papers of the liquids community are still largely flowing off to rheology, fluid mechanics or physical chemistry reservoirs. The core of the field remains solid-state materials with a potential for use in the microelectronics and computing industries. The most significant pioneer specialist journal was the seemingly strangely titled *Philosophical Magazine* (U.K., Taylor and Francis) one of the earliest scientific journals (founded in 1791, when physics was often termed "natural philosophy"). It was also one of the first to recognize just how important solid state physics was becoming and thereby committed itself to it wholeheartedly by the 1950s. It has lost its early lead to the quick-to-press *Solid State Communications* (U.K., Pergamon, 1963) and to the appropriately solid and very "un-micro" *Physical Review B: Condensed Matter and Materials Physics* (American Institute of Physics for the American Physical Society, 1970).

SUPERCONDUCTIVITY

As if giving us the transistor and microchip technology weren't enough, solid-state physics also provided us with major advances in superconductivity, a strange and yet highly useful collapse of electrical resistance at lower temperatures. While virtually every letters journal in pure and applied physics reported significant papers in superconductivity early on, the solid-state sections of the *Physica C* (North Holland, 1988) and the *Zeitschrift fuer Physik D* (1979), now being transformed into the *European Physical Journal B* (Germany, EDP and Springer Verlag, 1998) deserve special mention. *Superconductor Science and Technology* (U.K., Institute of Physics, 1988) holds the lead going into the next century.

OPTICS

We have long understood visible light, and have gotten really good at generating it in many of its differing electromagnetic spectrum shades, including ones we don't see. Through using the strengths of each variety in reflectance and absorption, we've explored a lot of new materials. The *Journal of the Optical Society of America* (American Institute of Physics for the Optical Society of America, 1930) and its companion, *Optics Letters* (American Institute of Physics for the Optical Society of America, 1977) have been dominant for much of this century in this endeavor. Yet, they hold a historical debt to a strong Continental European tradition whose best current representative is *Optics Communications* (North Holland, 1969).

LASERS

Now if you could focus and rhythmically choreograph light beam emissions like a Rockettes' kick line, you'd have a laser. Tune it to just the wavelengths and level of intensity you need for the task at hand and you end up with the incredible tool used more and more over the last thirty years. American leaders in making this tool and finding uses for it have included the

IEEE Photonics Technology Letters (U.S., Insitute of Electrical and Electronics Engineering, 1989) and the *Journal of Lightwave Technology* (Optical Society of America and Institute of Electrical and Electronics Engineers, 1983). Its most enduring counterpart internationally has been *Applied Physics B: Lasers and Optics* (Germany, Springer Verlag, 1981).

ACOUSTICS

Hearing is really a case of sensing vibrations in the air. The generation, detection and channeling of these Doppler waves are what constitutes acoustics. Guitars, earthquakes, shock waves from explosions, underwater noises from submarine propellers, and car engine knock all have behaviors that can be modeled and studied as acoustic phenomena. The *Journal of the Acoustical Society of America* (American Institute of Physics for the Acoustical Society of America, 1929) and the *Journal of Sound and Vibration* (U.K., Academic Press, 1964) played on for much of the century. On the Continent, *Acustica* (Germany, Hirzel, 1951) sounded a similar note.

ULTRASOUND

Along with sonar, the biggest advance in applied acoustics has been ultrasound. While its medical uses are perhaps the best known, its physical sciences and engineering applications are also important. *Ultrasonic Imaging* (U.S., Academic Press, 1979) and the *IEEE Transactions on Ultrasonics, Ferroelectrics and Frequency Control* (U.S., Institute of Electrical and Electronics Engineers, 1986) became the dominant players by the end of this century.

PHYSICS IN MEDICINE AND BIOLOGY

Medical imaging like CAT and MRI scanning, ultrasound in obstetrics, fiber optic assistance for microsurgery, and vastly improved radioactive and beam therapies have made the 20th century a spectacular time for medical physicists and biomedical engineers. Two American journals deserve special recognition: *Medical Physics* (American Institute of Physics for the American Association of Physicists in Medicine, 1974) and *IEEE Transactions on Medical Imaging* (U.S., Institute of Electrical and Electronics Engineers, 1982). *Physics in Biology and Medicine* (U.K., Institute of Physics for the Institute of Physics and Engineering in Medicine) earns similar honors internationally.

GENERAL CHEMISTRY

Although the French, Dutch, and Swiss fielded very reputable general chemistry titles, the Germans and British dominated the European scene. Despite the fact that the British and German flagship journals devolved into entire families of publications, increasingly specialized by topic or type of paper featured, they maintained some general titles of continuing prominence. *Chemical Communications* (U.K., Royal Society of Chemistry, 1970) is one of the big contenders, while *Angewandte Chemie—International Edition* (Wiley-VCH for the German Chemical Society, 1888) is arguably the best representative on the Continental side. But both the Brits and the Germans have been gathering coalitions, including some from the second tier chemical powers, and a number of new ventures await measured review. For North America and the rest of the world, however, the *Journal of the American Chemical Society* (1879), has reigned supreme for the entire century.

GENERAL ORGANIC CHEMISTRY

The Germans effectively made carbon-containing "organic" compounds chemistry's biggest specialty for almost 200 years. The eponymic *Justus Liebigs Annalen der Chemie* (1832), now being transformed into the *European Journal of Organic Chemistry* (Germany, Wiley-VCH, for a consortium of European chemical societies) was its journal avatar. Two other journals, one national, the other multinational, have been its perennial leaders since the Second World War. These are the *Journal of Organic Chemistry* (American Chemical Society, 1936), and *Tetrahedron Letters* (U.K., Pergamon Press, 1959) respectively.

BIO-ORGANIC AND MEDICINAL CHEMISTRY

A good deal of organic chemistry came via the quest for drugs (and curiously enough, also via the search for dyes for cloth). The *Journal of Medicinal Chemistry* (American Chemical Society, 1963), the *Journal of Pharmaceutical Sciences* (American Chemical Society and American Pharmaceutical Association, 1912), and *Chemical and Pharmaceutical Bulletin* (Pharmaceutical Society of Japan, 1953) were particularly notable in documenting this search.

NATURAL PRODUCTS

Some people forget that drug discovery via organic chemistry began with the analyses of plants, and to a lesser degree, animal materials ground up with a mortar and pestle. Indeed, a surprising amount of information has surfaced from anthropological investigations of native remedies. While this approach has flowered once again in popular culture, it worth noting that these journals never forgot those roots: the *Journal of Natural Products* (American Society of Pharmacognoscy and American Chemical Society, 1938), *Planta Medica* (German Society for Pharmaceuticals, 1953), and the *Journal of Ethnopharmacology* (Switzerland, Elsevier, 1979).

SYNTHETIC ORGANIC CHEMISTRY

When crude natural products would not do, *Synthesis* (Germany, Thieme, 1969) and its companion *Synlett* (Germany, Thieme, 1990) have shown that one can make a living on this veritable specialty via reliable from-scratch recipes. The *Journal of the Chemical Society—Perkin Transactions I* (U.K., Royal Society of Chemistry, 1972) is aptly named for the discoverer of one of the first synthetic dyes for cloth, mauve, and proudly continues the British and Commonwealth tradition.

HETEROCYCLIC CHEMISTRY

Ringed structures matter a great deal in organic chemistry, and perhaps surprisingly, rings that include non-carbon "hetero" elements matter more than most purely carbon ones. Two journals corralled enduring interest. These are *Heterocycles* (Japan, Sendai Institute of Heterocyclic Chemistry, 1973) and the *Journal of Heterocyclic Chemistry* (U.S., HeteroCorporation, 1964).

POLYMER CHEMISTRY

In the Academy award winning film, *The Graduate,* an uncle advises his nephew, played by Dustin Hoffman, that the best chance at a financially rewarding occupation in the long run could be expressed in one word: Plastics. The avuncular advisor was right on the money with this variety of very long organic compounds. Readers of *Macromolecules* (American Chemical Society, 1968) took this advice long ago, even if Dustin Hoffman's character did not. And where did the uncle hear about polymers? When he was

Dustin Hoffman's age, he probably was reading the pioneering journals *Macromolecular Chemistry and Physics* (Switzerland, Huthig and Wepf, 1947), and the *Journal of Polymer Science* (U.S., Wiley, 1946).

GENERAL INORGANIC CHEMISTRY

The periodic table is filled with over 100 elements that are not carbon, including all the minerals, metals and earths, and many gases, yet these account for only about 10 percent of chemistry, albeit a very important 10 percent. For the last 200 years chemists interested in these had to fight for time and attention with organic chemistry. This specialized field was pioneered among journals by the *Zeitschrift fuer Anorganische und Allgemeine Chemie* (Germany, Wiley-VCH, 1892), not surprising given a historically strong interest among a persistent minority of Germans who did not opt for organic chemistry. But it was chiefly sustained by *Inorganic Chemistry* (American Chemical Society, 1962) and by the *Journal of the Chemical Society—Dalton Transactions* (U.K., Royal Society of Chemistry, 1972).

ORGANOMETALLICS

Just when the banquet of advances in largely synthetic carbon-based chemistry seemed to shrink the taste among new chemists for inorganic chemistry further, newly concocted metal-containing organic compounds became very appetizing in the 1960s. Inorganic chemistry claimed the field before the organic chemists realized its appeal. The *Journal of Organometallic Chemistry* (Switzerland, Elsevier, 1963) set the table for this explosively growing field. *Organometallics* (American Chemical Society, 1982) and *Polyhedron* (U.K., Pergamon, 1982) made it haute cuisine.

THEMATIC INORGANIC SPECIALTIES

Each of the following made pioneering contributions to their self-named thematic subspecialties. The *Journal of Coordination Chemistry* (U.S., Gordon and Breach, 1971) focused on complexes where the structure and behavior of these otherwise organic compounds were strictly determined or "coordinated" by the fairly rigid chemical bonds of the metal atoms occupying their dead centers. The *Journal of Inorganic Biochemistry* (U.S., Elsevier, 1971) showed that, while most of life's fluids other than water are carbon-based, the inorganic ions dissolved in those fluids, and, in water, play a vital role, as do certain vitamins, hormones and proteins, which are essentially coordination or organometallic compounds. The *Journal of Solid State Chemistry* (U.S., Academic Press, 1969) is focused on the sturdy foundation provided by semi-metallic and quasi-crystalline compounds that modulate the flow of electricity as it passes though them. These compounds are found in many electronic devices, including some computer chips and electronic sensors.

INORGANIC SUBSTANCE SPECIALTIES

Some of the individual squares, or rows of squares, in the ubiquitous periodic table have developed their own champion journals. These include the *Journal of Fluorine Chemistry* (Switzerland, Elsevier, 1971), *Phosphorous, Sulfur, Silicon and Related Elements* (U.S., Gordon and Breach, 1976), and *Transition Metal Chemistry* (Netherlands, Kluwer, 1975).

PHYSICAL ORGANIC CHEMISTRY

Why are some chemical structures much more frequently encountered in nature than others that would seem just as likely, given the same atomic building blocks as starting materials? Why do some molecules fall apart readily when others remain stable, even under extreme conditions? Quandaries like these faced by organic chemists were often solved by consultation with physical and theoretical chemists. The *Journal of Molecular Structure* (Netherlands, Elsevier, 1967), the *Journal of the Chemical Society—Perkin Transactions II* (U.K., Royal Society of Chemistry, 1972) and the *Journal of Physical Organic Chemistry* (U.K., Wiley, 1988), were venues where synthetically inclined chemists met their more architecturally inclined peers to jointly work on answers.

CHEMICAL KINETICS AND CATALYSIS

Where are the molecular bottlenecks or energy barriers that cause some reactions to proceed only with great force, or only under harsh conditions, or cause them to stall out before completion? Most of the time, these dilemmas are posed by organic chemists, explained by physical chemists, and remedied with facilitating, catalytic compounds by inorganic chemists working with metals, coordination compounds, or organometallics. The *International Journal of Chemical Kinetics* (U.S., Wiley, 1969), the *Journal of Catalysis* (U.S., Academic Press, 1962) and the *Journal of Molecular Catalysis* (Switzerland, Elsevier, 1975) got reactions restarted for the latter decades of this century.

GENERAL PHYSICAL CHEMISTRY

Once again, this was a field effectively invented by the Germans, with not one, but three historically prominent entries: two rival *Zeitschrifts fuer Physikalische Chemie,* and one *Berichte der Bunsengesellschaft.* These contended with a prominent British title, the *Faraday Society Transactions* (1905). Only the status of the world-leading American entry, the *Journal of Physical Chemistry* (American Chemical Society, 1896) was uncontested in regional leadership. How then to choose from among all these contenders from Britain and the Continent? By good fortune, this discrimination proved unnecessary for the British have joined the Germans, Dutch and Italians in forming the new *Physical Chemistry-Chemical Physics* (U.K., Royal Society of Chemistry) as a consolidated and worthy heir to both the Faraday and Bunsen family of publications. Third place goes to *Chemical Physics Letters* (North Holland, 1967).

PHOTOCHEMISTRY

Three journals shed light on this field. First and foremost was *Photochemistry and Photobiology* (U.K., Pergamon, 1962). The *Journal of Luminescence* (North Holland, 1970) and the *Journal of Photochemistry* (Switzerland, Elsevier, 1972) have since added to the illumination, but did not dim the brightness of the pioneer.

COLLOIDS AND SURFACES

The field started with an analysis of long-lived globules, emulsions, and suspensions in liquids (think pigments in oil paint or egg yolk in mayonnaise) and in air (think of water droplets in fog or soot particles in smoke). The field has since deliberately spread itself very thin by extending its expertise to wet and dry coatings on solids, and even including some biological membranes. The connection among these disparate objects is that the chemical and physical behavior of the droplets, coatings or membranes is often more substantially determined by their respective surfaces, not by their content or by the layers behind them. The pioneering and most inclusive of journals has been the *Journal of Colloid and Interfacial Science* (U.S., Academic Press, 1946). In slick wet coatings work, *Langmuir* (named after the Nobel Prizewinner Irving Langmuir, U.S., American Chemical Society, 1985) has since glided past its forebear. And for specially coated chips, so vital to microelectronics and sensors, *Thin Solid Films* (Switzerland, Elsevier, 1967) is transparently the leader.

MODELING MOLECULES

Theoretical Chemistry Accounts (Germany, Springer, 1962) pioneered the field even before computer graphics made it easier to visualize molecules. When the personal computer arrived on the scene, the *Journal of Computational Chemistry* (U.S., Wiley, 1980) really clicked with readers now able to execute programs on their desktops. And, while it has long had an experimentalist following among physicists, *Molecular Physics* (U.K., Taylor and Francis, 1958) has been revamping itself into a major forum for chemical theoreticians and molecular visualizers.

GENERAL ANALYTICAL CHEMISTRY

Virtually all types of chemists require someone who will tell them what their product is made of, and in what proportions. The tradition that began most notably with *Fresenius' Journal of Analytical Chemistry* (Germany, Springer, 1862), was sustained principally by *Analytical Chemistry* (American Chemical Society, 1947) and *Analytica Chimica Acta* (Netherlands, Elsevier, 1947) in this century.

ANALYTICAL SEPARATIONS SCIENCE

Chromatography is the archetypal means of separating components by size, and has both gas-based and liquid-based separation systems. The *Journal of Chromatography* (Netherlands, 1958) was the massive archive of record for much of the second half of the century, although the *Journal of Chromatographic Science* (U.S., Preston, 1963) and *LC-GC-Magazine of Separation Science* (U.S., Aster, 1983) are the quality leaders today.

SPECTROSCOPY AS A SIGNAL DETECTION APPROACH TO ANALYSIS

Applied Spectroscopy (U.S., Society for Applied Spectroscopy, 1951) and the *Journal of Molecular Spectroscopy* (U.S., Academic Press, 1957) are the longstanding leaders in molecular spectroscopy for analytical chemistry reasons. A special mention should be made of the *Journal of Analytical*

Atomic Spectrometry (U.K., Royal Society of Chemistry, 1986) for domi-
nating its niche, and thereby reclaiming atomic-level work from exclusive
control by physicists doing fundamental structural and energy shift studies.

OTHER ANALYTICAL TECHNIQUES

Nuclear magnetic resonance fundamentally altered organic structural determinations before it ever became a sexy tool in medical diagnosis, and the
Journal of Magnetic Resonance (U.S., Academic Press, 1969) led the way.
Fragmentation at high energies turned out to be productive for reducing particularly complicated molecules and mixtures to identifiable pieces, with
some key results archived in the massive pioneer, *International Journal of
Mass Spectrometry* (1968). Finally, the gargantuan *Journal of Electroanalytical Chemistry* (Netherlands, Elsevier, 1959) ably represented a very
old technique that is seeing a revival owing to great potential in surface science.

GENERAL EARTH SCIENCE

Of all the offspring of the protean *Journal of Geophysical Research,
Geophysical Research Letters* (American Geophysical Union, 1974) has
been the most dominant. *Earth and Planetary Science Letters* (Netherlands,
Elsevier, 1966) has become the closest international analogue, albeit one
with more of a solid-earth emphasis than the AGU titles. *Geophysical Journal* (U.K., Blackwell for the Royal Astronomical Society, the German Geophysical Society and the European Geophysical Society, 1911) has increasingly become the official Continental response to these two titans.

MONITORING TECHNOLOGY FOR EARTH SCIENCE

Global studies have been vastly furthered by three disparate developments that enable us to locate and measure geophysical phenomena better.
Three journals are emblematic of this progress: the *Bulletin of the Seismological Society of America* (1911), *Photogrammetric Engineering and Remote Sensing* (American Society of Photogrammetry and Remote Sensing,
1934), and *Remote Sensing of the Environment* (U.S., Elsevier, 1969).

GENERAL AND BOUNDARY LAYER METEOROLOGY

The *Bulletin of the American Meteorological Society* (1920) is the ances-
tral title of that group's veritable dynasty of journals. The *Quarterly Journal
of the Royal Meteorological Society* (U.K., 1871) has represented ably

Great Britain for many decades, while *Boundary Layer Meteorology* (Netherlands, Kluwer, 1970) has emerged as the best title among several Continental European claimants.

UPPER ATMOSPHERIC DYNAMICS

The *Journal of Atmospheric Sciences* (American Meteorological Society, 1962), *Tellus* (Denmark, Munksgaard for the Swedish Geophysical Society, 1949) and the *Journal of Atmospheric and Solar-Terrestrial Physics* (U.K., Pergamon, 1950) covered the field from on high.

ATMOSPHERIC CHEMISTRY AND AIR POLLUTION

Atmospheric Environment (U.K., Pergamon, 1967) was the pioneer in this field, with the *Journal of Atmospheric Chemistry* (Netherlands, Kluwer, 1983) rising in influence in recent decades. The *Journal of the Air and Waste Management* (U.S., Air Pollution Control Association, 1987) is arguably the best journal of amelioration.

GENERAL CLIMATOLOGY
AND ANTHROPOGENIC CLIMATIC CHANGE

The *Journal of Climate* (American Meteorological Society, 1962) has the longest track record in this field, but it will be sorely pressed by two more recent journals in this area of heightened concern. Foremost among them are *Global Biogeochemical Cycles* (American Geophysical Union, 1987) and *Climate Dynamics* (Germany, Springer, 1987).

TRADITIONAL GLACIOLOGY, PALEOCLIMATOLOGY,
AND QUATERNARY RESEARCH

Three multidisciplinary titles have long held sway. These are the *Journal of Glaciology* (British Glaciological Society, 1947), *Quaternary Research* (U.S., Academic Press, 1970) and a journal with a title almost as long as the longer time frame it covers—*Paleogeography, Paleoclimatology, Paleoecology* (Netherlands, Elsevier, 1965).

PREDOMINANTLY PHYSICAL OCEANOGRAPHY

The *Journal of Physical Oceanography* (American Meteorological Society, 1971), *Limnology and Oceanography* (American Society of Limnology and Oceanography, 1956), and the *Journal of Marine Research* (U.S., Sears

Foundation and Yale University Press, 1973) represent the best American entries, and arguably, the best in the world.

HYDROLOGY

This field, which largely deals with fresh (non-saline) surface and (under) groundwater has been long a concern of many nations. Therefore it is not surprising that there are leaders from the U.S., the U.K. and the European continent. These are respectively *Water Resources Research* (U.S., American Geophysical Union, 1965), *Water Research* (U.K., Pergamon Press for the International Association of Water Pollution Research, 1967), and the most international, the *Journal of Hydrology* (Netherlands, Elsevier, 1963).

GENERAL GEOLOGY AS THE MOST TRADITIONAL OF THE SOLID EARTH SCIENCES

One is between a rock and a hard place deciding which three general geology journals have been most influential in this century. Longevity alone as a sorting factor is not much help since a great many candidates are easily over a hundred years old. Nonetheless, the *American Journal of Science* (Yale University Press, 1818) and the *Geological Society of America Bulletin* (1889) are perhaps the best on this side of the Atlantic and the *Geological Magazine* (U.K., Cambridge University Press, 1864) on the other.

STRUCTURAL GEOLOGY AND TECTONICS

Questions regarding the fundamental processes that shaped larger regional features like mountain ranges and the distribution of the continents over the oceans, finally achieved some resolution through a revolutionary reconceptualization by Wegener in this century. Three titles have assumed the mantle of leadership, *Tectonophysics* (Netherlands, Elsevier, 1964), the *Journal of Structural Geology* (U.K., Pergamon, 1979) and *Tectonics* (American Geophysical Union, 1982).

GENERAL MINERALOGY AND PETROLOGY

The *American Mineralogist* (Mineralogical Society of America, 1916) has been the leader in North America, while *Contributions to Mineralogy and Petrology* (Germany, Springer, 1947) and *Geochimica et Cosmochimica Acta* (U.K., Pergamon, 1950) have been enduring multinational gems.

VOLCANOLOGY, IGNEOUS, AND METAMORPHIC PETROLOGY

The *Journal of Volcanology and Geothermal Research* (Netherlands, Elsevier, 1976) and the *Bulletin of Volcanology* (Germany, Springer for the International Association of Volcanology and Chemistry of the Earth's Interior, 1961) did not run out of new magmatic material or events to report and analyze. The mineralogical journal with the greatest emphasis on rocks of igneous origin and their metamorphed progeny, the *Journal of Petrology* (U.K., Clarendon Press of Oxford University, 1960) studied the remnant evidence of volcanic and other diagenic processes better than any other specialized title.

SEDIMENTATION AND PHYSICAL GEOGRAPHY CAUSED BY WEATHERING

Three journals captured the role of the wind and waters in the shaping of the earth's surface and in the laying down of deposits. Two are based on stratigraphic analysis. These are *Sedimentology* (U.K., Blackwell for the International Association of Sedimentologists, 1962) and the *Journal of Sedimentary Research* (U.S., Society for Sedimentary Geology, 1931). The other is based on the historical topography of larger regions: *Earth Surface Processes and Landforms* (U.K., Wiley for the British Geomorphological Research Group, 1976).

GENERAL PALEONTOLOGY

Three journals share the role of sustaining the field through a century where popular interest has blown hot and cold, and where most funding was provided unromantically by petroleum companies. The leading American title, the *Journal of Paleontology* (U.S., Society of Economic Paleontologists and Mineralogists, 1927) has been more than matched by the British *Paleontology* (Palaeontological Association, 1957) and the European *Lethaia* (Norway, Scandinavian University Press, 1968). The strength of British and Continental journals has a good deal to do with the fact that they are less fractionated by biological subspecialty defections than their American counterparts.

GENERAL ECONOMIC GEOLOGY

Economic Geology (U.S., Society of Economic Geologists, 1905), *Geophysical Prospecting* (U.K., Blackwell for the European Association of Exploration Geophysicists, 1953), and *Exploration and Mining Geology* (U.K., Pergamon for the Canadian Institute of Mining and Metallurgy, which published this journal's predecessors, since 1908) have been the century's leaders in the geology and geophysics of prospecting and mining.

GENERAL ORE GEOLOGY AND ANALYSIS

Among the most important journals not specifically targeted at fuels were *Mineralium Deposita* (Germany, Springer for the Society of Geology Applied to Mineral Deposits, 1966), *Ore Geology Reviews* (particularly good for metals, Netherlands, Elsevier, 1986), and *Clays and Clay Minerals* (including their uses in manufacturing and building materials, U.S., Pergamon for the Clay Mineral Society, 1968).

FOSSIL FUEL GEOLOGY

The *AAPG Bulletin* (American Association of Petroleum Geologists, 1918) has been the world's leader in the key energy "mineral," oil, with the *Journal of Petroleum Geology* (U.K., Scientific Press Ltd., 1978) a good second choice, and with both journals also covering natural gas. The leading title for solid combustible fuels (peat, bitumen, lignite, and anthracite) has been the *International Journal of Coal Geology* (Netherlands, Elsevier, 1980).

GEOCHEMISTRY AND CHEMICAL PROCESSING OF FOSSIL FUELS

Virtually all fossil fuels in nature exude chemical traces that aid in discovering deposits worth profitable extraction, with those traces also having tell-tale components that indicate something of the natural history of the deposit. Before geochemistry progressed, most fuel-source findings were dependent on paleontologists checking sites for fossils that were related to coal, oil, and gas deposits. Now, in addition to exploratory seismological studies, geochemical journals handle much of this and report chemical analyses that determine the types of refinement or handling necessary for the raw materials to be used as a clean burning energy source, or in an industrial process. *Organic Geochemistry* (U.S., Pergamon, 1977) has been the leader in the initial discovery and characterization aspects of fuels, and of the organic material and soil components that are precursors or indicators of fossil fuels, while *Fuel* (U.K., IPC Science and Technology Press, 1952) and *Energy & Fuels* (American Chemical Society, 1987) have dominated in advising on processing for clean combustion.

REFERENCES AND SUGGESTED READINGS

Alvarez, Pedro, and Antonio Pulgarin. "The Diffusion of Scientific Journals Analyzed through Citations." *Journal of the American Society for Information Science* 48: 953-958, 1997.

Bensman, Stephen J. and Stanley J. Wilder. "Scientific and Technical Serials Holdings Optimization in an Inefficient Market." *Library Resources and Technical Services* 42 (3): 147-242, 1998.

Bonitz, Manfred. "The Scientific Talents of Nations." *Libri* 47 (4): 206-213, 1997.

Bottle, R.T., and others. *Information Sources in Chemistry*. London: Bowker-Saur, 1993.

Braun, Tibor. "On Some Historical Antecedents of the Belief in the Decline of British Science." *Journal of Information Science* 19: 401, 1993.

Braun, Tibor, Hajnalka Maczelka, and A. Schubert. "World Flash on Basic Research. Scientometric Indicators, Datafiles, Summary Statistics, and Trendlines of Major Geopolitical Regions, 1980-1989." *Scientometrics* 25(2): 211-218, 1992.

Burnham, Paul D. "Private Liberal Arts Colleges and the Costs of Scientific Journals: A Perennial Dilemma." *College and Research Libraries* 59: 406-420, 1998.

Chrzastowski, Tina. "Information Sources in Surface and Colloid Chemistry." *Science and Technology Libraries* 9 (3): 75-96, 1989.

Chrzastowski, Tina E. "National Trends in Academic Serials Collections, 1992-1994" *Science and Technology Libraries* 16 (3-4): 191-207, 1997.

Cromer, Donna E. "English: The *Lingua Franca* of International Scientific Communication." *Science and Technology Libraries* 12 (1): 21-34, 1991.

Davis, Elisabeth B. *Guide to Information Sources in the Botanical Sciences*. Englewood, CO: Libraries Unlimited, 1996.

Davis, Elisabeth B. *Using the Biological Literature: A Practical Guide*. New York: Marcel Dekker, 1995.

Derksen, Charlotte R. M., and Michael Mark Noga. "The World of Geoscience Serials: Comparative Use Patterns." in *International Initiatives in Geoscience In-*

formation. Geoscience Information Society. 26th Meeting, 1991. Geoscience Information Society, 1992.

Diodato, Virgil P. *Dictionary of Bibliometrics.* Binghamton, NY: The Haworth Press, Inc., 1994.

Diodato, Virgil P. "The Use of English Language in Non-U.S. Science Journals: A Case Study of Mathematics Publications, 1970-1985." *Library and Information Science Research* 12: 355-371, 1990.

Duranceau, Ellen Finnie. "Exchange Rates and the Serials Marketplace." *Serials Review* 21 (3): 83-96, 1995.

Edelman, Hendrik. "Precursor to the Serials Crisis: German Science Publishing in the 1930s." *Journal of Scholarly Publishing* 25 (April): 171-178, 1994.

Garfield, Eugene. *Essays of an Information Scientist, v.1-14.* Philadelphia: ISI Press, 1977-1992. *Relevant papers in every volume from the master.*

Garfield, Eugene. "What Citations Tell Us About Canadian Research." *Canadian Journal of Information and Library Science* 18 (December): 14-35, 1993.

Hamaker, Charles A. "The Least Reading for the Smallest Number at the Highest Price." *American Libraries* 19: 764-768, 1988.

Harter, Stephen P., and Thomas E. Nisonger. "ISI's Impact Factor as a Misnomer: A Proposed New Measure to Assess Journal Impact." *Journal of the American Society for Information Science* 48: 1146-1148, 1997.

Havemann, Frank. "Changing Publication Behaviour of East and Central European Scientists and the Impact of their Papers." *Information Processing and Management* 32: 489-496, 1996.

Henderson, Albert. "The 160 Million Dollar Question: What Happens to the Federal Money Paid for University Research Libraries?" *Against the Grain* 9: 28-29, November, 1997.

Henderson, Albert. "A Solution to the Futility of Cost-Effective Librarianship." *Science and Technology Libraries* 12 (1): 99-107, 1991.

Hooydonk, Guido van. "Cost and Citation Data for 5399 Scientific Journals in Connection with Journal Price-Setting, Copyright Laws, and the Use of Bibliometric Data for Project Review." *The Serials Librarian* 27 (1): 45-58, 1995.

Hughes, Janet A. "Use of Faculty Publication Lists and ISI Citation Data to Identify a Core List of Journals with Local Importance." *Library Acquisitions: Practice and Theory* 19: 403-413, 1995.

Hurd, Julie M., Deborah D. Blecic, and Rama Vishwanatham. "Information Use by Molecular Biologists: Implications for Library Collections and Services." *College and Research Libraries* 60 (1): 31-43, 1999.

Hurt, Charlie Deuel. *Information Sources in Science and Technology.* Englewood, CO: Libraries Unlimited, 1994.

Journal Citation Reports. Philadelphia: Institute for Scientific Information, annual.

Knoche, Michael. "Scientific Journals Under National Socialism." *Libraries and Culture* 26: 415-426, 1991.

Kronick, David A. "Bibliographic Dispersion of Early Periodicals." *The Serials Librarian* 12 (3-4): 55-59, 1987.

Kronick, David A. *Literature of the Life Sciences.* Metuchen, NJ: Scarecrow Press, 1985.

Kronick, David A. *Scientific and Technical Periodicals of the Seventeenth and Eighteenth Centuries: A Guide.* Metuchen, NJ: Scarecrow Press, 1991.

Le Coadic, Yves F. and Serge Chambaud. "Politics and Policies in the Scientific and Technical Information Sector in France." *Journal of Information Science* 19 (6): 473-479, 1993.

Liang, Diane F. *Mathematics Journals: An Annotated Guide.* Lanham, MD: 1992.

Machlup, Fritz, and Kenneth Leeson. *Information Through the Printed Word: The Dissemination of Scholarly, Scientific, and Intellectual Knowledge. v.2. The Journals.*

Maizell, Robert E., *How to Find Chemical Information.* New York: Wiley, 1998.

McCain, Katherine W. "Core Journal Networks and Collection Maps: New Bibliometric Tools for Serials Research and Management." *Library Quarterly* 61: 311-336, 1991.

McCain, Katherine W. "Biotechnology in Context: A Database Filtering Approach to Identifying Core and Productive Non-Core Journals Supporting Multidisciplinary R & D." *Journal of the American Society for Information Science* 46: 306-317, 1995.

Meadows, A.J. *The Scientific Journal.* London: Aslib, 1979.

Nisonger, Thomas E. *Management of Serials in Libraries.* Edgewood, CO: Libraries Unlimited, 1998.

Olden, Anthony and Michael Wise, eds. *Information and Libraries in the Developing World, 3v.* London: Library Association Publishing, 1990-1994.

Peek, Robin, Jeffrey Pomerantz, and Stephen Paling. "The Traditional Scholarly Journals Legitimize the Web." *Journal of the American Society for Information Science 49* (11): 983-989, 1998.

Primack, Alice Lefler. *Journal Literature of the Physical Sciences.* Lanham, MD: Scarecrow Press, 1992.

Pruett, Nancy Jones and George McGregor. *Scientific and Technical Libraries.* 2v. Orlando, FL: Academic Press, 1986.

Rice, Barbara A. "Selection and Evaluation of Chemistry Periodicals." *Science and Technology Libraries* 4 (1): 43-59, 1983.

Richards, Pamela Spence. "Scientific Information for Stalin's Laboratories: 1945-1953." *Information Processing and Management* 32: 77-88, 1996.

Rioux, Margaret A. "Staying Afloat in a Sea of Knowledge: Information Sources in Applied Ocean Physics." *Science and Technology Libraries* 13 (2): 113-135, 1992.

Rousseau, R. and vanHooydonk, Guido. "Journal Production and Journal Impact Factors." *Journal of the American Society for Information Science* 47: 775-780, 1996.

Royle, Pam. "A Citation Analysis of Australian Science and Social Science Journals." *Australian Academic and Research Libraries* 25: 162-171, 1994.

Sapp, Gregg. "Subject Coverage in General and Specialized Mathematics Journals." *The Serials Librarian* 16 (3-4): 93-117, 1989.

Saunders, LaVerna. "ARL's SPARC Alliance Bears Fruit: ARL/ACS Electronic Publishing Venture." *Information Today* 15 (8): 25, 1998.

Schad, Jasper G. "Scientific Societies and Their Journals: Issues of Cost and Relevance." *Journal of Academic Librarianship* 23: 406-407, 1997.

Schaffner, Ann C. "The Future of Scientific Journals: Lessons from the Past." *Information Technology and Libraries* 13: 239-247, 1994.

Schmidt, Karen. "Information Resources in Animal Behavior." *Science and Technology Libraries* 12 (1): 69-83, 1991.

Shaw, Dennis F. *Information Sources in Physics*. London: Bowker-Saur, 1994.

Smith, B., Shirley V. King, Ian Stewart. "Survey of Demand for Japanese Scientific and Technical Serial Literature." *Interlending and Document Supply* 15 (October): 111-117, 1987.

Stankus, Tony. "Avoiding a Rush to a Verdict of Guilty: The Treatment of Third World Science by First World Publishers and Librarians." *RQ* 35: 467-475, 1996.

Stankus, Tony. "Could Long Term Shifts in Publishing Sector Dominance Among the Top 100 Physical Science Journals Slow Rates of Invoice Inflation?" *Science and Technology Libraries* 15 (3): 77-89, 1995.

Stankus , Tony. *Electronic Expectations: Science Journals on the Web*. New York: The Haworth Press, Inc., 1999.

Stankus, Tony, Bernard S. Schlessinger, and Rashelle Schlessinger. " English Language Trends in German Basic Science Journals." *Science and Technology Libraries* 1 (3): 55-66, 1981.

Stankus, Tony, William C. Littlefield, and Kevin Rosseel. "Is the Best Japanese Science in Western Journals?" *The Serials Librarian* 14 (1/2): 95-107, 1988.

Stankus, Tony. "Journal Divorces: With and Without Custody Fights and Remarriage." *Technicalities* (17 (7): 11-13, 1997.

Stankus, Tony. "The Journals of German University and Engineering School Scientists Before and After National Reunification." *Science and Technology Libraries* 16(1): 35-47, 1996.

Stankus, Tony. *Making Sense of Journals in the Life Sciences: From Specialty Origins to Contemporary Assortment*. New York: The Haworth Press, Inc., 1992.

Stankus, Tony. *Making Sense of Journals in the Physical Sciences: From Specialty Assortment to Contemporary Assortment*. New York: The Haworth Press, Inc., 1992.

Stankus, Tony. "Making the Scientist a Library Ally in the Real Research Journal Funding Wars: Those With Our Treasurers and With Our Own Mistaken Notions." *Library Acquisitions: Practice and Theory* 14 (1): 113-119, 1991.

Stankus, Tony. "Mergers, Acquisitions, and Euros." *Technicalities* 19 (3): 4.

Stankus, Tony and Kevin Rosseel. "The Rise of Eurojournals: Their Success Can Be Ours." *Library Resources and Technical Services* 31: 215-224, 1986.

Stankus, Tony., ed. *Scientific and Clinical Literature for the Decade of the Brain*. Binghamton, NY: The Haworth Press, Inc., 1993.

Stankus, Tony. *Scientific Journals: Improving Library Collections Through Analysis of Publishing Trends*. New York: The Haworth Press, Inc., 1990.

Stankus, Tony. *Scientific Journals: Issues in Library Selection and Management*. New York: The Haworth Press, Inc., 1987.

Stankus, Tony. "Sacred Cows, Cash Cows, and Mad Cow Disease." *Technicalities* 16 (6): 2-3, 1996.

Stankus, Tony and Virgil C. Diodato. "Selecting Multispecialty Mathematics Research Journals via Their Underlying Subject Emphases." *Science and Technology Libraries* 4 (1): 61-78, 1983.

Stankus, Tony. *Special Format Serials and Issues: Annual Reviews of . . ., Advances in . . ., Symposia on . . ., Methods of. . . .* New York: The Haworth Press, Inc., 1996.

Stankus, Tony and Carolyn Virginia Mills. "Which Life Science Journals will Constitute the Locally Sustainable Core Collection of the 1990s and Which will Become "Fax Access" Only? Predictions Based on Citation and Price Patterns, 1979-1989." *Science and Technology Libraries* 13 (Fall): 73-114, 1992.

Stern, David. "Pricing Models: Past, Present, and Future?" *The Serials Librarian* 36 (1-2): 301-319, 1999.

Tallent, Ed. "Project Muse." *Library Journal* 124 (March1, 1999): 119.

Teferra, Damtew. "The Status and Capacity of Science Publishing in Africa." *Journal of Scholarly Publishing* 27 (October): 28-36, 1995.

Tenopir, Carol, and King, Donald Ward. "Trends in Scientific Scholarly Journal Publishing in the United States." *Journal of Scholarly Publishing* 28(3): 135-170, 1997.

Walcott, Rosalind. "Serials Cited by Marine Sciences Research Center Faculty, University at Stony Brook, 1986-1991." *Science and Technology Libraries* 14(3): 15-33, 1994.

Wiggins, Gary. *Chemical Information Sources,* New York: McGraw-Hill, 1991.

Wilkinson, Sophie L. "Behind the Scenes at Journals." *Chemical and Engineering News* 77 (37): 25-31, September 13, 1999.

Wyatt, H. V. *Information Sources in the Life Sciences.* London: Bowker-Saur, 1994.

Young, Jeffrey R. "Stanford-based High Wire Press Transforms the Publication of Scientific Journals." *The Chronicle of Higher Education* 43 (36):A21, May 16, 1997.

Zhang Haiqi and Shigeaki Yamazaki. "Citation Indicators of Japanese Journals." *Journal of the American Society for Information Science* 49: 375-379, 1998.

Zipp, Louise S. "Core Serial Titles in an Interdisciplinary Field: The Case of Environmental Geology" *Library Resources and Technical Services* 43 (1): 28-36, 1999.

Zipp, Louise S. "Identifying Core Geologic Research Journals." *In Changing Gateways: The Impact of Technology on Geoscience Information Exchange.* Geoscience Information Society. 29th Meeting, 1994, Seattle, Washington. Geoscience Information Society, 1995.

Zitt, Michel, Francois Perrot, and Remi Barre. "The Transition from "National" to "Transnational" Model and Related Measures of Countries' Performance." *Journal of the American Society for Information Science* 49: 30-42, 1998.

Chapter 17

Journals of the Century in Engineering and Computer Science

Carol S. Robinson

Identifying the most influential engineering and computer science journals is like trying to hit a moving target while blindfolded. Even with unobstructed vision, the frequent appearance of new journals in fields that are hard to categorize made 20th century engineering and computer science librarianship challenging.

Nonetheless, there were some guideposts in designating the most enduring research, trade and popular titles. I placed great value on longevity. Impact factors as published in the Institute of Scientific Information's *Journal Citation Reports* often proved valuable. Sometimes, however, the *JCR*'s coverage of areas of engineering was spotty, or dissimilar areas were grouped together. Ultimately, my many years of experience in collections and reference was my best guide.

Most often I selected journals published by not-for-profit research and professional associations, usually American ones. I believe these journals of the century have every prospect of being among the journals of the next century, along with new titles published in areas not yet imagined, in formats familiar and unfamiliar.

After looking at general engineering, I will discuss the main branches of engineering, followed by any subdivisions. Neither food and agricultural nor biochemical and genetic technology were included to any great extent in this paper. They were assigned to other authors in the sections on allied health sciences and agriculture/veterinary medicine and the life sciences portion of the basic sciences paper.

This chapter originally appeared in *The Serials Librarian* 39(4): 119-132, 2001.

GENERAL ENGINEERING

The *Encyclopaedia Britannica Online* defines engineering as "the application of scientific principles to the optimal conversion of natural resources into structures, machines, products, systems, and processes for the benefit of humankind." Given this definition it might be seen as ironic that the first, and for a long time the only, use of the word *engineering* was in the context of military engineering, which is defined by the *Encyclopaedia Britannica Online* as "the art and practice of designing and building military works and of building and maintaining lines of military transport and communications. In its earliest uses the term engineering referred particularly to the construction of engines of war and the execution of works intended to serve military purposes." Out of military engineering grew civil engineering; the other three main branches, mechanical, electrical and chemical, came into existence in response to scientific discoveries and societal concerns. Each branch has distinct subdivisions as well as areas which cross these boundaries.

Two trade titles that have endured without even a name change are *Engineer* (U.K., Miller-Freeman, 1856) and *Engineering: For Innovators in Technology, Manufacturing and Management* (U.K., sponsored by the Design Council; published by Gillard Welch Ltd., 1866). Demonstrating its ability to keep up with the times, *Engineer* is now available online. A third trade title of lasting significance is *ENR: Connecting the Industry Worldwide* (U.S., McGraw-Hill, 1874). By far the oldest engineering research title can be traced back to the *Philosophical Transactions of the Royal Society of London* (U.K., the Society, 1665). Another enduring research title is *VDI-Z: Zeitschrift des Vereins Deutscher Ingenieure für Maschinenbau und Metallbearbeitung* (Germany, VDI, 1857).

CIVIL ENGINEERING

Civil engineering is the conception, design, construction, and management of residential and commercial buildings and structures, water supply facilities, and transportation systems for goods and people, as well as the control of the environment for the maintenance and improvement of the quality of life. Although the term was not used until the 18th century, it is apparent that civil engineers have been plying their trade since ancient times. Branches of civil engineering include, but are not limited to: geotechnical engineering, also known as engineering geology or geological engineering, construction engineering, structural engineering, environmental engineering, water resources engineering and transportation engineering.

The *Proceedings of the Institution of Civil Engineers* (U.K., ICE, 1837), the oldest civil engineering periodical in the world, is now published in six separate parts. The titles of the parts of the Proceedings—*Civil Engineering; Geotechnical Engineering; Municipal Engineer; Structures and Buildings; Transport; and Water, Maritime and Energy*—reflect many of the areas which fall into the category of civil engineering. Equally if not more important are the periodical publications of the American Society of Civil Engineers (ASCE). The ASCE began publishing its *Proceedings* (U.S., ASCE, 1873) in the latter 19th century. It now publishes 30 titles, 14 of which can be considered directly linked to the original proceedings. Today, both ICE and ASCE have online versions of their journals.

AEROSPACE ENGINEERING

Certainly the publications of the American Institute of Aeronautics and Astronautics (AIAA) are among the most significant in the field; its publication, the *AIAA Journal: Devoted to Aerospace Research and Development* (U.S., AIAA, 1963), consistently ranks among the top three aerospace journals in ISI's *Journal Citation Reports*. Four other AIAA titles—*Journal of Aircraft* (U.S., AIAA, 1963), *Journal of Guidance, Control, and Dynamics* (U.S., AIAA, 1978), *Journal of Propulsion and Power* (U.S., AIAA, 1985), and *Journal of Spacecraft and Rockets* (U.S., AIAA, 1964)—have almost always been in each year's top ten titles for the last decade. Another society publication which regularly ranks in the top ten is the *IEEE Transactions on Aerospace and Electronic Systems* (U.S., IEEE, 1957). *Progress in Aerospace Sciences* (U.S., Pergamon, 1961) is the highest ranking commercial publication in the field.

CONSTRUCTION ENGINEERING/ STRUCTURAL ENGINEERING

In 1747 the Ecole Nationale des Ponts et Chausses was founded in France to provide training in bridge and road building. Its *Annales des Ponts et Chausses* (France, Elsevier, 1831-1971; resumed 1976) was important enough for British engineers to learn French. Aside from the journals published by the ICE and the ASCE on this topic, the American Concrete Institute publishes two titles, *ACI Materials Journal* (U.S., ACI, 1929) and *ACI Structural Journal* (U.S., ACI, 1929) which consistently rank in the top ten in the *JCR*. Although it has only been published since 1991, *Indoor Air: International Journal of Indoor Air Quality and Climate* (Denmark, sponsored by International Society of Indoor Air Quality and Climate; published by Munksgaard, 1991) was ranked number one after only five years and has maintained that rank through 1998.

ENVIRONMENTAL ENGINEERING

Although it might seem that environmental engineering is a new branch of engineering, it has actually existed for at least a hundred years. Previously known as sanitary engineering, it began with a focus on clean water and disposal of wastes; today environmental engineering covers pollution of all types. For the past seven years *Environmental Science and Technology* (U.S., American Chemical Society, 1967) has been ranked first or second in environmental engineering by the *JCR*. This illustrates one of the difficulties of categorizing journals since the primary subject of the journal is environmental chemistry, and chemistry is a science. Other top titles include: *Ambio* (Sweden, Royal Swedish Academy of Sciences, 1972), *Journal of Environmental Engineering* (U.S., ASCE, 1956), *Water Environment Research* (U.S., Water Environment Federation, 1929) and the *Journal of the Air & Waste Management Association* (U.S., Air & Waste Management Association, 1951).

GEOTECHNICAL ENGINEERING

Geotechnical Engineering has been recognized by the ISI as a branch of engineering for only the past two years. In both years, *Geotechnique* (U.K., sponsored by the ICE; published by Telford, 1948) was ranked as the top title in the field. In prior years it was always in the top twenty in the broader category of civil engineering. *Rock Mechanics and Rock Engineering* (Austria, Springer, 1929) and the *Canadian Geotechnical Journal* (Canada, sponsored by the Canadian Geotechnical Society; published by the National Research Council of Canada Press, 1963) continue to be significant titles in the field.

TRANSPORTATION ENGINEERING

Transportation engineering has a branch for every mode of transportation as well as at least one professional society. Although transportation engineering is considered by most to be a part of civil engineering, many aspects involve a mechanical engineering component. The major civil engineering societies each publish a journal which covers all aspects of transportation: *Journal of Transportation Engineering* (U.S., ASCE, 1873) and *Proceed-*

ings of the Institution of Civil Engineers—Transport (U.K., ICE, 1837). *Transportation Research, Parts A-F* (U.S., Elsevier, 1967) is another important title covering the entire field.

Automotive engineering has the *Society of Automotive Engineers Transactions* (U.S., SAE, 1905) as well as *Automotive Engineering International* (U.S., SAE, 1905) and *SAE Off-Highway Engineering* (U.S., SAE, 1991). One section of the Institution of Mechanical Engineers' proceedings is devoted to automotive engineering: *Proceedings of the Institution of Mechanical Engineers, Part D, Journal of Automobile Engineering* (U.K., IMechE, 1989). As has been mentioned earlier, *Journal Citation Reports—Science Edition* does not cover engineering thoroughly. For many years there were fewer than ten titles listed in the category of transportation; however, every year since 1991 the *IEEE Transactions on Vehicular Technology* (U.S., IEEE, 1967) has been ranked number one.

Railroad engineering has the *American Railway Engineering Association Bulletin* (U.S., AREA, 1900) and *Proceedings of the Institution of Mechanical Engineers, Part F, Journal of Rail and Rapid Transit* (U.K., IMechE, 1847). A trade title which has been around for a long time is *Railway Age* (U.S., Simmons-Boardman, 1856).

WATER RESOURCES ENGINEERING

Water resources engineering includes the issue of water quality, the relationship between surface, soil and groundwater as well as the practical aspects of water management. Once again, the top journal in the field is published by a scientific society, not a commercial publisher. *Water Resources Research* (U.S., American Geophysical Union, 1965) has been ranked number one every year since 1991. Another society publication is the *Journal of the American Water Works Association* (U.S., American Water Works Association, 1881). Only twice since 1991 has *Water Research* (U.K., sponsored by International Association on Water Quality; published by Elsevier, 1967) not been the second ranked title in the field.

MECHANICAL ENGINEERING

Mechanical engineering was originally concerned with engines, machines and manufacturing. It came into its own with the Industrial Revolution, a time when new sources of power and new machines were developed. Today, mechanical engineering includes, but is not limited to: biomedical engineering, mechanics and materials, fluid mechanics, heat transfer, energy conversion and conservation, and manufacturing. Mechanical engineering may also include environmental engineering and transportation, which I chose to include under civil engineering. The establishment of the Institution of Mechanical Engineers in 1847 and the American Society of Mechanical Engineers in 1880 reflected the growing importance of this area of engineering. As with civil engineering, the publications of these two organizations cover all aspects of the field. The IMechE began publishing its *Proceedings* (U.K., IMechE, 1847) the same year it was founded although the first volume was not completed until 1849. Today they publish 12 sections of their proceedings, two of which began in 1999. ASME also began publishing its *Transactions* (U.S., ASME, 1980) the year it was founded; today there are 17 titles which continue the numbering of the original *Transactions*. Both IMechE and ASME have online versions of their publications.

BIOMEDICAL ENGINEERING

Biomedical engineering is the use of engineering techniques to solve medical problems. Although I have chosen to include it in mechanical engineering, there are large electrical and electronic engineering and computer science and materials science and engineering components. This is an area of engineering which has been in existence for around fifty years. Two of the first titles to be published in the area are: *IEEE Transactions on Biomedical Engineering* (U.S., IEEE, 1953) and the *ASAIO Journal* (U.S., sponsored by American Society for Artificial Internal Organs; published by Lippincott Williams & Wilkins, 1955). Both the *Journal of Biomedical Materials Research* (U.S., Wiley, 1966), the official journal of the Society for Biomaterials the European Society for Biomaterials, and the Japanese Society for Biomaterials, and the *Journal of Biomechanics* (U.K., Elsevier, 1968), a publication of the European Society of Biomechanics and the American Society of Biomechanics, began publication in the 1960's. IMechE and ASME each publish a title in the field: *Proceedings of the Institution of Mechanical Engineers, Part H, Journal of Engineering in Medicine* (U.K., IMechE, 1971) and *Journal of Biomechanical Engineering* (U.S., ASME, 1977). The *IEEE Transactions Medical Imaging* (U.S., IEEE, 1982) consistently ranks in the top ten in the *JCR*.

ENERGY CONVERSION AND CONSERVATION

This is another area of engineering where most of the frequently cited titles are society publications. Since 1995 the *AAPG Bulletin* (U.S., American Association of Petroleum Geologists, 1917) has ranked in the top five of the *JCR*. Other titles consistently near the top are: *Combustion and Flame* (U.S., sponsored by the Combustion Institute; published by Elsevier, 1957), *Energy and Fuels* (U.S., American Chemical Society, 1987), and *Progress in Energy and Combustion Science* (U.S., Pergamon, 1975). Other society publications are: *Journal of Power and Energy* (U.K., IMechE, 1990), the *Journal of Solar Energy Engineering* (U.S., ASME, 1980), the *Journal of Energy Engineering* (U.S., ASCE, 1956) and the *IEEE Transactions on Energy Conversion* (U.S., IEEE, 1952). The latter two titles illustrate the "interconnectedness" of engineering. Nuclear engineering is comprehensively covered in *Nuclear Science and Engineering: Research and Development Related to Peaceful Utilization of Nuclear Energy* (U.S., American Nuclear Society, 1956) and the *IEEE Transactions on Nuclear Science* (U.S., IEEE, 1954).

MANUFACTURING, INDUSTRIAL AND QUALITY CONTROL ENGINEERING

Manufacturing engineering deals with product design and improvement, while industrial engineering deals with the management of the people and equipment involved in the manufacturing process. Quality control is a shared concern of both specialties. Although there is very little consistency in the rankings for manufacturing and industrial engineering journals, the *IEEE Transactions on Advanced Packaging* (U.S., IEEE, 1978) has consistently ranked in the top five in the manufacturing section of the *JCR*. There are, nonetheless, a number of notable manufacturing engineering titles, including two from the Society of Manufacturing Engineers, namely, *Manufacturing Engineering* (U.S., SME, 1932) and *Journal of Manufacturing Systems* (U.S., sponsored by SME; published by Elsevier, 1982).

The Institute of Industrial Engineers publishes two titles which are consistently ranked: *IIE Solutions* (U.S., IIE, 1969) and *IIE Transactions: Industrial Engineering Research and Development* (U.S., sponsored by IIE; published by Kluwer, 1969). In response to the increasing automation of manufacturing processes, journals like the *IEEE Transactions on Robotics and Automation* (U.S., IEEE, 1985) have been published.

As mentioned, quality control engineering is linked to both manufacturing and industrial engineering. Some of the most significant titles in the field are the *Journal of Product Innovation Management* (U.S., sponsored by the Product Development and Management Association; published by Elsevier, 1984), the *Journal of Quality Control* (U.S., American Society for Quality Control, 1969), the *Journal of Testing and Evaluation* (U.S., American Society for Testing and Materials, 1973), and *Materials Evaluation* (U.S., American Society for Nondestructive Testing, 1942).

There are a number of titles which cover all three areas of engineering. The *International Journal of Machine Tools and Manufacture: Design, Research and Application* (U.K., Elsevier, 1961) is one; *Composites, Part A, Applied Science and Manufacturing* (U.K., Elsevier, 1969) is another. Two IEEE titles also fit in here: the *IEEE Transactions on Semiconductor Manufacturing* (U.S., IEEE, 1988) and the *IEEE Transactions on Computer-Aided Design of Integrated Circuits and Systems* (U.S., IEEE, 1982).

MATERIALS ENGINEERING

Materials engineering involves developing processes for the preparation and production of materials and designing materials for specific applications. Areas of materials engineering include, but are not limited to, semiconductors, metals, ceramics, textiles, and polymers. There are general materials journals as well as those focused on specific materials or materials of interest to a particular industry. Two of the most important titles in the general category are *JOM: The Journal of the Minerals, Metals and Materials Society* (U.S., Minerals, Metals and Materials Society, 1949) and *Advanced Materials and Processes* (U.S., ASM International, 1941). Other titles of significance include the *Journal of Materials Research* (U.S., Materials Research Society, 1986) and the *MRS Bulletin* (U.S., Materials Research Society, 1976).

The Minerals, Metals and Materials Society and ASM International are jointly responsible for two titles—*Metallurgical and Materials Transactions, A, Physical Metallurgy and Materials Science* (U.S., ASM International, 1970) and *Metallurgical and Materials Transactions B—Process Metallurgy and Materials Processing Science* (U.S., ASM International, 1975)—which traditionally focus on metals, while the Minerals, Metals and Materials Society and the IEEE are responsible for the *Journal of Electronic Materials* (U.S., Minerals, Metals and Materials Society, 1971). One of the top ceramic journals is the *Journal of the American Ceramic Society* (U.S., ACS, 1918); another is the *Journal of the European Ceramic Society* (U.K., sponsored by ECS; published by Elsevier, 1985). In the area of textiles, the *Textile Research Journal* (U.S., Textile Research Institute, 1930) is one of the most significant titles. Polymers are one of the few areas where the top journals are not published by or for societies; the only exception is *Macromolecules* (U.S., American Chemical Society, 1968). Other important titles are *Progress in Polymer Science: An International Review Journal* (U.K.,

Elsevier, 1967) and *Macromolecular Rapid Communications* (Germany, Wiley, 1980).

NAVAL ARCHITECTURE AND MARINE ENGINEERING

Traditionally, naval architecture has been concerned with the design and construction of ships, and marine engineering has referred to the power plant which drives the ship. One of the oldest publications in the field is the *Transactions of the Institution of Engineers and Shipbuilders in Scotland* (U.K., the Institution, 1857). The *Transactions of the Royal Institution of Naval Architects* (U.K., RINA, 1860) began publication only three years later. The American equivalent, the *Society of Naval Architects and Marine Engineers Transactions* (U.S., SNAME, 1893) did not begin publication until 1893, the same year the society was founded. SNAME now also publishes the *Journal of Ship Research* (U.S., SNAME, 1957) and the *Journal of Ship Production* (U.S., SNAME, 1985). Another society publication of lasting interest is the *Institute of Marine Engineers Transactions* (U.K., IMarE, 1889). Today the society also publishes the *Marine Engineers Review* (U.K., IMarE, 1967) and the *Journal of Offshore Technology* (U.K., IMarE, 1993). *Marine Technology and SNAME News* (U.S., SNAME, 1964) and the *Naval Architect* (U.K., RINA, 1971) combine news and research articles.

CHEMICAL ENGINEERING

Chemical engineering has existed for as long as man has used the processes of fermentation and evaporation. Until the middle of the 19th century the manufacturing of chemicals was more of a craft than a science. The combination of a growing demand for chemicals produced safely and efficiently and the growth of the petroleum industry with its need for separation processes led to the development of the field of chemical engineering as a separate discipline. Some of the areas covered by chemical engineering today are the development of clean energy sources, advances in medical science and biotechnology, the improvement of the environment and the creation and production of new materials. Chemical engineering is another discipline in which the top ranked titles are not society publications, nor are they even journal titles. Since 1991 the most consistently ranked journal title is the *AIChE Journal* (U.S., American Institute of Chemical Engineers, 1955). While other AIChE journals, e.g., *Chemical Engineering Progress* (U.S., AIChE, 1947), *Environmental Progress* (U.S., AIChE, 1982), *Pro-*

cess Safety Progress (U.S., AIChE, 1982), and *Biotechnology Progress* (U.S., AIChE, 1985) may not be highly ranked, they do reflect the breadth of the discipline. *Industrial and Engineering Chemistry Research* (U.S., American Chemical Society, 1962) and *Chemistry and Industry* (U.K., Society of Chemical Industry, 1881) are also significant titles in general chemical engineering.

PETROLEUM ENGINEERING

One could argue that the field of petroleum engineering began with the drilling of the first oil well in Titusville, Pennsylvania, in 1859. Petroleum engineering is defined as the development and production of oil and natural gas reservoirs. Petroleum engineering does not include exploration for new oil fields. The top ranked title in the field is the *AAPG Bulletin* (U.S., American Association of Petroleum Geologists, 1917). In spite of the fact that it is published by an American society it is truly international in scope. Two other important titles are the *Bulletin of Canadian Petroleum Geology* (Canada, Canadian Society of Petroleum Geologists, 1953) and the *Journal of Petroleum Geology* (U.K., Scientific Press, Ltd., 1963). The Society of Petroleum Engineers publishes *JPT: Journal of Petroleum Technology* (U.S., SPE, 1919), which is usually ranked among the top five titles. As with chemical engineering, the society's other publications—*SPE Drilling & Completion* (U.S., SPE, 1961), *SPE Production and Facilities* (U.S., SPE, 1961), and *SPE Reservoir Evaluation and Engineering* (U.S., SPE, 1961)—reflect the breadth of the field.

ELECTRICAL AND ELECTRONICS ENGINEERING

Electrical engineering is concerned with the practical applications of electricity while electronics engineering deals with the electromagnetic spectrum and electronic devices such as vacuum tubes, electronic circuits and transistors. The invention of the telegraph in 1837 was the first practical use of electricity but it wasn't until 1864 that Maxwell demonstrated the basic laws of electricity mathematically; this may be regarded as the real beginning of the discipline. The American Institute of Electrical Engineers was founded in 1884; the Institute of Radio Engineers was founded in 1912. In 1963 these two societies merged to become the Institute of Electrical and Electronics Engineers, an organization with over 274,000 members today which publishes over 30 percent of the world's literature on electrical engineering and computer science.

In the 1998 *JCR* the Institute of Electrical and Electronics Engineers published 8 of the top 10 cited journals, 40 of the top 60 journals in electrical and electronics engineering, and had the number one ranked journals in telecommunications, computer science and manufacturing. The previous two years, however, the top title was *Progress in Quantum Electronics* (U.K., Pergamon, 1969), followed by the *Institute of Electrical and Electronics Engineers Proceedings* (U.S., IEEE, 1913). There is no consistency in the order of the IEEE publications which have been ranked in the top 10 since 1995, but there is some consistency in the titles. The *IEEE Electron Device Letters* (U.S., IEEE, 1980) appears in all four years, as does the *IEEE Journal of Quantum Electronics* (U.S., IEEE, 1965). The *IEEE Transactions on Information Theory* (U.S., IEEE, 1953) and the *IEEE Transactions on Pattern Analysis and Machine Intelligence* (U.S., IEEE, 1979) appear in the top ten in three of the last four years.

In addition to the titles mentioned above, the IEEE publishes titles which support more traditional areas of electrical and electronics engineering. Some examples are: *IEEE Transactions on Antennas and Propagation* (U.S., IEEE, 1952), *IEEE Transactions on Broadcasting* (U.S., IEEE, 1955), *IEEE Transactions on Consumer Electronics* (U.S., IEEE, 1952), *IEEE Transactions on Control Systems Technology* (U.S., IEEE, 1993), *IEEE Transactions on Industrial Electronics* (U.S., IEEE, 1953), *IEEE Transactions on Power Delivery* (U.S., IEEE, 1986), and *IEEE Transactions on Power Systems* (U.S., IEEE, 1986).

COMPUTER SCIENCE AND ENGINEERING

The *Encyclopedia Britannica Online* defines computer science as "the study of computers, including their design (architecture) and their uses for computations, data processing, and systems control." It goes on to say that it " . . . includes engineering activities such as the design of computers and of the hardware and software that make up computer systems. It also encompasses theoretical, mathematical activities, such as the design and analysis of algorithms. . . ."

As is true with so many other areas of engineering, most of the influential journal literature is published by professional societies. The top two organizations are the Association for Computing Machinery and the Institute of Electrical and Electronics Engineers. The ACM was founded in 1947 as the first "educational and scientific computing" society with the purpose of disseminating research efforts in computer science. Today, there are more than 80,000 members worldwide. The ACM is composed of 36 Special Interest Groups (SIGs) ranging from artificial intelligence to university and college computing services. The ACM publishes 28 titles and most SIGs publish at least one journal. The premiere journals are the *Journal of the ACM* (U.S., ACM, 1958) and the *Communications of the ACM* (U.S., ACM, 1954). The *JCR* divides computer science into seven sections. Between 1995 and 1998 the *Communications of the ACM* was ranked either one, two or three in hardware and architecture, number one or two in software, graphics, and programming, and between 1996 and 1998 was ranked first or third in theory and methods. In those same three years the *Journal of the ACM* ranked between number one and number five in hardware and architecture, between first and sixth in software, graphics and programming, between two and six in theory and methods, and fourth or ninth in information systems. Another important title from the ACM is *ACM Computing Surveys* (U.S., ACM, 1969).

The IEEE today consists of 10 regions, 36 technical societies, 4 technical councils, 1,200 society chapters, and 300 sections. Many of these subdivisions also publish journals. For the generalist, the *IEEE Transactions on Computers* (U.S., IEEE, 1952) and *Computer* (U.S., IEEE Computer Society, 1966) are the top titles. Some of the significant specialized titles are discussed next.

The *IEEE Transactions on Systems, Man and Cybernetics* (U.S., IEEE, 1971) is one of the top five cybernetics titles for the period 1995-1998. For the same four years the *IEEE Transactions on Neural Networks* (U.S., IEEE, 1990) ranks in the top five in two separate categories, hardware and architecture and theory and methods. The *IEEE Transactions on Software Engineering* (U.S., IEEE, 1975) appears in the top five for those same years in the category of software, graphics and programming, and the *IEEE Transactions on Image Processing* (U.S., IEEE, 1992) is ranked in the top five for the last three years. In the same period, the *IEEE/ACM Transactions on Networking* (U.S., IEEE & ACM, 1993) has been ranked no lower than 6th.

Other influential titles which may not appear high in the rankings are: *Signal Processing* (Netherlands, sponsored by the European Association for Signal Processing; published by Elsevier, 1979), *Byte* (U.S., Byte Publications, 1975), the *IBM Systems Journal* (U.S., IBM, 1962), the *IBM Journal of Research and Development* (U.S., IBM, 1957), and the *Bell Labs Technical Journal* (U.S., Lucent Technologies, 1922).

APPENDIX

Many of the most distinguished engineering societies publish an extended family of high quality journals. Mention of each and every one of these journals could not be readily incorporated into the narrative of this article without sacrificing readability. Nonetheless, whether clearly incorporated into the text or not, the following journals are commended to the reader's attention.

AMERICAN SOCIETY OF CIVIL ENGINEERS (ASCE)

Journal of Aerospace Engineering (US, ASCE, 1996).
Journal of Bridge Engineering (US, ASCE, 1996).
Journal of Cold Region Engineering (US, ASCE, 1987).
Journal of Computing in Civil Engineering (US, ASCE, 1987).
Journal of Composites for Construction (US, ASCE, 1997).
Journal of Construction Engineering and Management (US, ASCE, 1867).
Journal of Energy Engineering (US, ASCE, 1956).
Journal of Engineering Mechanics (US, ASCE, 1983).
Journal of Environmental Engineering (US, ASCE, 1956).
Journal of Geotechnical and Geoenvironmental Engineering (US, ASCE, 1983).
Journal of Hydraulic Engineering (US, ASCE, 1983).
Journal of Hydrologic Engineering (US, ASCE, 1996).
Journal of Infrastructure Systems (US, ASCE, 1995).
Journal of Irrigation and Drainage (US, ASCE, 1983).
Journal of Management in Engineering (US, ASCE, 1985).
Journal of Materials in Civil Engineering (US, ASCE, 1989).
Journal of Professional Issues in Engineering Educational and Practice (US, ASCE, 1991).
Journal of Structural Engineering (US, ASCE, 1983).
Journal of Surveying Engineering (US, ASCE, 1983).
Journal of Transportation Engineering (US, ASCE, 1873).
Journal of Urban Planning (US, ASCE, 1983).
Journal of Water Resources Planning and Management (US, ASCE, 1983).
Journal of Waterway, Port, Coastal and Ocean Engineering (US, ASCE, 1983).
Practice Periodical of Hazardous, Toxic and Radioactive Waste Management (US, ASCE, 1997).
Practice Periodical on Structural Design and Construction (US, ASCE, 1996).

AMERICAN SOCIETY OF MECHANICAL ENGINEERS (ASME)

Journal of Applied Mechanics (US, ASME, 1934).
Journal of Architectural Engineering (US, ASME, 1995).
Journal of Biomedical Engineering (US, ASME, 1977).

Journal of Dynamic Systems, Measurement and Control (US, ASME, 1971).

Journal of Electronic Packaging (US, ASME, 1989).

Journal of Energy Resources Technology (US, ASME, 1979).

Journal of Engineering Mechanics and Technology (US, ASME, 1973).

Journal of Fluid Engineering (US, ASME, 1973).

Journal of Heat Transfer (US, ASME, 1959).

Journal of Manufacturing Science and Technology (US, ASME, 1959).

Journal of Mechanical Design (US, ASME, 1982).

Journal of Offshore Mechanics and Arctic Engineering (US, ASME, 1987).

Journal of Performance of Constructed Facilities (US, ASME, 1987).

Journal of Pressure Vessel Technology (US, ASME, 1974).

Journal of Solar Energy Engineering (US, ASME, 1980).

Journal of Tribology (US, ASME, 1984).

Journal of Turbomachinery (US, ASME, 1986).

Journal of Vibration and Acoustics (US, ASME, 1990).

Mechanical Engineering (US, ASME, 1908).

INSTITUTION OF CIVIL ENGINEERS—UK (ICE)

Proceedings of the Institution of Civil Engineers: Civil Engineering (UK, ICE, 1837).

Proceedings of the Institution of Civil Engineers: Geotechnical Engineering (UK, ICE, 1837).

Proceedings of the Institution of Civil Engineers: Municipal Engineering (UK, ICE, 1837).

Proceedings of the Institution of Civil Engineers: Structures and Buildings (UK, ICE, 1837).

Proceedings of the Institution of Civil Engineers: Transport (UK, ICE, 1837).

Proceedings of the Institute of Civil Engineers: Water, Maritime and Energy (UK, ICE, 1837).

INSTITUTION OF MECHANICAL ENGINEERS—UK (IMechE)

Proceedings of the Institution of Mechanical Engineers—Part A—Journal of Power and Energy (UK, IMechE, 1990).

Proceedings of the Institution of Mechanical Engineers—Part B—Journal of Manufacture Engineering (UK, IMechE, 1989).

Proceedings of the Institution of Mechanical Engineers—Part C—Journal of Mechanical Engineering Science (UK, IMechE, 1983).

Proceedings of the Institution of Mechanical Engineers—Part D—Journal of Automobile Engineering (UK, IMechE, 1989).

Proceedings of the Institution of Mechanical Engineers—Part E—Journal of Process Mechanical Engineering (UK, IMechE, 1989).
Proceedings of the Institution of Mechanical Engineers—Part F—Journal of Rail and Rapid Transport (UK, IMechE, 1989).
Proceedings of the Institution of Mechanical Engineers—Part G—Journal of Aerospace Engineering (UK, IMechE, 1989).
Proceedings of the Institution of Mechanical Engineers—Part H—Journal of Engineering in Medicine (UK, IMechE, 1989).
Proceedings of the Institution of Mechanical Engineers—Part J—Journal of Engineering Tribology (UK, IMechE, 1994).

SOCIETY OF AUTOMOTIVE ENGINEERS—US (SAE)

Aerospace Engineering (US, SAE, 1983).
Automotive Engineering International (US, SAE, 1905).
SAE Off-Highway Engineering (US, SAE, 1991).

TRANSPORTATION RESEARCH (ELSEVIER)

Transportation Research, Part A, Policy and Practice (US, Elsevier, 1967).
Transportation Research, Part B, Methodological (US, Elsevier, 1967).
Transportation Research, Part C, Emerging Technologies (US, Elsevier, 1967).
Transportation Research, Part D, Transportation and Environment (US, Elsevier, 1967).
Transportation Research, Part E, Traffic Psychology and Behavior (US, Elsevier, 1967).

CLUSTER VI:
LIFE, HEALTH, AND AGRICULTURE

In contrast to the often rigidly hierarchical publishing patterns of the dominant national Anglo-American physical sciences and engineering organizations for much of the twentieth century, journal start-ups in the life sciences were often improvisational. They came from a plethora of competing specialty societies, sometimes several even within the same country. Often, there was not much initial thought for their long term financial stability. A degree of toleration for chaos, as much as a fundamental concern with all living things, is what holds this cluster together.

Overall, this balkanization of organizations and subspecialties fostered a tremendous financial need for alliances between the differing sectors of the publishing industry. Therefore, joint ventures were three times more common in the life, health, and agricultural sciences than in the physical sciences and engineering, and indeed are the most distinctive feature of this cluster when compared to all the others within this book. University presses (notably Oxford, Cambridge, Chicago, and Rockefeller) appeared substantially more often in the life sciences than in the physical, also making common cause with societies more often. The major not-for-profit medical specialty boards in the U.S. also frequently signed on with for-profits, most notably with some historically American-owned firms (Lippincott, Williams and Wilkins, Saunders, and Mosby) that are now parts of the expanded Elsevier and Kluwer. And while Blackwell has done very well in Britain, both Karger and Springer have sustained loyalties in central Europe. Overall, this was almost as great a cluster for the Dutch, Nordics, and Germans as was seen in the physical sciences.

Part of the reason for the success of European for-profits like Elsevier was ironically their heavy investment in branch editorial offices in the Asian Pacific countries. They forwarded locally produced manuscripts to their international headquarters in continental Europe. This active outreach foreshadowed the time when Asian scientists would recover from World War II's effects and become economically able to contribute to the world's knowledge base in exploding fields like biochemistry, genetics, brain sciences, and pharmacology.

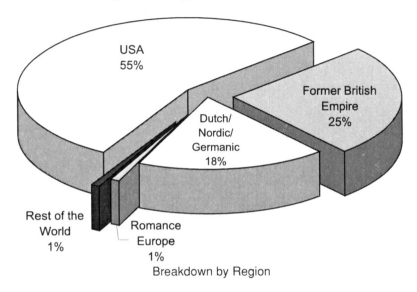

Breakdown by Region

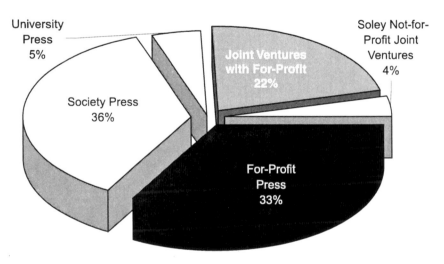

Breakdown by Publishing Sector

Chapter 18

Journals of the Century in the Basic Sciences, Part II: Life Sciences

Tony Stankus

GENERAL BIOLOGY

By the century's end, there were few truly influential journals that attempted to deal with all levels of biological activity—from the whole Ecosphere, down to the individual living animal or plant, down to the single DNA molecule. Research journals that stayed within narrower subject ranges tended to do better, and readers did not cross boundaries that often. The *Proceedings of the Royal Society of London B—Biological Sciences* (1905) published the widest scope of topics and succeeded at attracting more interest across all three levels of biological study more often than most. The *FASEB Journal* (Federation of American Societies for Experimental Biology) had more modest goals. It revamped itself from the rather eclectic *Federation Proceedings* (1942) into a real competitor serving two levels particularly well: the mid-level of the physiology and pharmacology community and the microscopic level of cellular and molecular workers. *Cell* (U.S., Cell Press, 1974), however, was the most spectacularly successful life sciences journal founded in this century, despite its intended microscale appeal. It epitomized the accelerating post-WWII trend in biology to add molecular arguments in debates at larger scales of biological activity. Not only is *Cell* cited by more journals at its own molecular and cellular level of biology than any other, its also become more cited by journals at larger levels of biological organization than anyone had anticipated, given its primary scope. Getting a paper into *Cell* is at least as important for biologists today as getting a paper into any of the three major multiscience journals: *Nature, Science,* and the *Proceedings of the National Academy of Sciences of the USA.*

This chapter originally appeared in *The Serials Librarian* 39(1): 122-144, 2000.

BIOCHEMISTRY

Historically, organic chemists and biochemists were members of the same fraternity. The terms biological chemist and biochemist came into use largely because "organic chemists" quickly achieved and sustained such astonishing success with synthetically derived drugs, dyes, industrial solvents, fuels, and polymers that they were lured away from their original intent on the chemical probing of life processes. Indeed, up to the 1950s, there were many more synthetically inclined organic chemists who never dealt with biological specimens than there were biochemists of any kind. But the biochemists and their allies in natural products isolation, hospital lab testing, nutrition, and agricultural breeding, persisted. Breakthroughs in understanding nucleic acids, proteins, lipids and carbohydrates began to swell their ranks. Today, biochemistry has become much larger than organic chemistry as both a discipline and as a literature. Three journals deserve special mention. Two nationally sponsored journals particularly exemplified this dramatic turnaround: the *Journal of Biological Chemistry* (American Society for Biological Chemistry and Molecular Biology, 1905) and *Biochemical Journal* (U.K., Portland Press for the Biochemical Society, 1906). Another journal, while not a current leader, became the paradigm of post-WWII internationalism, publishing hundreds of thousands of papers from literally over a hundred countries: *Biochimica et Biophysica Acta* (Netherlands, Elsevier, 1947).

MOLECULAR BIOLOGY: NUCLEIC ACIDS AND PROTEINS IN THE LIFE OF THE CELL

Molecular biology made its name by stressing two categories of biochemical substances (nucleic acids and proteins) that had an overarching role in the transmission of the genetic code and in the biosynthesis and regulation of most other biochemicals. While the *Journal of Molecular Biology* (U.K., Academic Press, 1959) evolved into the Anglo-American pioneer, and the *EMBO Journal* (U.K., Oxford University Press for the European Molecular Biology Organization, 1982) became its most obvious Continental European competitor, both owe a debt to *Nucleic Acids Research* (U.K., Oxford University Press, 1974) , which sustained a focus on the central problem of how DNA and RNA interact with each other to make proteins and then modulate their activity.

OTHER INDIVIDUAL BIOCHEMICAL/MOLECULAR BIOLOGY SUBSTANCE JOURNALS

While the *Journal of Lipid Research* (U.S., Lipid Research Inc., 1959), and *Carbohydrate Research* (Netherlands, Elsevier, 1965), are enduring and honorable pioneers, blending in agricultural, nutritional, and industrial processing interests in some cases, they all seem starved for attention relative to the ongoing explosion of new titles in proteins, many of which are now bioengineered for pharmaceutical purposes. The *Journal of Peptides Research* (1969) from Denmark's Munksgaard (peptides are the building blocks of proteins) represents perhaps the best combination of longevity and ongoing performance in what is now a very crowded field.

GENERAL MICROBIOLOGY AND BACTERIOLOGY

In the American South, there is a monument to the boll-weevil, a persistent pest of cotton crops, which forced the ultimately beneficial diversification of that region's agriculture. In the land of cells and genetics, there ought to be one to *E. Coli* and another for *Salmonella typhimurium,* for all the biology they taught us indirectly while we were originally trying to eradicate them. Three titles dominated the century in fundamental discoveries: the *Journal of Bacteriology* (American Society for Microbiology, 1916), *Microbiology* (U.K., Society for General Microbiology, 1947), and the *Archives of Microbiology* (Germany, Springer, 1930).

APPLIED MICROBIOLOGY AND BIOTECHNOLOGY

Not only did we learn to tolerate some microbes, we learned where they lived, what they needed to thrive, and how to put them to work creating useful byproducts. *Applied and Environmental Microbiology* (American Society for Microbiology, 1953) *Applied Microbiology & Biotechnology* (Germany, Springer, 1973) and *Nature Biotechnology* (U.S., Macmillan, 1983) proudly displayed their exemplary employment records.

GENERAL VIROLOGY

If molecular biology was built on studies of nucleic acids and proteins, what could have been better teachers than viruses, which are purely nucleic acids jacketed with protective protein covers? Their lectures could be found between the covers of the *Journal of Virology* (American Society for Microbiology, 1967), *Virology* (U.S., Academic Press, 1955), and the *Journal of General Virology* (U.K., Society for General Microbiology, 1967).

BASIC SCIENCE ASPECTS OF IMMUNOLOGY

Once again, we began a field with the idea of understanding why some people get diseases, while others do not. We began with bacterial or viral diseases, and found connections to allergies. We wondered why some suffer badly while others have mild symptoms; why some have recurrences, while others get it only once. We discovered that many diseases (juvenile diabetes and lupus, for instance) initially assigned to causes other than exaggerated immune responses are actually autoimmune disorders. We found that this self-destruction involves mistakes in nucleic acids and proteins, often entangled in antigen-antibody complexes. Over time these complexes could be induced in the laboratory and serve as useful markers for particular proteins and nucleic acid sequences in basic studies of cell biology. Traditional leaders in the basic science sector of immunology included the *Journal of Immunology* (American Association of Immunologists, 1916), the *European Journal of Immunology* (Germany, Wiley-VCH, 1971), and *Molecular Immunology* (U.K., Pergamon, 1964).

FROM MICROSCOPIC ANATOMY TO GENERAL CELL BIOLOGY

Before it was possible to explore cells molecularly, there was a long tradition of isolating, culturing, staining and then observing their microanatomy on slides. Most of the journals that pioneered these studies now go beyond the study of their internal structures and deal with all manner of cellular topics. In the U.S., the *Journal of Cell Biology* (Rockefeller University Press, 1955) remains the best among many. In England, it is the *Journal of Cell Science* (founded as the *Quarterly Journal of Microscopial Science* in 1853) and among the many German-speaking nations, the now-all-English *Cell and Tissue Research* (Springer, 1924) has remained supreme by blending medically concerned histology with basic cell biology.

PHYSIOLOGY AND BIOCHEMISTRY OF THE CELL

The astonishing success of *Cell,* mentioned earlier, dramatically refocused energies away from microscopy and towards an intense analysis of biochemical and molecular events in the cell. The *Journal of Cellular Phys-*

iology (U.S., Wiley for the Wistar Institute, 1932) with its longstanding connections to the clinical testing and pharmaceutical communities, weathered the changes intact better than most. *Molecular Biology of the Cell* (American Society for Cell Biology, 1989) and *Molecular and Cellular Biology* (American Society for Microbiology, 1981), by contrast, represented drastic and ultimately successful reorganizations of journal strategies among long-established publishers.

FROM ANATOMIC EMBRYOLOGY TO DEVELOPMENTAL BIOLOGY

Embryos were objects of experimental manipulation sooner than were individual cells largely because some of them were easier to keep alive in the lab, or at least tough to kill inadvertently. The pioneer journal was founded by Wilhelm Roux in Germany in 1895, and is now known as *Development, Genes & Evolution* (Springer). The British journal *Development* (Company of Biologists, 1953) followed a similar path from the *Journal of Embryology and Experimental Morphology*. In the U.S., *Developmental Biology* (Academic Press for the Society for Developmental Biology, 1959) represented a successful transition from largely anatomical to more modern means, and remains a prominent player today.

FROM AGRICULTURAL BREEDING TO BIOCHEMICAL GENETICS AND MOLECULAR DEVELOPMENTAL BIOLOGY

It's hard for some to believe that genetics predated the formal identification of chromosomes and the discovery of DNA, but it got its start by breeding for agricultural advantage and by analyzing failures of health that ran in families. While it had worthwhile predecessors and some older competitors, *Genetics* (Genetics Society of America, 1916) remains the best traditional journal from the Americas, with *Molecular & General Genetics (*Germany, Springer, 1909) a similarly venerable Continental entry with continuing currency. Cold Spring Harbor Laboratories (run by DNA discoverer and Nobel Laureate James Watson) and the Genetical Society of Great Britain hybridized genetics and embryology to give birth to *Genes and Development* (1987), the hi-tech leader going into the next century.

CHANGE IS NOT ALWAYS GOOD: GENETIC MUTATION RESEARCH

One of the fundamental breakthroughs in our understanding of diseases caused by environmental factors including diet, smoking, occupational exposure to chemicals and to radiation, came when we realized that we were actually damaging chromosomes, and causing mutations when those damaged chromosomes reproduced themselves. The pioneer journal was the massive and now multisectional *Mutation Research* (Netherlands, Elsevier, 1964). It has been surpassed somewhat by *Mutagenesis* (Oxford University Press for the UK Environmental Mutagen Society, 1986) and decisively by *Environmental and Molecular Mutagenesis* (U.S., Wiley for the Environmental Mutagen Society, 1979).

THE BASIC SCIENCE UNDERLYING POISONING, OUT OF CONTROL CELLS, AND BIRTH DEFECTS

Taking a cue from mutation research journals, some traditional clinical fields like poison control, oncology and the study of birth defects have seen their journals vastly transformed. *Toxicology and Applied Pharmacology* (U.S., Academic Press for the Society of Toxicology, 1959), *Cell Growth & Differentiation* (*American Association for Cancer Research*, 1990), and *Teratology* (U.S., Wiley for the Teratology Society, 1968) now analyze cause and effect at the much finer level of molecular mishap.

DON'T LIKE THE DESTINATION YOUR GENES ARE TAKING YOU? LOOK AT THE MAP, REBUILD THE ROAD

The major general journals of science, genetics, biochemistry and molecular biology featured most of the breakthrough papers on particularly newsworthy gene sequencings and recombinations. But three other journals archived many of the follow-up papers that mapped other genes in their native state and demonstrated new methods for multiplying and altering genetic material. These most prominently included *Gene* (Netherlands, Elsevier, 1977), *Genomics* (U.S., Academic Press, 1987), and *Genome Research*, the successor to *PCR Methods and Applications* (U.S., Cold Spring Harbor Laboratories Press, 1991).

GENERAL PHYSIOLOGY OF ADULT ORGANISMS

Finding the right experimental laboratory animals most appropriate for the physiological phenomenon being probed was essential to a wider understanding of cross-species principles, including many operating in humans. *Pfluegers Archiv—European Journal of Physiology* (Germany, Springer, 1868) showed the way for Continental Europe, much as the *Journal of Physiology* (Cambridge University Press for the Physiological Society of Great Britain and Ireland, 1867) and the *American Journal of Physiology* (American Physiological Society, 1858) did for their audiences.

IS THE BRAIN THE HEAD OF THE BODY?
THE RISE OF NEUROSCIENCE

A longstanding debate initiated in modern times among doctors by Pflueger (the German famed for the *Archives* noted above) concerned which of the several organ systems was the master controller of the body. The science that underlies that debate goes on today, and it involves many more participants than just physicians. Influential journals open to all types of neuroscientists and neuroscience topics include the current leaders, the *Journal of Neuroscience* (U.S., Society of Neuroscience, 1981) and the *European Journal of Neuroscience* (Blackwell for the European Neuroscience Association, 1989). Both owe a tremendous debt to *Brain Research* (Netherlands, Elsevier, 1966), the mother of all general neuroscience journals.

TRADITIONAL NEUROSCIENCE SPECIALTIES:
NEUROANATOMY, NEUROPHYSIOLOGY,
NEUROPSYCHOLOGY

Some neuroscience specialties are actually older than the grand general journals of neuroscience. The *Journal of Comparative Neurology* (an American microanatomy entry from Wiley, 1904) and the *Journal of Neurophysiology* (American Physiological Society, 1938) are cases in point. Journals that stress the brain biology underlying higher mental processes multiplied throughout this century. As far back as the Civil War, papers were written by battlefield doctors dealing with disorders in thinking, memory and perception among soldiers with head injury. Now much work can be done by basic scientists dealing with experimentally damaged animal brains, or with damaged and undamaged human subjects using noninvasive imaging, with papers in journals like the leading *Journal of Cognitive Neuroscience* (U.S., MIT Press for the Cognitive Neuroscience Institute, 1989).

THE CHEMISTRY, BIOCHEMISTRY AND CELLULAR BIOLOGY OF THE BRAIN

The hottest specialty journal of any type in the neurosciences is *Neuron* (U.S., Cell Press, 1988), the molecular and cellular neuroscience first cousin of the great journal, *Cell*. It had important forebears in the *Journal of Neurochemistry* (U.S., Raven, 1956) and in *Psychopharmacology* (Germany, Springer Verlag, 1960), a journal, for both lab scientists and psychiatrists, that pioneered in counteracting brain dysfunctions like mood disorders and psychoses via deliberate chemical interventions.

HORMONES: RIVALS AND PARTNERS OF THE NERVOUS SYSTEM AS PHYSIOLOGICAL REGULATORS

When laypersons argue the importance of endocrine system, they're likely to mention clinical topics like growth, weight regulation, diabetes, the promotion of differences between the sexes in appearance, and reproduction. But these tasks and the consequences of deficiencies in their performance represent only part of a much wider list of roles played by hormones. Journals like *Endocrinology* (U.S., Endocrine Society, 1917), the *Journal of Endocrinology* (U.K., Society for Endocrinology, 1939), and *General and Comparative Endocrinology* (U.S., Academic Press, 1961) made the basic science case for even more pervasive involvement, and in many species other than humans.

YOU CAN'T HAVE ONE FUNCTION WELL WITHOUT THE OTHER: NEUROENDOCRINOLOGY

Hormones and Behavior (U.S., Academic Press, 1969), *Neuroendocrinology* (Switzerland, Karger, 1966), and the *Journal of Neuroendocrinology* (U.K., Blackwell, 1989) became emblematic of the finding that the endocrine and nervous systems are mutually interacting coregulators.

HORMONES AND REPRODUCTION

The *Biology of Reproduction* (U.S., Society for the Study of Reproduction, 1969) is the protean basic science journal in this field.

MOLECULAR ENDOCRINOLOGY

It was only a matter of time before virtually all topics in endocrinology, behavioral ones included, involved biochemical levels of analysis and interpretation. *Molecular Endocrinology* (U.S., Endocrine Society, 1987), *Molecular and Cellular Endocrinology* (North Holland, 1974), and the *Journal of Molecular Endocrinology* (U.K., Society for Endocrinology, 1988) began to view the field as ripe for interpretation as a nucleic acid and protein drama.

ANIMALS STUDIED FOR THEIR OWN SAKE: GENERAL ZOOLOGY

While their use in uncovering general biological principles was important, animals continued to have their own unique stories to tell. Veritable arks of insight included the *Journal of Zoology* (U.K., Academic Press for the Zoological Society of London, 1833), the *American Zoologist* (Society for the Study of Integrative and Organismal Biology, 1961) and the *Canadian Journal of Zoology* (National Research Council, 1937).

COMPARATIVE ANATOMY

Studies of the inner architecture of animals became more microscopic over the course of the century, but still taught big lessons in journals like the historically crucial *Annals of Anatomy* (Germany, Fischer for the Anatomische Gesellschaft, 1886), and the ongoing leaders of today, the *Journal of Morphology* (U.S., Wiley for the Wistar Institute, 1887) and *Zoomorphology* (Germany, Springer, 1924).

ADAPTIVE PHYSIOLOGY

Some of the best stories of physiological adjustments in animals for survival are to be found in the British-based *Journal of Experimental Biology* (Company of Biologists, 1923), the American *Physiological and Biochemi-*

cal Zoology (University of Chicago Press, 1928), and the Continental pioneer, the *Journal of Comparative Physiology* (Germany, Springer, 1924).

ADAPTIVE BEHAVIOR IN WILD ANIMALS: ETHOLOGY

Does it seem far-fetched in this day of computer controlled, video monitored labs populated by specially bred rats, that seemingly instinctive behaviors observed in freely roaming wild animals still have lessons these have for our own species? The Nobel Prizes in Medicine given to ethologists Tinbergen, Meyer, and Lorenz suggest that it does not. Leading journals for workers like them included the *Journal of Comparative Psychology* (American Psychological Association, 1947), *Animal Behaviour* (U.K., Academic Press for the Association for the Study of Animal Behaviour and the Animal Behavior Society, 1953) and *Behavioral Ecology and Sociobiology* (Germany, Springer, 1976).

INTEGRATING STUDIES OF ADAPTIVE ANIMAL PHYSIOLOGY AND BEHAVIOR

It became apparent that in some cases adaptive physiology and adaptive behavior were tightly linked, had evolved together over time, and ought to be probed in tandem. While many topics were initially suggested by observation in the wild, many studies were furthered in the lab with captured animals in journals like *Physiology and Behavior* (U.S., Pergamon, 1966), *Psychobiology* (U.S., Psychonomic Society, 1964) and a pioneer in long-range studies, *Brain, Behavior and Evolution* (Switzerland, Karger, 1968).

ORNITHOLOGY

Birds have more journals than any other vertebrates, but *The Auk* (American Ornithologists Unions, 1884), *Ibis* (British Ornithologists Union, 1859), and the *Journal fuer Ornithologie* (Germany, Friedlaender for the German Ornithological Society, 1853), flew somewhat above the rest of this large flock.

MAMMALOGY

The *Journal of Mammology* (American Society of Mammalogists, 1919) had fewer rivals in leading its compact pack, which notably included *Mam-*

mal Review (Blackwell for the Mammal Society of the British Isles, 1954) and the *Zeitschrift fuer Saugertierkunde* (Paul Parey for the German Society for Mammal Studies, 1926).

HERPETOLOGY

Copeia (American Society of Ichthylogists and Herpetologists, 1913) covered fish, reptiles, and amphibians as well collectively as any journal devoted to any single one of these three phyla. But *Herpetologica* (U.S., Herpetologist's League, 1936) and the *Journal of Herpetology* (U.S., Society for the Study of Amphibians and Reptiles, 1958) also did quite well with just the latter two.

ICHTHYOLOGY AND FISHERIES

The *Journal of Fish Biology* (U.K., Academic Press, 1969), the *Transactions of the American Fisheries Society* (1885), and the *Canadian Journal of Fisheries and Aquatic Sciences* (National Research Council, 1938) schooled us well.

GENERAL ENTOMOLOGY

Given that there are more known species of beetles alone than there are of all the known vertebrates put together, it is not surprising that there are literally hundreds of journals and bulletins related to insects and their kin. While most nations (including many underdeveloped countries) sponsor one or more titles, those published in the U.S. are among the world's most influential, with the *Annals of the American Entomological Society* (1908) the most cited currently among general titles. Other general leaders include *Entomologia Experimentalis et Applicata* (Kluwer for the Netherlands Entomological Society, 1958), and the *Canadian Entomologist* (Entomological Society of Canada, 1868).

INSECT PHYSIOLOGY, BIOCHEMISTRY AND MOLECULAR BIOLOGY

The *Journal of Insect Physiology* (U.K., Pergamon, 1957) is arguably the first journal to go beyond traditional emphases on identification, classification, biogeography and damage control. It has since been joined by its own offspring, *Insect Biochemistry and Molecular Biology* (U.K., Pergamon, 1971), and another very strong British contender, *Physiological Entomology* (Blackwell for the Royal Entomological Society of London, 1976).

INSECT ECOLOGY AND BEHAVIOR

It is little appreciated just how much we have learned from the life cycles and interactions of insects with their environment and each other. *Ecological Entomology* (Blackwell, for the Royal Entomological Society of London, 1976), *Environmental Entomology* (Entomological Society of America, 1972), and *Insectes Sociaux* (France, Masson for the International Union for the Study of Social Insects, 1954), have been among the greatest workers in these veritable colonies.

OTHER LAND-BASED INVERTEBRATES, INCLUDING INSECT RELATIVES

The *Journal of Arachnology* (American Arachnological Society, 1973) dealt largely with spiders and scorpions. *Experimental and Applied Acarology* (Netherlands, Elsevier, 1985) and *Acarologia* (France, Marc Vachon, 1959) gained in importance as ticks and mites were shown to have considerable public health significance.

OTHER INVERTEBRATES, MOSTLY AQUATIC

While *Invertebrate Biology* (American Microscopial Society, 1895) also deals with larger and land-based invertebrates, its strengths have largely been aquatic and microscopic animals. While neither all crustaceans nor all molluscs are aquatic, most are. *Crustaceana* (Netherlands, Brill, 1960) and the *Journal of Molluscan Studies* (Oxford University Press for the Malacological Society of London, 1895) have left an indelible watermark on their respective literatures.

WORMS

Of the many kinds of worms, two large families have wriggled to the top. The *Journal of Nematology* (U.S., Society of Nematologists, 1969) and the *Journal of Helminthology* (U.K., London School of Hygiene and Tropical Medicine, 1923) are among the leaders in more basic science studies, although frankly, many of these organisms are regarded as parasites to be eradicated. A generally more beneficent view of their role in soil ecology can be found in *Pedobiologia* (Germany, Gustav Fischer, 1961).

PARASITOLOGY

While not all parasites are invertebrates or microscopic, most are, and are studied for reasons of eradication, with more molecular means than ever before. Traditional leaders include basic science titles like the *Journal of Parasitology* (American Society of Parasitologists, 1914) and *Parasitology* (Cambridge University Press for the British Society of Parasitology, 1908). *Molecular and Biochemical Parasitology* (Netherlands, Elsevier, 1980) is among the first to infiltrate and engorge on the flow of biotech funding.

BOTANY AS THE FIRST PLANT SCIENCE

Academic plant studies began with identification and classification, based on anatomy, growing habits, means of reproduction and natural range. All of these approaches have since subdivided into their own specialties, but general botanical journals remain of enduring importance. In the U.S., the *American Journal of Botany* (Botanical Society of America, 1914) and the *International Journal of Plant Sciences* (U.S., University of Chicago Press, 1876) have been deeply rooted. In Europe, the *Annals of Botany* (U.K., Academic Press, 1804) has become a perennial leader.

PLANT PHYSIOLOGY

Aggressive, experimental studies soon began to change botany from being merely a passive, descriptive science. Most often the goal was to learn what optimized productive growth, increased tolerance of stress, and enhanced resistance to disease. *Plant Physiology* (American Association of Plant Physiologists, 1976) has remained the consistent American leader, as have the *Journal of Experimental Botany* (U.K., Society for Experimental Biology, 1950) and *Planta* (Germany, Springer, 1925) for constituencies abroad.

PLANT CELLULAR AND MOLECULAR BIOLOGY

It was only a matter of time before the lessons of cell culture and genetic engineering exploded on the plant science scene, where progress has actually been made much more quickly than with animals or humans. *The Plant Cell* (American Society of Plant Physiologists, 1989), *The Plant Journal for Cell and Molecular Biology* (U.K., Blackwell for the Society for Experimental Biology, 1991), and *Plant Cell, Tissue and Organ Culture* (Netherlands, Nijhoff-Junk, 1981) were the most successful offshoots of the new movement.

TREES AND FORESTRY

Trees: Structure and Function (Germany, Springer, 1986), *Tree Physiology* (Canada, Heron Publishers, 1986), and the *Canadian Journal of Forest Research* (Canada, National Research Council, 1971) stood tall for their specialty.

LARGER FUNGI, SYMBIOTIC PLANTS AND ALGAE

Journals that dealt with mushrooms like *Mycologia* (Mycological Society of America and the New York Botanical Garden, 1909), with mosses and lichens like *The Bryologist* (American Bryological and Lichenological Society, 1895), and with aquatic algae, like the *Journal of Phycology* (Phycological Society of America, 1965) gave us insights into less familiar, but important members of the plant kingdom, and their sometimes unusual living arrangements.

PLANT BIOGEOGRAPHY

Different plants thrive in different regions of the world, and tracking their spread and relative abundance tells us a lot about both the adaptability of plants and changes in regional climatic conditions. The *Journal of Biogeography* (U.K., Blackwell, 1974), *Plant Ecology* (Netherlands, Kluwer for the International Society for Plant Geography and Ecology, 1948), and the *Journal of Vegetation Science* (Sweden, Opulus Press for the International Association for Vegetation Science, 1990) gave us the lay of the land.

FROM TRADITIONAL FIELD BIOLOGY TO MODELING OF ECOLOGICAL AND EVOLUTIONARY PROCESSES

Both plant and animal studies benefited from itinerant naturalists, hiking in the woods, or out on the range, or canoeing over the waters. Their serendipitous working style of patient observation and inference, particularly when joined with findings in paleontology and systematics, foreshadowed the development of ecology and evolution as more formal disciplines. High-concept natural history journals today now favor papers with testable hypotheses that have an a priori orientation towards advancing modern ecological and evolutionary theory. Despite their relative antiquity, the *American Naturalist* (University of Chicago Press for the American Society of Naturalists, 1867) and the *Journal of Natural History* (U.K., Taylor and Francis, 1840) are becoming more rigorously programmatic today, with increasing emphasis on more quantitative methods. But the *American Midland Naturalist* (Notre Dame University Press, 1909) continues to do quite well using more traditional approaches that still allow for unexpected but real finds in the field that cause us to stop, enjoy, and reflect, even as we learn.

GENERAL LAND-BASED ECOLOGY

While pollution does concern many ecologists, ecology is actually a much larger subject than environmental contamination. It encompasses how plants and animals interact with each other and exploit their environment to best advantage. Three titles have exceptionally broad scope and influence. These are *Ecology* (Ecological Society of America, 1920), *Oecologia* (Germany, Springer, 1924), and *Oikos* (Denmark, Munksgaard for the Nordic Society Oikos, 1949).

FRESHWATER ECOLOGY

Watery environments, and the journals that monitor them ecologically, constitute a special niche refreshed most notably by *Freshwater Biology* (U.K., Blackwell for the Freshwater Biology Association, 1971), the *Journal of the North American Benthological Society* (U.S., 1982), and *Hydrobiologia* (Netherlands, Kluwer, 1948).

MARINE ECOLOGY

Marine Biology (Germany, Springer, 1967), the *Journal of Experimental Marine Biology & Ecology* (North-Holland, 1967), and *Marine Ecology—Progress Series* (Germany, Inter-Research, 1979) proved well worth their salt.

OTHER ECOLOGICAL NICHE JOURNALS

Biotropica (U.S., Association for Tropical Biology, 1962), *Polar Biology* (Germany, Springer, 1982), the *Journal of Range Management* (American Society of Range Management, 1948), and the *Journal of Arid Environments* (U.K., Academic Press, 1978) blew steadily hot or cold, over grassland or barren land, as called for, uncovering unusual adaptations and interrelations.

CONSERVATION BIOLOGY AND WILDLIFE MANAGEMENT

Preserving a diversity of species as well as the habitats that sustain them remained the focus of *Biological Conservation* (U.K., Elsevier, 1968), the *Journal of Applied Ecology* (Blackwell for the British Ecological Society, 1964), and *Journal of Wildlife Management* (U.S., Wildlife Society, 1937).

ENVIRONMENTAL POLLUTION: DETECTION, DOCUMENTATION OF ILL EFFECTS, AND REMEDIATION

In the 20th century, we finally took a sustained look at what our factories and factory farms were doing harmfully to the earth and its creatures. *Environmental Science and Technology* (American Chemical Society, 1967), *Environmental Pollution* (U.K., Elsevier, 1970), and *Ambio* (Royal Swedish Academy of Sciences, 1972) documented our concerns and actions with much greater sophistication in quantitative analytical determinations, investigative pathology, and restorative technology.

BIOLOGICAL CLASSIFICATION AS A PREDECESSOR TO MODERN EVOLUTIONARY THEORY

Evolution had many more fathers than just Charles Darwin. Many of them were classifiers, systematizers, and taxonomists who began by simply sorting out relationships among contemporary organisms but soon found their work used to create evolutionary family trees, whether they personally anticipated or believed in a particular theory of evolution or not. Some of these evolutionary pioneers included Linnaeus, one of the first great categorizers of plants; Cuvier, a man of both fossil animal and contemporary animal classification; Willi Hennig of insect fame; and Ferdinand Cohen, who systematized bacteria, fungi, and some unicellular creatures.

Their efforts evolved into journals like *Systematic Botany* (American Society of Plant Taxonomists, 1952), the *Journal of Zoological Systematics and Evolutionary Research* (Germany, Blackwell, 1963), *Systematic Entomology* (Blackwell for the Royal Entomological Society of London, 1976), and the *International Journal of Systematic Bacteriology* (American Society for Microbiology for International Association of Microbiological Societies, 1951). Only one journal really encompasses all of these organisms, and has done so only after revamping from a zoological-only approach, *Systematic Biology* (U.S., Taylor and Francis for the Society of Systematic Biologists, 1952).

BIOLOGICAL PALEONTOLOGY

Three journals have taken on the sexier, biological side of paleontology. That all three are American may have to do with this country's fascination with dinosaurs, and occurs in spite of the fact that most fossils are less dramatically derived from plants and invertebrates than from Tyrannosaurus Rex. For all their academic formality, *Paleobiology* (U.S., Paleontological Society, 1975), the *Journal of Vertebrate Paleontology* (U.S., Society of Vertebrate Paleontology, 1981), and *Palaios* (U.S., Society of Economic Paleontologists and Mineralogists, 1986) have something of an academician's Jurassic Park about them.

EVOLUTION

Evolution (U.S., Society for the Study of Evolution, 1947), the *Journal of Evolutionary Biology* (Switzerland, Birkaehauser for the European Society of Evolutionary Biology, 1988), and the *Biological Journal of the Linnean Society* (U.K., Academic Press for the Zoological Society of London, 1848) lead in incorporating all manner of data from the traditional academic feeder disciplines into general evolutionary studies.

BIOCHEMICAL AND MOLECULAR EVOLUTION

Even the historically-inclined feeder disciplines relating to evolution have found themselves molecularized with protein and nucleic acid-based studies in the *Journal of Molecular Evolution* (Germany, Springer, 1971) and *Molecular Biology & Evolution* (U.S., University of Chicago Press, 1983). *Origins of Life and Evolution of the Biosphere* (Netherlands, Kluwer for the International Society for the Study of the Origin of Life, 1984) goes even farther, discussing the pre-biological conditions which fostered the rise of the earliest life forms whose protein and nucleic acid interactions began evolution in the first place.

REFERENCES AND SUGGESTED READINGS

Alvarez, Pedro, and Antonio Pulgarin. "The Diffusion of Scientific Journals Analyzed through Citations." *Journal of the American Society for Information Science* 48: 953-958, 1997.

Bensman, Stephen J. and Stanley J. Wilder. "Scientific and Technical Serials Holdings Optimization in an Inefficient Market." *Library Resources and Technical Services* 42 (3): 147-242, 1998.

Bonitz, Manfred. "The Scientific Talents of Nations." *Libri* 47 (4): 206-213, 1997.

Bottle, R.T., and others. *Information Sources in Chemistry.* London: Bowker-Saur, 1993.

Braun, Tibor. "On Some Historical Antecedents of the Belief in the Decline of British Science." *Journal of Information Science* 19: 401, 1993.

Braun, Tibor, Hajnalka Maczelka, and A. Schubert. "World Flash on Basic Research. Scientometric Indicators, Datafiles, Summary Statistics, and Trendlines of Major Geopolitical Regions, 1980-1989." *Scientometrics* 25(2): 211-218, 1992.

Burnham, Paul D. "Private Liberal Arts Colleges and the Costs of Scientific Journals: A Perennial Dilemma." *College and Research Libraries* 59: 406-420, 1998.

Chrzastowski, Tina. "Information Sources in Surface and Colloid Chemistry." *Science and Technology Libraries* 9 (3): 75-96, 1989.

Chrzastowski, Tina E. "National Trends in Academic Serials Collections, 1992-1994" *Science and Technology Libraries* 16 (3-4): 191-207, 1997.

Cromer, Donna E. "English: The Lingua Franca of International Scientific Communication." *Science and Technology Libraries* 12 (1): 21-34, 1991.

Davis, Elisabeth B. *Guide to Information Sources in the Botanical Sciences.* Englewood, CO: Libraries Unlimited, 1996.

Davis, Elisabeth B. *Using the Biological Literature: A Practical Guide.* New York: Marcel Dekker, 1995.

Derksen, Charlotte R. M., and Michael Mark Noga. "The World of Geoscience Serials: Comparative Use Patterns." in *International Initiatives in Geoscience Information.* Geoscience Information Society. 26th Meeting, 1991. Geoscience Information Society, 1992.

Diodato, Virgil P. *Dictionary of Bibliometrics.* Binghamton, NY: The Haworth Press, Inc., 1994.

Diodato, Virgil P. "The Use of English Language in Non-U.S. Science Journals: A Case Study of Mathematics Publications, 1970-1985." *Library and Information Science Research* 12: 355-371, 1990.

Duranceau, Ellen Finnie. "Exchange Rates and the Serials Marketplace." *Serials Review* 21 (3): 83-96, 1995.

Edelman, Hendrik. "Precursor to the Serials Crisis: German Science Publishing in the 1930s." *Journal of Scholarly Publishing* 25 (April): 171-178, 1994.

Garfield, Eugene. *Essays of an Information Scientist,* v.1-14. Philadelphia: ISI Press, 1977-1992. *Relevant papers in every volume from the master.*

Garfield, Eugene. "What Citations Tell Us About Canadian Research." *Canadian Journal of Information and Library Science* 18 (December): 14-35, 1993.

Hamaker, Charles A. "The Least Reading for the Smallest Number at the Highest Price." *American Libraries* 19: 764-768, 1988.

Harter, Stephen P., and Thomas E. Nisonger. "ISI's Impact Factor as a Misnomer: A Proposed New Measure to Assess Journal Impact." *Journal of the American Society for Information Science* 48: 1146-1148, 1997.

Havemann, Frank. "Changing Publication Behaviour of East and Central European Scientists and the Impact of their Papers." *Information Processing and Management* 32: 489-496, 1996.

Henderson, Albert. "The 160 Million Dollar Question: What Happens to the Federal Money Paid for University Research Libraries?" *Against the Grain* 9: 28-29, November, 1997.

Henderson, Albert. "A Solution to the Futility of Cost-Effective Librarianship." *Science and Technology Libraries* 12 (1): 99-107, 1991.

Hooydonk, Guido van. "Cost and Citation Data for 5399 Scientific Journals in Connection with Journal Price-Setting, Copyright Laws, and the Use of Bibliometric Data for Project Review." *The Serials Librarian* 27 (1): 45-58, 1995.

Hughes, Janet A. "Use of Faculty Publication Lists and ISI Citation Data to Identify a Core List of Journals with Local Importance." *Library Acquisitions: Practice and Theory* 19: 403-413, 1995.

Hurd, Julie M., Deborah D. Blecic, and Rama Vishwanatham. "Information Use by Molecular Biologists: Implications for Library Collections and Services." *College and Research Libraries* 60 (1): 31-43, 1999.

Hurt, Charlie Deuel. *Information Sources in Science and Technology.* Englewood, CO: Libraries Unlimited, 1994.

Journal Citation Reports. Philadelphia: Institute for Scientific Information, annual.

Knoche, Michael. "Scientific Journals Under National Socialism." *Libraries and Culture* 26: 415-426, 1991.

Kronick, David A. "Bibliographic Dispersion of Early Periodicals." *The Serials Librarian* 12 (3-4): 55-59, 1987.

Kronick, David A. *Literature of the Life Sciences.* Metuchen, NJ: Scarecrow Press, 1985.

Kronick, David A. *Scientific and Technical Periodicals of the Seventeenth and Eighteenth Centuries: A Guide.* Metuchen, NJ: Scarecrow Press, 1991.

Le Coadic, Yves F. and Serge Chambaud. "Politics and Policies in the Scientific and Technical Information Sector in France." *Journal of Information Science* 19 (6): 473-479, 1993.

Liang , Diane F. *Mathematics Journals: An Annotated Guide.* Lanham, MD: 1992.

Machlup, Fritz, and Kenneth Leeson. *Information Through the Printed Word: The Dissemination of Scholarly. Scientific, and Intellectual Knowledge. v.2. The Journals.*

Maizell, Robert E., *How to Find Chemical Information*. New York: Wiley, 1998.

McCain, Katherine W. "Core Journal Networks and Collection Maps: New Bibliometric Tools for Serials Research and Management." *Library Quarterly* 61: 311-336, 1991.

McCain, Katherine W. "Biotechnology in Context: A Database Filtering Approach to Identifying Core and Productive Non-Core Journals Supporting Multidisciplinary R & D." *Journal of the American Society for Information Science* 46: 306-317, 1995.

Meadows, A.J. *The Scientific Journal*. London: Aslib, 1979.

Nisonger, Thomas E. *Management of Serials in Libraries*. Edgewood, CO: Libraries Unlimited, 1998.

Olden, Anthony and Michael Wise, eds. *Information and Libraries in the Developing World, 3v*. London: Library Association Publishing, 1990-1994.

Peek, Robin, Jeffrey Pomerantz, and Stephen Paling. "The Traditional Scholarly Journals Legitimize the Web." *Journal of the American Society for Information Science* 49 (11): 983-989, 1998.

Primack, Alice Lefler. *Journal Literature of the Physical Sciences*. Lanham, MD: Scarecrow Press, 1992.

Pruett, Nancy Jones and George McGregor. *Scientific and Technical Libraries*. 2v. Orlando, FL: Academic Press, 1986.

Rice, Barbara A. "Selection and Evaluation of Chemistry Periodicals." *Science and Technology Libraries* 4 (1): 43-59, 1983.

Richards, Pamela Spence. "Scientific Information for Stalin's Laboratories: 1945-1953." *Information Processing and Management* 32: 77-88, 1996.

Rioux, Margaret A. "Staying Afloat in a Sea of Knowledge: Information Sources in Applied Ocean Physics." *Science and Technology Libraries* 13 (2): 113-135, 1992.

Rousseau, R. and vanHooydonk, Guido. "Journal Production and Journal Impact Factors." *Journal of the American Society for Information Science* 47: 775-780, 1996.

Royle, Pam. "A Citation Analysis of Australian Science and Social Science Journals." *Australian Academic and Research Libraries* 25: 162-171, 1994.

Sapp, Gregg. "Subject Coverage in General and Specialized Mathematics Journals." *The Serials Librarian* 16 (3-4): 93-117, 1989.

Saunders, LaVerna. "ARL's SPARC Alliance Bears Fruit: ARL/ACS Electronic Publishing Venture." *Information Today* 15 (8): 25, 1998.

Schad, Jasper G. "Scientific Societies and Their Journals: Issues of Cost and Relevance." *Journal of Academic Librarianship* 23: 406-407, 1997.

Schaffner, Ann C. "The Future of Scientific Journals: Lessons from the Past." *Information Technology and Libraries* 13: 239-247, 1994.

Schmidt, Karen. "Information Resources in Animal Behavior." *Science and Technology Libraries* 12 (1): 69-83, 1991.

Shaw, Dennis F. *Information Sources in Physics*. London: Bowker-Saur, 1994.

Smith, B., Shirley V. King, Ian Stewart. "Survey of Demand for Japanese Scientific and Technical Serial Literature." *Interlending and Document Supply* 15 (October): 111-117, 1987.

Stankus, Tony. "Avoiding a Rush to a Verdict of Guilty: The Treatment of Third World Science by First World Publishers and Librarians." *RQ* 35: 467-475, 1996.

Stankus, Tony. "Could Long Term Shifts in Publishing Sector Dominance Among the Top 100 Physical Science Journals Slow Rates of Invoice Inflation?" *Science and Technology Libraries* 15 (3): 77-89, 1995.

Stankus, Tony. *Electronic Expectations: Science Journals on the Web.* New York: The Haworth Press, Inc., 1999, in press.

Stankus, Tony, Bernard S. Schlessinger, and Rashelle Schlessinger. " English Language Trends in German Basic Science Journals." *Science and Technology Libraries* 1 (3): 55-66, 1981.

Stankus, Tony, William C. Littlefield, and Kevin Rosseel. "Is the Best Japanese Science in Western Journals?" *The Serials Librarian* 14 (1/2): 95-107, 1988.

Stankus, Tony. "Journal Divorces: With and Without Custody Fights and Remarriage." *Technicalities* (17 (7): 11-13, 1997.

Stankus, Tony. "The Journals of German University and Engineering School Scientists Before and After National Reunification." *Science and Technology Libraries* 16(1): 35-47, 1996.

Stankus, Tony. *Making Sense of Journals in the Life Sciences: From Specialty Origins to Contemporary Assortment.* New York: The Haworth Press, Inc., 1992.

Stankus, Tony. *Making Sense of Journals in the Physical Sciences: From Specialty Assortment to Contemporary Assortment.* New York: The Haworth Press, Inc., 1992.

Stankus, Tony. "Making the Scientist a Library Ally in the Real Research Journal Funding Wars: Those With Our Treasurers and With Our Own Mistaken Notions." *Library Acquisitions: Practice and Theory* 14 (1): 113-119, 1991.

Stankus, Tony. "Mergers, Acquisitions, and Euros." *Technicalities* 19 (3): 4.

Stankus, Tony and Kevin Rosseel. "The Rise of Eurojournals: Their Success Can Be Ours." *Library Resources and Technical Services* 31: 215-224, 1986.

Stankus, Tony., ed. *Scientific and Clinical Literature for the Decade of the Brain.* Binghamton, NY: The Haworth Press, Inc., 1993.

Stankus, Tony. *Scientific Journals: Improving Library Collections Through Analysis of Publishing Trends.* New York: The Haworth Press, Inc., 1990.

Stankus, Tony. *Scientific Journals: Issues in Library Selection and Management.* New York: The Haworth Press, Inc., 1987.

Stankus, Tony. "Sacred Cows, Cash Cows, and Mad Cow Disease." *Technicalities* 16 (6): 2-3, 1996.

Stankus, Tony and Virgil C. Diodato. "Selecting Multispecialty Mathematics Research Journals via Their Underlying Subject Emphases." *Science and Technology Libraries* 4 (1): 61-78, 1983.

Stankus, Tony. *Special Format Serials and Issues: Annual Reviews of . . ., Advances in . . ., Symposia on . . ., Methods of. . . .* New York: The Haworth Press, Inc., 1996.

Stankus, Tony and Carolyn Virginia Mills. "Which Life Science Journals will Constitute the Locally Sustainable Core Collection of the 1990s and Which will Become "Fax Access" Only? Predictions Based on Citation and Price Patterns, 1979-1989." *Science and Technology Libraries* 13 (Fall): 73-114, 1992.

Stern, David. "Pricing Models: Past, Present, and Future?" *The Serials Librarian* 36 (1-2): 301-319, 1999.

Tallent, Ed. "Project Muse." *Library Journal* 124 (March1, 1999): 119.

Teferra, Damtew. "The Status and Capacity of Science Publishing in Africa." *Journal of Scholarly Publishing* 27 (October): 28-36, 1995.

Tenopir, Carol, and King, Donald Ward. "Trends in Scientific Scholarly Journal Publishing in the United States." *Journal of Scholarly Publishing* 28(3): 135-170, 1997.

Walcott, Rosalind. "Serials Cited by Marine Sciences Research Center Faculty, University at Stony Brook, 1986-1991." *Science and Technology Libraries* 14(3): 15-33, 1994.

Wiggins, Gary. *Chemical Information Sources.* New York: McGraw-Hill, 1991.

Wilkinson, Sophie L. "Behind the Scenes at Journals." *Chemical and Engineering News* 77 (37): 25-31, September 13, 1999.

Wyatt, H. V. *Information Sources in the Life Sciences.* London: Bowker-Saur, 1994.

Young, Jeffrey R. "Stanford-based High Wire Press Transforms the Publication of Scientific Journals." *The Chronicle of Higher Education* 43 (36):A21, May 16, 1997.

Zhang Haiqi and Shigeaki Yamazaki. "Citation Indicators of Japanese Journals." *Journal of the American Society for Information Science* 49: 375-379, 1998.

Zipp, Louise S. "Core Serial Titles in an Interdisciplinary Field: The Case of Environmental Geology" *Library Resources and Technical Services* 43 (1): 28-36, 1999.

Zipp, Louise S. "Identifying Core Geologic Research Journals." In *Changing Gateways: The Impact of Technology on Geoscience Information Exchange.* Geoscience Information Society. 29th Meeting, 1994, Seattle, Washington. Geoscience Information Society, 1995.

Zitt, Michel, Francois Perrot, and Remi Barre. "The Transition from "National" to "Transnational" Model and Related Measures of Countries' Performance." *Journal of the American Society for Information Science* 49: 30-42, 1998.

Chapter 19

Journals of the Century
in Medicine and Surgery

Lucretia W. McClure

The race to publish is important to both clinicians and scientists. The changes and developments in medicine are frequent and often dramatic. Patients demand the best in treatment and knowing the most recent information is essential to the physician. Since the first journal containing medical papers, the *Philosophical Transactions of the Royal Society of London,* was begun in 1665, the journal has been the best method for transmitting the newest information to a wide audience. Today, electronic versions of journals give added efficiency and speed.

In his *Introduction to the History of Medicine,* Fielding H. Garrison declared in 1929 that no modern science has so many periodicals as medicine. In contrast to the 18th century that had few medical journals, "our own time, particularly our own country, has literally swarmed with medical journals, many of which are, as the Germans say, *Eintagsfliegen*—of ephemeral duration."[1] One wonders what Garrison would say about the proliferation of publications today.

In the first series of the *Index Catalogue of the Library of the Surgeon-General's Office,* started in 1880, some 8,289 titles were indexed. Checking the title or subject "medical sciences" in *Ulrich's International Periodicals Directory* for 1999 provides a total of 15,476 titles. The list for dentistry totals 884. The National Library of Medicine receives more than 20,000 serial titles. It would seem we have an overwhelming number of publications in medicine, yet there is no indication that new journals will cease to emerge. New fields, new techniques, and new societies deem that new titles are necessary.

Medical writers of the 19th century were verbose, provincial—publishing in such titles as the *Georgia Blister and Critic,* the *Quarterly Review of Narcotic Inebriety,* the *Divine Science of Health,* the *Indiana Scalpel,* and

---

This chapter originally appeared in *The Serials Librarian* 39(3): 133-145, 2001.

the *Dental Jarius*. John Shaw Billings' critique, in 1876, along with his creations, the *Index Catalogue* and the *Index Medicus,* did much to raise the standards in medical literature.

Garrison points out that the best of the American journals came from New York, Philadelphia, and Boston. In his opinion, the *American Journal of the Medical Sciences* was the best of the American monthly publications. The best of the medical weeklies included the *Boston Medical and Surgical Journal,* the *Medical News* (Philadelphia), the *New York Medical Journal,* and the *Medical Record.*

Billings divided medical journal literature into three classes: (1) those not connected with a medical school and drawing contributions from a wide field, (2) those relying mainly on the faculty of a medical school and its hospital clinics, and (3) those devoted to advocating the interests of a school and attacking those of rival institutions. "Of the first class, some compare favourably with the best of the journals of other countries, of the last class, some are as bad as, but not worse than, the worst."[2] This statement might be made today: the good journals are better than ever, the mediocre still flourishing.

The differences today include the advent of electronic journals, Web sites offering medical resources and information, and the impact of the high cost of scientific and medical titles. The pricing situation forces libraries and institutions to consider other ways of publishing and holding copyrights. An additional factor is the startling announcement by Harold Varmus of the National Institutes of Health concerning the plan to post data from NIH research on a Web site, open to all. Clearly, a review of journals fifty years hence might well find a vastly different publishing scene.

The story of medical publishing in many ways parallels the rise of disciplines, the establishment of new specialties and societies, and the discovery of new techniques. In contrast with the basic sciences that had a long history of publishing in Europe and other countries, clinical medicine has seen most of its tremendous advances and growth in the 20th century, primarily in the United States. At one time, physicians believed they must train in Europe in order to complete their education. Today, the world looks to the United States for the most advanced training. Before World War II, the most respected medical titles were published in Germany, Britain, France, Sweden, etc. Today, a high percentage of the most-read titles world-wide are published in America.

The growth of specialties in the late 19th and early 20th centuries spawned many new journals, and interestingly enough, a few societies were formed after a specialized journal had been established and began to flourish. Reading the editors' words in the first issues of many titles, one is struck by the similarity of reasons for needing another journal in a world already overflowing with more titles than any individual could read. Those editors did apologize, but at the same time emphasized the need to publish a journal over which the society could maintain control along with the hope that communication among those vitally interested in the subject would be enhanced.

Journals come in many formats: reports of original research, abstracts of conferences, news and quick communications, and reviews. Selecting the best in clinical medicine means primarily choosing those with reports of original research. To select a "top three" is to leave out significant journals. Perhaps it is better to describe the titles as representative of many important and substantive titles. In order to recognize the journals of lasting value, I have based choices on the most frequently cited and what I believe to be the most-read journals. The list will first recognize the weekly medical journals. Following will be two sections: surgery and such related areas as anesthesia and radiology, and clinical medicine. No attempt is made to select titles for the many sub-specialties. There are also surgical counterparts of medical disciplines that will be included in the medical list.

THE WEEKLIES

Four weekly general medical journals are set apart by virtue of their world-wide readership and frequency of publication. The *New England Journal of Medicine* is said by many to be the best-known medical title in the world. It is highly respected and considered authoritative. The journal, published by the Massachusetts Medical Society, started with this title in 1928, continuing the *Boston Medical and Surgical Journal,* one of those recognized earlier by Garrison. The Boston title, begun in 1828, was formed by the union of the *New England Medical Review and Journal* and the *Boston Medical Intelligencer,* but had its beginning with the *New England Journal of Medicine and Surgery and the Collateral Branches of Science.* Boston has produced medical news and information through these titles since 1812. The *Lancet* (U.K., Lancet Publishing of Elsevier Science, 1823), the British counterpart, is also recognized for its longevity and quality. These two journals are the most cited in clinical medicine.

Two of the quartet are the official organs of the American and British Medical Associations. The *JAMA, The Journal of the American Medical Association,* was established in 1883, becoming simply the *JAMA* in 1960. The journal has grown in stature under recent editors and is recognized worldwide as is its British counterpart, the *BMJ, British Medical Journal* (U.K., 1857). Like *JAMA,* it dropped the full title and became simply *BMJ* in 1988. It also had a variety of titles dating back to 1840.

Each of the general titles offers a variety of items as well as the peer-reviewed article. Many practitioners who read primarily in their fields of expertise, scan some or all of the weeklies to keep current on the world of medicine, the issues of the day, the discussions carried out in the letters, and the special features, such as *JAMA*'s "A Piece of My Mind." The titles also enjoy a wide readership among the general public.

SURGERY AND RELATED AREAS

Surgery is as old as medicine. While advances were made from the earliest days, often as the result of experiences during a war, it was a primitive and often brutal practice. By the end of the 19th century, however, great changes were taking place, the most astonishing being the discovery of anesthesia. The *Annals of Surgery* (U.S., Lippincott Williams & Wilkins, 1885) is the oldest journal in English devoted exclusively to surgery. It is the journal of both the American and European Surgical Associations, as well as a number of other associations. Some sixty years later, the *Journal of Neurosurgery* (U.S., American Association of Neurological Surgeons, 1944) appeared, a title "fathered" by Dr. John F. Fulton to disseminate new developments in neurological surgery inspired during wartime. According to the editorial in the first issue, there had been only one other neurological journal, the *Zentralblatt für Neurochirurgie*, established in 1936 in Berlin. Today, there are many titles in the specialty. Early in the 20th century, the *British Journal of Surgery* (U.K., Blackwell Science with the British Journal of Surgery Society, 1913) was established. Complicating the review of surgical titles is that surgical specialties continue to change and narrow.

ANESTHESIA

The major development that presaged the improvement in surgery was, of course, the discovery of anesthesia. When ether was introduced as the anesthetic for an operation at the Massachusetts General Hospital on October 16, 1846, a new era of surgery had arrived. No longer was the fastest surgeon the best one. Surgeons could take on more complicated and more invasive operations.

Three top anesthesiology journals are the organs of societies. *Anesthesiology* was established in 1940 (U.S., Lippincott Williams & Wilkins for the American Society of Anesthesiologists). *Anesthesia and Analgesia* was started under an earlier title, *Current Researches in Anesthesia and Analgesia,* in 1922 (U.S., Lippincott Williams & Wilkins for the International Anesthesiology Research Society). The third title, *Pain,* is much newer. It was begun in 1975 with the goal of bringing together knowledge for many separate disciplines involved in the problems of pain (Netherlands, Elsevier Science for the International Association for the Study of Pain).

EMERGENCY MEDICINE

Emergency medicine did not become a specialty until 1979, and there are relatively few titles in this discipline. The *American Journal of Respiratory and Critical Care Medicine* was started in 1917 as the *American Review of Tuberculosis.* Several title changes occurred until this title was established in 1994 by the American Thoracic Society (American Lung Association). The journal, *Critical Care Medicine,* was established in 1973 by the Society of Critical Care Medicine with this in mind: that many people who die of injury or illness each year could be saved if the knowledge already available was more widely known (U.S., Lippincott Williams & Wilkins). The *Journal of Trauma: Injury, Infection, and Critical Care* is the organ of the American Association for the Surgery of Trauma founded in 1938, long before the journal, to improve the care of the injured (U.S., Lippincott Williams & Wilkins for the Association, 1961).

ORTHOPEDICS

Two of the most important journals in orthopedics are the *Clinical Orthopaedics and Related Research* and the *Journal of Bone and Joint Surgery. Clinical Orthopaedics* was established in 1953 (U.S., Lippincott Williams & Wilkins). The *Journal of Orthopaedic Surgery,* as it was originally, was started in 1919, becoming the *Journal of Bone and Joint Surgery* in two sections, American and British, in 1949. The highest readership is recorded by the American version. Each section is the organ of the American/British Orthopaedic Associations (U.S., Journal of Bone and Joint Surgery Publishing). *Spine* is a more recent title, one that clearly reflects the need to understand and treat spinal disabilities and diseases (U.S., Lippincott Williams & Wilkins for the Cervical Spine Research Society and others, 1976).

RADIOLOGY

With Roentgen's discovery of the X-ray in 1895, surgeons had another tool to advance their art. Along with anesthetics, the introduction of X-rays changed the opportunities for successful surgery, for the X-ray gave surgeons the ability to see the fracture or the foreign object in the film. Radiology has expanded to include nuclear medicine, magnetic resonance imaging, and ultrasound. *Radiology* is the widely-read journal of the Radiological Society of North America (U.S., 1923). *AJR, American Journal of Roentgenology* started as the *American Journal of Roentgenology* in 1913, adding radium therapy, then nuclear medicine to its title. In 1976, it returned to the original title with the initials (U.S., American Roentgen Ray Society). A third title, the *International Journal of Radiation Oncology, Biology, Physics,* was started in 1975 to address the issues of radiation oncology (U.S., Elsevier Science for the American Society for Therapeutic Radiology and Oncology).

TRANSPLANTATION

The use of anesthesia and the X-ray transformed the practice of surgery in earlier days. One of the major revolutions in the 20th century was organ transplantation. While the journal pool in the subject is not large, there are journals of note. *Transplantation* was started in 1963, successor to the *Transplantation Bulletin* (U.S., Lippincott Williams & Wilkins for the Transplantation Society) and the *Transplantation Proceedings* (U.S., Elsevier Science for the Transplantation Society) in 1969. The third title, *Bone Marrow Transplantation,* was started seventeen years later (U.K., Nature Publishing Group for the European Group for Blood and Marrow Transplantation, 1986).

DENTISTRY

Just as in all areas of surgery, the changes and advances in dentistry have been dramatic. From the days of the traveling dentist who went from village to village to help offer relief from the aching tooth, dentistry continues to use new technology and new drugs to help ease distress. The *Journal of Dental Research* was launched in 1919 as the official organ for the American Association for Dental Research and the International Association for Dental Research. *Oral Surgery, Oral Medicine, Oral Pathology, Oral Radiology, and Endodontics* started in 1948 with a shorter title (U.S., Mosby for the American Academy of Oral and Maxillofacial Radiology and others). As with other scientific disciplines, dentistry has many specialties and the *Journal of Periodontology* reflects the importance of these to dentistry (U.S., American Academy of Periodontology, 1930).

GENERAL INTERNAL MEDICINE
AND CLINICAL INVESTIGATION

In addition to the weekly medical titles cited above, there are a number of internal medicine titles of note. *Annals of Internal Medicine* (1927), the publication of the American College of Physicians/American Society of Internal Medicine, heads the list. Another standard is the *American Journal of Medicine*, the so-called "green journal" in reference to its cover color (U.S., Excerpta Medica for the Association of Professors of Medicine, 1946). The third title, the *Journal of Laboratory and Clinical Medicine*, was designed to bring medical discovery and application together (U.S., Mosby for the Central Society for Clinical Research, 1915). It is interesting that the *American Journal of the Medical Sciences*, Garrison's choice, is not included in this list.

FUNDAMENTAL MEDICAL RESEARCH
AND EXPERIMENTAL MEDICINE

The American Society for Clinical Investigation grew out of the need for more clinical studies, and the *Journal of Clinical Investigation* was established in 1924. Some twenty-eight years earlier, the *Journal of Experimental Medicine* was founded to publish results of investigations in medical science (U.S., Rockefeller University Press, 1896). A third title in this section is recent, having been started in 1995. *Nature Medicine*, one of the cluster of *Nature* titles, should be recognized because of its rapid acceptance. Its impact indicates the growing interest and demand for information on molecular medicine (U.S., Nature American).

CARDIOLOGY

Physicians have always been keenly interested in the heart and cardiovascular activities. Since Harvey described the circulation of the blood in the 17th century, the operation of this organ and its relation to health has been at the forefront of medical concern. The American Heart Association established the journal *Circulation* in 1950 to span the field, addressing the research scientist, the specialist, and the practicing physician. Soon after, 1953, the Association launched its companion, *Circulation Research*, in response to the great interest in cardiovascular research (Lippincott Williams & Wilkins for the Association). Two other titles in this field are the *Journal of the American College of Cardiology*, started in 1983 (Elsevier Science for the College), and the *American Journal of Cardiology,* at one time a publication of the American College of Cardiology, now an independent publication (Excerpta Medica, 1958).

CLINICAL NEUROLOGY

Many 19th century journals combined neurology and psychiatry as exemplified by the *Journal of Nervous and Mental Disease,* 1874. As neurology expanded in the 20th century, titles no longer included psychiatry. The journal *Neurology* was the first American journal devoted entirely to neurology (Lippincott Williams & Wilkins for the American Academy of Neurology, 1951) and the *Annals of Neurology* (U.S., Lippincott Williams & Wilkins for the American Neurological Association and the Child Neurology Society) was started in 1977. The third title, *Stroke, A Journal of Cerebral Circulation,* is a publication of the American Heart Association (Lippincott Williams & Wilkins, 1970).

DERMATOLOGY

As with many medical societies, the Society for Investigative Dermatology planned a journal to emphasize research as well as clinical reports. It began publishing the *Journal of Investigative Dermatology* (after absorbing *Advances in Biology of Skin*) in 1938 (U.S., Blackwell Science for the Society and the European Society for Dermatological Research). The *Journal of the American Academy of Dermatology* (U.S., Mosby for the Academy) was started in 1979. A third title is a publication of the American Medical Association, the *Archives of Dermatology.* It was established in 1920 as the *Archives of Dermatology and Syphilology,* another subject combination that was once common.

GASTROENTEROLOGY

Gastroenterology is the official organ of the American Gastroenterological Association with publication from 1943 (Saunders for the Association). It was fitting that its first issue was dedicated to William Beaumont, the physician who had the opportunity to study the exposed stomach of a wounded soldier in 1822. It would be nearly forty years before *Hepatology* appeared, emphasizing the need for a separate title on the liver (U.S., Saunders for the American Association for the Study of Liver Diseases, 1981). The British counterpart to *Gastroenterology* is the more descriptive title, *Gut*. It includes both gastroenterology and hepatology (U.K., BMJ Publishing for the British Society of Gastroenterology, 1960).

GERIATRICS

The study of aging as a discipline is recent in medical annals. Treating patients within the context of age has been a development of the 20th century. The American Geriatrics Society launched its *Journal* in 1953 (Lippincott Williams & Wilkins for the Society). Two titles reflect the scientific study of aging. The first, *Neurobiology of Aging*, was started in 1980 (U.S., Elsevier Science) and *Mechanisms of Ageing and Development* in 1972 (U.K., Elsevier Science).

HEMATOLOGY

The journals *Circulation* and *Circulation Research* could be included in hematology as well as in cardiology where they have been cited. Other major titles in this field include *Blood*, the journal of the American Society of Hematology (Saunders for the Society, 1946). Its British counterpart, the *British Journal of Haematology*, was begun a decade later (Blackwell Science for the British Society for Haematology and the European Haematology Association, 1955). The third title is published in Germany, *Thrombosis and Haemostasis* (Schattauer for the International Society on Thrombosis and Haemostasis, 1957). Its earlier title was *Thrombosis et Diathesis Haemorrhagica*.

INFECTIOUS DISEASES

Great strides have been made in the fight against communicable diseases. The discovery of penicillin and other antibiotics was one of the major achievements of the 20th century, one that changed the practice of medicine. Despite the advances, new threats have come from AIDS, swine flu, ebola, etc. The journals of note are *Infection and Immunity* (U.S., American Society for Microbiology, 1970), the *Journal of Infectious Diseases* (U.S., University of Chicago Press for the Infectious Diseases Society of America, 1904), and the same Society's *Clinical Infectious Diseases*, 1979. At least one AIDS title should be mentioned because of the impact of this disease upon world health. *AIDS (Acquired Immune Deficiency Syndrome)* was begun in 1986 (U.S., Lippincott Williams & Wilkins).

OBSTETRICS AND GYNECOLOGY

One of the oldest areas of medicine, obstetrics saw many new developments in the 20th century. The long established *American Journal of Obstetrics and Gynecology* dates from 1868, if you include its forerunner, the *American Journal of Obstetrics and Diseases of Women and Children* (Mosby for the American Gynecological and Obstetrical Society and others, 1920). *Obstetrics and Gynecology,* the journal of the American College of Obstetricians and Gynecologists, was begun in 1953 (Elsevier Science). The journal *Fertility and Sterility* (U.S., Elsevier Science for the American Society for Reproductive Medicine and others) was introduced in 1950 to bring together reports and experiences from various scientists, ranging from anatomists to veterinarians. The development of in vitro fertilization and other reproductive techniques has broadened the field.

ONCOLOGY

No word is more dreaded then the word cancer; no disease has been more studied and debated throughout the world. *Cancer Research,* the journal of the American Association for Cancer Research, was started in 1941 to make research results in cancer widely known. *Cancer,* started shortly after in 1948, is the publication of the American Cancer Society (Wiley Liss for the Society). A third title, *Journal of Clinical Oncology,* is the publication of the American Society of Clinical Oncology (Lippincott Williams & Wilkins for the Society, 1983).

OPHTHALMOLOGY

The prevention of blindness has been the focus of both the researcher and the clinician in ophthalmology. The Association for Research in Vision and Ophthalmology established a journal, *Investigative Ophthalmology and Visual Science,* in 1962 (U.S.). The *Archives of Ophthalmology* was established in 1929 by the American Medical Association, and, the oldest of the three, *Ophthalmology,* began in 1904 as the *Transactions of the Ophthalmological Division of the American Academy of Ophthalmology and Oto-Laryngology* (U.S., Elsevier Science for the American Academy of Ophthalmology).

OTOLARYNGOLOGY

One of the earliest specialties in medicine was otolaryngology. In 1896, the journal *Laryngoscope* was established for practitioners dealing with the nose, throat, and ear (U.S., Lippincott Williams & Wilkins for the American Laryngological, Rhinological, and Otological Society). The *Archives of Otolaryngology—Head and Neck Surgery* began in 1925 as the official journal of the American Academy of Facial Plastic and Reconstructive Surgery and others (American Medical Association). A third title, *Hearing Research,* brings into print the research of the physiology, morphology, and psychophysics of audiology (Netherlands, Elsevier Science, 1978).

PEDIATRICS

In the years before pediatrics became a specialty, children were often treated as small adults. Abraham Jacobi began lecturing on pediatrics in 1857, and it was due to his efforts that the New York Medical College offered the first pediatric clinic in 1860. The *Journal of Pediatrics* (U.S., Mosby) was started for the American Academy of Pediatrics in 1932, but became an independent publication when the Academy established the journal *Pediatrics* sixteen years later in 1948. The British title *Archives of Disease in Childhood* is the publication of the Royal College of Paediatrics and Child Health (BMJ Publishing for the College, 1926).

PSYCHIATRY

For centuries, the treatment of the insane was inhumane. Patients were often chained or caged, with no hope and no treatment. In 1798, Philippe Pinel struck off the chains at Bicetre, placing the patients in hospitals and earning the designation of founder of the "open door" school of psychiatry. The consideration for and treatment of the mentally ill have changed dramatically since that time. The *Archives of General Psychiatry* was established in 1959 by the American Medical Association. The *American Journal of Psychiatry* was started as the *American Journal of Insanity,* changing to the more appropriate title in 1921 (American Psychiatric Association, 1844). The *British Journal of Psychiatry,* formerly the *Journal of Mental Science* and its predecessor, the *Asylum Journal of Mental Science,* dates from 1853 (Royal College of Psychiatrists).

PULMONARY DISEASES

Once the focus of diseases of the respiratory system was tuberculosis. When new drugs provided successful treatment of tuberculosis, there were still many other cardiopulmonary diseases of concern. *Chest: The Cardiopulmonary and Critical Care Journal,* the publication of the American College of Chest Physicians, started as *Diseases of the Chest* in 1935. The *Annals of Thoracic Surgery* began in 1965 (U.S., Elsevier Science for the Society of Thoracic Surgeons and the Southern Thoracic Surgical Association) and the *Journal of Thoracic and Cardiovascular Surgery* in 1931 as *Journal of Thoracic Surgery* (U.S., Mosby for the American Association for Thoracic Surgery and the Western Thoracic Surgical Association).

RHEUMATOLOGY

Although this is a small field in terms of the number of journals, it concerns a disease that has long been a serious affliction to many. *Arthritis and Rheumatism* is the publication of the American College of Rheumatology (U.S., Lippincott Williams & Wilkins for the College, 1958), and *the Journal of Rheumatology* is a Canadian publication (Journal of Rheumatology Publishing, 1974). The *Annals of the Rheumatic Diseases* is an official publication of the European League Against Rheumatism (EULAR) (U.K., BMJ Publishing, 1939).

UROLOGY

The *Journal of Urology* was established in 1917 to encompass the experimental, medical and surgical aspects of the urinary tract, the kidney, urine, etc. (U.S., Lippincott Williams & Wilkins for the American Urological Association). The journal *Kidney International* was begun much later in 1972 in response to the expanding field of nephrology (U.S., Blackwell Science for the International Society of Nephrology). The *American Journal of Kidney Diseases* is the official publication of the National Kidney Foundation (U.S., Saunders for the Foundation, 1981).

TROPICAL MEDICINE

This field has only a few journal titles, but the diseases of tropical countries have long been of great interest. Ancient diseases such as leprosy continue to be studied and the health of populations around the world besieged by AIDS and malaria is a global concern. The *American Journal of Tropical Medicine and Hygiene* was so named in 1952, being formed by the union of the *American Journal of Tropical Medicine* and the *Journal of the National Malaria Society* (U.S., The Society). The *Transactions of the Royal Society of Tropical Medicine and Hygiene* (U.K, The Society) began in 1907. The *Annals of Tropical Medicine and Parasitology* began in 1907 as successor to the *Memoirs of the Liverpool School of Tropical Medicine* (U.K., Carfax for the Liverpool School).

REFERENCES

1. Fielding H. Garrison. *An Introduction to the History of Medicine.* 4th ed, rev. and enl. Philadelphia: Saunders, 1929: 785-6.

2. John S. Billings. "Literature and Institutions." In: *A Century of American Medicine* by Edward H. Clark, Henry J. Bigelow, Samuel D. Gross et al. Philadelphia: Henry C. Lea, 1876: 339.

Chapter 20

Journals of the Century in Pharmacy, Physical Therapy, and Nutrition

Julia Whelan
Patricia Durisin
Vivienne Piroli

This article will look at the journal literature of three professions closely related to the practice of medicine. As one of the series in "Journals of the Century," the goal is to highlight the most enduring and influential journals which have made outstanding contributions to their respective professions. The intent is not to provide a core journal list, a task which others have already undertaken (see the Reference list). The growth of the journal literature in these fields reflects the scientific advancement and innovation as these emerging professions aimed to establish their separate identities, standards and practices.

Three authors wrote this article. Julia Whelan, Head of Reference, Sheppard Library, Massachusetts College of Pharmacy and Health Sciences, Boston, wrote the section on Pharmacy journals. Patricia Durisin, Reference/Instruction Coordinator, Simmons College Beatley Library in Boston, wrote about Physical Therapy journals. Vivienne Piroli, Periodicals Librarian at Simmons College, wrote about journals in Nutrition.

PHARMACY JOURNALS

History

The formative era of pharmaceutical journalism was 1794-1844. During this time period there was widespread recognition of the utility of scientific periodicals, proliferation of professional societies and organizations to sponsor these publications, as well as advances in the printing trades and transportation which enhanced their marketing.[1] In the United States, the

This chapter originally appeared in *The Serials Librarian* 39(4): 103-118, 2001.

first colleges of pharmacy in Philadelphia (1821) and Boston (1823) were established, evidence of an effort to centralize knowledge and elevate pharmacy practice by creating standards for the ethical and scientific practice of the profession.[2] Journals soon followed as a means of disseminating pharmacists' evolving views as to what constituted professional practice. The first journal in the U.S., and the first pharmacy journal in the English language, started as the *Journal of the Philadelphia College of Pharmacy* in 1825. In 1835 it became the *American Journal of Pharmacy,* preceding its British counterpart by almost 20 years.[3] This journal also represents the only one of the early titles sponsored by the colleges of pharmacy which survived into the 1990's. The journal advanced the profession by representing it as a unique, scientifically based occupation elevated above the commercialized drug trade.

Twentieth century milestones for the profession and consequently for its journal literature were the 1906 Food and Drug Act and 1914 Harrison Narcotic Act. Both laws served to increase the professional stature of the pharmacist, demonstrating a new trust in the pharmacist to enforce the laws and protect the public health.[4] Towards the close of the century, the OBRA '90 legislation elevated the profession by mandating that pharmacists engage in drug utilization review and patient counseling activities. As pharmacists attempted to demonstrate to Congress that the trust placed in them was not misplaced, a new concept of pharmaceutical care developed and influenced pharmaceutical education and publishing towards an increased emphasis on clinical practice.[5]

Pharmaceutical journal publishing has been a mercurial arena. Constant name changes, mergers and splits reflect disparate factions and the changes within the profession. For an example, one can follow the circuitous path and hotly debated name changes of the *Annals of Pharmacotherapy* (the title since 1992) which has former titles such as *DICP: Annals of Pharmacotherapy* (1989-1991), then *Drug Intelligence and Clinical Pharmacy* (1969-1988), and earlier, *Drug Intelligence* (1967-1969). The early 20th century saw the rise of independent pharmacy journals and commercialization of pharmacy publications, reflecting the commercialization of the profession, competition between publishers, and the fact that editors were businessmen rather than pharmacists. The mid-1960s found the profession educated in the science and medicine of drug therapy and development, but without a specialized journal for community pharmacists that provided professional and impartial information on drugs. *Annals of Pharmacotherapy* (Harvey Whitney Books, 1967) was founded by Donald E. Franke to fill this void and exemplified the shift in the 1960s to a clinical orientation for pharmacy practice.[6] Dr. Franke, whose Audit of Pharmaceutical Service in Hospitals steered the profession toward its current clinical orientation, was one of the great leaders of 20th century American pharmacy. Franke's work with the American Society of Hospital Pharmacists (ASHP) brought that profession out of isolation and integrated the pharmacist into the health care team.[7] The Society has since become one of the most respected publishers of drug information. In 1964, Franke launched a new index and abstracting service, *International Pharmaceutical Abstracts (IPA),* through ASHP. Available in both print and electronic formats, IPA is the only index devoted to in-depth indexing of all the literature of pharmacy.

Europe

The evolution of pharmacy journals in Europe is a mirror image of the U.S. saga. In Europe, pharmacy was a well-established profession and articles by pharmacists were sought by medical journals.[8] Great Britain's oldest pharmacy journal still in publication is *The Pharmaceutical Journal* (Pharmaceutical Society of Great Britain, 1841). For a period it was titled *The Pharmaceutical Journal and the Pharmacist* but the term "pharmacist" has never been adopted by the English dispensing professionals who still prefer the designation "chemist."[9] The emphasis in *Pharmaceutical Journal* is news, letters, continuing education, and advertisements. A sister publication, *The International Journal of Pharmacy Practice* (Pharmaceutical Society of Great Britain, 1991) is an academic health services research journal, emphasizing original research papers.[10]

Journal Types

As with many other fields, pharmacy has spawned a wide variety of journal types. Some of the dynamic journal spectra can be characterized as research versus practice; peer review versus immediate publication; rated by impact factor based on citation analysis or rated by scholars within the discipline; supported by pharmaceutical industry or independent. The relevance of citation analysis based impact factors to the discipline of pharmacy has been widely discussed. While this rating scheme has often been given importance in the promotion of academics and the funding of research, there are numerous critics of the sole use of impact factors in evaluating scientific quality and importance of publications. Some of the negative attributes of impact factors are:

- They are biased toward popular fields so specialty journals automatically receive lower scores;

- *Science Citation Index* (the index used to generate the impact factors) has a limited (144 pharmacy titles) journal list and includes self-citations and editorials in its calculations;
- Analysis is based on the assumption that all valuable data is published in the leading journals;
- Impact factors measure scientific utility rather than scientific quality;
- This schema is dominated by American scientists publishing in American journals.[11]

There have been other efforts to measure the quality of the research reported in pharmacy journals, notably studies by Gagnon, Ilersich et al., and Argo et al. [12,13,14]

Some tension exists between the research pharmacy journals and the medical journals as they compete for readers, authors and respect. However, it is clear that the major medical journals are essential reading to pharmacists in almost every discipline.[15,16] Medical titles that are important to the field of pharmacy are: *JAMA, New England Journal of Medicine, Annals of Internal Medicine, British Medical Journal,* and *Lancet.*

Another genre of pharmacy journal is the state and regional publications. After initial growth, there are now a steady number of regional and state publications; as of 1971, there were 68+ in the U.S. largely performing the function of newsletters.[17]

Clinical Pharmacy and Therapeutics

As a result of forces both within the profession and mandated by law, the practice of clinical pharmacy has grown until it is currently the vision of the profession's future. With the articulation of the practice concept of pharmaceutical care, the pharmacist is positioned educationally to become an equal partner in the health care team and the drug therapy expert.

Annals of Pharmacotherapy (Harvey Whitney Books, 1967) has been mentioned in the history section both in regards to its exemplary status as a harbinger of the profession's focus on clinical practice and its many name changes which reflected identity struggles within the profession. This highly respected monthly is focused on providing an interdisciplinary perspective on issues in drug therapy. The editors emphasize reports of research and clinical experiences as well as critical reviews.

A more recent but strong contributor in clinical pharmacy is the title *Pharmacotherapy: The Journal of Human Pharmacology and Drug Therapy* (American College of Clinical Pharmacy, 1981). Articles report on original research, practice innovations, case reports, or provide therapeutic reviews. *Clinical Pharmacology and Therapeutics* (American Society for Pharmacology and Experimental Therapeutics, 1960) has a cross-disciplinary scope, publishing articles in pharmacokinetics, pharmacodynamics and drug action, molecular therapeutics, genomics, pharmacoepidemiology, pharmacology and therapeutics.

American Journal of Health System Pharmacy: AJHP: Official Journal of the American Society of Health System Pharmacists (American Society of Health System Pharmacists, 1943) started as mimeographed sheets titled *The Bulletin of the American Society of Hospital Pharmacists*. As the society has evolved and changed its name, the journal has followed suit. In 1994, AJHP merged with the society's research publication, Clinical Pharmacy, in a move editors felt was consistent with pharmacy's evolution as a clinical profession. Published semi-monthly, AJHP provides information on new drugs, results of clinical trials evaluating drug therapy and adverse effects.

Not mincing any words with its title, *Drugs* (ADIS International, 1971) represents one of the many outstanding pharmacy publications from ADIS Press of New Zealand. A monthly, *Drugs* provides a regular program of review articles covering the most important aspects of clinical pharmacology and therapeutics.

An enduring weekly from the Netherlands, *Pharmaceutisch Weekblad, Scientific Edition* (Royal Netherlands Pharmaceutical Society, 1864), publishes in all fields of the pharmaceutical sciences, but the editorial emphasis is on pharmacy practice. Observational and experimental articles are included. Most articles are in English although articles in French and German are accepted.

Several newsletters have developed an international reputation for scholarly reviews in clinical pharmacy as well as performing current awareness, news reporting functions. Sister publications *Inpharma Weekly* (ADIS, 1975) and *Reactions Weekly* (ADIS, 1980) offer evaluative reviews on drug therapy and adverse reaction topics. *The Medical Letter on Drugs and Therapeutics* (Medical Letter, 1959) also provides unbiased, critical evaluations of drugs.

Medicinal Chemistry/Pharmaceutics

Just as the pharmacy practitioners find the core medical journals essential periodicals, medicinal chemists rate most highly the general chemistry periodicals. Titles such as the *Journal of the American Chemical Society, Journal of Organic Chemistry, Journal of Biological Chemistry, Journal of* the *Chemical Society, Science, Tetrahedron, Analytical Chemistry, Angewandte Chemie* are basic resources.[18]

More closely affiliated with medicinal chemistry, the *Journal of Pharmaceutical Sciences* (American Pharmaceutical Association, 1940) is known for high quality primary research in the pharmaceutical sciences. The previous title of this journal was *Journal of the American Pharmaceutical Association, Scientific Edition.* The American Chemical Society co-sponsors this journal. Added features are brief reports on research, reader discussion in the Open Forum section as well as book reviews.

Journal of Medicinal Chemistry (American Chemical Society, 1958) is a bi-weekly whose broad scope is to publish studies on the relationship between molecular structure and biological activity or mode of action.

Archiv der Pharmazie (Wiley-VCH, 1822) is a monthly, written in English, devoted to reporting research and development in all fields of pharmaceutical chemistry. This journal was forced to stop publication during the Nazi regime, but was revived in 1950.[19]

Chemical & Pharmaceutical Bulletin (Pharmaceutical Society of Japan, 1953) was previously titled the *Pharmaceutical Bulletin.* Now monthly issues contain English language articles in all areas of pharmaceutical chemistry. *Arzneimittel Forschung/Drug Research* (Editio Cantor, 1951) contains high quality scientific studies in English and German on drugs in research. Some studies of newly marketed drugs are sometimes included.

The *Journal of Pharmacokinetics and Biopharmaceutics* (Kluwer, 1973) publishes studies dealing with the disposition or action of drugs over time in humans or animals. The experimental and theoretical papers published here have helped it become one of the most respected journals in pharmacokinetics.

Natural Products

In the specialized field of pharmacognosy, the development of medicinal agents derived from natural products, several journals have withstood the test of time. The *Journal of Natural Products* (American Society of Pharmacognosy and the American Chemical Society, 1938) includes studies on the chemistry, biochemistry and biology of naturally occurring compounds. The journal was previously published by the Lloyd Library and Museum and was titled *Lloydia.* From the same era, the journal *Planta Medica: Journal of Medicinal Plant Research* (Thieme Verlag, 1935) began publishing scientific research in phytochemistry, pharmacology, plant biochemistry, and related fields. Most articles are in English. The *Journal of Ethnopharmacology: An Interdisciplinary Journal Devoted to Research on*

Indigenous Drugs (Elsevier, 1979) focuses on scientific study of the traditional medicines used around the globe both in the past and present.

Pharmacology

In the field of pharmacology, which focuses on the study of the actions of drugs on the body, there are many outstanding journals. *Annual Review of Pharmacology and Toxicology* (Annual Reviews, 1961) is one of the most important. The reviews filter and synthesize the primary research of the past year. *Pharmacological Reviews* (Williams and Wilkins, 1949) is published by the American Society of Pharmacology and Experimental Therapeutics but includes editors from the British Pharmacological Society and the Scandinavian Pharmacological Society. It has been ranked at the top of impact factor analysis consistently in the 1990s.[20]

Journal of Pharmacology and Experimental Therapeutics (Williams and Wilkins, 1909) is a leader in publishing studies which deal with the whole spectrum of research on interactions of chemicals with biological systems. This journal is another of the many publications of the American Society of Pharmacology and Experimental Therapeutics. The readership includes pharmacologists, biochemists and toxicologists.

The *British Journal of Pharmacology* (British Pharmacological Society, 1946) publishes studies in all fields of experimental pharmacology including neuroscience, biochemical, cellular and molecular pharmacology. The twice-monthly issues are international in coverage and appeal to researchers across a variety of disciplines.

Journal of Clinical Pharmacology (American College of Clinical Pharmacology, 1960) invites manuscripts that deal with the effects of drugs in human beings. Studies that include both animals and humans or bridge the gap between animal and human applications are also included.

Notable for its proud lineage and its wide scope, the *Journal of Pharmacy and Pharmacology* (Royal Pharmaceutical Society of Great Britain, 1864) can be traced back to 1864 although with many name changes, additions and deletions.[21] Original research articles and review articles which contribute to the development or evaluation of medicines are considered. The transactions of the British Pharmaceutical Conference are also published by this journal. One section is devoted to natural product research.

Miscellaneous

Some journals worthy of mention don't fit neatly into the categories above. *Pharmacy in History* (American Institute of the History of Pharmacy, 1959), is a quarterly journal offering articles on a wide range of topics related to the history of pharmacy. Illustrations, international coverage and the scholarship of the authors enhance its appeal.

American Journal of Pharmaceutical Education (American Association of Colleges of Pharmacy, 1937) is the official publication of the American Association of Colleges of Pharmacy. Lengthy, peer-reviewed research articles on topics related to pharmacy education are supplemented by shorter reports and news items.

Drug Information Journal: Official Publication of the Drug Information Association (Pergamon, 1966) is a quarterly of interest to anyone involved with drug information from pharmacists who specialize in drug information practice, to pharmaceutical industry workers, hospital administrators and librarians.

Pharmacy Administration

This fairly new discipline finds many of the multidisciplinary titles such as *New England Journal of Medicine, American Journal of Public Health* and *JAMA* of great importance.[22] More pharmacy specific journals of importance to this group are: *Annals of Pharmacotherapy, American Journal of Hospital Pharmacy,* and the *American Journal of Pharmaceutical Education*. Important titles focused on this field include *The Journal of Pharmaceutical Marketing and Management* (The Haworth Press, Inc., 1986), a quarterly addressing issues in management, administration and marketing both in the pharmaceutical industry and pharmacy practice. The *Journal of Social and Administrative Pharmacy* (Swedish Pharmaceutical Press, 1983) covers topics such as the role of pharmacists in health care, the drug supply chain, patient drug use and misuse, economic issues and more.

Retail Pharmacy

These commercial publications appeal to the practicing retail pharmacist providing summaries of research, reviews of new drugs and important therapeutic topics, political and economic news, advertisements, and colorful illustrations.

American Druggist (Hearst, 1871), started as *New Remedies, a Quarterly Retrospect of Therapeutics, Pharmacy and Allied Subjects*. Its many transformations include numerous titles (in the 1920s it was even subtitled the "Pharmaceutical Business Paper"), changes from a medical journal to a pharmaceutical journal (1884), and an editorial shift from the scientific to the practical aspects of pharmacy (1891).[23] *American Druggist* was very similar to its British counterpart *Chemist and Druggist* (Pharmaceutical Society of North Ireland, 1859), a trade journal intended to be practical and useful to the retail pharmacist. *NARD Journal* (National Association of Retail Druggists, 1902), having endured almost the entire century, stresses the business and management of pharmacies.

Drug Topics (Medical Economics, 1857) began as a house organ for pharmaceutical manufacturer McKesson & Robbins. In the mid 20th century the editors began reporting scientific news in addition to articles on drugs and dosage forms.

A newer entry in this arena is *US Pharmacist* (Jobson, 1976), which bills itself as the journal of drug therapy for the nation's pharmacists and also adds a subtitle, "the journal for pharmacists' education." Consequently, it includes continuing education modules, patient teaching aids and reviews of new drugs. Of note is a current feature, "cyberpharmacist," which examines relevant information available on the internet.

JAPhA: Journal of the American Pharmaceutical Association (American Pharmaceutical Association, 1912), formerly *American Pharmacy,* is the official journal of the American Pharmaceutical Association, the national professional association of pharmacists. Departments include "science & practice," and reviews. The current journal is an outgrowth of the movement to create a recognized pharmaceutical profession. The merger of the Association's *Annual Proceedings* and *Bulletin* into this monthly publication were a celebrated achievement.[24]

We stand on the shoulder of giants. Any discussion of the literature of pharmacy must include mention of the great 20th century bibliographers who have written in this area. Winifred Sewell, author of *Guide to Drug Information*,[25] Theodora Andrews with her *Guide to the Literature of Pharmacy and the Pharmaceutical Sciences*,[26] and more recently Bonnie Snow *(Drug Information: A Guide to Current Resources)*[27] are the masters of pharmacy literature. Their works will aid the reader looking for more comprehensive and detailed bibliographies.

PHYSICAL THERAPY

The roots of the physical therapy profession in North America can be traced back to the first World War, when both the United States and Canadian armies recruited (mostly female) physical therapy reconstruction aides to help care for and rehabilitate wounded and disabled soldiers. After the war ended, these women saw a need to professionalize the occupation of physical therapy and to gain autonomy in the medical field. In the United States, Mary McMillan, a reconstruction aide and advocate of the profession, led the way to the founding of the American Women's Physical Therapeutic Association (1921) and became its first president. The association was renamed (after several name changes such as the American Physiotherapy Association) to its current American Physical Therapy Association, or APTA, in 1947.[28] In Canada, Ethel Cartwright was elected president of the Canadian Association of Massage and Remedial Gymnastics in 1920.[29] Even before the war, Great Britain's Society of Trained Masseuses (1894) was created with the same intent of legitimizing the occupation of physical therapy, whose practitioners were known as 'rubbers' or 'masseuses.'[30] Because these early societies and associations were fundamental in the development and advancement of the profession, it is no surprise that they also publish or produce significant journals in the field.

Physical therapy has come a long way since the early 1900s. According to the American Physical Therapy Association, more than 90,000 male and female physical therapists practice in the United States today and the profession is expected to continue growing through the year 2008.[31, 32] The literature of physical therapy has also grown over time, due to the professional journals in the field. The most significant journals of the century will be profiled here. These journals were chosen based upon their duration over time, inclusion in significant indexes *(Index Medicus, CINAHL, Excerpta Medica, EMBASE)*, and rankings in research conducted by Brandon and Hill,[33] Bohannon,[34] Wakiji[35] and others. The World Wide Web address of each journal is included for further information about each title and, in some cases for tables of contents and abstracts of included articles. The many important journals from related or sub-disciplines such as rehabilitation, orthopedics and sports physical therapy are not included here, although each has significant titles that physical therapists frequently read, cite, and publish in.

The most well known and widely recognized journal of the profession is *Physical Therapy,* the Journal of the American Physical Therapy Association (APTA, 1921). This journal originated as the *P.T. Review,* a bimonthly publication of the American Women's Physical Therapeutic Association. In 1926, it became *Physiotherapy Review,* and in 1962 adopted its current title.[36] According to the first issue of the *P.T. Review* (March, 1921), the publication aimed to "secure a medium through which physicians and aides can more easily get in touch."[37] Today, *Physical Therapy* is not only a communication medium for the professional community, but is also a peer-reviewed research publication that documents the evolution and expansion of the scientific and professional body of knowledge related to physical therapy.[38] *Physical Therapy* is available online at: http://internet.apta.org/pt_journal/. APTA and its sections publish several other journals that are important to the field, such as *PT Magazine* (1993), *Neurology Report* (1994), and *Journal of Orthopaedic and Sports Physic Therapy* (1979).

Physiotherapy, the journal of the Chartered Society of Physiotherapy (1915), is an international, scholarly journal that publishes original scientific and clinical research as well as theories and ideas that challenge traditional physiotherapy practice. This journal facilitates continuing education for physiotherapists and related professions. Members of the Society can view articles online at: <http://www.csp.org.uk/>. The Society also publishes *Physiotherapy Frontline* (1994), a magazine billed as a companion to the journal. The Canadian Physiotherapy Association publishes *Physiotherapy Canada,* another peer-reviewed research journal of note.

The American Congress of Rehabilitation Medicine and the American Academy of Physical Medicine and Rehabilitation jointly produce *Archives of Physical Medicine and Rehabilitation* (W. B. Saunders, 1920). This journal has changed names several times since its inception as the *Journal of Radiology,* published by the Radiological Society of North America (1920-25).[39] This is a significant journal in the field, as it publishes research-based articles covering physical and pharmaceutical agents for people with disabilities and chronic illness. Visit <http://www.archives-pmr.org/> for citations and abstracts of current and previous articles.

The *American Journal of Physical Medicine and Rehabilitation* (Lippincott Williams & Wilkins, 1921) is the official journal of the Association of Academic Physiatrists which publishes peer-reviewed research articles concerning clinical problems and current treatment methods and equipment. This journal also includes case studies, literature reviews and organizational news and reports in its issues. A unique feature of this journal is the ability to gain Continuing Medical Education credits by reading the CME articles and completing the self-assessment exam. To find out more, go to: <http://www.physiatry.org/publications/>.

NUTRITION

Nutrition and dietetics are fields that have made their way into professional occupations in the last one hundred years. While both have fascinated and engaged many scientists from the Middle Ages onward it was not until the advent of the Crimean War and the Civil War that nutrition and dietetics became considerations in preserving the well being of humans. Florence Nightingale considered the feeding and diets of the sick to be crucial elements of nursing science.[40] World War I highlighted the need for food conservation and the post war era saw an increase in demand for home economists.[41] As care of the sick and household management were considered women's work, it is not surprising that women dominated nutrition and dietetics professions. In 1917 the American Dietetic Association was founded with the intention of shaping and monitoring the nutrition of the public. Shortly thereafter in 1928 the American Institute of Nutrition (now the American Society for Nutritional Sciences) came into being with the purpose of being a research society which would improve the quality of life through nutrition research. The American College of Nutrition was founded in 1959 "to promote scientific endeavor in the field of nutritional sciences."[42] Today these societies continue to encourage research and discussion on the topics of nutrition and dietetics. Through membership, their journals, and other publications they continue to inform and stimulate debate and research in the public and scholarly domains.

The journals featured in this section endeavor to highlight the most influential and enduring journals of the past century. The list is selective and therefore cannot act as a core list for either discipline.[43] Neither does the list focus on journals that are catchy or popular, hence the omission of titles such as, *Garlic Times: The Newsletter of Lovers of the Stinking Rose,* or, *Light 'N' Delightful: The Newsletter for Real Losers.*[44] Instead the list focuses on journals that are indexed in popular science, health, and medical indices, have made contributions to the fields of nutrition science and dietetics, and continue to be leaders in influencing the course of research and advocates for public health.

Journal of Nutrition Education (Society for Nutrition Education, 1969) as its title suggests is directed at educators of nutrition science. Since the journal's inception in 1969, it has aimed to be the pre-eminent journal in guiding research and public policy on nutrition education. Its longevity and viability are maintained by the Society's commitment to producing and disseminating new knowledge in applied nutritional sciences. This journal continues to be influential in stimulating research and debate on nutritional practices and policies.

American Journal of Clinical Nutrition (American Society for Clinical Nutrition Inc., 1952) is probably the most influential and important journal in the field of nutrition. As testament to its influence it is the most highly cited peer reviewed journal of any in ISI's category of nutrition and dietetics. It publishes the latest in clinical studies dealing with human nutrition. Its articles are worldwide in scope and cover topics relative to eating disorders, disease, minerals and vitamins, as well as energy and metabolism. Proceedings of international conferences are occasionally included in supplements to the journal. Subscribers to this journal also have the added benefit of access to its electronic version (<http://www.ajcn.org/>). Complementary to this title is the *European Journal of Clinical Nutrition* (Stockton Press, 1976). Although a relative newcomer in comparison to its American cousin, this journal has a similar scope, looking at the theoretical aspects of nutrition, the relationship of nutrition to disease, eating behaviors, and nutrition education. Again the studies are related to nutrition in humans. Subscribers also have access to the electronic version of this title (<http://www.stockton-press.co.uk/ejcn/contents.html>), although the subscription rate to *European Journal of Clinical Nutrition* is significantly greater than the *American Journal of Clinical Nutrition*.

Nutrition Reviews (International Life Sciences Institute, 1942) could easily be billed as the nutrition journal for the busy professional. Edited at Tufts University, this journal offers its subscribers reviews of recent research and discussion on matters relating to nutrition science. Topics covered include nutrition and dietetics as well as food science and matters of public policy. It offers commentary on nutrition issues worldwide. Contributors to the journal review hundreds of nutrition science and related publications to identify issues of critical importance to the profession. On occasion the journal publishes papers and excerpts from conference proceedings and also acts as a supplement to other journals in the field of nutrition science. The International Life Sciences Institute makes abstracts of the journal's content available electronically at http://www.ilsi.org/pubs/nrlist.html.

Journal of the American Dietetic Association (American Dietetic Association, 1925) is the official publication of the American Dietetic Association and one of the longest running dietetics and nutrition journals in the U.S. It aims to be a pre-eminent forum for the publication of original research. Its scope is not limited to dietetics but covers topics such as nutrition and diet therapy, nutrition education and administration, and community nutrition. The journal solicits articles and research from practitioners and scholars in the field and subjects all contributions to rigorous peer review in order to keep the standard of the journal consistently high and to support the professional development of the Association and its members. Access to the tables of contents and abstracts are available at <http://www.eatright.org/journal/>.

British Journal of Nutrition (CABI Publishing, 1947) is one of four journals published by the Nutrition Society in Britain. In spite of its title and origins it is very much international in scope, thus widening its area of appeal. Its cost, however, is a mitigating factor in promoting it in academic settings. The journal itself focuses on original research in the areas of human, general, clinical, and animal nutrition. The journal also accepts research on specialized subjects in an effort to recognize all areas of nutrition science and will occasionally issue supplements dealing with particular topics of note. Its process of peer review contributes to its goal of advancing the scientific study of nutrition as it is applied to health in humans and animals. The full text of articles prior to 1999 is freely available through the publisher's Web site, <http://nutrition.cabweb.org/BJN/journals/contents.asp>, in both PDF and HTML formats. More recent articles are available through the Ingenta journal service.

Journal of Nutrition (American Institute of Nutrition, 1928) is the official monthly publication of the American Society for Nutritional Sciences. Its longevity and quality continue to make it a leader in the field of nutrition science. Like the other pre-eminent journals it too draws its contributions from an international arena and has a worldwide audience. Its focus is the publication of original research in human and animal nutrition. It publishes articles on areas such as advances in nutrition science, human nutrition and metabolism, nutrient requirements, and nutritional epidemiology. Critical reviews and specialized topics are published in supplements on a regular basis. Subscribers to the journal can register for online access to the full text of articles at <http://www.nutrition.org/>.

Journal of the American College of Nutrition (American College of Nutrition, 1982) is a relative newcomer to the plethora of nutrition and dietetics journals. The American College of Nutrition was founded much earlier, in 1959, with the purpose of promoting and enhancing scientific research in the field of nutritional science. The *Journal of the American College of Nutrition* carries on this goal today highlighting the importance of nutrition education. Articles focus on research useful to practitioners, physicians, and other healthcare professionals. The journal contains critical reviews, book reviews, and commentaries on pertinent topics. Abstracts from the annual meeting of the College are published in the October issue. The current year abstracts are available online at <http://www.am-coll-nutr.org/jacn/jacn.htm>.

Nutrition Today (William and Wilkins, 1966) is aimed at dieticians, nutritionists, and physicians. However, articles are written in such a way as to appeal to the lay reader also. The tone of the journal is informative and lively and the content topical. The articles are written by leading nutritionists and scientists with the aim of demystifying some of the current nutritional concepts, controversies, and practices. It also serves to encourage and endorse sound nutritional and public health policies and practices. Online access to the abstracts is available through: <http://www.nursingcenter.com/ journals/catch.cfm?id=AC9F81F5% 2D1522%2D11D3%2D8EB0% 2D009 0276F330E>.

REFERENCES

1. Glenn Sonnedecker, "The Beginning of American Pharmaceutical Journalism," *Pharmacy in History* 33, no. 2 (1991): 63.

2. Edward Kremers, *Kremers and Urdang's History of Pharmacy.* Edited by Glenn Sonnedecker. (Philadelphia: Lippincott, 1976), 193.

3. Sonnedecker, "The Beginning of American Pharmaceutical Journalism," 64.

4. Kremers, *Kremers and Urdang's History of Pharmacy,* 126-133.

5. David B. Brushwood, Carmen A. Catizone, and John M. Coster, *OBRA 90: Impact on Pharmacy Practice* (East Islip, N.Y.: Glaxo Pharmacy Affairs and National Association of Boards of Pharmacy, 199u), 1-6.

6. Kremers, *Kremers and Urdang's History of Pharmacy,* 437.

7. Kremers, *Kremers and Urdang's History of Pharmacy,* 253.

8. Sonnedecker, "The Beginning of American Pharmaceutical Journalism," 64.

9. Kremers, *Kremers and Urdang's History of Pharmacy,* 432.

10. Kevin Taylor and Geoffrey Harding, "Publishing in the PJ—Why Bother?," *The Pharmaceutical Journal* 258, no. Feb 22 (1997): 269.

11. Per O. Seglen, "Why the Impact Factor of Journals Should Not Be Used for Evaluating Research," *British Medical Journal* 314, no. 7079 (1997): 498-502.

12. J.P. Gagnon, "Ratings of Scholarly Journals in Five Pharmacy Disciplines," *American Journal of Pharmaceutical Education* 50, Summer (1986): 124-134.

13. Lane A. Ilersich, Richard R. Arlen, Terrence R. Ozolins et al., "Quality of Reporting in Clinical Pharmacy Research," *American Journal of Pharmaceutical Education* 54, no. 1 (1990): 126-131.

14. Karen E. Argo, Carole A. Bradley, Nicole Mittmann et al., "Sensitivity Analysis in Health Economic and Pharmacoeconomic Studies: An Appraisal of the Literature," *Pharmacoeconomics* 11, no. 1 (1997): 75-88.

15. Gagnon, "Ratings of Scholarly Journals in Five Pharmacy Disciplines," 124-134.

16. Alan P. Wolfgang, Charlotte A. Jankel, John A. McMillan et al.,"Faculty Ratings of Journals in Pharmacy Administration," *American Journal of Pharmaceutical Education* 57, no. 1 (1993): 35-38.

17. G.P. Provost, "State Pharmaceutical Journals: Legitimate Need or Ego Fulfillment?," *American Journal of Hospital Pharmacy* 28, no. Mar (1971): 153.

18. Gagnon, "Ratings of Scholarly Journals in Five Pharmacy Disciplines," 129.

19. Kremers, *Kremers and Urdang's History of Pharmacy,* 429.

20. Guy Hasegawa, "Indicators of Journal Quality or Value," *American Journal of Health-System Pharmacy* 53, (1996): 1530.

21. Kremers, *Kremers and Urdang's History of Pharmacy,* 432.

22. Wolfgang et al., "Faculty Ratings of Journals in Pharmacy Administration," 35.

23. Kremers, *Kremers and Urdang's History of Pharmacy,* 436.

24. Kremers, *Kremers and Urdang's History of Pharmacy,* 433.

25. Winifred Sewell, *Guide to Drug Information* (Hamilton, IL: Drug Intelligence Publications, 1976).

26. Theodora Andrews, *Guide to the Literature of Pharmacy and the Pharmaceutical Sciences* (Littleton, CO: Libraries Unlimited, 1986).

27. Bonnie Snow, *Drug Information: A Guide to Current Resources.* 2nd ed. (Lanham, MD: Scarecrow Press, 1999).

28. Wendy Murphy, *Healing the Generations: A History of Physical Therapy and the American Physical Therapy Association* (Alexandria, VA: American Physical Therapy Association, 1995).

29. Ruby Heap, "Training Women for a New 'Women's Profession': Physiotherapy Education at the University of Toronto, 1917-1940," *History of Education Quarterly* 35, no. 2 (1995): 135-158.

30. Heap, "Training Women."

31. *American Physical Therapy Association.* Accessed 13 July 2000. <http://www.apta.org>.

32. U.S. Department of Labor, Bureau of Labor Statistics, "Physical Therapists," *Occupational Outlook Handbook* (Washington, D.C.: The Bureau, 2000), 207.

33. Brandon, Alfred N. and Dorothy R. Hill, "Selected List of Books and Journals in Allied Health," *Bulletin of the Medical Library Association* 82, no. 3 (1994): 247-263.

34. Richard W. Bohannon, "Core Journals of Physiotherapy," *Physiotherapy* 85, no. 6 (1999): 317-321.

35. Eileen M. Wakiji, "Mapping the Literature of Physical Therapy," *Bulletin of the Medical Library Association* 85, no. 3 (1997): 284-288.

36. Murphy, *Healing the Generations.*

37. "Yesterday's Journals Lead to New Horizons," *Physical Therapy* 66, no. 5 (1986): 697-704.

38. *Ulrich's International Periodicals Directory* (New York: Bowker, 2000).

39. Glenn Gritzer & Arnold Arluke, *The Making of Rehabilitation: A Political Economy of Medical Specialization, 1890-1980* (Berkeley: University of California Press, 1985).

40. American Dietetic Association, *Essays on History of Nutrition and Dietetics* (Chicago, Illinois: American Dietetic Association, 1967).

41. University of Massachusetts, School of Public Health and Health Sciences, Department of Nutrition, *History of Nutrition at UMass,* <http://www.umass.edu/sphhs/nutrition/history.html> (Amherst, MA: University of Massachusetts, 2000).

42. American College of Nutrition, *Objectives,* <http://www.am-coll-nutr. org/can-purp.htm> (American College of Nutrition).

43. Bill Katz, *Magazines for Libraries* (New York, NY: Bowker, 2000), 702.

44. Ulrich's.

Chapter 21

Journals of the Century in Agriculture and Veterinary Medicine

Sandra Sinsel Leach
Ann Viera

Tony Stankus conceived the "Journals of the Century" project to identify journals with the greatest impact as measured by their reputation, influence, and durability in specific categories within disciplines. Depending on the specialty, various selection criteria were used to compile this list of agriculture and veterinary medicine journals. Significant weight was given to bibliometric data, as reported by the Institute for Scientific Information's *Journal Citation Reports*. Evaluations were then supplemented with information from published lists, OCLC holdings records, our experience with the journals, and guidance from faculty in the College of Agricultural Sciences and Natural Resources and the College of Veterinary Medicine at the University of Tennessee in Knoxville. Scholarly journals are emphasized, although important trade publications are occasionally included. Titles were eliminated from consideration if they were (1) annuals, monographic serials, or irregulars, (2) regional, (3) primarily review journals, which by their nature are cited more frequently, (4) primarily proceedings or statistics, (5) abstracting or indexing services, or (6) no longer published. We also eliminated journals identified by Stankus in his lead article.[1] With few exceptions, journals listed must have begun publication by 1992 to be included as influential in the twentieth century. During the 1990s the increased specialization of research areas fostered the publication of journals covering narrow aspects of a discipline. If these titles are important and frequently cited, they are occasionally recognized as choices in the lists.

This chapter originally appeared in *The Serials Librarian* 39(2): 105-119, 2000.

AGRICULTURE

Life as we knew it in the twentieth century depended upon agriculture. Our food and much of our clothing in the foreseeable future will depend upon it as well. Agriculture encompasses "the broad industry engaged in the production of plants and animals for food and fiber, the provision of agricultural supplies and services, and the processing, marketing, and distribution of agricultural products."[2] Farming was the basis of agriculture throughout the century. Although its profile has been transformed through agribusiness, biotechnology, chemistry, and engineering, the farm and farming still characterize our concept of agriculture.

Farming

Farm Journal (U.S., Farm Journal Inc., 1877) and *Progressive Farmer* (U.S., Progressive Farmer, Inc., 1886) started and ended the century as farm advisors and consultants to hundreds of thousands of families who own and operate farms and ranches, or who live in the country. *Successful Farming* (U.S., Meredith Corporation, 1902) hasn't been at it quite as long, and reaches fewer subscribers, but all three offer advice, practical tips and feature articles to the practicing farmer.

Agricultural Biotechnology

Biotechnology applies the techniques of biology and engineering to organisms for the development of commercial processes and products. *Bioresource Technology* (Netherlands, Elsevier, 1979) incorporated several waste journals in 1991 and now leads the field in reporting research developments in biomass and biotransformation. The *Journal of Horticultural Science and Biotechnology* (U.K., Headley Brothers, 1919) reflects the increasing importance of plant genetics. *Postharvest Biology and Technology* (Netherlands, Elsevier, 1991) reports exclusive research in the specialized and increasingly important field of postharvest handling and treatment of agricultural products.

Agricultural Entomology

Control of insects to prevent losses from plant and human diseases is a primary concern to agriculturists. *Insect Molecular Biology* (U.K., Royal Entomological Society/Blackwell Science, 1992) is widely held and the most highly cited primary research journal in entomology. Its original research articles report on the structure, function, mapping, organization, expression, and evolution of insect genomes. The Entomological Society of America (ESA) publishes four research journals, all of which are frequently cited. The *Journal of Economic Entomology* (ESA, 1908) is of most importance to agriculture. It carries articles on insect behavior and physiology and on insect control. The *Bulletin of Entomological Research: containing original and review articles on economic entomology* (U.K., CABI Publishing, 1910) has carried original research papers with international scope for nine of the century's ten decades.

Agricultural Research

Much effort has gone into agricultural research in an attempt to improve production and solve problems, and stunning progress has been made during this century. While nearly every journal in this article reports research, the *Australian Journal of Agricultural Research* (Australian Academy of Sciences/CSIRO Publishing, 1950), *Experimental Agriculture* (U.K., Cambridge University Press, 1965), and *The Journal of Agricultural Science* (U.K., Cambridge University Press, 1905) cover pure and applied research on agricultural systems, including work in tropical regions.

Conventional Forestry Practices

Forestry is the science and business of growing, conserving, or managing trees and natural resources in forests. *Agricultural and Forest Meteorology: an international journal* (Netherlands, Elsevier, 1964) is an important specialized journal reporting basic and applied research of special interest to foresters. The *European Journal of Forest Pathology/Europäische Zeitschrift für Forstpathologie* (Germany, Blackwell Science, 1971) publishes articles in English, French, and German on pathological problems in international forests. *Forest Science: a quarterly journal of research and technical progress* (Society of American Foresters, 1955) reports research on all aspects of forestry and forest management. These journals, which view trees and forests as crops for harvest, have been challenged in recent years by journals that promote forests as ecosystems that can be preserved only via highly sensitive management. These challengers will be reviewed later.

AGRICULTURAL ECONOMICS—POLICY AND INDUSTRY

The business of agriculture concerns the interrelationships of farm producers, distributors, manufacturers, and wholesalers as analyzed by government agencies, universities, extension services, experiment stations, conservation services, investors, and consumers of agricultural products.

Agribusiness

Two journals with international scope offer information on agribusiness marketing systems to economists, analysts, and researchers. *Agribusiness: an international journal* (U.S., Wiley, 1985) serves the nonfarm sectors with refereed articles on the economic aspects of industrial food systems. *Journal of International Food & Agribusiness Marketing* (U.S., The Haworth Press, Inc., 1989) emphasizes the exchange of information on marketing theory among scholars, practitioners, and policymakers with articles on marketing practices and technology and the exporting and importing of food between and among developing and developed countries. *Feedstuffs: the weekly newspaper for agribusiness* (U.S., Miller Publishing) has been informing farm businesses of international issues in the political, economic and safety aspects of commodities since 1929.

Agricultural Economics and Policy

Agricultural economics is concerned with farm production, prices, and management and is a research emphasis in colleges of agriculture and the United States Department of Agriculture and similar international agencies. In recent years, agricultural economics also encompasses the study of natural resources and rural development beyond farming, but two journals are so heavily cited as to elbow out the newcomers. The economics of natural resources will become increasingly important in the future. The *American Journal of Agricultural Economics* (American Agricultural Economics Association, 1919) and the *Journal of Agricultural Economics* (U.K., The Agricultural Economics Society, 1928) are respected and widely indexed journals of their respective societies. They facilitate scholarly exchange with research and issue articles, conference proceedings, book reviews, and letters. *Food Policy* (U.K., Pergamon, 1976) is another highly cited journal in this category that focuses on international aspects of the politics, safety, and economics of food, agriculture, and nutrition.

AGRICULTURAL ENGINEERING—
CHEMISTRY AND PHYSICS

Agricultural Engineering

Agricultural engineering includes the design and construction of agricultural equipment and buildings, agricultural and food products processing systems, biosystems engineering, waste management, and soil and water engineering. Three societies began publications for their members in the late 1950s and today are citation leaders in published research. The American Society of Agricultural Engineers (ASAE) is a prolific publisher of standards and communications for its multinational membership. The *Transactions of the American Society of Agricultural Engineers* (ASAE, 1958) reports on machinery, irrigation, electronics, robotics, energy, and food and processing engineering. *Canadian Agricultural Engineering* (Canadian Society for Engineering in Agricultural, Food, and Biological systems, 1959) publishes scientific and technical papers in English or French on agricultural, food, and biosystems engineering as well as general papers on education, extension, or research methodology related to these areas. The *Journal of Agricultural Engineering Research* (U.K., European Society of Agricultural Engineers/Academic, 1956) emphasizes original research articles on farm tractors and equipment, cultivation systems, soil drainage and irrigation, crop production and storage, fertilizer application and hydroponics, and postharvest methods.

Agricultural Chemistry

Agricultural chemistry is a broad field covering chemical composition and processes of many aspects of agriculture. It is often included in other subject categories in this article. *Bioscience, Biotechnology, and Biochemistry* (Japan Society for Bioscience, Biotechnology, and Agrochemistry, 1924) publishes original articles in English on the broad array of agricultural concerns. The *Journal of Agricultural and Food Chemistry* (American Chemical Society, 1953) publishes original research on food and agricultural biochemistry pertaining to humans and animals. *Journal of AOAC International* (U.S., AOAC International, 1915) publishes basic and applied research in the analytical sciences related to foods, drugs, agriculture, and the environment.

Agrochemicals: Pesticides and Fertilizer

Agrochemicals include fertilizers, fungicides, herbicides, insecticides, and other chemical materials used in agricultural production and on farms.

Pesticide Science (U.K., Society of Chemical Industry/Wiley, 1970) covers the research and development of products for pest control and crop protection and is the most widely indexed and cited journal in the pesticide field. *Pesticide Biochemistry and Physiology: an international journal* (U. S., Academic, 1971) includes articles on biocontrol agents as well. The primary surviving fertilizer journal is *Nutrient Cycling in Agroecosystems* (Netherlands, Kluwer, 1980), which publishes articles on the effects of carbon and nutrients in ecological, agronomic, environmental, and economic terms.

Agrophysics

Agrophysics is the study of physical properties and conditions in soil and plant production, environments, and interactions. The recognized trade journal in this field, *International Agrophysics* (Polish Academy of Sciences, Institute of Agrophysics, 1985) publishes refereed articles in English.

AGRICULTURAL EXTENSION AND EDUCATION

The U.S. Department of Agriculture pioneered the concept of extension services, which provide practical, research-based information to people who have identified their own problems and opportunities. The extension philosophy has spread internationally, and programs now serve farmers, homemakers, youth, and communities. *The Journal of Agricultural Education* (American Association for Agricultural Education, 1959) covers trends and research in agricultural education, while the *Journal of Extension* (U.S., National Association of Land Grant Colleges and State Universities, 1963), now available only online <http:/joe.org/>, brings refereed feature articles to extension personnel and agricultural educators. The *Journal of International Agricultural and Extension Education* (U.S., Association of International Agricultural and Extension Educators, 1994) aims to disseminate research and increase knowledge on agricultural and extension education in developing countries.

AGRONOMY

Agronomy is the scientific management of land to practice effective soil conservation and to maximize crop production.

Agronomy

Agronomy Journal: an international journal of agriculture and natural resource sciences (American Society of Agronomy/Springer, 1907) explores soil-plant relationships though articles on various aspects of production agriculture. *Journal of Agronomy and Crop Science/Zeitschrift für Acker- und Pflanzenbau* (Germany, Blackwell Science, 1853) publishes original research articles in German and English. It has not been highly cited in recent years as publishing competition increased in the areas of crop and soil sciences, but it is respected and deserves listing for its duration and survival.

Crop Production

Raising plants as a product of the soil is a core agricultural activity. Best practices and current research are reported on all aspects of field crop production, including genetics, metabolism, ecology, quality, and utilization in *Crop Science: a journal serving the international community of crop scientists* (Crop Science Society of America/Springer, 1961). *Field Crops Research: an international journal* (Netherlands, Elsevier, 1978) is equally well cited; it also encompasses soil studies and water management. Three journals focusing on weeds trade citation positions over recent years, but the winner appears to be *Weed Science* (U.S., Weed Science Society of America, 1952), which covers all aspects of weeds and their control.

Soil Science

Three clear leaders in this crowded publication category cover the scientific study of soils. Many subscribers, original research articles, and an essential relationship to the literature of agriculture have made *Soil Science: an interdisciplinary approach to soils research* (U.S., Lippincott Williams & Wilkins, 1916), *Soil Biology and Biochemistry* (U.K., Pergamon, 1969), and *Soil Science Society of America (SSSA) Journal* (SSSA/Springer, 1936) the most highly cited journals over a period of years.

CONSERVATION AND SUSTAINABLE PRACTICES

Originally linked to the need to preserve soil, conservation now extends to the preservation and wise management of many natural resources, including forests, wildlife, nonagricultural plants, water, air, and open spaces. Sustainable agricultural practices are perhaps the hope of the future, and are being widely promoted in developing countries for the production of food and economic development.

Agriculture and the Environment

Three outstanding journals feature this intersection of agricultural production and the larger natural system. The clear leader in reputation and impact is *Journal of Environmental Quality* (American Society of Agronomy, 1972), which ASA publishes cooperatively with the Crop Science Society of America and the Soil Science Society of America. *Agriculture, Ecosystems and Environment* (Netherlands, Elsevier, 1974) emphasizes the impact of agricultural production, while *Journal of Environmental Science and Health. Part B: Pesticides, Food Contaminants, and Agricultural Wastes* (U.S., Dekker, 1965) looks at the effects of various contaminants on the ecosphere.

Conservation

The general topics of environmental management, sustainable technology and the use of natural resources are treated in conservation journals. *Conservation Biology* (U.S., Society for Conservation Biology/Blackwell Science, 1986) is widely indexed and has been frequently cited during its relatively brief existence. Original research articles are charmingly illustrated with line drawings. The *Journal of Soil and Water Conservation* (U.S., Soil and Water Conservation Society, 1946) is the pioneer, carrying both research and feature articles on a variety of conservation issues and developments.

The future will be monitored by the *Journal of Agricultural and Environmental Ethics* (Netherlands, Kluwer, 1988), which injects the notion of moral issues into conservation discourse.

Sustainable Agriculture

Sustainable agriculture seeks to substitute alternative farming practices for intrusive methods and chemicals to improve environmental and social conditions on farms. *Biological Agriculture and Horticulture: an international journal for sustainable production systems* (U.K., A B Academic Publishers, 1982) promotes biological husbandry, which relies on natural processes for the maintenance of soil fertility and pest and disease control. *Ecological Engineering: the journal of ecotechnology* (Netherlands, Elsevier, 1991) is a young journal reflecting the new fields of bioengineering and synthetic ecology, and it is gaining attention in the scholarly literature. The *Journal of Sustainable Agriculture: innovations for the long-term and lasting maintenance and enhancement of agricultural resources, production, and environmental quality* (U.S., Haworth, 1990) aims to promote the study of sustainable agriculture to solve problems of resource depletion and environmental misuse.

Organic Cultivation

The Henry A. Wallace Institute for Alternative Agriculture was established in 1983 to promote environmentally sound farming methods. Its *American Journal of Alternative Agriculture* (1986) reports research, policy, opinions, and news. Robert Rodale was an early prophet for the sustainable movement. His *Organic Gardening* (U.S., Rodale Press, 1942) guided generations of farmers and gardeners attempting to produce healthier crops.

Sustainable Forestry and Forest Policy

The ecological use of forests is important to all farmers worldwide, but is essential to the efforts of lesser-developed nations in combating hunger and poverty. *Agroforestry Systems* (Netherlands, International Council for Research in Agroforestry/Kluwer, 1982) publishes research on systems that combine farming and forestry. *Forest Ecology and Management* (Netherlands, Elsevier, 1976) features applications of biology, ecology, and social policy to forest management. The Food and Agriculture Organization (FAO) of the United Nations publishes *Unasylva: an international journal of forestry and forest products* (Italy, FAO, 1947) in separate English, French and Spanish editions to keep alive the international dialogue on sustainable forest planning, policy and science.

FOOD

Food is material used by the bodies of humans and animals to sustain vital biological processes and to provide energy for activity. Food science and technology concerns the basic principles of converting raw food materials into acceptable consumer products.

Food Processing and Food Industries Trade Literature

Food engineering technology promotes the manufacture, preservation, storage, and distribution of food products. Trade journals report developments and trends in processes, ingredients, and packaging. *Food Technology* (U.S., Institute of Food Technologists, 1947) and *Prepared Foods* (U.S., Cahners Business Information, 1895), are well-established publications that inform the industry on technical and commercial aspects of the business. *Food Manufacture* (U.K., Miller Freeman, Ltd., 1927) serves a similar purpose for Europe.

Food Science and Technology Scholarly Journals

Food science and technology as a discipline is the application of basic sciences and engineering to aspects of food manufacture and processing, including composition, storage and distribution. Food scientists are especially interested in the sensory and nutritional qualities of food, but not necessarily in the roles of nutritional processes in health. It is therefore a delicate process to identify the focus of the journals in these frequently combined and interrelated areas. Approximately twenty-five journals in this competitive field enjoy very high rates of citation and impact. Without doubt the citation leader for several years has been *Chemical Senses* (U.K., Association for Chemoreception Sciences/Oxford University Press, 1974), which provides an international forum for chemoreception research and indicates how important the field of sensory perception has become to food technologists. The *Journal of Food Science* (U.S., Institute of Food Technologists, 1936) served an important scholarly need for the specialist during much of the century by publishing research on all basic and applied areas of food science. A newcomer heralds the future, *Trends in Food Science and Technology* (U.K., Elsevier, 1990), which quickly moved near the top of the cited journals list.

Cereal Science

Both *Journal of Cereal Science* (U.S., Academic, 1983) and *Cereal Chemistry* (American Association of Cereal Chemists, 1924) advance scientific concepts by reporting significant, reviewed research in the functional and nutritional qualities of cereal grains and their products.

PLANTS AND PLANT SCIENCE

Plants are organisms that lack locomotion, have cell walls of cellulose, and have nutritive systems that form carbohydrates through photosynthetic action on chlorophyll. The scientific study of plants has resulted in advances for agriculture and horticulture that have improved the food supply as well as the aesthetics of plants for the ornamentals industry and for people who grow plants for pleasure and beauty.

Professional Horticulture

Horticulture is the science of cultivating flowers, fruits, vegetables, ornamental plants, or turfgrass. The *Journal of the American Society for Horticultural Science* (ASHS) (ASHS, 1903) has reported horticultural discoveries throughout the century and serves as the Society's communications vehicle for primary research. *HortScience* (also ASHS, 1966) is nearly as frequently cited, although it also serves more general needs of the membership with feature articles, book reviews, and society news. *Scientia Horticulturae* (Netherlands, International Society for Horticultural Science/Elsevier, 1973) serves similar purpose for the European society.

Home Gardening

The cultivation of flowers, herbs, vegetables, fruit, and other plants in home gardens has grown to explosive proportions over the course of the twentieth century. Home horticulture is a hobby, business, necessity, or passion for millions of people and three fine magazines have championed the cause. *The Garden* (U.K., Royal Horticultural Society, 1866) features English gardens worth visiting, but its international coverage has inspired avid gardeners with news of plants, designs, tips and calendars of events. The *American Gardener* (American Horticultural Society, 1922) evolved over the years to a similarly attractive publication which currently covers developments and issues in garden design, plant selection, horticulture and the environment. The beautiful *Fine Gardening* (U.S., Taunton, 1988) treats gardening as a fine craft, and offers well-illustrated, practical articles by writers with experience, expertise, or both.

Plant Pathology

Plant pathology deals with diseases and pests of plants. The *European Journal of Plant Pathology* (Netherlands, European Foundation for Plant Pathology/Kluwer, 1895) covers the entire field including mycology, viruses, entomology, nematology, and weeds. *Biological Control: theory and application in pest management* (U.S., Academic, 1991) reflects the rise and importance of biological control and quickly occupied its niche as the leader in the reporting of research on natural enemies for the control of plant pests. *Plant Pathology* (British Society for Plant Pathology/Blackwell Science, 1952) continues the official record previously published by the Ministry of Agriculture, Fisheries and Food for England and Wales and covers all areas of plant pathology. The Society is particularly supportive of younger researchers.

Plant Science

The plant science field is crowded with highly cited journals, many of which were covered in Stankus's "Journals of the Century in the Basic Sciences." Two titles are of particular interest to agriculture. *Molecular Plant-Microbe Interactions* (American Phytopathological Society/APS Press, 1988) reports research on molecular genetics and molecular biology of plants and microbes. *Plant Physiology: an international journal devoted to physiology, biochemistry, cellular and molecular biology, biophysics, and environmental biology of plants* (American Society of Plant Physiologists, 1926) is one of the pioneers in reporting of plant science research.

FARM ANIMAL SCIENCE AND VETERINARY MEDICINE

Meat Animal Science

Animal science is the part of agriculture that studies livestock husbandry and the processing of two main categories of products from cattle, poultry, sheep, goats, and swine: meat and milk. Horses are also considered livestock and are in a separate category below. The top three journals that deal with meat animals are the *Journal of Animal Science* (American Society of Animal Science, 1942), *Animal Science* (British Society of Animal Science, 1944), and *Livestock Production Science (*Netherlands, European Association for Animal Production/Elsevier, 1974).

Poultry Science

Poultry Science (U.S., Poultry Science Association, 1921) is the premier journal devoted to the production and distribution of poultry and related products. *British Poultry Science* (Carfax Publishing Limited, 1960), despite its name, is the other major international journal publishing articles on all aspects of the industry—from poultry anatomy to meat and egg yields—with sixty per cent of the refereed articles originating outside of the U.K.

Dairy Science

Journal of Dairy Science (American Dairy Science Association, 1917) and the *Journal of Dairy Research* (U.K., Hanna Research Institute & Institute of Food Research/Cambridge University Press, 1929) are the two most distinguished journals in dairy science. They publish articles on both aspects of dairying—care of the dairy cow and milking, and the production of milk and milk products.

Animal Breeding Genetics

Genetics is the study of inheritance in plants and animals. "Genetics is genetics," explained one of our animal science professors, so it is not surprising that *Theoretical and Applied Genetics* (Germany, Springer, 1929), a journal focusing primarily on plant genetics, is regarded highly by animal geneticists. Also held in high regard are *Journal of Heredity* (American Genetic Association, 1910) and *Journal of Animal Breeding and Genetics/Zeitschrift für Tierzüchtung und Züchtungsbiologie* (Germany, Blackwell Science, 1924).

Animal Nutrition

Animal nutrition researchers are concerned with optimizing the feeding of farm, laboratory, and companion animals. The *Journal of Nutrition* (American Society for Nutritional Sciences, 1928), the *British Journal of Nutrition* (Nutrition Society/Cambridge University Press, 1947), and *Animal Feed Science Technology* (Netherlands, Elsevier, 1976) are the optimal journals.

Animal Reproductive Technology

Much of the complex science of reproduction, a series of events that must be properly timed, has been generated during the past 25 years.[3] Animal reproduction specialists, who are called theriogenologists, regard two journals as crucial: *Biology of Reproduction* (U.S., Society of the Study of Reproduction/Allen Press, 1969) and *Theriogenology: an international journal of animal reproduction* (Netherlands, Elsevier, 1974).

Endocrinology

For animal endocrinologists, the aforementioned *Biology of Reproduction, Endocrinology* (U.S., The Endocrine Society, 1917) and *Journal of Re-

production and Fertility (U.K., Journals of Reproduction & Fertility, Ltd., 1960), are important journals.

Farm and Domestic Animal Behavior

Applied Animal Behaviour Science: an international scientific journal reporting on the application of ethology to animals used by man (Netherlands, Elsevier, 1975) and *Animal Welfare* (U.K., Universities Federation for Animal Welfare, 1992) are the two journals in which veterinary behaviorists and animal science personnel find the best research. The *Journal of Animal Science* and *Animal Science,* listed above, have specific sections on "Environment and Behavior." Stankus discussed other animal behavior journals.

Equines

Equine Veterinary Journal (British Equine Veterinary Association, 1968) is by far the leading source of articles on equine husbandry and medicine, followed by *Journal of Equine Veterinary Science* (U.S., Veterinary Data, 1981), and *Equine Veterinary Education* (U.K., Equine Veterinary Journal, Ltd., 1989).

General Veterinary Medicine and Surgery

Journal of the American Veterinary Medical Association (American Veterinary Medical Association, 1877), *The Veterinary Journal* (U.K., Baillière Tindall, 1875), and the *Veterinary Record* (British Veterinary Association, 1888), are the three oldest and most venerable journals. They publish articles on all aspects of animal medicine for "real doctors [who] treat more than one species," a slogan seen on T-shirts at the veterinary college.

Veterinary Pathology

Natural and experimental diseases in domestic animals and other vertebrates are the purview of veterinary pathologists. Because useful comparisons can be made between humans and animals, comparative pathology is a strong component of this huge, multidisciplinary, interspecies specialty. Traditionally it constitutes a separate department in veterinary colleges. Consequently, veterinary pathologists publish in a wide range of journals, with *American Journal of Pathology* toplisted. In veterinary pathology, three journals stand out. *Veterinary Pathology* (American College of Veterinary Pathologists, 1964) and *Toxicologic Pathology* (U.S., Society of Toxicologic Pathologists, 1973) are the two most important titles to veterinary pathologists as the century ends. Also esteemed due to the classic articles published in the first part of the century is *Journal of Comparative Pathology* (U.K., Harcourt Publishers, 1888).

Zoo, Exotics, and Wildlife

Until the mid-1980s, articles on the medicine and diseases of all aspects of captive animals were published in an annual issue of the *Journal of the American Veterinary Medical Association,* and a few other general veterinary journals focused primarily on domestic animals. *The Journal of Zoo and Wildlife Medicine* (American Association of Zoo Veterinarians, 1971) has become the principal source of peer-reviewed articles on zoo or captive animals in the U.S. Much of the exotic animal literature is covered by *Journal of Avian Medicine and Surgery* (U.S., Association of Avian Veterinarians, 1980). The *Journal of Wildlife Diseases* (U.S., Wildlife Disease Association, 1965) finishes the century as the foremost journal on free ranging wildlife.

Laboratory Animals

Laboratory Animal Science (American Association for Laboratory Animal Science, 1950) and *Laboratory Animals* (U.K., Royal Society of Medicine Press, 1966) are the two key titles covering the care and well being of experimental animals. For the last several years, a relatively new journal, *ATLA: alternatives to laboratory animals* (U.K., Fund for the Replacement of Animals in Medical Experiments, 1973) has led the other two in impact. This is probably due to increased interest in the three R's: replacement, reduction, and refinement and other ways of finding alternatives to animal subjects.

Aquaculture

The *North American Journal of Aquaculture* (American Fisheries Society, 1938), *Aquaculture* (Netherlands, Elsevier, 1972), and *Journal of Fish Diseases* (U.K., Blackwell Science, 1978) are the leaders in underwater agriculture, which pertains to the raising of fish, shellfish, and vegetation in fresh water.

NOTES

1. Tony Stankus, "Journals of the Century in the Basic Sciences," *The Serials Librarian.* Vol. 39:2 (2000).
2. Ray V. Herren and Roy L. Donahue, *The Agriculture Dictionary.* (Albany, N.Y.: Delmar Publishing, 1991), 10.
3. H. Joe Bearden and John W. Fuquay, *Applied Animal Reproduction,* 3rd ed. (Englewood Cliffs, N.J.: Prentice Hall, 1992).

BIBLIOGRAPHY

Bearden, H. Joe and John W. Fuquay. *Applied Animal Reproduction,* 3rd ed. Englewood Cliffs, N. J.: Prentice Hall, 1992.

Blood, D. C. and V. P. Studdert. *Saunders Comprehensive Veterinary Dictionary,* 2nd ed. London: W.B. Saunders, 1999.

Gibb, Mike. *Keyguide to Information Sources in Veterinary Medicine.* London: Mansell, 1990.

Herren, Ray V. and Roy L. Donahue. *The Agriculture Dictionary.* Albany, N.Y.: Delmar Publishing, 1991.

Journal of Animal Science, Diamond Jubilee Issue 57, Supplement 2 (July 1983).

Katz, Bill and Linda Sternberg Katz. *Magazines for Libraries.* N. Y.: Bowker, 1997.

Olsen, Wallace C. *The Literature of Animal Science and Health.* Ithaca, N.Y.: Cornell University Press, 1993.

Stankus, Tony. "Journals of the Century in the Basic Sciences," *The Serials Librarian.* Vol. 39:2 2000.

Index of Journal Titles

Fyiane Nsilo-Swai

Titles are in alphabetical order with [ISSN:s] for their print editions or URLs for those primarily accessed via the Web. Page numbers followed by the letter "t" indicate tables.

A and U: Architecture and Urbanism [ISSN:0389-9160], 134
AAPG Bulletin [ISSN:0149-1423], 366, 378-379, 382
ABA Banking Journal [ISSN:0194-5947], 194, 206-207
Academe [ISSN:0190-2946], 21
Academy of Management Journal [ISSN:0001-4273], 210
Acarologia [ISSN:0044-586X], 402
Accounting Review [ISSN:0001-4826], 195-196
ACI Materials Journal [ISSN:0889-325X], 375
ACM Computing Surveys [ISSN: 0360-0300], 384
Acta Mathematica [ISSN:0001-5962], 345
Acta Musicologica [ISSN:0001-6241], 82
Acta Poloniae Historica [ISSN:0001-6829], 257
Acta Sociologica [ISSN:0001-6993], 49
Acustica [ISSN:0001-7884], 355
Administration in Social Work [ISSN:0364-3107], 11, 14
Administrative Science Quarterly [ISSN:0001-8392], 211, 276t
Adult Education Quarterly [ISSN:0741-7136], 21
Advanced Materials and Processes [ISSN:0882-7958], 380
Advertising Age [ISSN:0001-8899], 194, 216
Adweek [ISSN:0199-2864], 216
Aerospace Power Journal www.airpower.maxwell.af.mil, 316
Africa [ISSN:0001-9720], 142
African Archaeological Review [ISSN:0263-0338], 149
African Arts [ISSN:0001-9933], 125
Afterimage {ISSN:0300-7472], 138
Agribusiness [ISSN:0742-4477], 446
Agricultural and Forest Meteorology [ISSN:0168-1923], 445
Agricultural History [ISSN:0002-1482], 258-259
Agricultural History Review [ISSN:0002-1490], 259
Agriculture, Ecosystems and Environment [ISSN:0167-8809], 450
Agroforestry Systems [ISSN:0167-4366], 451
Agronomy Journal [ISSN:0002-1962], 449

AIAA Journal: Devoted to Aerospace Research and Development [ISSN:0001-1452], 375

AICHE Journal [ISSN:0001-1541], 381

AIDS [ISSN:0269-9370], 421

Air Force Journal of Logistics www.il.hq.af. mil/aflma/lgj/afjl.home.html, 316-317

Air Force Law Review [ISSN:0094-8381], 317

Air Force Magazine [ISSN:0730-6784], 317-318

Air Power History [ISSN:1044-016X], 318

Airman [ISSN:0002-2756], 318-319

AJR: American Journal of Roentgenology [ISSN: 0361-803X], 418

All Hands [ISSN:0002-5577], 304-305, 310

Ambio [ISSN:0044-7447], 376, 406

American Anthropologist [ISSN:0002-7294], 142, 144

American Antiquity [ISSN:0002-7316], 147, 149

American Archivist [ISSN:0360-9081], 69

American Art [ISSN:0890-4901], 126

American Art Journal [ISSN:0002-7359], 126

American Ceramics [ISSN:0278-9507], 137

American Craft [ISSN:0194-8008], 137

American Criminal Law Review [ISSN:0164-0364], 228

American Druggist [ISSN:0190-5279], 434

American Economic Review [ISSN:0002-8282], 46, 202-203

American Educational Research Journal [ISSN:0002-8312], 24

American Ethnologist [ISSN:0094-0496], 144

American Gardener [ISSN:1087-9978], 453

American Historical Review [ISSN:0002-8762], 245, 251

American Jewish History [ISSN:0164-0178], 176

American Journal of Agricultural Economics [ISSN:0002-9092], 446

American Journal of Alternative Agriculture [ISSN:0889-1893], 451

American Journal of Archaeology [ISSN:0002-9114], 146

American Journal of Botany [ISSN:0002-9122], 403

American Journal of Cardiology [ISSN:0002-9149], 420

American Journal of Clinical Nutrition [ISSN:0002-9165], 438-439

American Journal of Comparative Law [ISSN:0002-919X], 232, 274t

American Journal of Criminal Law [ISSN:0092-2315], 228

American Journal of Education [ISSN:1077-7032], 20

American Journal of Health-System Pharmacy [1079-2082], 431

American Journal of Human Biology [ISSN:1042-0533], 143

American Journal of International Law [ISSN:0002-9300], 231, 274t, 276t

American Journal of Kidney Diseases [ISSN:0272-6386], 424

American Journal of Law and Medicine [ISSN:0098-8588], 232

American Journal of Legal History [ISSN:0002-9319], 236

American Journal of Medicine [ISSN:0002-9343], 419

American Journal of Obstetrics and Gynecology [ISSN: 0002-9378], 422

American Journal of Orthopsychiatry [ISSN:0002-9432], 10, 12-13

American Journal of Pharmaceutical Education [ISSN:0002-9459], 434

American Journal of Physical Anthropology [ISSN:0002-9483], 143

American Journal of Physical Medicine and Rehabilitation [ISSN:0894-9115], 437

American Journal of Physiology [ISSN:0002-9513], 397
American Journal of Political Science [ISSN:0092-5853], 273t, 276t, 281
American Journal of Primatology [ISSN:0275-2565], 143
American Journal of Psychiatry [ISSN:0002-953X], 423
American Journal of Psychology [ISSN:0002-9556], 32
American Journal of Respiratory and Critical Care Medicine [ISSN:1073-449X], 417
American Journal of Science [ISSN:0002-9599], 364
American Journal of Sociology [ISSN:0002-9602], 45-47, 48, 276t, 279
American Journal of Tropical Medicine and Hygiene [ISSN:0002-9637], 425
American Journal on Mental Retardation [ISSN:0895-8017], 26
American Libraries [ISSN:0002-9769], 59, 64
American Midland Naturalist [ISSN:0003-0031], 405
American Mineralogist [ISSN:0003-004X], 364
American Naturalist [ISSN:0003-0147], 141, 405
American Neptune [ISSN:0003-0155], 305
American Philosophical Quarterly [ISSN:0003-0481], 153-154
American Political Science Review [ISSN:0003-0554], 273t, 276t, 280
American Presbyterians [ISSN:0886-5159], 176
American Psychologist [ISSN:0003-066X], 32
American Railway Engineering Association Bulletin [ISSN:0096-0268], 377
American Sociological Review [ISSN:0003-1224], 47-48, 276t, 279
American Zoologist [ISSN:0003-1569], 399
Anales del Instituto de Investigaciones Esteticas [ISSN:0185-1276], 128
Analysis [ISSN:0003-2638], 153
Analytica Chimica Acta [ISSN:0003-2670], 361
Analytical Chemistry [ISSN:0003-2700], 361, 432
Ancient MesoAmerica [ISSN:0956-5361], 128
Anesthesia and Analgesia [ISSN:0003-2999], 416-417
Anesthesiology [ISSN:0003-3022], 416
Angewandte Chemie—International Edition [ISSN:0044-8249], 356, 432
Animal Behaviour [ISSN:0003-3472], 400
Animal Feed Science and Technology [ISSN:0337-8401], 455
Animal Science [ISSN:1357-7298], 454, 456
Animal Welfare [ISSN:0747-5144], 456
Annalen der Physik [ISSN:0003-3804], 353
Annales des Pointes et Chausses [ISSN:0152-9668], 375
Annales, Histoire, Sciences Sociales [ISSN:0395-2649], 249
Annales Historique de la Revolution Francaise [ISSN:0003-4436], 253-254
Annals of Anatomy [ISSN:0940-9602], 399
Annals of Botany [ISSN:0305-7364], 403
Annals of Internal Medicine [ISSN:0003-4819], 419, 430
Annals of Mathematics [ISSN:0003-486X], 345
Annals of Neurology [ISSN:0369-5134], 420
Annals of Pharmacotherapy [ISSN:1060-0280], 428, 430, 434
Annals of Pure and Applied Logic [ISSN:0168-0072], 345
Annals of Surgery [ISSN:0003-4932], 416
Annals [of the] Entomological Society of America [ISSN:0013-8746], 401

Annals of the Rheumatic Diseases [ISSN:0003-4967], 424
Annals of Thoracic Surgery [ISSN: 0003-4975], 424
Annals of Tropical Medicine and Parasitology [ISSN: 0003-4983], 425
Annual Review of Pharmacology and Toxicology [ISSN:0362-1642], 433
Anthropological Linguistics [ISSN:0003-5483], 145
Antike Kunst [ISSN: 0003-5688], 123
Antiquity [ISSN:0003-598X], 146
Aperture [ISSN:0003-6420], 138
Applied and Environmental Microbiology [ISSN:0099-2240], 393
Applied Animal Behaviour Science [ISSN:0168-1591], 456
Applied Microbiology and Biotechnology [ISSN:0175-7598], 393
Applied Physics A: Materials Science and Processing [ISSN:0947-8396], 353
Applied Physics B: Lasers and Optics [ISSN:0946-2171], 355
Applied Physics Letters [ISSN:0003-6951], 353
Applied Spectroscopy [ISSN:0003-7028], 361
Apollo [ISSN:0003-6536], 120, 123
Aquaculture [ISSN:0044-8486], 457
Archaeology [ISSN:0003-8113], 146
Archaeology in Oceania [ISSN:0003-8121], 149
Architectura [ISSN:0044-863X], 133
Architectural Design [ISSN:0003-8504], 134
Architectural History [ISSN:0066-622X], 132-133
Architectural Record [ISSN:0003-858X], 133, 134
Architectural Review [ISSN:0003-861X], 134
Architecture [ISSN:0746-0554], 133
Architecture d'Aujourd'hui [ISSN:0003-8695], 134
Archiv der Pharmazie [ISSN:0365-6233], 432
Archive for Rational Mechanics and Analysis [ISSN:0003-9527], 347
Archiv für Musikwissenschaft [ISSN:0003-9292], 83
Archiv für Reformationsgeschichte/Archive for Reformation History
    [ISSN:0341-8375], 251
Archives of American Art Journal [ISSN:0003-9853], 126
Archives of Asian Art [ISSN:0066-6637], 127
Archives of Dermatology [ISSN:0003-987X], 420
Archives of Disease in Childhood [ISSN:0003-9888], 423
Archives of General Psychiatry [ISSN:0003-990X], 423
Archives of Microbiology [ISSN:0302-8933], 393
Archives of Ophthalmology [ISSN:0003-9950], 422
Archives of Otolaryngology—Head and Neck Surgery [ISSN: 0886-4470], 423
Archives of Physical Medicine and Rehabilitation [ISSN:0003-9993], 437
Archivo Espanol de Arte [ISSN:0004-0428], 129
Armed Forces and Society [ISSN:0095-327X], 273t, 290
Armed Forces Journal International [ISSN:0196-3597], 291
Armor [[ISSN:0004-2420], 299
Army [ISSN:0004-2455], 300
Army Quarterly and Defense Journal [ISSN:0004-2552], 300-301
Ars Orientalis: The Arts of Islam and the East [ISSN:0571-1371], 123
Art Bulletin [ISSN:0004-3079], 117-118, 123, 124

Art Criticism [ISSN:0195-4148], 120-121
Art Documentation [ISSN:0730-7187], 72
Art History [ISSN:0141:6790], 118
Art in America [ISSN:0004-3214], 126
Art Journal [ISSN:0004-3249], 117-118
Art Nexus [0120-713X], 129
Art on Paper [ISSN:1089-7909], 131
Artes de Mexico [ISSN:0300-4953], 128-129
Artforum [ISSN:0004-3532], 120, 125
Arthritis and Rheumatism [ISSN:0004-3591], 424
Artibus Asiae [ISSN:0004-3648], 127
Artibus et Historiae [ISSN:0391-9064], 130
ARTnews [ISSN:0004-3273], 125, 127
Arts and the Islamic World [ISSN:0264-1828], 123
Arts d'Afrique Noire [ISSN:0337-1603], 125
ArtsCanada [ISSN:0004-4113], 127
Arzneimittel Forschung / Drug Research [ISSN:0004-4172], 432
ASAIO Journal [ISSN:1058-2916], 378
Asian Music [ISSN:0044-9202], 97
Aslib Proceedings [ISSN:0001-253X], 72
Assemblage [ISSN:0889-3012], 133
Astronomy and Astrophysics [ISSN:0004-6361], 349
Astrophysical Journal [ISSN:0004-637X], 349
ATLA: Alternatives to Laboratory Animals [ISSN:0261-1929], 457
Atmospheric Environment [ISSN:0957-1272], 363
Auk [ISSN:0004-8038], 400
Australian Journal of Agricultural Research [ISSN:0004-9409], 445
Australian Social Work [ISSN:0312-407X], 14
Automatica [ISSN:0005-1098], 348
Automotive Engineering International [ISSN:0307-6490], 377, 387t
Aviation Weekly and Space Technology [ISSN:0005-2175], 319

Banking Strategies [ISSN:1091-6385], 207
Barron's [ISSN:1077-8039], 209
Behavior and Philosophy [ISSN:1053-8348], 156
Behavioral and Brain Sciences [ISSN:0140-525X], 32
Behavioral and Social Sciences Librarian [ISSN:0163-9269], 72
Behavioral Ecology and Sociobiology [ISSN:0340-5443], 400
Bell Labs Technical Journal [ISSN:1089-7089], 384
Berkeley Women's Law Journal [ISSN:0882-4312], 235
Biblical Archaeological Review [ISSN:0078-9444], 147
Billboard [ISSN:0006-2510], 101
Biochimica et Biophysica Acta [ISSN:0006-3002], 392
Biological Agriculture and Horticulture [ISSN:0144-8765], 450
Biological Conservation [ISSN:0006-3207], 406
Biological Control [ISSN:1049-9644], 453
Biological Journal of the Linnean Society [ISSN:0024-4066], 407

Biology of Reproduction [ISSN:0006-3363], 399, 455
Biometrika [ISSN:0006-3444], 349
Bioresource Technology [ISSN:0960-8524], 444
Bioscience, Biotechnology, and Biochemistry [ISSN:0916-8451], 447
Biotechnology Progress [ISSN:8756-7938], 382
Biotropica [ISSN:0006-3606], 406
Blood [ISSN:0006-4971], 421
BMJ: British Medical Journal [ISSN:0959-8146], 415
Bolletino d'Arte [ISSN:03944-4573], 122, 123
Bone Marrow Transplantation [ISSN:0268-3369], 418
Booklist [ISSN:0006-7385], 65
Boston College Environmental Affairs Law Review [ISSN:0190-7034], 229
Bottom Line [ISSN:0888-045X], 67
Boundary Layer Meteorology [ISSN:0006-8314], 363
Brain, Behavior and Evolution [ISSN:0006-8977], 400
Brain Research [ISSN:0006-8993], 39, 397
Brio [ISSN:0007-0173], 104
British Journal for the Philosophy of Science [ISSN:0007-0882], 169
British Journal of Haematology [ISSN:0007-1048], 421
British Journal of Nutrition [ISSN:0007-1145], 439, 455
British Journal of Pharmacology [ISSN:0007-1188], 433
British Journal of Political Science [ISSN:0007-1234], 273t, 280
British Journal of Psychiatry [ISSN:0007-1250], 423
British Journal of Social Work [ISSN:0045-3102], 14-15
British Journal of Surgery [ISSN:0007-1323], 416
British Poultry Science [ISSN:0007-1668], 454
Bruckmanns Pantheon [ISSN:0720-0056], 121
Bryologist [ISSN:0007-2745], 404
Bulletin Monumental [ISSN:0007-473X], 124
Bulletin of Canadian Petroleum Geology [ISSN:0007-4802], 382
Bulletin of Entomological Research [ISSN:0007-4853], 445
Bulletin of the American Meteorological Society [ISSN:0003-0007], 362
Bulletin of the American Schools of Oriental Research [ISSN:0003-097X], 148
Bulletin of the History of Medicine [ISSN:0007-5140], 264
Bulletin of the Medical Library Association [ISSN:0025-7338], 73
Bulletin of the Seismological Society of America [ISSN:0007-4853], 362
Bulletin of Volcanology [ISSN:0285-8900], 365
Bulletin van het Rijksmuseum [ISSN:0165-9510], 117
Burlington Magazine [ISSN:0007-6287], 120
Business and Society Review [ISSN:0893-4398], 199-200
Business Lawyer [ISSN:0007-6899], 226, 227
Business Marketing [ISSN:1087-948X], 217
Byte [ISSN:0360-5280], 384

Cahiers d'Histoire [ISSN:0008-008X], 250
California Law Review [ISSN:0008-1271], 225
Cambridge Opera Journal [ISSN:0954-5867], 107

Canadian Agricultural Engineering [ISSN:0045-432X], 447
Canadian Art [ISSN:0825-3854], 127
Canadian Entomologist [ISSN:0008-347X], 401
Canadian Geotechnical Journal [ISSN:0008-3674], 376
Canadian Journal of Fisheries and Aquatic Sciences [ISSN:0706-652X], 401
Canadian Journal of Forest Research [ISSN:0045-5067], 404
Canadian Journal of History/Annales Canadienne [ISSN:0008-4107], 247
Canadian Journal of Sociology/Cahiers Canadiens de Sociology [ISSN:0318-6431], 49
Canadian Journal of Zoology [ISSN:0008-4301], 399
Cancer [ISSN:0008-543X], 422
Cancer Research [ISSN:0008-5472], 422
Carbohydrate Research [ISSN:0008-6215], 393
Cardozo Arts and Entertainment Law Journal [ISSN:0736-7694], 230-231
Casabella [ISSN:0008-7181], 134
Cataloging and Classification Quarterly [ISSN:0163-9374], 67
Catholic Historical Review [ISSN:0008-8080], 176, 263
Cell [ISSN:0092-8674], 391, 394
Cell and Tissue Research [ISSN:0302-766X], 342, 394
Cell Growth and Differentiation [ISSN:1044-9522], 396
Central European History [ISSN:0008-9389], 256
Ceramics Monthly [ISSN:0009-0328], 137
Chemical and Pharmaceutical Bulletin [ISSN:0009-2363], 356, 432
Chemical Communications [ISSN:1359-7345], 356
Chemical Engineering Progress [ISSN:0009-2460], 381
Chemical Physics Letters [ISSN:0009-2614], 360
Chemical Senses [ISSN:0379-8640], 452
Chemist and Druggist [ISSN:0009-3033], 434-435
Chemistry and Industry [ISSN:0009-3068], 382
Chest [ISSN:0012-3692], 424
Child Development [ISSN:0009-3924], 36
Child Welfare [ISSN:0009-4021], 10, 11, 13
Chinese Sociology and Anthropology [ISSN:0009-4625], 49
Choice [ISSN:009-4978], 65
Christian History [ISSN:0891-9666], 176
Chronicle of Higher Education [ISSN:0009-5982], 21
Church History [ISSN:0009-6407], 176, 263
Circulation [ISSN:0009-7322], 419, 421
Circulation Research [ISSN:0009-7330], 419, 421
Classical and Quantum Gravity [ISSN:0264-9381], 353
Clays and Clay Minerals [ISSN:0009-8604], 366
Climate Dynamics [ISSN:0010-0277], 363
Clinical Infectious Disease [ISSN:1058-4838], 421
Clinical Orthopedics and Related Research [ISSN:0009-921X], 417
Clinical Pharmacology and Therapeutics [ISSN:0009-9236], 431
Cognition [ISSN:0010-0277], 36, 157
Cognitive Psychology [ISSN:0010-0285], 36-37
Collection Building [ISSN:0160-4953], 67

Collection Management [ISSN:0146-2679], 67
College and Research Libraries [ISSN:0010-0870], 63, 70
College and Research Libraries News [ISSN:0099-0086], 70
Columbia Business Law Review [ISSN:0898-0721], 227
Columbia Human Rights Law Review [ISSN:0090-7944], 230
Columbia Journal of Environmental Law [ISSN:0098-4582], 229
Columbia Journal of Transnational Law [ISSN:0010-1931], 232, 274t
Columbia Law Review [ISSN:0010-1958], 224-225
Columbia—VLA Journal of the Law and the Arts [ISSN:0888-4226], 231
Combustion and Flame [ISSN:0010-2185], 379
Commentarii Mathematici Helvetici [ISSN:0010-2571], 347
Communications in Mathematical Physics [ISSN:0010-3616], 350
Communications of the ACM [ISSN:0001-0782], 384
Communications on Partial Differential Equations [ISSN:0360-5302], 347
Communications on Pure and Applied Mathematics [ISSN:0010-3640], 345
Comparative Education Review [ISSN:0010-4086], 22
Comparative Political Studies [ISSN:0010-4140], 273t, 282
Comparative Politics [ISSN:0010-4159], 273t, 276t, 282
Composites Part A: Applied Science and Manufacturing [ISSN:1359-835X], 380
Computer Music Journal [ISSN:0148-9267], 90-91
Computers in Libraries [ISSN:1041-7915], 66
Computerworld [ISSN:0010-4841], 200-201
Connaisance des Artes [ISSN:0293-9274], 136
Connoisseur [ISSN:0010-6275], 120
Conservation Biology [ISSN:0888-8892], 450
Consortium on Revolutionary Europe, 1750-1850 [OCLC:31281105], 253
Constitutional Commentary [ISSN:0742-7115], 228
Contemporary Sociology [ISSN:0094-3061], 48
Contributions to Mineralogy and Petrology [ISSN:0010-7999], 364-365
Copeia [ISSN:0045-8511], 401
Coptic Church Review [ISSN:0273-3269], 176
CPA Journal [ISSN:1094-9348], 197
Criminology [ISSN:0011-1384], 53
Critica d'Arte [ISSN:0011-1511], 122
Critical Care Medicine [ISSN:0090-3493], 417
Critical Sociology [ISSN:0896-9205], 51
Crop Science [ISSN:0011-183X], 449
Crustaceana [ISSN:0011-216X], 402
Current Anthropology [ISSN: 0011-3204], 142
Current History [ISSN:1087-948X], 246-247

Database [ISSN:0095-0033], 68
Defense www.defenselink.mil/pubs/almanac, 291-292
Defense and Foreign Affairs Strategic Policy [ISSN:0277-4933], 292
Delaware Journal of Corporate Law [ISSN:0364-9490], 227
Design Issues [ISSN:0747-9360], 136
Development [ISSN:0950-1991], 395

Development, Genes and Evolution [ISSN:0949-944X], 342, 395
Developmental Biology [ISSN:0012-1606], 395
Developmental Psychology 0012-1649], 36
Diogenes [ISSN:0392-1921], 169
Discrete Mathematics [ISSN:0012-365X], 346
Dispute Resolution Journal [ISSN:1074-8105], 213
Dix-Septieme Siecle [ISSN:0012-4273], 252
Documents to the People [ISSN:0270-5095], 70
Domus [ISSN:0012-5377], 135
Down Beat [ISSN:0012-5768], 101-102
Drug Information Journal [ISSN:0092-8615], 434
Drug Topics [ISSN:0012-6667], 435
Drugs [ISSN:0012-6667], 431
Duke Mathematical Journal [ISSN:0012-7094], 346
Dumbarton Oaks Papers [ISSN:0070-7546], 124

Early Music [ISSN:0306-1078], 88-89
Earth Surface Processes and Landforms [ISSN:0197-9337], 365
East Central Europe/L'Europe du Cenre Est/Eine Wissenschaftliche Zeitschrift
    [ISSN:0084-3037], 256-257
East European Quarterly {ISSN:0012-8449], 257
Ecological Engineering [ISSN:0925-8574], 450
Ecological Entomology [ISSN:0307-6946], 402
Ecology [ISSN:0012-9658], 405
Ecology Law Quarterly [ISSN:0046-1121], 229
Econometrica [ISSN:0012-9682], 203-204
Economic Geology [ISSN:0013-0109], 366
Economic History Review [ISSN:0013-0117], 259
Economic Indicators [ISSN:0013-0215], 202
Economist [ISSN:0013-0613], 204
Education [ISSN:0013-1172], 20
Educational and Psychological Measurement [ISSN:0013-1644], 25
Educational Technology Research and Development [ISSN: 1042-1629], 22-23
Educational Theory [ISSN:0013-2004], 24
Eighteenth Century [ISSN: 0193-5380], 253
Eighteenth Century Studies [ISSN:0013-2586], 253
Elementary School Journal [ISSN:0013-5984], 23
EMBO Journal [ISSN:0261-4189], 392
Endocrinology [ISSN:0013-7227], 398, 455-456
Energy and Fuels [ISSN:0887-0624], 367, 379
Engineer [ISSN:0046-1989], 374
Engineering [ISSN:0013-7782], 374
English Historical Review www3.oup/co.uk/enghis/, 245, 248
English Journal [ISSN:0013-8274], 23
ENR [ISSN:0891-9526], 374
Entomologia Experimentalis et Applicata [ISSN:0013-8703], 401
Environmental and Molecular Mutagenesis [ISSN:0893-6692], 396

Environmental Entomology [ISSN:0046-225X], 402
Environmental Law [ISSN:0046-2276], 229
Environmental Progress [ISSN:0278-4491], 381
Environmental Science and Technology [ISSN:0013-936X], 376, 406
Equine Veterinary Education [ISSN:0957-7734], 456
Equine Veterinary Journal [ISSN:0425-1644], 456
Ethics [ISSN:0014-1704], 158, 273t, 276t
Ethnomusicology [ISSN:0014-1836], 95
European Journal of Clinical Nutrition [ISSN:0954-3007], 438-439
European Journal of Forest Pathology/Europaische Zeitschrift fuer
    Forspathologie [ISSN:0300-1237], 445
European Journal of Immunology [ISSN:0014-2980], 394
European Journal of Neuroscience [ISSN:0953-816X], 397
European Journal of Organic Chemistry [ISSN:1434-193X], 356
European Journal of Political Research [ISSN:0304-4130], 282-283
European Photography [ISSN:0172-7028], 138
European Physical Journal A: Nuclear Structure, Reactions, and Heavy Ion
    Physics [ISSN:1434-6001], 343, 350, 352
European Physical Journal B: Solid and Condensed State, Statistical, General,
    Mesoscopic, Hydrodynamic, and Interdisciplinary Physics [ISSN:1434-6028],
    343, 350, 354
Europhysics Letters [ISSN:0295-5075], 350
Exceptional Children [ISSN:0014-4029], 26
Experimental Agriculture [ISSN:0014-4797], 445
Experimental and Applied Acarology [ISSN:0168-8162], 402
Exploration and Mining Geology [ISSN:0964-1823], 366

Families in Society [ISSN:1044-3894], 10, 11
Far Eastern Economic Review [ISSN:0014-7591], 204-205
Farm Journal [ISSN:0014-8008], 444
FASEB Journal [ISSN:0892-6638], 391
Federal Reserve Bulletin [ISSN:0014-9209], 207-208
Feedstuffs [ISSN:0014-9624], 446
Feminist Studies [ISSN:0046-3663], 162
Fertility and Sterility [ISSN:0015-0282], 422
Field Artillery www.army.mil/FAMAG, 301
Field Crops Research [ISSN:0378-4290], 449
Fine Gardening [ISSN:0896-6281], 453
Filosofia [ISSN:0015-1823], 170
Financial Analysts Journal [ISSN:0015-198X], 208
Flash Art [ISSN:0394-1493], 125
FM: Financial Management [ISSN:0046-3892], 208
Fontes Artis Musicae [ISSN:0015-6191], 104-105
Food Manufacture [ISSN:0015-1823], 452
Food Policy [ISSN:0015-1823], 446
Food Technology [ISSN:0015-6639], 452
Foreign Affairs [ISSN:0015-7120], 273t, 274t, 276t, 284

Forest Ecology and Management [ISSN:0378-1127], 451
Forest Science [ISSN:0015-749X], 445
Fortitudine [ISSN:0362-9910], 313-314
French Historical Studies [ISSN:0016-1071], 256
Fresenius Journal of Analytical Chemistry [ISSN:0937-0633], 361
Freshwater Biology [ISSN:0046-5070], 405
Fuel [ISSN:0016-2361], 367
Fundamenta Mathematicae [ISSN:0016-2736], 345

GA Document: Global Architecture [ISSN:0913-1639], 134
Garden [ISSN:0308-5457], 453
Gastroenterology [ISSN:0016-5085], 420
Gazette des Beaux-Arts [ISSN:0016-5530], 121
Gender and Society [ISSN:0891-2432], 52
Gene [ISSN:0378-1119], 396
General and Comparative Endocrinology [ISSN:0016-6480], 398
Genes and Development [0890-9369], 395
Genetics [ISSN:0016-6731], 395
Genome Research [ISSN:1088-9051], 396
Genomics [ISSN:0888-7543], 396
Geochimica et Cosmochimica Acta [ISSN:0016-7037], 365
Geological Magazine [ISSN:0016-7568], 364
Geological Society of America Bulletin [ISSN:0016-7606], 364
Geophysical Journal [ISSN:0275-9128], 362
Geophysical Prospecting [ISSN:0016-8025], 366
Geophysical Research Letters [ISSN:0094-8276], 362
Geotechnique [ISSN:0016-8505], 376
Geschichte in Wissenschaft und Unterricht [ISSN:0016-9056], 267
Geschichte und Gesellschaft [ISSN:0340-613X], 250
Gesta [ISSN:0016-920X], 124
Gifted Child Quarterly [ISSN:0016-9862], 26
Global Biogeochemical Cycles [ISSN:0886-6236], 363
Government Information Quarterly [ISSN:0740-624X], 70
Goya [ISSN:0017-2715], 129
Gramophone [ISSN:0017-310X], 109-110
GRG Journal: General Relativity and Gravitation [ISSN:0001-7701], 353
Guerres Mondiales et Conflits Contemporarines [ISSN:0755-1584], 254-255
Gut [ISSN:0017-5749], 420-421

Harvard Business Review [ISSN:0017-8012], 211
Harvard Civil Rights—Civil Liberties Law Review [ISSN:0017-8039], 222, 230
Harvard Educational Review [ISSN:0017-8055], 20
Harvard Environmental Law Review [ISSN:0147-8257], 229
Harvard International Law Journal [ISSN:0017-8063], 232
Harvard Journal of Law and Public Policy [ISSN:0193-4872], 233
Harvard Law Review [ISSN:0017-811X], 222, 223-224, 225, 226

Harvard Theological Review [ISSN:0017-8160], 175
Harvard Women's Law Journal [ISSN:0270-1456], 235
Hastings Center Report [ISSN:0093-3252], 159
Hastings Communications and Entertainment Law Journal [ISSN:1061-6578], 231
Hastings Constitutional Law Quarterly [ISSN:0094-5617], 227, 228
Hearing Research [0378-5955], 423
Herpetologica [ISSN:0018-0831], 401
Hesperia [ISSN:0018-098X], 148
Heterocycles [ISSN:0385-5414], 357
Histoire de l'Arte [ISSN:0992-2059], 118
The Historian [ISSN:0018-2370], 246
Historical Journal [ISSN:0018-246X], 248, 276t
Historical Magazine of the Protestant Episcopal Church [ISSN:0018-2486], 176
Historical Reflections/Reflexions Historique [ISSN:0315-7997], 247
Historical Research [ISSN:0950-3471], 248
Historische Zeitschrift [0018-2613], 244-245
History and Theory [ISSN:0018-2656], 261
History of Photography [ISSN:0308-7298], 138
History of Political Thought [ISSN:0143-781X], 262, 276t, 283
History of Religions [ISSN: 0018-2710], 176
History Teacher [ISSN:0018-2745], 266
History Today [ISSN:0018-2753], 248
History Workshop Journal [ISSN:1363-3554], 265
Horizons [ISSN:0360-9669], 175
Hormones and Behavior [ISSN:0018-506X], 398
Horn Book Magazine [ISSN:0018-5078], 71
HortScience [ISSN:0018-5345], 453
HR Magazine [ISSN:1047-3149], 213
Human Biology [ISSN:0018-7143], 143
Human Resource Management [ISSN:0090-4848], 214
Human Studies [ISSN:0163-8548], 160
Hydrobiologia [ISSN:0018-8158], 405
Hypatia [ISSN:0887-5367], 161

Ibis [ISSN:0019-1019], 400
IBM Journal of Research and Development [ISSN:0018-8646], 384
IBM Systems Journal [ISSN:0018-8670], 384
Icarus [ISSN:0019-1035], 349
ID: International Design [ISSN:0894-5373], 135-136
IEEE—ACM Transactions on Networking [ISSN:1063-6692}, 384
IEEE Electron Device Letters [ISSN: 0741-3106], 383
IEEE Journal on Quantum Electronics [ISSN:0018-9197], 383
IEEE Photonics Technology Letters [ISSN:1041-1135], 355
IEEE Transactions on Advanced Packaging [ISSN:1521-3323], 379
IEEE Transactions on Aerospace and Electronic Systems [ISSN: 0018-9251], 375
IEEE Transactions on Antennas and Propagation [ISSN:0018-926X], 383

IEEE Transactions on Biomedical Engineering [ISSN:0018-9294], 378
IEEE Transactions on Broadcasting [ISSN: 0018-9316], 383
IEEE Transactions on Computer-Aided Design of Circuits and Systems [ISSN:0278-0070], 380
IEEE Transactions on Computers [ISSN:0018-9340], 384
IEEE Transactions on Consumer Electronics [ISSN: 0098-3063], 383
IEEE Transactions on Control Systems Technology [ISSN:1063-6536], 383
IEEE Transactions on Energy Conversion [ISSN:0885-8969], 379
IEEE Transactions on Image Processing [ISSN:1057-7149], 384
IEEE Transactions on Industrial Electronics [ISSN:0278-0046], 383
IEEE Transactions on Information Theory [ISSN:0018-9448], 383
IEEE Transactions on Medical Imaging [ISSN:0278-0062], 355, 378
IEEE Transactions on Pattern Analysis and Machine Intelligence [ISSN:0162-8828], 383
IEEE Transactions on Power Delivery [ISSN:0885-8977], 383
IEEE Transactions on Power Systems [ISSN:0885-8959], 383
IEEE Transactions on Robotics and Automation [ISSN:1042-296X], 379
IEEE Transactions on Semiconductor Manufacturing [ISSN:0894-6507], 380
IEEE Transactions on Software Engineering [ISSN:0098-5589], 384
IEEE Transactions on Systems, Man, and Cybernetics Part A: Systems and Humans [ISSN:1083-4427], 384
IEEE Transactions on Systems, Man, and Cybernetics Part B: Cybernetics [ISSN:1083-4419], 384
IEEE Transactions on Ultrasonics, Ferroelectrics, and Frequency Control [ISSN:0885-3010], 355
IEEE Transactions on Vehicular Technology [ISSN:0018-9545], 377
IFLA Journal [ISSN:0340-0352], 64
IIE Solutions [ISSN:1085-1259], 379
IIE Transactions [ISSN:0740-817X], 379
IMA Journal on Applied Mathematics [ISSN:0272-4960], 345
IMA Journal of Numerical Mathematics [ISSN:0272-4979], 348
Image [ISSN:0536-5465], 138
Inc. [ISSN:0162-8968], 205-206
Indian Journal of Social Work [ISSN:0019-5634], 14
Indiana University Mathematics Journal [ISSN:0022-2518], 348
Indoor Air [ISSN:0905-6947], 375-376
Industrial and Engineering Chemistry Research [ISSN:0888-5885], 382
Industrial and Labor Relations Review [ISSN:0019-7939], 212
Infantry [ISSN:0019-9532], 301-302
Infection and Immunity [ISSN:0019-9567], 421
Information Outlook [ISSN:1091-0808], 72
Information Processing and Management [ISSN:0306-4573], 66
Information Science Abstracts [ISSN:0020-0239], 68
Information Technology and Libraries [ISSN:0730-9295], 66
Inorganic Chemistry [ISSN:0020-1669], 358
Inpharma Weekly [ISSN:0156-2703], 431
Insect Biochemistry and Molecular Biology [ISSN:0905-1748], 401-402
Insect Molecular Biology [ISSN:0962-1075], 444

Insectes Sociaux [ISSN:0020-1812], 402
Institute of Marine Engineers Transactions [ISSN:0268-4152], 381
Institutional Investor [ISSN:0020-3580], 209-210
Instrumentalist [ISSN:0020-4331], 97-98
Interior Design [ISSN:0020-5508], 136
Interiors [ISSN:0164-8470], 136
Internal Auditor [ISSN:0020-5745], 196
International Agrophysics [ISSN:0236-8722], 448
International Economic Review [ISSN:0020-6598], 205
International Information and Library Review [ISSN:1057-2317], 64
International Journal of American Linguistics [ISSN:0020-7071], 145
International Journal of Chemical Kinetics [ISSN:0538-8066], 359
International Journal on Control [ISSN:0020-7179], 348
International Journal of Machine Tools and Manufacture [ISSN:0890-6955], 380
International Journal of Mass Spectrometry [ISSN:1387-3806], 362
International Journal of Pharmacy Practice [ISSN:0961-7671], 429
International Journal of Plant Sciences [ISSN:1058-5893], 403
International Journal of Radiation Oncology, Biology, and Physics [ISSN:0360-3016], 418
International Journal of Thermophysics [ISSN:0195-928X], 351
International Organization [ISSN:0020-8183], 274t, 276t, 284-285
International Review of African American Art [ISSN:1045-0920], 130
International Review of Social History [ISSN:0020-8590], 265-266
International Social Work [ISSN:0020-8728], 14
Inventiones Mathematicae [ISSN:0020-9910], 345
Invertebrate Biology [ISSN:1077-8306], 402
Investigative Ophthalmology and Visual Science [ISSN:0146-0404], 422
Isis [ISSN:0021-1753], 264

JAMA: Journal of the American Medical Association [ISSN:0098-7484], 415, 430, 434
JAPhA: Journal of the American Pharmaceutical Association [ISSN:1086-5082], 435
Jahrbuch des Deutschen Archaeoloschen Istituts [ISSN:0070-4415], 123
Jahrbuecher fuer Geschichte Osteuropas [ISSN:0021-4019], 257
Jane's Defence Weekly [ISSN:0265-3818], 292-293
Jane's Intelligence Review {ISSN:1350-6226], 292-293
Jane's International Defence Directory www.directories@janes.com.uk, 292-293
Japan Architect [ISSN:0021-4302], 134
Jewish Art [ISSN:0792-0660], 130
JMR: Journal of Marketing Research [ISSN:0022-2437], 218
Joint Force Quarterly [ISSN:1070-0692], 293
JOM: Journal of the Minerals, Metals, and Materials Society [ISSN:1047-4838], 380
Journal for the Scientific Study of Religion [ISSN:0021-8294], 175
Journal of Abnormal Psychology [ISSN:0021-843X], 35, 36
Journal of Academic Librarianship [ISSN:0099-1333], 70

Journal of Accountancy [ISSN:0021-8448], 198
Journal of Accounting, Auditing, and Finance [ISSN:0148-558X], 196
Journal of Accounting Research [ISSN:0021-8456], 196
Journal of Adolescent and Adult Literacy [ISSN:1081-3004], 23
Journal of Advertising [ISSN:0091-3367], 217
Journal of Aerospace Engineering [0893-1321], 385t
Journal of Aesthetics and Art Criticism [ISSN:0021-8529], 120
Journal of Agricultural and Environmental Ethics [ISSN:1187-7863], 450
Journal of Agricultural and Food Chemistry [ISSN:0021-8561], 447
Journal of Agricultural Economics [ISSN:0021-851X], 446
Journal of Agricultural Education [ISSN:1042-0541], 448
Journal of Agricultural Engineering Research [ISSN:0021-8634], 447
Journal of Agricultural Science [ISSN:0021-5896], 445
Journal of Agronomy and Crop Science/Zeitschrift fuer Acker-und-Pflanzbau
    [ISSN:0931-2250], 449
Journal of Aircraft [ISSN:0021-8689], 375
Journal of Algebra [ISSN:0021-8693], 346
Journal of Analytical Atomic Spectroscopy [ISSN:0267-9477], 361-362
Journal of Animal Breeding and Genetics/Zeitschrift fuer Tierzuchtung und
    Zuchtungsbiologie [ISSN:0931-2668], 455
Journal of Animal Science [ISSN:0021-8812], 454, 456
Journal of Anthropological Research [ISSN:0091-7710], 144
Journal of Applied Ecology [ISSN:0021-8901], 406
Journal of Applied Mechanics [ISSN:0021-8936], 385t
Journal of Applied Physics [ISSN:0021-8979], 353
Journal of Applied Psychology [ISSN:0021-9010], 33-34
Journal of Arachnology [ISSN:0161-8202], 402
Journal of Architectural Engineering [ISSN:1076-0431], 385t
Journal of Arid Environments [ISSN:0140-1963], 406
Journal of Atmospheric and Solar-Terrestrial Physics [ISSN:1364-6826], 363
Journal of Atmospheric Chemistry [ISSN:0167-7764], 363
Journal of Atmospheric Sciences [ISSN:0022-4928], 363
Journal of Avian Medicine and Surgery [ISSN:1082-6742], 457
Journal of Bacteriology [ISSN:0021-9193], 393
Journal of Biogeography [ISSN:0305-0270], 404
Journal of Biological Chemistry [ISSN:0021-9258], 392, 431-432
Journal of Biomechanics [ISSN:0021-9290], 378
Journal of Biomedical Engineering [ISSN:0148-0731], 385t
Journal of Biomedical Materials Research [ISSN:0021-9304], 378
Journal of Bone and Joint Surgery [ISSN:0021-9355], 417
Journal of Bridge Engineering [ISSN:1084-0702], 385t
Journal of British Studies [ISSN:0021-9371], 255
Journal of Business and Finance Librarianship [ISSN:0896-3568] , 72
Journal of Business Ethics [ISSN:0167-4544], 200
Journal of Business Strategy [ISSN:0275-6668], 215-215
Journal of Canadian Art History/Annales d'Histoire de l'Art Canadien
    [ISSN:0315-4297], 127
Journal of Catalysis [ISSN:0021-9017], 359

Journal of Cell Biology [ISSN:0021-9525], 394
Journal of Cell Science [ISSN:0021-9533], 394
Journal of Cellular Physiology [ISSN:0021-9541], 394-395
Journal of Chemical Physics [ISSN:0021-9606], 352
Journal of Chemical Thermodynamics [ISSN:0021-9614], 351
Journal of Chromatography [ISSN:0021-9673], 361
Journal of Climate [ISSN:0894-8755], 363
Journal of Clinical Investigation [ISSN:0021-9738], 419
Journal of Clinical Oncology [ISSN:0732-183X], 422
Journal of Clinical Pharmacology [ISSN:0091-2700], 433
Journal of Cognitive Neuroscience [ISSN:0898-929X], 397-398
Journal of Cold Region Engineering [ISSN:0887-381X], 385t
Journal of Colloid and Interface Science [ISSN:0021-9797], 360
Journal of Combinatorial Theory Series A: Structures, Designs, and Applications
    of Combinatorics [ISSN:0097-3165], 346
Journal of Combinatorial Theory Series B: Graph Theory and Matroid Theory
    [0095-8956], 346
Journal of Comparative Neurology [ISSN:0092-7317], 397
Journal of Comparative Pathology [ISSN:0021-9975], 457
Journal of Comparative Physiology A: Sensory, Neural and Behavioral
    Physiology [ISSN:0174-1578], 400
Journal of Comparative Physiology B: Biochemical, Systemic, and
    Environmental Physiology [ISSN:0340-7594], 400
Journal of Comparative Psychology [ISSN:0735-7036], 34-35, 400
Journal of Composites for Construction [ISSN:1090-0268], 385t
Journal of Computational Chemistry [ISSN:0192-8651], 361
Journal of Computing in Civil Engineering [ISSN:0887-3801], 385t
Journal of Construction Engineering and Management ISSN:0733-9364], 385t
Journal of Consulting and Clinical Psychology [ISSN:0022-006X], 35-36
Journal of Contemporary Health Law and Policy [ISSN:0882-1046], 233
Journal of Contemporary History [ISSN:0022-0094], 249
Journal of Coordination Chemistry [ISSN:0095-8972], 358
Journal of Corporation Law [ISSN:0360-795X], 226, 227
Journal of Counseling Psychology [ISSN:0022-0167], 34
Journal of Criminal Law and Criminology [ISSN:0885-2731], 228
Journal of Dairy Research [ISSN:0022-0299], 455
Journal of Dairy Science [ISSN:0022-0302], 455
Journal of Decorative and Propaganda Arts [ISSN:0888-7314], 136
Journal of Dental Research [ISSN:0027-0345], 418
Journal of Design History [ISSN:0952-4649], 136
Journal of Differential Equations [ISSN:0022-0396], 347
Journal of Differential Geometry [ISSN:0022-040X], 346
Journal of Documentation [ISSN:0022-0418], 68
Journal of Dynamical Systems, Measurement, and Control [ISSN:0022-0434],
    386t
Journal of Economic Entomology [ISSN:0022-0493], 445
Journal of Economic History [ISSN:0022-0507], 259-260
Journal of Education for Library and Information Science [ISSN:0748-5786], 66

Journal of Educational Psychology [ISSN:0022-0663], 25
Journal of Educational Research [ISSN:0022-0671], 25
Journal of Electroanalytical Chemistry [ISSN:0022-0728], 362
Journal of Electronic Defense [ISSN:0192-429X], 293
Journal of Electronic Materials [ISSN:0361-5235], 380
Journal of Electronic Packaging [ISSN:1043-7398], 386t
Journal of Endocrinology [ISSN:0022-0795], 398
Journal of Energy Engineering [ISSN:0733-9402], 379, 385t
Journal of Energy Resources Technology [ISSN:0195-0738], 386t
Journal of Engineering for Gas Turbines and Power [ISSN:0742-4795]
Journal of Engineering Materials and Technology [ISSN:0094-4289]
Journal of Engineering Mechanics [ISSN:0733-9399], 385t, 386t
Journal of Environmental Engineering [ISSN:0733-9372], 376, 385t
Journal of Environmental Quality [ISSN:0047-2425], 450
Journal of Environmental Science and Health Part B; Pesticides, Food
    Contaminants, and Agricultural Wastes [ISSN:0047-2433], 450
Journal of Equine Veterinary Science [ISSN:0737-0806], 456
Journal of Ethnopharmacology [ISSN:0378-8741], 357, 432-433
Journal of European Economic History [ISSN:0391-5115], 260
Journal of Evolutionary Biology [ISSN:1010-061X], 407
Journal of Experimental and Theoretical Physics [ISSN:1063-7761], 350
Journal of Experimental Biology [ISSN:0022-0949], 399
Journal of Experimental Botany [ISSN:0022-0957], 403
Journal of Experimental Education [ISSN:0022-0973], 25
Journal of Experimental Marine Biology and Ecology [ISSN:0022-0981], 405
Journal of Experimental Medicine [ISSN:0022-1007], 419
Journal of Experimental Psychology: Animal Behavior Processes [ISSN:0097-
    7403], 37
Journal of Experimental Psychology: Applied [ISSN:1076-898X], 37
Journal of Experimental Psychology: General [ISSN:0096-3445], 37
Journal of Experimental Psychology: Human Perception and Performance
    [ISSN:0096-1523], 37
Journal of Experimental Psychology: Learning, Memory and Cognition
    [ISSN:0278-7393], 37
Journal of Experimental Social Psychology [ISSN:0022-1031], 38
Journal of Finance [ISSN:0022-1082], 209
Journal of Fish Biology [ISSN:0022-1112], 401
Journal of Fish Diseases [ISSN:0140-7775], 457
Journal of Fluid Mechanics [ISSN:0022-1120], 351
Journal of Fluids Engineering [ISSN:0098-2202], 386t
Journal of Fluorine Chemistry [ISSN:0022-1139], 359
Journal of Food Science [ISSN:0022-1147], 452
Journal of Forensic Sciences [ISSN:0022-1198], 143
Journal of General Virology [ISSN:0022-1317], 394
Journal of Geotechnical and Geoenvironmental Engineering [ISSN:1090-0241],
    385t
Journal of Glaciology [ISSN:0022-1430], 363
Journal of Government Information [ISSN:1352-0237], 70

Journal of Graph Theory [ISSN:0394-9024], 346
Journal of Guidance, Control, and Dynamics [ISSN:0731-5090], 375
Journal of Heat Transfer [ISSN:0022-1481], 386t
Journal of Helminthology [ISSN:0022-149X], 402-403
Journal of Heredity [ISSN:0022-1303], 455
Journal of Herpetology [ISSN:0022-1511], 401
Journal of Heterocyclic Chemistry [ISSN:0022-152X], 357
Journal of Higher Education [ISSN:0022-1546], 21
Journal of Horticultural Science and Biotechnology [ISSN:1462-0316], 444
Journal of Human Evolution [ISSN:0047-2484], 143
Journal of Hydraulic Engineering [ISSN:0733-9429], 385t
Journal of Hydrologic Engineering [ISSN:1084-0699], 385t
Journal of Hydrology [ISSN:0022-1694], 364
Journal of Immunology [ISSN:0022-1767], 394
Journal of Imperial and Commonwealth History [ISSN:0308-6534], 254
Journal of Infectious Diseases [ISSN:0022-1899], 421
Journal of Information Science [ISSN:1352-7460], 66
Journal of Infrastructure Systems [ISSN:1076-0342], 385t
Journal of Inorganic Biochemistry [ISSN:0162-0134], 358-359
Journal of Insect Physiology [ISSN:0022-1910], 401-402
Journal of Intellectual Property Law www.lawsch.uga.edu/jipl, 231
Journal of Interdisciplinary History [ISSN:0022-1953], 260-261
Journal of International Agricultural and Extension Education [ISSN:1077-0755], 448
Journal of International Food and Agribusiness Marketing [ISSN:0897-4438], 446
Journal of Investigative Dermatology [ISSN:0022-202X], 420
Journal of Irrigation and Drainage [ISSN:0733-9437], 385t
Journal of Laboratory and Clinical Medicine [ISSN:0022-2143], 419
Journal of Law and Economics [ISSN:0022-2186], 235-236
Journal of Law Reform www.law.umich.edu/pubs/journals/mjlr, 230
Journal of Legal Education [ISSN:0022-2208], 236
Journal of Legal Studies [ISSN:0047-2530], 222, 236
Journal of Library Administration [ISSN:0193-0826], 67
Journal of Lightwave Technology [ISSN:0733-8724], 355
Journal of Linguistic Anthropology [ISSN:1055-1360], 145
Journal of Lipid Research [ISSN:0022-2275], 393
Journal of Luminescence [ISSN:0022-2313], 360
Journal of Magnetic Resonance [ISSN:1053-1807], 362
Journal of Mammology [ISSN:0022-2372], 400
Journal of Management in Engineering [ISSN:0742-597X], 385t
Journal of Manufacturing Science and Technology [ISSN: 1087-1357], 386t
Journal of Manufacturing Systems [ISSN:0278-6125], 379
Journal of Marine Research [ISSN:0022-2402], 363-364
Journal of Marketing [ISSN:0022-2429], 218
Journal of Marriage and the Family [ISSN:0022-2445], 52
Journal of Materials in Civil Engineering [ISSN:0899-1561], 385t
Journal of Materials Research [ISSN:0884-2914], 380

Journal of Mathematical Analysis and Its Applications [ISSN:0022-247X], 347
Journal of Mathematical Physics [ISSN:0022-2488], 350
Journal of Mathematical Sociology [ISSN:0022-250X], 50
Journal of Mechanical Design [ISSN:1050-0472], 386t
Journal of Medicinal Chemistry [ISSN:0095-9065], 356, 432
Journal of Memory and Language [ISSN:0749-596X], 37
Journal of Military History [ISSN:0899-3718], 294
Journal of Modern History [ISSN:0022-2801], 246, 249, 276t
Journal of Molecular Biology [ISSN:0022-2836], 392
Journal of Molecular Catalysis A: Chemical [ISSN:1381-1169], 359
Journal of Molecular Catalysis B: Enzymatic [ISSN:1381-1177], 359
Journal of Molecular Endocrinology [ISSN:0952-5041], 399
Journal of Molecular Evolution [ISSN:0022-2844], 407
Journal of Molecular Spectroscopy [ISSN:0022-2802], 361
Journal of Molecular Structure [ISSN:0022-2860], 359
Journal of Molluscan Studies [ISSN:0260-1230], 402
Journal of Morphology [ISSN:0362-2525], 399
Journal of Music Theory [ISSN:0022-2909], 91-92
Journal of Music Therapy [ISSN:0022-2917], 100
Journal of Natural History [ISSN:0022-2933], 405
Journal of Natural Products [ISSN:0163-3864], 357, 432
Journal of Near Eastern Studies [ISSN:0022-2968], 148
Journal of Negro Education [ISSN:0022-2984], 22
Journal of Nematology [ISSN:0022-300X], 402
Journal of Neurochemistry [ISSN:0022-3042], 398
Journal of Neuroendocrinology [ISSN:0953-8194], 398
Journal of Neurophysiology [ISSN:0449-282X], 397
Journal of Neuroscience [ISSN:0270-6474], 397
Journal of Neurosurgery [ISSN:0022-3085], 416
Journal of New Music Research [ISSN:0929-8215], 92
Journal of Nutrition [ISSN:0022-3166], 440, 455
Journal of Nutrition Education [ISSN:0022-3182], 438
Journal of Offshore Mechanics and Arctic Engineering [ISSN:0892-7219], 386t
Journal of Offshore Technology [ISSN:0968-784x], 381
Journal of Organic Chemistry [ISSN:0022-3263], 356, 431-432
Journal of Organometallic Chemistry [ISSN:0022-328X], 358
Journal of Orthopaedic and Sports Physical Therapy [ISSN:0190-6011], 437
Journal of Paleontology [ISSN:0022-3360], 365
Journal of Parasitology [ISSN:0022-3395], 403
Journal of Pediatrics [ISSN:0022-3476], 423
Journal of Peptides Research [ISSN:1397-002X], 393
Journal of Performance of Constructed Facilities [ISSN:0887-3828], 386t
Journal of Periodontology [ISSN:0022-3492], 418
Journal of Personality [ISSN:0022-3506], 38
Journal of Personality and Social Psychology [ISSN:0022-3514], 35, 38
Journal of Petroleum Geology [ISSN:01410-6421], 366, 382
Journal of Petrology [ISSN:0022-3530], 365
Journal of Pharmaceutical Marketing and Management [ISSN:0883-7597], 434

Journal of Pharmaceutical Sciences [ISSN:0022-3549], 356, 432

Journal of Pharmacokinetics and Biopharmaceutics [ISSN:0090-486X], 432

Journal of Pharmacology and Experimental Therapeutics [ISSN:0020-3565], 433

Journal of Pharmacy and Pharmacology [ISSN:0022-3573], 433

Journal of Philosophical Logic [ISSN:0022-3611], 167

Journal of Philosophy [ISSN:0022-362X], 162-163

Journal of Photochemistry [ISSN:0047-2670], 360

Journal of Phycology [ISSN:0022-3646], 404

Journal of Physical Chemistry A: Molecules, Spectroscopy, Kinetics, Environmental and General Theory [ISSN:1089-5639], 360

Journal of Physical Chemistry B: Condensed Matter, Materials, Surfaces, Interfaces, and Biophysical Chemistry [1089-5647], 360

Journal of Physical Oceanography [ISSN:0022-3670], 363

Journal of Physical Organic Chemistry [ISSN:0894-3230], 359

Journal of Physics B: Atomic Molecular and Optical Physics [ISSN:0022-3700], 352

Journal of Physiology [ISSN:0022-3751], 397

Journal of Political Economy [ISSN:0022-3808], 203, 277t

Journal of Polymer Science [ISSN:0022-3832], 358

Journal of Pressure Vessel Technology [ISSN:0094-9930], 386t

Journal of Product Innovation Management [ISSN:0737-6782], 379

Journal of Professional Issues in Engineering Education and Practice [ISSN:1052-3928], 385t

Journal of Propulsion and Power [ISSN:0748-4658], 375

Journal of Religion [ISSN:0022-4189], 175

Journal of Reproduction and Fertility [ISSN:0022-4251], 455-456

Journal of Research in Music Education [ISSN:0022-4294], 98-99

Journal of Rheumatology [ISSN:0315-162X], 424

Journal of Roman Archaeology [ISSN: 1047-7594], 148-149

Journal of Sedimentary Research A: Sedimentary Petrology and Processes [ISSN:1073-130X], 365

Journal of Sedimentary Research B: Sedimentary Geology [ISSN:1073-1318], 365

Journal of Ship Production [ISSN:9756-1417], 381

Journal of Small Business Management [ISSN:0047-2778], 206

Journal of Social and Administrative Pharmacy [ISSN:0281-0662], 434

Journal of Social History ISSN:0022-4529], 265

Journal of Social Service Research [ISSN:0148-8376], 10, 11, 12

Journal of Social Work Education [ISSN:1043-7797], 10, 11, 12

Journal of Soil and Water Conservation [ISSN:0022-4561], 450

Journal of Solar Energy Engineering [0199-6231], 379, 386t

Journal of Solid State Chemistry [ISSN:0022-4596], 359

Journal of Sound and Vibration [ISSN:0022-460X], 355

Journal of Spacecraft and Rockets [ISSN:0022-4650], 375

Journal of Statistical Physics [ISSN:0022-4715], 351

Journal of Strategic Studies [ISSN:0140-2390], 294

Journal of Structural Engineering [ISSN:0733-9445], 385t

Journal of Structural Geology [ISSN:0191-8141], 364

Journal of Surveying Engineering [ISSN:0733-9453], 385t
Journal of Sustainable Agriculture [ISSN:1044-0046], 451
Journal of Symbolic Logic [ISSN:0022-4812], 345
Journal of Taxation [ISSN:0022-4863], 198, 234
Journal of Testing and Evaluation [ISSN:0090-3973], 379-380
Journal of the Acoustical Society of America [ISSN:0001-4966], 355
Journal of the Air and Waste Management Association [ISSN:1096-2247], 363, 376
Journal of the American Academy of Dermatology [ISSN:0190-9622], 420
Journal of the American Academy of Religion [ISSN:0002-7189], 175
Journal of the American Ceramic Society [ISSN:0002-7820], 380
Journal of the American Chemical Society [ISSN:0002-7863], 356, 431-432
Journal of the American College of Cardiology [ISSN:0735-1097], 419-420
Journal of the American College of Nutrition [ISSN:0731-5724], 440
Journal of the American Dietetic Association [ISSN:0662-8223], 439
Journal of the American Geriatrics Society [ISSN:0002-8614], 421
Journal of the American Musicological Society [ISSN:0402-012X], 84-85, 93
Journal of the American Society for Information Science [ISSN:0044-7870], 63, 66
Journal of the American Statistical Association [ISSN:0162-1459], 349
Journal of the American Veterinary Medical Association [ISSN:0003-1488], 456, 457
Journal of the American Water Works Association [ISSN:0008-150X], 377
Journal of the Chemical Society—Dalton Transactions [ISSN:0300-9246], 358, 431-432
Journal of the Chemical Society—Perkin Transactions I [ISSN:0300-922X], 357, 431-432
Journal of the Chemical Society—Perkin Transactions II [ISSN:0300-9580], 359, 431-432
Journal of the Copyright Society of the USA [ISSN:0886-3520], 231
Journal of the European Ceramic Society [ISSN:0955-2219], 380
Journal of the History of Ideas [ISSN:0022-5037], 163, 262, 276t
Journal of the History of Philosophy [ISSN:0022-5053], 163
Journal of the North American Benthological Society [ISSN:0887-3593], 405
Journal of the Optical Society of America A: Optics, Image Science, and Vision [ISSN:0740-3232], 354
Journal of the Optical Society of America B: Optical Physics [ISSN:0740-3224], 354
Journal of the Royal Anthropological Institute [ISSN:1359-0987], 144
Journal of the Royal Musical Association [ISSN:0269-0403], 85
Journal of the Royal Statistical Society [ISSN:0964-1998], 349
Journal of the Society for Army Historical Research [ISSN:0037-9700], 302
Journal of the Society of Architectural Historians [ISSN:0037-9808], 132
Journal of Thoracic and Cardiovascular Surgery [ISSN:0022-5223], 424
Journal of Transportation Engineering [ISSN:0733-947X], 376-377, 385t
Journal of Trauma—Injury, Infection, and Critical Care [ISSN:1079-6061], 417
Journal of Tribology [ISSN:0742-4787], 386t
Journal of Turbomachinery [ISSN:0889-504X], 386t

Journal of Urban Planning and Development [ISSN:0733-9488], 385t
Journal of Urology [ISSN:0022-5347], 424
Journal of Vegetation Science [ISSN:1100-9233], 404
Journal of Vertebrate Paleontology [ISSN:0272-4634], 407
Journal of Vibration and Acoustics [ISSN:1048-9002], 386t
Journal of Virology [ISSN:0022-538X], 393-394
Journal of Volcanology and Geothermal Research [ISSN:0377-0273], 365
Journal of the Warburg and Courtauld Institutes [ISSN:0075-4390], 119
Journal of Water Resources Planning and Management [ISSN:0733-9496], 385t
Journal of Waterway, Port, Coastal, and Ocean Engineering [ISSN:0733-950X],
    385t
Journal of Wildlife Management [ISSN:0022-541X], 406
Journal of Youth Services in Libraries [ISSN:0894-2498], 71
Journal of Zoological Systematics and Evolutionary Research [ISSN:0947-5745],
    407
JPT: Journal of Petroleum Technology [ISSN:0149-2136], 382

Kidney International [ISSN:0085-2538], 424
Kirkus Reviews [ISSN:0042-6598], 65
Konsthistorisk Tidskrift [ISSN:0023-3609], 118
Kunstchronik [ISSN:0023-5474], 122

Laboratory Animal Science [ISSN:0023-6764], 457
Laboratory Animals [ISSN:0023-6772], 457
Labour History Review [ISSN:0961-5652], 261
The Lancet [ISSN:0140-6736], 415, 430
Langmuir [ISSN:0743-7463], 360
Language [ISSN:0097-8507], 145
Language Arts [ISSN:0360-9170], 23
Language in Society [ISSN:0047-4045], 145
Language Learning [ISSN:0023-8333], 22
Laryngoscope [ISSN:0023-852X], 423
Latin American Antiquity [ISSN:1045-6635], 128, 149
Latin American Music Review [ISSN:0163-0350], 97
Law and Contemporary Problems [ISSN:0023-9186], 233
Law and History Review [ISSN:0738-2480], 236
Law and Human Behavior [ISSN:0147-7307], 233
Law and Social Inquiry [ISSN:0897-6546], 236
Law and Society Review [ISSN:0023-9216], 237, 276t
Law Library Journal [ISSN:0023-9285], 72
LC-GC: Magazine of Separation Science [ISSN:0888-9090], 361
Leatherneck [ISSN:0023-981X], 314
Leonardo [ISSN:0024-094X], 130
Lethaia [ISSN:0024-1164], 365-366
L'Homme [ISSN:0439-4216], 144
Libraries and Culture [ISSN:0894-8631], 65

Library Acquisitions: Practice and Theory [ISSN:0364-6408], 67
Library Administration and Management [ISSN:0888-4463], 67
Library and Information Science Research [ISSN:0740-8188], 67
Library Hi-Tech [ISSN:0737-8831], 66
Library Journal [ISSN:0000-0027], 58, 59, 63, 64, 71
Library Literature [ISSN:0024-2373], 68
Library Quarterly [ISSN:0024-2519], 67
Library Resources and Technical Services [ISSN:0024-2527], 69
Library Trends [ISSN:0024-2594], 67
Libri [ISSN:0024-2667], 64
Limnology and Oceanography [ISSN:0024-3590], 363
Linguistics and Philosophy [ISSN:0165-0157], 166-167
LISA: Library and Information Science Abstracts [ISSN:0024-2179], 68
Livestock Production Science [ISSN:0301-6226], 454
L'Oeil [ISSN:0029-862X], 121
Long Range Planning [ISSN:0024-6301], 215

Macromolecular Chemistry and Physics [ISSN:1022-1352], 358
Macromolecules [ISSN:0024-9297], 357-358, 380
Magazine Antiques [ISSN: 0161-9284], 136-137
Mammal Review [ISSN:0305-1836], 400-401
Manufacturing Engineering [ISSN:0361-0853], 379
Marg [ISSN:0972-1444], 127
Marine Biology [ISSN:0025-3162], 405
Marine Corps Gazette ISSN:0025-3170], 314-315
Marine Ecology—Progress Series [ISSN:0173-9565], 405
Marine Engineers Review [ISSN:0047-5955], 381
Marine Technology and SNAME News [ISSN:0025-3324], 381
Mariner's Mirror [ISSN:0025-3359], 305-306
Marines [ISSN:1056-9073], 315
Master Drawings [ISSN:0025-5025], 131
Materials Evaluation [ISSN:0025-5327], 380
Mathematische Zeitschrift [ISSN:0025-5874], 346
Mechanical Engineering [ISSN:0025-6501], 386t
Mechanisms of Ageing and Development [ISSN:0047-6374], 421
Medical Letter on Drugs and Therapeutics [ISSN:0025-732X], 431
Medical Physics [ISSN:0094-2405], 355
Melody Maker [ISSN:0025-9012], 102
Metallurgical and Materials Transactions A: Physical Metallurgy and Materials
    Science [ISSN:1073-5623], 380
Metallurgical and Materials Transactions B: Process Metallurgy and Materials
    Processing [ISSN:1073-5615], 380
Meteoritics and Planetary Science [ISSN:1086-9379], 349
Metropolitan Museum Journal [ISSN:0077-8958], 117
Metropolitan Museum of Art Bulletin [ISSN:0026-1521], 117
Methodist History [ISSN:0026-1238], 176
MHQ: The Quarterly Journal of Military History [ISSN:1040-5992], 294-295

Michigan Law Review [ISSN:0026-2234], 225
Microbiology [ISSN:0026-2617], 393
Military Law Review [ISSN:0026-4040], 295
Military Review [ISSN:0026-4148], 302-303
Military Technology [ISSN:0722-3226], 295
Mind [ISSN:0026-4423], 157
Mineralium Deposita [ISSN:0026-4598], 366
Minerva [ISSN:0736-718X], 295-296
MIS Quarterly: Management Information Systems [ISSN:0276-7783], 201
Mitteilungen des Kunshistorisches Institutes in Florenz [ISSN:0342-1201], 124
Molecular and Biochemical Parasitology [ISSN:0166-6851], 403
Molecular and Cellular Biology [ISSN:0270-7306], 395
Molecular and Cellular Endocrinology [ISSN:0303-7207], 399
Molecular and General Genetics [ISSN:0026-8926], 395
Molecular Biology and Evolution [ISSN:0737-4038], 407
Molecular Biology of the Cell [ISSN:1059-1524], 395
Molecular Endocrinology [ISSN:0888-8809], 399
Molecular Immunology [ISSN:01610-5980], 394
Molecular Physics [ISSN:0026-8976], 361
Molecular Plant-Microbe Interactions [ISSN:0027-4224], 454
Monthly Labor Review [ISSN:0098-1818], 212
Monthly Notices of the Royal Astronomical Society [ISSN:0035-9017], 349
Mouvement Social [ISSN:0027-2671], 266
MRS Bulletin: Materials Research Society [ISSN:0883-7694], 380
Muqarnas [ISSN:0732-2992], 123
Music and Letters [ISSN:0027-4224], 85-86
Music Educators Journal [ISSN:0027-4321], 99
Musical Quarterly [ISSN:0027-4631], 86
Musik und Kirche [ISSN:0027-4771], 110-111
Musikforschung [ISSN:0027-4801], 87-88
Mutagenesis [ISSN:0267-8357], 396
Mutation Research [ISSN:0165-1298], 396
Mycologia [ISSN:0027-5514], 404

NATO's Nations and Partners for Peace www.monch.com, 296
National Defense [ISSN:0092-1491], 296
National Geographic [ISSN:0027-9358], 142, 145
National Tax Journal [ISSN:0028-0283], 198-199, 234
Nature [ISSN:0028-0836], 39, 141, 343, 391, 419
Nature Biotechnology [ISSN:1087-0156], 393
Nature Medicine [ISSN:1078-8956], 419
Naval Architect [ISSN:0306-0209], 381
Naval Aviation News [ISSN:0028-1417], 306
Naval Engineers Journal [ISSN:0028-1925], 306-307
Naval Forces [ISSN:0722-8880], 307
Naval History [ISSN:1042-1920], 307-308
Naval Law Review [ISSN:1049-0272], 308

Naval Research Logistics [ISSN:0894-069X], 308-309
Naval Review [ISSN:0077-6238], 309-310
Naval War College Review [ISSN:0028-1484], 310
Near Eastern Archaeology [ISSN:1094-2076], 147
Nederlands Kunsthistorisch Jaarboek/Netherlands Yearbook for History of Art
    [ISSN:0169-6726], 128
Neurobiology of Aging [0197-4580], 421
Neuroendocrinology [ISSN:0028-3835], 398
Neurology [ISSN:0025-3878], 420
Neurology Report [ISSN:1085-049X], 436-437
Neuron [ISSN:0896-6273], 398
New Art Examiner [ISSN:0886-8115], 120
New Criterion [ISSN:0734-0222], 120
New England Journal of Medicine [ISSN:0028-4793], 415, 430, 434
New York Review of Books [ISSN:0028-7504], 65
New York Times Book Review [ISSN:0028-7806], 65
New York University Review of Law and Social Change [ISSN:0048-7481], 230
NKA: Journal of Contemporary African Art [ISSN:1075-7163], 125-126
Nineteenth Century Music [ISSN:0148-2076], 88, 89-90
North American Journal of Aquaculture [ISSN:1522-2055], 457
Notes [ISSN:0027-4380], 73, 105-106
Notre Dame Journal of Formal Logic [ISSN:0029-4527], 168
Nuclear Fusion [ISSN:0029-5515], 351
Nuclear Physics A: Nuclear and Hadronic Physics [ISSN:0375-9474], 352
Nuclear Physics B: Physical Mathematics, Field Theory, Statistical, and Particle
    Physics [ISSN:0550-3213], 352
Nuclear Science and Engineering [ISSN:0029-5639], 379
Nucleic Acids Research [ISSN:0305-1048], 392
Numerische Mathematik [ISSN:0029-599X], 348
Nutrient Cycling in Agroecosystems [ISSN:1385-1314], 448
Nutrition Reviews [ISSN:6029-6643], 439
Nutrition Today [ISSN:0029-666X], 440

Obstetrics and Gynecology [ISSN:0029-7844], 422
Oceania [ISSN:0029-8077], 142
October [ISSN:0162-2870], 120
Online [ISSN:0146-5422], 68
Online and CD-ROM Review [ISSN:1353-2642], 68
Opera Quarterly [ISSN:0736-0058], 107-108
Ophthalmology [ISSN:0161-6420], 422
Optics Communications [ISSN:0030-4018], 354
Optics Letters [ISSN:0146-9592], 354
Oral Surgery, Oral Medicine, Oral Pathology, Oral Radiology, and Endodontics
    [ISSN:1079-2104], 418
Ore Geology Reviews [ISSN:0169-1368], 366
Organic Gardening [ISSN:0163-3449], 451
Organic Geochemistry [ISSN:0146-6380], 367

Organizational Behavior and Human Decision Processes [ISSN:0749-5978], 34
Organometallics [ISSN:0276-7333], 358
Oriental Art [ISSN:0030-5278], 127
Osteuropa [ISSN:0030-6428], 257-258
Oud Holland [ISSN:0030-672X], 128
Oxford Art Journal ISSN:0142-672X], 119
Oxford Studies in Ancient Philosophy [ISSN:0265-7651], 155

Pacific Philosophical Quarterly [ISSN:0276-0750], 158-159
Paedagogica Historica [ISSN:0030-9230], 24
Pain [0304-3954], 417
Palaios [ISSN:0883-1351], 407
Paleobiology [ISSN:0094-8373], 407
Palaeogeography, Palaeoclimatology, Palaeoecology [ISSN:0031-0182], 363
Palaeontology [ISSN:0031-0239], 365-366
Paragone [ISSN:0031-1650], 122
Parameters [ISSN:0031-1723], 303
Parasitology [ISSN:0964-7570], 403
Parliamentary Affairs [0031-2290], 263, 277t
Parliamentary History [ISSN:0264-2824], 262-263
Past and Present [ISSN:0031-2746], 247-248, 276t
Peabody Journal of Education [ISSN:0161-956X], 20
Pedobiologia [ISSN:0031-4056], 403
Perception and Psychophysics [ISSN:0031-5117], 37
Personality and Social Psychology Bulletin [ISSN:0146-1672], 38-39
Personnel Psychology [ISSN:0031-5826], 34
Perspectives of New Music [ISSN:0031-6016], 93-94
Pesticide Biochemistry and Physiology [ISSN:0048-3575], 448
Pesticide Science [ISSN:0031-613X], 447-448
Pflugers Archiv: European Journal of Physiology [ISSN:0031-6768], 397
Pharmaceutical Journal [ISSN:0031-6873], 429
Pharmaceutisch Weekblad [ISSN:0031-6911], 431
Pharmacological Reviews [ISSN:0031-6997], 433
Pharmacotherapy [ISSN:0277-0008], 430
Pharmacy in History [ISSN:0031-7047], 433-434
Phi Delta Kappan [ISSN:0031-7217], 20
Properties [ISSN:0958-6644], 353
Philosophical Review [ISSN:00312-8108], 162
Philosophical Studies [ISSN:0031-8116], 154
Philosophical Transactions of the Royal Society of London [ISSN:0962-8428],
    271, 374, 413
Philosophy [ISSN:0031-8191], 162
Philosophy and Phenomenological Research [ISSN:0031-8205], 159-160
Philosophy of Science [ISSN:0031-8248], 168-169
Phosphorous, Sulfur, Silicon, and Related Elements [ISSN:0308-664X], 359
Photochemistry and Photobiology [ISSN:0031-8655], 360
Phronesis [ISSN:0031-8868], 154-155

Physica C: Superconductivity [ISSN:0921-4534], 354
Physical Chemistry—Chemical Physics [ISSN:1463-9076], 360
Physical Review A: Atomic, Molecular and Optical Physics [ISSN:1094-1622], 352
Physical Review B: Condensed Matter and Materials Physics [ISSN:0163-1829], 354
Physical Review C: Nuclear Physics [ISSN:0556-2813], 352
Physical Review D: Particles and Fields [ISSN:0556-2821], 352
Physical Review E: Statistical Physics, Plasma, Fluids, and Related Interdisciplinary Topics [ISSN:1063-651X], 351
Physical Review Letters [ISSN:0031-9007], 350
Physical Therapy [ISSN:0031-9023], 436
Physics in Medicine and Biology [ISSN:0031-9155], 355
Physics Letters B: Nuclear and Particle Physics [ISSN:0370-2693], 352
Physics of Fluids [ISSN:0031-9171], 351
Physics of Plasmas [ISSN:1070-664X], 351
Physiological and Biochemical Zoology [ISSN:1522-2152], 399-400
Physiological Entomology [ISSN:0307-6962], 402
Physiology and Behavior [ISSN:0031-9384], 400
Physiotherapy [ISSN:0031-9406], 437
Physiotherapy Canada/Physiotherapie Canada [ISSN:0300-0508], 437
Physiotherapy Frontline [ISSN:1356-9791], 437
Piano and Keyboard [ISSN:1067-3881], 109
Plant Cell [ISSN:1040-4651], 404
Plant Cell, Tissue, and Organ Culture [ISSN:0167-6857], 404
Plant Ecology [ISSN:1385-0237], 404
Plant Journal for Cell and Molecular Biology [ISSN:0960-7412], 404
Plant Pathology [ISSN:0032-0862], 453-454
Plant Physiology [ISSN:0032-0889], 403, 454
Planta [ISSN:1432-2048], 403
Planta Medica [ISSN:0032-0943], 357, 432
Plasma Physics and Controlled Fusion [ISSN:0741-3335], 351
Polar Biology [ISSN:1432-2056], 406
Policy and Practice of Public Human Services [ISSN:0033-3816], 13
Political Science Quarterly [ISSN:0032-3195], 271, 274t, 276t, 280-281
Political Theory [ISSN:0090-5917], 274t, 276t, 283
Polyhedron [ISSN:0277-5387], 358
Population and Development Review [ISSN:0098-7921], 52
Population Studies [ISSN:0032-4728], 52
Postharvest Biology and Technology [ISSN:0925-5214], 444
Poultry Science [ISSN:00325791], 454
Practice Periodical on Hazardous, Toxic, and Radioactive Waste Management [ISSN:1090-025X], 385t
Practice Periodical on Structural Design and Construction [ISSN:1084-0680], 385t
Prepared Foods [ISSN:0747-2536], 452
Presidential Studies Quarterly [ISSN:0360-4918], 281
Print Quarterly [ISSN:0265-8305], 131
Proceedings of the American Mathematical Society [ISSN:0002-9939], 347

Proceedings of the Institution of the Civil Engineers: Civil Engineering [ISSN:1353-2618], 375, 386t

Proceedings of the Institution of Civil Engineers: Geotechnical Engineering [ISSN:1353-2618], 375, 386t

Proceedings of the Institution of Civil Engineers: Municipal Engineering [ISSN:0965-0903], 375, 386t

Proceedings of the Institution of Civil Engineers: Structures and Buildings [ISSN:0965-0911], 375, 386t

Proceedings of the Institution of Civil Engineers: Transport [ISSN:0965-092X], 375, 376-377, 386t

Proceedings of the Institution of Civil Engineers: Water, Maritime, and Energy [ISSN:0965-0946], 375, 386t

Proceedings of the Institution of Mechanical Engineers Part A: Journal of Power and Energy [ISSN:0957-6507], 378, 386t

Proceedings of the Institution of Mechanical Engineers Part B: Journal of Manufacture Engineering [ISSN:0954-4054], 378, 386t

Proceedings of the Institution of Mechanical Engineers Part C: Journal of Mechanical Engineering Science [ISSN:0954-4062], 378, 386t

Proceedings of the Institution of Mechanical Engineers Part D: Journal of Automobile Engineering [ISSN:0954-4070], 377-378, 386t

Proceedings of the Institution of Mechanical Engineers Part E: Journal of Process Mechanical Engineering [ISSN:0954-4089], 378, 387t

Proceedings of the Institution of Mechanical Engineers Part F: Journal of Rail and Rapid Transport [ISSN:0954-4097], 377-378, 387t

Proceedings of the Institution of Mechanical Engineers Part G: Journal of Aerospace Engineering [ISSN:0954-4100], 378, 387t

Proceedings of the Institution of Mechanical Engineers Part H: Journal of Engineering in Medicine [ISSN:0954-4119], 378, 387t

Proceedings of the Institution of Mechanical Engineers Part I: Journal of Systems and Control Engineering [ISSN:0959-6518], 378

Proceedings of the Institution of Mechanical Engineers Part J: Journal of Engineering Tribology [ISSN:1350-6501], 378, 387t

Proceedings of the National Academy of Sciences of the USA [ISSN:0027-8424], 344, 391

Proceedings of the Royal Society of London B—Biological Sciences [ISSN:0080-4649], 391

Proceedings of the Western Society for French History [ISSN:0099-0329], 255

Progress in Aerospace Sciences [ISSN:0376-0421], 375

Progress in Quantum Electronics [ISSN:0079-6727], 383

Progressive Farmer [ISSN:00330760], 444

Psychobiology [ISSN:0889-6313], 34, 400

Psychological Bulletin [ISSN:0033-2909], 32-33

Psychological Methods [ISSN:1082-989X], 33

Psychological Record [ISSN:0033-2933], 156-157

Psychological Review [ISSN:0033-295X], 32, 33

Psychological Science [ISSN:0956-7976], 33

Psychometrika [ISSN:0033-3123], 37-38

Psychopharmacology [ISSN:0033-3158], 398

Psychophysiology [ISSN:0048-5772], 35
Public Art Review [ISSN:1040-2111], 132
Public Libraries [ISSN:0163-5506], 71
Public Library Quarterly [ISSN:0161-6846], 71
Public Opinion Quarterly [ISSN:0033-362X], 274t, 276t, 282

Qualititative Sociology [ISSN:0162-0436], 50-51
Quarterly Journal of Economics [ISSN:0033-5533], 203
Quarterly Journal of Mathematics [ISSN:0033-5606], 346
Quarterly Journal of the Royal Meteorological Society [ISSN:0035-9009], 362-363
Quaternary Research [ISSN:0033-5894], 363

RACAR: Revue d'Art Canadienne/Canadian Art Review [ISSN:0315-9906], 119
Race and Class [ISSN:0306-3968], 51-52
Radiology [ISSN:0033-8419], 418
Railway Age [ISSN:0033-8826], 377
Rare Books and Manuscripts Librarianship [ISSN:0884-450X], 69-70
Reactions Weekly [ISSN:0114-9954], 431
Reading Teacher [ISSN:0034-0561], 23
Records Management Quarterly [ISSN:1050-2343], 70
Reference and User Services Quarterly [ISSN:1094-9054], 68-69
Reference Librarian [ISSN:0276-3877], 69
Reference Services Review [ISSN:0090-7324], 69
Renaissance Quarterly [ISSN:0034-4338], 124, 251
Renaissance Studies [ISSN:0269-1213], 252
Research in Phenomenology [ISSN:0085-5553], 160
Research Strategies [ISSN:0734-3310], 66-67
Review of Educational Research [ISSN:0034-6543], 24-25
Review of General Psychology [ISSN:1089-2680], 33
Review of Higher Education [ISSN:0162-5748], 21
Revue d'Histoire Moderne et Contemporaine [ISSN:0048-8033], 249-250
Revue de l'Art [ISSN:0035-1326], 121
Revue du Louvre [ISSN:0035-2608], 117
Revue Historique [ISSN:0035-3264], 245
Revue Philosophique [ISSN:0035-3833], 170
Rivista Storica Italiana [ISSN:0035-7073], 251
Rock Mechanics and Rock Engineering [ISSN:0723-2632], 376
Rolling Stone [ISSN:0035-791X], 103
Rural Sociology [ISSN:0036-0112], 52

SAE Transactions—Journal of Aerospace [ISSN:0096-736X], 377, 387t
School Library Journal [ISSN:0362-8930], 71
School Library Media Research www.ala.org/aasl/slmr, 71
Science [ISSN:0193-4511], 33, 39, 141, 343, 391, 432

Science and Technology Libraries [ISSN:0194-262X], 72
Science Education [ISSN:0036-8326], 24
Scientia Horticulturae [ISSN:0304-4238], 453
Sculpture [ISSN:0889-728X], 131-132
Sculpture Review [ISSN:0747-5284], 132
Sea Power [ISSN:0199-1337], 311
Sedimentology [ISSN:0037-0746], 365
Semiotica [ISSN:0037-1998], 166
Serials Librarian [ISSN:0361-526X], 1, 7, 69
Serials Review [ISSN:0098-7913], 69
SIAM Journal on Applied Mathematics [ISSN:0036-1399], 345
SIAM Journal on Control and Optimization [ISSN:0363-0129], 348
SIAM Journal on Mathematical Analysis [ISSN:0363-0129], 347
SIAM Journal on Numerical Analysis [ISSN:0036-1429], 348
Signal [ISSN:0037-4938], 297
Signal Processing [ISSN:0165-1684], 384
Signs [ISSN:0097-9740], 161-162
Simiolus [ISSN:0037-5411], 119
Sixteenth Century Journal [ISSN:0361-0160], 252
Slavic Review [ISSN:0037-6779], 258, 276t, 279
Slavonic and East European Review [ISSN:0037-6795], 258
Sloan Management Review [ISSN:0019-848X], 211-212
Smith College Studies in Social Work [ISSN:0037-7317], 5, 13
Smithsonian Studies in American Art [ISSN:0890-4901], 126
Social Forces [ISSN:0037-7732], 48
Social History [ISSN:0307-1022], 265
Social Problems [ISSN:0037-7791], 54
Social Psychology Quarterly [ISSN:0190-2725], 53
Social Service Review [ISSN:0037-7961], 10, 11
Social Work [ISSN:0037-8046], 10, 11, 14
Social Work Research [ISSN:1070-5309], 10, 11, 12
Social Worker/le Travailleur Social [ISSN:0037-8089], 14
Society of Naval Architects and Marine Engineers Transactions [ISSN:0081-
    1661], 381
Sociological Methods and Research [ISSN:0049-1241], 50
Sociology of Education [ISSN:0038-0407], 20-21, 53
Sociology of Health and Illness [ISSN:0141-9889], 53
Soil Biology and Biochemistry Research [ISSN:0038-0717], 449
Soil Science [0038-075X], 449
Soil Science Society of America Journal -SSSA Journal [ISSN:0361-5995], 449
Solar Physics [ISSN:0038-0938], 349
Soldiers [ISSN:0093-8440], 303-304
Solid State Communications [ISSN:0038-1098], 354
Source [ISSN:0737-4453], 118
Soviet Sociology [ISSN:0038-5824], 49
SPE Drilling and Completion [ISSN:1064-6671], 382
SPE Production and Facilities [ISSN:1064-668X], 382
SPE Reservoir Evaluation and Engineering [ISSN:1094-6470], 382

Spine [ISSN:0362-2436], 417
Stanford Law Review [ISSN:0038-9765], 225
Storia dell'Arte [ISSN:0392-4513], 122
Strad [ISSN:0039-2049], 108
Strategic Finance [ISSN:1524-833X], 197
Strategic Management Journal [ISSN:0143-2095], 215
Stroke [ISSN:0034-2499], 420
Studi Storici [ISSN:0039-3037], 251
Studia Logica [ISSN:0039-3215], 168
Studies in Iconography [ISSN:0148-1029], 119
Studies in Medieval and Renaissance History [ISSN:0081-8224], 252
Submarine Review [OCLC:12184742], 311-312
Successful Farming [ISSN:0039-4432], 444
Superconductor Science and Technology [ISSN:0953-2048], 354
Supreme Court Review [ISSN:0081-9557], 227
Surface Warfare Magazine [ISSN:0145-1073], 312
Survey of Current Business [ISSN:0039-6222], 202
Survival [ISSN:0039-6338], 297
Synlett [ISSN:0936-5214], 357
Synthese [ISSN:0039-7857], 157-158
Synthesis [ISSN:0039-7881], 357
Systematic Biology [ISSN:1063-5157], 407
Systematic Botany [ISSN:0363-6445], 407
Systematic Entomology [ISSN:0307-6970], 407

I Tatti Studies: Essays in the Renaissance [ISSN:0393-5949], 124
Tax Law Review [ISSN:0040-0041], 234
Taxes [ISSN:0040-0181], 199
Teacher Librarian [ISSN:1481-1782], 71
Teachers College Record [ISSN:0040-9475], 5, 20
Teaching History [ISSN:0230-1383], 266-267
Technical Services Quarterly [ISSN:0731-7131], 69
Tectonics [ISSN:0278-7407], 364
Tectonophysics [ISSN:0040-1951], 364
Tellus—Series A: Dynamic Meteorology and Oceanography [ISSN:0280-6445],
    363
Teratology [ISSN:0090-3709], 396
TESOL Quarterly [ISSN:0039-8322], 22
Tetrahedron Letters [ISSN:0040-4039], 356, 432
Textile Research Journal [ISSN:0040-5175], 380
Theological Studies [ISSN:0040-5639], 175
Theology Today [ISSN:0040-5736], 175
Theoretical and Applied Genetics [ISSN:0040-5752], 455
Theoretical Chemistry Accounts [ISSN:1432-881X], 361
Theriogenology [ISSN:0093-691X], 455
Thin Solid Films [ISSN:0040-6090], 361
Thrombosis and Haemostasis [0340-6245], 421

TLS: Times Literary Supplement [ISSN:0307-661X], 65
Topoi [ISSN:0167-7411], 163-164
Topology [ISSN:0040-9383], 347
Toxicologic Pathology [ISSN:0192-6233], 457
Toxicology and Applied Pharmacology [ISSN:0041-008X], 396
Transactions of the American Fisheries Society [ISSN:0002-8487], 378, 401
Transactions of the American Society of Agricultural Engineers [ISSN:0001-2351], 378, 447
Transactions of the Institution of Engineers and Shipbuilders in Scotland [ISSN:0020-3289], 378, 381
Transactions of the Royal Institution of Naval Architects [ISSN:0035-8967], 378, 381
Transactions of the Royal Society of Tropical Medicine and Hygiene [ISSN:0035-9303], 378, 425
Transition Metal Chemistry [ISSN:0340-4285], 359
Transplantation [ISSN:0041-1337], 418
Transplantation Proceedings [ISSN:0041-1345], 418
Transportation Research—Part A: Policy and Practice [ISSN:0965-8564], 377, 387t
Transportation Research—Part B: Methodological [ISSN:0191-2615], 377, 387t
Transportation Research—Part C: Emerging Technologies [ISSN:0968-090X], 377, 387t
Transportation Research—Part D: Transportation and Environment [ISSN:1351-9209], 377, 387t
Transportation Research—Part E: Logistics and Transportation [ISSN:1366-5545], 377, 387t
Transportation Research—Part F: Traffic Psychology and Behavior [ISSN:1366-5545], 377
Tree Physiology [ISSN:0829-318X], 404
Trees [ISSN:0931-1890], 404
Trends in Food Science and Technology [ISSN:0924-2244], 452

Ultrasonic Imaging [ISSN:0161-7346], 355
Umbrella [ISSN:0160-0699], 130
Unasylva [ISSN:0041-6436], 451
University of Chicago Law Review [ISSN:0041-9494], 225
University of Pennsylvania Law Review [ISSN:0041-9907], 225
U.S. Banker [ISSN:0148-8848], 208
U.S. Naval Institute Proceedings [ISSN:0041-798X], 312-313
U.S. Pharmacist [ISSN:0148-4818], 435
USAF Weapons Review [ISSN:0274-6824], 319-320

VDI-Z: Zeitschrift des Vereins Deutscher Ingenieure fuer Maschinenbau und Metallbearbeitung [ISSN:0042-1766], 374
Veterinary Journal [ISSN:1090-0233], 456
Veterinary Pathology [ISSN:0300-9858], 456-457
Veterinary Record [ISSN:0042-4900], 456

Victorian Studies [ISSN:0042-5222], 254
Vie des Arts [ISSN:0042-5435], 127-128
Vierteljahrsschrift für Sozial und Wirstschaftsgeschichte [ISSN:0042-5699], 266
Vierteljahrshefte für Zeitgeschichte [ISSN:0042-5702], 256
Vingtieme Siecle [ISSN:0294-1759], 254
Virginia Journal of International Law [ISSN:0042-6571], 232, 275t
Virginia Tax Review [ISSN:0735-9004], 234
Virology [ISSN:0042-6822], 394
VOYA: Voice of Youth Advocates [ISSN:0160-4201], 71

War and Society [ISSN:0729-2473], 298
War in History [ISSN:0968-3445], 298
Water Environment Research [ISSN:1061-4303], 376
Water Research [ISSN:0043-1354], 364, 377
Water Resources Research [ISSN:0043-1397], 364, 377
Weed Science [ISSN:0043-1745], 449
William and Mary Bill of Rights Journal [ISSN:1065-8254], 227-228
Wilson Library Bulletin [ISSN:0043-5651], 64
Winterthur Portfolio [ISSN:0084-0416], 137
Woman's Art Journal [ISSN:0270-7993], 129-130
Women's Rights Law Reporter [ISSN:9985-8269], 235
Workforce [ISSN:1092-8332], 214
World Air Power Journal [ISSN:0959-7050], 320
World of Music [ISSN:0043-8774], 95-96

Yale Journal of International Law [ISSN:0889-7743], 232
Yale Law and Policy Review [ISSN:0740-8048], 234
Yale Law Journal [ISSN:0044-0094], 224
Yearbook for Traditional Music [ISSN:0740-1558], 96-97
Yearbook of Physical Anthropology [ISSN:0096-848X], 143

Zeitschrift fuer Angewandte Mathematik und Mechanik [ISSN:0044-2267], 350
Zeitschrift fuer Anorganische und Allgemeine Chemie [ISSN:0044-2313], 358
Zeitschrift fuer Kunstgeschichte [ISSN:0044-2992], 121-122
Zeitschrift fuer Philosophische Forschung [ISSN:0044-3301], 170
Zeitschrift fuer Saugertierkunde [ISSN:0044-3468], 401
Zodiac [ISSN:0394-9230], 135

Subject Index

Aby, Stephen H., 46
Academy of Management, 210
accounting, 195-199
Africa, 77, 125-126, 142, 146, 149. *See also* Egypt
African Americans
  anthropology and, 143
  education and, 22
  religion and, 173, 177, 184-185
  sociology and, 51
  in visual arts, 130
agriculture, 443-458
  agronomy, 447, 448-450
  animal science, 454-457
  aquaculture, 457
  biotechnology, 393, 444, 447
  business and economics, 445-446, 448
  chemistry, 447-448
  ecology, 448, 449-451
  education, 448
  entomology, 444-445
  food, 446, 447, 451-452
  forestry, 445, 451
  history of, 258-259
  horticulture, 453
  physics, 448, 454
  plant science, 452-454
  selection criteria for, 443
  veterinary science, 456-457
American Academy of Advertising, 217
American Academy of Political and Social Science, 271
American Anthropological Association, 95
American Arbitration Association, 213
American Bankers Association, 207

American Bar Association, 222
American College of Nutrition, 440
American Economic Association (AEA), 202-203
American Historical Association, 243, 245, 246
American Institute of Aeronautics and Astronautics (AIAA), 375
American Library Association, 63, 64
American Marketing Association, 218
American Medical Association, 415
American Musicological Society, 84, 93
American Philosophical Association, 154
American Physical Therapy Association, 436
American Political Science Association, 271
American Psychological Association, 233
American Schools of Oriental Research, 147, 148
American Society for Legal History, 236
American Society of Civil Engineers (ASCE), 375, 385
American Society of Comparative Law, 232
American Society of Hospital Pharmacists, 429
American Society of International Law, 231
American Society of Mechanical Engineers (ASME), 378, 385-386
American Society of Naval Engineers (ASNE), 306-307

anatomy, 399
Andrews, Theodora, 435
anesthesiology, 416
animal science, 454-456
anthropology, 94-97, 141-146
aquaculture, 457
Arabic language articles, 169
archaeology, 123, 128, 141, 145-149
architecture, 124, 126, 127, 132-135
Aristotle, 155, 271, 283
art. *See* visual arts
Asia. *See also* Japan
    arts in, 77, 97, 126-127
    China, 49-50, 126-127, 142, 204-205
    India, 14, 31, 126-127, 334, 339
    publishing industry in, 2, 77, 389-390
    Singapore, 338
Association for Computing Machinery,
    383-384
Association for Investment Management
    and Research (AIMR), 208
Association of the U.S. Army, 300
astronomy, 349
auditing, 196-197
Australia
    science, 338, 445
    social sciences, 14, 31, 142, 149,
        261, 298
Austria, 351, 376

bacteriology, 393
Bahaism, 181
Baker, Donald R., 11
Bank Administration Institute, 207
banking, 206-208
Banks, Joseph A., 49
Bartlett, Clifford, 104
Baskind, Frank R., 10
Belgium, 24
Bentley College, 200
Bible, 147-148, 182-183
Billings, John Shaw, 414
biology, 344, 391-407. *See also*
    ecology
    anatomy, 399
    anthropology and, 143

biology *(continued)*
    biochemistry, 392-395, 398,
        447-449, 454
    biotechnology, 393, 444, 447
    botany, 403-407, 452-454
    endocrinology, 398-399, 455-456
    ethology, 400, 456
    genetics, 143, 395-396, 444, 449,
        454-455
    molecular, 392, 399, 403-404,
        407-408, 419, 454
    neuroscience, 32, 35, 397-398, 416,
        420
    physics, 355
    physiology, 34-35, 394-395, 397,
        399-402
    zoology, 399-403, 406-407, 457
Blackwell Publishers, 78, 190, 200,
    241, 322, 389
Blake, Virgil L. P., 61-62, 63
Bloch, Marc, 247, 249
Boas, Franz, 145
Bobinski, George S., 61
botany, 403-407, 452-454
Braude, Lee, 45
Braudel, Fernand, 249
Brazil, 316
Breasted, James Henry, 148
Brill, 78
Britain. *See* Great Britain
British Association for the
    Advancement of Science, 327
British Parliament, 262-263
British Psychological Society, 31
Broderick, Dorothy, 60
Brown, James Duff, 58-59
Buchanan, Anne L., 278, 280-282, 285
Budd, John, 61
Buddhism, 180, 181
Bureau of Economic Analysis, 202
Bureau of Labor Statistics, 212-213
Burgin, Robert, 60
Bury, John Bagnell, 248
Bush, Irene R., 12
business, 189-220. *See also* publishing
    industry
    accounting, 195-199
    agriculture, 446, 448

business *(continued)*
    banking, 206-208
    economics, 51-52, 193-195, 201-205,
        235-236, 259-260, 446
    entrepreneurship, 205-206
    ethics, 199-200
    finance, 206-210
    history of, 189-190, 259-260
    human resources, 34, 213-214
    information technology, 200-201
    international, 206
    investment, 209-210
    labor, 212-213
    law, 226-227, 235-236
    in libraries, 72
    management, 197, 200-201, 210-215,
        385
    marketing, 216-218, 446
    pharmacy, 434-435
    selection criteria for, 193-195
    strategy, 214-215
    taxation, 198-199, 234
Butchvarov, Panayot, 164
Butterfield, Herbert, 248

Cambridge University, 245, 248, 322,
        389
Canada
    religion, 186
    sciences
        life, 399, 401, 404, 423, 437, 447
        physical, 376, 382
    social sciences, 14, 31, 49, 71-72,
        247, 285, 338
    visual arts, 119, 127-128
Caputo, Richard K., 10
Cartwright, Ethel, 436
Catholicism, 174-176, 178-180,
        182-187, 263. *See also*
        religion
Center for Business Ethics, 200
chemistry, 356-362
    agriculture, 447-448, 454
    biochemistry, 392-395, 407-408,
        447-449, 454
    engineering, 381-382

chemistry *(continued)*
    environmental, 376
    journal selection criteria, 325,
        341-343
    medicine, 431-432
children
    education, 23-24, 26
    librarianship and, 65, 71
    medicine, 422, 423
    psychology, 36
    social work, 12-13, 15
    sociology, 52
China, 49-50, 126-127, 142, 204-205
Christenson, James A., 277, 284
Christianity. *See* religion
Churchill, Winston, 341
Clapham, John Harold, 248
class, 51-52, 261. *See also* labor;
        Marxism
climatology, 363
Cnaan, Ram A., 10, 11, 12-13, 14, 15
Colbert, Jean Baptiste, 326
Colombia, 129
Columbia University, 223, 224-225,
        229, 271
Commerce Clearing House, 190
computer science, 373, 378, 383-384
Conklin, Barbara, 10
Copyright Society of the U.S.A., 231
Cornell University, 211, 212
Crania Americana (Morton), 143
Crawford, O. G. S., 146
Crespi, Scott Gregory, 229, 231, 232
Crewe, Ivor, 278, 280, 282-285
criminology, 51, 53, 228
Cuvier, Georges, 406

Darwin, Charles, 406
Davis, Charles H., 61, 62
Davis, John B., 193
De Pauw, Linda Grant, 295
Dead Sea Scrolls, 148
Deigh, John, 158
Delevie, Ari S., 34
demography, 51-52
Denmark, 363, 375-376, 393, 405

dentistry, 413, 418
Department of Defense (DoD), 291-292,
    293, 317
Department of Labor, 212
Discourse on the Origin of Inequality
    (Rousseau), 57
Doreian, Patrick, 29
Drucker, Peter, 210
*Drug Information: A Guide to Current
    Resources* (Snow), 435
Duke University, 233
Durisin, Patricia, 427

earth sciences, 362-367, 376, 379, 382,
    407
Eaton, Gale, 60
Ecole Nationale des Ponts et Chausses,
    375
ecology, 404-406
    agriculture, 449-451
    environmental engineering for, 376
    insects, 402
    law, 229
    wildlife, 406, 457
Econometric Society, 204
economics, 51-52, 193-195, 201-205,
    235-236, 259-260, 446. *See
    also* business
education, 19-27
    curriculum, 23-24
    general education, 20-21
    higher and adult, 21, 23
    history of, 6, 7, 24
    multicultural and comparative, 22
    of music, 91, 92, 97-100, 109
    philosophy of, 24
    psychology of, 25
    of religion, 175-176, 184-185
    research, 24-25, 26
    of science, 385, 434, 438, 448
    selection criteria for, 19-20
    of social sciences, 12, 20-21, 53,
        66-67, 71-72, 236, 266-267
    special, 25-26
    technology of, 22-23
Egypt, 146, 148, 248

Elsevier, 63, 389
engineering, 321-323, 373-387
    aerospace, 375, 385, 387
    agricultural, 447
    chemical, 381-382
    civil, 374-377, 379, 385-387
    computer science, 373, 378, 383-384
    electrical and electronic, 375,
        377-379, 380, 382-384
    environmental, 376, 450-451
    food, 451-452
    general, 374
    history of, 321-323
    management, 385
    marine, 381
    mechanical, 376, 377-381, 385-387
    medical, 377, 378, 381-382, 385
    online, 374, 375, 378
    pedagogy, 385
    petroleum, 382
    selection criteria for, 373
England. *See* Great Britain
English. *See* language: publication
        issues concerning
entomology, 401-402, 407, 444-445
environment. *See* ecology
ethics
    business and, 199-200
    environmental, 450
    law, 232
    military affairs and, 303
    philosophy and, 156-159, 161-163
    science, 457
ethnicity. *See also* African Americans;
        Judaism
    anthropology and, 141, 143-145, 149
    education and, 22, 25
    Latinos, 149, 184
    music and, 82-84, 86, 94-97
    Native Americans, 141, 143-145, 186
    religion and, 184, 186
    sociology and, 51-52
    visual arts and, 130
ethology, 400, 456
Europe. *See also* history; *specific
        countries*
    agriculture, 445, 447
    biology, 392, 394, 397, 399, 407

Europe *(continued)*
  economic history, 260
  engineering, 378
  health, 414, 421, 424, 429, 438-439
  publishing industry and, 2-3, 8, 79, 191, 241-242, 323, 390
  science journal history, 321-322, 329-330, 333-334, 336-339, 342-343, 389-390
  sciences, physical, 349-350, 352, 354, 356, 366
  visual arts, 117
European Strategic Planning Federation, 215
evolution, 143, 146, 406-408

Fairchild, Muir S., 316
Feather, John, 60
Febvre, Lucien, 247, 249
Federal Reserve Board, 201, 207-208
Feehan, Patricia E., 60
feminism. *See* women
finance, 206-210. *See also* business
Financial Accounting Standards Board (FASB), 195
Financial Management Association International, 208
food, 437-440, 446, 447, 451-452. *See also* nutrition
Food and Drug Act (1906), 428
forestry, 404, 445, 451
FORTRAN, 335
France. *See also* Europe
  architecture, 134
  French language in international publications
    arts, 92, 105, 127-128
    issues concerning, 30, 330, 335, 337, 414
    philosophy, 155, 163, 166, 167, 169
    science, 431, 445, 447, 451
    social sciences, 14, 24, 149, 251, 253-257, 266
  mathematics, 346
  science, 329-330, 334, 349-350, 375, 402

France *(continued)*
  social sciences, 144, 245, 249-250, 252-255, 266, 271
  visual arts, 117-118, 121, 124-125, 136
Franke, Donald E., 428-429
Franklin, Benjamin, 326
French Academy of Science, 326
Fyfe, Janet, 243

Garand, James C., 278, 281-282, 284-285
Garrison, Fielding H., 413-414, 415
genetics, 143, 395-396, 444, 449, 454-455
geology, 362-367, 376, 379, 382, 407
George, Tracey E., 226-228, 231-235
Georgetown University, 228
Germany. *See also* Europe
  agriculture, 445, 449, 455
  archaeology, 123
  architecture, 133
  astronomy, 349
  biology, 393-395, 397-401, 403-407
  chemistry, 356-358, 360-361
  earth sciences, 363, 365, 366
  engineering, 374, 381
  German language in international publications
    arts, 92, 105, 124, 128
    issues concerning, 30, 335, 414
    philosophy, 155, 163
    science, 431, 449
    social sciences, 24, 149, 244, 251, 254, 256-257
  history, 241, 244-245, 250, 256-258, 266-267
  library and information science, 64
  mathematics, 345-348
  medicine, 414, 416, 421, 432
  military affairs, 295, 296, 307
  music, 83-84, 87-88, 95-96, 110-111
  philosophy, 166-167, 170
  physics, 349-350, 352-355
  publishing industry and, 3, 8, 79, 191, 241-242, 323, 390

Germany *(continued)*
  science journal history, 321, 329-330,
    333-334, 338, 342-343
  visual arts, 115, 121-122, 123, 138
Giles, Michael W., 275, 277-278,
    281-282, 284-285
Goedeken, Edward A., 243
Goehlert, Robert, 279-280
Goodall, Jane, 142
Graduate, The, 357
Gragg, W. Lee, II, 60
graphs, 1-3
  Business and Law, 191
  Helping Professions, 8
  Life, Health and Agriculture, 390
  Music, Museums, and Methodists, 79
  Physical Sciences and Engineering,
    323
  War and Peace, 242
Great Britain. *See also* Europe
  agriculture, 444-450, 453-457
  anthropology, 144, 145
  archaeology, 146
  architecture, 132-133, 134
  astronomy, 349
  biology, 392-407, 457
  chemistry, 256-362, 382
  earth sciences, 362-367
  economics, 204, 209-210, 215
  engineering, 374-379, 380-383
  food, 452
  history, 245-249, 252, 254, 258-264,
    266-267
  library and information science, 58,
    64-68, 72
  mathematics, 345-349
  medicine, 413, 415-418, 421, 423-425
  military affairs, 292-294, 296-298,
    300-302, 305-306, 309-310,
    320
  music, 85-86, 88, 102, 104, 108
  nutrition, 439-440
  pharmacy, 429, 433, 435
  philosophy, 153, 155, 157-159, 162,
    165-166, 169
  physics, 350-355
  political science, 262-263, 271, 280,
    283

Great Britain *(continued)*
  psychology, 31
  publishing industry and, 2-3, 8, 79,
    191, 241-242, 323, 390
  science, general, 343
  science history, 321, 327, 329-330,
    334, 338
  social work, 14-15
  sociology, 49-53, 264-266
  veterinary medicine, 456-457
  visual arts, 118-120, 123, 127, 131,
    136, 138
Green, Robert R., 10, 11, 12, 13, 14
Greenspan, Alan, 201
Grout, Donald, 84
Guide to Drug Information (Sewell), 435
*Guide to the Literature of Pharmacy
    and the Pharmaceutical
    Sciences* (Andrews), 435
Guthrie, Chris, 226-228, 231-235

Hardesty, Larry, 29
Harper, William Rainey, 147
Harrison Narcotic Act (1914), 428
Harvard University, 189, 223-224, 225
Havener, W. Michael, 60
Haworth Press, 7, 63, 71, 72
health. *See* medicine; nutrition;
    physical therapy; psychology
Hegel, Georg, 164-165, 170, 261, 283
Heidegger, Martin, 170
Heil, John, 153
hepatology, 421
herpetology, 401
Hérubel, Jean-Pierre V. M., 243, 278,
    280-282, 285
Hinduism, 180, 181
Hirohito, Emperor, 332
Hispanics, 149, 184. *See also* Latin
    America
history, 241-268. *See also* science
    journal history
  agriculture, 258-259
  archaeology, 123, 128, 141, 145-149
  chronological periods, 251-253

history *(continued)*
contemporary, 246-247, 249, 254-255, 257
of economics, 259-260
of education, 6-7, 24
of Europe, 255-258
general, 246-251
of Germany, 241, 244-245, 250, 256-258, 266-267
of Great Britain, 245-249, 252, 254-255, 258-264, 266-267
of history journals, 243-246
interdisciplinary, 250, 253-255, 260-261
labor, 261
of Latin America, 149
of law, 189-190, 236
of library science, 65
Marxist, 247, 265
of medicine, 264, 413-415, 427-429, 433-436
military, 294-295, 298, 302-303, 305-308, 311-312, 318
of music, 81, 89, 91-93, 106
pedagogy, 266-267
of philosophy, 159, 163-165, 169
philosophy of, 261-262
of politics, 262-263, 283-284
of religion, 173-174, 176, 178, 263
of Russia and Soviet Union, 257-258
of science, 264
selection criteria for, 243-244
of sociology, 45-47, 264-266
of visual arts, 115, 117-119, 121-122, 130
of women, 265
Hoffman, Dustin, 357
horticulture, 453
Hrdlicka, Aleš, 143
human resources, 213-214
Husserl, Edmund, 159
hydrology, 364, 405, 449, 450

Ilersich, Lane A., 430
immunology, 394

India, 14, 31, 126-127, 334, 339
Asia, 14
Institute for Scientific Information (ISI), 46, 272
Institute of Electrical and Electronics Engineers (IEEE), 321, 382-384
Institute of Historical Research, 248
Institute of Internal Auditors, 196
Institution of Civil Engineers (ICE), 375, 386
Institution of Mechanical Engineers (IMechE), 377, 378, 386-387
International Association of Music Libraries, Archives and Documentation Centres (IAML), 104-105
International Musicological Society (IMS), 82
international relations, 271, 272, 284-286
Internet. *See* online journals
Introduction to the History of Medicine (Garrison), 413
investment management, 209-210
Islam, 122-123, 180-181
Israel, 130, 148
Italy. *See also* Europe
architecture, 135
English language publications from, 124, 125, 260, 451
philosophy, 155, 170
science, 330, 349-350, 451
social sciences, 149, 250-251, 254, 260
visual arts, 122, 124, 125

Jane's Information Group, 241, 292
Japan
architecture, 134
English language publications from, 134, 331-333, 338, 356-357, 378, 432, 447
Japanese language publications, 134, 330-335
science, 330-335, 338, 356-357, 378, 432, 447
visual arts and, 126-127, 134

John Paul II, Pope, 178
Johns Hopkins University, 339
Johnson administration, 6
Jones, Malcolm, 104
Judaism
    education and, 178
    Israel, 130, 148
    religion and, 173, 176, 179, 183-187
    science and, 321, 331-332
    visual arts and, 130

Kant, Immanuel, 170
Katz, Bill, 158, 160, 163, 165-166,
        169-170, 279
Katz, Linda Sternberg, 158, 160, 163,
        165-166, 169-170, 279
Kennan, George, 284
Keselman, H. J., 31, 34
Kester, Diane D., 60
Kim, Mary T., 62
Kingsbury, Mary, 59-60
Kirk, Stuart A., 10, 11, 13-14, 15
Klein Lecture series, 205
Kluwer, 78, 389
Kockelmans, Joseph J., 159
Kohl, David F., 61, 62
Koulack, David, 31, 34

labor, 212-214, 261
Lang, Paul Henry, 86
language
    anthropology, 144-145
    education, 22
    mathematics, 350
    philosophy, 156-158, 166-167, 168
    psychology, 37
    publication issues concerning, 30,
        48, 58, 77, 330-335, 337, 414
Laselle, Charles, 210
Latin America. *See also* Spanish
        language publications
    archaeology, 149
    arts, 77, 97, 128-129
    military affairs, 316
    publishing industry in, 2-3, 77, 339

Latin language, 155
Latinos, 149, 184. *See also* Latin America
law
    constitutional, 227-228
    criminal, 228
    economic, 226-227, 235-236
    education, 236
    environmental, 229
    general, 222-225
    health, 232-233
    history of, 189-190, 236
    human rights, 230
    intellectual property and
        entertainment, 230-231
    interdisciplinary, 236
    international, 231-232
    librarianship and, 72
    military affairs, 295, 308, 317
    public policy, 227-228, 233-234
    selection criteria for, 221-223,
        225-226, 238n.15
    society and, 236-237
    taxation, 234
    women's issues, 235
Leakey family, 142, 145
Levi-Strauss, Claude, 144
Lewis & Clark College, 229
Lexis, 221
library and information science (LIS),
        57-75
    archives, 69-70
    book reviews, 65
    children's services, 65, 71
    future of, 58, 73
    general interest, 64-66
    government documents, 70
    history of, 7, 58-60, 65
    library types, 70-73
    music, 73, 92, 103-106
    online, 58, 64, 68-69, 71, 73
    rare books, 69-70
    research, 66-67
    science journals and, 336-337,
        339-341
    selection criteria for, 57-58, 60-64
    selection tools, 65
    special functions, 67-69
    technology, 66, 200-201

Liebowitz, S. J., 194
Lindgren, James, 226, 228, 231-233,
    236-237
Lindsay, Duncan, 10, 11, 13-14, 15
linguistics. *See* language
Linnaeus, Carl, 406
Locke, John, 283
Louttit, C. M., 30
Lycan, William, G., 166

Mace, Kenneth C., 37
Maguire, Carmel, 60
mammalogy, 400-401
Mann, Richard, 233
Marine Corps Association, 313
marketing, 216-218, 446
Marras, A., 156
Martin, Fenton, 279-280
Marxism, 247, 250, 251, 265, 283
mathematics, 344-349
    journal selection criteria, 325,
        341-343
    in military affairs, 308
    philosophy and, 157-158, 165-168
    in physics, 350
    in psychology, 37-38
    in sociology, 50
Maximilian II, King (Bavaria), 244
McBride, William L., 159
McDonald, Steven, 60
McMillan, Mary, 435-436
medicine, 413-442. *See also* biology;
        pharmacy
    and anthropology, 143
    chemistry, 431-432
    clinical, 415, 417, 419-425
    dentistry, 413, 418
    engineering, 377-378, 382, 385
    ethics, 159
    general, 413
    history of, 264, 413-415
    law, 232-233
    librarianship and, 73
    online, 414
    physical therapy, 435-437
    and physics, 355

medicine *(continued)*
    psychiatry, 12-13, 31, 398, 423
    religion and, 182
    selection criteria for, 415
    sociology and, 53
    surgery related, 415, 416-418
    weekly journals, 415-416
Meltzer, H., 34
Mendelsohn, Henry N., 10
meteorology, 362-363
Mexico, 128-129
microbiology, 393, 395, 421
Midwest Political Science Assocation,
    281
military affairs, 289-320
    Army, 294, 298-304
    aviation, 306, 315-320
    defense, 290-298, 316-319
    foreign language journals, 302-303,
        316
    history, 294-295, 298, 302-303,
        305-308, 311-312, 318
    international concerns, 291-293,
        296-297, 303, 307, 310
    law, 295, 308, 317
    Marines, 305, 313-315
    Navy, 305-313
    selection criteria for, 289-290
    society and, 290, 298
    strategy, 294, 296-297, 300, 302-303,
        307, 316
    technology, 293, 295, 297, 319
    women, 295-296
MIT Press, 78
Mitchell, William J., 109
Mizell, Francie, 278, 281-282, 284-285
molecular biology, 392, 399, 403-404,
    407-408, 419, 454
Monch, 241
Monod, Gabriel, 245
Moore, G. E., 153
morality. *See* ethics
Morton, Samuel, 142-143
Moser, Paul K., 157
Moses, Claire G., 162
music, 81-113
    American music, 86
    ancient, 84

music *(continued)*
  contemporary and popular, 84, 86,
      93-95, 100-103
  early, 87, 88-89
  education, 91-92, 97-100, 109
  electronic, 90-91, 92
  ethnomusicology, 82-84, 86, 94-97
  folk, 96-97
  history, 89, 91-93, 106
  history of journals, 81
  interdisciplinary, 83, 85, 86, 92
  international, 82, 85, 104-105,
      108-109
  librarianship and bibliography, 73,
      103-106
  musicology, 81, 82-88
  nineteenth century, 89-90
  non-Western, 84, 86, 91
  opera, 107-108
  performance, 106-110
  religious, 110-111, 184
  technology, 90-91, 92, 109-110
  theory, 90-94
  therapy, 100
  traditional, 96-97
  twentieth century, 83, 84, 87, 89
Music Educators National Conference
    (MENC), 98, 99
Music Library Association, 105, 106
mycology, 404, 453
Myers, Roger A., 34

National Academy of Sciences, 344
National Association of Social
    Workers, 9
National Defense Industrial Association
    (NDIA), 296
National Library of Medicine, 413
National Tax Association, 198-199, 234
Native Americans, 141, 143-145, 186
Naval Society, 309
Naval War College, 310
Navy League of the United States, 311
Netherlands. *See also* Europe
  agriculture, 444-445, 448-451,
      453-457

Netherlands *(continued)*
  biology, 392, 393, 396, 397, 399, 407
  botany, 399, 453
  business, 200
  chemistry, 359-362
  earth sciences, 362-366
  ecology, 405
  engineering, 384
  mathematics, 345, 346
  medicine, 417, 423, 431
  music, 92
  philosophy, 154-155, 157-158, 160,
      163-164, 166-168
  physics, 349, 352, 354
  political science, 282-283
  psychology, 36
  visual arts, 117, 119, 123, 128
  zoology, 401, 402, 403
neuroscience, 32, 35, 397-398, 416,
    420-421. *See also* psychology
New York University, 196, 230, 234
New Zealand, 338, 431
Newman, William S., 109
Nisonger, Thomas E., 272, 278, 284-285
Nobel Prize, 328-329, 330, 331, 344
Norris, Pippa, 278, 280, 282-285
North Atlantic Treaty Organization
    (NATO), 296
Northwestern University, 228
Norway, 49, 118, 365
Nour, Martyvonne Morton, 60
nuclear engineering, 379
nutrition, 437-440, 446. *See also* food

Oceania, 125-126, 142, 149
O'Connor, Daniel, 61
Oltmanns, Gail, 29
On the Origin of Species (Darwin), 145
oncology, 396, 422
online journals
  anthropology, 146
  business, 219-220
  engineering, 374, 375, 378
  law, 238-239
  library and information science, 58,
      64, 68-69, 71, 73

online journals *(continued)*
  medicine, 414, 436-437
  military affairs, 289
  philosophy, 155, 157, 162, 164
  political science, 282, 283, 287-288
  religion, 180
  science, 339
Oriental Institute, 148
ornithology, 400
Osaka University, 205
Oxford University, 245, 322, 389

paganism, 180
paleontology, 365-366, 407
Palmer, J. P., 194
Patterson, David, 278, 281-282, 284-285
petroleum, 366-367, 382
pharmacy, 427-435
  administration, 434
  history of, 427-429
  journals, 428, 430-434
  pharmacology, 391, 396, 398
  retail, 434-435
  selection criteria for, 429-430
philosophy, 153-171
  analytic, 153-154, 160, 163
  ancient, 154-155, 170
  behaviorism, 155-157
  deconstruction, 151
  epistemology, 153-154, 156-158,
    160, 162-163, 165
  ethics, 156, 157, 158-159, 161,
    162-163
  existentialism, 151, 159-161
  feminist, 161-162, 165
  general, 162-163, 165, 170
  of history, 261-262
  history of, 159, 163-164, 165, 169
  idealism, 151, 164-166
  interdisciplinary, 163, 165-166
  language/linguistics, 156-158,
    166-167, 168
  logic, 154, 157-159, 165, 167-168
  mathematics, 157-158, 165, 167-168
  metaphysics, 151, 155, 157, 162-166
  methodology, 160, 168

philosophy *(continued)*
  of mind, 153-154, 157, 162-163
  online, 155, 157, 162, 164
  phenomenology, 151, 159-161, 165
  of political science, 283-284, 285
  pricing of journals, 152-153
  of psychology, 155-157
  of science, 151, 154, 157-158, 160,
    167-169
  selection criteria for, 151-152
  semantics, 153, 166, 167, 168
  structuralism, 151
physical therapy, 435-437
physics, 349-355, 361, 377, 385, 448,
  454
physiology, 34-35, 394-395, 397,
  399-402
Piroli, Vivienne, 427
plant science, 403-404, 452-454
Plato, 155, 164, 271, 283
Poland, 130, 168, 257, 345, 448
political science, 271-288
  American, 281-282
  comparative, 282-283
  general, 280-281
  international, 262-263, 284-286
  online, 282, 283
  selection criteria for, 271-279,
    285-286
  tables, 273-277
  theory, 283-284, 285
Pollard, Cecil, 110
pollution, 363, 376, 406, 447. *See also*
  ecology
Portugal, 302-303, 316. *See also*
  Europe
Princeton University, 93
Principles of Geology (Lyell), 145
Protestantism, 110, 173-177, 179-180,
  182-187. *See also* religion
psychiatry, 12-13, 31, 398, 423
psychology, 29-44
  abnormal, 35-36
  applied, 33-34
  clinical, 35-36
  cognitive, 36-37
  developmental, 36
  experimental, 36-37

psychology *(continued)*
  general, 31-33, 39
  music therapy, 100
  neuroscience, 32, 35, 397-398, 416,
      420-421
  organizational, 34
  personality, 38-39
  philosophy of, 155-157
  physiological, 34-35
  psychiatry, 12-13, 31, 423
  quantitative, 37-38
  and religion, 182
  selection criteria for, 29-31
  social, 38-39, 53
publishing industry
  Business and Law, 189-191
  graphs, 1-3, 8, 79, 191, 242, 323, 390
  Helping Professions, 5-8, 45-47,
      58-60
  language issues, 30, 48, 58, 77,
      330-335, 337, 414
  Life and Health Sciences, 389-390,
      413-415, 427-429
  Music, Museums, and Methodists,
      79, 81, 115, 159, 163-165,
      169, 173-174
  Physical Sciences, 321-323, 326-343.
      See also science journal history
  War and Peace, 241-245
Purdue University, 256

race, 51-52. *See also* ethnicity
radiology, 417-418
Reed-Elsevier, 63
religion, 173-187
  for academics and clergy, 175-176,
      183
  and art, 182
  Bible studies, 147-148, 182-183
  Catholicism, 174-176, 178-180,
      182-187, 263
  conservative, 178-179, 186-187
  Eastern, 180-181
  ecumenical, 174, 181, 185
  education, 175-176, 184-185
  history of, 173-174, 176, 178, 263

religion *(continued)*
  humor, 187
  interdisciplinary, 174, 175, 181-182
  Jewish journals, 176, 179, 183-187.
      See also Judaism
  journals of record, 176-181
  laity, 177-179, 185-186
  liberal, 174, 178-179, 186-187
  music, 110-111, 184
  New Age, 180
  new faiths, 179-180
  preaching, 183
  Protestantism, 110, 173-177,
      179-180, 182-187
  social issues, 174, 178-179, 186-187
  worship and liturgy, 184
Rescher, Nicholas, 164
Roentgen, Wilhelm, 417
Roettger, Walter B., 275, 280-282
Rousseau, Jean-Jacques, 57, 283
Royal Musical Association, 85, 86
Ruben, Douglas H., 158, 160, 167, 170
Russ, Raymond C., 156
Russell, Bertrand, 153
Russia
  English language translations, 49-50,
      142, 333-334, 338, 350
  Russian language publications, 254,
      330-334, 338
  science and, 330-334, 338, 350
  social sciences and, 49-50, 142, 254,
      258
Rutgers University, 235

Sage Publications, 7
Salzman, Eric, 86
Sapir, Edward, 145
Schirmer, Rudolph, 86
Schliemann, Heinrich, 328
Schumm, George F., 167
science. *See also* science journal
      history; *specific sciences*
  general journals, 39, 141-142, 339,
      343-344, 391
  language issues, 330-335

science *(continued)*
  philosophy of, 151, 154, 157-158,
    160, 167-169
science journal history
  chronology of, 326-339
  Europe, 321-322, 329-330, 333-334,
    336-339, 342-343, 389-390
  for-profit, 322, 333, 335-337, 339
  Japan, 330-335, 338
  language issues, 330-335
  librarians and, 336-337, 339-341
  not-for-profit, 333, 335-336, 339
  Russia, 330-334, 338
  United States, 321, 330, 331, 335-339
  universities and, 327, 329-330,
    333-337, 339-341
Seltzer, Daniel, 226, 228, 231-233,
    236-237
Sewell, Winifred, 435
Shmuely, Yochi, 10
Sigelman, Lee, 277, 284
Singapore, 338
Sklar, Lawrence, 168
Small, Albion W., 45-46, 47
Smart, John C., 19
Smelser, Neil J., 46, 50
Snow, Bonnie, 435
social work, 9-15
Society for American Archaeology, 147
Society for Human Resource
    Management, 213
Society for Military History, 294-295
Society for Nautical Research, 305
Society for Personality and Social
    Psychology, 38
Society of Automotive Engineers
    (SAE), 377, 387
Society of Ethnomusicology, 95
Society of Manufacturing Engineers, 379
sociology, 45-55
  class and, 51-52
  criminology, 51, 53
  demography, 51-52
  education and, 20-21, 53
  ethnicity and, 51-52
  families and, 52
  health and, 53
  history of, 7, 45-47

sociology *(continued)*
  psychology and, 53
  research, 50-51
  rural, 52
  selection criteria for, 46-47
  social problems and, 54
  theory, 47-50
  of women, 52
solar energy, 379, 386
Somit, Albert, 275, 280-282, 285
Sonneck, Oscar, 86
Spain, 129. *See also* Europe; Spanish
    language publications
Spanish language publications
  archaeology, 149
  forestry, 451
  military affairs, 302-303, 316
  philosophy, 169
  science, 330
  visual arts, 129
Stanford University, 339
Stankus, Tony, 443
Stieg, Margaret, 244
Strategic Planning Society, 215
Strunk, Oliver, 84
Sweden, 128, 345, 376, 404, 406, 434.
    See also Europe
Switzerland. *See also* Europe
  arts, 82-83, 123, 127
  mathematics, 347
  science, 357-361, 398, 400, 407

Tanenhaus, Joseph, 275, 280-282, 285
taxation, 198-199, 234
Taylor & Francis, 322
Temperley, Harold, 248
Thomson, 190
Thomson, J. M., 88
Tjoumas, Renee, 61-62
Tong, Rosemarie, 161

Union of Soviet Socialist Republics
    (USSR). *See* Russia
United Kingdom. *See* Great Britain
United Nations, 285

United States Air Force, 315
United States Air Force Weapons
    School, 319
United States Army War College, 303
United States Naval Institute, 307,
    312-313
United States Supreme Court, 222, 224,
    225, 227
University of California, 164, 229
University of Chicago, 11, 189, 196,
    227, 322, 389
University of Georgia, 231
University of Michigan, 214
University of Minnesota, 228
University of Pennsylvania, 205
University of Tennessee, 443
University of Texas, 228
University of Virginia, 234
University of Washington, 93
Unsworth, Michael E., 290

Van Orden, Phyllis, 61
Varmus, Harold, 414
Vatican II, 174, 184
veterinary science, 456-457
Virchow, Rudolph, 327, 328
visual arts, 115-139
    African American, 130
    architecture, 124, 126, 127, 132-135
    art history, 117-119, 121-122, 130
    connoisseurship, 119-120
    crafts, 137
    criticism, 120-121, 125
    decorative, 136-137
    drawing, 130-131
    history of journals, 115
    iconography, 119
    interior design, 121, 135-136
    Islamic, 122-123
    in libraries, 72
    museum serials, 116-117
    periods, 122-125
    photography, 126, 137-138

visual arts *(continued)*
    prints, 131
    public, 132
    regional, 115, 125-129
    sculpture, 126, 131-132
    selection criteria for, 115-116
von Sybel, Heinrich, 244-245

Walter de Gruyter, 78
Warner, Harold D., 37
Wenner, Jann, 103
Werner, Andreas, 193, 194
West Virginia University, 206
Whelan, Julia, 427
Wicca, 180
Widener University, 227
Wiley, 322, 339
Wilson, H. W., 243
Wittgenstein, Ludwig, 153
women
    feminism, 161-162, 165, 180, 182,
        265, 283
    gynecology, 422
    in helping professions, 5, 6
    history and, 265
    law and, 235
    military affairs and, 295-296
    philosophy and, 161-162, 165
    religion and, 180, 182
    social work and, 15
    sociology and, 51-52
    in visual arts, 129-130
World Peace Foundation, 284
Wright, G. Ernest, 147
Wright, Gerald C., Jr., 275, 277, 282,
    285

Yale University, 91, 224, 225
youth. *See* children

zoology, 399-403, 406-407, 457

Order a copy of this book with this form or online at:
http://www.haworthpressinc.com/store/product.asp?sku=4700

JOURNALS OF THE CENTURY

_____in hardbound at $49.95 (ISBN: 0-7890-1133-6)

_____in softbound at $29.95 (ISBN: 0-7890-1134-4)

COST OF BOOKS_____

OUTSIDE USA/CANADA/
MEXICO: ADD 20%____

POSTAGE & HANDLING_____
(US: $4.00 for first book & $1.50
for each additional book)
Outside US: $5.00 for first book
& $2.00 for each additional book)

SUBTOTAL_____

in Canada: add 7% GST____

STATE TAX____
(NY, OH & MIN residents, please
add appropriate local sales tax)

FINAL TOTAL____
(If paying in Canadian funds,
convert using the current
exchange rate, UNESCO
coupons welcome.)

❏ **BILL ME LATER:** ($5 service charge will be added)
(Bill-me option is good on US/Canada/Mexico orders only;
not good to jobbers, wholesalers, or subscription agencies.)

❏ Check here if billing address is different from
shipping address and attach purchase order and
billing address information.

Signature_____

❏ **PAYMENT ENCLOSED: $_____**

❏ **PLEASE CHARGE TO MY CREDIT CARD.**

❏ Visa ❏ MasterCard ❏ AmEx ❏ Discover
❏ Diner's Club ❏ Eurocard ❏ JCB

Account # _____

Exp. Date_____

Signature_____

Prices in US dollars and subject to change without notice.

NAME_____

INSTITUTION_____

ADDRESS_____

CITY_____

STATE/ZIP_____

COUNTRY_____ COUNTY (NY residents only)_____

TEL_____ FAX_____

E-MAIL_____

May we use your e-mail address for confirmations and other types of information? ❏ Yes ❏ No
We appreciate receiving your e-mail address and fax number. Haworth would like to e-mail or fax special
discount offers to you, as a preferred customer. **We will never share, rent, or exchange your e-mail address
or fax number.** We regard such actions as an invasion of your privacy.

Order From Your Local Bookstore or Directly From
The Haworth Press, Inc.
10 Alice Street, Binghamton, New York 13904-1580 • USA
TELEPHONE: 1-800-HAWORTH (1-800-429-6784) / Outside US/Canada: (607) 722-5857
FAX: 1-800-895-0582 / Outside US/Canada: (607) 722-6362
E-mail: getinfo@haworthpressinc.com
PLEASE PHOTOCOPY THIS FORM FOR YOUR PERSONAL USE.
www.HaworthPress.com

BOF02